Architecture of Topic

Studies in Generative Grammar

Editors
Norbert Corver
Harry van der Hulst

Founding editors
Jan Koster
Henk van Riemsdijk

Volume 136

Architecture of Topic

Edited by
Valéria Molnár
Verner Egerland
Susanne Winkler

DE GRUYTER
MOUTON

ISBN 978-1-5015-2496-7
e-ISBN (PDF) 978-1-5015-0448-8
e-ISBN (EPUB) 978-1-5015-0438-9
ISSN 0167-4331

Library of Congress Control Number: 2019931402

Bibliographic information published by the Deutsche Nationalbibliothek
The Deutsche Nationalbibliothek lists this publication in the Deutsche Nationalbibliografie;
detailed bibliographic data are available on the Internet at http://dnb.dnb.de.

© 2021 Walter de Gruyter, Inc., Boston/Berlin
This volume is text- and page-identical with the hardback published in 2019.
Typesetting: Integra Software Services Pvt. Ltd.
Printing and binding: CPI books GmbH, Leck

www.degruyter.com

Acknowledgements

This volume grew out of an international workshop held at the University of Lund in December 2014 on the topic of the *Architecture of Topic* and a long lasting cooperation between the University of Lund and the University of Tübingen. We would like to thank all participants of the workshop for the substantial discussions of relevant topic-related issues and for their contributions and participation in the reviewing process. We would also like to gratefully acknowledge the fruitful dialogues on the architecture of topic and on issues of experimentation with the following linguists: Werner Abraham, Elisabet Engdahl, Hans-Martin Gärtner, Beata Gyuris, Jutta Hartmann, Arthur Holmer, Shinichiro Ishihara, Dianne Jonas, Andreas Nolda, Christer Platzack and Kerstin Schwabe.

A special thank you goes to our project manager, Lara Wysong, for discussing the design of this book with us and for her ongoing support in bringing it to its conclusion. Particular gratitude goes to De Gruyter assistance, to Kirsten Brock and to Dianne Jonas for copy-editing substantial parts of this text.

We are also grateful to *Elisabeth Rausing Minnesfond* (Sweden), *Kungliga Humanistiska Vetenskapssamfundet i Lund* (Sweden) and the German Science Foundation (Deutsche Forschungsgemeinschaft DFG) under the grants SFB 833 and RTG 1808 for supporting the research that is presented in this book.

This volume is dedicated to the memory of our colleague and friend, Michael S. Rochemont, who passed away on July 3rd, 2018. Michael's work has made a deep and lasting impact on the research of information structure, focus and topic and on the scientific discipline of linguistics as a whole.

Contents

Acknowlegements —— V

Valéria Molnár, Verner Egerland, Susanne Winkler
Exploring the Architecture of Topic at the Interface of Grammar and Discourse —— 1

Part I: Semantic and Discourse-pragmatic Correlates of Topicality

Michael Rochemont
Topics and Givenness —— 47

Roland Hinterhölzl
The Role of Topics in Licensing Anaphoric Relations in VP-ellipsis —— 67

Werner Frey, André Meinunger
Topic Marking and Illocutionary Force —— 95

Mara Frascarelli
Topics, Conversational Dynamics and the Root/Non-root Distinction: Adverbial Clauses at the Discourse-syntax Interface —— 139

Part II: Variation in the Grammatical Encoding of Topicality: Clause-internal, Clause-external and Null Topics

Peter W. Culicover, Susanne Winkler
Why Topicalize VP? —— 173

Kordula De Kuthy, Andreas Konietzko
Information-structural Constraints on PP Topicalization from NPs —— 203

Nomi Erteschik-Shir
Stage Topics and their Architecture —— 223

Halldór Ármann Sigurðsson
Topicality in Icelandic: Null Arguments and Narrative Inversion —— 249

Verner Egerland
Apropos the Topic – On Topic-introducing Expressions in Swedish —— 273

Valéria Molnár, Hélène Vinckel-Roisin
Discourse Topic vs. Sentence Topic – Exploiting the Right Periphery of German Verb-second Sentences —— 293

Part III: Topics from the Diachronic Perspective

Augustin Speyer
Topichood and the Margins of the German Clause from a Historical Perspective —— 337

Valéria Molnár
Stylistic Fronting at the Interface of Syntax and Discourse —— 373

Index —— 425

Valéria Molnár, Verner Egerland, Susanne Winkler
Exploring the Architecture of Topic at the Interface of Grammar and Discourse

1 Introduction

The investigation of the *Architecture of Topic* in linguistic theory follows the programme of bringing the different strands of information structure research together and integrating the insights of this research into a new and complete picture. Topics are regarded as "sorting keys" to file and access information (Kuno 1972), and are also claimed to be "one of the means available in the language to organize or classify the information exchanged in linguistic communication – they are signals for how to construct the context set, or under which entries to classify the new proposition" (Reinhart 1981: 80). The notion of *topic* is often regarded as complementary to the notion of *focus*, contributing to a binary division of sentences corresponding to the basic requirements of information structure (IS): (i) anchoring the message in discourse, and (ii) guaranteeing informativeness in discourse.[1] According to this view, topics are important means for establishing coherence, while the focused part adds new information to the common ground of the discourse participants.

In the decades since Chomsky (1972) and Jackendoff (1972), most attention has been paid to the notions of focus, its discourse-semantic features and its cross-linguistic and language-specific manifestation in grammar (cf. Molnár and Winkler 2006). In this volume, we will therefore highlight the concept of topic and argue that *topic* is one of the basic primitives of IS besides *focus* and (according to recent proposals also) *contrast*.[2] We agree with Reinhart (1981: 68), who claims that "[C]larifying what sentence-topics are is not just a matter

---

[1] See also Strawson's (1964: 96) two general principles of communication, *the principle of the presumption of knowledge* and *the principle of relevance*, which "intends, in general, to give or add information about what is a matter of standing or current interest or concern".
[2] The linguistic relevance of the notion of *contrast* is discussed in Molnár (2002, 2006), Frey (2006, 2010), Repp and Cook (2010), Kučerová and Neeleman (2012), and Neeleman and Vermeulen (2012).

Valéria Molnár, Verner Egerland, Lund University
Susanne Winkler, Eberhard Karls University Tübingen

https://doi.org/10.1515/9781501504488-001

of intellectual curiosity; several other linguistic phenomena depend on or interact with this pragmatic relation".

Linguistically, it is a highly relevant concept which is vital for the interpretation of the boldfaced items in English sentences like (1)–(4), as well as for the explanation of the difference between these cases and example (5) (instances of topichood are underlined):

(1) [CONTEXT: *What about Hurricane Irma?*]
It swept across the northern Caribbean and Florida in September 2017, leaving a trail of devastation in its path.

(2) *As for Hurricane Irma, it was the most powerful storm ever recorded in the Atlantic ocean.*

(3) *Cuba Hurricane Irma devastated, (but the strength of the hurricane diminished gradually over the US mainland.)*

(4) *In Miami, Hurricane Irma left more than 1 million homes without electricity.*

(5) *There was an extremely powerful storm in the northern Carribbean and Florida in September 2017.*

Examples (1)–(4) above illustrate different types of "sorting keys" for the organization of information in the sentence, also signalling contextual givenness in (1), and expressing some kind of shift in (2), contrast in (3), and frame-setting in (4). Sentence (5) seems to be different since it lacks this sorting possibility in its structure. As examples (1)–(4) above demonstrate, topics differ not only in their discourse-semantic properties but also in their formal realization, making use of various types of sentence-initial constituents and special structures in English. Both the language-specific properties of topics in English and the cross-linguistic variation of topicality have received a considerable amount of attention in linguistic research.

However, it is far from clear whether the notion of *topic* can be established as a language universal, justified by a common functional feature or grammatical property. This problem can also provide an explanation for the latest strand of research, which raises doubt about the theoretical status and applicability of this concept. Recently a special issue of *The Linguistic Review* (edited by van Bergen and de Hoop 2009) and a few articles (e.g. Büring 2016 and Roberts

2011) have been devoted to the topic issue.[3] These influential analyses focus on the difficulties with the operationalization of the notion topic[4] and point out that the linguistic relevance of topic is still highly controversial: "there is very little consensus among linguists on any (...) specific definition. Multiple properties contributing to topichood have been described, but none of these properties seems either necessary or sufficient to classify something as a topic" (van Bergen and de Hoop 2009: 173). A serious objection to the notion of topic is that it has not been treated uniformly in linguistic research: "There is no agreed-upon way to identify topics across languages, and therefore inconsistent claims about their properties abound" (Büring 2016: 85).

In contrast to the above-mentioned sceptical views, the present investigation of the architecture of topic aims to close this gap and provide arguments for a uniform treatment of the notion of topic. After a short overview of the theoretical foundation of topicality in discourse and grammar suggested in linguistic theory and an introduction of relevant concepts of information structure research in section 2, section 3 discusses the linguistic relevance of topicality. Section 4 focuses on the burning issues of topicality research. In 4.1 and 4.2. the two crucial dimensions of topicality are explored, with specification of the discourse-semantic features and presentation of the most important topic markers of grammar (in morphology, syntax, and phonology). Subsection 4.3 provides a discussion of the possibility of a uniform, universally valid topic definition despite the great cross-linguistic variation, connecting this question to the issue of topic typology. The open questions and the challenges for future research in the field of topicality are summarized in section 5. Section 6 introduces the papers included in this volume, which highlight relevant topic-related theoretical aspects of information structure research and investigate different discourse-semantic and grammatical properties of topichood in various languages.

---

3 Although focus is the dominating notion in information-structural research in edited volumes and handbooks (Féry and Ishihara 2016), some of them also include deeper discussion of topics (e.g. Krifka and Musan 2012; Neeleman and Vermeulen 2012; von Heusinger; Maienborn and Portner 2012).
4 Cf. Büring (2016: 81) concerning the problems with the operationalization tests, referring back to Roberts' (2011) work: "none of the topic tests seems sufficient or necessary to identify topics, nor is it clear that they actually test for the same thing".

2 Information Structure in Linguistic Theory

The strategies of anchoring topicality in grammar and/or discourse are widely debated and the architecture of topic is a highly relevant theoretical issue. The concept of *topic* has been controversially discussed for almost six decades and still has not found a uniform treatment. The key theoretical question is whether information structure can be accounted for in the theory of Generative Grammar or whether a widening of the perspective is necessary. In the generative framework "[l]anguage is not properly regarded as a system of communication. It is a system for expressing thought, something quite different" (Chomsky 2000: 75). Here, the modelling of the internal language faculty and the mapping between the components of *Grammar* are in the centre of interest: the basic component, known as the computational system (narrow syntax), generates internal representations and maps them into the *sensory-motor interface* (the phonological system) and the *conceptual-intentional interface* (formal-semantic system). In contrast, *Discourse Grammar* regards language as a means of *communication* and the focus lies on the context-dependent aspects of meaning and their means of expression. This approach requires the study of the interface between Grammar and Discourse.

The proponents of the formal grammar approach to information structure assume that information-structural notions are integrated into the formal system of language. According to their view, the syntax-semantics interface is responsible both for the representation of scopal relations and for the interpretation of information-structural and discourse notions. The opposite position, which is assumed by the proponents of the discourse grammar approach to information structure, assigns the explanation of different discourse functions, among them those expressed by these notional pairs of information structure, to (Discourse-)pragmatics, which either interfaces with LF (Logical Form) or forms a separate component (cf. Winkler 2005: 25–26). Even though it remains an open question whether information-structural notions should be integrated into the formal system of language or should be represented in the pragmatic component primarily governed by contextual factors, there is agreement concerning the nature of "informational meaning", which is defined as context-dependent meaning that is crucial for the theoretical treatment of topicality. The exploration of informational meaning requires attention to the influence of context on linguistic structures and to the dynamic character of communication. Language as a means of communication provides the necessary syntactic, prosodic, and morphological means to meet the communicative demands of a particular context or discourse.

The main goal of this volume is to show that the analysis of information structure and its basic concepts requires an interface approach and the integration of different perspectives: in addition to the grammatically coded syntactic and prosodic properties, it is important to take into account the discourse-semantic dimension in the analysis of topicality. This dimension has been elaborated in influential linguistic approaches in the last decades and the proposals are based on relevant linguistic concepts which are necessary for the analysis of information structuring. These concepts will be presented below in more detail.

As suggested by Vallduví (1992: 13), *information* "as viewed in information theory is by definition a reduction of uncertainty: the information carried by two sentences with equal propositional content is different when the reduction of uncertainty they bring along to the hearer's knowledge-store is different". *Communication* "can be seen as continuous change of the common ground" according to Krifka and Musan (2012: 2). The notion of *Common Ground* (CG) is defined by Krifka (2007: 15) as "information that is mutually known to be shared and continuously modified in communication". Since the main task of communication is "*transfer of information* and its optimization relative to the temporary needs of interlocutors" (Krifka 2007: 15), it is relevant to structure information and provide clearly recoverable instructions. As Prince (1986: 208) claims, "[i]nformation in a discourse does not correspond to an unstructured set of propositions; rather, speakers seem to form their utterances so as to structure the information they are attempting to convey, usually or perhaps always in accordance with their beliefs about the hearer: what s/he is thought to know, what s/he is expected to be thinking about".

In order to meet the communicative demands of interlocutors, packaging instructions are necessary and must be recoverable from the overt structure of any language. *Information packaging* is a concept originally suggested by Chafe (1976), and is structurally represented by syntactic, morphological, or prosodic means, or a combination of these, as is usually the case. They indicate "how information conveyed by linguistic means fits into the (hearer's mental model of the) context or discourse" (Vallduví and Engdahl 1996: 460). The basic idea of "information packaging" is illustrated by Vallduví and Engdahl with the following examples:

(6)   *She hates chocolate.*

(7)   *Chocolate she hates.*

The claim is that (6) and (7) have the same propositional content – they are truth-conditionally equivalent. The difference between (6) and (7) is not in *what* they say about the world, but *how* they say what they say about the world. These sentences embody two different packaging instructions with the same propositional content.

Even if information packaging by foregrounding and backgrounding different parts of the information takes care of "those aspects of optimization of message that respond to the temporary state of the addressee's mind" in updating the common ground, in certain cases it also affects the "message itself" and has truth-conditional consequences (Krifka 2007: 14). Krifka (2007: 13–14) argues that it is crucial to distinguish between two dimensions of the *Common Ground* (CG): *CG content* and *CG management*. The dimension of the CG that indicates how the *CG content* should develop is subsumed under *CG management*, the dimension that is concerned with the truth-conditionally relevant information is subsumed under the *CG content*. This distinction seems especially relevant for different uses of focus, where in addition to the pragmatic use, the semantic use can also be attested. Focus can be used for information packaging in answers to questions "guiding the direction into which communication should develop" (Krifka 2007: 21). Different options can be indicated in English by placement of accent as in (8), quoted from Krifka (accented syllables are marked by capital letters, the focused constituent (F) is in square brackets):

(8) a. A. *What did John show Mary?*
    B. *John showed Mary the [PICtures]$_F$.*
  b. A. *Who did John show the pictures?*
    B. *John showed [MAry]$_F$ the pictures.*

Focus is claimed in these cases to be related to a "set of alternatives" (cf. Rooth's 2016 *Alternative Semantics*, Krifka 2007), also called "F-alternatives" by Büring (2016: 66), defined as a set of propositions containing a variable for the focused constituent. Focusing in these semantic approaches is considered as a kind of operation *asserting the exclusion* of alternatives (as opposed to contrastive topics, which *question* alternatives; cf. Büring 2016). This view thus does not correspond to (although it is compatible with) other focus definitions based on phonological criteria (Chomsky 1972), a syntactic feature (Jackendoff 1972; Rizzi 1997), or contextual newness.[5] The truth-conditional relevance of focusing

---

[5] Chomsky (1972) regards focus essentially as a *phonological* phenomenon; with the phrase "containing the intonation center", however, he also takes the functional property of focus into consideration by claiming that the focus constituent represents *new information*. Jackendoff (1972) integrates focus into the syntactic theory by introducing a *syntactic marker F* and argues that *two systems of rules* make use of the syntactic marker F: one in semantics and one in

in Hungarian (with a designated focus position) has already been argued for by Szabolcsi (1981). Focus affecting the truth-conditional content of the CG occurs, however, in other languages, too. This type of truth-conditionally relevant focus is discussed in research primarily in connection with the focus- sensitive particles *only* and *even* in English (cf. Jackendoff 1972; Rooth 1985; Krifka 2007). The claim is that the truth-conditions of (9a) and (9b) differ depending on the association of the focus particle with either *pictures* in (9a) or *Mary* in (9b):

(9) a. *John only showed Mary the [PICtures]$_F$.*
　 b. *John only showed [MAry]$_F$ the pictures.*
　　 (Krifka 2007)

As will be argued in the following sections, an account of topichood also requires that both dimensions of the CG, *CG management* and *CG content*, are taken into consideration (see presentation of papers in sections 4 and 6). The conversational moves performed by the participants for signalling topics are motivated by the communicative goals in discourse, whereas certain aspects of topichood (like its effect on presuppositions and anaphora interpretation; see Reinhart 1981: 69) could be claimed to belong to CG content as they affect the truth-conditions of the sentence.

3 On the Linguistic Relevance of Topicality

The notion of "sentence topic" is most often included among the basic notions of information structure in linguistic theory, despite terminological confusion and controversy concerning the relevance of this concept. Depending on the character of the theoretical approaches, several terminological pairs have been used for the binary division of the sentence with respect to the requirements of linguistic communication into a part responsible for the anchoring of the message in the discourse and a part adding new information to the common ground (see section 1 above, footnote 1). The former notion has been called "psychological subject" (von der Gabelentz 1891), "theme" (Prague school of functional linguists following Mathesius 1929, 1975), "topic" (Dahl 1969; Reinhart 1981), and "link" (Vallduví 1992), while its complementary notion has been referred to

---

phonology. The [F]-feature is still present in the "universal syntactic structure" (cf. the cartographic approach of Rizzi 1997).

as "psychological predicate", "comment", "rheme", or "focus". Whereas focus as "the phrase containing the intonation center" (in a few languages also bound to designated positions) and "represent[ing] new information" (Chomsky 1972) or "indicat[ing] the presence of alternatives that are relevant for the interpretation of linguistic expressions" (Krifka 2007: 18) is operationalizable, the large language-internal and also cross-linguistic diversity of topics presents an immense challenge for linguistic research.

Concerning the issue of the linguistic relevance of topichood, many approaches refer to a strong intuition that it is necessary to have a concept for organizing and storing of information (e.g. Krifka 2008; Büring 2016; Roberts 2011). This is clearly stated by Roberts (2011: 1908):

> Quite often in making an utterance, a speaker in some way brings our attention to an entity that is relevant at that point in the discussion, in order to tell us something about it. The relevant entity may be an individual or it may be a situation or event. In any such case, we say that the entity to which our attention is drawn is the Topic of the utterance.

However, the identification of topics is not a straightforward matter. As Krifka (2007: 40) argues "[t]his presupposes that information in human communication and memory is organized in a certain way so that it can be said to be 'about' something. This does not follow from a general definition of information. For example, relational databases or sets of possible worlds, both models for information, do not presuppose any relation of aboutness". Büring (2016: 83–84) supports this view by claiming that "there is no reason to assume *a priori* that information should be structured into aboutees and their properties (...)".

A different way of approaching this problem is to look at its observable effects in languages in order to decide whether they fulfil the criteria of *necessary descriptive concepts*. Marga Reis (1982: 172) defines the criteria of the necessary descriptive concepts as follows: "Ein Konzept K ist beschreibungsrelevant /-notwendig für eine Einzelsprache L genau dann, wenn es in der (optimalen) Grammatik von L mindestens einmal wesentlich auftritt, d.h. für die Formulierung mindestens einer sprachlichen Gesetzmäßigkeit von L benutzt werden muß" [A concept has descriptive relevance for an individual language L iff it appears at least once in the (optimal) Grammar of L, i.e. it must be used for the formulation of at least one language rule of L; translation by Molnár, Egerland, and Winkler].

The concept of topichood is exploited for the explanation of a whole range of phenomena in grammar, such as the function of morphological markers (like *wa* in Japanese), the interaction with syntactic constraints in, for example, Chinese, the use of certain syntactic structures like in English (e.g. hanging topic, left dislocation and topicalization, illustrated above in the introductory examples (2)–(4)), the effect of certain prosodic patterns ('hat pattern', 'fall-rise' in the case of contrastive topics; cf. Büring 1997, 2016), as well as for the interpretation of discourse-semantic phenomena (see e.g. Reinhart 1981). Consequently, the topic must be accessible to sentence grammar. These facts suggest that the topic is a "necessary descriptive concept" in the sense of Marga Reis' definition.

4 Burning Issues of Topichood

In addition to the two questions concerning the *anchoring of topic (and other concepts of IS) in linguistic theory* and the *linguistic relevance of topichood* discussed above, there are at least three burning issues in topic research. These three domains are related to the *operationalization* of topics and will be individually discussed in sections 4.1 to 4.3:
(i) the *discourse-semantic* properties and dimensions of topichood,
(ii) the *grammatical* (syntactic and phonological) coding of topichood, and
(iii) the possibility of *a uniform definition of topichood* and the specification of its *language-specific features*, connected to the question of the *typology* of topics.

4.1 The Discourse-Semantic Dimension of Topichood

The question which specific discourse-semantic properties enter into topichood has received different answers in research. The type of answers are relevant for the type of topic definition suggested in different approaches as well as for the identification of features that make the realization of optimal topics possible.

(i) Aboutness
In regard to the topic definition, most attention has been paid to the *aboutness*-relation, which is also typical for predicative constructions. According to Hockett (1958/²1963: 201), "[t]he most general characteristic of predicative constructions is suggested by the terms «topic» and «comment» for their ICs [intermediate constituents]: the speaker announces a topic and then says something about it. Thus *John / ran away; That new book by Thomas Guernsey / I haven't read yet*. In English and the familiar languages of Europe, topics are usually also subjects, and comments are predicates: so in *John / ran away*". É. Kiss (2002: 9) also captures

topichood in relation to predication, arguing that the topic "foregrounds an individual (a person, an object, or a group of them) from among those present in the universe of discourse as the subject of the subsequent predication". Similarly, topic is regarded by Gundel (1988: 210) as "the domain within which the main predication holds". According to her, an entity E is "the topic of a sentence (...) S, iff in using S the speaker intends to increase the addressee's knowledge about, request information about, or otherwise get the addressee to act with respect to E".

Whereas the notion of aboutness is regarded as a primitive in several other approaches without a deeper theoretical anchoring (see e.g. Kuno 1972; Dik 1978), Reinhart (1981) elaborates the aboutness-relation by exploiting the notions of *pragmatic aboutness* and *context set* suggested by Strawson (1964). In this model a *discourse* is regarded as "a joint-procedure of constructing a context-set" containing a set of propositions accepted to be true by the participants. Reinhart integrates the concept of topic into this theory of linguistic communication, claiming that "[s]entence-topics, within this view, are one of the means available in the language to organize, or classify the information exchanged in linguistic communication – they are signals for how to construct the context set, or under which entries to classify the new proposition" (Reinhart 1981: 80). To explain the organization of the context set, Reinhart uses the metaphor of a library catalogue which information is stored on file cards with particular headings. Thus in examples (6) *She hates chocolate* and (7) *Chocolate she hates* discussed above, the identical propositional content needs different entries, since (6) provides information about *the subject referent* and (7) about *chocolate*. A definition of topics in the same vein is suggested by Krifka (2007: 41): "The topic constituent identifies the entity or set of entities under which the information expressed in the comment constituent should be stored in the CG content". The notion of *link*, partly corresponding to the notion of topic, receives a similar definition in the instruction-based model developed by Vallduví (1990: 58): "A link is an address pointer in the sense that it directs the hearer to a given address (...) in the hearer's knowledge-store, under which the information carried by the sentence is entered". Portner and Yabushita (2001) also suggest to relate topicality to an update procedure quite similar to Reinhart's (1981) notion of aboutness and to Vallduví's (1992) notion of link: the information conveyed by the utterance updates the discourse referent corresponding to its topic (if it has one).

The definition of topics based on the notions of predication and aboutness has been advocated in a large number of accounts of information structure over the last two decades (e.g. Lambrecht 1994; Molnár 1991, 1998; Chiarcos 2010; Bianchi and Frascarelli 2010). However, this influential definition of topicality has also received criticism, not least because of the difficulties of its operationalization as pointed out by Roberts (2011: 1928): "In all its instantiations in the literature, the notion of aboutness remains relatively vague, and as we saw, the tests proposed to check for aboutness give slightly different results for language".

(ii) Frame-setting
Another influential view of topichood is proposed by Chafe (1976: 51). He regards frame-setting as the decisive function of topics and claims that "'real' topics (in topic-prominent languages) are not so much 'what the sentence is about' as the *frame* within which the sentence holds". According to Chafe (1976: 50) "What the topic appears to do is to limit the applicability of the main predication to a certain restricted domain (...) *the topic sets a spatial, temporal, or individual framework* within which the main predication holds". Frame-setting is also discussed by Krifka (2007) as a possible topic function carried out by different types of adverbials. These "set the frame in which the following expression should be interpreted" and "systematically restrict the language (...) in certain ways" (Krifka 2007: 46), as illustrated in examples (10) and (11):

(10) A: *How is John?*
 B: { *Healthwise / As for his health* }, *he is* [*FINE*]$_F$.

(11) A: *How is business going for Daimler-Chrysler?*
 B: [*In GERmany*]$_{Frame}$ *the prospects are* [*GOOD*]$_F$,
  but [*in AMErica*]$_{Frame}$ *they are* [*losing MOney*]$_F$.

The function of frame-setting mainly by temporal and local adverbials is also considered by Jacobs (1984) as essential for the definition of topics. In a later work, Jacobs (2001: 656) defines frame-setting as follows: "Frame-setting: In (X Y), X is the frame for Y iff X specifies a domain of (possible) reality to which the proposition expressed by Y is restricted". However, Jacobs not only distinguishes *frame-setting* from *addressation* (the corresponding dimension to the intuitive notion of aboutness) but adds two more dimensions to the topic-comment partition: *predication* (a closely related dimension to aboutness) and the dimension called *informational separation*. According to Jacobs the functional diversity of the topic-comment partition can only be captured by taking all these dimensions of TC (topic-comment) into consideration. He also argues that a uniform definition of topic is impossible, since the specific patterns of topic-related constructions in different languages show different values.

(iii) Givenness

A crucial feature of *aboutness-* and *frame-related* approaches to topichood is their interest in defining topics "in terms of their effect on the ongoing discourse" (Reinhart 1981: 78), thereby focusing on the relation of topics to the complementary part of the sentence (comment or focus). Reinhart's analogy with a library catalogue also makes it understandable why new entries should be possible. This view is, however, not generally accepted in research where the context-dependence of the topic constituent – "a property of the referents denoted by linguistic expression in a given context" (Reinhart 1981: 61) – is often claimed to have definitional relevance. In these approaches the topic corresponds simply to known or given information of the sentence (see Gundel 1974; Chafe 1976; Clark and Haviland 1977; Clark and Clark 1977; Lambrecht 1994; Büring 1997; Haftka 1995; etc.). Context-dependence is, however, not generally required as an obligatory topic correlate. Büring (2016: 82) claims, referring to Aissen (1992: 51) in example (12), that "the topic marking in Tzozil is only used to *establish* the aboutee, not to refer back to it". The marking of topic by the prefix *a* and the suffix *e* occurs when the topic is new or shifted:

(12) [context: Something had landed at the foot of the tree (...) There was a straw mat (...) They untied it...]
<u>A</u> <u>ti</u> <u>tzeb</u> *san-antrex*   *un-e,*   *iyik'ik*   *la ech'el un.*
TOP DET girl San Andres   ENC-ENC   they.took   cl away ENC
'They took the San Andres girl with them.'

Frey (2004) has a similar view: "Indefinite DP may be an aboutness topic. If so, it has a specific interpretation". He illustrates this possibility by example (13), which contains the indefinite DP *ein Student* as topic in the first position of the German middle field:

(13) *Heute hat ein Student leider   während der Vorlesung geschlafen.*
today has a student unfortunately during the lecture   slept
'Unfortunately, a student slept during the lecture today.'

The optionality of context-dependence of topichood is claimed by many other linguists, too (cf. Sasse 1987; Molnár 1991, 1998; Frey 2004; Endriss 2009; Krifka, Musan 2012 and Rochemont 2016). However, it is also pointed out that topics are frequently associated with the discourse status given. Consider Krifka (2007: 41): "in many cases, topic constituents are 'old' in the sense of being inferable from the context. But there are certainly cases of new topics". Rochemont (in this volume: 64) also argues in his analysis of the relation between topic and givenness that "[n]othing prevents a topic from being Given in virtue of an available discourse antecedent/topic, but nothing requires it either. Topics may be New (and/or shifted), familiar or salient".

(iv) Referentiality
Referentiality is also often regarded as an important requirement for topichood. According to Dahl (1974: 7), "[i]n a sentence with a topic-comment structure, then, we say something – expressed in the comment – about someone or something – represented by the topic. To be able to say something about an entity, we must first pick it out for our listener, in other words we must *refer* to it". Topicality, defined as the "notional subject" of the clause, is also assumed in research on Hungarian (a language with designated topic position(s)) to be bound to referentiality or genericity and thus "only entities and classes of entities that can be presupposed to exist (...) can be predicated about" (É. Kiss 1992: 68).

This widely accepted view led to the exclusion of quantified DPs (and sentence adverbials), which are regarded as non-referential entities (cf. Frey 2004: 97). However, this claim has been called into question in several works, motivated both by cross-linguistic evidence and by theoretical considerations. Horn (1989: 501) shows that the Japanese (topic) particle *wa* can associate with quantifiers (14) and Büring (2016) analyses quantified DPs with a fall-rise contour as contrastive topics in (15) (marked by CT):

(14) Zenin wa repooto o das-anakatta
 all top report acc hand-in-neg
 'Not everyone handed in the report.'
 (Horn 1989)

(15) ALLE$_{CT}$ Politiker sind NICHT$_F$ korrupt.
 all politicians are not corrupt
 'Not all politicians are corrupt.'
 (Büring 2016)

Krifka (2007: 42) also argues that quantified DPs can be topics and his view is based on the following definition of topics: "The topic constituent identifies the entity or set of entities under which the information expressed in the comment constituent should be stored in the CG [Common Ground] content". He illustrates this possibility by examples (16) and (17), which contain quantified expressions as topic candidates, and claims that "[t]he quantifier in such sentences expresses the extent to which the comment holds for the elements of the set":

(16) *Every zebra in the zoo was sick.*

(17) *Most zebras in the zoo were sick.*

Interestingly, from the semantic perspective most attention has been devoted to the relevance of topichood for scope taking, motivated by the quantificational and/or operator character of topichood. It is assumed that topics have a kind of operator function and create widest scope (cf. Huang 1982; É. Kiss 1987). The relevance of topics for scope taking is also discussed in terms of the *de re* and *de dicto* distinction suggested in the framework of epistemic logic (cf. Hintikka 1973), where not only quantifiers but also epistemic operators (related to propositional attitudes) are claimed to have scope. "*De re* in Latin means 'about the thing' and *de dicto* means 'about what is said' (...) in the *de re* case, what is important is 'the **thing** in the actual world', i.e. what the description refers to in our world, but in the *de dicto* case the important thing is what the description **says** about the object it refers to" (Allwood, Andersson, and Dahl 1977: 115, boldfacing by Molnár, Egerland, and Winkler). This distinction is especially relevant for the resolution of scope ambiguities occurring in the presence of several scopal expressions (operators and/or quantifiers) in a sentence like in (18). This example contains an expression of propositional attitude *believe* (indicated by B_a, i.e. *a believes*) and a quantified expression *all Nobel prize-winners*. In the semantic structure of the example shown in (18a,b) F corresponds to 'is a Nobel prize-winner'; the examples also contain an additional expression G corresponding to 'is an idiot':

(18) *John <u>believes</u> that <u>all Nobel prize-winners</u> are idiots.*
    a. $B_a (\forall x\, F(x) \to G(x))$
    b. $\forall x\, (F(x) \to B_a(G(x)))$

Following Hintikka's semantics, Allwood, Andersson, and Dahl (1977: 114) argue that the sentence with the wide scope of the epistemic operator B_a over the proposition p can be interpreted as "in all worlds consistent with a's beliefs (B_a) p holds". This is the case in the *de dicto* reading (18a), expressing that "in all John's belief worlds, all Nobel prize-winners (i.e. the individuals that are Nobel prize-winners in those worlds) are idiots". In contrast, the *de re* option in (18b), where the quantified expression has wide scope (crucial for its topicality), should be interpreted as "for every Nobel prize-winner (who is a Nobel prize-winner in the actual world) he believes that this individual is an idiot" (Allwood, Andersson, and Dahl 1977: 115).

In Beghelli and Stowell's (1997) model, semantically conditioned scopal mechanisms are proposed, where each kind of expression participates in those processes that suit its particular semantic properties. According to their analysis the functional projections of the sentence representing different types of quantifiers are hierarchically ordered in Logical Form in English (instead of the traditional movement rule called Quantifier Raising). In this structure (19) each quantifier acquires its scope by moving into the specifier of the required functional category.[6] As the proposed order in (19) shows, referential phrases (RefP) occupy the leftmost position. Szabolcsi (1997) argues that the preverbal structure of the Hungarian sentence corresponds to the hierarchy of functional projections represented in English in LF (illustrated in (20)). Crucially, the Topic is identified with the referential phrase:

(19) **[RefP** [AgrSP **[DistP [ShareP** [AgrP/VP]]]]]

(20) [**Topic**=RefP [Quantifier=DistP [Focus=ShareP [Pred.Operator=AgrP/VP]]]]

Topics are thus claimed to have (discourse-)semantic effects. As noted by Reinhart (1995: 80), topichood has relevance for anaphora resolution: unstressed pronouns have a strong tendency to refer to the topic, which is the preferred antecedent in anaphora resolution:

(21) [context: *Max was on his way home from school, worrying about how things were going to turn out. After a while he ran into Felix, and...*]
 a. *he proposed they go to a pub.* (*he* refers to Max, not Felix)
 b. *the guy proposed they go to a pub.* (*the guy* refers to Felix, not Max)

Neeleman and Vermeulen (2012: 16) argue that topics also have direct (or indirect) relevance for truth-value judgments as the contrast below between (22a) and (22b) shows. The referential failure results in a presupposition failure only

---

[6] Inverse scope is accounted for with recourse to reconstruction, which is claimed, however, to only undo semantically insignificant movements.

in (22a), but not in (22b), where the referential expression *King of France* is part of the predicate:

(22) a. *As for the King of France, he visited the exhibition yesterday.*
     b. *As for the exhibition, it was visited by the King of France yesterday.*

Abrusán and Szendrői (2011) have a similar view and call the referent that is used to evaluate the truth value of a proposition a *pivot*. Topichood is claimed to be relevant for the choice of the pivot and truth-value judgments, since the default choice is the topic. This supports the assumption that the topic should be integrated into sentence grammar.

(v) Topic vs. focus and contrast
One of the central issues concerning the discourse-pragmatic dimension of topichood is the relation of topics to other primitives of information structure. Especially the relation between topic and focus seems to be controversial. Concerning this relation we find two opposite views in research: while certain approaches claim that they are complementary categories (see e.g. Büring 1997; É. Kiss 2006; Heycock 2008), an overlap between topic and focus is held to be possible in others (Uhmann 1991; Molnár 1991; 1998; Krifka 2007; Büring 2016). As instances of the potential co-occurrence of topic and focus, cases are mentioned in which the *topic creates a part of a maximal focus domain* like in example (23) or where the *focus is part of the topic* (cf. Büring: "partial topic") as in example (24) (focus is indicated by *F*, topic by *T*, and comment by *K* for *Kommentar* in German):

(23) Q: *Gibt's was$_i$ Neues?*
        is there anything new
        'What's the news?'
     A: Ja. [F$_i$ [$_T$ *XENja*] [$_K$ *promoVIERT*]], (*und Marianne heiratet.*)
        yes   Xenja   gets a PhD   and Marianne marries
        'Yes. Xenja will get a PhD and Marianne will marry'
        (Uhmann 1991)

(24) Q: *Where are the unicorns?*
     A: [SOME]$_T$ *unicorns are* [*in the GARden*]$_F$.
        (Büring 1995)

Molnár (1998) analyses contrastive topics (indicated by *CT* below) as "topics in focus". These topics are also regarded as a kind of focus (with shifting function) by Büring (2016), when he comments on example (25):

(25) Q: *Where did Fritz buy this book?*
A: *BERTIE$_{CT}$ bought it at HARTLIEB$_{F's}$.*
(Büring 2016)

However, as emphasized by Molnár (1998), the correlation of topic and focus is not unrestricted. There are several important cases where the focus status of a constituent prevents it from serving simultaneously as a topic; a case in point is a structure where the first NP is a narrow focus associated with the nuclear accent of the sentence, like the noun phrase *a bicycle* in the cleft example (26-A):

(26) Q: *Did you buy a car?*
A: *No. It was only A BICYCLE that I bought.*

It goes without saying that this type of focus reading conflicts with topichood, since it is not possible for the nuclear focus of the sentence to assume the function of the pragmatic predication and at the same time form the element which is predicated about. However, the topiclessness of the sentence does not necessarily mean that the information-structural partition of the sentence on other levels must also be absent. In the cleft sentence (26-A) above, used as a reply to a question like (26-Q), the information of the sentence is divided into two parts where the relative clause (*that I bought*) forms the background as the counterpart to the focus (*bicycle*).

Another problematic case for the co-occurrence of focus and topic is when the potential topic of the sentence is the focus exponent (extending the focus domain over a larger part or the whole sentence) as in (27). These sentences – referred to as *thetic sentences* (as opposed to *categorical* ones) – are appropriate answers to questions like (27-Q), which "avoid imposing any presuppositions to which the answer could refer" (Sasse 1987: 521):[7]

(27) Q: *What's this noise?*
A: *The CAT is miaowing.*
(Sasse 1987)

---

[7] Elaborating Brentano's ideas (1973/1974), Kuroda (1972: 154) argues for the distinction of two fundamental judgment types, categorical and thetic judgments, characterized as follows: "the categorical judgment is assumed to consist of two separate acts, one the recognition of that which is to be made the subject, and the other, the act of affirming or denying what is expressed by the predicate about the subject". He also claims that these two types of judgments are realized in Japanese with different markers, *wa* (for categorical judgments) and *ga* (for thetic judgments). According to Kuroda, the categorical judgment (corresponding to the topic-comment division) is thus only an option.

(vi) Topic vs. illocutionary force

In recent topic research much attention has been devoted to the relation between topics and another relevant pragmatic concept, in particular speech acts (or illocutions). The idea that the topic can be a speech act goes back to Jacobs (1984), who claims in a theoretical framework based on illocutionary semantics that certain instances of topichood (see examples (28)–(30) with accented topics) create illocutions. According to him, the topic in these cases should be regarded as a FRAME operator – the illocutionary operator referring to topicality as opposed to the illocutionary operator ASSERTION, which he regards as responsible for the partition of the sentence into TOP and PRÄD:

(28) *Was Péter betrifft, so wird er dieses Jahr káum verreisen.*
 what Peter concerns so will he this year not go away
 'As for Peter, he will not go away this year.'

(29) *Die Gérda, die mag ich wirklich nicht*
 the Gerda this like I really not
 'Gerda, I don't like her at all.'

(30) *Den Franz-Jósef hat Petra nicht gewählt.*
 the Franz-Josef has Petra not chosen
 'Franz-Josef, Petra has not chosen.'

Krifka (2001: 25) argues in a similar manner that "topic selection is a speech act itself, an initiating speech act that requires a subsequent speech act (...) about the entity that was selected". Bianchi and Frascarelli (2010: 51) also assume illocutionary force for certain types of topics, identifying ABOUTNESS-topics (A-topics) as a Shift operator where "the speaker's conversational move is to signal a shift in the direction of the conversation, and hence the necessity to access a different file card in the propositional CG".

A further important task for the clarification of the relation between topichood and illocutionary force is also the examination of the force-related conditions for the distribution of topics. Since topics belong to the range of information-structural phenomena that affect conversational dynamics (Krifka's 2007 *CG management*), Bianchi and Frascarelli (2010: 51) claim that "topics are expected to appear only in clauses endowed with illocutive force, which realize a speech act implementing a conversational move" – suggesting the *Interface Root Restriction (IRR)*. However, they point out that different types of topics behave differently in this respect and the language-specific differences also have an impact on the dependence of topichood on illocutionary force.

4.2 Grammatical Coding of Topicality

As pointed out by Reinhart (1981: 62), "[t]he identification of the topic expression of a given sentence is an interesting instance of the interaction of syntactic, semantic and pragmatic considerations". Although the topic is claimed to be a pragmatic concept, semantic, syntactic, phonological, and morphological properties of the sentence may also influence or restrict the choice of the sentence topic.

(i) Topic vs. morphology
In Asian languages (e.g. Japanese, Korean) the information-structural status of constituents can be morphologically marked. Kuno (1972) analyses the particle *wa* in Japanese as a topic particle (which often co-occurs with the focus particle *ga* in the sentence). According to Kuno (1972: 270) "[*wa*] marks either the *theme* or the *contrasted element* of the sentence. The theme must be either anaphoric (i.e. previously mentioned) or generic, while there is no such constraint for the contrasted element". Kuno (1972: 271) illustrates non-contrastive *wa* in examples (31) and (32) and contrastive *wa* in example (33):

(31) <u>Kuzira wa</u> honyuu-doobutu desu. [generic]
     whale   mammal   is
     'A whale is a mammal.'

(32) <u>John wa</u> watakusi no tomoati desu. [anaphoric]
     John   I   's friend   is
     'John is my friend.'

(33) <u>Ame wa</u>   hutte   imasu ga, <u>yuki wa</u> hutte   imasen.
     rain   falling is   snow   falling is-not
     'Rain is falling, but snów is nót falling.'

The particle *nun* in Korean is also traditionally regarded as a topic marker in (34) (see Choe 1995: 282), or together with intonational prominence as in (35) as a marker of contrastive topic (CT) (see Büring 2016: 69):

(34) <u>Chelswu-nun</u>   CA-   N-   TA
     Chelswu- TOP   sleep PRES DEC
     'Chelswu sleeps.'
     'Speaking about Chelswu, he sleeps.'

(35) (*Who did what?*)
　　　[*JOE-* **nun**]_CT ca　　-ko　SUE-　**nun**　nol-　assta.
　　　 Joe　CT　　　sleep and Sue　　CT　　play PAST

It is, however, pointed out by Hetland (2007) that the particle *nun* with prominent constituents is not a necessary condition for topic status and its function should rather be captured in terms of marking alternatives typical for contrast.

(ii) Topic in syntax

Cross-linguistically, the most important formal property of topicality seems to be its syntactic position in the linear and hierarchical structure of the sentence, indicated both by empirical evidence and motivated by regularities in cognitive mechanisms (cf. Givón 1992). It is argued in several approaches to information structure that the topic preferably occurs in the left-peripheral position of the sentence, preceeding the focus (Givón 1992; Jacobs 1997; Vallduví and Engdahl 1996; É. Kiss 1987, 2002; etc.). In some theories topics are even claimed to be bound to the sentence-initial position. In a functional framework Halliday regards the topic as "the point of departure for the clause as a message" (Halliday 1967: 212) or as "the peg on which the sentence is hung" (Halliday 1970: 161). Chomsky (1965: 221) argues in an early version of generative grammar that "[i]t might be suggested that Topic-Comment is the basic grammatical relation of surface structure corresponding (roughly) to the fundamental Subject-Predicate relation of deep structure. Thus we might define the Topic-of the Sentence as the leftmost NP immediately dominated by S in the surface structure, and the Comment-of the Sentence as the rest of the string". Even if the left-peripheral position is relevant for topichood, most works do not assume a one-to-one correlation between this position and topic function.

Molnár (1991, 1998) argues that sentence-initiality can only be regarded as a necessary but by no means sufficient formal condition of topicality. Compatibility with the topic interpretation has further formal prerequisites, such as the syntactic category of the left-peripheral constituent and certain semantic properties (see the discussion above in 4.1). The judgments are somewhat controversial not only concerning the relevance of semantic properties for topichood, but also with respect to the syntax of topic. The obligatory character of the clause-initial position is estimated differently and there is no agreement on the types and number of potential syntactic positions for topics. According to an influential proposal made by Frey (2004), the prototypical topic position is not sentence-initial, but is located in the left periphery of the middle field of the

German sentence, preceding the sentence adverbial (as in example (13) above). In the analysis of Italian and Hungarian several topic positions are assumed in front of the focus constituent, and thus only one of them can be sentence-initial (Bianchi and Frascarelli 2010; É. Kiss 2002; etc.; see also Frascarelli and Hinterhölzl 2007 concerning German).

It is often pointed out both in language-specific and in typological studies that the default case for the choice of topic is the subject of the sentence (Li and Thompson 1976; Molnár 1991; Reinhart 1981; etc.). In V2-languages (e.g. German and Swedish) the Spec-CP-position at the left edge is, however, not bound to subjects, and different constituents (objects, adverbials) can be moved to this position, i.e. "topicalized". The functional effect of topicalization varies depending on language-specific properties of this movement, which are related, for example, to the type of the moved constituent and the basic word order type of the language. Whereas topicalization of non-pronominal non-subjects in German (an OV-language) from the middle field requires contrast only in special cases, it is most often marked in Swedish (a VO-language) (see Molnár and Winkler 2010).

As shown in several investigations, other special movements or structures are also used in different languages for the expression of *marked topics*. Topicalization in English can realize not only contrastive foci (35a) but also topics obligatorily bound to contrastive effects (cf. Prince 1984: 214) as in example (35b). Cleft structures in, for example, English and Swedish are also claimed to be compatible with topicality if they contain the nuclear focus in the later part of the sentence. This is illustrated by Hedberg's (2000) example (36) with a so-called "comment-clause cleft" and Huber's (2006) example with a so-called "continuous topic *it*- cleft" (37):

(35) a. *WITH ROSA Felix went to the beach.*
   b. <u>*With Rosa*</u>, *Felix went to the BEACH.*
   (Reinhart 1981)

(36) *It was the Greeks who first made wine (...)*

(37) (*Peter är min bäste vän.*)
   Peter is my best friend
   Det var han som hjälpte mig när   jag var SJUK.
   it   was him REL helped me when I   was sick

In addition to sentence-internal positions, left-peripheral structures outside the core sentence are frequently claimed to host the topic. The two main structures are left dislocation (LD) and hanging topic (HT). In LD there is no pause between the dislocated phrase and the rest of the clause, and the resumptive pronoun (RP) is a weak *d*-pronoun which appears in the prefield of the clause (38). In contrast, the typical features of HT include a pause between the hanging topic and the rest of the clause, and the resumptive element is a personal pronoun which can appear in the prefield or in the middle field of the clause (39) (see Frey's discussion and examples (38) and (39) in 2004: 207):

(38) *Den   Hans, den   mag jeder.*
     the-acc H.   RP-acc likes everyone
     'Hans, him everyone likes.'

(39) *Den   Hans, jeder   mag ihn*
     the-acc H.   everyone likes him
     'Hans, everyone likes him.'

The language-specific functional behaviour of potential topic-related structures is, however, a challenge for information structure research. Contrastive analyses of different languages show that similar structures differ with respect to their functional potential and that identical discourse functions can be rendered by different structures. As mentioned above, topicalization in English is obligatorily related to contrast, whereas this correlation is only optional in German (cf. Molnár and Winkler 2010). Frey (2004) accounts for the functional differences in the distribution of topicalization (TOP), LD, and HT in English and German, claiming that LD-Ger corresponds to TOP-Eng and HT-Ger to LD-Eng. Bianchi and Frascarelli (2010) discuss the functional and (partly also) formal differences between LD in English and clitic left dislocation (CLLD) in Italian, where CLLD can take over the functions carried by both TOP and LD in English. The differences in the function of clefts in English, German, and Swedish and their various relevance for topichood are discussed by Huber (2002, 2006).

(iii) Topic and prosodic patterns
A significant grammatical criterion for the characterization of the concept of topic is its phonological marking and, within this criterion, primarily the presence vs. the absence of a pitch accent (although the intonation contour can also be decisive).

As discussed by Molnár (1998), topics can be prosodically unmarked and in this case realized with low or middle pitch intonation contours. The most uncontroversial variant appears in sentences where the topic-comment division (TCD) correlates with the distribution of given (thematic) and new (rhematic, focal) elements in the clause. In optimal cases, the topic is not only thematic, but the TCD also corresponds to the subject-predicate structure, like in example (40-A) in the context of (40-Q) (the nuclear accent is marked by É. Kiss by an apostrophe preceding the predicate):

(40) Q: *Hogy döntött a bizottság a tervezetek ügyében?*
      how decided the committee the plans concerning
      'How did the committee decide concerning the plans?'
   A: *A bizottság 'elfogadta a javaslatot.*
      the committee accepted the proposal-ACC
      'The committee accepted the proposal.'
      (É. Kiss 1987)

Topics can, however, be prosodically marked in different ways. The binary division – the topic-comment structure – of the sentence can also be signalled by dividing the sentence into two accent domains. This is possible in integrated focus structures, i.e. with a maximal focus domain motivated by the all-new character of the utterance in the context of general information questions like in example (41). In these cases, the pitch accent (marked by capital letters) is assumed to mark primarily the categorical character (the topic-comment structure) of the sentence (as opposed to the example for theticity (see (27)), where the sentence-initial pitch accent is the nuclear accent of the sentence, marking the focus exponent):

(41) Q: *What's this noise?*
   A: *The CAT is MIAOWing.*
      (Sasse 1987)

Besides the prosodic marking of the topic-comment articulation, additional semantic and pragmatic effects can be triggered by a special prosodic pattern called "Wurzelakzent", "I-Kontur", "fall-rise", or "B-accent" in research. This bitonal L*+H or tritonal L*+H L pattern (low-high (low)) accent in the framework of autosegmental phonology has specific discourse-semantic features typical for contastive topics (see (42)–(44)).

One relevant semantic effect of the L*+H prosodic pattern (assigned to the constituent marked by v in Jacobs' work or to the constituent marked by CT (contrastive topic) in Büring's analyses) is scope inversion as shown by examples (42) and (43) below:

(42) √ALle Grass-Romane kann man \NICHT empfehlen.
 all Grass novels can one not recommend
 'Not all Grass novels can be recommended.'
 (Jacobs 1997)

(43) ALLE$_{CT}$ Politiker sind NICHT korrupt.
 all politicians are not corrupt
 'Not all politicians are corrupt.'
 (Büring 2016)

In examples (42) and (43), negation takes scope over the universal quantified expression leading to scope inversion, with the interpretation of the sentences being that *not all Grass novels can be recommended* and *not all politicians are corrupt*.

Further, CT-marking leads to a specific conventional implicature (also called "Residual Topic" by Büring 1997). This specific "Topic Implicature" only implies, but does not exclude, other relevant alternatives. "The idea is that from the mere existence of such non-excluded alternatives, a hearer can deduce that the speaker must find these alternatives potentially relevant, and at least possible (otherwise she would have explicitly excluded them, i.e. have used a focus instead)" (Büring 2016: 65). In Büring's (2003 and 2016) model, this type of implicature is conceptualized as a special strategy of inquiry by means of discourse trees. Alternative questions are claimed to arise in discourse among the CT-alternatives which are unresolved and where "at least one must be pertinent to the conversation" (Büring 2016: 65). Consider example (44):

(44) (*Do you remember where you were when you first heard about Chernobyl?*)
 I$_{CT}$ was at HOME$_F$.

"Using the CT-marking on the first person subject here [44] adds the implication that someone else's whereabouts (at the time of their learning about Chernobyl) are a pertinent question" (Büring 2016: 69).

The investigation of the formal and functional properties of this complex contour is especially dominant in recent topic research and is claimed to be the essential feature of topichood (see Büring 2016). There is, however, a caveat. This prosodic pattern is related to a certain discourse-semantic effect, but not necessarily to topichood (cf. Molnár 1998). This is illustrated by examples (45) and (46) below, where elements (a negation particle and a finite verb) are CT-marked which cannot carry the topic-function. In these cases the fall-rise contour or "I-Kontur" is only connected with "adversativity" (Jacobs

1997: 104) and indicates open questions, in contrast to Büring's and Jacobs' claim.[8]

(45) Ich habe NICHT_CT getrunken, weil ich TRAURIG_F bin.
I have not drunk because I sad am
'I didn't drink because I am sad.'
(Büring 2016)

(46) Man √MUSS das Buch \NICHT mögen (, aber man KANN).
one must the book-acc not like but one can
'You must not like the book, but you may.'
(Jacobs 1997)

A further piece of evidence for the non-topical character of this accent pattern, called *B-accent* by Jackendoff (1972) or recently *RFR (rise-fall-rise)* by Büring (2016), is that it can occur as a single accent in the sentence as in examples (47) and (48). As the nuclear accent of the sentence (marking the nuclear focus), the constituent carrying RFR is not compatible with topichood (see the discussion of the focus-restriction of topichood above):

(47) (*Did you feed the animals?*) *I fed the cat*_RFR.

(48) (*Do you want a glass of water?*) *I'll have a beer*_RFR.
(Büring 2016: 75)

The issue of prosodically marked topics, referred to as "Topics, English style", has already been discussed by Chafe (1976: 49–53). There he suggests that these instances must be distinguished from "real topics" ("Topics, Chinese style") attested in topic-prominent languages. He regards prominent topics in left dislocation (49) and topicalization structures of English (50) as "double foci of contrast", containing "possible pairings of theatrical events with certain times":

---

8 Cf. Jacobs (1997: 104): "[Mit Bürings Ansatz] wird (...) zum ersten Mal eine plausible Analyse des pragmatischen Effekts der I-Topikalisierung vorgeschlagen. Es wird erfaßt, daß die *erste Hervorhebung* bei I-Topikalisierung einen *Alternativenbezug* beinhaltet (...), aber auch, daß dieser Alternativenbezug nicht denselben Status hat wie der mit dem Fokus verbundene". [Büring's approach provides a plausible analysis of the pragmatic effects of I-topicalization for the first time. It proposes that the first highlighting in I-topicalization is related to alternatives. However, it also suggests that this relation to alternatives does not have the same status as the alternatives related to the concept of focus.] (translated by Molnár, Egerland, and Winkler).

(49) *As for the pláy, John saw it yésterday.*

(50) *Yésterday, John saw the pláy.*

Concluding the prosodic features of topicality, the following aspects of the proposed analysis should be emphasized: (i) Topics can remain unaccented, but they can also carry different types of accents which fulfil various functions. (ii) Crucially, the topic accent can never be the nuclear accent of the sentence, since the nuclear accent realizes the focus (the focus exponent or the nuclear, narrow focus) of the sentence, which is not compatible with topicality.

(iv) Variation and the limits of topic coding

As the discussion above has shown, topichood has been captured in linguistic research in many different ways. In addition to considerable cross-linguistic variation, topics have frequently been defined on the basis of different functional criteria. In particular the notion of aboutness vs. frame-setting and the non-contrastive vs. contrastive character have been evaluated differently by linguists. A further controversial issue of topic research is related to the number of possible topics in a sentence. This issue has two different aspects: (i) The first one concerns the question whether topics are obligatory and always overt or whether they can be absent or only covert. (ii) The other problematic question is the number of overt topics, i.e. whether the number of sentence topics should be restricted to a unique occurrence or whether multiple topics are possible.

The answers to the first question differ. Molnár (1998) proposes that topicality should be ruled out by "the focus-restriction of topic", that is when the clause-initial element contains the nuclear accent. This is typical for two cases: (i) when the nuclear accent indicates a narrow ("emphatic") focus, and (ii) when the nuclear accent is assigned to the focus exponent on the left periphery in thetic statements and the sentence has a maximal focus domain. Thetic sentences are often claimed in research not only to be monolithic structures but also to be topicless (Sasse 1987; Drubig 1992; Rosengren 1997). However, this view has been questioned; see, for instance, Krifka (2007: 43): "sentences may have no topic constituent at all, under which condition they are called **thetic**, following Marty (1884). But as already Marty [a follower of Brentano] had indicated, this does not mean that such sentences are about nothing. While they lack a topic constituent, they do have a topic denotation, typically a situation that is given in the context, as in [*The HOUSE is on fire*]$_{Comment}$". According to Krifka, the topic-comment division is thus obligatory even if the overt realization of topics is not required.

The views are also divided over the second question, which concerns the uniqueness of topics. The restriction to a single topic in the sentence is functionally or grammatically motivated. This view is expressed by Reinhart's (1981) metaphor for explaining aboutness topics as an entry in a library catalogue, Vallduví's (1992) link specified as an address-pointer, and Büring's (1997, 2016) prosodically anchored topic definition, which provide explanations for why at most one topic per sentence can occur. However, restricted occurrences of two or more topics are sometimes accepted in the case of an ordered set of n-elements by É. Kiss (2002) and also by Krifka (2007):

(51) *As for Jack and Jill, they married last year.*

Krifka (2008: 266) argues that a possible way to handle these cases where "a relation between two file cards is expressed (...) is to introduce a new file card that contains information concerning both Jack and Jill".

However, based on syntactic and semantic facts several linguists suggest that topichood is not restricted to a unique occurrence, but that multiple topics are also possible in languages like German, Italian, and Hungarian. Frey (2004: 99) defends the view that "[a] German clause can have more than one topic" with the following motivation: "Since only a topic can be coreferential with a cataphoric pronoun, it follows that the main clause in [52] contains two topics" (Frey 2004: 100):

(52) *Da   sie$_1$ ihn$_2$ mag,   wird Maria$_1$ Hans$_2$ wahrscheinlich helfen.*
      since she   him   likes   will   M.   H.   probably   help

Multiple topics are also held to be possible in Hungarian by Lipták (2011) and Gyuris (2016). They discuss the topical field of the Hungarian sentence in detail, where the different topic types "A-topics" (term for *aboutness topics*) and "R-topics" (term for *Rahmentopik, delimitation*) can occur at the same time, with different constraints on their order.

Frascarelli and Hinterhölzl (2007) as well as Bianchi and Frascarelli (2010) argue for the existence of multiple topics in Italian, taking syntactic and prosodic evidence into consideration. They distinguish several topic types, "A-topics" (aboutness topics), "C-topics" (contrastive topics), and "G-topics" (given topics), which are ordered in a strict hierarchy in the C-domain (as opposed to the free recursion analysis of TOP-projection in Rizzi's 1997 cartographic model). The three topic types are not only different with respect to their functions but are also related to different prosodic patterns (L*+H, H*, and L*).

Moreover, only G-topics are claimed to be recursive (marked by * on the projection FamP below):

(53) [ShiftP A-Topic [ContrP C-Topic [FocP [FamP* G-Topic [FinP [IP
     L*+H   H*   L*

The discussion shows that the answers to both questions (concerning the obligatory character of topichood as well as the uniqueness issue) are central to the current research and they are accordingly addressed in the contributions of this book.

4.3 Topic Typology: Universal Topic Features and Cross-Linguistic Variation

(i) Definition – universal characterization of topics

After having accounted for the discourse-semantic and grammatical properties of topichood, the question arises whether it is possible to provide a uniform definition of the concept of topic despite the diversity of its cross-linguistic features and considerable differences in its theoretical analyses. In recent research, the answer is not seldom negative (see Jacobs 2001; Roberts 2011; Büring 2016). Similarly to Jacobs' (2001) sceptical view discussed above (see section 4.1.), Roberts (2011: 1908, also quoted by Büring 2016) calls into question a possible generalization: "[although] there may be many common factors, in the end it appears that what these various conventions realize is a family of closely related notions, rather than a syntactic or pragmatic universal". Moreover, Büring (2016: 85) warns against attempts to provide a unified definition: "the notion of 'topic' (without 'contrastive') should be used with great caution"; he makes "a plea to refrain from using the notion altogether, and [to] characterize 'topic'-markings independently". However, as argued by Molnár (2006: 207) elaborating Chafe's idea (suggested only for "Topics, Chinese style"), a uniform account of topichood seems plausible:

> Topics serve, namely, in one sense or another to optimally restrict the domain of the main predication in the sentence drawing the speech participants' attention to a certain entity. They can fulfil this function in two different ways: Either in an unmarked way by choosing a salient entity already in the focus of attention of the hearer/speaker, or by directing attention to this entity by highlighting the entity, in which case the co-occurrence with focus should be thinkable.

Moreover, even if the pragmatic dimension is considered to have crucial relevance for the definition of topichood, the notion of topic is claimed to be closely related to grammar, being dependent on the presence of certain formal features (see also Molnár 1998). For most investigated languages the left periphery of the sentence plays a decisive role in the realization of topichood, whereas the prosodic patterns show a greater variability since topics can remain unaccented and are compatible with different accent types.

(ii) Topic typology

Not only the universal definition of topics is a challenge for linguistic research, but also the description of the limits of the variation and the specification of different topic types attested in various languages.

Sentence topic vs. discourse topic
An important distinction concerning the notion of topic is the domain that topichood is related to. The role of topic in the discourse structure has been investigated in a large number of theories in recent decades (Daneš 1967; Klein and von Stutterheim 1991, 2002; Roberts 1996; Büring 2003, 2016; Chiarcos 2010, 2011; Givón 1983; the *Centering Theory* of Grosz, Joshi and Weinstein 1995). The definition of 'discourse topics' seems, however, to be a challenge for the theory on information structure. Stede (2004: 242) mentions four different groups of theoretical approaches, which "are not entirely unrelated but nonetheless quite distinct". The notion of discourse topic is defined (i) in terms of aboutness, (ii) as an over-arching 'theme', (iii) as an 'ideal question' that readers can construct, or (iv) as a proposition that readers have to actively construct.

Crucially, topichood on the discourse level has an impact on the global stucture of the text, whereas the sentence-internal structuring into topic and comment is a local issue. Consequently, the definitions of two topic types – 'discourse topics' and 'sentence topics' – are based on different criteria (cf. Molnár and Vinckel-Roisin in this volume). For sentence topics the appropriate marking of topichood within the sentence (aboutness or frame-setting for the predication) is essential, and the correlation with discourse-semantic features like givenness and familiarity (and also referentiality, specificity) of the entity as well as early mentioning in the left periphery is preferable. In contrast, discourse topics operate beyond the sentence level and their operationalization requires the consideration of more complex discourse properties, like for example persistency of certain elements (i.e. their occurrence in a large number of segments of the text) to indicate relevance for the whole text (Givón 1983).

Types of sentence topics
The cross-linguistic diversity of sentence topics as well as the range of possible topic types within specific languages have led to different categorizations of topics in different approaches. The typology of topics suggested in research is based on different criteria, including different pragmatic properties and various aspects of grammatical coding. The most often mentioned aspects of categorization are the distinction between (i) sentence-external and sentence-internal topics, (ii) aboutness-topics vs. frame-setters, (iii) topics bound to givenness vs. context-independent topics, and (iv) contrastive topics vs. non-contrastive topics. The proposed topic types or distinctions are generally based on specific properties of topic-related structures attested in a certain language. A further problem for the establishment of a topic typology is the combination and/or overlap of different discourse-semantic and grammatical features: both aboutness-topics and frame-topics can be given or new, non-contrastive or contrastive, and sentence-externally or sentence-internally realized. The tripartite division of topichood suggested by Frascarelli and Hinterhölzl (2007) and Bianchi and Frascarelli (2010) motivated both by the syntactic distribution and specific prosodic patterns is an attempt at a systematic analysis of different possible topic types in Italian, German, and English (see (53) above in 4.2). However, the function and grammatical features of A-(*aboutness*)-topics, C-(*contrastive*)-topics, and G-(*given*)-topics in different languages need more investigation. An important question in recent research is also the compatiblity of different topic types with root contexts.

5 Inventory of Claims and Problems

In this introduction to the *Architecture of Topic* we have pointed out the burning issues of topic research. This included the question of the linguistic relevance of topic, its theoretical anchoring in linguistic theory (in Grammar or Discourse), as well as the discourse-semantic and cross-linguistically attested grammatical properties of this concept. We have argued for the linguistic relevance of topic and discussed the arguments which support or refute the usefulness of a uniform definition of topics. We have proposed an approach where topichood is regarded as an inherently discourse-semantic concept – as a pragmatic restrictor in the utterance that the predication can be based on. We have argued for the possibility of delimiting the discourse-semantic domain of topicality and regarding it as applicable in all languages, but we have also accounted for the necessity of the differentiation of this concept, distinguishing topicality on the level of discourse and sentence. Further, it has also seemed relevant to identify various topic types motivated by their close relation to different discourse properties. Last but not least, we have also claimed in our interface approach that the discourse-semantically anchored concept of topichood is dependent on linguistic realization and requires various linguistic means in different languages. According to our view, a satisfactory theoretical and empirical analysis of topichood presupposes that both the interplay of discourse and grammar and the relation between universal topic features and cross-linguistic variation are taken into consideration.

In the previous four sections we have provided an overview of the most important results of linguistic theory including a set of open questions and challenges for future research. Concerning the question related to the *discourse-semantic properties of topichood*, the question of the context-dependence of topic (and its relation to givenness), our analysis included the following issues: the relation between topic and focus and topic and contrast, the relevance of referentiality, and the possibility of quantification, as well as the dependence of topicality on illocutionary force (and the root character of the sentence).

The *grammatical coding of topichood* focused on the morphological, syntactic, and prosodic means of topicality in different languages. In the syntactic structure of many European languages, the left periphery (outside or inside the core sentence) is regarded as relevant, leading also to the topic-focus order. The prosodic patterns of topicality show considerable variation, and the topic prosody seems only to respect the restriction that the topic cannot carry the nuclear accent of the sentence. Morphology also plays an important role in signalling topicality, by providing means for different types and degrees of determination (in the article and pronominal system in several European languages) and by providing morphological markers in Asian languages.

Several *other controversial questions* were addressed in connection with topicality. As we have seen, there are different proposals concerning the issue whether the topic is an obligatory or optional category, whether its realization should be overt, excluding covert instances. The question concerning the number of possible topics in a sentence is also open, since it is argued both for the view that topic is a unique category and for the opposite claim that multiple topics are acceptable. Further, both the possibility of a universally valid topic concept and the typology of topicality constitute one of the core challenges of this research field, since topics within and across languages show different discourse-semantic properties closely related to their grammatical coding.

6 Contributions to the Architecture of Topic Volume

The goal of this volume is to address the above-mentioned questions related to topicality and provide comprehensive answers by studying the interface between discourse and grammar. The mapping of grammatical (syntactic and prosodic) structures and discourse-semantic interpretations is of central relevance in all the articles, although the points of departure for the analyses differ. They apply different perspectives, including contrastive studies of modern languages, studies on diachronic development, and typological generalizations. They also take into consideration various types of empirical data – introspective data, semi-spontaneously produced data, experimental data, and language corpora. The basic underlying idea is that there are universal properties of topichood but that there may be cross-linguistic variation at the same time. The main goal is to provide a uniform definition of topicality but also to show the range of the discourse-semantic and grammatical variation of topics in different European languages. An additional aim is to show that the concept of topic is necessary for the description and explanation of a number of discourse-semantic phenomena.

The articles of this volume are presented and structured according to the central rationale that topicality at the grammar-discourse interface can be analysed from two perspectives, departing from either linguistic functions or linguistic forms. Whereas in several works information-structural and semantic notions and functions (such as givenness, discourse anaphoricity, binding relations, topicality, and illocutionary force) serve as a point of departure or tertium comparationis, showing various grammatical representations in different languages (see the articles of Rochemont, Hinterhölzl, Frey and Meinunger, Frascarelli in PART I), others concentrate on certain forms and structures such as topicalization, left dislocation, "unbracketing", right dislocation, certain clause types, and topic positions whose realizations fulfil information-structural and other discourse-semantic functions (cf. the articles of Culicover and Winkler, De Kuthy and Konietzko, Erteschik-Shir, Sigurðsson, Egerland, Molnár and Vinckel-Roisin in PART II). The investigations of the semantic and pragmatic correlates of topicality on the one hand and the special grammatical strategies of topic realization on the other not only focus on modern languages but also include studies of diachronic change (see the articles of Speyer, Molnár in PART III).

(i) PART I – Semantic and Discourse-Pragmatic Correlates of Topicality

The first two papers of this section concentrate on different discourse-pragmatic and semantic correlates of topicality. They also account for the prosodic and syntactic coding of different topic types, analysing instances of (de)accentuation and secondary occurrences of focus.

In his article *Topic and Givenness*, **Michael Rochemont** explores the relationship between topics and givenness, and specifically, the hypothesis that deaccenting is directly a function of topichood. He argues that the givenness condition on topics and the one on deaccenting derive from distinct notions of givenness and should not be confused. He suggests that two forms of givenness should be distinguished, one based on familiarity, the other on salience. Where relevant, topics depend on one form of givenness (familiarity), which also yields the requirement that topics are referential. In contrast, the other form of givenness (salience) requires deaccenting, which is dependent on coreference to or entailment by a discourse antecedent (Schwarzschild's GIVENness). Rochemont also advances a new procedure for GIVENness calculation, which yields an account not only of non-focused deaccented expressions but also of the specific deaccenting of Second Occurrence Focus expressions.

Roland Hinterhölzl addresses the role of topics in the licensing of anaphoric relations in his paper on *The Role of Topics in Licensing Anaphoric Relations in VP-ellipsis*. He argues that the C-domain plays a crucial role in accounting for valid and invalid cases of coreference. In particular, it is argued that a contrastive topic rather than focus as proposed by Rooth (1992) accounts for the presence of sloppy and strict readings in cases of VP-ellipsis. The discussion of the data is exclusively concerned with anaphoric relations in English (with a minor comparison of parallel facts in German). As far as the architecture of topics is concerned, it is argued that even in languages like English, where discourse-given elements remain in their positions, these elements enter into an Agree-relation with a Topic head in the C-domain. The paper thus provides strong cross-linguistic evidence for the presence of topic positions in the C-domain even in languages like English that are not discourse configurational like Italian or German. A further relevant claim of the paper is that a syntactic account of coreference is superior to a pragmatic account in terms of a complex evaluation of binding alternatives at LF as it is generally assumed in the standard approach.

The next two papers of the second section (in PART I) investigate the relation between topicality and another relevant discourse-pragmatic dimension – illocutionary force. In order to account for the complexity of cases they both argue for the differentiation of topicality on the one hand and for a more fine-grained distinction of different sentence types on the other.

The main claim of **Werner Frey and André Meinunger's** article *Topic Marking and Illocutionary Force* is that only certain types of topic require illocutionary force in German and English (e.g. left dislocation) whereas the conditions of topic marking are flexible in other cases of topicality (e.g. can be achieved by topicalization). The investigation includes four types of topic marking constructions and three types of embedded clauses. A three-way distinction is suggested: some of the instances of topic marking (e.g. in the case of *aboutness topics*) are weakly root sensitive, i.e. they have an intermediate status, others can only be hosted by a clause with full illocutionary force, and still others may occur in any kind of clause. The analysis shows that the three-way distinction is also valid for other non-truth-functional/non-descriptive phenomena (e.g. question tags, expressive interjections, modal particles, expressively coloured expressions). A central theoretical goal of the paper is to characterize the property of being weakly root sensitive (relating it to the concept of 'common ground management') and thereby to gain some insights about the semantic/pragmatic properties which a clause must have in order to make the marking of an aboutness topic possible.

In her paper *Topics, Conversational Dynamics and the Root/Non-root Distinction: Adverbial Clauses at the Discourse-syntax Interface*, **Mara Frascarelli** analyses the occurrence of different topic types in Italian (Aboutness-Shift Topic, Contrastive Topic, and Givenness Topic) in adverbial clauses, investigating original Italian data. A novel perspective sheds new light on the syntactic mapping and the formal properties of central vs. peripheral adverbial clauses, and the proposal is embedded in a cartographic framework. Frascarelli argues for the dependence of different instances of topicality on clause complexity (based on the root/non-root distinction) and for the Interface Root Restriction, according to which phenomena that affect the conversational dynamics must occur in clauses endowed with illocutionary Force. Based on the assumption of lack of Force in "central" adverbial clauses, the exclusion of A(boutness)-Topics and the presence of C(ontrastive)- and G(iven)-Topics can be accounted for.

(ii) PART II – Variation in the Grammatical Encoding of Topicality: Clause-Internal, Clause- External, and Null Topics

The first two articles in PART II investigate specific instances of topicalization and their relation to the pragmatic function of topicality in different Germanic languages.

Peter Culicover and Susanne Winkler discuss different discourse constraints on VP topicalization in English and German in their article *Why Topicalize VP?*, and also address questions related to the syntactic analysis of the phenomenon. In their contrastive analysis they are especially interested in the explanation of the language-specific differences in the field of VP topicalization. The key aspect of their proposal is that the explanation for this movement does not have to do with what is in initial position. The constituent in initial position must be interpreted in such a way that the sentence is coherent with the preceding discourse, and this can happen in a number of ways. What is crucial is that what is left behind in final position is in focus. According to their hypothesis there are two motivations for VP topicalization: (i) movement of the VP to the left satisfies the need to isolate focus at the right edge of the sentence (as suggested in Culicover and Winkler 2008); (ii) the topicalized constituent connects to the previous discourse and therefore falls under general constraints of discourse coherence.

In their paper *Information-structural Constraints on PP Topicalization from NPs* **Kodula De Kuthy and Andreas Konietzko** account for PP extraction from complex NPs in German such as *[Aus Tübingen]$_i$ haben [mehrere Studenten t$_i$] am Forschungswettbewerb teilgenommen* ('From Tübingen have several students in the research contest participated'). Extractions from complex NPs are difficult to capture since they are subject to various restrictions related to the syntactic status of the extracted PP, the semantic relation between the verb and the complex NP, as well as the type of verb involved. The authors argue that supposedly syntactic restrictions on extraction from NPs follow from particular information-structural conditions. As a result of this detailed information-structural analysis it is shown that the topicalized PP (or parts of this PP) always functions as a contrastive topic, while the remnant NP always functions as the focus of the entire sentence. They can also show that such specific conditions of the information structure of PP topicalization impose requirements on the preceding context of the construction, for example that the appropriate alternative sets for the fronted PP and the remnant NP have to be introduced. In order to account for the discourse properties of the construction, they present an account anchored in the *Questions under Discussion* (QUD) approach to information structure. The proposed QUD analysis is based on attested data from corpora, which is supplemented by experimental evidence.

The two papers of the second section (in PART II) address the controversial question concerning the obligatory vs. optional character of topic realization. **Nomi Erteschik-Shir** argues in her article *Stage Topics and their Architecture* that all-focus sentences in English and Danish have implicit "stage" topics indicating the spatio-temporal parameters of the sentence, the here-and-now of the discourse. Such stage topics can provide the main topic of the sentence and can also appear as the topics of subordinate clauses. It is also argued in this paper that the properties of stage topics seem to require a non-syntactic account of IS. It is claimed that they are superior to syntactic theories of IS such as Rizzi (1997) and the following research based on his initial insights that require a plethora of often language-specific IS features to explain word order across languages. Erteschik-Shir strongly argues that pursuing her line of thought may lead to a simpler computational system, freeing it from the onus of explaining gradient data and (cross-linguistic) variation. At the same time, she also claims that a coherent view of information structure and its integration into a model of grammar is required to fulfil this mission.

Halldór Ármann Sigurðsson concentrates in his paper *Topicality in Icelandic: Null Arguments and Narrative Inversion* on topicality in Icelandic grammar and discusses the discourse-pragmatic and syntactic constraints on the null realization of topics. Null topics appear in several phenomena from different periods of Icelandic: referential third person *pro* drop in Old Icelandic, diverse types of topic drop in Old and Modern Icelandic, and Narrative Inversion (declarative VS clauses), also in both Old and Modern Icelandic. These phenomena all involve Aboutness Topics, Given Topics, or both, thus showing that distinct types of topicality are active in Icelandic. However, in contrast to Italian, Icelandic does not provide evidence that different topic types have different structural correlates. This fact indicates that topicality types are not generally structuralized in language (while not excluding that a topicality hierarchy may be PF-licensed by externalization properties specific to languages like Italian). It is also suggested that topicality is presumably a universally available phenomenon, but it is plausibly an interface third factor phenomenon (in the sense of Chomsky 2005), not provided by Universal Grammar but interacting with it in the shaping of externalized grammar, differently so in different languages.

The two papers of the third section (in PART II) investigate strictly edge-related instances of topic marking. Exploring the interface between syntax, discourse structure, and salience, they concentrate on the establishment of certain relations between the local topic of the clause and the discourse topic. In his article *Apropos the Topic – On Topic-introducing Expressions in Swedish*, **Verner Egerland** investigates the syntactic and discourse-semantic properties of Swedish "topic markers" such as *apropå* 'apropos' and *beträffande* 'concerning'. He argues that these expressions have a different syntactic behaviour than other syntactic construction types like topicalization, left dislocation, or hanging topic on the left periphery of the clause. They are claimed to represent a fourth construction type. Egerland also convincingly shows that the topic markers *apropå* and *beträffande* also differ in their information-structural functions: they lexicalize pragmatical features such as *aboutness* and *givenness* in different ways.

In their study *Discourse Topic vs. Sentence Topic – Exploiting the Right Periphery of German Verb-second Sentences* **Valéria Molnár and Hélène Vinckel-Roisin** discuss different types of topichood and their relation to the edge positions of the German sentence at the syntax-discourse interface. Special attention is paid to the discourse-pragmatic properties of two right-peripheral structures, 'extraposition' and 'right-dislocation', and their relevance for the expression of topichood on the discourse level. The analysis is based on the key notion of 'mental salience' and its different types as suggested by Chiarcos (2010) in the *Mental Salience Framework*. On the basis of a corpus collected from German contemporary newspapers (*Frankfurter Allgemeine Zeitung* and *Süddeutsche Zeitung*), they show that these two right-peripheral syntactic strategies can have the same discourse function, despite different syntactic and prosodic/typographic features. They indicate that the referent of the right-peripheral constituent (NP or PP) is salient and highly relevant for the whole discourse. It functions as the 'discourse topic referent', i.e. the discourse referent that is most stably activated in the mental representation of each discourse segment. They show that both investigated strategies are relevant 'forward-looking' devices imposing certain constraints on the subsequent (or previous) discourse segment(s).

(iii) PART III – Topics from the Diachronic Perspective

The last part of the volume includes two investigations of diachronic development and variation in the field of topicality.

Based on historical corpora, **Augustin Speyer** claims in his article *Topichood and the Margins of the German Clause from a Historical Perspective* that both the left periphery (the prefield) and the right periphery (the postfield) in German clauses have been subject to changes in the history of German. The changes can be linked to changes in the correlation to information-structural values: in both cases, the correlation to information-structural values is loosened up. According to Speyer's analysis, the content of the two clause-peripheral positions, the left-peripheral prefield and the right-peripheral postfield of the German sentence, is determined by information-structural constraints. A closer look into the history of German reveals that the prefield, which is often seen as the topic position, started as a position specialized for familiar aboutness topics in pre-Old High German, but it became more permissive over time, eventually allowing anything that establishes a link to the context. Likewise, the postfield, a designated position for constituents bearing presentational focus, widened its application range to anything that bears some focus (including contrastive foci). The development of the fields towards less information-structural specialization is interpreted as a process of 'bleaching', in that the semanto-pragmatic feature content of elements that are compatible with the fields has been reduced, until only few features are left.

In the paper *Stylistic Fronting at the Interface of Syntax and Discourse*, **Valéria Molnár** presents a novel analysis of the discourse-semantic properties of the phenomenon called "Stylistic Fronting", comparing Icelandic with Romance languages and challenging the widely held view that Stylistic Fronting has no discourse-semantic effects in Icelandic, but is related to topic or focus interpretation in Romance. It is argued that Stylistic Fronting (SF) is not simply triggered by formal features but has relevance for information structure in both Romance and Scandinavian. The impact of SF on discourse interpretation is, however, dependent on the type of syntactic derivation. In Icelandic, the "stylistic" movement can be either a locally (and information-structurally) restricted "formal movement" (*STYL-Inversion*) into the subject gap without changing the IS-properties of the moved constituent or a "true" discourse-triggered movement (*STYL-Preposing*) with an obligatory contrastive effect. Since SF also seems to vary with respect to syntactic properties and discourse interpretation in Romance, the triggers and interpretive properties of SF in Scandinavian seem not to be as different from those in Romance as generally suggested in the literature.

References

Abrusán, Márta & Kriszta Szendrői. 2011. Experimenting with the King of France. In *Logic, Language and Meaning*. 18th Amsterdam Colloqium. Amsterdam, The Netherlands, December 19–21, 2011, 102–111. Springer.
Aissen, Judith L. 1992. Topic and Focus in Mayan. *Language* 68(1). 43–80.
Allwood, Jens, Lars-Gunnar Andersson & Östen Dahl. 1977. *Logic in Linguistics*. Cambridge: Cambridge University Press.
Beghelli, Fillipo & Tim Stowell. 1997. Distributivity and negation. The syntax of *each* and *every*. In Anna Szabolcsi (ed.), *Ways of scope taking*, 71–107. Kluwer Academic Publishers.
Bergen, Geertje van & Helene de Hoop. (eds.). 2009. Topics cross-linguistically. *The Linguistic Review* 26 (2/3).
Bianchi, Valentina & Mara Frascarelli. 2010. Is topic a root phenomenon? *Iberia: An International Journal of Theoretical Linguistics* 2. 43–88.

Büring, Daniel. 1995. The great scope inversion conspiracy. In Mandy Simons and Teresa Galloway (eds.), *Proccedings of SALT 5* (1995), 37–53. Austin, Texas.
Büring, Daniel. 1997. *The 59th street bridge accent*. London: Routledge.
Büring, Daniel. 2003. On d-trees, beans, and b-accents. *Linguistics and Philosophy* 26(5). 511–545.
Büring, Daniel. 2016. (Contrastive) Topic. In Caroline Féry & Shinichiro Ishihara (eds.), *The Oxford handbook of information structure*, 64–85. Oxford: University Press.
Chafe, Wallace L. 1976. Givenness, contrastiveness, definiteness, subjects, topics, and point of view. In Charles Li (ed.), *Subject and topic*, 25–55. New York: Academic Press.
Chiarcos, Christian. 2010. *Mental salience and grammatical form. Toward a framework for salience in natural language generation*. Potsdam: University dissertation. http://www.academia.edu/785120/Mental_Salience_and_Grammatical_Form_Toward_a_Framework_for_Salience_Metrics_in_Natural_Language_Generation (accessed 24 July 2017).
Chiarcos, Christian. 2011. The mental salience framework: Context-adequate generation of referring expressions. In Christian Chiarcos, Berry Claus & Michael Grabski (eds.), *Salience. Multidisciplinary perspectives on its function in discourse*, 105–140. Berlin & New York: Mouton de Gruyter.
Choe, Hyon Sook. 1995. Focus and topic movement in Korean and licensing. In Katalin É. Kiss (ed.), Discourse-configurational languages, 269–334. Oxford: Oxford University Press.
Chomsky, Noam. 1965. *Aspects of the theory of syntax*. Cambridge, MA: The MIT Press.
Chomsky, Noam. 1972. Deep structure, surface structure, and semantic interpretation. Studies on Semantics in Generative Grammar, 62–119. The Hague: Mouton.
Chomsky, N. 2000. *On nature and language*. New York: Cambridge. University Press.
Chomsky, Noam. 2005. Three factors in language design. *Linguistic Inquiry* 36. 1–22.
Clark, Herbert H. & Susan E. Haviland. 1977. Comprehension and the given-new contract. In Freedle, Roy O. (ed.), *Discourse production and comprehension*, 1–40. Norwood, NJ: Ablex Publishing.
Clark, Herbert H. & Eve V. Clark. 1977. *Psychology and language*. New York: Harcourt, Brace Jovanovich.
Culicover, Peter & Susanne Winkler. 2008. English focus inversion. *Journal of Linguistics* 44(3). 625–658.
Dahl, Östen. 1969. *Topic and comment* (Acta Universitatis Gothoburgansis, volume 4). Almqvist & Wiksell.
Dahl, Östen. 1974. Topic-comment structure revisited. In Östen Dahl (ed.), *Topic and comment, contextual boundedness and focus* (Papiere zur Textlinguistik 6), 1–24. Hamburg: Helmut Buske Verlag.
Daneš, František. 1967. Order of elements and sentence intonation. In *To Honor Roman Jakobson: Essays on the occasion of his seventieth birthday, 11 October 1966*, 500–512. The Hague, Paris: Mouton de Gruyter.
Dik, Simon C. 1978. *Functional grammar* (North-Holland Linguistic Series 37). Amsterdam: North-Holland Publishing Company.
Drubig, Bernhard. 1992. Zur Frage der grammatischen Repräsentation thetischer und kategorischer Sätze. In Joachim Jacobs (ed.), *Informationsstruktur und Grammatik*, 142–195. Opladen: Wetsdeutscher Verlag.
É. Kiss. 1987. *Configurationality in Hungarian*. Budapest: Akadémiai Kiadó.
É. Kiss, Katalin. 1992. Move-alpha and scrambling in Hungarian. In István Kenesei & Csaba Pléh (eds.), *Approaches to Hungarian, vol. 4: The structure of Hungarian*, 67–98. Szeged: JATE.

É. Kiss, Katalin. 2002. *The syntax of Hungarian*. Cambridge: Cambridge Academic Press.
É. Kiss, Katalin 2006. Focussing as predication. In Valéria Molnár & Susanne Winkler (eds.), *The architecture of focus* (Studies in Generative Syntax 82), 169–193. Berlin & New York: Mouton de Gruyter.
Endriss, Cornelia. 2009. *Quantificational topics. A scopal treatment of exceptional wide scope phenomena*. Dordrecht: Springer.
Féry, Caroline & Shinichiro Ishihara (eds.). 2016. *The Oxford handbook of information structure*. Oxford: Oxford University Press.
Frascarelli, Mara & Roland Hinterhölzl. 2007. Types of topics in German and Italian. In Kerstin Schwabe & Susanne Winkler (eds.), *On information structure, meaning and form: generalizations across languages* (Linguistik aktuell/Linguistics Today 100), 87–116. Amsterdam & Philadelphia: John Benjamins.
Frey, Werner. 2004. A medial topic position for German. *Linguistische Berichte* 198. 153–190.
Frey, Werner. 2006. Contrast and movement to the German prefield. In Valéria Molnár & Susanne Winkler (eds.), *The architecture of focus*, 235–264. Berlin & New York: Mouton de Gruyter.
Frey, Werner. 2010. A-bar movement and conventional implicatures: About the grammatical encoding of emphasis in German. *Lingua* 2010 (120–6). 1416–1435.
Gabelentz, Georg von der. 1891. *Die Sprachwissenschaft, ihre Aufgaben, Methoden und bisherigen Ergebnisse*. Leipzig: Tauchnitz.
Givón, Talmy. 1983. *Topic continuity in discourse*. Amsterdam & Philadelphia: John Benjamins.
Givón, Talmy. 1992. The grammar as referential coherence as mental processing instructions. *Linguistics*. 30(1). 5–56.
Grosz, Barbara J., Aravind K. Joshi & Scott Weinstein. 1995. Centering: A framework for modelling the local coherence of discourse. *Computational Linguistics* 21(2). 203–225.
Gundel, Jeanette K. 1974. *The role of topic and comment in linguistic theory*. Austin: University of Texas at Austin PhD dissertation.
Gundel, Jeanette. 1988. Universals of topic-comment. In Michael Hammond, Edith Moravcsik & Jessica R. Wirth (eds.), *Studies in syntactic typology*, 209–239. Amsterdam & Philadelphia: John Benjamins.
Gyuris, Beata. 2016. Topiktests und Topikpositionen im Ungarischen: Ergebnisse und theoretische Bewertung einer Korpusanalyse. In Martine Dalmas, Cathrine Fabricius-Hansen & Horst Schwinn (eds.), *Variation im europäischen Kontrast. Untersuchungen zum Satzanfang im Deutschen, Französischen, Italienischen, Norwegischen, Polnischen und Ungarischen*, 157–188. Berlin & New York: Mouton de Gruyter.
Haftka, Brigitta. 1995. Syntactic positions for topic and contrastive focus in the German Middlefield. In Inga Kohlhoff (ed.), *Proccedings of the Göttinger Focus Workshop* (Arbeitsberichte des Sonderforschungsbereichs 340 Nr. 69), 1–24. University of Tübingen.
Halliday, Michael A. K. 1967. Notes on transitivity and theme in English. Part 2. *Journal of Linguistics* 3(2). 199–244.
Halliday, Michael A. K. 1970. Language structure and language function. In John Lyons (ed.), *New horizons in linguistics*, 140–165. Harmondsworth: Penguin.
Hauser, Marc D., Noam Chomsky & Tecumseh W. Fitch. 2002. The faculty of language: What is it, who has it, and how did it evolve? *Science* 198. 1569–79.
Hedberg, Nancy. 2000. The referential status of clefts. *Language* 76. 891–920.

Hetland, Jorunn. 2007. The Korean particle *nun*, the English fall-rise accent and the thetic/categorical judgments. In Kerstin Schwabe & Susanne Winkler (eds.), *On information structure, meaning and form*, 117–127. Amsterdam & Philadelphia: John Benjamins.

Heusinger von, Klaus, Claudia Maienborn & Paul Portner (eds.). 2012. *Semantics: An international handbook of natural language meaning*. (Handbücher zur Sprach- und Kommunikationswissenschaft/[Handbooks of Linguistics and Communication Science] 33.1.). Berlin & New York: De Gruyter Mouton.

Heycock, Caroline. 2008. Japanese *-wa*, *-ga*, and information structure. In Shigeru Miyagawa & Mamoru Saito (eds.), *The Oxford handbook of Japanese linguistics*, 54–83. Oxford: Oxford University Press.

Hintikka, Jaakko. 1973. *Logic, language-games and information*. Oxford: Clarendon Press Oxford.

Hockett, Charles, F. 1958. 1963. *A course in modern linguistics*. New York: Macmillan.

Horn, Laurence R. 1989. *A natural history of negation*. Chicago: Chicago University Press.

Huang, C. T. James. 1982. Move *wh* in a language without *wh*-movement. *Linguistic Review* 1. 369–417.

Huber, Stefan. 2002. *Es-Clefts und det-Clefts. Zur Syntax, Semantik und Informationsstruktur von Spaltsätzen im Deutschen und Schwedischen* (Lunder germanistische Forschungen 64). Stockholm: Almquist & Wiksell International.

Huber, Stefan. 2006. The complex functions of *it*-clefts. In Valéria Molnár & Susanne Winkler (eds.), *The architecture of focus*, 549–578. Berlin & New York: Mouton de Gruyter.

Jackendoff, Ray. 1972. *Semantic interpretation in generative grammar*. Cambridge, MA: MIT Press.

Jacobs, Joachim. 1984. Funktionale Satzperspektive und Illokutionssemantik. *Linguistische Berichte* 91. 25–58.

Jacobs, Joachim. 1997. I-Topikalisierung. *Linguistische Berichte* 168. 91–133.

Jacobs, Joachim. 2001. The dimensions of topic-comment. *Linguistics* 39. 641–681.

Klein, Wolfgang & Christiane von Stutterheim. 1991. Text structure and referential movement. *Arbeitsberichte des Forschungsprogramms Sprache und Pragmatik* 22. 1-32.

Klein, Wolfgang & Christiane von Stutterheim. 2002. Quaestio and L-perspectivation. In Carl Friedrich Graumann & Werner Kallmeyer (eds.), *Perspective and perspectivation in discourse*, 59–88. Amsterdam & Philadelphia: John Benjamins.

Krifka, Manfred. 2001. Quantifying into question acts. *Natural Language Semantics* 9(1). 1–40.

Krifka, Manfred. 2007. Basic notions of information structure. In Caroline Féry, Gisbert Fanselow & Manfred Krifka (eds.), *Interdisciplinary studies on information structure* 6, 13–55. Potsdam.

Krifka, Manfred. 2008. Basic notions of information structure. *Acta Linguistica Hungarica* 55. 243–276.

Krifka, Manfred & Renate Musan. 2012. Information structure: overview and linguistic issues. In Manfred Krifka & Renate Musan (eds.), *The expression of information structure* (The Expression of Cognitive Categories 5), 1–43. Berlin & New York.

Kučerová, Ivana & Ad Neeleman. 2012. Introduction. In Ivana Kučerová and Ad Neeleman (eds.) *Contrast and positions in information structure*, 1–26. Cambridge: Cambridge University Press.

Kuno, Susumo, 1972. Functional sentence perspective. *Linguistic Inquiry* 3. 269–320.

Kuroda, S.-Y. 1972. The categorical and the thetic judgment: Evidence from Japanese syntax. *Foundations of Language* 9. 153–185.

Lambrecht, Knud. 1994. *Information structure and sentence form. Topic, focus, and the mental representation of discourse referents*. Cambridge: Cambridge University Press.

Li, Charles N. & Sandra A. Thompson. 1976. Subject and topic: a new typology of language. In Charles N. Li (ed.), *Subject and topic* (Syntax and Semantics 12), 457–489. London & New York: Academic Press.

Lipták, Anikó. 2011. The structure of the topic field in Hungarian. In Paola Benincà & Nicola Munaro (eds.), *Mapping the left periphery. The cartography of syntactic structures* (Oxford Studies in Comparative Syntax, volume 5), 163–198. Oxford: Oxford University Press.

Marty, Anton. 1884. Über subjektslose Sätze und das Verhältnis der Grammatik zu Logik und Psychologie. *Vierteljahresschrift für wissenschaftliche Philosophie*.

Mathesius, Vilém. 1929 (1975). Zur Satzperspektive im modernen Englisch. *Archiv für das Studium der neueren Sprachen und Literaturen* 155. 202–210.

Mathesius, Vilém. 1975. *A functional analysis of present day English on a general linguistic basis*. Hague & Paris: Mouton de Gruyter.

Molnár, Valéria. 1991. *Das TOPIK im Deutschen und im Ungarischen* (Lunder germanistische Forschungen 58). Stockholm: Almquist & Wiksell International.

Molnár, Valéria. 1998. Topic in focus. On the syntax, phonology, semantics and pragmatics of the so-called 'constrastive topic' in Hungarian and German. *Acta Linguistica Hungarica*, vol. 45 (1–2), 1–77. Dordrecht: Kluwer Academic Publishers & Budapest: Akadémiai Kiadó.

Molnár, Valéria. 2002. Contrast – From a contrastive perspective. In Hilde Hasselgård, Stig Johansson, Bergliot Behrens & Cathrine Fabricius-Hansen (eds.), *Information structure in a cross-linguistic perspective*, 147–162. Amsterdam & New York: Rodopi.

Molnár, Valéria. 2006. On different kinds of contrast. In Valéria Molnár & Susanne Winkler (eds.), *The architecture of focus*, 197–233. Berlin & New York: Mouton de Gruyter.

Molnár, Valéria & Susanne Winkler (eds.). 2006. *The architecture of focus* (Studies in Generative Syntax 82). Berlin & New York: Mouton de Gruyter.

Molnár, Valéria & Susanne Winkler. 2010. Edges and gaps. Contrast at the interfaces. *Lingua* 120(6). 1392–1415.

Neeleman, Ad & Reiko Vermeulen. 2012. The syntactic expression of information structure. In Ad Neeleman & Reiko Vermeulen (eds.), *The syntax of topic, focus, and contrast*, 1–38. Berlin & New York: Mouton de Gruyter.

Portner, Paul & Katsuhiko Yabushita. 1998. The semantics and pragmatics of topic phrases. *Linguistics & Philosophy* 21. 117–157.

Portner, Paul & Katsuhiko Yabushita. 2001. Specific indefinites and the information structure theory of topics. *Journal of Semantics* 18(3). 221–297.

Prince, Ellen F. 1984. Topicalization and left-dislocation: A functional analysis. In Sheila J. White & Virginia Teller (eds.), *Discourses in reading and linguistics* (Annuals of the New York Academy of Sciences 433), 213–225. New York: New York Academy of Sciences.

Prince, Ellen F. 1986. On the syntactic marking of open proposition. *Chicago Linguistic Society* 86. 208–221.

Reinhart, Tanja. 1981. Pragmatics and linguistics: An analysis of sentence topics. *Philosophica* 27(1). 53–94.

Reinhart, Tanja. 1995. Interface strategies. *OTS Working Papers in Linguistics*. Universiteit Utrecht.

Reis, Marga. 1982. Zum Subjektbegriff im Deutschen. In Werner Abraham (ed.), *Satzglieder im Deutschen. Vorschläge zur syntaktischen, semantischen und pragmatischen Fundierung*, 171–211. Tübingen: Gunter Narr Verlag.

Repp, Sophie & Philippa Cook. 2010. Contrast as an information-structural notion in grammar. [Special Issue]. *Lingua* 120(6). 1333–1457.

Rizzi Luigi. 1997. The fine structure of the left periphery. In Liliane Haegeman (ed.), *Elements of grammar: A handbook of generative syntax*, 281–337. Dordrecht: Kluwer Academic Publishers.

Roberts, Craige, 1996. Information structure in discourse: Towards an integrated formal theory of pragmatics. *Papers in Semantics*, OSU *Working Papers in Linguistics*, vol. 49. Columbus, OH: The Ohio State University.

Roberts, Craige. 2011. Topics. In Claudia Maienborn, Klaus von Heusinger & Paul Portner (eds.), *Semantics: an international handbook of natural language meaning, vol. 1+2*, (Handbücher zur Sprach- und Kommunikationswissenschaft 33 [Handbooks of Linguistics and Communication Science 33]). 1908–1934. Berlin & New York: Mouton De Gruyter.

Rochemont, Michael. 2016. Givenness. In Caroline Féry & Shinichiro Ishihara (eds.), *The Oxford handbook of information structure*. 41–63. Oxford: Oxford University Press.

Rochemont, Michael. (this volume). Topic and givenness.

Rooth, Mats. 1985. Association with focus. University of Massachusetts, Amherst PhD thesis.

Rooth, Mats. 1992. A theory of focus interpretation. *Natural Language Semantics* 1. 75–116.

Rooth, Mats. 2016. Alternative semantics. In Caroline Féry & Shinichiro Ishihara (eds.), *Oxford handbook of information structure*, 128–146. Oxford: Oxford University Press.

Rosengren, Inger. 1997. The thetic/categorical distinction revisited once more. *Linguistics* 35(3). 439–480.

Sasse, Hans-Jürgen. 1987. The thetic/categorical distinction revisited. *Linguistics* 25. 511–580.

Schwarzschild, Roger. 1999. Givenness, AvoidF and other constraints on the placement of accent. *Natural Language Semantics* 7. 141–177.

Stede, Manfred. 2004. Does discourse processing need discourse topic? *Theoretical Linguistics*. 30(2–3). 241–253.

Strawson, P. F. 1964. Identifying reference and truth values. *Theoria* 30(2). 96–118.

Szabolcsi, Anna. 1981. Compositionality in focus. *Folia Linguistica* XV/1–2. 141–61.

Szabolcsi, Anna. 1997. Strategies for scope taking. In Anna Szabolcsi (ed.), *Ways of scope taking*, 109–154. Dordrecht: Kluwer Academic Publishers.

Uhmann, Susanne. 1991. *Fokusphonologie: Eine Analyse deutscher Intonationskonturen im Rahmen der nicht-linearen Phonologie* (Linguistische Arbeiten 252). Tübingen: Niemeyer Max Verlag.

Vallduví, Enric. 1990. *The informational component*. Pennsylvania: University of Pennsylvania PhD dissertation.

Vallduví, Enric. 1992. *The informational component*. New York & London: Garland.

Vallduví, Enric & Elisabeth Engdahl. 1996. The linguistic realization of information packaging. *Linguistics* 34. 459–519.

Winkler, Susanne. 2005. *Ellipsis and focus in generative grammar* (Studies in Generative Grammar 81). Berlin & New York: Mouton de Gruyter.

Part I: **Semantic and Discourse-pragmatic Correlates of Topicality**

Michael Rochemont
Topics and Givenness

Abstract: In this article I explore the relationship between topics, givenness and deaccenting, and specifically, the hypothesis that deaccenting is directly a function of topichood. I argue that, where relevant, topics depend on one form of givenness (familiarity) and deaccenting on another (salience). Familiarity yields the requirement that topics are referential. Salience yields the requirement that deaccenting is dependent on coreference to or entailment by a discourse antecedent (Schwarzschild's GIVENness). I argue for a novel theory of GIVENness calculation, which yields an account not only of non-focused deaccented expressions but also of the specific deaccenting of Second Occurrence Focus expressions.

Keywords: deaccenting, definiteness, familiarity, F-marked, focus, given, givenness, G-marked, prosody, salience, second occurrence focus (SOF), topic

1 Introduction

It is not uncommon in studies of topic to claim that a topic must be given, or old information. Since deaccenting is also generally dependent on givenness, it might seem reasonable to propose that deaccenting is a function of topichood (e.g., Erteschik-Shir 1997; Lambrecht 1994). But there are several types of givenness, with different properties and functions. It must be asked then whether the reduction of deaccenting to topichood is indeed legitimate, that is, whether both notions depend on the same form of givenness. It is not at all clear to me that they do, at least not in any general way. As we will see, a topical constituent may be given in the sense that it is functionally dependent (through Common Ground Content) on the discourse topic of the surrounding discourse, without being given in the sense required for deaccenting. While a refined analysis of topics might propose a sub-type of topic with a givenness requirement that matches that for deaccenting, this would not change the force of my argument here, that topichood generally does not suffice to license deaccenting.

I proceed by distinguishing two forms of givenness, familiarity and salience. I argue that deaccenting is conditioned by salience (Rochemont 2016), whereas topics are generally familiar (Gundel 2003). Building from a proposal

---

Michael Rochemont, University of British Columbia

https://doi.org/10.1515/9781501504488-002

by Selkirk (2008), I then propose a formulation of salience-based givenness that is capable of characterizing the deaccenting of not only given non-focused expressions but also Second Occurrence Focus (SOF).

2 Two Types of Givenness

Following Prince (1981) and most recently Rochemont (2016), I distinguish for present purposes two types of givenness: salience-based (Prince's givenness$_S$) and familiarity-based (Prince's givenness$_K$). Both are evident in the following modified example modeled from Chafe (1976). (I will use small caps to mark pitch accents and underscoring to mark deaccenting. Sentences in braces provide context for target sentences.)

(1)   {John and Mary recently went to the beach.}
   a. *They brought some $_{PICNIC}$ supplies, but they didn't drink the $_{BEER}$ because it was $_{WARM}$.*
   b. *They brought some $_{BEER}$, but they didn't $_{DRINK}$ <u>the beer</u> because it was $_{WARM}$.*

Speakers of most varieties of English (known exceptions include Hawaiian English (Vanderslice and Pierson 1967), Caribbean English (Gumperz 1982), Singapore English (Deterding 1994; Low 2006) and Malaysian English (Gut and Pillai 2014) systematically distinguish the pronunciation of the italicised sentences in (1a,b). These two sentences, though segmentally identical, form a minimal pair: in (a) 'beer' is intonationally prominent (pitch accented), while in (b) 'beer' can be deaccented (it can show a complete lack of pitch prominence). Patently, what makes deaccenting possible in the second conjunct in (1b) is the prior mention of beer in the first conjunct (where 'the beer' is accented at first mention, as in (1a)). In (1a) there is no such prior mention in the first conjunct. I will refer to the notion of givenness required for deaccenting as "salience", to be implemented formally as *Givenness* following Schwarzschild (1999). I refer to the notion of givenness that licenses the use of the definite *the beer* in (1b) as "familiarity".

Distinguishing these two notions of givenness is essential to deciding whether topichood can serve as a conditioning factor for deaccenting. The givenness condition on topics is usually appealed to capture the need for a topic to be referential so that the topic may serve as that element of a proposition against which its truth value is assessed, or equivalently in the file card metaphor, as the file card on which the "comment" is entered. (The ability of a topic to be replaced by a pronoun without loss of acceptability/interpretability is seen by many as a hallmark of topichood.) A topical constituent in a sentence may also be given in the sense that that constituent links the sentence to the prior discourse by identifying in some way with the topic that encompasses the discourse, including the local utterance (Roberts 2011). But in both these cases, it seems that the type of givenness associated with topichood is a function of familiarity rather than salience. In particular, while topics may be restricted to referential expressions, deaccenting is not (section 2.1). And while a discourse topic may "antecede" a sentence topic in a broad variety of ways, including functional dependence of the type seen in (1a), deaccented expressions may not; the latter may only identify with an antecedent, topic or not, through coreference or entailment (section 2.2).

2.1 Topichood and (In)Definiteness

Topics must be referential. Assuming that *as for/concerning* mark intended topics in English (e.g., Reinhart 1982; Roberts 2011), the contrast below shows that non-referential phrases qualify as poor topics in contrast to those that are referential.

(2) a. *As for/concerning Bill/the boy/my best friend/beavers/a few of my friends,* (...)
    b. **as for/concerning many people/someone/a boy/no one/everything,* (...)

The quantified and indefinite phrases in (2b) do not refer, but the definite referring expressions in (2a) (including generics and partitives) do refer, suggesting that the best topics are familiar in the sense of Heim (1982). In the *file card metaphor*, definites are associated with existing file cards (hence familiar), indefinites are not (hence novel), and require the introduction of a new file card (see also Erteschik-Shir 1997, 2007). Proponents of such a view impose restrictions on candidate topics, requiring them to be familiar, and so excluding indefinite phrases to one degree or another. For instance, Gundel (2003) prohibits indefinites generally from serving as topics, with possible exceptions for specific indefinites. But if deaccenting depends on topichood and topics cannot be indefinite, then it is falsely predicted that indefinites (and especially non-specific indefinites) cannot be deaccented. In both examples in (3), the deaccented *an apple* is a non-referring indefinite – no discourse referent has been introduced by the first instance of *an apple* that the second instance refers to.

(3) a. *Whenever John eats an ₐₚₚₗₑ, Mary ᵦᵤᵧₛ an apple.*
    b. *Mary buys an ₐₚₚₗₑ whenever John ₑₐₜₛ an apple.*

Erteschik-Shir (2007) requires only that non-specific indefinites not be topics, unless they are restrictive (contrastive) topics. But non-restrictive non-specific indefinites can be deaccented.[1]

(4) {*Have you ever been asked to give a job talk?*}
    Yes, but I've never been ₁ₙₜₑᵣᵥᵢₑw₁ₑ in a job talk.

Moreover, Erteschik-Shir requires that the subjects of individual level predicates must be topics. But whether such a subject may be deaccented is not a function of subject/topic-hood but of salience. (That subjects generally must be accented when discourse new has been argued by many researchers.) Without enriching the context beyond the question, only (5b) can be answered by (6b).

(5) a. *Did you learn something today?*
    b. *Did you learn something about beavers today?*

(6) a. *Yes. BEAVERS are ₁ₙₜₑₗₗ₁gₑₙₜ.*
    b. *Yes. Beavers are ₁ₙₜₑₗₗ₁gₑₙₜ.*

If the subjects of individual level predicates must indeed be topics, (5/6) show that topichood is independent of deaccenting and cannot serve to condition it. If topics are always given, in the sense of being familiar, then this is independent of their potential for being salient, as seen in (6). As a consequence, topichood cannot be a conditioning factor for deaccenting.

2.2 Topichood and Entailment

As noted earlier, topical constituents (sentence topics) can also be given in virtue of bearing a relation to a discourse topic. These relations can vary broadly,

---

[1] Nomi Erteschik-Shir (p.c.) points out to me that this argument may not hold in a framework where only focused constituents bear accents and all other units are not accented. For arguments that non-focussed constituents may bear accents, see Rochemont (2013b).

so long as the topical phrase is construed as bearing a set relation of some sort to the discourse topic (Daneš 1974; Ward 1985).

(7) {A: *Tell me about your siblings.*}
B: *My sister, I live with. And my brother, I barely talk to.*

Deaccenting, on the other hand, is more restricted. As I review below, previous research has shown that deaccenting is licensed only by coreference to or entailment from a discourse antecedent (and we know from examples like (3) that the antecedent might not even be a discourse referent). A preliminary indication that this is so arises from the observation that the topical phrases in (7B/8B) cannot be deaccented if they appear in situ, as in (8B'). Instead they must be accented (as discourse new) as in (8B).

(8) {A: *Tell me about your siblings.*}
B: *I live with my $_{SISTER}$, and I barely talk to my $_{BROTHER}$.*
B': *#I $_{LIVE}$ with <u>my sister</u>, and I barely $_{TALK}$ to <u>my brother</u>.*

To summarize, the givenness requirement for topics does not seem at all equivalent to that for deaccenting. Deaccenting applies irrespective of definiteness and under stricter semantic relations to a discourse antecedent than topics generally bear. In the terms expressed here, topics depend on familiarity, whereas deaccenting depends on salience. The discussion of examples (3–8) gives ample reason to be sceptical of the claim that topichood generally conditions deaccenting. For this reason, in what follows I will pursue an account of deaccenting that does not depend on the notion of topic. Rather, following previous researchers, I will use deaccenting as a probe into the proper notion of givenness that is required for prosodic marking of salience. To distinguish this notion from the familiarity-based notion, I will refer to this salience-based notion as *GIVENness*.

3 Deaccenting and GIVENness

Before proceeding, two widely recognized caveats are in order about the relation of deaccenting to GIVENness. First, however defined, GIVENness is a necessary but not sufficient condition for deaccenting, as is widely noted. In particular, a focused phrase, if GIVEN (Second Occurence Focus (SOF) aside – see below), is not deaccented. For instance, in (9) neither *tea* (9a) nor *John* (9b) can be deaccented, though both are patently GIVEN in the respective prior sentence.

(9) a. *{Do you like coffee or tea?} I like $_{TEA}$. (# I $_{LIKE}$ tea.)*
    b. *John's mother slapped Mary, and then she slapped J$_{OHN}$. (#... $_{SLAPPED}$ John.)*

Second, deaccenting is mandatory for GIVEN non-focused constituents only in post-nuclear position; in pre-nuclear position constituents that are GIVEN may be accented or not, as in (10).

(10) *{Mary met a student from her class at a social event.}*
    a. *The student/$_{STUDENT}$ asked her to $_{DANCE}$.*
    b. *She $_{DANCED}$ with the student/#$_{STUDENT}$.*

Given this distribution, judgments about the availability of deaccenting are more reliable when candidates appear in post-nuclear position. I will endeavour throughout to structure examples in this fashion wherever possible, re-fashioning examples from the literature when needed.

It is readily shown that deaccenting is limited by entailment from or coreference to a discourse antecedent. Thus, coreference suffices for deaccenting in (11), and hyponymy in (12), but hypernymy, functional dependence, meronymy, and holonomy fail in (13–16), respectively (Rochemont 2016).

(11) *John's sister doesn't $_{LIKE}$ John / him / the bastard.*

(12) a. *Where are those groceries I paid for? Actually, J$_{OHN}$ bought them.*
    b. *John traps gorillas and he also $_{TRAINS}$ animals.*
    c. *John had a sister before M$_{ARY}$ had a sibling.*

(13) a. *#John traps animals and he also $_{TRAINS}$ gorillas.*
    b. *#John had a sibling before M$_{ARY}$ had a sister.*

(14) a. *When I boarded the $_{BUS}$, I thought I recognized the $_{DRIVER}$.*
    b. *# When I boarded the $_{BUS}$, I thought I $_{RECOGNIZED}$ the driver.*

(15) a. *#If you knock on the $_{DOOR}$, you can $_{ENTER}$ the room.*
    b. *#When the engine $_{DIED}$, I $_{JUNKED}$ my car.*
    c. *#John takes pictures of $_{STEEPLES}$, and he $_{PAINTS}$ churches, too.*
    d. *#If I give you the $_{OARS}$, you have to $_{FIND}$ the rowboat.*

(16) a. #*If you want to enter the $_{ROOM}$, you have to $_{KNOCK}$ <u>on the door</u>.*
   b. #*My car broke $_{DOWN}$. I forgot to $_{OIL}$ <u>the engine</u>.*
   c. #*John takes pictures of $_{CHURCHES}$, and he $_{PAINTS}$ <u>steeples</u>, too.*
   d. #*When I got out of the $_{ROWBOAT}$, I $_{FORGOT}$ <u>the oars</u>.*

All #'d examples in (13–16) are improved if the accent is shifted to the deaccented phrase. Accenting marks the respective phrases as discourse new.

Furthermore, deaccenting a constituent when the antecedent must be inferred can lead to an inference of coreference or entailment, as in (17–18). (In these examples I have used single quotation marks for the intended antecedents for deaccenting.)

(17) a. *John 'called' Mary 'a Republican' and then $_{SHE}$ <u>insulted</u> $_{HIM}$.*
   b. #*John 'insulted' Mary and then $_{SHE}$ <u>called</u> $_{HIM}$ <u>a Republican</u>.*

(18) a. *On my way home, 'a dog' barked at me. I was really $_{FRIGHTENED}$ by <u>the fierce German Shepherd</u>.*
   b. *Did you see 'Dr. Cramer' to get your root canal? Don't remind me. I'd like to $_{STRANGLE}$ <u>the butcher</u>.*
   c. *'My neighbour' is a funny character. Still, I really $_{LIKE}$ <u>John</u>.*
   d. *'The crowd' approached the gate. The guards were $_{AFRAID}$ of <u>the women</u>.*
   e. *'The children' were up late. I'm reluctant to $_{WAKE}$ <u>the boys</u>.*

In all these cases, when the accent is shifted to the deaccented expression, the interpretation of entailment or coreference is lost.

Finally, let me point out that deaccenting is not limited to cases of repetition or predictability, as many experimental studies assume. None of the examples in (12–18) involve repetition. Rochemont (2016) uses the example below to argue that predictability is equally flawed as a determinant of the possibility for deaccenting.

(19) a. *The $_{CHICKEN}$ pecked at the $_{GROUND}$ with its_____.*
   b. *The $_{CHICKEN}$ pecked at the $_{GROUND}$ with its $_{BEAK}$/ # at the $_{GROUND}$ with <u>its beak</u>.*

Although the lexical item in (19b) that appears in the position of the dash in (19a) is fully predictable, as (19b) shows this item is not deaccentable in virtue of this predictability.

Schwarzschild (1999) proposes a definition for GIVEN and a system for determining when a GIVEN constituent must be deaccented. He assumes that focus and discourse new are identified though F-marking, and that GIVENness identifies deaccenting as the complement of focus accenting.

(20) Definition of GIVEN (Schwarzschild 1999: 151):
An utterance U counts as GIVEN iff it has a salient antecedent A and
a. if U is of type e, then A and U corefer;
b. otherwise, modulo ∃-type shifting, A entails the Existential F-Closure of U.

GIVENness: If a constituent is not F-marked, it must be GIVEN
AVOID F: F-mark as little as possible, without violating GIVENness

∃-type shifting is an operation that raises non-propositional constituents to the type of a proposition by filling missing argument slots with variables and existentially closing them. Existential F-closure removes F-marked constituents from a proposition, replacing each with a variable and existentially closing the result. Recursively applying the procedure in (20) to each node in the syntactic representation of a sentence will yield an F-marked representation constrained by GIVENness and AVOID F that is sensitive to the discourse context the sentence appears in. Assuming that a *wh*-question makes salient a proposition derived by existentially closing the *wh*-variable, then in (21), the question makes salient a proposition to the effect that ∃X [*John voted for* X]. The answer, with F-marking of *Mary*, produces a proposition that matches that for the question, where the F-marked phrase bears an accent and all else is deaccented under entailment by the propositional antecedent made salient by the question. Question answer congruence is satisfied as a result.

(21) Who did John vote for?   ∃x [he voted for x]
[He [voted for [M$_{ARYF}$]]]   ∃X [he voted for X]

Avoid F guarantees that F-marking applies to the minimum extent possible to satisfy the requirements of GIVENness. In (21) this restricts F-marking to *Mary*. F-marking more broadly in this example would violate AVOID F since all constituents apart from *Mary* are indeed GIVEN under the definition in (20).

While effective across much of the relevant empirical landscape, Schwarzschild's proposal faces at least two difficulties.[2] The first is that F-marking as construed in this analysis is almost exclusively identified with

---

[2] See Rochemont (2016) for fuller discussion of these and other problems for Schwarzschild's proposal.

discourse new expressions. In particular, a GIVEN constituent may be F-marked solely in service of the mandatory F-marking of a discourse new constituent that contains it. This restriction of F-marking to constituents that are (contained in) discourse new expressions proves problematic for the analysis, as Beaver and Clark (2008: 20–22) observe, in cases where the motivation for F-marking is solely to indicate the association of a constituent with a focus sensitive operator irrespective of its role in satisfying GIVENness.

(22) {Brady taught semantics and ...}
    a. *the students were glad that B$_{RADY}$ taught semantics.*
    b. *the students were glad that Brady taught $_{SEMANTICS}$.*
    c. *the students were $_{GLAD}$ that Brady taught semantics.*

Because the emotive predicate in (22a, b) responds to the position of sentence stress in the predicate's complement, the interpretations of these examples differ: (22a) expresses the students' preference for Brady, rather than someone else, to teach semantics, whereas (22b) expresses their preference for Brady to teach semantics rather than some other subject. But in Schwarzschild's system not only are each of the elements of the clausal complement to the predicate in both examples (22a, b) GIVEN, the clausal complement itself is GIVEN and hence grammatically unmarked and predicted to be deaccented, as in (22c). AVOID F rules out any further internal F-marking within these clausal complements, and so does not license F-marking of *Brady* in (22a) or *semantics* in (22b). One way to capture such cases is to allow F-marking to distinguish alternatives-based focus (henceforth 'Focus') constituents from discourse new (henceforth 'New') ones.

Other studies point to this same conclusion. Katz and Selkirk (2011) show experimentally that when Focused and New constituents co-occur in the domain of a focus sensitive operator, the accent marking the focus has greater excursion, duration and intensity than that marking the new constituent, regardless of order. This implies that F-marking distinguishes between focused and new constituents, as argued in Kratzer and Selkirk (2007), Selkirk (2008), and Rochemont (2013b). Consider (23).

(23) {*Did John do anything odd at the reception?*} Yes – *He only introduced B$_{ILL}$ to S$_{UE}$.*
    a. *He didn't introduce anyone else to Sue.*
    b. *He didn't introduce Bill to anyone else.*
    c. *He didn't make any other introductions.*
    d. *He didn't do anything else.*

Rochemont observes that in the context indicated, the utterance *He only introduced Bill to Sue* is multiply ambiguous, as the possible continuations in (23) indicate: *only* may associate with just *Bill* (23a), with just *Sue* (23b), with both *Bill* and *Sue* (23c), or with the VP (23d). But in Schwarzschild's analysis all of these constituents (and more) are F-marked, as below.

(24) He only [introduced$_F$ B$_{ILLF}$ to S$_{UEF}$]$_F$

Representation (24) does not distinguish among the various ambiguities evident in (23). If F-marking marks the Focus that *only* associates with and NEW constituents are unmarked (Kratzer and Selkirk 2007), then four distinct representations are called for, as in (25), corresponding to each of the interpretations invoked in (23a-d) respectively.

(25) a. He only [introduced B$_{ILLF}$ to S$_{UE}$].
 b. He [only [introduced B$_{ILL}$ to S$_{UEF}$].
 c. He only [introduced B$_{ILLF}$ to S$_{UEF}$].
 d. He only [introduced B$_{ILL}$ to S$_{UE}$]$_F$.

Both (22) and (23) give reason to think that Focus and New should be distinguished. One possible conclusion is that F-marking should be restricted.

The second problem for Schwarzschild's proposal has to do with the complementarity it imposes on the relation of focus (as new) to givenness. As other researchers have noted (e.g., Kučerová and Neeleman 2012; Reich 2012), the facts of Second Occurrence Focus (SOF) seem to argue against the view that focus and givenness are in complementary distribution. Briefly, if a SOF is a focus that must be given, then givenness cannot be the complement of focus. The SOF in the following examples is underscored.

(26) A: *Everyone already knew that Mary only eats $_{VEGETABLES}$.*
 B: *If even P$_{AUL}$ knew that Mary only eats <u>vegetables</u>, then he should have suggested a different $_{RESTAURANT}$.*

(27) A: *The provost and the dean aren't taking any candidates other than Susan and Harold seriously.*
 B: *Even the $_{CHAIRMAN}$ is only considering <u>younger</u> candidates.*

(28) *Mary only talked to John's $_{MOTHER}$. Even J$_{OHN}$ only talked to his <u>mother</u>.*

In each of (26–28), the SOF behaves as a focus in associating with the focus sensitive operator *only* and in bearing some measure of relative prosodic prominence (e.g., Beaver et al. 2007; Féry and Ishihara 2009; Baumann et al. 2010), though deaccented. Example (27) from Rooth (2004) shows that it is givenness that is at stake and not simply repetition. Comparing (26) with (29) shows that a SOF must be given.

(29) *Mary is a fussy eater. Even P$_{AUL}$ knows that Mary only eats $_{VEGETABLES}$.*

The givenness condition on SOF is only necessary, not sufficient. A focus may readily be given and still not bear SOF prosody, as in (30).

(30) *Who did John's mother hug? She hugged J$_{OHN}$.*

A full analysis of SOF must therefore address the question what specifically conditions SOF prominence over Focus accenting in cases of SOF, given that both SOF and a primary focus may be given. The important point for now is that a SOF must be given, and this seems to contradict the complementarity that Schwarzschild's system imposes on focus/new and givenness generally. As with the first difficulty for Schwarzschild's analysis noted above, a feasible solution to the problem brought by SOF is to distinguish discourse new accenting and focus accenting: Given is seen to be in complementary distribution with New but not with Focus. As Selkirk (2008) proposes, this leaves three distinct relevant categories of information structure (Given, New and Focused), each with distinctive prosodic expression. SOF too has a distinctive prosody – it displays reduced focus prominence whose specific expression is relativized to the positional variation in expression of deaccenting (Féry and Ishihara 2009 and below). In the next section I examine the mapping between these categories of information structure and their prosodic expression, with a proposal for corresponding revisions to Schwarzschild's analysis of GIVENness outlined in (20).

4 More on Second Occurrence Focus and Defining GIVEN

It is clear in example (30) that the need to mark focus through prosodic prominence outweighs the need to mark givenness through prosodic reduction. But SOF shows us that this resolution of the conflict cannot generally hold, since with SOF deaccenting is not completely overridden by the need for focus prominence. Rather both requirements (focus prominence and givenness deaccenting) find equally compromised expression, even in cases where a SOF can bear a pitch accent. In particular, Féry and Ishihara (2009) argue that, as with given non-focused phrases in pre-nuclear position generally, SOF can bear pitch prominence when pre-nuclear, though weaker in instrumentally observable force than a primary focus in parallel position. I think a similar argument might be made on the basis of (31).

(31) A: *John has always depended on his parents. It was them that he turned to for comfort when he needed it.*
B: *Yeah, and it was $_{THEM}$/them/*'em (that) he turned to for $_{MONEY,\ TOO}$.*

The previously focused pivot in the cleft in B's utterance is a pronoun. Evidence that it remains prominent when deaccented is that it cannot alternate with a reduced (cliticized) pronoun as though it were entirely unfocused. (An instrumental study would be necessary to determine how the accented pronoun variant in B's statement might compare with that in A's utterance.) Though for clarity I will continue to restrict examples to deaccenting in post-nuclear position, by "SOF prosody" I mean to include not only the reduced prominence displayed by SOF when deaccented but also when potentially accented as well. Following Féry and Ishihara (2009) (see also Selkirk 2008), I take it that the specific manifestation of SOF prosody is a function of the competition between prosodic prominence for focus and prosodic reduction for givenness, the varying character of its expression (pitch accent vs. prosodic reduction) being tied to the differing domains for mandatory and optional deaccenting.

So, what specifically conditions SOF prosody over Focus accenting in cases of SOF, given that both SOF and a primary focus may be given? Space does not permit me the luxury of reviewing here in detail the various proposals on offer in the literature (e.g., Rooth 2010; Büring 2015; Selkirk 2008; Beaver and Velleman 2011). Instead I will simply outline a new approach, referring interested readers to the critical review in Beaver and Velleman (2011) and leaving a more comprehensive comparison to another occasion. In the paradigmatic examples of SOF in (26–28), it is patently true that the SOF is simply part of a larger constituent that is given in the preceding sentence, and that includes the SOF as given. This might lead one to hypothesize that what marks a phrase in need of the special prosody of a SOF is that it is Given as a focus, i.e., that it and its focus domain are Given (Selkirk 2008). However, not all cases of SOF follow the pattern of (26–28). Rooth (1992) discusses (32):

(32) *People who ₍GROW₎ rice generally only ₍EAT₎ rice.*
    (= the only thing rice-growers eat is rice)

In (32) the SOF *rice* is not given as a focus in that it is not a focus in its discourse prior use. Being a prior focus can therefore not be a conditioning factor for SOF.

Alternatively, one might seek to predict SOF prosody by means of nested domains of application of Focus Prominence, the phonological rule that gives greatest relative prosodic prominence to a contrastive focus within its syntactically determined prosodic domain (Büring 2015). If the domain of a SOF is properly contained within the domain of another (primary, or first occurrence) focus, then Focus Prominence is satisfied for both the SOF and the primary focus within their respective domains: the SOF bears primary prominence within the contained domain and so long as this prominence is weaker than that borne by the primary focus in the broader (containing) domain, Focus Prominence is satisfied for both foci. In this sort of approach, no special account of SOF is needed – its existence and nature follows from the independently required Focus Prominence rule. As a focus the SOF must bear prominence in its domain, but it cannot bear prominence as great as that of another focus in whose domain it's own domain is contained. Problems with this approach arise in cases where the primary focus appears within the SOF's domain. In (32) again, assuming that v/VP is the domain of the underscored SOF, the accented Focus is contained in this domain, even assuming its own domain is the entire sentence. Focus Prominence is satisfied for the accented focus at the level of IP, but not for the SOF, which does not bear the relatively greatest prominence in its vP focus domain.

Appealing though the initial account might seem, it does not appear possible to reduce the manifestation of SOF prosody to Focus Prominence without depriving Focus Prominence of its predictive force.

This conclusion is reinforced by (33), which is ambiguous. It has not only the reading that rice-growers feed rice exclusively to their pets, but also the SOF reading that rice-growers feed exclusively rice to their pets (where *pets* is simply New and not Focused).

(33) *People who ₍GROW₎ rice only ₍FEED₎ rice to their ₍PETS₎.*[3]

---

[3] A reviewer asks whether the sentence remains ambiguous (with either *rice* or *pets* the focus associate of *only*) when *rice* is replaced by a pronoun (*it/that*). My judgment is that *only* cannot associate with *it*, but can associate with *pets* (or *that*). The reason, I think, may be that *it* cannot bear any level of prosodic prominence (cf. **I saw IT, not IT.*).

In the SOF reading, *rice* bears relatively weaker prominence than both *feed* and *pets*, these latter both contained within the focus domain of *rice*. (This example also poses problems for Beaver and Velleman's analysis, which distinguishes only two levels of prominence, where (33) in the SOF interpretation shows the need for at least three.) In addition to an example like (33), it has not been previously observed that multiple pronunciations are possible for Rooth's original example (32), shown in (34–35). (In general, accenting of constituents in the relative clause is not a pre-condition for accenting in the predicate phrase, as these examples show.[4] I include them for completeness.)

(34) a. *People who $_{GROW}$ rice only eat $_{RICE}$.*
 b. *People who grow $_{RICE}$ only eat $_{RICE}$.*

(35) a. *People who $_{GROW}$ rice only $_{EAT\ RICE}$.*
 b. *People who grow $_{RICE}$ only $_{EAT\ RICE}$.*

Any analysis that that is designed to require SOF prosody in (32) is already empirically inadequate, given (34–35). The crucial variants in (35) illustrate that SOF prosody is not mandatory for the given focus *rice*, even when *eat* is contrastively focused.

I propose a new analysis, adapting Selkirk's (2008) proposal to a revised implementation of Schwarzschild's (1999) basic framework summarized in (20). Selkirk proposes four distinct information structural categories (Focused, New, SOF, Given), each with distinctive prosody (focus pitch accented, New pitch accented, SOF prosody, deaccented) and syntactic marking (F, unmarked, G, F+G, respectively). These alignments are displayed in the chart below.

Table 1.

Semantics	Focused	Given	New	SOF
Syntax	F-marked	G-marked	unmarked	F-+G- marked
Prosody	nuclear accent (ι)	deaccented	accented (φ)	SOF prosody

---

4 As (35b) shows, there need be no contrastive accent on *grow* even when it is contrasted with *rice*. (See the discussion of anticipatory accenting in American farmer examples in Rochemont 2013a.) A reviewer asks how it is possible that *grow* can be accented in (34a) without a corresponding contrast on *eat* in the main clause. This can arise in different ways depending on utterances that may precede (34a). For example, consider (i).
(i) *Some people grow rice, others buy it. But people who GROW rice only eat RICE.*

The revisions to Schwarzschild's GIVENness proposal are summarized in (36), now replacing (20). In the syntax, information structure feature attachment applies freely, subject to the condition that a well-formed (i.e., prosodically and semantically interpretable) output must result. I assume that a constituent α is F-marked only if Focused, G-marked only if GIVEN, and unmarked only if New.

(36) An utterance of U counts as GIVEN iff it has a salient antecedent A and
   a. if U is type e then A and U corefer;
   b. otherwise, modulo existential type shifting, A entails the Existential F-closure of U.

Existential F-closure of U $=_{df}$ the result of replacing all non-G-marked F-marked constituents in U with variables, removing all other non-G-marked constituents, and existentially closing the result, modulo existentialtype shifting.

G-marking Condition: F-marked α is G-marked only if (i) α is GIVEN, and (ii) the focus domain of α is GIVEN.

The definition for focus domain is borrowed from Büring (2015).

(37) focus domain $=_{df}$ P is the domain of a focus F and its operator O iff P is the smallest vP/IP that marks the scope position of O.

The revised procedure of Existential F-closure in (36) disregards New constituents, so that only GIVEN and Focused constituents are obliged to seek discourse antecedents in checking for GIVENness. This change allows us to keep the basic insight Selkirk brings in the form of the G-marking Condition, but now understanding GIVEN in a substantially different way, while recognizing the distinction between Focus (as alternatives) and New.

Let us apply this analysis now to some representative examples from the preceding discussion. (38)–(43) repeat several examples, annotated for their interpretation so as to properly describe their prosodic characteristics as described earlier. In each case the focus domain (fd) is the bracketed string in the representation. (39)–(42) illustrate how the domain of SOF *rice* may be
GIVEN if the main verb is Focused, and (40)–(41) show how *rice* may not be a SOF when the verb is simply New.

(38) (26B)[5] ι(*If even P$_{AUL}$ knew that Mary only eats vegetables*)ι (...)
(...) that Mary only [eats$_G$ vegetables$_{F,G}$]
Paul is F-marked because it associates with *even*
vegetables is F-marked because it associates with *only*
vegetables is GIVEN
eats vegetables is GIVEN (fd = ∃x (x eats vegetables))

(39) (32) *People who $_{GROW}$ rice only $_{EAT}$ rice*
(...) only [eat$_F$ rice$_{F,G}$]
eat is F-marked because it is a focused alternative to *grow*
rice is F-marked because it associates with *only*
F-marked *rice* may be G-marked because ∃;x ∃V (x V rice) is GIVEN

(40) (34a) *People who $_{GROW}$ rice only eat $_{RICE}$.*
(...) only [eat rice$_F$]
rice is F-marked because it associates with *only*
rice is GIVEN, but cannot be G-marked because its fd [*eat rice*] is not GIVEN (only *rice* is GIVEN)

(41) (34b)[6] *People who grow $_{RICE}$ only eat $_{RICE}$.*
(...) only [eat rice$_F$]
rice is F-marked because it associates with *only*
F-marked *rice* is not G-marked, though GIVEN, because its fd [*eat rice$_F$*] is not GIVEN (only *rice* is GIVEN)

(42) (33) *People who grow rice only $_{FEED}$ rice to their $_{PETS}$.*
(...) only [feed$_F$ rice$_{F,G}$ to their pets]
feed is F-marked because it is a focused alternative to *grow*
rice is F-marked because it associates with *only*
F-marked *rice* is G-marked because [feed$_F$ rice$_G$ to their pets] is GIVEN ∃x∃V (x V rice)

(43) (22) {Brady taught semantics and ...}
  i. the students were [glad that B$_{RADYF}$ [taught semantics]$_G$].
  ii. the students were [glad that Brady$_G$ taught$_G$ SEMANTICS$_F$].
  iii. the students were [$_{GLAD}$ that [Brady taught semantics]$_G$].

---

5 The subscripted ι represents the boundary of a prosodic Intonation Phrase.
6 In examples (i), where the fd *eat rice* is GIVEN, SOF prosody on *rice* is possible.
(i) a. *People who eat RICE ONLY eat rice.*
     b. *People who eat RICE only eat rice.*

i) *Brady* is F-marked because it associates with *glad*
    Brady is not G-marked because although ∃x(x *taught semantics*) is GIVEN, the fd [*glad that x taught semantics*] is not GIVEN
ii) *semantics* is F-marked because it associates with *glad*
    semantics is not G-marked because *glad that Brady taught semantics* is not GIVEN
iii) *Brady taught semantics* is G-marked (and deaccented)
    glad is New (unmarked) and accented (as the sole accentable candidate in a New constituent (i.e., VP).

Recall that I have assumed the necessary but not sufficient conditions in (44).

(44) A node α is
  – F-marked only if α is a FOCUS
  – G-marked only if α is GIVEN
  – F- and G-marked only if both α and the focus domain of α are GIVEN
  – unmarked only if α is not GIVEN

The prosodic representations are conditioned by phonological constraints. The most important of these for present purposes is the constraint requiring discourse new phrases to bear a pitch accent. This constraint will block a derivation like that provided for (40) but in which *rice* is tagged as [F+G] instead of [F]. The conditions given in (44) are met in this case for this feature specification, but the resulting representation cannot be implemented prosodically because the VP *eat rice* is New and so must bear an accent. This can be satisfied in the manner of (38c) or by accenting *eat* as New (rather than Focused, as in (38b)) – see Féry and Samek-Lodovici (2006) and Rochemont (2013a).

5 Conclusion

I have argued that the givenness condition on topics and that on deaccenting derive from distinct notions of givenness and should not be confused. I have distinguished two forms of givenness, one based on familiarity, the other on salience. I have also advanced a new procedure for calculating Givenness, the salience based notion. This procedure supplies an account not only of deaccenting generally but also of SOF. It relies on a modification to Schwarzschild's procedure that distinguishes between Focused and discourse New constituents. This revision supplemented by Selkirk's proposal for identifying contexts where SOF is possible repairs the difficulties noted for Schwarzschild's account and extends to previously unobserved variations in the expression of SOF.

Nothing prevents a topic from being Given in virtue of an available discourse antecedent / topic, but nothing requires it either. Topics may be New (and/or shifted), familiar or salient. Not so with deaccenting. Deaccenting must be tied solely to a salient antecedent; familiarity does not suffice. It might be proposed that topichood is merely a necessary but not sufficient condition on deaccenting, but it remains that topichood by itself must be adapted to stricter conditions (namely coreference / entailment) to be the controlling factor in deaccenting, and creating a type of topic with these attributes amounts to positing again a notion of givenness that is distinct for putative topics that support deaccenting and those that do not. I prefer to think of salience as a separate category of information structure (Givenness) that can interact with topic or focus but that is in complementary distribution with New.

References

Baumann, Stefan, Doris Mücke & Johannes Becker. 2010. Expression of second occurrence focus in German. *Linguistische Berichte* 221. 61–78.

Beaver, David, Brady Clark, Edward Flemming, T. Florian Jaeger & Maria Wolters. 2007. When semantics meets phonetics: acoustical studies of second occurrence focus. *Language* 83. 245–276.

Beaver, David & Brady Clark. 2008. *Sense and sensitivity*. Walden, MA: Wiley-Blackwell.

Beaver, David & Dan Vellemann. 2011. The communicative significance of primary and secondary accents. *Lingua* 121. 1671–1692.

Büring, Daniel. 2015. A Theory of Second Occurrence Focus. *Language Cognition and Neuroscience* 30 (1–2). 73–87.

Chafe, Wallace. 1976. Givenness, contrastiveness, definiteness, subjects, topics, and point of view. In Charles Li (ed.), *Subject and topic*, 25–55. New York: Academic Press.

Daneš, František. 1974. Functional sentence perspective and the organization of the text. In František Daneš (ed.), Papers on functional sentence perspective, 106–128. Prague: Academia.

Deterding, David. 1994. The intonation of Singapore English. *Journal of the International Phonetic Association* 24(02). 61–72.

Erteschik-Shir, Nomi. 1997. *The dynamics of focus structure*. Cambridge: Cambridge University Press.

Erteschik-Shir, Nomi. 2007. *Information structure: the syntax- discourse interface*. Oxford: Oxford University Press.

Féry, Caroline & Shinichiro Ishihara. 2009. The phonology of second occurrence focus. *Journal of Linguistics* 45. 285–313.

Féry, Caroline & Vieri Samek-Lodovici. 2006. Focus projection and prosodic prominence in nested foci. *Language* 82. 131–150.

Gumperz, John. 1982. *Discourse strategies*. Cambridge: Cambridge University Press.
Gundel, Jeannete K. 2003. Information structure and referential givenness/newness: how much belongs in the grammar? In Stefan Müller (ed.), *Proceedings of the HPSG03 Conference, Michigan State University, East Lansing*, 122–142. Stanford: CSLI.
Gut, Ulrike & Stefanie Pillai. 2014. Prosodic marking of information structure by Malaysian speakers of English. *Studies in Second Language Acquisition* 36. 283–302.
Heim, Irene.1982. *The semantics of definite and indefinite noun phrases*. Amherst: University of Massachusetts PhD dissertation.
Katz, Jonah & Elisabeth O. Selkirk. 2011. Contrastive focus vs. discourse-new: Evidence from phonetic prominence. *Language* 87. 771–816.
Kratzer, Angelika & Elisabeth O. Selkirk. 2007. Phase theory and prosodic spell-out: the case of verbs. *The Linguistic Review* 24. 93–135.
Kučerová, Ivona & Ad Neeleman. 2012. Introduction. In Ivona Kučerová and Ad Neeleman (eds.), *Contrasts and positions in information structure*, 1–23. Cambridge: Cambridge University Press.
Lambrecht, Knud. 1994. *Information structure and sentence form*. Cambridge: Cambridge University Press.
Low, Ee Ling. 2006. A cross-varietal comparison of deaccenting and given information: implications for international intelligibility and pronunciation teaching. *TESOL Quarterly* 40. 739–761.
Prince, Ellen. 1981. Toward a taxonomy of given-new information. In Peter Cole (ed.), *Radical pragmatics*, 223–256. New York: Academic Press.
Reich, Ingo. 2012. Information structure and theoretical models of grammar. In Manfred Krifka & Renate Musan (eds.), *The expression of information structure*, 401–447. Berlin & New York: Mouton de Gruyter.
Reinhart, Tanya. 1982. *Pragmatics and linguistics: an analysis of sentence topic*. Bloomington, IN: Indiana University Linguistics Club.
Roberts, Craige. 2011. Topics. In Claudia Maienborn, Klaus von Heusinger, & Paul Portner (eds.), *Semantics: an international handbook of natural language meaning, vol. 1+2* (Handbücher zur Sprach- und Kommunikationswissenschaft 33/ [Handbooks of Linguistics and Communication Science] 33), 1908–1934. Berlin & New York: Mouton de Gruyter.
Rochemont, Michael. 2013a. Discourse new, F-marking and normal stress. *Lingua* 136. 38–62.
Rochemont, Michael. 2013b. Discourse new, focused and given. In Johan Brandtler, Valéria Molnár & Christer Platzack (eds.), *Approaches to Hungarian, vol.* 13, 199–228. Amsterdam & Philadelphia: John Benjamins.
Rochemont, Michael. 2016. Givenness. In Caroline Féry & Shinichiro Ishihara (eds), *The Oxford handbook of information structure*, 41–63. Oxford: Oxford University Press.
Rooth, Mats. 1992. A theory of focus interpretation. *Natural Language Semantics* 1. 75–116.
Rooth, Mats. 2004. Comments on Krifka's paper. In Hans Kamp & Barbara H. Partee (eds.), *Context-dependence in the analysis of linguistic meaning*, 475–487. Amsterdam: Elsevier.
Rooth, Mats. 2010. Second occurrence focus and relativized stress F. In Caroline Féry & Malte Zimmerman (eds.), *Information structure: theoretical, typological and experimental perspectives*. 15–35. Oxford: Oxford University Press.
Schwarzschild, Roger. 1999. Givenness, AvoidF and other constraints on the placement of accent. *Natural Language Semantics* 7. 141–177.

Selkirk, Elisabeth O. 2008. Contrastive focus, givenness and the unmarked status of "discourse-new". *Acta Linguistica Hungarica* 55. 331–346.

Terken, Jacques & Julia Hirschberg. 1994. Deaccentuation and persistence of grammatical function and surface position. *Language and Speech* 37. 125–145.

Vanderslice, Ralph & Laura Shun Pierson. 1967. Prosodic features of Hawaiian English. *Quarterly Journal of Speech* 53. 156–166.

Ward, Gregory L. 1985. *The semantics and pragmatics of preposing*. Philadelphia: University of Pennsylvania dissertation. [Reprinted in 1988, New York: Garland.]

Roland Hinterhölzl
The Role of Topics in Licensing Anaphoric Relations in VP-ellipsis

Abstract: This paper addresses the role of topics in the licensing of anaphoric relations. I demonstrate that the C-domain plays a crucial role in accounting for valid and invalid cases of coreference. In particular, I argue that discourse anaphors are bound by a context operator, implying that the mechanism that corresponds to coreference is syntactically encoded. The crucial empirical evidence comes from the licensing of strict and sloppy readings in VP-ellipsis that follow from an alternative analysis of the role of focus binding proposed by Rooth (1992). I propose a topic hypothesis that requires that a coreferential expression enters into an Agree-relation with a topic head in the C-domain. Impossible cases of coreference are ruled out as violations of the locality constraint imposed by the syntactic Agree-relation.

Keywords: binding, contrastive topic, contrastive focus, coreference, Coreference Rule, Dahl's puzzle, discourse update, Interface Rule, parallelism requirement, VP-ellipsis

1 Introduction

This paper starts out with a discussion of the traditional distinction between two types of anaphoric relations, binding and coreference. I dispute a prominent approach, initiated by Reinhart (1983) and further developed by Heim (1998), Fox (2000), Büring (2005), Reinhart (2006), and Roelofsen (2008), which assumes that only one type of anaphoric relation, namely binding, is syntactically encoded (and thus subject to rules of syntactic well-formedness), while coreference is not syntactically encoded and thus not constrained by rules of grammar.

Alternatively, I argue that coreference also involves a binding relation that is mediated by a functional head in the C-domain. The empirical arguments for this approach come from a revised treatment of anaphoric relations in VP-ellipsis in terms of focus binding in the account of Rooth (1992). The discussion of the data is exclusively concerned with anaphoric relations in English (a minor comparison of parallel facts in German aside). As far as the architecture of topics is concerned,

---

Roland Hinterhölzl, Università Ca'Foscari, Venezia

https://doi.org/10.1515/9781501504488-003

I thus argue that even in languages like English, where discourse-given elements remain in their base positions, these elements enter into an Agree-relation with a Topic head in the C-domain.

1.1 Binding and Coreference

To see what is at issue, let us consider how standard cases of binding and coreference are treated in generative syntax (cf. Büring 2005; Heim and Kratzer 1998). A pronoun bound by a referential expression as in (1a) or by a quantified expression as in (1b) is interpreted as a variable bound by an operator with the relevant configuration created by Quantifier Raising (QR) of the antecedent and predicate abstraction, as is illustrated in (1c,d), respectively.

(1) a. *John$_1$ admires his$_1$ teacher*
　　b. *Every student$_1$ admires his$_1$ teacher*
　　c. John λx. x admires x's teacher
　　d. Every student λx. x admires x's teacher (quantifiers are of type ((e,t) (e,t), t))

A coreferential pronoun, in contrast to a bound pronoun, is interpreted as a referential pronoun that is freely assigned a value via an assignment function from the domain of entities in the model, as is familiar from cases of cross-sentential anaphora and illustrated in (2a). Applying the same procedure as in (2a) to the pronoun *his* in (2b) yields a coreferent pronoun: if the possessive pronoun is assigned the value *John*, it accidentally corefers with the subject, without involving any binding relation.

(2) a. *Peter met Mary yesterday. He gave her a present* (he = Peter, her = Mary)
　　b. *John admires his teacher* (his = John)

From this approach it follows that cases of illicit (accidental) coreference as in (3a) are not ruled out in the syntax (in terms of a violation of the binding theory) but require an extra pragmatic principle that regulates the interaction between cases of binding and cases of coreference. Reinhart's (1983) Coreference Rule states that coreference is ruled out if it yields exactly the same interpretation as its binding alternative. For instance, coreference between the subject and the object pronoun in (3a) is ruled out, since there is a licit binding relation in (3b) that yields the very same interpretation. Coreference in (3c) is not ruled out, since the binding alternative in (3d) does not have the same interpretation, stating that only John is a self-admirer, while (3c) expresses the proposition that only John and no other person is such that he admires John.

(3) a. *John admires him (him = John)
    b. John admires himself (binding alternative to (3a))
    c. Only John admires him (him = John)
    d. Only John admires himself

This approach works quite well for standard licit and illicit cases of coreference and has been widely accepted in the field. But we will see in section 2.1 that it runs into a number of problems in cases of VP-ellipsis.

1.2 The Alternative Proposal

Coreferential expressions, including coreferent pronouns, should be considered topics in the broadest sense. They presuppose an antecedent in the discourse to which they refer back. In other words, they behave like discourse anaphors. So far this has not been taken into consideration in standard accounts of coreference. In the terminology of Frascarelli and Hinterhölzl (2007), discourse anaphors count as familiar topics. Familiar topics in Italian and German undergo movement to a licensing position in the C-domain. No such movement is visible in a language like English. Nevertheless, I argue in the present paper for the conjecture in (4).

(4) Topic hypothesis: A coreferential expression enters into an Agree-relation with a licensing head in the C-domain (in all languages)

In particular, I argue that discourse anaphors are bound by a context operator (cf. Hinterhölzl 2013) implying that the mechanism that corresponds to coreference is syntactically encoded. Assuming that functional heads and not DPs are the real antecedents of bound pronouns (Kratzer 2009), I propose that a discourse anaphoric pronoun is in an Agree-relation with a functional head in the C-domain, F_{given}, that introduces a λ-operator binding the pronoun. The external argument A of this head is then retrieved from the context under the condition that A is the most salient discourse referent (DR) matching the φ-features of F_{given}.

In this way, illicit cases of coreference can be reduced to illicit cases of co-binding in the syntax, by adopting an absolute version of Fox's Rule H and Principle B of the binding theory, as is illustrated in (5) and (6).[1]

(5)   a. *John voted for him.* *John = him   b. *Only John voted for him.* ^{ok} John = him

(6)   a. <John> λx. x voted for x   b. <John> λx. No y (y ≠ John) y voted for x

(5a) is ungrammatical, because the (prepositional) object pronoun can neither be interpreted as a bound pronoun (bound by the subject) nor as a discourse anaphor coreferent with the subject. The bound pronoun interpretation is ruled out by Principle B of the binding theory and coreference is ruled out for the following reason: For the pronoun to be coreferent with *John* the latter must be an established discourse referent in the context, indicated by <John> in (6). If the subject in (5) is to be read as being coreferent with this discourse antecedent, it needs to be bound by the lambda-operator introducing this referent, as is illustrated in (6a). However, as we will see below, co-binding of both the subject and the pronoun to the discourse antecedent is not possible without the pronoun being bound by the subject. Thus the ungrammaticality of a coreference relation between the pronoun and the subject is reduced to a violation of the binding theory.

It is important to note that the same problem does not arise in the grammatical (5b). As is illustrated in (6b), the subject in this case is not co-bound by the discourse operator, since it is bound by a separate operator. Hence, the object pronoun can be bound by the discourse operator and coreference is possible, giving rise to the reading that *John* was the only individual in the context that voted for John.

It is clear that this account presupposes that possible violations of the Binding principles A, B and C are restricted to antecedents in A-positions, but this assumption has become a standard one since Aoun (1985). A better alternative would be to assume that violations of the Binding principles are restricted to

---

[1] An anonymous reviewer points out that (5b) is rather unnatural and that the intended reading is only present in (i) below. It must be noted that cases of coreferent pronouns require an appropriate context that (pre-)establishes an appropriate discourse referent, as in (ii) below. In the present paper, I will use coreferent pronouns, since only pronouns give rise to sloppy and strict readings in cases of VP-ellipsis, as we will see in sections 2 and 3, and the availability of certain anaphoric relations in VP-ellipsis serves as core argument against the standard approach.

    (i)   *Only John voted for John.*
    (ii) Context: *John's popularity is going down massively.*
             Only John (himself) voted for him.

antecedents with formal features. Given that the discourse operator introduces a DP that does not come from the lexicon but is inserted from the semantic interface, <John> in (5) only possesses semantic features, but can be taken to lack formal features. I leave this issue open for further research.

In the subsequent sections, I develop the alternative account in more detail and argue in particular that it is superior to the standard account when it comes to explaining the anaphoric relations in cases of VP-ellipsis. Section 2 is concerned with standard accounts of VP-ellipsis and the phenomenon of parallelism, which is at the basis of possible anaphoric relations in VP-ellipsis. Section 3 discusses the difficulties that the standard account has in explaining the different anaphoric relations in cases of VP-ellipsis. In particular, we will address the problems it faces with respect to strict readings (Dahl's puzzle). In section 4, the alternative account is developed. The distinction between binding and coreference is dismissed and replaced by a distinction between pronouns whose formal features are deleted under identity with a syntactic antecedent (syntactic anaphor) and those whose formal features remain active during the derivation and are interpreted in the selection of the respective discourse referent (discourse anaphor). In section 5, we return to Dahl's puzzle and show how it can be accounted for in the alternative approach. Section 6 explores the question of identity and parallelism in VP-ellipsis and investigates in more detail the information structure of the two conjuncts. I argue that identity can be stated on two levels: on the propositional level or on the speech act level. These observations will lead us to revise Rooth's account of semantic parallelism, replacing binding by a contrastive focus with binding by a contrastive topic. Section 7 summarizes the paper.

2 Identity and Parallelism in VP-ellipsis

There is a lot of literature on how to account for the phenomenon of and the restrictions on VP-ellipsis that I cannot fully do justice to in this paper. See Reich (2012) for an overview of the relevant literature. Summarizing somewhat the main lines of discussion, some authors propose that there is just a semantic or anaphoric relation between the ellipsis site and the antecedent; that is to say, the gap is to be treated as a null pronoun (cf. Hardt 1993, 1999). Others insist on the fact that there is strong evidence that VP-ellipsis is sensitive to syntactic structure and thus requires a syntactic account that makes use of syntactic identity (at some level) and of phonological deletion. Note in this respect that VP-ellipsis is sensitive to change of voice and to syntactic islands, as is illustrated in (7). In (7a), the ellipsis site cannot be interpreted as *look into this problem*. The examples in (7) are taken from Reich (2012).

(7) a. *This problem was looked into by John, and Bob did Δ, too
    b. * Dogs, I understand, but cats, I don't know a single person who does Δ

If we adopt a deletion approach the identity condition on VP-ellipsis must be stated on a syntactic level, which interfaces with semantic interpretation, that is at LF, because of the phenomenon of antecedent contained deletion, as May (1995) has argued. As is illustrated in (8), only QR of the direct object in (8a) derives the relevant configuration for copying the correct VP structure, avoiding an infinite regress.

(8) a. *Sandy hit everyone that Bill did Δ*
    b. Sandy [everyone that Bill did Δ] [hit t]

One of the crucial issues of the theory of VP-ellipsis is the definition and explanation of semantic effects of parallelism between the antecedent and the ellipsis site, to which we turn in the following section.

2.1 Effects of Parallelism in VP-ellipsis

It is well known that all kinds of constituent ellipsis show parallelism effects. Consider the famous chicken-argument by Sag (1976) (which goes back to John Ross and George Lakoff), illustrated in (9). Let us first observe that the sentence in (9a) is ambiguous between the reading *the chicken are ready to start eating* and the reading *the chicken are ready to be eaten*. The point of the argument is that if the first conjunct is interpreted as *the chicken are ready to be eaten* so must the second conjunct, giving rise to the awkward interpretation *the children are ready to be eaten*.

(9) a. *The chicken are ready to eat*
    b. *and the children are Δ, too*

Similar observations hold for quantifier scope, as discussed in detail in Fox (2000). First note that a sentence like *some girl hit everyone* is ambiguous between a wide scope reading of the existential quantifier (meaning there is some girl for which it holds that she hit everyone) and a narrow scope reading (meaning for everyone there is some girl or other that hit him). Fox points out that if the existential quantifier in (10a) is interpreted with narrow scope in the first conjunct, it is also interpreted with narrow scope in the second conjunct. The same holds true for the wide scope interpretation of the existential quantifier. Fox also notes that the existential subject in the first conjunct in (10b) can only be interpreted with narrow scope. He surmises that QR of the quantifier *everyone* in the second conjunct is forbidden to apply because it does not give rise to a different interpretation as the subject is a referential DP, thus by parallelism of interpretation the subject may not be interpreted with narrow scope in the first conjunct either.

(10) a. *Some girl hit everyone and some boy did Δ, too*
b. *Someone hit everyone and then Bill did Δ*

We can conclude from these data that the identity condition does indeed operate at LF and that it requires strict syntactic identity of the elided VP and its antecedent. Note furthermore that anaphoric relations in standard cases of VP-ellipsis give rise to the so-called sloppy (11a) and strict reading (11b).

(11) John scratched his arm and Bill did Δ, too
 a. also Bill scratched his own arm (sloppy reading)
 b. also Bill scratched John's arm (strict reading)

The above discussed requirements on identity and parallelism in cases of VP-ellipis are the reason why it is generally assumed that the first conjunct in (11) is ambiguous such that the availability of the strict and sloppy reading are derivable as a parallelism effect. One of the best developed theories on semantic parallelism in VP-ellipsis and the one that is most widely accepted in the field is the account by Rooth (1992) to which we turn now.

2.2 Syntactic and Semantic Parallelism

Rooth (1992) imposes two conditions on the parallelism effects in cases of VP-ellipsis. The conjuncts must be parallel in syntactic form and in semantic interpretation, where syntactic parallelism is given, if the elided VP is a copy of the antecedent VP and semantic parallelism is given, if the target sentence (the second conjunct) contrasts with the antecedent sentence. The notion of *contrast* is crucial in Rooth's account, which submits that the subject in cases of VP-ellipsis is focused, giving rise to focus alternatives. In this account the target sentence S2 contrasts with the antecedent sentence S1, if the proposition expressed by the antecedent clause entails some proposition in the set of alternatives to S2, as is illustrated in (12).

(12) *John said that he is brilliant before* [*Bill*]$_F$ *did* Δ

In (12), the strict reading *Bill said that John is brilliant* has as its focus alternative the proposition that *John said that John is brilliant*, which is implied by the first conjunct just in case no binding relation between the matrix subject and the embedded pronoun is assumed. The sloppy reading *Bill said that Bill is brilliant* has as its focus alternative the proposition *John said that he /himself is brilliant* just in case the first conjunct involves a binding relation that is replicated via focus binding in the second conjunct.

This is exactly what seems to be needed to explain the parallelism effects in VP-ellipsis. Note, however, that Rooth's account inherits the problems of the standard account that we will discuss in detail in Section 3. Furthermore, even though Rooth's account is on the right track as far as the definition of semantic parallelism is concerned, it makes assumptions about the information structure of cases of VP-ellipsis that are not entirely correct and will need to be revised, as we will see in Section 4. In the following section, I discuss in detail how the two readings in (11) are derived in the standard approach and point out the most important problems connected with this account.

3 Anaphoric Relations and VP-ellipsis

The standard explanation for the ambiguity of (13) in the account that distinguishes between coreference and binding is that the first conjunct is amenable to two semantically equivalent syntactic analyses, as is illustrated in (14a,b). Under the condition (16), these representations give rise to the following representation of the second conjunct, with (15a) representing the sloppy and (15b) the strict reading.

(13) *John visited his mother and Peter did* Δ, *too*
    a. Peter visited Peter's mother   b. Peter visited John's mother

(14) a. John λ_1 did t_1 visit his$_1$ mother   b. John$_1$ did visit his$_1$ mother
       (binding)   (coreference)

(15) a. Peter λ_1 did [t_1 visit his$_1$ mother]   b. Peter$_2$ did [visit his$_1$ mother]

(16) No LF-representation must contain both bound occurrences and free occurrences of the same index (Heim and Kratzer 1998: 254)

One might in fact argue that the presence of sloppy and strict readings in cases of VP-ellipsis provides empirical support for the distinction between binding and coreference. Note, however, that at a closer glance strict readings as derived in Reinhart's (1983) approach are incompatible with the above observed effects of parallelism.

3.1 Coreference and VP-ellipsis

Heim (1998) shows that Reinhart's (1983) Coreference Rule, ruling out the strict reading of (17) specified in (17c), is not compatible with standard accounts of VP-ellipsis. The reason is that the possessive pronoun in the first conjunct cannot (accidentally) corefer with the subject (17b), since there is a licit binding alternative using an anaphor that yields the very same interpretation (*John loves his own mother*). Thus the problem is that the second conjunct is ambiguous, while the first conjunct is necessarily unambiguous, violating the constraint on parallelism. Note, furthermore, that an anaphor in the first conjunct can never give rise to a strict reading in the second conjunct in the standard account.

(17) a. *John loves his mother and Peter does Δ, too*
 b. * his = John (coreference in the first conjunct is ruled out)
 c. *Peter loves John's mother too*

One way out here would be to assume that coreference in the first conjunct is not ruled out by its binding alternative in Reinhart's pragmatic approach, since coreference gives rise to a different interpretation in the second conjunct that is not obtainable from its binding alternative. However, Heim (1998) argues that the coreference rule must operate locally on the smallest clause containing the pronoun, otherwise the impossible strict reading in (18) could not be ruled out.

(18) *John saw him and Bill did Δ, too* (* Bill did see John)

She also points out that strict readings are not restricted to referential pronouns, but also occur with bound pronouns, as is illustrated in (19). Here the second clause in (19) admits the reading given in (19b), a clear case of strict pronoun interpretation, since the possessive pronoun does not covary with the local subject *the teacher* but with the higher subject *every student*.

(19) a. *No student said he liked his paper, but every student thought the teacher would*
    b. Every student x thought that the teacher would like x's paper

Furthermore, Heim points out that cases of illicit co-binding, as in (20), are not captured by Reinhart's theory. In (20), it is not possible to interpret the two pronouns as simultaneously bound by the c-commanding quantifier in the higher clause, without the embedded subject binding the object pronoun, as is indicated by super- and subscripted numbers, for binder and (co-)bindees respectively.

(20) * *Every man^1 said that he$_1$ called him$_1$* (co-binding)

In the following subsection, we will discuss how these problems can be remedied in the standard approach.

3.2 Alternative Accounts within the Standard Approach

In this section, I briefly outline two accounts, the one by Heim (1998) and the one by Reinhart (2006), that address the above problem maintaining the distinction between binding and coreference. Furthermore, I will point out additional problems of the standard account that will lead us to abandon the latter.

The solution to these problems proposed in Heim (1998) involves a novel notion of *codermination* that covers both binding and coreference as well as cases of co-binding, as is illustrated in (21). Furthermore, Heim also invokes an extended version of Principle B of the binding theory as given in (22). The core of her account is the exceptional rule of codetermination (ERC) in (23). In this proposal coreference becomes a matter of syntax with the essential result that coreferent but not co-bound coarguments are allowed in violation of condition B, if the relevant LF is semantically different from its binding alternative.

(21) Codetermination
    Let C be a context, let LF be a logical form and let A and B be two DPs in LF, we say that
    A and B are codetermined in LF/C iff:
    A binds B in LF, or
    A and B corefer in C, or
    there is a third DP which is codetermined with A and B in LF/C

(22) Heim's Condition B
Pronouns cannot be codetermined with their coarguments

(23) ERC
Let LF be a logical form in which a pronoun is codetermined but not bound by one of its coarguments. Then LF is (marginally) allowed, in violation of condition B, if it is semantically distinguishable from its binding alternative in the given context

Getting rid of Reinhart's Rule of Coreference, strict and sloppy readings in cases of VP-ellipsis can be dealt with again in terms of baseline accounts of the latter, since the ERC requiring distinct interpretations only comes into play if there is a violation of Principle B, as is the case in (4ac) but not in (17). My assessment of this proposal is that the solution works but comes at a high price, since Principle B can be violated in specific cases and more importantly since the solution requires a complex system of coindexing involving different types of indices for binders and bindees.

The problem with the strict reading in cases of VP-ellipsis and Heims's account of it are specifically addressed in Reinhart (2006), who introduces the Interface Rule, a revised version of her Coreference Rule, which states that coreference is only excluded if it would allow for a reading that is excluded by the respective binding alternative. As Roelofsen (2008) points out this solution solves the problem with strict readings in standard cases of VP-ellipsis as in (17), but runs into problems when confronted with Dahl's puzzle that I will discuss in detail below. A solution to Dahl's puzzle along the lines of Reinhart's interface rule is proposed by Roelofsen in (2009).

I will not discuss these accounts in any detail here, since they rely on two mechanisms, namely a) the complex indexing system of Heim (1998), and b) the comparison of binding alternatives that our alternative account can do without, as I argue below. Heim's observations about co-binding and the possibly non-referential character of pronouns obtaining a strict interpretation in cases of VP-ellipsis, however, are important for our account, as I argue that illicit cases of coreference reduce to illicit cases of co-binding.

Returning to the illicit case of co-binding in (20), Fox (2000) proposes an elegant solution to this problem with the economy condition in (24).

(24) Rule H
A pronoun P can be bound to an antecedent A only if there is no closer antecedent B such that it is possible to bind P to B and get the same semantic interpretation

Note that Rule H is preferable to Heim's codetermination rule, since it avoids that condition B can be violated sometimes and since it also accounts for Dahl's puzzle. Dahl (1973) noted that cases of VP-ellipsis involving two pronouns in the elided VP allow for only three of the four logically possible interpretations derived by combining sloppy and strict readings, as is illustrated in (25).

(25) *Max said that he called his mother and Bob did too.*
    a. *[Bob]$_F$ too said that Max called Max's mother* (strict-strict)
    b. *[Bob] $_F$ too said that Bob called Bob's mother* (sloppy-sloppy)
    c. *[Bob] $_F$ too said that Bob called Max's mother* (sloppy-strict)
    d. **[Bob] $_F$ too said that Max called Bob's mother* (strict-sloppy)

Within the complex indexing system outlined above, we have to consider the following possible logical forms of the first conjunct. For instance, (26b) is ruled out because it is equivalent to (26a), which involves a more local binding relation. Also, (26f), which underlies the ungrammatical strict-sloppy pattern, is ruled out since it is equivalent to, but less economical than (26d), if it is assumed that a binding relation is more economical than a relation of coreference.

(26) a. $[Max]^1$ t_1 said $[he_1]^2$ t_2 called his$_2$ mother (25b)
    b. $[Max]^1$ t_1 said $[he_1]^2$ t_2 called his$_1$ mother (25b)
    c. Max said that he called his mother (he = his = Max) (25a)
    d. Max said $[he]^2$ t_2 called his$_2$ mother (he = Max) (25b)
    e. $[Max]^1$ t_1 said $[he_1]^2$ t_2 called his mother (his = Max) (25c)
    f. $[Max]^1$ t_1 said he called his$_1$ mother (he = Max) (25d)

Note further that approaches based on indices predict that in a sequence of VP-ellipses, each ellipsis site is resolved sloppily, if the first one is. This is so because a sloppy pronoun requires binding and, given our assumptions about indices in (16), the bound index is no longer available for accidental coreference. However, Dahl (1974) presents an example in which the strict reading *Bill's wife is realizing that Bill is a fool* may follow the sloppy reading *Bill does not realize that Bill is a fool*, as is illustrated in (27).

(27) *John realizes that he is a fool, but Bill does not, even though his wife does.*

To conclude this section, we have seen that the standard account that distinguishes referential pronouns from bound pronouns and uses a complex system of indices faces serious problems in cases of VP-ellipsis. In the following section, I present an alternative account of coreferent pronouns in terms of variables bound by a context operator.

4 The Alternative Account

In the alternative account, the distinction between binding and coreference is given up and coreference is reduced to a binding relation to a context operator. Illicit cases of coreference can be reduced to illicit cases of co-binding in the syntax, by adopting an absolute version of Fox's Rule H, given in (28) and the Binding Principle B in (29). The crucial point of the principle in (28) is that the necessity of comparing interpretations evaporates.

(28) Absolute Ban on Co-binding
A DP A cannot be bound by DP C across an intervening DP B, if B itself is bound by C.

(29) Principle B
A pronoun P cannot be bound by one of its co-arguments.

The working of the principle in (28) is illustrated again in (30) and (31). As noted above, (30a) is ungrammatical, because both binding of the (prepositional) object pronoun by the subject and coreference with it are ruled out. Direct binding of the object pronoun by the subject is ruled out by the Binding Principle in (29), since subject and object are arguments of the same predicate (are co-arguments).

Let us explore how coreference between the two can be excluded in the alternative account. For the pronoun to be coreferent with *John* the latter must be an established discourse referent in the context, indicated by <John> in (31). If the subject in (31) is to be read as coreferent with this discourse antecedent, it needs to be co-bound by the lambda-operator introducing this referent, as is illustrated in (31a). However, co-binding in (31a) is ruled out by the principle in (28). The same problem, however, does not arise in the grammatical (30b), as is illustrated in (31b). In this case, the subject is not (co-)bound by the discourse operator, hence the object pronoun can be bound by the discourse operator and coreference is possible, giving rise to the reading that *John* was the only individual in the context that voted for John.

(30) a. *John voted for him.* b. *Only John voted for him.*
     *John = him   ok John = him

(31) a. <John> λx. x voted for x   b. <John> λx. No y (y ≠ John) y voted for x

The advantage of this account is that illicit cases of coreference via the independently necessary rule of co-binding can be reduced to standard cases of violations of the binding theory and possible cases of coreference can be accounted for without taking into consideration binding alternatives and the difficult issue of whether the latter give rise to alternative representations at LF that are semantically equivalent or not. Of course the approach will stand or fall depending on whether it can account for the presence of strict readings in cases of VP-ellipsis. This issue is discussed in more detail in the following subsection.

4.1 Strict Readings without Coreference

Note first that the rule in (28) implies that the first conjunct in (32) is unambiguous, allowing only for the sloppy reading in a standard account like Rooth's account of VP-ellipsis.

(32) *John visited his mother and Peter did Δ, too*

To account for the presence of the strict reading, we may assume that VP-ellipsis involves the conjunction of two speech acts (rather than of two propositions). After processing of the first conjunct the context is updated, and *John* is added to the stack of given DRs. (33) shows the representation of the strict reading in the present account, which meets the two requirements on parallelism of Rooth (1992): the proposition *John visited John's mother* is an element of the focus-value of (32) and the elided VP is a copy of the antecedent VP.

(33) < John> λ x. [$_F$ Peter] did [visit x's mother]

Is there any evidence for the assumption that in VP-ellipsis the conjunction of two assertions is involved? Krifka (1999) assumes that the conjuncts in VP-ellipsis constitute separate speech acts on the basis that pronouns in the second conjunct pick up referents in the first conjunct: "the second answer can have anaphoric elements that refer to the first answer, which shows that it should be interpreted after the context is updated with the first answer" (Krifka 1999), as is illustrated in (34).

(34) *What did the Permaneders eat?*
     Péter ate pàsta and his wife ate polènta

However, there are problems with a simple minded up-dating approach that will be discussed in detail in the following two sections.

4.2 Problems with the Updating Account

There are basically two types of problems with this account. One problem is technical and involves the treatment of pronouns in the grammar and that will be discussed in this section. The other problem points to the necessity of revising Rooth's proposal and will be taken up in section 6.

Note first that the strict reading cannot be derived in the present account if it is assumed that copying occurs at LF where the bound pronoun in the first conjunct is converted to a variable (bound by the subject). Note that under these assumptions the pronoun co-varies with the trace of the subject in VP and can never give rise to a strict reading, as is illustrated in (35).

(35) John λ x. x visited x's mother

This unwanted consequence can be remedied if it is assumed that what is copied into the ellipsis site is the pronoun with or without its φ-features. This proposal is based on two rather plausible assumptions, namely that a) syntactic anaphors lack φ-features, but discourse anaphors contain φ-features, and b) that syntactic anaphors obtain φ-features in the Agree-relation with their antecent. Given these assumptions one may propose the following mapping condition between pronouns and variables.

(36) **Mapping condition between pronouns and variables:**
A pronoun that shares formal φ-features with another DP A (in an Agree-relation) is mapped onto the same variable that A is mapped onto at LF

This mapping condition would then make the following prediction: discourse anaphors can only be bound by non overt antecedents, assuming, as we already did above, that a discourse antecedent enters the computation only with semantic features. This makes for a potentially interesting prediction. However, there is independent evidence that what is copied into the ellipsis site is always the pronoun **with** its φ-features.

Consider the following case of constituent ellipsis in German. (37) only allows for the strict reading *also Mary loves his mother*. The sloppy reading *also Mary loves her mother* is out. The intuition here is that the sloppy reading is out since the φ-features of subject and possessive pronoun in the object do not match.

However, if syntactic anaphors are copied into the ellipsis site without their φ-features, the sloppy reading cannot be excluded on anybody's account.

(37) Hans liebt seine Mutter und Maria auch.
   a. John λ x. x loves x's mother and Maria λx. x loves x's mother
   b. * Maria^i loves his^i mother
   c. <John> λy. Maria λx. x loves y's mother (strict reading)

The sloppy reading is excluded if it is assumed that re-binding by *Maria* requires an Agree-relation in which the φ-features of antecedent and pronoun are matched. Thus, I make the following proposal: a) the φ-features of the pronoun are always copied into the ellipsis site, and b) the φ-features of the pronoun can be deleted under identity with those of its antecedent, giving rise to a bound pronoun, or remain visible for the rest of the computation, building the basis for a coreferent pronoun when the latter enters into an Agree-relation with a discourse operator.

4.3 Updating and Speech Acts

Having resolved this (important) technical issue, let us now consider the main problem with the above assumed updating account. Consider the following case of VP-ellipsis in (38), which clearly allows for a strict reading of the possessive pronoun.

(38) *John visited his mother before Peter did*

Given the nature of the type of embedded clause containing the ellipsis site – it is a central adverbial clause in the terminology of Haegeman (2002) – it cannot be argued that the before-clause in (38) constitutes a separate speech act, implying that updating must be independent of the utterance of speech acts. As an alternative, I propose that discourse referents are updated after the processing of each clause, whether it is a main clause constituting a speech act or it is an embedded clause constituting only a proposition. Evidence for this assumption comes from the observation that even discourse antecedents in central embedded clauses give rise to de-accenting, as is illustrated in (39). Assuming that de-accentuation is a phonological correlate of d-linking, that is, of discourse anaphors, (39a) can be analysed as given in (39b).

(39) a. *If John does not come in time, Mary will hit_m (him)*
   b. If John does not come in time, <John> Mary will hit_m

To summarize the last two sections, we have argued that pronouns in cases of VP-ellipsis are not ambiguous between a bound and a referential construal. Due to the principle in (28) only a bound variable interpretation is admitted in the first conjunct. The strict reading in the present account is due to an update of discourse referents that occurs after every clause that provides the relevant antecedent for the discourse operator binding the pronoun in the second conjunct. The difference between bound pronouns and referential pronouns in the standard theory is replicated in the present account by assuming that the φ-features are deleted with bound pronouns but remain visible and interpretable in the interface with referential pronouns. What remains to be shown is why re-binding of the pronoun by the context operator does not violate the parallelism constraint. We consider this issue in the following section.

5 Returning to Dahl's Puzzle

To remind us of the case at hand, only three of the four possible readings are available if the ellipsis site contains two positions for pronominal variables, as is illustrated again in (40).

(40) *Max said that he called his mother and Bob did too.*
   a. $[Bob]_F$ *too said that Max called Max's mother* (strict-strict)
   b. $[Bob]_F$ *too said that Bob called Bob's mother* (sloppy-sloppy)
   c. $[Bob]_F$ *too said that Bob called Max's mother* (sloppy-strict)
   d. *$[Bob]_F$ *too said that Max called Bob's mother* (strict-sloppy)

Dahl's puzzle is explained in the present system by syntactic parallelism of binding relations: focus binding in the ellipsis site needs to be parallel to the binding relations in the antecedent clause. In (40) there are two binding relations in the antecedent clause: one between the matrix subject and the embedded subject and one between the embedded subject and the possessive pronoun.

Note that the proposition (*Max said Max called Max's mother*) is an element of the focus value of (40b), since the embedded subject and the possessive pronoun covary with the matrix subject in the ellipsis site via parallel binding relations in the antecedent site. The two mixed readings differ in that there is a parallel binding relation in the antecedent site between matrix and embedded subject for (40c), but there is no such parallel relation between the matrix subject and the possessive pronoun in the antecedent site for (40d).

This account raises the question of why parallelism of binding relations is required for obtaining sloppy readings but not for obtaining strict readings. To answer this question let us go back to Heim's observation that strict readings are also possible with bound pronouns, given again in (41a), where the second conjunct can be interpreted as specified in (41b). As is evident in (41), the relevant binding relation between the matrix subject and the embedded possessive pronoun in the second conjunct is not paralleled by a corresponding binding relation in the first conjunct.

(41) a. *No student said he liked his paper, but every student thought the teacher would*
b. Every student x thought that the teacher would like x's paper

Given these observations, I would like to put forward the following generalisation given in (42) to account for the grammaticality of (41b) and the ungrammaticality of (40d). In (41b), the binder *every student* (including its trace in the vP) is outside of the ellipsis-site. In (40d), however, both the trace of the matrix antecedent *Bob* and the possessive pronoun to receive a sloppy reading are contained in the ellipsis-site, while the antecedents of pronouns to receive a strict reading are always necessarily outside of the ellipsis-site in the present account. Thus Dahl's puzzle in (40) is reduced to the independently given availability of the strict reading in (41). I consider this as strong evidence in favour of the present account.

(42) Only binding relations properly contained in the ellipsis site need to be paralleled by corresponding binding relations in the antecedent clause.

Let us finally tackle the second challenge to the standard account posed by Dahl. The relevant example is given again in (43).

(43) *John realizes that he is a fool, but Bill does not, even though his wife does*

The problem with the strict reading in the third conjunct in (43) is the differential representation of coreference and binding, pronoun versus variable, in the standard account. Furthermore, the use of a complex indexing system with the restriction on index assignment in (16) makes it impossible to derive the strict reading *his wife does realize that Bill is a fool*, as we have seen. In the present account that operates without indices, the problem does not arise: the pronoun *he* in *x realizes that he is a fool* is copied with its φ-features into the ellipsis-site and the pronoun may receive a strict reading by entering into an Agree relation with F_{given} in terms of its interpretable φ-features and is in this way subject to re-binding by an operator outside of the ellipsis site voiding any requirement of a strict parallelism effect in binding relations with the antecedent, as is illustrated in (44). In (44), the Agree relation between the functional head and the pronoun is indicated via co-indexing only for ease of exposition.

(44) <Bill> F_i even though his wife does x realize that he$_i$ is a fool

To summarize this section, I have shown that Dahl's puzzle can be accounted for in a much simpler fashion without considering binding alternatives. Furthermore, I have argued that the switch between strict and sloppy readings is allowed– as long as semantic parallelism is respected – by the independently needed mechanism of copying a pronoun **with** its Φ features into the ellipsis site and by the important empirical generalisation that only binding relations properly contained in the ellipsis site must be matched by parallel binding relations in the antecedent site. As became evident in the examples discussed, including those comprising Dahl's puzzle, binding relations in the antecedent site need not to be matched with parallel binding relations in the ellipsis site.

The latter observation makes a lot of sense since the ellipsis site, becaue it is phonologically null, is highly ambiguous. It thus seems to be a cogent strategy to interpret only the ellipsis site as parallel to the antecedent site (but not vice versa). Different and also contrastive interpretations, as we will see in the next section, are possible in the second conjunct if these interpretations are indicated by lexical material that necessarily is added outside of the ellipsis site. In the following section, we will have a closer look at the parallelism constraint in VP-ellipsis. We will see that in standard cases of VP-ellipsis the information structural value of the ellipsis-site differs from that of the antecedent cite. In this case parallelism or semantic identity is observed at the propositional level. We will also discuss special cases in which parallelism or semantic identity is observed at the speech act level. The latter cases will lead us ultimately to revise Rooth's classical analysis replacing focus binding with binding by a contrastive topic.

6 Contrast and Contrastive Topics in VP-ellipsis

In the final section, I address the question of whether Rooth's analysis of the information structure of standard cases of VP-ellipsis is correct. Remember that in Rooth's account, a case of VP-ellipsis like (45a) is analysed as given in (45b), in which the subject in the second conjunct is necessarily focused, raising the question of what type of focus is at stake in cases of VP-ellipsis.

(45) a. *John visited his mother and Peter did too*
   b. John visited his mother and [Peter]$_F$ did Δ, too

The intuition behind standard cases of VP-ellipsis like (45) is that what *Peter* does is contrasted with what *John* does in some sense, as is also assumed by Rooth, implying the presence of a contrastive focus. Note, however, that the analysis of cases of VP-ellipsis as containing two contrastive foci in (46) is out, since these sentences can be uttered out of the blue, as is illustrated in (47). In the context of (47), the whole first conjunct has to be assumed to be focused. Note furthermore, as is also evident in (47) that while the antecedent site is typically part of the focus domain, the ellipsis site is necessarily given to meet the requirement of deletion under identity.

(46) [John]$_F$ visited his mother and [Peter]$_F$ did Δ, too

(47) *What's going on here?*
   [First, John insulted his mother]$_F$ and then [Peter]$_F$ did Δ, too

Moreover, the question arises that if there is no parallelism in terms of contrastive foci, what is contrasted in cases of VP-ellipsis. In the following section, I outline an alternative account that draws heavily from Krifka's (1999) account (cf. also Winkler and Konietzko 2010).

6.1 The Role of Contrastive Focus and Contrastive Topic in VP-ellipsis

Krifka (1999) argues that stressed additive particles like *too*, *also* and *auch* behave differently from their unstressed versions associated with focus and argues that they associate with a contrastive topic (CT), where he defines a CT as a constituent that refers to an entity about which information is required at the current point of the discourse, but there are other entities for which information of a similar type is required. He furthermore assumes that a stress that identifies a focus within the topic indicates the presence of such alternatives (Krifka 1999).

The analysis of CTs is a much debated issue. I follow Molnár (1998: 135) that a CT can only occur in obligatory combination with an additional focus in the sentence. Furthermore, a CT seems to involve a selective focus within the topic constituent and another selective focus within the comment, while contrastive focus is (mostly) corrective. See Molnár (2006), Frascarelli and Hinterhölzl (2007), and Bianchi, Bocci and Cruschina (2013) for further discussion of this issue.

It is also generally assumed that a CT presupposes a Question under Discussion (QUD) (cf. Roberts 1996; Büring 1997) for which each sentence connected to the topic provides a partial congruent answer, as is illustrated in (48). I use two types of accent to indicate that *Peter* and *Per* constitute CTs and *pasta* and *polenta* constitute contrastive foci in the context of (47). C in (48) indicates the comment part of the utterance.

(48) *What did Peter and Per eat?*
  a. *Péter ate pàsta (and)* [$_{CT}$ Peter] [$_C$ he ate pasta]
  b. *Pér ate polènta*

Furthermore, I adopt the distinctiveness condition on contrastive answers (Krifka's 1999 (48)), as given in (49). Note that (49) rules out the non-distinctive answer to (50a) in (50b) requiring an answer like (50c).

(49) If [T_F ...C_F] is a contrastive answer to a question Q, then there is no alternative T' to T such that the speaker is willing to assert [T' C]

(50) a. *What did Peter and Per eat?*
  b. * *Péter ate pàsta, and Pér ate pàsta*
  c. *Peter and Per ate pàsta*
  d. *Péter ate pàsta and Pér ate pasta, too*
  e. *Péter ate pàsta and Pér did Δ, too*

Based on (49), Krifka (1999) defines the role of the additive particle in the following way: it cancels the implicature of distinctiveness and constitutes the real focus in the second conjunct. Note, futhermore, that (50d), where the VP is de-accentuated, may be considered the basis of VP-ellipsis in (50c). Following this argumentation, I propose that the focus of the second conjunct in (50d) is the additive particle, indicating an affirmation or denial of the respective proposition. The analysis of the second conjunct of (50d) is given in (51). Note that the focus on the particle presupposes that someone else ate pasta, suggesting the alternative requirement on parallelism in (52).

(51) [Pér]_CT ate pasta, [too]_F

(52) Alternative Requirement on Parallelism (ARP):
The first conjunct must entail the presupposition of the second conjunct

Based on the ARP in (52), we can assume that a standard case of VP-ellipsis as in (53a) has the information structural representation given in (53b).

(53) a. *John visited his mother and Peter did too*
 b. [John]_CT [visited his mother]_F and [Peter]_CT did Δ [too]_F

What is important in (53b) is that the two conjuncts have different information structures. The part that is deleted in the second conjuncts constitutes given (or presupposed) information but is asserted as new information in the first conjunct, suggesting that parallelism is computed on the propositional level in cases like (53a). Some evidence for this analysis comes from a re-interpretation of the phenomenon of vehicle change addressed in the following section.

6.2 Vehicle Change and Parallel Interpretation

Fiengo and May (1994) argue that the identity condition on VP-ellipsis cannot be strictly syntactic, since VP-ellipsis displays a phenomenon of switching from a name or pronoun to another pronominal representation (called vehicle change), as is illustrated in (54).

(54) a. *Mary voted for Ben and he did, too*
 b. *Mary thinks that Ben will win and he does, too*
 c. *Ben voted for himself and Mary did, too*

To avoid violations of Principle C in (54a, b), it is assumed that a name can be replaced with an anaphor or a pronoun in these cases. Likewise in (54c) to obtain the strict reading an anaphor (a bound pronoun) must be taken to be changeable into a pronominal representation, in standard terminology into a referential pronoun. The big question behind vehicle change is why these changes are available and licit in cases of VP-ellipsis but unavailable in other cases.

I would like to argue based on my judgments on parallel cases of stripping in German (for stripping in German cf. Konietzko 2016) that vehicle change crucially involves contrastive focus on the element to be changed, as is illustrated in (55).

(55a, b) are completely parallel in judgment to (54a, b). (55c) with the anaphor *sich* in German only allows for the sloppy reading. A strict reading, however, is marginally possible to my ear, if a pronoun is reinforced with the focus particle *selbst*.

(55) a. *Maria hat für [Hans]*$_{CF}$ *gestimmt und er (selber) auch*
  Mary has for John   voted   and he himself too
  'Mary voted for John and he (himself) did too'
  b. *Maria glaubt dass [Hans]*$_{CF}$ *gewinnt und er (selber) auch*
   Mary thinks that John   wins   and he himself too
   'Mary thinks that John will win and he (himself) does too'
  c. *?? Hans hat für [ihn]*$_{CF}$ *selbst gestimmt und Maria auch*
   John has for him   himself voted   and Mary too
   'John has voted for himself and Mary did too'

According to our assumptions what is copied into the ellipsis cite is the verb plus the name or the pronoun (with its φ-features), leading to violations of the BT or to wrong interpretations. Note, however, that if it is assumed that the contrastive focus information is copied into the ellipsis site as well, both the subject and the object are bound by a separate operator in (56). Given that variables bound by two different operators can covary, as is illustrated in (57a) (if co-variation is to be excluded (57b) must be used in English), no violation of the binding theory is expected in (56).

(56) [he]$_{CT}$ voted for [Ben]$_{CF}$ [too]$_F$

(57) a. *everyone loves everyone*
  b. *everyone loves everyone else*

This analysis raises the question of how parallelism is computed in cases like (54) and (55). In a Rooth-style analysis, one would have to assume that every proposition that is an element of the focus value of the first conjunct entails a proposition that is an element of the focus value of the second conjunct and vice versa, leading to wrong results.

Alternatively, I would like to make the following suggestion: the identity condition is also stateable at the level of the assertion comprising information structural distinctions and not just at the level of the proposition as seems to be the default in standard cases of VP-ellipsis. The presupposition of (56) is that someone else voted for Ben rather than for another person. This is implied by the first conjunct *Mary voted for Ben rather than for someone else* guaranteeing a parallel interpretation in our account. The informal LF of (54a) in this analysis is given in (58).

(58) for Mary the speaker asserts that it was Ben (and not someone else) that she voted for and for Ben, the speaker asserts that it was Ben as well (and not someone else) that he voted for

If this account of the data in (54) and (55) is on the right track, it forms an important argument against Rooth's analysis. Recall that most cases of VP-ellipsis involve identity on the propositional level such that the two conjuncts can have an independent and possibly different information structure, as is illustrated again in (59). While *ate pasta*, as is also indicated by the obligatory accent on the object, is part of the focus domain in the first conjunct, *ate pasta* is necessarily given, de-accented and thus deletable in the second conjunct.

(59) a. *Péter ate pàsta and Pér ate pasta, too*
    b. *Péter ate pàsta and Pér did Δ, too*

Furthermore, note that the accent on *Per* in (59a) cannot correspond to a CF since the latter would require identity of assertion, contrary to fact. A CT on the other hand – contrary to a contrastive focus (CF)–can be assumed to scope outside of the assertion, as is illustrated in (60), and can either allow for identity at the propositional level or at the speech act level.

(60) [CT [$_{Assertion}$ ...CF...]]

There is evidence for this distinction between CTs and CFs in VP-ellipsis and for the structure assumed in (60) coming from German data discussed in Konietzko and Winkler (2010). They show that in cases of bare argument deletion a CT precedes sentence adverbs and negation, while a CF follows these elements, as is illustrated in (61) and (62). The context of (61) requires the presence of CTs, which must be realized in a high position in the clause, while the context in (62) does not trigger the obligatory presence of a CT topic and is compatible with a CF, as is indicated in (62). In this context, however, a CT topic is also admissible suggesting that the relevant QUD can always be accomodated as well.

(61) *Will both of the siblings go to France?*
    a. *Maria wird wohl fahren, aber [Hans]$_{CT}$ vermutlich   nicht*
       Mary will PART go-there but John   presumably   not
       'Mary will go there but John will probably not do it'

    b. *Maria wird wohl fahren, aber vermutlich   (Hans) nicht (Hans)
       Maria will PART go   but presumably John not   John

(62) *Will Maria go to France?*
    a. *Maria wird wohl nicht fahren, aber vermutlich   [Hans]$_{CF}$*
       Maria will PART not go,   but presumably John
    b. *Maria wird wohl nicht fahren, aber [Hans]$_{CT}$ vermutlich schon*
       'Mary is likely not to go there but presumably John will'

To summarize this section, the role of contrastive focus (CF) in the account of Rooth (1992) has to be replaced with the role of contrastive topic to arrive at a comprehensive account of the information structure involved in VP-ellipsis. As far as anaphoric relations are concerned, focus binding has to be replaced with binding by a contrastive topic. Everything else remains the same, including the solution to Dahl's puzzle in the alternative account. The present analysis of coreference in terms of binding by a context operator thus provides further support for the role of CTs in VP-ellipsis, as argued for by Krifka (1999), and is in line with recent work by Winkler and Konietzko (2010) on bare argument ellipsis in German.

7 Conclusions

This paper set out to tackle the traditional distinction between binding and coreference, arguing that coreference is to be replaced by a binding relation to a discourse operator. I have shown that the alternative approach can account in a much simpler way for the anaphoric relations found in cases of VP-ellipsis, including Dahl's puzzle. In particular, it explains the presence and absence of strict readings without appealing to a complex index system and without necessitating the comparison between binding alternatives. Instead it shows that sloppy and strict readings are possible since the antecedent site makes at the same time available a binding relation and a discourse antecedent. The latter is then available as antecedent for re-binding an appropriate pronoun without violating the parallelism constraint to obtain the strict reading, since it is shown that only binding relations properly contained in the ellipsis site need to be paralleled by appropriate binding relations in the antecedent site.

    Finally, I argued that the crucial element that allows for focus binding in VP-ellipsis contexts is a CT and not a CF, as proposed by Rooth (1992). The most important point is, however, the conclusion that a simple account of coreference and of anaphoric relations in VP-ellipsis is achieved by the assumption that a syntactic head in the C-domain, a familiar topic in the framework of Frascarelli and Hinterhölzl (2007), enters into an Agree-relation with discourse given elements that are spelled out in their base position. I have thus provided strong cross-linguistic evidence for the presence of topic positions in the C-domain even in languages like English that are not discourse configurational like Italian or German. Furthermore, the paper argues that contrastive topics play a crucial role in the licensing of anaphoric relations in cases of VP-ellipsis and shows that a syntactic account of coreference is superior to a pragmatic account in terms of a complex evaluation of binding alternatives at LF, as it is generally assumed in the standard approach.

References

Aoun, Joseph. 1985. *A grammar of anaphora* (Linguistic Inquiry Monograph 11). Cambridge, MA: MIT Press.
Bianchi, Valentina, Giuliano Bocci & Silvio Cruschina. 2013. Focus fronting and its implicatures. In Enoch Aboh (ed.), *Romance languages and linguistic theory: selected papers from Going Romance 2013*. Amsterdam & New York: John Benjamins.
Büring, Daniel. 2005. Bound to bind. *Linguistic Inquiry* 36(2). 259–274.
Büring, Daniel. 1997. *The meaning of topic and focus: The 59th Street bridge accent*. London: Routledge.
Dahl, Östen. 1973. On so-called sloppy identity. *Synthese* 26. 81–112.
Dahl, Östen. 1974. *How to open a sentence: abstraction in natural language*. (Logical Grammar Reports 12). Göteborg. University of Göteborg.
Fiengo, Robert & Robert May. 1994. *Indices and identity*. Cambridge, MA: MIT Press.
Fox, Dany. 2000. *Economy and semantic interpretation*. Cambridge, Ma: MIT Press.
Frascarelli, Mara & Roland Hinterhölzl. 2007. Types of topics in German and Italian. In Kerstin Schwabe & Susanne Winkler (eds.), *On information structure, meaning and form*, 87–116. Amsterdam & New York: John Benjamins.
Haegeman, Liliane. 2012. *Adverbial clauses, main clause phenomena, and composition of the left periphery*. New York: OUP.
Hardt, Dan. 1993. Verb phrase ellipsis: Form, meaning and processing. Philadelphia: University of Pennsylvania dissertation.
Hardt, Dan. 1999. Dynamic interpretation of verb phrase ellipsis. *Linguistics and Philosophy* 22. 185–219.
Heim, Irene. 1998. Anaphora and semantic interpretation: a reinterpretation of Reinhart's approach. In Uli Sauerland & Orin Percus (eds.), *The interpretive tract*. Cambridge, MA: MIT Working Papers in Linguistics 25. 205–246.
Heim, Irene & Angelika Kratzer. 1998. *Semantics in generative grammar*. Oxford: Blackwell.
Hinterhölzl, Roland. 2013. Economy conditions and coreference: From minimal pronouns to referential acts. *Working Papers in Scandinavian Syntax* 91. 1–35. University of Lund.

Konietzko, Andreas. 2016. *Bare argument ellipsis and focus*. Amsterdam & New York: John Benjamins.
Kratzer, Angelika. 2009. Making a pronoun. *Linguistic Inquiry* 40(2). 187–237.
Krifka, Manfred. 1999. Additive particles under stress. Austin: University of Texas manuscript.
Molnár, Valéria. 1998. Topic in focus: on the syntax, phonology, semantics and pragmatics of the so-called "contrastive topic" in Hungarian and German. *Acta Linguistica Hungarica* 45. 89–166.
Molnár, Valéria. 2006. On different kinds of contrast. In Valéria Molnár & Susanne Winkler. (eds.), *The architecture of focus*, 197–233. Berlin & New York: Mouton de Gruyter.
Reich, Ingo. 2012. Ellipsis. In Claudia Maienborn, Klaus von Heusinger & Paul Portner (eds.), *Semantics: an international handbook of natural language meaning*. Volume 3, 1849–1874. Berlin & New York: Mouton de Gruyter.
Reinhart, Tanja. 1983. *Anaphora and semantic interpretation*. London: Croom Helm.
Reinhart, Tanja. 2006. *Interface strategies*. Cambridge, MA: MIT Press.
Roelofsen, Floris. 2008. *Anaphora resolved*. Amsterdam: University of Amsterdam dissertation.
Roelofsen, Floris. 2009. Free variable economy. In Arndt Riester & Torgrim Solstad (eds.), *Proceedings of Sinn and Bedeutung* 13, 415–424. Stuttgart: University of Stuttgart.
Rooth, Mats. 1992. Ellipsis redundancy and reduction redundancy. In Steve Berman & Arild Hestvik (eds.), *Proceedings of the Stuttgart workshop on ellipsis, 1–26*. Stuttgart: University of Stuttgart.
Sag, Ivan. 1976. *Deletion and logical form*. Cambridge, MA: MIT dissertation.
Winkler, Susanne & Andreas Konietzko. 2010. Contrastive ellipsis: Mapping between syntax and information structure. *Lingua* 120. 1436–1457.

Werner Frey, André Meinunger
Topic Marking and Illocutionary Force

Abstract: The main goal of the paper is to determine whether topic marking of a constituent of a clause requires that the clause have independent illocutionary force. To do so, four types of topic marking constructions and, in addition to independent clauses, three types of dependent clauses are investigated. It is shown that for the constructions that mark an aboutness topic it holds that in order for a clause to allow the marking, the clause does not need to have the capability to perform a speech act; however, it also holds that these topic markings cannot occur in just any type of dependent clause. The topic markings with this intermediate status are called weakly root-sensitive. A three-way distinction can be found. Next to the weakly root-sensitive markings there exist one type of topic marking which can only be hosted by a clause with full illocutionary force and one type that may occur in any kind of clause.

Other non-truth-functional/non-descriptive phenomena (e.g. question tags, interjections, modal particles, expressively coloured expressions) are also studied to determine their distribution. Among them a three-way distinction can be found as well. Some of the phenomena are weakly root-sensitive, i.e. they have the intermediate status, others can only be hosted by a clause with full illocutionary force, and still others may occur in any kind of clause.

The paper aims to characterise the property of being weakly root-sensitive and thereby gain some insights about what semantic/pragmatic properties a clause must have in order that marking of an aboutness topic may occur in it. In this regard, the concept of a judge (cf. Krifka 2017) is crucial.

The paper arrives at a classification of three types of non-descriptive phenomena and of three types of clauses as well as correlations between these two classifications.

Keywords: adverbial clauses, dependent clauses, expressives, illocution, integration, judgement phrase, left dislocation, root phenomena (weak, strong), speech act, topic marking constructions

---

Werner Frey, André Meinunger, ZAS, Berlin

https://doi.org/10.1515/9781501504488-004

1 Introduction

It can easily be agreed on that it is an interesting and challenging task to determine which expressions are root-sensitive and why they are. This paper will argue that it is equally important to ask to what degree an expression is root-sensitive. Thus, the goal of this paper is twofold. One goal is to show that in German, topic-marking constructions and other expressives (i.e. expressions with an evaluative/emotional component which is not-at-issue) differ with regard to their root-sensitivity. Some of the expressives are what we call strongly root-sensitive, i.e. they may only occur in clauses with an independent illocution. Some of them are weakly root-sensitive, i.e. they may occur in root clauses and in a restricted set of embedded clauses, which, as we will show, do not need to have illocutionary force. And some of the expressives are not root-sensitive at all, i.e. they may occur in any kind of clause. The other goal of the paper is to arrive at some understanding of what the difference is between being strongly root-sensitive, being weakly root-sensitive and not being root-sensitive.

We begin by specifying the four constructions which have been related to topicality (cf. e.g. Altmann 1981; Jacobs 2001; Frey 2004; Averintseva-Klisch 2009; Krifka 2008; Frascarelli and Hinterhölzl 2007) and which will be studied in this paper:

(i) **Topic marking by the particle *jedenfalls* 'for one'**

The following considerations reveal that *jedenfalls* marks an aboutness topic. Frey (2004) argues for the thesis in (1).

(1) In the middle field of the German clause, directly above the base position of sentential adverbials (SADVs), there is a designated position for topics (in the aboutness sense): all topical phrases occurring in the middle field, and only these, occur in this position.[1]

The term "SADV" refers to adverbials which express the speaker's estimation of the eventuality, e.g. *zum Glück* 'luckily', *anscheinend* 'apparently', *wahrscheinlich* 'probably'.[2] Evidence for (1) for example is given by a context which forces a certain expression to be understood as an aboutness topic, (2), and by non-referential expressions, (3) (for further evidence, see Frey 2004):

---

1 The middle field of a German clause corresponds to the region between the C-domain to the left and the verbal elements at the right edge of the clause.
2 A list of the abbreviations used can be found at the very end of this article.

(2) *Ich erzähle dir etwas über Hans.*
   I   tell   you something about Hans
   a. *Nächstes Jahr wird den Hans zum Glück eine vornehme*
      next   year will the-ACC Hans luckily   a   fine
      Dame heiraten.
      lady marry
   b. #*Nächstes Jahr wird zum Glück den Hans eine vornehme Dame heiraten.*

(3) a. **Während des Vortrags haben mindestens zwei leider*
       during   the lecture   have at.least   two unfortunately
       einen Apfel gegessen.
       an-ACC apple   eaten
   b. *Während des Vortrags haben leider mindestens zwei einen Apfel gegessen.*
   c. **Heute hat fast jeder erfreulicherweise gearbeitet.*
      today has almost everyone fortunately   worked
   d. *Heute hat erfreulicherweise fast jeder gearbeitet.*

The context in (2) states that the next sentence will be about Hans. Thus, it requires that if *Hans* occurs in the following sentence, it has to be an aboutness topic. The expression *Hans* may occur in the prefield, i.e. in front of the finite verb in a verb-second clause, or in the middle field following the finite verb. The prefield in German may host elements of different information-structural statuses. Crucially, however, if *Hans* occurs in the middle field it has to precede a SADV as the sentences (2a,b) demonstrate. Thus, the sentences (2) confirm one part of (1): there is a position above the position of SADVs which an aboutness topic has to occupy if it occurs in the middle field. The examples (3a,c) confirm the other part of (1). According to, for example, Reinhart (1981) and Jacobs (2001), quantificational phrases cannot be aboutness topics. The sentences (3a,c) show that quantificational phrases, i.e. non-topics, cannot appear in the middle field in front of a SADV.

With the help of the topic position characterised in (1) it can be established that the particle *jedenfalls* marks the constituent it is attached to as an aboutness topic, (4a,b). In addition (4c) proves that *jedenfalls* cannot be attached to a quantified phrase.

(4) a. *Heute wird Hans jedenfalls glücklicherweise helfen.*
       today will Hans for.one   luckily   help
   b. **Heute wird glücklicherweise Hans jedenfalls helfen.*
   c. **Heute wird keiner jedenfalls helfen.*
      today will nobody for.one   help

(ii) **German Left-Dislocation (GLD)**

In the German literature, the term 'Linksversetzung' (Left Dislocation) is used to refer to the following construction:

(5) Den   Hans$_1$, → den$_1$ mag   jeder t$_1$
     the-ACC   Hans   ResP-ACC   likes everyone

This construction will be called 'German Left Dislocation' (GLD) here to avoid its identification with the English construction called 'Left Dislocation', which has rather different properties from GLD and resembles the German Hanging Topic construction to be introduced below. Many authors assume that the primary function of GLD is to mark a sentence topic, e.g. Altmann (1981); Jacobs (2001); Grohmann (2003); Frey (2005). According to Frey (2005), GLD promotes a non-topic occurring in the preceding text to an aboutness topic. In his influential study, Altmann (1981) lists the following main characteristics of GLD: (i) progredient intonation on the left peripheral phrase and no pause between it and the rest of the clause (indicated by "→" in (5)); (ii) the resumptive pronoun (ResP) appearing in the construction is a form of the weak d-pronoun (i.e. of the pronoun which in the nominative case is *der, die* or *das* depending on gender); (iii) the ResP occurs in the prefield of the clause; (iv) if the left peripheral phrase is a DP, it agrees with the ResP in case. Note however that not all authors subscribe to property (iii). Some linguists assume that in a GLD the ResP may appear in the middle field (e.g. Grewendorf 2002; Frey 2005). Also in the present paper only Altmann's characteristics (i), (ii) and (iv) will be adopted.

(iii) **The German Hanging Topic construction (GHT)**

GLD has to be differentiated from the construction in (6), which is often referred to as 'Free Theme' or the 'Hanging Topic construction'. In this paper, the term 'German Hanging Topic construction' (GHT) will be used:

(6) Hans, ↓ jeder   mag   ihn.
     Hans   everyone likes him

Many authors assume that, like for GLD, it also holds for GHT that its primary function is to mark a sentence topic (e.g. Altmann 1981; Jacobs 2001; Grohmann 2003). However, Frey (2005) argues that GHT has the function of establishing a new discourse topic. Altmann (1981) notes the following main characteristics of GHT: (i) there is a pause between the left peripheral phrase and the rest of the clause (indicated by "↓" in (6)); (ii) the resumptive element shows up in the form of a personal pronoun, a d-pronoun (which can, but does not have to, be weak), a definite description or an epithet; (iii) the resumptive element may appear either in the prefield or in the middle field of the clause; (iv) if the left peripheral phrase is a DP, it is in the nominative or in the same case as the resumptive element (or even in the same case as a previously mentioned coreferring DP).

It is clear that, given these characteristics, the analysis of an example as GLD is not conclusive in written language; it could also be analysed as GHT. Therefore, it is helpful to find a further criterion to distinguish GLD from GHT. This criterion is offered by binding phenomena (cf. e.g. Vat 1981; Grohmann 2003; Frey 2005):

Operator binding:
(7) a. *Seinen$_1$ Doktorvater,* → *den verehrt jeder Linguist$_1$.* (GLD)
        his-ACC supervisor   ResP-ACC admires every linguist
    b. **Sein$_1$/*Seinen$_1$ Doktorvater, jeder Linguist$_1$ verehrt ihn.* (GHT)
        his-NOM/his-ACC supervisor   every linguist admires him

Principle C-effects:
(8) a. **Das neue Buch von Peter$_1$,* → *das   will   er$_1$ bald*
        the-ACC new book by Peter   ResP-ACC wants he soon
        veröffentlichen. (GLD)
        (to) publish
    b. *Das   neue Buch von Peter$_1$, er$_1$ will es   bald*
        the-NOM/ACC new book by Peter he wants it-ACC soon
        veröffentlichen. (GHT)
        (to) publish

As demonstrated by (7) and (8), GLD shows binding effects, but GHT does not. (7a) demonstrates that with GLD, an operator appearing in the clause may bind a pronoun inside the left dislocated phrase. As (7b) shows, this is not possible in a construction which is unambiguously a GHT construction. Furthermore Principle C-effects are induced for an R-expression inside the left peripheral phrase of a GLD structure, cf. (8a), but not for an R-expression inside the left peripheral phrase of a GHT construction, cf. (8b). Note that to get binding effects it is necessary that there be no pause between the dislocated element and the rest of the clause. If sentences like (7a) and (8a) are spoken with a pause between the preceding phrase and the rest, the binding effects disappear. Thus, the progredient intonation without a pause is a necessary condition for GLD.

The binding criterion proves that Altmann (1981) was right in restricting the ResP of a GLD structure to d-pronouns which are weak:

(9) *Seinen₁ Doktorvater, diesen/diesen Mann verehrt jeder Linguist₁.
 his-ACC supervisor this-ACC/this man admires every linguist

If, as illustrated in (9), the resumptive expression is a strong d-pronoun or a definite description (or, as could be shown, any other expression different from a weak d-pronoun), the binding option disappears.

(iv) **Right Dislocation**

Another construction we will consider is right dislocation, (10). It is sometimes seen as a topic marking construction (e.g. Frascarelli and Hinterhölzl 2007; de Vries 2009; Averintseva-Klisch 2009).

(10) *Maria hat ihn heute in der Stadt getroffen, den Chef.*
 Maria has him today in the city met the-ACC boss

A pronominal form in the core of the clause is coreferential with a referential expression which appears in the right periphery of the clause. To be more concrete, the referential expression occurs in the right outer domain of the German clause, and not in the so-called postfield, which is structurally closer to the clause; cf. e.g. Zifonun, Hoffman, and Strecker (1997); Averintseva-Klisch (2009); Truckenbrodt (2016).

The paper will study the constructions (i)–(iv) regarding their root-sensitivity. It will be shown that (i) and (ii) are weakly root-sensitive, that (iii) is strongly root-sensitive, and that (iv) is not root-sensitive. An obvious goal of the paper is to gain some understanding of why topic marking constructions and expressives in general have the very property regarding root-sensitivity they have. To see this, one has to get an idea what the relevant differences are between independent and dependent clauses which may host strongly root-sensitive expressions, dependent clauses which may host weakly root-sensitive expressions and the remaining dependent clauses. For this purpose it will be crucial for us what Krifka (2017) has proposed regarding speech acts and judgements. Krifka (2017) follows Peirce (cf. Tuzet 2006) and Frege (1918) in assuming three different acts which take part in the emergence of a statement:

(11) i. the conception of a thought – the thinking
 ii. the appreciation of the truth of the thought – the judging
 iii. the manifestation of the judgement – the asserting

(11i) refers to the forming of a proposition, which has truth conditions. (11ii) refers to the forming of a judgement, which is a private act. (11iii) refers to the forming of an assertion, which is a public act. Krifka (2017) takes subjective epistemics like *probably* or reportative evidentials like the German modal verb *sollen* (literally "ought", meaningwise "is supposed to") as prominent elements which exemplify the act of judging.

According to Krifka (2017), a speaker S asserts a simple proposition φ in order to introduce φ to the common ground (CG). Importantly, a speaker S asserts a judgement about a proposition φ also to introduce φ in some form to the CG. By asserting a judgement the speaker for example might weaken his commitment to the truth of φ by referring to a private act since this can make him more protected from possible social sanctions. Thus, Krifka (2017) assumes that the CG contains the information about who is committed to the truth of a proposition φ and whether φ is qualified by a subjective epistemic or an evidential. We will argue that the same applies to any other qualification by a judge.

The present paper assumes that clauses which can host strongly root-sensitive expressions encode a speech act, cf. (11iii) (which naturally can be extended to other speech acts). Embedded clauses which may host weakly, but not strongly, root-sensitive expressions are assumed to encode a judgement and a judge, cf. (11ii), but not to encode a speech act. The remaining embedded clauses, which may only host expressions that are not root-sensitive, just encode a proposition without further layers.

Thus, we assume that, for example, the marking of an aboutness topic can straightforwardly be conceived of as involving a judgement and a judge in the sense of Krifka (2017). It is a judge who conceives of a property as being prominently related to a certain object, which can be identified independently of the property. In the case of an assertion involving topic marking with a proposition φ, the speaker intends that it is recorded in the CG that he relates the open φ to the referent of the topic.

Likewise, modal particles (henceforth MPs) arguably involve a judge. It is a judge who, for example by means of the particle *ja*, indicates that he takes a proposition as being already known albeit not as being necessarily in the conscious awareness of others. Using the MP *denn* triggers the evaluation that the instantiation of an open proposition is highly relevant and context related for hearer and speaker.

The paper is structured as follows. Section II studies the root-sensitivity of different expressive expressions, among them most notably the topic marking constructions listed above. In section III some syntactic properties of the different types of dependent clauses are discussed which can be shown to be sensitive to the different degrees of root-sensitivity of expressives. Section IV introduces the notions of a judge and a judgement and, following Krifka (2017), argues that judgement operators are not speech act operators. Rather, they indicate a qualification of a proposition and scope under speech act operators. Section V reconsiders some expressives which operate on the illocutionary level and some which operate on the level of a judgement. Ties between the hierarchy in (11) and the different types of clauses which have been found to be relevant are established. Section V also contains a short comparison with the results of Bianchi and Frascarelli (2010) and the results of Jacobs (2018). A brief summary concludes the paper.

2 Degrees of Root-Sensitivity of Topic Markings and Other Expressives

With the notion 'root phenomena' (RPs) one standardly refers to phenomena which only occur in root clauses and in the restricted set of so called root-like dependent clauses. Often the dependent clauses which may show RPs are vaguely ascribed the property of having some illocutionary potential. The pioneers of the research on RPs, Hooper and Thompson (1973), already identified the pertinent subordinate structures: assertive argument clauses, non-restrictive relative clauses and certain adverbial clauses. Subsequently the main focus of research was first on argument clauses, especially on complement clauses of non-negated verbs of saying, of expressing a doxastic attitude (*glauben – believe, hoffen – hope, einfallen – occur to*) and of perception (hören – hear, *fühlen – feel*) (cf. e.g. Meinunger 2004, 2006 and references quoted therein). Standard examples of non-root-like dependent clauses are the object clauses of factive verbs and of predicates which are inherently negative (*leugnen – to deny, unmöglich sein – to be impossible*). Later the availability of RPs in non-restrictive relative clauses and certain adverbial clauses was discussed more vividly. Haegeman (2003) and much work after, for example, distinguishes central adverbial clauses (CACs), which do not allow RPs, and peripheral adverbial clauses (PACs), which do. Frey (2012) applied this distinction to German adverbial clauses; cf. the lists in (12).

(12) i. CACs: e.g. temporal, factual conditional, manner adverbial clauses
　　 ii. PACs: e.g. adversative, concessive adverbial clauses, German *da*-causal clauses

A well-known German RP is the occurrence of a MP (e.g. Thurmair 1989; Coniglio 2011); cf. the unstressed element *ja* in (13). It is not licensed in the complement clause of a factive verb, (13b), in a restrictive relative clause, (13c), or in a CAC, (13d,e).

(13) a. *Fritz kommt ja gleich.*
    Fritz comes MP soon
  b. **Maria bedauert, dass Fritz ja gleich kommt.*
    Maria regrets that Fritz MP soon comes
  c. **Sie spricht mit jemandem, der ja vorher gekommen ist.*
    she talks with someone who MP before come is
  d. **Maria war aufgeregt, als Fritz ja kam.*
    Maria was nervous when Fritz MP came
  e. **Fritz kam, ohne dass er ja eingeladen war.*
    Fritz came without that he MP invited was

However, a MP is legitimate in the complement clause of a verbum dicendi like *meinen*, (14a), or in a PAC, (14b,c).

(14) a. *Maria meint, dass Fritz ja gleich kommt.*
    Maria thinks that Fritz MP soon comes
  b. *Maria ist aufgeregt, da Fritz ja gleich kommt.*
    Maria is nervous since Fritz MP soon comes
  c. *Maria ist aufgeregt, obwohl Fritz ja gleich kommt.*
    Maria is nervous although Fritz MP soon comes

According to the received view, RPs are seen as a homogeneous class, i.e. they may appear in root clauses and in the members of the fixed class of embedded root-like clauses. However, there is evidence that one has to distinguish between what here are called weakly root-sensitive elements (or weak root elements) and strongly root-sensitive elements (or strong root elements) (Frey 2012). The weak RPs are legitimate in all root contexts, while the strong ones can be found only in a very few contexts. The occurrence of the MP *ja* is a weak RP. The MP occurs in root clauses and in the root-like dependent clauses which are standardly identified as such. As mentioned already, these are the complement clauses of non-negated verbs of saying, of expressing a doxastic attitude and of perception as well as PACs. Weak RPs are possible in clauses which appear in positions that can be argued to be an integral part of their host clause (Frey 2012). The German prefield is such a position. Strong root elements are different. They only occur in independent clauses and in a very small set of dependent clauses which show signs of being semantically dependent but syntactically independent of the clause they relate to (Frey 2012). Following the terminology of Frey (2012), the latter will be called non-integrated dependent clauses (NonIC). German examples of NonICs are given in (15). See section III of a discussion of main differentiating properties of CACs, PACs and NonICs.

(15) NonICs: e.g. continuative relative clauses, so-called free *dass*-clauses, verb-first causal and concessive clauses and so-called pragmatic adverbial clauses, which appear outside of the core of the clause they relate to.

An example of a strongly root-sensitive element is constituted by tag questions like German *nicht wahr?* ('right?' literally "not true") or *habe ich recht?* ('am I right'). A tag adds to an assertion a question for the hearer with a strong bias toward a support of the speaker's assertion. In English, the most prominent tags are so-called verb-polarity markers. (16b) reveals that these cannot be associated with the complement of a mental attitude verb. They have to relate to the main clause, which has independent illocutionary force, cf. (16a).

(16) a. *Bill hopes that Mary will come, doesn't he?*
    b. **Bill hopes that Mary will come, won't she?*

The same applies to German question tags. (17) demonstrates that these are not tolerable in an object clause of a verbum dicendi, (17a), or in a PAC, (17b), but they are in a continuative relative clause, (17c). Crucially (17c) is fine with the tag relating to the *wobei*-clause only, asking for certainty as to whether Max got the second degree.³

---

3 One might wonder why in (17b) the tag test is applied to the preposed subordinate clause. The reason is that a postposed concessive becomes a NonIC if the right intonation (i.e. sentence accent for the concessive and a pause preceding the concessive) is supplied (cf. e.g. Frey 2012). With the relevant clause in the prefield, matters are clear: the concessive in (17b) is a PAC. Thus (17b) should be contrasted with preposed clauses which contain modal particles, for example (i):

(i)   [Obwohl Max ja das zweite Examen hat], hat er sich   noch nicht
         although Max MP the second exam   has has he himself still not
         beworben.
         applied

    MPs are licensed in these environments, proving that they have a different status than tags.

(17) a. *Maria hat erzählt, [dass Max das zweite Examen hat,
       Maria has told   that Max the second exam has
       nicht wahr].
       not true
    b. ??/*[Obwohl Max das zweite Examen hat, nicht wahr], hat
          although Max the second exam has not true has
    c.   er sich   noch nicht beworben.
          he himself still not applied
          Max hat sich   noch nicht beworben, [wobei   er doch das
          Max has himself still not applied   whereby he MP the
          zweite Examen hat, nicht wahr?]
          second exam has not true

The same contrast is shown by integrated causal verb-final clauses on the one hand and syntactically independent causal verb-first clauses on the other. Again, the well-formed example has a reading in which the tag is restricted to the semantically dependent clause.

(18) a. *[Weil Maria sehr begabt ist, hab ich recht], wird sie
         since Maria very talented is have I right will she
         schnell promovieren.
         quickly graduate
    b. Maria wird schnell promovieren, [ist sie doch sehr begabt, hab
       Maria will quickly graduate   is she MP very talented have
       ich recht?]
       I right
       'Maria will graduate quickly. Because she is highly talented, am I right?'

Thus, in their distribution tags are much more restricted than weak RPs.
   Yet in some cases it seems that the tag may target the apparent embedded clause.

(19) a. *I suppose she isn't coming, is she?*
    b. #*I suppose she isn't coming, don't I?*

However, it has been argued that in these cases what appears to be the matrix is not an embedding clause but an epistemic adverbial which comes as a modifier to the actual assertion, one argument being that this pattern is only possible with a subgroup of assertive predicates in combination with a first person singular subject (e.g. Giorgi and Pianesi 2005). Thus these sentences are monoclausal and the tag operates on the basic claim (i.e. *she isn't coming*).

German tags are definitely fine in sentence-final position.

(20) a. *Hans glaubt, dass Maria Otto getroffen hat, nicht wahr?*
       Hans believes that Maria Otto met has not true
    b. *Hans glaubt, Maria hat OTTO getroffen, nicht wahr?*
       Hans believes Maria has Otto met not true

Note, however, that what is challenged here by using the tag is the matrix content, i.e. that Hans believes what Maria did. Neither the realisation of the subordinate clause as a verb-second or verb-final clause nor the information structure (i.e. whether the subordinate contains a narrow or a wider focus) has any effect on this. This is confirmed by the oddness of (21). Here the matrix cannot felicitously be offered to the hearer inviting him to refute or rather confirm.

(21) a. #*Ich glaube/weiß dass Maria Otto getroffen hat, nicht wahr?*
       I believe/know that Maria Otto met has not true
    b. ??*Ich vermute, Maria hat OTTO getroffen, nicht wahr?*
       I assume Maria has Otto met not true

Knowing or believing (= taking as true) is not compatible with doubting it or offering it for challenge. To the extent that for some people (21b) sounds marginally possible, it means that the speaker is requiring the hearer to confirm that his assumption is correct rather than inviting the hearer to challenge Otto's coming.

Another strict RP we would like to mention here is the German interjection *Mann*. It cannot appear in a CAC, (22a), or a PAC, (22b), but it can appear in a NonIC, (22c):

(22) a. **Ohne dass Max viel gearbeitet hat, Mann, hat*
       without that Max much worked has man has
       er die Prüfung brillant gemeistert.
       he the exam brilliantly mastered
    b. **Obwohl Max echt wenig gearbeitet hat, Mann, hat er*
       although Max MP little worked has man has he
       die Prüfung brillant gemeistert.
       the exam brilliantly mastered

c. *Max hat die Prüfung brillant gemeistert, wobei er*
   Max has the exam brilliantly mastered whereby he
   echt wenig gearbeitet hat, Mann.
   MP little worked has man

Crucially again, the interjection in (22c) can be understood as being related only to the content of the continuative relative clause.

Note that all the RPs considered so far, strong or weak, do not contribute to the truth conditions of the clauses in which they appear but have effects on the use of these clauses. This means they do not belong to the content side, but to the expressive side. They are non-cognitive or non-descriptive. Gutzmann (2013) gives a rather comprehensive list of such expressive linguistic items; the first two on the list have already been discussed:

(23) Modal (and other) particles (*ja, eh, denn, halt, gel/wa*)
   Interjections (*Huch, Mann, damn*)
   Pejorative epithets (*dieser Idiot Hans* 'that idiot Paul')
   Expressive attributive adjectives (*dein verdammter Hund* 'your damn dog')
   Expressively coloured expressions (*Köter* 'cur', *Kraut* for Germans)
   Formal vs. familiar pronouns (*du* vs. *Sie* in German)
   Ethical, personal dative (*Dass du mir ja nicht zu spät kommst,* literally "that you me (ethical dative) ja (=MP) not too late come", meaning "Don't be late!"
   Focal accent
   Exclamative or unexpectedness intonation (*Obama won the Nobel Prize!*)
   Verum operator (*Karl HAT sein Buch beendet* 'Carl did finish his book')
   Appositives and parentheses (*Egon, ein ehemaliger Spion,* 'Egon, a former spy')
   Topicalisation(s) in English and German
   Diminutives (*Hansi*)
   Non-inflected verbs as substitutes for actions (*dich in den Arm nehm,* literally "you in the arm take")

It turns out that while some of the phenomena listed in (23) are (strongly or weakly) root-sensitive, most are not root-sensitive at all, i.e. most phenomena on Gutzmann's list are clearly legitimate inside any embedded clause. A CAC such as a temporal clause, for example, can host expressive nouns or adjectives, (24a,b), appositive elements, (24c), and focussed constituents, and is insensitive toward the familiar vs. formal pronoun use, (24e), or the presence of a diminutive, (24f).

(24) a. *Als   ein Köter Maria entgegenkam,* (...)
       when   a   mutt   Maria toward.came
   b. *Als   dein verdammter Hund auf mich zuging,* (...)
       when   your damn   mutt up me   to.came
   c. *Als   Kehler, ein Spion, aus dem Flugzeug stieg,* (...)
       when   Kehler a   spy   out the aircraft stepped
   d. *Ich war in der U-Bahn,   als ich MaRIa traf.*
       I   was in the underground when I   Maria met
   e. *Als   dein/Ihr   Kind auf mich zuging,* (...)
       when   your-INFORMAL/your-FORMAL child up me   to.came
   f. *Als   dein Hund/Hündchen   auf mich zuging,* (...)
       when   your dog/dog-DIMINUTIVE   up me   to.came

Hence, at this point we can conclude that some expressives are strongly or weakly root-sensitive, while others are not root-sensitive. Note that as shown in (24d) non-root-sensitivity also holds for the information-structural marking of new information focus.

Note that Gutzmann's (2013) list of expressives contains another classic example of a RP: English topicalisation. (25) indicates that English topicalisation is root-sensitive. Given our more fine-grained distinction we can say that (25a) shows that English topicalisation is weakly root-sensitive.

(25) a. **Mary regrets that this book, John read.*
   b. *Mary said that this book, John read.*

Let us now in turn test the root-sensitivity of the constructions (i)–(iv) starting with the marking of an aboutness topic with the particle *jedenfalls*. This construction is a RP, more precisely, it is a weak RP. This is demonstrated in (26):

(26) a. **Maria leugnete, dass [Fritz jedenfalls] kommen wird.*
       Maria denied   that Fritz for.one   come   will
   b. *Maria denkt, dass [Fritz jedenfalls] kommen wird.*
       Maria thinks that Fritz for.one   come   will
       'Maria thinks that Fritz for one will come.'
   c. **Als   Fritz jedenfalls freundlich auf mich zuging, habe ich*
       when   Fritz for.one   friendly   up me   to.came have I
       mich gefreut.
       REFL been.glad

d. *Während mich Fritz jedenfalls freundlich gegrüßt hat, ist*
   while   me   Fritz for.one   friendly   greeted has has
   Maria grußlos   vorbeigegangen.
   Maria without.greeting passed.by
e. *Maria wurde befördert, worüber   sich Fritz jedenfalls sehr*
   Maria was   promoted about.which REFL Fritz for.one   very
   gefreut   hat.
   been.glad has

The constituent *Fritz jedenfalls* may appear in the clausal complement of a doxastic verb, (26b), and in a PAC, (26d), but not in the complement clause of an inherently negative verb, (26a), or in a CAC, (26c). It is to be expected that it may appear in a NonIC, (26e).

We get the same result for the construction (ii), GLD. It is weakly root-sensitive too.

(27) A: *Haben Sie auch Otto eingeladen?*
        have you also Otto invited
   a. B: **Nein, weil   jeder   bedauern würde, der Otto, dass*
          no   because everybody regret   would the Otto that
         der dabei   ist.
          ResP thereby is
   b. B: *Ja, weil   jeder   denkt, der Otto, dass der   dabei*
         yes because everybody thinks the Otto that ResP thereby
         sein sollte.
         be   should
   c. B: *Ja, weil   jeder   denkt, der Otto, der sollte*
         yes because everybody thinks the Otto ResP should
         dabei   sein.
         thereby be

GLD may not occur in the complement clause of an emotive factive verb, (27a), but it is fine in the clausal complement of a verb of a mental attitude, (27b,c) (recall the remarks on the positions of the GLD's RP in the introductory section).

However, in another context for weak RPs, PACs, GLD cannot appear, cf. (28).

(28) **Otto ist sehr sportlich, der Max, während der   sehr musikalisch ist.*
      Otto is very athletic   the Max while   ResP very musical   is

We see the reason for this in the different statuses of complementisers of adverbial clauses on the one hand (e.g. *während* 'while', *obwohl* 'although', *weil* 'because') and mere indicators of subordination (*dass* 'that' or *ob* 'if') on the other. The former seem to have semantic and formal commonalities with prepositions, thus with P°-elements, whereas the mere indicators of subordination are just pure C°-elements. Whatever the crucial difference is and how the distinctness must be properly formalised, it appears that the pure C°-items in principle tolerate material to their left which still belongs to the clause they head. So in informal, dialectical registers (mostly in Southern German varieties) interrogatives, (29a), topical constituents, (29b,c), and the *je*-constituent of a correlative construction can precede these items, (29d); cf. Bayer (2001) and Meinunger (2011). Something similar is not possible with a 'prepositional' complementiser, (29e,f).

(29) a. *Ich weiß nicht, für wen dass er sich entschieden hat.*
       I know not for whom that he REFL decided has
   b. *Den Peter, dass ich getroffen habe, freut mich.*
      the Peter that I met have pleases me
      'That I met Peter pleases me.'
   c. *Der Hans, ob kommt, weiß ich nicht.*
      the Hans if comes know I not
   d. *Je mehr Städte dass er kennt, desto mehr liebt er Stuttgart*
      the more cities that he knows all.the more loves he Stuttgart
   e. **Die Maria obwohl nicht gekommen ist, war Peter fröhlich.*
      the Maria although not come is was Peter happy
   f. **Die Maria weil gekommen ist, war Peter fröhlich.*
      the Maria because come is was Peter happy

Furthermore, if a 'prepositional' complementiser co-occurs with a C-element, the former always precedes the latter, which again means that the C-element is fine with clause-mate material to its left: *bis dass* 'until that' / *dass bis, *trotzdem dass* 'despite that' / *dass trotzdem.

GLDed constituents presumably target other positions than interrogative or relative expressions or 'prepositional'-like complementisers. Yet what we want to point out is that adverbial complementisers never allow clause-mate material to precede them whereas pure subordinators occasionally do. We conclude that adverbial complementisers, or in general openers of non-selected clauses, do not provide space for any co-constituents before them.

We expect that a weak RP like GLD can appear in contexts for strong RPs. However, a GLD may not appear with a continuative relative clause, (30). The reason is likely to be the same as for the impossibility of its occurrence in a

PAC: the left periphery of a continuative relative clause does not offer a position for the GLDed-phrase.

(30) *Alle sind zur Feier eingeladen, seinen₁ Doktorvater,
 all are to.the party invited his doctoral.supervisor
 worüber den jeder Promovend₁ informiert hat.
 about.what ResP every doctorand informed has

With regard to our other example of a NonIC the situation is somewhat different. A causal verb-first clause marginally offers the space for a GLDed-phrase, (31).

(31) ?Viele Professoren waren gekommen, seinen₁ Doktorvater,
 many professors were come his doctoral.supervisor
 hat den doch jeder Promovend₁ dabei haben wollen.
 has ResP MP every doctorand thereby have wanted
 'Many professors had come, the reason being that every doctorand had wanted his supervisor to be present.'

The reading of a verb-first causal clause emerges through a pragmatic procedure triggered by context, verb placement and mainly through the presence of the particle *doch*. The clause is not a 'prepositional' adverbial clause, and like other verb-first clauses, such as matrix yes-no questions, imperatives or narrative declarative verb-first clauses, it is in principle compatible with a preceding GLDed phrase; hence the somewhat marginal acceptability of (31).

Let us next consider (iii), GHT. We find an important difference to GLD. GHT cannot figure in the complement of root-inducing verbs like *denken* or *sagen*. So, GHT seems to be a strong RP.

(32) A: *Wir sollten auch Otto einladen.*
  we should also Otto invite
 a. B: **Ja, auch weil* Max gemeint hat, der Otto, dass er
   yes also because Max thought has the Otto that he
   dabei sein sollte.
   thereby be should
 b. B: **Ja, Maria hat gesagt, der Otto, er möchte kommen.*
   yes Maria has said the Otto he wants come

In addition, GHT cannot appear in a PAC. However, this does not tell us anything further because, as we have seen, this also holds for the weak RP GLD, most likely for reasons independent of root-sensitivity. Let us next have a look at our examples of NonICs, i.e. at continuative relative clauses and at causal verb-first clauses. Can a GHT appear in such constructions? For the causal verb-first clauses the answer is yes, cf. (33a). With a continuative relative clause, however, a GHT is not possible, (33b).

(33) a. *Ich freue mich auf meinen Slowenien-Urlaub – Slowenien, gibt es doch dort wunderbar unberührte, herrliche Landschaften.*
'I am looking forward to my holidays in Slovenia – Slovenia since there are marvelously untouched gorgeous landscapes.'
b. *Ich freue mich auf meinen Slowenien-Urlaub, (*Slowenien), wobei ich dort noch niemals war.*
'I am looking forward to my holidays in Slovenia though I never have been there before.'

What could be the reason why a GHT is not possible with a continuative relative clause? If we assume that a hanging topic belongs to the structure of the following clause, the reason for the ungrammaticality of (33b) is the same as that for the ungrammaticality of (30). The continuative relative clause simply does not offer a position for the hanging topic.[4]

Overall, we have seen that the crucial data showing the difference between the weak root constructions (i) (marking of an aboutness topic with the help particle) and (ii) (GLD) on the one hand, and the strong root construction (iii) (GHT) on the other are the examples (26b) and (27b,c) versus (32).

Next we can see that right dislocation, our construction (iv), is not root-sensitive at all. In (34a) we find the construction with the complement clause of an inherently negative verb, and in (34b) it appears with a CAC. Obviously, we do not need to illustrate that right dislocation also may appear in the remaining types of dependent clauses considered here.

---

4 However, another explanation has to be given if we follow Frey (2005) in the analysis of GHT. According to Frey (2005), the dislocated phrase of GHT does not belong to the syntactic structure of the following clause. It is a syntactic orphan, i.e. it stands in isolation. Thus, in this view the dislocated phrase of GHT, in contrast to the dislocated phrase of GLD, is not in need of a syntactic position made available by the following clause. Note, however, that (33b) with GHT is not good might be due to another property, which Frey (2005) ascribes to the semantics of this construction. According to Frey (2005), a GHT establishes a new discourse topic, which the following clause elaborates. Arguably this goes against the nature of a continuative relative clause, which, as the name suggests, continues the current discourse unit and does not start a new one.

(34) a. *Max hat verneint, dass sie vorbeigekommen ist, die Chefin.*
       Max has denied   that she by.passed   is the boss-FEM
   b. *Max war beschäftigt, als sie hereinkam,   die Chefin.*
       Max was busy   when she in.came   the boss-FEM

So, we have found that four constructions which in the literature are often discussed in relation to topic marking differ in terms of root-sensitivity. The marking by a particle and GLD are weakly root-sensitive, GHT is strongly root-sensitive, and right dislocation is not root-sensitive at all. In the remainder of the paper we want to make some sense out of these differences. In order to do so, we first have to understand the relevant properties of the environments in which strong RPs, weak RPs and root-insensitive phenomena occur. Next, we have to get some understanding of the relevant distinctions between the four topic constructions which make them behave the way they do.

3 Three Types of Dependent Clauses and their Properties

In the following we will discuss some properties of three different types of dependent clauses, which are all not complement clauses (Holler 2008; Frey 2012). These are the above-mentioned CACs, PACs and NonICs. Examples of CACs are temporal adverbial clauses, event-related conditionals, local clauses and clauses of manner. Standard examples of PACs are adversatives and concessives. Examples of NonICs are continuative w-relatives, so-called free *dass*-clauses, verb-first causal clauses and so-called pragmatic adverbial clauses. In the following paragraphs, a temporal clause will serve as an instance of a CAC, an adversative clause will represent PACs, and a w-relative will serve as an example of a NonIC.

In (35) it is shown how our representatives of the three classes of dependent clauses behave regarding binding into them by a quantified DP sitting in the main clause. As (35a) reveals, a temporal adverbial clause does allow it, while (35b) and (35c) show that an adversative adverbial and a continuative w-relative, respectively, do not.

(35) a. *Keiner$_1$ hat protestiert, als   er$_1$ unterbrochen wurde.*
         no.one has protested   when he   interrupted was

b. *Jede Kollegin₁ ist letzten Sonntag am Institut
  every colleague has last Sunday at.the institute
  gewesen, während sie₁ doch sonst bei schönem Wetter
  been while she MP otherwise in beautiful weather
  einen Ausflug macht.
  an excursion makes
c. *Jede₁ hat die Prüfung bestanden, worüber sie₁ sich
  every has the exam passed about.what she REFL
  gefreut hat.
  been.glad has

Thus, with regard to binding the CAC stands alone in allowing it, and the PAC and the NonIC pattern together in not allowing it. The next property to consider is the positioning of these clauses in the prefield of a German clause. The prefield is a genuine part of its clause. Thus, it is a position of integration. Here the pattern among the three types of clauses is different. (36) demonstrates that the CAC and the PAC may occupy the prefield, whereas the NonIC may not.

(36) a. *Als Max unterbrochen wurde, hat er protestiert.*
  when Max interrupted was has he protested
  b. *Während Maria doch sonst bei schönem Wetter einen*
  while Maria MP otherwise in beautiful weather an
  Ausflug macht, ist sie letzten Sonntag am Institut
  excursion makes has she last Sunday at.the institute
  gewesen.
  been
  c. **Worüber sich Max gefreut hat, hat er die Prüfung*
  about.what REFL Max been.glad has has he the exam
  bestanden.
  passed

Another property of the three types of dependent clauses which shows that CACs and PACs go together to the exclusion of NonICs concerns the possibility of being embedded together with the related clause.

(37) a. *Hans erzählte, [dass Max protestierte, als er unterbrochen*
  Hans told that Max protested when he interrupted
  wurde].
  was

b. *Hans erzählte, [dass Maria klug ist, während ihr Bruder*
      Hans told   that Maria intelligent is while her brother
      fleißig ist].
      diligent is
   c. **Hans erzählte, [dass Eva die Schachpartie gewann, worüber*
      Hans told   that Eva the chess.match won   about.what
      sich Oskar ärgerte].
      REFL Oskar annoyed.was

We see that a CAC and a PAC can be embedded together with their host clauses, (37a,b), whereas a NonIC cannot, (37c).

Frey (2012) argues that data like (35)–(37) yield two main insights about the structural relations of CACs, PACs and NonICs with their host clauses. First, CACs can be in the c-command domains of sentence constituents belonging to the host clause, but this does not hold for PACs and NonICs. Second, CACs and PACs both belong to the structure of the matrix clause, while NonICs do not.

According to Frey (2012), the licensing of CACs, PACs and NonICs is very different. A CAC is licensed in the standard way inside its host's TP by the verb or by one of its functional projections. A PAC is also syntactically licensed inside its host. However, it is licensed locally in very high positions by the host's Force-projection. This difference explains why PACs, in contrast to CACs, show signs of non-integration like the opaqueness for binding by an element of the host. That a PAC is syntactically licensed inside its host after all, albeit in a very high position, captures that it may be positioned in the prefield of a verb-second clause. This treatment of CACs and PACs distinguishes this account from proposals like that of Pasch et al. (2003: 398), who make a sharp distinction between the semantics of CACs and PACs but treat them syntactically on a par.

Frey (2012) goes on to argue that PACs and NonICs also have very different licensing conditions. Some evidence consists in the fact that a PAC may appear in the prefield of its host, whereas a NonIC may not, (36b,c), and in the fact that a PAC can be embedded with its host clause, while a NonIC cannot, (37b,c). Whereas a PAC receives its syntactic licensing by the Force-projection of its host, according to Frey (2012), a NonIC is not part of the syntactic structure of its associated clause – it is syntactically a true orphan in the sense of Haegeman (1991). Thus, syntactically a NonIC constitutes an independent sentence. Frey (2012) assumes that a NonIC has a force which is anchored to the speaker independently of the host. A NonIC has its own illocutionary force. Its licensing as a dependent clause happens solely semantically in the discourse by a coherence relation which connects it with its associated clause.

The different ways of licensing of CACs, PACs and NonICs correspond to further basic differences between these clauses. Here we will have a look at differences in the prosodic behaviour of the combination of main clauses and dependent clauses (cf. Frey and Truckenbrodt 2015). In a wide focus context, CACs can carry the sentence accent of the entire utterance, cf. (38a), while an utterance with a PAC requires separate sentence stress on the host clause, cf. (39) (Brandt 1990; Frey 2012).

(38) *What did Elsa tell you?*
    a. *Peter wird kommen, sobald er etwas ZEIT hat.*
    b. *Peter wird KOMMEN, sobald er etwas ZEIT hat.*
       Peter will come as.soon.as he some time has

(39) *What did Elsa tell you?*
    a. *#Peter wird kommen, während Maria KEINE Zeit hat.*
    b. *Peter wird KOMMEN, während Maria KEINE Zeit hat.*
       Peter will come while Maria no time has

The contrast between (38a) and (39a) confirms that a PAC is – loosely speaking – less deeply integrated than a CAC. However there are also prosodic indications of the integration of a PAC. When either the host clause or the PAC is contextually given, the constraint that a constituent marked as given should not be assigned sentence stress (the constraint '*Stress-given' in Truckenbrodt 2015) can in principle remove sentence stress from them, as in (40) and (41).

(40) *Peter wird kommen. [Er wird kommen]$_G$ während Maria KEINE*
    Peter will come he will come while Maria no
    Zeit hat.
    time has

(41) *Maria hat keine Zeit. Während [sie keine Zeit hat]$_G$ wird*
    Maria has no time while she no time has will
    Peter aber KOMmen.
    Peter but come
    'Maria has no time. While she has no time, Peter will come, though.'

The host clause and the PAC form a unit under one single root node. The constraint 'each root sentence requires at least one sentence stress' requires sentence stress only once in the entire utterance, and so the stress may shift away from a given part to another part of the utterance.

This is different with a NonIC, illustrated here once more with a continuative w-relative. In (42) the host clause is contextually given. Nevertheless the constraint '*Stress-given' cannot remove sentence stress from the host clause (Frey and Truckenbrodt 2015). Thus, 'host + continuative w-relative' do not count as one utterance. With each sentence a separate utterance is performed.

(42) *Peter wird kommen.*
 Peter will come
 a. *#Ja, [er wird kommen]$_G$ worüber sich Maria FREUT.*
  yes he will come about.what REFL Maria is.glad
 b. *Ja, [er wird KOMmen]$_G$ worüber sich Maria FREUT.*
  yes, he will come about.what REFL Maria is.glad

In sum, the prosodic data in (38)–(42) confirm that a CAC occupies a structurally low position inside its host, while a PAC belongs to the host, but is not embedded deeply enough to be able to carry the sole sentence accent of 'host + PAC'. A NonIC is an independent clause, which constitutes its own prosodic domain.

4 Judgements Versus Speech Acts

Let us recapitulate our observations about the dependent clauses which may host strong RPs, the so-called NonICs. We have seen that NonICs in contrast to CACs and PACs may host question tags and interjections like *Mann*. Furthermore, we have observed that NonICs are syntactically rather independent of their host clauses. Some authors (e.g. Frey 2012) assume that they are completely autonomous syntactically. As we have seen, the syntactic independence of NonICs corresponds to their prosodic independence. A NonIC constitutes its own prosodic domain.

As already stated, Frey (2012) concludes that a NonIC has a Force-projection which is anchored to the speaker independently of the force of the host clause. This encodes that a NonIC has its own illocutionary force. This makes some sense. For example, the insertion of a question tag into a sentence requires that an assertion be performed with the sentence and it triggers that a conforming question regarding the proposition of the sentence is added.

Note also the examples in (43).

(43) a. *Nimmst du noch ein Dessert? Worüber ich mich*
take you one more dessert about.what I REFL
freuen würde.
be.glad would
b. *Wird Fritz auch eingeladen? Ist er doch ein guter Freund*
will.be Fritz also invited is he MP a good friend
des Hauses.
of.the house

The two sentences in (43a) and (43b) have different illocutionary force, showing the illocutionary independence of NonICs most clearly.

Note finally that the prosodic independence of NonICs may be seen as a confirmation of the assumption that NonICs have their own illocutionary force. This holds if we follow Truckenbrodt's (2015) claim in (44).

(44) Clauses that are speech acts are mapped to intonation phrases.

Above we have seen that PACs do allow weak RPs, but no strong ones. They are not syntactically independent and they need not be mapped to intonation phrases. These observations cast doubt on the truth of the popular claim in (45) (e.g. Hooper and Thomson 1973; Jacobs 1991; Haegeman 2004; Coniglio 2011).

(45) A clause may host a RP iff an illocutionary act is performed with the clause.

If (45) were true, it would remain opaque why PACs cannot host strong RPs and why they need not be mapped to intonation phrases. On the other hand, regarding their syntactic and semantic status, we obviously cannot treat PACs in the same way as we treat CACs. We have seen many differences. In particular PACs, in contrast to CACs, have the special capacity to host weak RPs.

Why has a condition like (45) so often been assumed? We believe it is because of data like in (46a,b).

(46) a. *Fritz hat ja/*denn das Buch gelesen.*
Fritz has MP/MP the book read
b. *Hat Fritz *ja/denn das Buch gelesen?*
c. *Fritz hat (*denn) das Buch geLEsen?*

(46a,b) illustrate that MPs, which according to our classification constitute a weak RP, are sensitive to sentence mood. This sometimes is taken as evidence that they can only occur in clauses with illocutionary force. Note, however, that we follow the standard distinction in the German tradition between sentence mood, on the one hand, and illocution or illocutionary force, on the other. The former is related to the concept of sentence type, which is the result of the interplay of grammatical features (such as w(h)-words, verbal mood, verb position and the like; for German see Altmann 1993 or Lohnstein 2000). Illocution is considered to be related to true speech acts (which change the world). We are claiming that weak RPs do not presuppose that the clauses they occur in must have illocutionary force and, hence, are performative. MPs, for example, are tied to sentence mood (declarative, interrogative, imperative), but not to specific speech acts. For example, *denn* is restricted to interrogative sentence mood, but it cannot appear in just any kind of question or inquisitive act. So the declaratives with a rising accent in (46c) and (65a), which are understood as a special yes-no question, do not tolerate the appearance of *denn*[5] (see also section 5 below).

We want to base our proposal for the treatment of strong and weak RPs on ideas developed in Krifka (2017). First we observe that weak RPs are not-at-issue expressions. In (47) this is illustrated with an epistemic sentence adverbial (subjective modal).

(47) A: *Es   wird   wahrscheinlich regnen.*
       it   will   likely   rain
   B: *Das glaube ich   nicht.*
       it believe I   not
   This cannot mean that B does not believe that it is likely that it will rain, it only means that B does not believe that it will rain.

---

5 Likewise, *denn* is not licensed in questions arising through tags ((60b) below). On the other hand, it is fine in orders or rhetorical questions, which are sometimes considered to be not inquisitive but assertive.

(i) *Könntest du   mir denn bitte   das Salz geben?*
    could   you   me MP   please the salt give
    roughly: 'Please, pass me the salt!'

(ii) *Wer will   denn nachts   um halb 4 Butter kaufen?*
     who wants MP   at.night at half 4 butter buy
     roughly: 'Nobody wants to buy butter at 3:30 a.m.'

Compare (47) with (48), in which an epistemic adjective occurs. Such an expression is at-issue.

(48) A: *Es ist wahrscheinlich, dass es regnet.*
  it is likely   that it will rain
  B: *Das glaube ich nicht.*
  it believe I not
  This can mean that B does not believe that it is likely that it will rain.

Krifka (2017) concludes from this observation that subjective modals are proposition-external. Epistemic sentence adverbials and the marking of an aboutness topic are equally not-at-issue. Regarding the latter, consider:

(49) A: *Hans jedenfalls wird mithelfen.*
  Hans for.one will assist
  'Hans, for one, will be assisting.'
  B: *Das glaube ich nicht.*
  This cannot mean that B does not believe that it especially holds of Hans – perhaps in contrast to others – that he will assist, it just means that B does not believe that Hans will assist. Thus B does not refute any additional nuance or expressive feature that comes along with the particle.

By means of this test it can be shown that all weak RPs are not-at-issue. With Krifka (2017) we can conclude from these observations that all weak RPs are proposition-external. Arguably, this semantic property is mirrored by the fact that in syntax, weak RPs are located outside TP. For example, according to, for example, Cinque (1999), sentence adverbials are positioned outside of TP, and the marking of an aboutness topic always seems to occur outside the TP; cf. e.g. Frey (2004) for German.

Furthermore, Krifka (2017) claims that subjective modals are not related to the speech act performed, i.e. they are neither operators modifying the strength of the commitment to the speech act nor do they qualify the speech act. One of Krifka's reasons for this claim is that subjective modals may occur in the complement of a propositional attitude clause (*John thinks that it will likely rain*), where they can become part of the embedded propositional attitude. Furthermore, Krifka observes that adverbials which are clearly speech act related can be 'added' in the following discourse, (50a). This is usually not possible with subjective modal adverbials, (50b).

(50) a. *It will rain. Honestly, it will rain.*
    b. *#It will rain. It likely will rain.*

Thus, Krifka reasons that subjective epistemics do not scope over speech acts, and that they are also not part of the proposition. Thus, he concludes that there must be a distinct semantic layer in-between.

We can apply this kind of reasoning to the other weak RPs. They all are not-at-issue and they all can become part of an embedded propositional attitude, i.e. they do not modify the speech act performed with the whole clause. Thus, we can conclude that weak RPs relate to a distinct layer between the speech act and the proposition.

Krifka points to writings of Frege and Peirce (cf. Tuzet 2006), where such a distinct layer is introduced. Frege (1918) explicitly differentiates between the following aspects involved in an assertion:

(51) i. das Fassen eines Gedankens – das Denken ('the grasping/conception of a thought – the thinking')
   ii. die Anerkennung der Wahrheit eines Gedankens – das Urteilen ('the appreciation of the truth of a thought – the judging')
   iii. die Kundgebung des Urteils – das Behaupten ('the manifestation of the judgement – the asserting')

Similar thoughts about the distinction between a thought, a private judgement on the truthfulness of the thought and a public assertion of this judgement were developed by Peirce. Thus, according to Krifka, Frege and Peirce envisage three distinct semantic operations:

(52) i. A thought/proposition φ which has truth conditions,
   ii. a judgement of a person x concerning a proposition φ, a private act,
   iii. an assertion of a person x of a proposition φ, a public act.

Krifka (2017) generalises Frege's and Peirce's partition to all speech acts and proposes representing the judgement and the speech act in the syntactic structure, the pertinent functional projections being called JP and ActP. Thus, he arrives at a general syntactic representation of these semantic partitions, standing hereby in what meanwhile can be called the tradition of the 'syntacticisation of discourse' (cf. e.g. Speas and Tenny 2003; Miyagawa 2012; Haegeman and Hill 2013).

According to Krifka (2017), the weakly root-sensitive subjective modals are semantically anchored to a judge; they express the degree of the confidence of the judge in the truth of a proposition. Syntactically they are related to JP.

Krifka (2017) subscribes to the commitment view of speech acts. Regarding assertions, the commitment view holds that in asserting a proposition φ the speaker expresses public responsibility for the truth of φ, backed by social sanctions if φ is false and the speaker has no excuse. To the CG shared by speaker and hearer it is added that the speaker is publicly committed to the truth of φ. The proposition φ itself is added to the CG as a conversational implicature. In line with this view, Krifka (2017) adds a fourth partition to (52), which is the dimension of the commitment of a participant in the dialogue. While the committer x equals the speaker in assertions, it equals the addressee in information seeking questions. According to Krifka, a question of speaker S to hearer H like *Is it raining or not?* does not change the set of shared propositions but restricts the continuations of the conversation to those in which either H commits to the proposition that it is raining or H commits to the proposition that it is not raining. As for syntax, Krifka assumes a commitment phrase CmP, whose head represents the commitment of a committer.

Thus, one arrives at the assumptions in (53).

(53) i. The TP encodes a proposition φ.
  ii. Above TP there can be a judgement phrase (JP), which encodes a judge and expresses an evaluation of the proposition φ by the judge.
  iii. Above JP there can be a commitment phrase (CmP), which encodes a committer and expresses public commitment of the committer.
  iv. Above CmP there can be a speech act phrase (ActP), which encodes the speaker and expresses the occurrence of a specific speech act.

For illustration let us take two other examples of weak RPs. The use of a MP presupposes a judgement. For example, with the MP *ja* the status of a proposition relative to the CG is evaluated and it is expressed that the proposition is assumed to be in principle available. Obviously also topic marking involves a judgement. A judger considers a statement to be essentially about a certain object; as a consequence the term which refers to this object is highlighted and marked a sentence topic.

Our observations concerning weak RPs lead to the general thesis in (54):

(54) Weak RPs relate semantically to a judge and are syntactically licensed by J^0.

An immediate consequence of (54) is that all clauses which allow weak RPs exhibit a JP and all clauses disallowing weak RPs don't.

In the syntactic structure (53) leads to the hierarchy in (55):

(55) ActP > CmP > JP > TP

The presence of the projections in (55) is implicationally top down, i.e. if a clause structure encodes the projection α in (55), it also encodes all projections below α. Thus, every independent clause contains an ActP, a CmP, a JP and a TP. What about dependent clauses? CACs are just TPs[6]; they express a proposition, but they do not allow any RPs. PACs express a proposition and they allow weak RPs. It follows that they are JPs.[7] NonICs also allow strong RPs. According to our considerations they have full illocutional force, i.e. they are ActPs and as such contain a CmP, a JP and a TP. The complements of mental attitude verbs allow weak RPs but not strong ones. Therefore, we assume that they have the categorial status of (a CP dominating) a JP. The complements of factive verbs do not allow any RPs. Thus, we assume that they have the categorial status of (a CP dominating) a TP. The same is true for the complements of all other verbs which do not induce an embedded root context. Are there dependent clauses which are CmPs? The answer likely is yes. The prime candidates are the complement clauses of speech predicates in certain languages. Although this goes beyond the topic of the present paper, one case in point should be mentioned. There are languages in which indexical shift occurs in the complements of attitude verbs and in the complements of speech predicates, and there are languages in which indexical shift only obtains in the scope of certain speech predicates (Sundaresan 2018). In Tamil, for example, index shift is allowed in the complement of a speech verb, but not in the complement of an attitude verb.[8] Note that there are no languages in which it is the other way round

---

6 This statement should not be taken literally since of course CACs are introduced by subordinators. We do not want to take a stand on whether these subordinators are prepositions, which would mean that CACs are PPs dominating a TP, or whether they are complementisers, which would mean that CACs are CPs dominating a TP.
7 The remarks of fn. 6 apply mutatis mutandis to PACs.
8 In the Tamil examples in (i) indexical shift becomes obvious in the number agreement on the verb (Sundaresan 2017).

(i) a. *Seetha₁ [taan₁ pootti-læ dʒej-čč-een-nnŭ] sonnaal*
Seetha ANAPH.NOM.SG contest-LOC win-PST-1SG-COMP say-PST-3FSG
'Seetha₁ said that she₁ won the contest.'
b. *??Seetha₁ [taan₁ pootti-læ dʒej-čč-een-nnŭ] nenččal*
Seetha ANAPH.NOM.SG contest-LOC win-PST-1SG-COMP think-PST-3FSG
'Seetha₁ thought that she₁ won.'

(Sundaresan 2017). We can assume that in the more liberal languages indexical shift is dependent on JP, while in the restrictive ones indexical shift is dependent on CmP. If speech verbs take CmP-complements and mental attitude verbs take JP-complements, the pattern follows. Thus, it might be worthwhile to consider the option that in some languages, speech verbs and only these take CmP-complements. However, in the following we will stick to the simple assumption that, at least in German, all root-inducing verbs just take JP-complements.

We arrive at the following listing of the categorial statuses of the different dependent clauses considered in the present paper:

(56) i. CAC: $[_{CP}$ TP]
  ii. PAC: $[_{CP}$ JP]
  iii. NonIC: ActP
  iv. complement of a mental attitude verb or of other root-inducing verbs: $[_{CP}$ JP]
  v. complement of a factive verb or of other not-root-inducing verbs: $[_{CP}$ TP]

How is the judge of a clause determined, i.e. how does J^0 get its value? We can assume that the licensing and valuation of J^0 has to occur under c-command in a strict local environment, i.e. the valuation occurs via the closest head. In the case of an independent sentence the judge equals the committer, cf. (57a). As already noted, the performer of the speech act might be different from the committer though. It follows that in this case the judge will be different from the speaker. This is what happens in information seeking questions, cf. (57b). Who is the judge of the complement clause of a mental attitude verb, i.e. how is the J-projection of the embedded clause licensed and valued? The answer is rather straightforward. The judge of the embedded clause equals the logical subject of the matrix verb and the J-projection is licensed by the matrix verb, (57c). Note that the J^0 of the embedded clause is in local configuration with its licenser.

(57) a. Peter: *It will likely rain.*   judge of main clause = Peter
  b. Mary to Peter: *Will it likely rain?*   judge of main clause = Peter
  c. Mary: *Peter thinks that it will likely rain.* judge of embedded clause = Peter

Let us next ask the question of who the judge of a PAC is and how the J-projection of a PAC is syntactically licensed and valued. A natural answer to the first question is (58).

(58) A PAC derives its judge from that source which also delivers the judge of the PAC's host.

Regarding the syntactic licensing of a PAC's JP, it follows from the considerations above that a PAC has to be base-generated structurally close to the syntactic representative of the source of its host's judge. We will make the following assumption:

(59) A PAC's base position is right-adjoined to its host's JP.

A PAC may also occur in the prefield of a V2-clause, cf. e.g. (36b). In the case of (36b) the PAC is moved to [Spec,ActP] from its JP-adjoined base position. If the PAC's host is an embedded JP, the PAC is right-adjoined to that JP, or if the PAC occurs in the prefield of the embedded JP, it is base-generated in [Spec,JP] of its host.

It follows that there is no binding from a constituent of a PAC's host into the PAC since the PAC is base-generated too high. It follows as well that the complex [host + PAC] cannot have just one nuclear accent inside the PAC since again the PAC is too high in its host's structure.

Note that it also follows that binding into a PAC should be possible from a position which is structurally higher than the PAC's host. (60) confirms this prediction.

(60) *Jede$_1$ fragte sich, warum Otto genommen wurde, obwohl sie$_1$*
everyone asked REFL why Otto taken was although she
doch die Richtige wäre.
MP the right would.be

The pronoun in (60) is inside the c-command domain of the subject of the highest clause.

Let us now consider the positioning of NonICs. We have seen that NonICs have full illocutionary force. Thus, we can assume that they are ActPs. In addition, it is a natural assumption that a NonIC constitutes a subsidiary speech act relative to the speech act performed with the NonIC's host. In contrast to Frey (2012), we assume here that in syntax this ancillary function of NonICs is mirrored by their being adjoined to their hosts. Since a NonIC constitutes a subsidiary speech act for another speech act, the host of a NonIC has to be an ActP too. We arrive at the assumption in (61).

(61) NonICs are ActPs which are adjoined to ActPs.

A consequence is that a NonIC cannot be embedded together with its host. Its host, being an ActP, cannot be embedded in the first place. Following Green (2000) and others (cf. section II), we formulate (62).

(62) An ActP cannot occur embedded in another syntactic structure.

Let's next consider strong RPs. (63) makes clear that a strong RP cannot occur in the prefield of a V2-clause. Thus it cannot be part of its host's syntactic structure.

(63) a. *Ich muss heute zum Amt, Mann.*
     I must today to.the department man
  b. **Mann, muss ich heute zum Amt.*
     man must I today to.the department
  c. *Maria wird gewinnen, wetten!*
     Maria will win let's bet
  d. **Wetten wird Maria gewinnen.*
     let's bet will Maria win

Next we note that a strong RP too can be considered to constitute its own speech act, albeit again a subsidiary speech act relative to the speech act with which it is associated. This assumption seems to be justified on grounds of the semantics/pragmatics of strong RPs and on the basis of their phonology. Thus, strong RPs have a certain semantic and pragmatic independence. Correspondingly they do not seem to be in need of syntactic licensing by the head of another syntactic structure. Therefore, we can assume (64).

(64) A strong RP constitutes a speech act and is adjoined to the ActP of its host.

An immediate consequence of (64) is that strong RPs can only occur with independent sentences and the restricted set of dependent clauses which are called NonICs in the present paper.[9]

---

[9] At first glance the following data seems to contradict the claim that strong RPs cannot appear embedded.

5 On the Correspondences between Root Phenomena and Types of Clauses

Our observations so far yield the following correspondences. GHT and other strong RPs need a host which encodes an independent illocutionary operator, i.e. which exhibits an ActP. GLD, the marking of an aboutness topic with a particle and other weak RPs need a host which is able to encode a judge, i.e. which has a JP. Finally, right dislocation and other expressives which are not root-sensitive may be hosted by a clause which encodes neither a speech act nor a judgement but just a proposition.

Let us start with the strong RPs. In syntactic theory it is sometimes assumed (cf. e.g. Speas and Tenny 2003 and Miyagawa 2012) that the fact that a clause has illocutionary force is encoded syntactically by a projection in the clause's left periphery. Here the relevant projection is called ActP. Given our observation, it is justified to assume that the hosting clause of a strong RP must have an Act-projection, which in the interpretation component is independently related to an illocutionary operator. If we look at our examples of strong RPs, we realise that they occur in an outermost position of the clause they belong to. This follows since they have to be locally licensed by Act^0, which is the highest head in its clause.

According to Frey (2005) a GHT introduces a new discourse topic. Thus it contributes to the structuring of the discourse. Therefore, it is of a very high level in terms of interpretative effect. We may assume that only clauses with illocutionary force can be used to structure the discourse. Therefore, it makes sense that in order for a phenomenon to be able to affect discourse structure it has to belong to a clause which is an ActP, i.e. it has to be a strong RP.

The other examples of strong RPs considered in this paper also affect discourse structure. As noted above, the insertion of a question tag demands that

(i) a. *Maria, ein Genie, wetten, hat den besten Vortrag gehalten*
       Maria a   genious let's bet has the best   talk   given
    b. *der bisher   größte – oder etwa nicht? – Bankenskandal*
       the until-now biggest or   MP   not   bank-scandal

Strong RPs may appear in appositional constructions and in non-restrictively interpreted attributes. Note, however, that at least regarding appositive constructions it has been noted for a long time that they behave as secondary messages that are not syntactically integrated in a standard way into their host (cf. e.g. de Vries 2006; Heringa 2012). (ib) indicates that for non-restrictive attributes the same has to be assumed.

an assertion be performed and it adds a conforming question to the discourse, which affects the continuing discourse. An interjection also has an effect on discourse structure. It not only expresses an emotional attitude of the speaker towards a speech act, but it also makes clear that the speaker considers her/his statement as highly relevant for the ongoing discourse by strengthening the illocutionary weight of the statement.

Let's move to weak RPs. A weak RP is not immediately dependent on a speech act. MPs, for example, are linked to sentence mood, but, as we have seen, they are not restricted in such a way that their host clause must constitute an independent speech act on its own (cf. for that matter also Jacobs 2018 on *ja*). Let us once more consider the particle *denn*. It is licensed by interrogative mood (cf. (46b)), but it is not licensed in just any question-like speech act. 'Rising declaratives' or tagged declaratives constitute inquisitive acts that do not provide a good host for *denn*, cf. (46c) and (65a,b). On the other hand, some open propositions do allow *denn*, without encoding independent speech acts, cf. (65c,d). Thus, it rather seems to be the case that *denn* is an operator which characterises the assessment of a proposition by a judge. The standard assumption about the meaning of the particle *denn*, which occurs in a question with the open proposition φ, is that it indicates that the speaker considers the answer to the question highly relevant. We propose to characterise the meaning of *denn* slightly different: a judge considers the true proposition φ', which has the open position of the proposition φ with which *denn* occurs instantiated, as highly relevant.

(65) a. *Du hast das Buch (*denn) gelesen?*
　　　　you have the book MP　　　read
　　b. *Peter hat das Buch (*denn) gelesen, oder?*
　　　　Peter has the book MP　　　read　　or
　　c. *Marias Frage　an Peter, ob　　er denn dabei war,*
　　　　Maria's question to Peter whether he MP at-that was
　　　　wollte　er nicht beantworten.
　　　　wanted he not　answer
　　d. *Finde mal heraus, wen　sie denn getroffen hat!*
　　　　find　MP out　　whom she MP　met　　has

MPs do not induce a discourse move, i.e. by themselves they do not structure the discourse, but rather have a more local interpretative effect. However, they can be said to constitute means to support CG-management.

Let us now consider the marking of an aboutness topic by a particle and by GLD. Unlike GHT these are clause-internal phenomena. Topic marking by a particle occurs below the so-called C-domain or, to use an alternative terminology, inside the middle field. The GLDed phrase of the GLD construction is positioned very high in the C-domain or, using the alternative terminology, in the 'Vor-Vorfeld' (pre-prefield). In line with this and in contrast to GHT, the marking of an aboutness topic by a particle and GLD have a rather local interpretative effect. They establish the aboutness topic of the clause they occur in. In addition, GLD demands that the topic it establishes be already given by the context. Topic marking expresses that a judge considers a property as being associated especially with a specific object. In addition it becomes part of the CG that the judge establishes this association. Topic marking does not induce a certain discourse move and it does not structure the discourse. Therefore, these markings are not directly linked to illocutionary acts. They have an effect on CG-management though.

Many, if not even most, expressive items, however, are not sensitive to the occurrence of an illocution or to the estimation by a judge. Right dislocation, focal constituents, diminutives, pejorative epithets and so on can appear anywhere. Non-root-sensitive phenomena are not dependent on illocutionary force or on a judgement, i.e. they are not concerned with discourse moves nor with the way information is assessed by a thinking mind.[10] They just facilitate the communication between speaker and hearer by marking what is new or given at a certain point in the communication, help to clarify the reference of an expression or make clear the emotional attitude of the speaker towards a referent. Note that non-root-sensitive phenomena do not have scope over the proposition they occur in. In contrast to topic marking or discourse particles they do not affect CG-management. For example, CG-information is not affected by indicating which part of a sentence is new and which part is given at a certain point in the conversation. Furthermore, although the fact that the speaker has used a pejorative epithet or diminutive to refer to an object might become part of the CG, i.e. it might get stored as an additional proposition in the CG, the use of these elements

---

10 We are aware of the fact that there are authors who think differently about right dislocation. Averintseva-Klisch (2009) is a case in point. She assumes that right dislocation has the function of introducing the discourse topic for the following passage of the text. We are sceptical about the correctness of this claim, though. Note, for example, that it is perfectly fine to end a text with a right dislocation construction.

does not affect how the proposition of the ambient clause should be judged epistemically or how it should be stored in the CG. Thus, an epithet for example does not have scope over the overall proposition.

Note also in this context that Krifka (2008) makes a crucial difference between CG-content and CG-management. CG-content refers to phenomena such as givenness, novelty, presuppositions etc. CG-management manifests the communicative interests and goals of the participants. Krifka proposes that CG-management is concerned with the way in which the CG-content should be treated.

Let us conclude this section with a short look at two other classifications of RPs and topic constructions in recent works of Jacobs (2018) and Bianchi and Frascarelli (2010), respectively.

Jacobs (2018) also proposes a three-fold split of expressions as far as their distribution in dependent (embedded) or independent clauses is concerned. He calls them MCP (Main Clause Phenomena) I, II and III. At first glance, this might look much like what we propose. However, Jacobs' (2018) division is crucially different. Jacobs' proposal and our proposal are not counter-proposals; in the end both classifications may turn out to be compatible to quite a large extent although not throughout. For the sake of clarification let us make a short comparison. Jacobs thus distinguishes MPC I, which are linguistic expressions that are licit in some embedded clauses such as pertinent adverbial clauses (presumably our PACs), complement clauses of verba dicendi and in appositive relative clauses, though not in restrictive relative clauses. His main illustrating element is the discourse particle *ja*. The second group (= MCP II) comprises expressions which are less restrictive than those of group I because they are legitimate in more environments; the example for an additional environment he gives is restrictive relative clauses. The MCP II elements are evaluative and epistemic adverbials (such as *leider* 'unfortunately'). An example of Jacobs' is given in (66).

(66) *Gestern rief jemand an, der sich leider / $^{??}$ja verwählt*
yesterday call someone PRT who REFL unfortunatly / MP misdialed
hat.
has

The third group comprises elements and structures which under no circumstances can be embedded: special verb-first clauses (yes-no questions, imperatives) and "marginal" constructions which lack a finite verb altogether (one of Jacobs' examples is infinitive commands: (*das Bild*) *nicht berühren!* 'Don't touch (the picture)!').

Recall that we do not propose a three-type division of main clause phenomena. We differentiate three types of use-conditional expressions and three types of dependent structures. We argue for a class of expressive items which are fine in any context, including regular embedded clauses. Hence these expressions cannot be typed and named main clause phenomena. We then divide main clause phenomena into two categories: strong ones and weak ones. Our notions of weakness and strictness (strength) do not fit with Jacobs' division between his MCP I and MCP II. If there is a potential correspondence, then Jacobs' MCP III and our strict main clause phenomena may cover similar expressions. Yet the concrete phenomena are pretty different, perhaps with the exception of the "unembeddable discourse particles" *doch* or *nochmal* in *Wie war doch/nochmal Ihr Name?* ('What was MP your name? / What was your name again?'). However, whereas Jacobs is interested in phenomena which do not embed at all, our interest has been phenomena which occur in independent clauses and in clauses which are syntactically autonomous while being dependent on a semantic or pragmatic level.

All in all, it seems that Jacobs' classification is by and large orthogonal to the one we propose.[11]

We also think it will be helpful to clarify the difference between our approach and the one advocated in Bianchi and Frascarelli (2010). What the two proposals have in common is the study of different types of topic constructions and the assumption that CG-management and illocutionary force play an essential role. Furthermore, Bianchi and Frascarelli also distinguish different types of topics. They propose a three-fold partition: (i) aboutness topics (which they call A-topics), (ii) contrastive topics (their C-topics) and (iii) givenness topics (G-topics).

The type (iii) just refers to constituents which are given. We would not subsume them under the notion topic but one certainly can do so. Such constituents do not show any signs of illocutionary dependency or any relation to CG-management, and hence they are not considered to be root-sensitive: they

---

11 However, we would like to note that at this point we are not fully convinced that an example like (66) shows that one has to separate MCP II from MCP I. First, the relative clause in (66) with *leider* does not seem to have the reading of a restrictive relative clause. The speaker has a certain person in mind who called and for whom it holds in addition that unfortunately has dialed the wrong number and who is not identifiable to the hearer. Second, the fact that the MP *ja* is not appropriate in the context of the non-restrictive relative clause in (66) might just be due to the fact that *ja* requests the hearer to retrieve information from the CG and that this is incompatible with the subject of the clause in question being a (specific) indefinite.

appear freely in any type of clause. In this respect, we fully agree with Bianchi and Frascarelli.

More intricate are Bianchi and Frascarelli's topic types (i) and (ii). A(boutness)-topics are argued to be root-sensitive; C-topics are considered to not be root-sensitive. Bianchi and Frascarelli agree with Haegeman (2004) and others that C-topics cannot appear in CACs, which they attribute to the status of these clauses as mere event modifiers. As such they are analysed as not denoting propositions. Complements of predicates which according to Bianchi and Frascarelli (2010) do select for propositions, however, may allow C-topics although these complements are not considered to be root-like. Thus sentences which comprise factive predicates (*be glad*) or inherently negative verbs like *conceal* are claimed to be well formed with C-topics:

(67) a. *I am glad that this unrewarding job, she has finally decided to give _ up.*
   b. *He tried to conceal from his parents that the maths exam he had not passed _, and the biology exam he had not even taken.*

Bianchi and Frascarelli take these data to show that this type of topic is not root-sensitive. Subsequent research has shown, however, that the data are not watertight. Haegeman and Ürögdi (2010) suggest that *glad* in (67a) is shifted to mean something like "glad to say" and coerces a verbum dicendi meaning (this shift from some true factives to assertive predicates is well attested; see Fabricius-Hansen and Sæbø 2004). We think that the same can also be carried over to the example in (67b). To conceal that something has not happened, is not the case or does not take place may very well mean that the subject of the concealing makes statements about the content of the embedded clause. For (67b) this reading seems especially natural because of the presence of *try*. Under this perspective the matrix verb in (67b) also acts a verb of saying and not as a canonical factive verb, which makes it likely to allow RPs.

As for A-topics, Bianchi and Frascarelli show that they are root-sensitive. However, the crucial difference between our approach and the one taken by them is that Bianchi and Frascarelli do not make the three-way distinction between dependent clauses we make. For them, clauses are either canonically embedded (as e.g. CACs) or illocutionarily independent. Furthermore, in contrast to our assumption they assume that PACs are illocutionarily independent. Another difference is that they propose that PACs are syntactically connected by some coordinating element with their host clauses. Instead we analyse aboutness topics as weakly root-sensitive, which means that they need not appear in illocutionarily independent clauses, and we analyse PACs as being part of the syntactic structures of their hosts. On the other hand, we classify GHT, an instance of hanging topics (a type which Bianchi and Frascarelli do not recognise as a special type of its own), as a type of topic that must appear in a syntactically independent clause.

What is similar in both approaches is that both assume different types of topics and a different distribution of the particular types across the dependency statuses of different types of clauses.

6 Summary

The paper argues for the following theses:
- It is necessary to distinguish between weakly and strongly root-sensitive phenomena. Strongly root-sensitive phenomena may only occur in clauses with independent illocutionary force, while weakly root-sensitive phenomena have a broader distribution, but they may not occur in just any kind of clause. They require that the clauses in which they occur exhibit the Judge-projection (JP). JP encodes an act of judging of the following proposition by a judge.
- Regarding their root-sensitivity, constructions which in the literature are often classified as topic constructions differ. The German Hanging Topic construction is strongly root-sensitive, German Left Dislocation and topic marking with a particle are weakly root-sensitive, and Right Dislocation is not root-sensitive.
- At least a threefold distinction among dependent clauses is necessary. There are (i) dependent clauses which may host strongly root-sensitive constructions, (ii) dependent clauses which may not host strongly root-sensitive constructions, but weakly root-sensitive ones, and (iii) clauses which may only host non-root-sensitive constructions. Clauses of type (i) have independent illocutionary force and encode a speech act, clauses of type (ii) encode a proposition and a judgement on the proposition, and clauses of type (iii) just encode a proposition.
- Other non-truth-functional/non-descriptive phenomena like tags, interjections, pejorative epithets, diminutives or the marking of information focus are also to be distinguished regarding strong root-sensitivity, weak sensitivity or non-root-sensitivity.

- Strongly root-sensitive phenomena have an effect on the organisation of the discourse, while weakly root-sensitive phenomena have an effect on common ground management.

References

Altmann, Hans. 1981. *Formen der "Herausstellung" im Deutschen*. Tübingen: Niemeyer.
Altmann, Hans. 1993. Satzmodus. In Jacobs, Joachim, Arnim von Stechow, Wolfgang Sternefeld & Theo Vennemann (eds.), *Syntax. Ein Internationales Handbuch der zeitgenössischen Forschung. Syntax*, 1006–1029. Berlin & New York: Mouton de Gruyter.
Averintseva-Klisch, Maria. 2009. *Rechte Satzperipherie im Diskurs. NP-Rechtsversetzung im Deutschen*. Studien zur deutschen Grammatik 78. Tübingen: Stauffenburg.
Bayer, Josef. 2001. Asymmetry in emphatic topicalization. In Caroline Féry & Wolfgang Sternefeld (eds.), *Audiatur Vox Sapientiae* (Studia grammatica 52), 15–47. Berlin: Akademie Verlag.
Bianchi, Valentina & Mara Frascarelli. 2010. Is topic a root phenomenon? Iberia: IJTL 2, 43–88.
Brandt, Margareta. 1990. *Weiterführende Nebensätze. Zu ihrer Syntax, Semantik und Pragmatik* (Lunder germanistische Forschungen 57). Stockholm: Almqvist & Wiksell.
Cinque, Guglielmo. 1999. *Adverbs and functional heads. A cross-linguistic perspective*. Oxford: Oxford University Press.
Coniglio, Marco. 2011. *Die Syntax der deutschen Modalpartikeln: Ihre Distribution und Lizenzierung in Haupt- und Nebensätzen* (Studia grammatica 73). Berlin: Akademie Verlag.
Fabricius-Hansen, Cathrine & Kjell Johan Sæbø. 2004. In a meditative mood: The semantics of the German reportative. *Natural Language Semantics* 12. 213–257.
Frascarelli, Mara & Roland Hinterhölzl. 2007. Types of topics in German and Italian. In Kerstin Schwabe & Susanne Winkler (eds.), *On information structure, meaning and form*, 87–116. Amsterdam & Philadelphia: John Benjamins.
Frege, Gottlob. 1918. Der Gedanke. Eine logische Untersuchung. *Beiträge zur Philosophie des Deutschen Idealismus*. 58–77. Deutsche Philosophische Gesellschaft. Erfurt: Stenger.
Frey, Werner. 2004. A medial topic position for German. *Linguistische Berichte* 198. 153–190.
Frey, Werner. 2005. Pragmatic properties of certain German and English left peripheral constructions. *Linguistics* 43(1). 89–129.
Frey, Werner. 2012. On two types of adverbial clauses allowing root-phenomena. In Lobke Aelbrecht, Liliane Haegeman & Rachel Nye (eds.), *Main clause phenomena: new horizons*, 405–429. Amsterdam & Philadelphia: John Benjamins.
Frey, Werner & Hubert Truckenbrodt. 2015. Syntactic and prosodic integration and disintegration in peripheral adverbial clauses and in right dislocation/afterthought. In Andreas Trotzke & Josef Bayer (eds.), *Syntactic complexity across interfaces*, 75–106. Berlin & New York: Mouton de Gruyter.

Giorgi, Alessandra & Fabio Pianesi. 2005. Credo (I believe): Epistemicity and the syntactic representation of the speaker. *University of Venice Working Papers in Linguistics* 15. 105–152.

Green, Mitchell S. 2000. Illocutionary force and semantic content. *Linguistics and Philosophy* 23, 435–473.

Grewendorf, Günther. 2002. Left dislocation as movement. In Simon Mauck & Jenny Mittelstaedt (eds.), *Georgetown University Working Papers in Theoretical Linguistics 2*. 31–81. Georgetown.

Grohmann, Kleanthes. 2003. *Prolific domains: on the anti-locality of movement dependencies*. Amsterdam & Philadelphia: John Benjamins.

Gutzmann, Daniel. 2013. Expressives and beyond. An introduction into varieties of use-conditional meaning. In Daniel Gutzmann & Hans-Martin Gärtner (eds.), *Beyond expressives. Explorations in use-conditional meaning* (Current Studies in the Semantics/Pragmatics Interface (CRiSPI) 28), 1–58. Leiden: Brill.

Haegeman, Liliane. 1991. Parenthetical adverbials: The radical orphan approach. In Shuki Chiba, Akira Ogawa, Yasuaki Fuiwara, Norio Yamade, Osamo Koma & Takao Yagi (eds.), *Aspects of modern English linguistics*, 232–254. Tokyo: Kaitakusha.

Haegeman, Liliane. 2003. Conditional clauses: external and internal syntax. *Mind and Language* 18. 317–339.

Haegeman, Liliane. 2004. The syntax of adverbial clauses and its consequences for topicalisation. *Antwerp Papers in Linguistics* 107. 61–90.

Haegeman, Liliane & Barbara Ürögdi. 2010. Referential CPs and DPs: an operator movement account. *Theoretical Linguistics* 36(2-3). 111–152.

Haegeman, Liliane & Virginia Hill. 2013. The syntacticization of discourse. In Raffaella Folli, Chrsitina Sevdali & Robert Truswell (eds.), *Syntax and its limits*, 370–390. Oxford: Oxford University Press.

Heringa, Hermanus. 2012. *Appositional constructions*. Utrecht: LOT.

Holler, Anke. 2008. German dependent clauses from a constraint-based perspective. Cathrine Fabricius-Hansen & Wiebke Ramm (eds.), *Subordination versus coordination in sentence and text*, 187–216. Amsterdam & Philadelphia: John Benjamins.

Hooper, Joan B. & Sandra A. Thompson. 1973. On the applicability of root transformations. *Linguistic Inquiry* 4. 465–497.

Jacobs, Joachim. 1991. On the semantics of modal particles. In Werner Abraham (ed.), *Discourse particles*, 141–162. Amsterdam & Philadelphia: John Benjamins.

Jacobs, Joachim. 2001. The dimensions of topic-comment. *Linguistics* 39(4). 641–681.

Jacobs, Joachim. 2018. Main clause phenomena in German. *Linguistische Berichte* 254. 131–182.

Krifka, Manfred. 2008. Basic notions of information structure. *Acta Linguistica Hungarica* 55. 243–276.

Krifka, Manfred. 2017. Assertions and judgments, epistemics and evidentials. Handout for the workshop: Speech acts: meanings, uses, syntactic and prosodic realization. ZAS, Berlin, May 2017. http://amor.cms.hu-berlin.de/~h2816i3x/Talks/CommitmentEpistemicsHandout.pdf (accessed on 15/8/2017).

Lohnstein, Horst. 2000. *Satzmodus – kompositionell. Zur Parametrisierung der Modusphrase im Deutschen*. Berlin: Akademie Verlag.

Meinunger, André. 2004. Verb position, verbal mood and the anchoring (potential) of sentences. In Horst Lohnstein & Susanne Trissler (eds.), *The syntax and semantics of the left periphery*, 311–341. Berlin & New York: Mouton de Gruyter.

Meinunger, André. 2006. The discourse status of subordinate sentences and some implications for syntax and pragmatics. In Valéria Molnár & Susanne Winkler (eds.), *The architecture of focus*, 459–487. Berlin & New York: Mouton de Gruyter.

Meinunger, André. 2011. Der Wortartenstatus des Elements 'je' in der komparativen Korrelativkonstruktion. *Zeitschrift für Germanistische Linguistik* 39(2). 217–231.

Miyagawa, Shigeru. 2012. Agreements that occur mainly in the main clause. In Lobke Aelbrecht, Liliane Haegeman & Rachel Nye (eds.), *Main clause phenomena. New horizons*, 79–11. Amsterdam & Philadelphia: John Benjamins.

Pasch, Renate, Ursula Brauße, Eva Breindl & Ulrich Hermann Waßner (eds.). 2003. *Handbuch der deutschen Konnektoren*. Berlin & New York: Mouton de Gruyter.

Reinhart, Tanya. 1981. Pragmatics and linguistics: An analysis of sentence topics. *Philosophica* 27. 53–94.Brill.

Speas, Peggy & Carol Tenny. 2003. Configurational properties of point of view roles. In A.-M. Di Sciullo (ed.), *Asymmetry in grammar*, 315–344. Amsterdam & Philadeplhia: John Benjamins.

Sundaresan, Sandhya. 2018. An alternative model of indexical shift: Variation and selection without context-overwriting. Ms. available under: https://ling.auf.net/lingbuzz/004115.

Thurmair, Maria. 1989. *Modalpartikeln und ihre Kombinationen*. Tübingen: Niemeyer.

Truckenbrodt, Hubert. 2015. Intonation phrases and speech acts. In Marlies Kluck, Dennis Ott & Mark de Vries (eds.), *Parenthesis and ellipsis. Cross-linguistic and theoretical perspectives*, 301–349. Berlin & New York: Mouton de Gruyter.

Truckenbrodt, Hubert. 2016. Some distinctions in the right periphery of the German clause. In Werner Frey, André Meinunger & Kerstin Schwabe (eds.), *Inner-sentential propositional proforms. Syntactic properties and interpretative effects*, 105–145. Amsterdam & Philadelphia: John Benjamins.

Tuzet, Giovanni. 2006. Responsible for truth? Peirce on judgement and assertion. *Cognitio* 7. 317–336.

Vat, Jan. 1981. Left dislocation, connectedness and reconstruction. *Groninger Arbeiten zur Germanistischen Linguistik* 20, 80–103. Reprinted in Elena Anagnostopoulou et al (eds.), (1979) *Materials on left dislocation*, 67–92. Amsterdam & Philadelphia : John Benjamins.

Vries, Mark de. 2006. The syntax of appositive relativization. On specifying coordination, false free relatives, and promotion. *Linguistic Inquiry* 37(2). 229–270.

Vries, Mark de. 2009. The left and right periphery in Dutch. *The Linguistic Review* 26. 91–327.

Zifonun, Gisela, Ludger Hoffmann & Bruno Strecker. 1997. *Grammatik der deutschen Sprache*. Berlin: & New York: Mouton de Gruyter.

List of Abbreviations

CAC   Central adverbial clause
CG   Common ground
GHT   German Hanging Topic

GLD	German Left Dislocation
MP	Modal particle
NonIC	Non-integrated dependent clause
PAC	Peripheral adverbial clause
ResP	Resumptive pronoun
RP	Root phenomenon
SADV	Sentential adverbial

Mara Frascarelli
Topics, Conversational Dynamics and the Root/Non-root Distinction: Adverbial Clauses at the Discourse-syntax Interface

Abstract: The composition and extent of the phrasal hierarchies in the left periphery of different clause types has been a major concern in recent research, mainly concentrating on the root/non-root distinction. This chapter intends to address this issue for adverbial clauses, assuming information structure and prosodic elicitation as diagnostics; specifically, the present analysis focuses on what Topic types are admitted in the C-domains of diverse adverbial clauses, through a systematic interface investigation based on original Italian data.

A novel perspective is thus proposed to shed new light on the syntactic mapping and the formal properties of (central vs. peripheral) adverbial clauses, embedding the relevant proposal in a cartographic framework of analysis.

Keywords: central adverbial clauses, conversational dynamics, discourse categories, interface analysis, peripheral adverbial clauses, prosody, root/non-root phenomena, topic

1 Root Phenomena under the Lens of Discourse Analysis: An Introduction

A number of recent works have examined the composition and extent of phrasal hierarchies of different clause types, distinguishing between root, root-like and (diverse types of) embedded clauses, and relevant phenomena (cf. Hooper and Thompson 1973; Emonds 1970, 1976, 2004; Haegeman 2002; Meinunger 2004; Heycock 2006).

Furthermore, recent works on the formal properties of discourse categories led to a clause-related distinction for different types of Topics (cf. Haegeman 2004; Frascarelli 2007; Krifka 2007; Bianchi and Frascarelli 2010; Frascarelli and Hinterhölzl 2007, 2016), Foci (cf., among others, Cruschina 2011; Bianchi and Bocci 2012; Bianchi 2013) and Contrast, often associated with either Focus or Topic, but also as an independent feature (Vallduví and Vilkuna 1998; Molnár 2006; Bianchi and

---

Mara Frascarelli, University of Roma Tre
https://doi.org/10.1515/9781501504488-005

Bocci 2012; Frascarelli and Ramaglia 2013; Bianchi 2013, 2015). The data examined in this respect, however, mainly concern declarative or interrogative clauses.

Based on the assumption that a systematic connection exists between the formal (syntax-prosody) and the semantic properties of discourse categories (cf. Frascarelli and Hinterhölzl 2007), this chapter uses information structure as diagnostics to define the root/non-root quality of adverbial clauses and provide a structural analysis in a cartographic approach (cf. Rizzi 1997 and subsequent works). For this purpose we propose a syntax-discourse investigation examining the acceptability of different types of Topic (*Aboutness-Shift* Topics, *Contrastive* Topics and *Familiar/Given* Topics) in diverse types of adverbial clauses, based on judgments collected by means of an original online survey. The investigation is based on original Italian data; however, cross-linguistic considerations will be also provided from the literature when relevant for the discussion.

The chapter is organized as follows. In section 2 we discuss the root/non-root distinction and illustrate the notion of Root phenomena, providing examples for the relevant distinction in different languages. In section 3 we present the discourse categories addressed in the current investigation and their role is discussed with respect to Conversational Dynamics. Section 4 provides a short survey on the major properties of adverbial clauses, focusing on their mixed properties, as is argued in recent works. In Sections 5 and 6 we present the interface analysis: interpretive judgments are analysed and confronted with their prosodic realizations.

Based on the evidence collected, we present a novel proposal on the syntactic mapping of adverbial clauses in section 7, supporting the necessity of a formal distinction for central and peripheral adverbials that can take into account their different interpretive (discourse-semantic and prosodic) properties.

2 The Root/Non-root Distinction[1]

2.1 What is a Root Clause?

To provide a clear-cut, uncontroversial definition of a Root clause is far from trivial. Since Emonds (1970, 1976), this quality has been attributed to those clausal domains that can host specific types of phenomena (like Left Dislocation) and the relevant "root restriction" has been connected to the availability of *assertive force* in these clauses.

---

[1] Please see the list of abbreviations used for glosses of non-English examples at the end of the chapter.

Hooper and Thompson (1973) made the point that this restriction only relies on semantic/pragmatic requirements and cannot be accounted for syntactically. In this sense, assertion is connected with illocutionary force,[2] a claim that is supported by the observation that "root transformations" are actually also allowed in syntactically embedded clauses whose content constitutes the main assertion:

(1) *It appears [that **this book** he read thoroughly].*
     (Hooper and Thompson 1973: 478)

This challenge was then taken up by different authors, who tried to elaborate a syntactic account for the relevant restriction. Emonds (1970, 1976) observed that for many speakers dependent clause contexts mimic the freedom of root structures in indirect discourse. However, root-like indirect discourse embedding is incompatible with most dependent clause positions (cf. Emonds 2004). In a similar vein, Haegeman and Ürögdi (2010) and Jiménez-Fernández and Miyagawa (2014) propose that non-root clauses contain an operator, which prevents some discourse categories from moving to the C-domain.

Based on an integrated, multi-layered perspective, Bianchi and Frascarelli (2010: 19) suggest that the restriction imposed on some phenomena to be realized in clausal domains (potentially) endowed with assertive force complies with plausible *interface requirements* and should be accounted for within the tradition of update semantics. The latter endorses a dynamic view of semantic interpretation, whereby the meaning of a sentence is its *update potential*: a function from an input context to an output context. The input context is the set of possible worlds that are compatible with the conversational Common Ground (CG), i.e. the set of propositions that are considered to be presupposed by all the participants in the conversation up to that point. The updating effect of an assertion is that the asserted proposition, when accepted by all the participants, is admitted into the CG, and thus discards from the input context all the possible worlds that are incompatible with it (technically, by intersection), yielding a "reduced" output context. (cf. Bianchi and Frascarelli 2010 for discussion).

Bianchi and Frascarelli's (2010) approach is assumed in the present analysis, so that a root clause is intended as a clausal domain endowed with update

---

[2] In fact, Hooper and Thompson (1973: 495) do not provide a clear definition of what constitutes an "asserted clause" and state that the assertion of a sentence is "its core meaning or main proposition", which "may be identified as the part that can be negated or questioned". The authors also provide a five-way division of predicates, which has later been resumed by different authors for further discussion and elaboration (cf., among others, Vikner 1995; Reis 1997; Meinunger 2004; Heycock 2006).

potential, and root phenomena can be thus either considered as operations triggering/connected with "conversational moves" or as "instructions" to the hearers on where the propositional content expressed by the assertion act should fit in the CG (cf. Krifka 2007 and footnote 4).

2.2 Two Types of Root Phenomena

In the literature, root phenomena are primarily instances of movement to the left periphery of the clause including operations like VP preposing (2a), Negative Constituent Preposing (2b), Topicalisation (2c), Left Dislocation (2d), Locative inversion (2e), Preposing around *be* (2f), Subject Auxiliary inversion (2b-2g), illustrated in the example below from English (cf., among others, Hooper and Thompson 1973; Heycock 2006), and V2 constructions in languages like German (3) (cf., among others, Gärtner 2002; Wiklund et al. 2009):

(2) a. *Mary promised that she would cook fish tonight, and cook fish she will.*
 b. *Never in my life have I told you lies!*
 c. *That movie you should watch.*
 d. *John, I never saw him at a scientific conference.*
 e. *On the wall hangs a portrait of my ancestors.*
 f. *Standing next to me was the bride's first man.*
 g. *Will Sara ever finish writing that paper of hers?*

(3) Dieses Buch wollte ich gestern lesen.
 this book want.PST.1SG I yesterday read.INF
 'Yesterday I wanted to read this book.'

Starting from this classification, Bianchi and Frascarelli (2012) provide evidence for the necessity of a *finer distinction* across left-peripheral root phenomena, based on the analysis of the distributional and scopal properties of constituents in the C-domain. Specifically, the authors identify and discuss *two types of Root phenomena*:

(i) Type I root phenomena like Left Dislocation (4) and Focus Fronting in Italian (5), which can occur in root clauses and in complements of bridge verbs (e.g., *say, think*),[3] but cannot occur under emotive and factive predicates (e.g.,

---

[3] In investigations dedicated to root phenomena, complements of bridge verbs play a major role since they have a "quasi-root" character; that is to say, they generally allow for the realization of root operations, while this is normally excluded in complements of factive or volitional verbs (cf., among others Bianchi and Frascarelli 2010; Gärtner 2002; Haegeman 2002;

be glad/sorry, regret, resent), or under volitional verbs (e.g., *hope, wish, would like*), as is shown in the following examples (from Bianchi and Frascarelli 2012):

(4) a. *I am glad [that **this unrewarding job**, she has finally decided to give it up]
    b. *I hope [that **the past** he will forget it soon], so as to bravely face the future.

(5) A: Di   sicuro sei   contento che   tua   sorella si
       of   certain be.2SG   glad   that your   sister   REFL
       fidanzi   with Gianni (...)
       get.engaged-SUBJ.2SG   con   Gianni (...)
       'For sure you are glad that your sister gets engaged with Gianni (....)'
    B: ?*No ,sono   contento [che CON   MARIO si
       no   be.PRS.1SG   glad   that with   Mario REFL
       fidanzi].
       get-engaged.SUBJ.2SG
       'No, I am glad that WITH MARIO she gets engaged.'

(ii) Type II root phenomena like English Topicalization (6) and V2 constructions, which can occur in root clauses and in complements to bridge verbs, but also in complements to volitional verbs, both with a Focus (7a) and a Contrastive Topic (7b) interpretation (from Bianchi and Frascarelli 2012):

(6) I **hope** that the past he will forget _, and the future he will face _ bravely.

(7) a. Ich wünschte, meine Fehler hätte   ich rechtzeitig
       I   wish.1SG   my   errors have.SUBJ.1SG I   in time
       erkannt,   nicht nur   meine Mängel.
       acknowledged   not   only   my   faults
       'I wish I had acknowledged my errors in time, not only my faults.'
    b. Ich wünschte, meine Fehler hätte   ich rechtzeitig
       I   wish.1SG   my   errors have-SUBJ.1SG I   in time
       erkannt   und meine   Wünsche   realisiert.
       acknowledged   and my   wishes   realised
       'I wish I had acknowledged my errors in time and my wishes realised.'

Emonds 2004; Meinunger 2004; Heycock 2006). Notice, however, that this distinction is not always clear-cut intra- and cross-linguistically. Volitionals like German *wollen*, for instance, behave like bridge verbs, but do not license V2 (cf. Penner and Badge 1991), whereas manner-of-speech verbs license V2, despite the fact that they are not bridge verbs. See references cited for details on this controversial issues, which are far beyond the scope of the present chapter.

As will be clear later, the distinction between the two types of root phenomena will play a crucial role in the study and understanding of imperative and adverbial clauses.

3 Discourse Categories and Conversational Dynamics

Frascarelli and Hinterhölzl (2007) propose a typology of Topics, based on the systematic correlation between their formal properties and their function in discourse, which is encoded in a strict hierarchy in the C-domain:

(8) [ForceP [ShiftP [ContrP [FocP [FamP [FinP [IP]]]]]]]

Assuming Frascarelli and Hinterhölzl's (2007) typology, Bianchi and Frascarelli (2010) show that the realization of discourse categories also depends on conversational dynamics. In particular, they provide evidence that a discourse category that triggers an update of the discourse context must occur in clauses endowed with context update potential. Supported by comparative data, this observation leads the authors to formulate the Interface Root Restriction (9), which provides a clear-cut distinction between Type I and Type II Root phenomena:

(9) *Interface Root Restriction* (Bianchi and Frascarelli 2010: 51)
Information Structure phenomena that affect the conversational dynamics (CG management) must occur in clauses endowed with illocutionary force that implement a conversational move.[4,5]

---

4 Following Krifka (2007), two dimensions of the CG are assumed, namely the CG content and the CG management. The CG content is the truth-conditional information accumulated up to a given point in the conversation. The CG management includes (i) the sequence of conversational moves (assertions, questions, etc.) performed by the speech act participants, which require illocutionary force, and (ii) the instructions that help the interlocutor determine the way in which the CG content develops and is organized (but do not constitute, in themselves, independent conversational moves).
5 Even though this restriction was not overtly stated as bi-conditional by the authors, it was intended as such. Hence, clauses endowed with illocutionary force are expected to host (all) information-structural phenomena. I thank a reviewer for pointing out this crucial aspect to me.

Since we address the acceptability of different types of Topics in adverbial clauses in this chapter, an overview on their discourse and formal properties is in order in the next sub-sections.

3.1 The Aboutness-shift (A-)Topic

The A-Topic connects Reinhart's (1981) aboutness ("what the sentence is about") with the property of being newly introduced or reintroduced to propose a shift in discourse. Assuming with Reinhart that the CG is divided into subsets of propositions that are stored under defining entries (so-called "file cards"), the A-Topic can be defined as the entry identifying the file card under which the proposition expressed in the sentence is stored. Consider for instance the following passage (from the naturalistic corpus used in Frascarelli 2007) in which the speaker, who is a radio speaker, is talking about her boss (introduced before and realised here as a null subject) and, at a certain point, she shifts to her abilities in her job through the clitic-left dislocation (CLLD) of the term *brava* ('good at') (glosses are only provided for the sentence under examination):

(10) *per il momento mi ha messo a far la speaker*
'By now he has given me the speaker role
dice che c'ho la voce per far la speaker perché sono brava-
he says that I have the right voice to be a speaker because I am good at -
"brava" non me lo dirà mai perché non è il tipo (...)
in fact he will never say "brava" to me, he is not that kind of person (...)'

(10′) **brava** non me   lo   dirà   mai
      good not me.IO.CL it.DO.CL say.FUT.3SG never
      'He will never say "brava" to me.'

Syntactically, the A-Topic is merged in the highest topic position in the C-domain (i.e., ShiftP in (8)) and, from an intonational viewpoint, it is associated with the complex L*+H tone (following a ToBi notation; cf. Pierrehumbert 1980); i.e., the topic shift is signalled by a rise in the F^0 contour that is aligned with the tonic vowel in its full extension, while the highest point is reached on the post-tonic vowel (cf. Frascarelli 2007: §3.1). The intonational contour of the sentence at-issue in (10) is provided in Figure 1 below.

As for its role in conversational dynamics, the A-Topic must be considered a conversational move insofar as topic selection is a *speech act itself* (cf. Krifka 2001: 25). In particular, it is an *initiating* speech act providing the entry (the 'file card') under which the subsequent speech act (an assertion, a question, a command, etc.) will be stored. As such, this operation is restricted to clauses endowed with illocutionary force and this means that the A-Topic qualifies as a Type I root phenomenon.

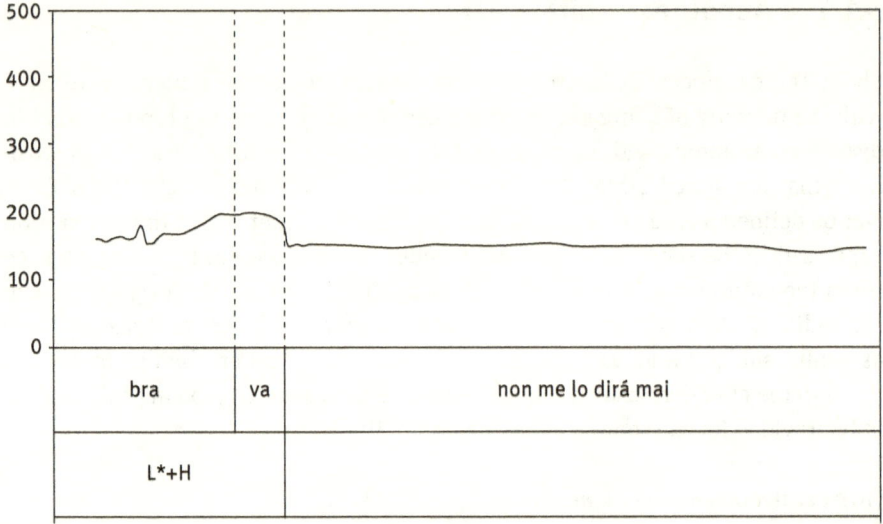

Figure 1: A-Topic.

3.2 The Contrastive (C-)Topic

C-Topics induce alternatives in the discourse that have no impact on the Focus value of the sentence (cf. Büring 2003).[6] Specifically, the C-Topic marking is used to "break down a complex proposition into a conjunction of simpler ones in which a predicate applies separately to each member of a salient set"

---

[6] In the Alternative Semantics approach (Rooth 1992; Beaver and Clark 2008), the crucial difference between Contrastive Topic and Focus is that the latter generates a set of *alternative propositions* (varying in the position of the focused element), while the former implies a set of *questions* hierarchically ordered by entailment relations. In particular, according to Büring (2003) the CT-congruence requirement states that every declarative clause containing a C-Topic must be the answer to a question belonging to a set of alternative questions – either explicitly asked or implicitly introduced – which are all part of a strategy to solve a super-question. Thus, a sentence like [*Fred*]$_{CT}$ *ate* [*THE BEANS*]$_F$ must be part of a "discourse-tree" entailing the super-question *Who ate what?* and the relevant sub-questions ({*What did Fred eat?, What did Mary eat?, ...*}).

4 Topics, Conversational Dynamics and the Root/Non-root Distinction — 147

(Bianchi and Frascarelli 2010: 72). Syntactically, the C-Topic is merged in the position immediately below the A-Topic in the C-domain (i.e., ContrP in (8)) and is characterized by a high tone that is aligned on the tonic vowel (H*).

This is illustrated in the following passage, in which a student was asked about how she liked an online English course. She thus dislocates the DP *il senso generale* as a (partial) C-Topic in order to break down a complex answer and contrast her capacity to understand the theory (i.e., the 'general meaning') with her ability to carry out the relevant exercises. As expected, this constituent is marked with a H* tone (cf. Figure 2 below):

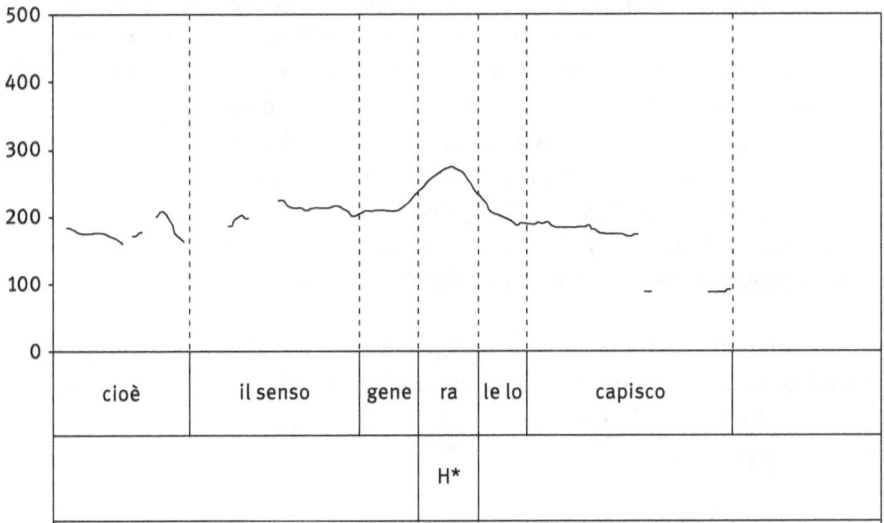

Figure 2: C-Topic.

(11) *I video per me almeno sono piuttosto lunghi da fare sezione per sezione*
'Videos are, for me at least, rather long to follow, section after section
cioè *il **senso generale** lo capisco*
that is to say, I understand the general meaning
ma poi quando vado a fare gli esercizi è pesante]
but then, when I go to do the exercises, it is hard'

(11') Cioè   il   **senso   generale**   lo   capisco
      that is DET sense   general   it.DO.CL   understand.1SG
      'I mean, I understand the overall meaning.'

C-Topics thus provide an instruction to the speaker, but do not constitute, in themselves, independent conversational moves. This means that, unlike A-Topics, C-Topics are not restricted to root domains, though the meaning of clauses containing C-Topics must remain at the propositional level (Bianchi and Frascarelli 2010). From this it follows that C-Topics qualify as Type II root phenomena.

3.3 The Familiar/Given (G-)Topic

G-Topics refer to given information in the discourse that is somehow salient to the conversation. Since their main function is the retrieval of given information, G-Topics can be considered as D-linked constituents (Pesetsky 1987), either in a 'strong' (Heim 1982) or in a 'familiar/weak' sense (Roberts 2003)[7], and can be used either for topic continuity, that is to say, to 'maintain' the current A-Topic (this is the case of the so-called *Aboutness G-Topics*), or to mention a constituent that is part of the background but was not proposed as a 'file card' (i.e., an A-Topic) in the previous context (these are what we call *Background G-Topics*). Syntactically, the G-Topic is merged in the lowest Topic position in the C-domain (i.e., FamP in (8)) and its tonic vowel is low-toned (L*).

In order to illustrate the distinction between an Aboutness and a Background G-Topic consider the following passage in which a student is talking about a self-learning course. The relevant DP (*l'autoapprendimento*) thus represent the current A-Topic:

(12) *Il problema di questo autoapprendimento è stato affrontare la grammatica*
'The problem of this self-learning course was the grammar part
lì ti trovi davanti ad argomenti nuovi nei quali avresti bisogno di qualcuno (...)
there you deal with new topics for which you would exactly need someone (...)
invece l'__autoapprendimento questo__ non- non me l'ha dato ecco.
while a self-learning course could not give it to me, that's it.'

---

[7] In particular, Roberts' (2003) notion of Familiarity refers to discourse referents that are (i) perceptually accessible in the utterance, (ii) globally familiar from shared cultural knowledge, (iii) contextually entailed to exist, or (iv) implied *via* "bridging".

(12') ***l'autoapprendimento*₍ₖ₎ *questo*ⱼ** pro₍ₖ₎ non me   lⱼ'
       DET self-learning   this   not me.IO.CL it.DO.CL
       ha   dato
       have.3SG   given
       'while self-learning did not give this to me'

As is clear, the dislocated subject *l'autoapprendimento* is an Aboutness G-Topic (connected with a *pro*), while the demonstrative *questo* resumes the information just given about the relevant course and is therefore a Background G-Topic. Both are low-toned (as is shown in Figure 3 below) and realized in the left periphery of the sentence. This means that, contrary to A- and C-Topics, G-Topics can be multiple and can also appear in the right periphery of the sentence (always assuming Merge in FamP and deriving its final position through IP-inversion to the C-domain; for details, cf. Frascarelli 2000; Cardinaletti 2002).

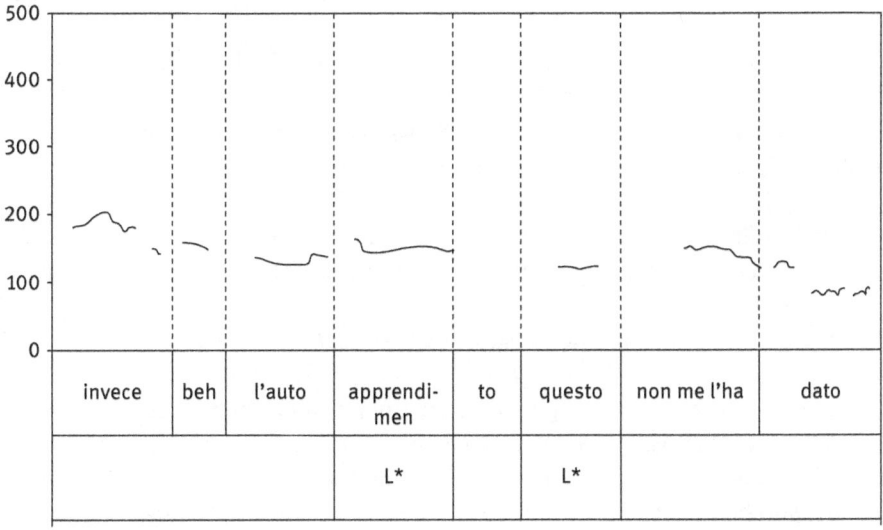

Figure 3: Multiple G-Topics.

Since givenness is calculated on the basis of the CG content, G-Topics clearly do not instantiate a conversational move and do not depend on illocutionary force: they simply refer to the existing CG content with a retrieval function. This implies that the G-Topic is *not* a root phenomenon (of any type) and is expected to be found in any type of subordinate clause (cf. Bianchi and Frascarelli 2010).

4 Adverbial Clauses: Major Properties and Background for Analysis

4.1 Central and Peripheral Adverbial Clauses

In her recent seminal investigation on adverbial clauses, Haegeman (2002 and subsequent work) provided evidence that adverbial clauses are not a homogenous group and that at least two types must be distinguished, namely *central* and *peripheral* adverbial clauses. The former modify the proposition expressed by the clause with which they are related, while the latter allow background propositions to be processed as the privileged discourse context for the proposition expressed in the associated clause.

It is argued that these two types of clauses differ in both external and internal syntax, and different explanations have been proposed to account for that. We assume Haegeman's distinction and intend to evaluate the author's analysis against the realisation of different types of Topics in central and peripheral clauses in Italian.

It is generally agreed that temporal and conditional adverbial clauses resist root phenomena (cf. section 2.2), such as argument fronting in English (cf. Hooper and Thompson 1973; Emonds 2004), as is shown in the following English examples (from Haegeman 2012: 155):

(13) a. *While this paper I was revising last week, I thought of another analysis.
 b. *When her regular column she began to write again, I thought she would be OK.
 c. *If these exams you don't pass, you won't get the degree.

In early discussions on root phenomena, Hooper and Thompson (1973) make the point that this restriction cannot be accounted for syntactically and offer a semantic-pragmatic account, arguing that it is based on the fact that phenomena depend on assertion, hence they are blocked in adverbial clauses. As a matter of fact, speech act adverbials and evaluative adverbs are incompatible with temporal and conditional adverbial clauses: Consider (14) and (15) below, respectively from Haegeman (2010) and Ernst (2007):

(14) *?When/if frankly he is unable to cope, we 'll have to replace him.

(15) *If they luckily arrived on time, we will be saved.

Assuming a structural approach to this issue, Haegeman (2006) proposes instead that argument fronting and speaker-related adverbs were dependent on the availability of the functional head Force, which is missing in adverbial clauses, whose left periphery is "reduced". Nevertheless, in later works the author pointed out the limits of such an approach, showing that the presence of illocutionary force *per sé* is not a sufficient condition for argument fronting in English. Haegeman (2008), 2010, 2012) then argues that the incompatibility between adverbial clauses and root phenomena (like the dislocation of arguments) depends on an *intervention effect*: since temporal and conditional clauses are derived by operator movement, this operation conflicts with argument fronting.

The hypothesis that adverbial clauses are derived by movement originates from Geis' analysis (1970, 1975), who noticed that a sentence like (16) is ambiguous between a high construal and a low construal of the temporal operator:

(16) *John left when Sheila said he should leave.*

Based on this observation, Larson (1987) proposed the following representations for high (17a) and low (17b) construal respectively, which is resumed and assumed in Haegeman's analysis:

(17) a. John left [$_{CP}$ when$_i$ [$_{IP}$ Sheila said [$_{CP}$ [$_{IP}$ he should leave]] t$_i$]]
 b. John left [$_{CP}$ when$_i$ [$_{IP}$ Sheila said [$_{CP}$ [$_{IP}$ he would leave t$_i$]]]]

As for conditional clauses, Haegeman (2010, 2012) draws from Bhatt and Pancheva (2006) the suggestion that conditional *if*-clauses can be analysed as free relatives of possible worlds, derived by the leftward movement of a world operator (for details, cf. Bhatt and Pancheva 2006). In the cartographic approach Haegeman, assumes, she proposes that the relevant world operator is associated with FinP. Accordingly, also in this case an argument fronted to the left periphery will lead to an intervention effect:

(18) [$_{CP}$ OP if [$_{TopP}$ this book [$_{FinP}$ OP [$_{IP}$ you ... [$_{VP}$ find ~~this book~~]]]]]

Even though an analysis of conditional clauses as underlyingly free relatives might seem harder to maintain, cross-linguistic comparative evidence shows that such a proposal is totally feasible and with substantial explicative value. Languages like Somali, for instance, provide clear evidence that both temporal and conditional clauses are in fact relative clauses, since they are headed by a generic element like 'time', 'way/manner', 'turn/condition', and present exactly the same (operator) properties shown by relative clauses headed by referential DPs (cf. Puglielli 1981; Puglielli and Frascarelli 2005; Frascarelli 2010):

(19) a. [gabartii [oo markaas guriga galaysá]] baan arkay.
     girl.AN COMP time.DET house.DET enter.PRG.RED FM.1SCL saw.1SG
     'I saw the girl when (lit.: that (discourse-given) time') she was coming home.'
  b. [sida Ahmed uu doonayó] ereyga u qor.
     manner.DET Ahmed SCL.3SG.M want.PRG.SUB word.DET to write.IMP
     'Write the word as (lit.: 'the way') Ahmed wants.'
  c. [haddii Cali uu yimaadó] waan la hadli lahaa.
     turn.AN Cali SCL.3SGM come.SUB DECL.SCL.1SG with talk had
     'If (lit.: '(given) the condition (that)') Cali came I would talk with him.'

Similar evidence can be found in typologically diverse languages, as is discussed in Puglielli and Frascarelli (2011). Consider the following examples from Turkish (Kornfilt 1997) and Maori (Bauer 1993), respectively:

(20) *Müdür [tatil-e çik-tiğ-i zaman] ofis kapa-n-ir.*
     boss holiday-DAT go-NOMIN-3SG.POSS time office close-REFL-HAB
     'When the boss is on holiday, the office is closed.'
     (lit.: 'the boss, the time of his going on holiday, the office is closed')

(21) [kia tae mai koe] ka kai taatou.
     time coming here you T/ASP eat we.INCL
     'When you arrive here, we will eat.'
     (lit.: 'the time of your arriving here, we eat')

Nevertheless, Bhatt and Pancheva (2006: 656) point out that not all adverbial clauses are derived by operator movement, as 'because' and 'since' are sentential functions and not quantifiers; that is, they do not bind positions inside their clause.

Rationale/reason adverbial clauses are indeed listed in Haegeman's works among peripheral adverbial clauses and this distinction correctly predicts that rationale clauses are compatible with argument fronting in English (differently from temporal and conditional clauses, cf. (13) above). Consider the following example (from Haegeman 2012: 159):

(22) *I think we have more or less solved the problem for donkeys here, because those we haven't got, we know about.*
     (Guardian, G2, 18.02.2003, p. 3, col. 2)

The class of peripheral adverbial clauses also includes adversative/concessive clauses, and argument fronting is permitted also in this case, as expected:

(23) *His face not many admired, while his character still fewer felt they could praise.*
(Quirk et al. 1985: 1378)

This contrast leads Haegeman (2008, 2012) to conclude that peripheral adverbial clauses are not so tightly related to the associated sentence as central clauses are and, in particular, that peripheral adverbial clauses are not derived by operator movement to the left periphery (cf. cited references for details).[8]

Nevertheless, argument fronting does not seem to always come 'for free' in peripheral adverbial clauses. As Lahousse (2003) argues, for instance, in languages like French, Stylistic Inversion in concessive and causal clauses requires the presence of an additional trigger (differently form temporal and conditional adverbial clauses). In (24), for instance, the adverbial *là* ('there') is the relevant trigger (from Lahousse 2003: 319):

(24) Un   nom   prédestiné,   parce-que **là**   renaîtrait   le
     a   name   predestine.PART   because   there   re-arise.COND.3SG the
     phénix.
     phoenix
     'A predestined name because there would be reborn the phoenix.'
     (Japrisot, *La dame dans l'auto avec des lunettes et un fusil*, 1966)

Furthermore, cross-linguistic evidence shows that rationale clauses also somehow show the morpho-syntactic properties DP-embedded clauses in some languages. Consider the following example from Maori (Bauer 1993):

(25) I   hoki   maatou   ki   te   kaainga   [i   te   mea   e   ua   ana]
     T/ASP   return   we.ESCL to   DET   home   from   DET   thing T/ASP rain   PST
     'We went back home because [lit.: from the thing that] it was raining.'

---

8 As a reviewer pointed out, it is interesting to notice that temporal and conditional clauses are given in fronted position in (13), while the examples provided for rationale and concessive clauses show them in the right periphery. This contrast leads to the suggestion that their information-structural relation with the matrix clause is different. In particular, central adverbial clauses seem to provide a "domain of application" for the associate sentence, whereas rationale/concessive clauses are "naturally" interpreted in the scope of the assertion expressed in the main clause. This intuition will be resumed and given a formal account in final section of this chapter.

Additional problems for a distinction based on operator movement and intervention effects seem to be provided by CLLD languages like Italian, in which topic dislocation is allowed in temporal and conditional clauses (cf. also Cinque 1990: 58), as well as in rationale and concessive clauses, without restrictions or additional triggers (cf. the original data examined in section 6). We reckon that this apparent drawback can be provided an explanation if a different perspective is assumed for analysis and two major questions are addressed.

4.2 What about Discourse? Diagnostics and Methodology

Most approaches to adverbial clauses have focused either on their pragmatic or on their morpho-syntactic properties. On the other hand, we think that an analysis of the phenomena occurring in left periphery of different clause types should be based on the discourse-related properties of their left peripheries. In particular:
1. *what kind(s) of Topic* can be hosted in the left periphery of adverbial clauses?
2. is there any variation in the type of discourse categories permitted based on independent core grammar properties of languages?

In order to answer these two major questions and provide an interface-based syntactic mapping of adverbial clauses, two tests have been designed for a *systematic comparative analysis* concerning the acceptability (expressed on a Likert scale from 0 to 4) of different types of Topic in diverse adverbial clauses. The relevant test was provided as an online survey, which permitted the collection of 198 full questionnaires. In a second step of the analysis, a selected number of respondents collaborated in the recording of a set of sentences taken from the tests, in order to check whether the intonational contours associated to the Topic was the one intended for the relevant context.

5 The Analysis of Data: Central Adverbial Clauses

5.1 The A-Topic in Temporal and Conditional Clauses

In order to test the possibility of having an A-Topic in the left periphery of temporal and conditional clauses, informants were asked to provide a judgment on the acceptability of a couple of sentences in which a Topic proposing a shift was realized either after or before the relevant complementizer (i.e., *when* 'quando' and *se* 'if'). This is shown in the following examples.[9]

(26) [*Un dirigente dice: Per il mio lavoro devo tenermi sempre informato e risolvere i problemi in tempo reale* (...)
'A manager says:' 'For my job I must always be informed and solve problems in real time (...)']
   a. *se l'   email, non la   leggessi   sempre, in una*
       if DET email NEG it.DO.CL.F read.SUBJ.2SG always   in a
       sola   giornata si   accumulerebbero   decine   di messaggi!
       single   day   REFL gather.COND.3PL dozens of messages
   b. *l'email, se non la leggessi in continuazione, in una sola giornata (...)*
      'If I didn't read my e-mail continuously, in a single day dozens of messages would gather.'

(27) [*Squilla il telefono. E' per Gianni, ma lui è uscito. Risponde la moglie e dice al suo amico: Mi dispiace, Gianni è uscito e* (...)
'The telephone rings. It's for Gianni, ma he is not at home. His wife answers and says to his friend: *I'm sorry, Gianni went out and* (...)]
   a. (...) *quando* **la**   **spesa,**   *la*   *va*   *a* *fare*   *lui,*
       when   DET shopping   it.DO.CL.F go.3SG to do.INF he
       non si   sa   mai   quanto   ci   mette.
       NEG IMPERS know.3SG never   how much in.it.CL take.3SG
   b. (...) **la spesa,** *quando la va a fare lui....*
      '(...) when he goes to do the shopping, you never know how long he can take.'

The prediction is that in the (a) sentences an A-Topic interpretation should be excluded for the dislocated constituent since it is located in 'a low' position in the C-domain (given the analysis of elements like *if* and *when* as (original) Operators, they should occupy a position that is lower than ShiftP and ContrP; cf. (8) above). As for the dislocated DP in the (b) sentences, even though it might be an A-Topic from a cartographic perspective, it should be also excluded by the IRR (9), since adverbial clauses are event modifiers and cannot host Type I root phenomena. In this respect, it should be noticed that the Topics in (26b)–(27b) cannot be located in the matrix ShiftP (i.e., in a position that is higher than the projection targeted by the fronted adverbial clause), since the realisation of clitic resumption (i.e., *la*

---

[9] For reason of space, glosses are only provided for the target sentences.

'IT.CL.F') shows that they are associated with the argument structure of the adverbial clauses.[10]

As expected, the (b) sentences were totally rejected by informants (they obtained 1 as a median value[11]) whereas, surprisingly, the (a) sentences were judged as fully acceptable (median value 4 for both types of central adverbials). However, after elicitation, the prosodic analysis showed that a *low tone* was associated with the relevant Topics. This means that acceptation was associated with a (*Background*) *G-Topic interpretation* (cf. Section 3.3). In other words, informants provided a positive judgment for the *only possible function* a Topic can have in that low position in the C-domain.

The analysis of interpretive and prosodic data thus leads to conclude that A-Topics are *excluded* in central adverbial clauses.

5.2 The C-Topic in Temporal and Conditional Clauses

To test the acceptability of C-Topics in adverbial clauses was not easy, since it is difficult to create (and parse) a context in which an adverbial clause provides an answer to a question belonging to a set of alternative questions (either explicitly asked or implicitly introduced), which are all part of a strategy to solve a super-question (as is required for CT-congruence, according to Büring's 2003 formulation). To the best of our capacities, a couple of sentences like (28a-b) and (29a-b) were proposed to informants. Notice that, since here and in the following couples of examples (from (28) to (37)) glosses and idiomatic translations are the same, to improve readability and save space glosses are only given for (a) and idiomatic translations for (b).

(28) [*Tutti hanno finito di mangiare, ma il piatto della piccola Sara è ancora pieno. La bimba chiede quale sia la condizione per mangiare il gelato alla fine e la mamma risponde:*
'Everybody has finished eating, except little Sara, whose dish is still full. The girl asks what is the condition to have an ice-cream at the end. Her mother replies:']
   a. *Se* **il pollo** *lo finisci e* **le zucchine** *le*
      if DET chicken it.DO.CL end.2SG and DET zucchini them.DO.CL.F

---

[10] In other words, the relevant Topics would have no syntactic role in the matrix sentence.
[11] In statistics and probability theory, a median is the number separating the higher half of a data sample, or a probability distribution, from the lower half. It is the most resistant statistic, having a breakdown point of 50%. A median is only defined on ordered one-dimensional data, and is independent of any distance metric dimensions (cf. Baayen 2008).

mangi almeno un po', avrai il gelato.
eat.2SG at least a bit have.FUT.2SG DET ice-cream
b. *Se **il pollo** lo finisci e mangi almeno un po' di **zucchine**, avrai il gelato.*
'If you finish your chicken and eat at least some zucchini, you'll have your ice-cream!'

(29) [*Negli ultimi tempi Leo ha problemi con lo studio e non riesce a passare gli esami. Un suo amico gli chiede perché è cominciato il problema e Leo risponde:*
'Leo is recently having problems in his studies and cannot pass his exams. One of his friends asks him why this problem started and Leo answers:']
   a. *Quando **il lavoro** finalmente lo trovi e **le lezioni***
      when DET job finally it.DO.CL.F find.2SG and DET lessons
     non le puoi seguire, comincia il problema!
     NEG them.DO.CL.F can.2SG follow.INF start.3SG DET problem
   b. *Quando **il lavoro** finalmente lo trovi e non puoi seguire **le lezioni**, comincia il problema!*
'When you finally find a job and you can't follow the classes, the problem starts!'

As is shown, these sentences realise two conjoined adverbial clauses introduced by the same C° head. In the (a) sentences a C-Topic is located in the left peripheries of both conjoined clauses, while in the (b) sentences a single C-Topic is proposed (in the first conjoined clause), while the second contrastive element is left in situ. The comparative judgment was aimed at checking whether the presence of a single C-Topic could influence acceptability.

The analysis of data shows that (a) sentences were generally refuted by informants (median value 1.5 for both types of central clauses), while (b) sentences scored 3 as a median value. Hence, the presence of a single C-Topic seems to improve acceptability. However, also in this case, when prosodic analysis is taken into account, it appears that this positive value is due to the fact that the informants provided a G-Topic (i.e., low-toned) interpretation for the dislocated constituent in the first sentence (i.e., *il pollo* in (28b) and *il lavoro* in (29b)). This means that in the presence of a clear CT context (as in the (a) sentences), informants' answers show that C-Topics cannot be realised in central adverbial clauses, whereas when a single dislocated constituent is realised (i.e., in the (b) sentences), the *intended* partial C-Topic could be re-interpreted as a G-Topic (conjured up *via* familiarity) and, as such, accepted.

This result thus supports our working hypothesis: central adverbial clauses are not propositions, hence a C-Topic cannot be realised in their C-domains.

5.3 The G-Topic in Temporal and Conditional Clauses

Based on the evidence indirectly obtained from the sentences dedicated to A- and C-Topics, we can already conclude that our predictions are fully borne out for G-Topics, that is to say, they are fully accepted in central adverbial clauses. As a matter of fact, informants regularly produced low-toned topics to "save the interpretation" of differently intended dislocated constituents.

Still, it is important to analyse in detail the results obtained for the sentences used to test G-Topics, since they allow for interesting considerations concerning the difference between their left- and right-hand realisation. Let us therefore consider the following sample sentences:

(30) [*Tutti hanno finito di mangiare, ma Sara ha lasciato tutte le verdure nel piatto. La mamma dice:*
'Everybody has finished eating, but Sara's vegetables are still lying in her dish. Her mother says:']
   a. *Non avrai il gelato se* **le zucchine** *non le*
      NEG have.FUT.2SG DET ice-cream if DET zucchini NEG them.DO.CL.F
     finisci!
     eat up.2SG
   b. *Non avrai il gelato se non le finisci,* **le zucchine***!*
     'You won't have your ice-cream if you don't eat up your zucchini!'

(31) [*Leo è preoccupato perché non riesce a passare la prova di livello e dice ad un suo amico:*
'Leo is worried because he cannot pass his proficiency test and says to one of his friends:']
   a. *È davvero un problema quando* **gli esami di lingua**
     be.3SG really a problem when DET exams of language
     non riesci a passarli!
     NEG can.2SG to pass.INF.them.DO.CL
   b. *È davvero un problema quando non riesci a passarli,* **gli esami di lingua***!*
     'It's really a problem when you can't pass language exams!'

Very consistently the (a) sentences scored value 4, while the (b) sentences obtained 2.5 as a median value. As for intonation, the relevant dislocated constituents are realised with a low tone, in either position. This means that they were correctly interpreted as G-Topics in both positions and, consequently, the question arises as to why a leftward location is better than right-dislocation.

In this respect, in a recent study Frascarelli and Hinterhölzl (2016) have shown that when G-Topics that are *not explicitly mentioned* in the previous context (hence, they are "weakly given", *familiar* G-Topics; cf. footnote 7), they are preferably realized in the left periphery of the sentence, whereas a right-peripheral realization is generally associated with a *strongly given* characterization (*à la* Heim 1982). This can provide a feasible explanation for the asymmetry at issue, since neither *zucchine* 'zucchini' in (30) nor *esami di lingua* 'language exams' in (31) are overtly mentioned in the relevant previous contexts: these entities are inferred and accommodated in the background via shared cultural knowledge. Hence, we can understand why a right-hand position is the most appropriate for the examples under exam, though a left-hand realisation is not rejected (but only considered as 'marginal').

We can thus conclude that the G-Topic is the only Topic type that is accepted in central adverbial clauses, thus supporting our working hypothesis. This means that argument fronting is not banned *per se* in adverbial clauses and that intervention effects can only provide a *concurrent* motivation for ungrammaticality.[12]

The ban on dislocated constituents in languages like English and the difference with respect to CLLD languages can be thus given a comprehensive explanation from an information-structural, discourse-based perspective. Specifically, it can be argued that in central adverbial clauses Left Dislocation and Topicalization are excluded in all languages because they implement, respectively, A- and C-Topics. As for G-Topics, English sentences like (13) cannot be 'saved' through a G-Topic interpretation due to core grammar properties of the language: as argued in Bianchi and Frascarelli (2010: 21), no leftward topic structure is devoted to mere givenness marking in English where the retrieval of given information is generally implemented through in situ destressing (cf. also Neeleman and Reinhart 1998; Schwarzschild 1999). Hence, the dislocation of G-Topics is not an option in (languages like) English.

Finally, notice that an operator analysis for central adverbial clauses also supports the analysis of CLLD constituents as a "different type of A'-dependency", which does *not* create intervention effects with wh-type movements.

Let us now consider the results obtained with peripheral adverbial clauses of the concessive and rationale type.

---

12 Furthermore notice that, operator movement could not be invoked to explain the ban on Left Dislocation, since LD Topics are resumed by pronouns in argument position.

6 The Analysis of Data: Peripheral Adverbial Clauses

6.1 The A-Topic in Concessive and Rationale Clauses

As in the case of central adverbials, the interpretive judgments expressed on peripheral adverbial clauses clearly show that A-Topics are not allowed in this clausal type. Specifically, when the *intended* A-Topic is located lower than the complementizer, it is realized with the intonation of a G-Topic (and, as such, it median value is 4); when the Topic is higher than the complementizer, it is rated 0 (hence, worse than with central adverbials). Consider the following examples:

(32) [*Sara parla con un'amica dei suoi impegni familiari che non le danno respiro. Dice: Non posso fare programmi (...)*
'Sara is talking with a friend about her familiar commitments, which are breath-taking. She says: 'I can't make plans (...)'']
  a. (...) *a volte   anche se* **il   biglietto,** *l'   ho   già*
     sometimes even if   DET ticket   it.DO.CL have.1SG already
     comprato,
     bought
     non posso   partire   a causa di un' emergenza.
     NEG can.1SG leave.INF because of a   urgency
  b. (...) *a volte,* **il biglietto***, anche se l'ho già comprato, non posso partire a causa di* (...)
     '(...) sometimes, even though I have already bought a ticket, I cannot leave for some urgency.'

(33) [*Un'amica che Leo e Sara non vedono da tempo li andrà a trovare. Leo propone di andare a cena fuori. Sara risponde:*
'A friend that Leo and Sara haven't seen for ages will visit them soon. Leo proposes to go outside for dinner. Sara replies:']
  a. *Va bene. Siccome* **la   carne,** *non la   mangia,*
     all right as   DET meat   NEG it.DO.CL.F eat.3SG
     propongo   di andare in pizzeria.
     propose.1SG of go.INF in pizza place
  b. *Va bene.* **La carne,** *siccome non la mangia, propongo di andare in pizzeria.*
     'OK. Since she doesn't eat meat, I propose a pizza place.'

We can thus conclude that A-Topics are not allowed in the C-domain of peripheral adverbial clauses as well: when a Topic is higher than complementizers like 'as/since' or 'even if/although', it is not accepted by informants, and when it is located in a lower position, the PF interface shows that its realization is low-toned. This means that, in the relevant contexts, informants can only accept an interpretation in which the dislocated constituent is a (familiar) G-Topic.

6.2 The C-Topic in Concessive and Rationale Clauses

To test the acceptability of C-Topics in peripheral adverbial clauses, sentences like the following were provided to informants:

(34) A: *Allora stasera ceniamo da Maria: ho detto che noi porteremo un pollo mentre lei deve solo friggere le patate. Lei ha detto che va bene, ma ha concluso con un "anche se (...)". Tu sai qual è il problema?*
'So, this evening we have dinner at Maria's place: I told her that we will bring a chicken and she has to prepare some French fries. She said this is fine, but she ended saying "even if (...)" Do you know what the matter is?'
B: *Non ti preoccupare, è contenta di cenare insieme (...)*
'Don't worry: she is happy to have dinner together (...)'
a. (...) *anche se* **il pollo** *non lo ama molto e*
    even if   DET chicken NEG it.DO.CL love.3SG much and
  le patate *non le   frigge quasi mai.*
    DET potatoes NEG them.DO.CL.F fry.3SG almost never
b. (...) *anche se* **il pollo** *non lo ama molto e non frigge quasi mai* **le patate** *a casa.*
'(...) even if she doesn't like chicken very much and she doesn't often fry potatoes.'

(35) A: *Per quale motivo non andiamo ad un ristorante con Elisa stasera?*
'Why are we not going to a restaurant with Elisa this evening?'
B: *Beh (...)*
'Well (...)'
a. (...) *siccome* **la carne** *non la   mangia e* **il pesce**
       since   DET meat   NEG it.DO.CL.F eat.3SG and DET fish
  non le   piace,   è   meglio una pizzeria.
   NEG her.IO.CL.F please.3SG be.3SG better a   pizza place

b. (...) *siccome* **la carne** *non la mangia e non le piace* **il pesce,** *è meglio una pizzeria.*
'(...) since she doesn't eat meat and she doesn't like fish, a pizza place is better.'

As is shown, also in this case the two adverbial clauses were proposed as conjoined under the same C° head, and in the (b) option only the first C-Topic was realised (cf. Section 5.2).

Interestingly, in the present case informants the (a) sentences (median value 3, for both types of peripheral clauses), and the relevant elicitations show that Topics were produced with the intonation associated with a C-Topic (H*), as intended. This makes a significant difference with respect to central adverbial clauses and can be taken as evidence that peripheral adverbial clauses have a propositional import, even though they are not endowed with illocutionary force. Hence, they cannot host an A-Topic in their C-domain, but a C-Topic is allowed. This result provides strong support for an (information-)structural distinction between central and peripheral adverbial clauses; the latter are propositions, while the former are event modifiers.

6.3 The G-Topic in Concessive and Rationale Clauses

Based on the indirect evidence obtained from the data discussed above, we can already claim that G-Topics are also permitted in peripheral adverbial clauses. Nevertheless, it is important to consider the relevant Likert results in detail.

(36) A: *Come mai non sei venuto al concerto ieri?*
'Why haven't you come to the concert yesterday?'
B: *Beh (...)*
'Well (...)'
a. (...) *anche se* **il biglietto** *ero riuscita a comprarlo,*
   even if   DET ticket   be.PST.3SG succeded to buy.INF.it.DO.CL
   ho   avuto un impegno   all'   ultimo momento.
   have.1SG had a   commitment to.DET last   moment
b. (...) *anche se ero riuscita a comprarlo,* **il biglietto**, *ho avuto un impegno (...)'*
'(...) even though I could buy the ticket, I had a last minute commitment.'

(37) [*Un'amica che Leo e Sara non vedono da tempo li andrà a trovare. Leo propone di andare ad un ristorante. Sara risponde:*

'A friend of Leo and Sara that they haven't seen for ages will visit them soon. Leo proposes to go to a restaurant. Sara replies:']

a. *Siccome **la carne** non la mangia,*
   as   DET meat NEG it.DO.CL.F eat.3SG
   forse meglio una pizzeria.
   maybe better a pizza place

b. *Siccome non la mangia, **la carne**, forse meglio una pizzeria.*
   'Since she doesn't eat meat, maybe better a pizza place.'

The results obtained support the considerations expressed in section 5.3 on the different discourse functions of left- and right-hand G-Topics, since left-dislocated G-Topics in the (a) sentences scored 4 on the Likert scale, while (b) sentences obtained 2 as a median value (in line with central adverbial clauses). This provides significant evidence that weakly given G-Topics are preferably realized in the left periphery of the sentence, whereas the right periphery is interpretively associated with elements overtly mentioned in the context.

Our general *interim* conclusion is therefore that argument fronting in adverbial clauses is *not* banned *per se*, but it depends on the *type* of Topic under exam. A-Topics are excluded – as expected in clauses not endowed with illocutionary force[13]–while G-Topics are always fine (in languages allowing for the dislocation of purely given information, like Italian). Hence, based on the behaviour of A- and G-Topics, no difference emerges between central and peripheral adverbial clauses.

However, the analysis of C-Topics offers a crucial divide between central and peripheral adverbial clauses, since only the latter can host a C-Topic in its C-domain. Peripheral adverbial clauses thus seem to qualify as propositions

---

13 A reviewer wonders whether explicitly performative rationale/concessive clauses (as in (i)) are compatible with this conclusion:

(i) *I'm still ready to defend my position, although I hereby acknowledge my failings.*

Since A-Topics are not allowed in a sentence like (i) – as is shown by the ungrammaticality of Left Dislocation in (ii) below – we must conclude that it is indeed not possible to propose/shift to a new topic within a rationale/concessive clause, despite the presence of a performative marker.

(ii) **I'm still ready to defend my position, although my failings, I hereby acknowledge them.*

We suggest that elements like *hereby* are 'lexically specified' as triggers of a performative reading (like performative verbs), but they do not require to be associated with a sentence endowed with illocutionary force. It might be argued that the illocutionary force of performative markers is 'presupposed', while in matrix clauses it is asserted. This interesting issue is however far from the purposes of the present work.

and, as such, cannot be analysed on a par with central adverbial clauses. A tentative structural analysis that can account for this difference will be offered in section 7.

7 Adverbial Clauses at the Interfaces: A Structured View to Discourse

In the light of the data examined, we suggest that relativization à la Kayne (1994) can provide an appropriate syntactic account for *central adverbial* clauses: the latter are (synchronically/diachronically) derived *via* promotion analysis: the adverbial clause is the complement of a D° head and the NP-head (a generic NP like 'time', 'way/manner', 'turn/condition', etc.) is an Operator sitting in Spec,CP, which can be overt or covert according to parametric variation. This is illustrated in (45):

(38) [$_{DP}$ [$_{D'}$ [$_{CP\ Central\ Adverbial}$ [NP-head]$_k$ [$_{C'}$ [$_{IP}$ ...VAR$_k$...]]]]]

Following Cinque's (1999) analysis of AdvPs, the relative/adverbial clause (a DP) is inserted in the Spec position of a functional projection in the split-IP domain, which is consistent with its modifying function (e.g., Spec,TP for a temporal adverbial clauses, Spec,MoodP$_{[+irrealis]}$ or Spec,ModP$_{[+possibility]}$ for conditional clauses, and so on).

As for peripheral adverbial clauses, on the other hand, we propose an analysis in terms of a clause that is *conjoined to its antecedent* through an "asymmetric conjunctive structure" (as is proposed in Puglielli and Frascarelli's 2005 for non-restrictive relative clauses, following Rebushi 2003):

(39) [$_{ConjP}$ [DP$_{+def}$]$_k$ [$_{Conj'}$ Conj° [$_{CP\ Periph.\ Adverbial}$ <OP$_k$> [$_{C'}$ [$_{IP}$... VAR$_k$ ...]]]]]]

Assuming the conjoined structure in (39) for peripheral adverbial clauses, we propose that in rationale/concessive clauses the 'antecedent' is a (covert/overt) definite DP (like 'the reason/rationale', 'the concession/allowance', etc.), while the Conj° head is an element like 'why', 'because', 'as', 'though'. The adverbial CP, on the other hand, is the second term (i.e., the Complement) of the relevant ConjP and contains an Operator that is a (covert) copy of the antecedent.

According to this proposal, peripheral adverbial clauses are not modifiers: they are not in a DP-embedded position and can qualify as *a propositional CPs* providing additional information about their antecedent DP. Specifically, adverbial clauses provide *background* information with respect to the relevant DP (a sort of definite descriptions, cf. Chierchia and McConnel-Ginet 1990; Doron 1994; Del Gobbo 2003). As such, they have a propositional import but they are not endowed with illocutionary force. This structural distinction can provide an explanation for the different positions in which central and peripheral adverbial clauses are preferably located by speakers (cf. footnote 8), to be addressed below.

As is shown in (38), central adverbial clauses are merged in the split IP-domain. However, they are rarely spelled out in their basic position, for both prosodic and interpretive reasons. On the PF side, this movement is feasibly due to "prosodic heaviness", which is a common interface trigger to target a peripheral position. Nevertheless, heavy constituents generally reach a *final* position in the sentence (cf. the "Heavy NP-Shift" phenomenon), so, why is fronting preferred in this case? It can be argued that movement of temporal/conditional clauses is connected with a discourse-related function which is encoded in the C-domain, namely with "frame-setting" (cf. Chafe 1976; Lambrecht 1994; Jacobs 2001; Krifka 2007; Carella 2015; Frascarelli 2017). Indeed, according to Chafe (1976) frame-setters have the function to *limit the truth-conditional validity* of the sentence they are associated with or, using Jacob's (2001) words, they specify a *domain of (possible) reality* to which the proposition is restricted. This is exactly the function of temporal and conditional clauses, and this is the reason why their fronted position is cognitively preferred like rationale and concessive clauses do.

Peripheral adverbial clauses, on the other hand, are not event modifiers, hence they are not merged as Specifiers of inflectional heads in the split IP-domain. They are propositions and, as such, adjoined to VP in the conjoined structure illustrated in (39), thus accounting (among other things) for their preferred post-matrix location.

This structural analysis can provide a comprehensive explanation for the discourse-semantic and syntactic properties associated to central and peripheral clauses. Indeed, the structure proposed for peripheral clauses is consistent with Bhatt and Pancheva's (2006: 656) observation that elements like 'because' and 'since' are sentential functions (not quantifiers) and do not bind positions inside their clause. At the same time, the two structures proposed in (38) and (39) include the presence of a variable within the relative clause, and this accounts for the operator properties shown by peripheral adverbial clauses in different languages (cf. Section 5.1 above). Finally, this proposal offers a promising cartographic re-elaboration of Geis's (1970, 1975) analysis of high and low construal of the temporal operator (cf. Section 2.1 above), to be further explored cross-linguistically and refined in future works.

Acknowledgments: This paper is the outcome of reflections deriving from previous joint works with different authors. In this respect, I wish to thank in particular Roland Hinterhölzl and Valentina Bianchi for precious discussion on several aspects of this paper, the audience of the *The Architecture of Topic* Workshop (University of Lund, SOL December 2014) where a first version of this idea was presented and discussed, and two anonymous reviewers whose criticism greatly helped improving my work. Usual disclaimers apply.

List of Abbreviations

Abbreviations used for glosses of non-English examples throughout the chapter (notice that present tense is unmarked).

AN	anaphoric determiner
CL	clitic pronoun
COMP	complementizer
COND	conditional mood
DECL	declarative marker
DET	determiner
DO	direct object
F	feminine
FM	focus marker
FUT	future tense
HAB	habitual aspect
IMP	imperative
IMPERS	impersonal subject clitic
INF	infinitive mood
IO	indirect object
M	masculine
NEG	negative marker
NOMIN	nominalizer
PL	plural
POSS	possessive marker
RG	progressive aspect
PST	past tense
RED	reduced paradigm
REFL	reflexive
SCL	subject clitic
SUB	subordinate verbal form
SUBJ	subjunctive mood
SG	singular

References

Baayen, R. Harald. 2008. *Analyzing linguistic data. A practical introduction to statistics using R*. Cambridge: Cambridge University Press.
Bauer, Winifred A. 1993. *Maori*. London: Routledge.
Beaver, David & Brady Clark. 2008. *Sense and sensitivity: how focus determines meaning*. Oxford: Blackwell.
Bhatt, Rajesh & Roumyana Pancheva. 2006. Conditionals. In Martin Everaert & Henk van Riemsdijk (eds.), *The Blackwell companion to syntax, Vol 1*, 638–687. Boston & Oxford: Blackwell.
Bianchi, Valentina. 2013. On focus movement in Italian. In Victoria Camacho-Taboada, Ángel L. Jiménez-Fernández, Javier Martín-González & Mariano Reyes-Tejedor (eds.), *Information structure and agreement*, 194–215. Amsterdam & Philadelphia: John Benjamins.
Bianchi, Valentina. 2015. Focus fronting and the syntax-semantics interface. In Ur Shlonsky (ed.), *Beyond functional sequence. The cartography of syntactic structures 10*, 60–712. Oxford: Oxford University Press.
Bianchi, Valentina & Giuliano Bocci. 2012. Should I stay or should I go? Optional focus movement in Italian. In Christopher Pinon (ed.), *Empirical issues in syntax and semantics 9*, 1–16. Paris: EISS.
Bianchi, Valentina & Mara Frascarelli. 2010. Is topic a root phenomenon? *Iberia* 2. 43–88.
Bianchi, Valentina & Mara Frascarelli. 2012. How to be rooted in a context. Presented at the 35th GLOW Colloquium, University of Potsdam.
Büring, Daniel. 2003. On D-trees, beans, and B-Accents. *Linguistics and Philosophy* 26. 511–545.
Cardinaletti, Anna. 2002. Against optional and zero clitics. Right dislocation vs. marginalization. *Studia Linguistica* 56. 29–57.
Carella, Giorgio. 2015. The limiting topic. *Annali di Ca' Foscari. Serie Occidentale* 49. 363–391.
Chafe, Wallace. 1976. Givenness, contrastiveness, definiteness, subjects, topics, and point of view. In Charles N. Li (ed.), *Subject and topic*, 25–55. New York: Academic Press.
Chierchia, Gennaro & Sally Mc Connel-Ginet. 1990. *Meaning and grammar*. Cambridge MA: MIT Press.
Cinque, Guglielmo. 1990. *Types of A'-dependencies*. Cambridge, MA: MIT Press.
Cinque, Guglielmo. 1999. *Adverbs and functional heads. A cross-linguistic perspective*. Oxford & New York: Oxford University Press.
Cruschina, Silvio. 2011. Fronting, dislocation and the syntactic role of discourse-related features. *Linguistic Variation* 11. 1–34.
Del Gobbo, Francesca. 2003. *Appositives at the interface*. Irvine: University of California PhD dissertation.
Doron, Edit. 1994. The discourse function of appositives. *IATL* 1, 53–62.
Emonds, Joseph. 1970. Root and structure-preserving transformations. Cambridge, MA: MIT PhD dissertation.
Emonds, Joseph. 1976. *A transformational approach to English syntax: Root, structure-preserving, and local transformations*. New York: Academic Press.
Emonds, Joseph. 2004. Unspecified categories as the key to root constructions. In David Adger, Cécile de Cat & Georges Tsoulas (eds), *Peripheries: syntactic edges and their effects*, 75–120. Dordrecht: Kluwer.

Ernst, Thomas. 2007. On the role of semantics in a theory of adverb syntax. *Lingua* 117. 1008–1033.
Frascarelli, Mara. 2000. *The syntax-phonology interface in focus and topic constructions in Italian* (Studies in Natural Language and Linguistic Theory 50). Dordrecht: Kluwer.
Frascarelli, Mara. 2007. Subjects, topics and the interpretation of referential pro. An interface approach to the linking of (null) pronouns. *Natural Language and Linguistic Theory*. 25. 691–734.
Frascarelli, Mara. 2010. Narrow focus, clefting and predicate inversion. *Lingua* 120. 2121–2147.
Frascarelli, Mara. 2017. Dislocations and framings. In Elisabeth Stark & Andreas Dufter (eds.), *Manual of Romance morphosyntax and syntax* (Manuals of Romance Linguistics 17), 472–501. Berlin & New York: Mouton de Gruyter.
Frascarelli, Mara & Francesca Ramaglia. 2013. Phasing contrast at the interfaces. In Victoria Camacho-Taboada, Ángel L. Jiménez-Fernández, Javier Martín-González & Mariano Reyes-Tejedor (eds.), *Information structure and agreement*, 55–82. Amsterdam & Philadelphia: John Benjamins.
Frascarelli, Mara & Roland Hinterhölzl. 2007. Types of topics in German and Italian. In Kerstin Schwabe & Susanne Winkler (eds.), *On information structure, meaning and form*, 87–116. Amsterdam & Philadelphia: John Benjamins.
Frascarelli, Mara & Roland Hinterhölzl. 2016. German scrambling meets Italian right-dislocation. Paper presented at the *42th Incontro di Grammatica Generativa*, University of Salento.
Gärtner, Hans-Martin. 2002. On the force of V-2 declaratives, *Theoretical Linguistics* 28. 33–42.
Geis, Michael Lorenz. 1970. *Adverbial subordinate clauses in English*. Cambridge, MA: MIT PhD dissertation.
Geis, Michael Lorenz. 1975. English time and place adverbials. *Working Papers in Linguistics* 18. 1–11.
Haegeman, Liliane. 2002. Anchoring to speaker, adverbial clauses and the structure of CP. *Georgetown University Working Papers in Theoretical Linguistics* 2. 117–180.
Haegeman, Liliane. 2004. Topicalization, CLLD and the left periphery. In Claudia Maienborn, Werner Frey & Benjamin Shaer (eds.), *ZAS Papers in Linguistics* 35. 157–192.
Haegeman, Liliane. 2006. Conditionals, factives and the left periphery. *Lingua* 116. 1651–1669.
Haegeman, Liliane. 2008. The syntax of adverbial clauses and the licensing of main clause phenomena. Truncation or intervention? Presented at *GLOW 31* (University of Newcastle).
Haegeman, Liliane. 2010. The internal syntax of adverbial clauses. *Lingua* 120. 628–648.
Haegeman, Liliane. 2012. *Adverbial clauses, main clause phenomena, and the composition of the left periphery*. Oxford: Oxford University Press.
Haegeman, Liliane & Barbara Ürögdi. 2010. Referential CPs and DPs: An operator movement account. *Theoretical Linguistics* 36(2/3). 111–152.
Heim, Irene. 1982. *The semantics of definite and indefinite noun phrases*. Amherst: University of Massachusetts at Amherst PhD dissertation.
Heycock, Caroline. 2006. Embedded root phenomena. In Martin Everaert & Henk van Riemsdijk (eds), *The Blackwell companion to syntax*, 174–209. Oxford: Basic Blackwell.
Hooper, Joan & Sandra Thompson. 1973. On the applicability of root transformations. *Linguistic Inquiry* 4. 465–497.
Jacobs, Joachim. 2001. The dimensions of topic-comment. *Linguistics* 39. 641–681.
Jiménez-Fernández, Ángel L. & Shigeru Miyagawa. 2014. A feature-inheritance approach to root phenomena and parametric variation. *Lingua* 145. 276–302.

Kayne, Richard S. 1994. *The antisymmetry of syntax.* Cambridge, MA: MIT Press.
Kornfilt, Jacqueline. 1997. *Turkish.* London: Routledge.
Krifka, Manfred. 2001. Quantifying into question acts. *Natural Language Semantics* 9. 1–40.
Krifka, Manfred. 2007. Basic notions of information structure. In Caroline Féry & Manfred Krifka (eds.), *Interdisciplinary studies on information structure*, 13–55. ISIS: Universitätverlag Potsdam.
Lahousse, Karen 2003. La distribution de l'inversion nominale en français dans les principals non interrogatives et les subordonnées circonstancielles. *Linguisticae Investigationes* 26. 123–158.
Lambrecht, Knud. 1994. *Information structure and sentence form. Topic, focus, and the mental representation of discourse referents.* Cambridge: Cambridge University Press.
Larson, Richard K. 1987. 'Missing prepositions' and the analysis of English free relative clauses. *Linguistic Inquiry* 18. 239–266.
Meinunger, André. 2004. Verb position, verbal mood and the anchoring (potential) of sentences. In Horst Lohnstein & Susanne Trissler (eds.), *The syntax and semantics of the left periphery*, 313–341. Berlin & New York: Mouton de Gruyter.
Molnár, Valéria. 2006. On different kinds of contrast. In Valéria Molnár & Susanne Winkler (eds.), *The architecture of focus*, 197–233. Berlin & New York: Mouton de Gruyter.
Neeleman, Ad & Tanya Reinhart. 1998. Scrambling at the PF interface. In Wilhelm Geuder & Miriam Butts (eds.), *The projections of arguments: lexical and compositional factors*, 309–353. Stanford: CSLI.
Penner, Zvi & Thomas Bader. 1991. Main clause phenomena in embedded clauses. The licensing of V2 clauses in Bernese Swiss German. *The Linguistic Review* 8. 75–95.
Pesetsky, David. 1987. Wh-in-situ: Movement and unselective binding. In Eric Reuland & Alice ter Meulen (eds.), *The representation of (in)definiteness*, 98–129. Cambridge, MA: MIT Press.
Pierrehumbert, Janet B. 1980. *The phonology and phonetics of English intonation.* Cambridge, MA: MIT PhD dissertation.
Puglielli, Annarita. 1981. Frase dichiarativa. In Annarita Puglielli (ed.) *Sintassi della Lingua Somala* (Studi Somali Series 2), 3–45. Roma: Ministero degli Affari Esteri.
Puglielli, Annarita & Mara Frascarelli. 2005. A comparative analysis of restrictive and appositive relative clauses in Cushitic languages. In Laura Brugè, Giuliana Giusti, Nicola Munaro, Walter Schweikert & Giuseppina Turano (eds.), *Contribution to the IGG XXX*, 279–303. Venezia: Cafoscarina.
Puglielli, Annarita & Mara Frascarelli. 2011. *Linguistic analysis: from data to theory.* Berlin & New York: Mouton De Gruyter.
Quirk, Randolph, Sidney Greenbaum, Geoffrey Leech & Jan Svartvik. 1985. *A comprehensive grammar of the English language.* London: Longman.
Rebushi, Georges. 2003. Generalizing the antisymmetric analysis of coordination to nominal modification. *Lingua* 115. 445–459.
Reinhart, Tania. 1981. Pragmatics and linguistics: an analysis of sentence topics. *Philosophica* 27. 53–94.
Reis, Marga. 1997. Zum syntaktisches Status unselbständiger Verbzweit Sätze. In Christa Dürscheid (ed.), *Sprache im Fokus*, 121–144. Tübingen: Niemeyer.
Rizzi, Luigi. 1997. The fine structure of the left periphery. In Liliane Haegeman (ed.), *Elements of grammar. Handbook in generative syntax*, 281–337. Dordrecht: Kluwer.
Roberts, Craige. 2003. Uniqueness in definite noun phrases. *Linguistics and Philosophy* 26. 287–350.

Rooth, Mats. 1992. A theory of focus interpretation. *Natural Language Semantics* 1. 75–116.
Schwarzschild, Roger. 1999. GIVENnes, AvoidF and other constraints on the placement of accent. *Natural Language Semantics* 7. 141–177.
Vallduví, Enric & Maria Vilkuna. 1998. On rheme and contrast. In Peter W. Culicover & Louise McNally (eds.), *The limits of syntax*, 79–108. San Diego: Academic Press.
Vikner, Sten. 1995. *Verb movement and expletive subjects in the Germanic languages*. Oxford & New York: Oxford University Press.
Wiklund, Anna Lena, Kristine Bentzen, Gunnar Hrafn Hrafnbjargarson & Þorbjörg Hróarsdóttir. 2009. On the distribution and illocution of V2 in Scandinavian that-clauses. *Lingua* 119. 1914–1938.

Part II: **Variation in the Grammatical Encoding of Topicality: Clause-internal, Clause-external and Null Topics**

Peter W. Culicover, Susanne Winkler
Why Topicalize VP?

Abstract: In this paper we are concerned with explaining the function of VP topicalization in English and German. Our particular focus will be on what licenses VP topicalization. We continue a line of research that we began in Culicover and Winkler (2008). There we argued that the linear ordering of a particular English construction, focus inversion, is explained in part by the fact that the subject is isolated on the right edge of the construction. This position is characterized by being the default locus of sentence accent, which is thereby interpreted as focus. So, while the syntax of this construction is non-canonical, it does not require a sentence-internal accent to convey focus.

The key aspect of this proposal is that the explanation for focus inversion does not have to do with what is in initial position. The constituent in initial position must be interpreted in such a way that the sentence is coherent with the preceding discourse, and this can happen in a number of ways. What is crucial is that what is left behind in final position is in focus.

Our proposal here is that VP topicalization in English and German is explained in the same way. Specifically, the topicalized constituent appears in a non-canonical position so that the focused element may fall under the default sentence accent.

We summarize our core hypothesis as follows:

Hypothesis
There are two motivations for VP-Top:
a. Movement of the VP to the left satisfies the need to isolate focus at the right edge of the construction (as in Culicover and Winkler 2008).
b. The topicalized constituent connects to the previous discourse and therefore falls under general constraints of discourse coherence.

Keywords: VP topicalization, syntax/information structure interface, movement of VP, focus isolation, focus inversion, movement to left edge; right edge alignment of focus, discourse function/discourse coherence, intonation, language comparison: English vs German

Peter W. Culicover, The Ohio State University
Susanne Winkler, University of Tübingen

https://doi.org/10.1515/9781501504488-006

1 Introduction

In this paper we are concerned with explaining the function of VP topicalization – henceforth VP-Top – in English and German. The construction is exemplified in (1) and (2). (1) suggests that the entire VP must topicalize in English (a generalization that we call into question below), while (2) shows that in German it is possible to topicalize not only the entire VP, but part of the VP.

(1) a. (...) *and buy the book, Fritz did.*
    b. * (...) *and buy Fritz did, the book.*

(2) a. Den   Mercedes 220 gekauft hat keiner.
       the.ACC Mercedes 220 bought has no.one.NOM
       'No one bought the Mercedes 220.'
    b. Gekauft hat den   Mercedes 220 keiner.
       bought has the.ACC Mercedes 220 no.one.NOM
       'No one bought the Mercedes 220.'
    c. Verkaufen wird   er seinen Mercedes 220 nie.
       sell.INF will   he his.ACC Mercedes 220 never
       'He will never sell his Mercedes 220.'
    d. Seinen Mercedes 220 zu verkaufen, versuchte er erst gar nicht.
       his.ACC Mercedes 220 to sell.INF   tried   he first even not
       'He didn't even try to sell his Mercedes 220.'
    e. Zu verkaufen versuchte er seinen Mercedes 220 erst gar nicht.
       to sell.INF tried   he his.ACC Mercedes 220 first even not
       'He didn't even try to sell his Mercedes 220.'

Our particular focus will be on what licenses VP-Top. To put it another way, we want to understand the syntactic and discourse conditions that govern the possibilities for VP-Top in these languages.

We continue here an approach that we began in Culicover and Winkler (2008). There we argued that the linear ordering of a particular English construction, focus inversion, is explained in part by the fact that the subject is isolated on the right edge of the construction. This position is characterized by being the default locus of sentence accent, which is thereby interpreted as focus.

The key aspect of this proposal is that the explanation for focus inversion does not have to do with what is in initial position. The constituent in initial position must be interpreted in such a way that the sentence is coherent with the preceding discourse, and this can happen in a number of ways. What is crucial is that what is left behind in final position is in focus.

Our proposal is that VP-Top in English and German is explained in much the same way. Specifically, the topicalized constituent appears in a non-canonical position so that the focused element may fall under default sentence accent assignment. The VP is a particularly suitable category to consider in this context, because it is more difficult to transfer to VP the classical grammatical or functional explanations motivated for DPs and PPs. In particular, unlike these categories, the VP does not denote a set of entities, it does not participate as readily in focus constructions such as clefting, and it does not generally satisfy the thematic requirements of a lexical noun.

We summarize our core hypothesis as follows:

Hypothesis
There are two motivations for VP-Top:
a. Movement of the VP to the left satisfies the need to isolate focus at the right edge of the construction (as in Culicover and Winkler 2008).
b. The topicalized constituent connects to the previous discourse and therefore falls under general constraints of discourse coherence.

A preliminary glance at VP-Top in (1) and (2) suggests that it functions very differently in the two languages. In English it is apparently necessary to move the entire non-finite VP, while in German it seems to be possible to move any part of the finite VP (including the V alone).

But this is just a first glance, and the literature and our own intuitions show that it is possible to strand parts of VP in English as well.

(3) a. (...) *and buy a book Fritz did that was about the disappearance of many species due to climate change.*
b. (...) *and claim Fritz did that the future of the human race itself was at stake.*

We argue that stranding of VP material, including direct objects, is possible in English as well as in German. We investigate the differences in syntactic structure in the two languages that account for the observed differences in the topicalization constructions. We also investigate the different discourse functions of VP-Top. We show that the differences between the two languages can be accounted for in terms of minimal, well-motivated differences in their basic syntactic structures and the conditions that these structures must satisfy. Specifically:

(4) a. The VP in English is head-initial, while the VP in German is head-final.

b. Spec,IP in English must be filled by the external argument, while Spec, IP in German may be filled by any phrasal category.
c. The complement of C⁰ in English is IP, while the complement of C⁰ in German subordinate clauses is VP.
d. Topicalization in English is adjunction to IP or CP, while topicalization in German is movement to Spec,IP.

We show how these differences in syntactic structure account for the observed syntactic properties of the VP-Top constructions in the two languages. Our approach contrasts with those that take the constructions in the two languages to be fundamentally different (cf. Ott 2017).

The structure of the paper is as follows. In section 2 we describe the prosodic form and discourse functions of VP-Top in English and relate these aspects of VP-Top to a plausible syntactic analysis. Section 3 then looks at the comparable discourse and intonation properties of VP-Top in German and makes a preliminary syntactic proposal that captures both the similarities and the differences between the two languages with minimal stipulation. Section 4 reviews the main points of our analysis and suggests some directions for future research.

2 English VP Topicalization

2.1 Types of English VP-Top

English VP topicalization occurs in a restricted range of syntactic and discourse contexts. On the one hand, it can appear in the second conjunct if the VP echoes or is construable from the first conjunct. (5) illustrates.

(5) a. *They said that Trump would win the election, and* [$_{VP}$ *win the election he did*].
   b. *Shamir, the man who said that Netanyahu was "the angel of destruction." It takes one to know one. And destroy he did.*[1]

VP-Top can be constructed with *and, but* and even marginally with *(even) though/although*, as illustrated in (6).

---

[1] http://972mag.com/shamir-and-netanyahu-it-takes-one-to-know-one/49784/

(6) a. *They said that he would win, and win he did.*
  b. *They said that he would win, but win he didn't.*
  c. *?They were convinced that he would win,* $\left\{\begin{array}{c}\text{(even)though}\\ \text{although}\end{array}\right\}$ *win he couldn't.*

Typically the topicalized material is given, and the subject and the material in focus that follows it is a comment on what is given. The VP may be given in the sense that it is what is being talked about, even if it has not been asserted but simply entertained.

Cases such as these are discussed at some length by Ward (1990). Ward proposes that VP-Top has two types of discourse function: (i) proposition affirmation, which comes in three varieties, and (ii) proposition suspension.[2] The types of proposition affirmation identified by Ward are:

- INDEPENDENT PROPOSITION AFFIRMATION affirms a proposition that is neither semantically entailed by nor presupposed in the prior discourse. An example given by Ward is:

  (7) *As members of a Gray Panthers committee, we went to Canada to learn, and learn we did.*

- CONCESSIVE AFFIRMATION affirms a proposition that stands in RHETORICAL OPPOSITION to another proposition conceded in the prior discourse (Horn 1991). An example given by Ward is:

  (8) *Waiting in long lines to pay someone else more money than they seem to be entitled to is lunacy. But wait in line they did Monday in Chicago and the Cook County suburbs, (...)*

- SCALAR AFFIRMATION affirms a proposition whose predicate is construable as a scale upon which the subject represents a high value. An example given by Ward is:

  (9) *Asked what he thought about during today's race on a sultry day, [Tour de France winner Greg LeMond said:] 'I didn't think. I just rode.' Ride he did.*

Regarding proposition suspension, it "involves suspending a speaker's commitment to belief in a previously evoked and salient proposition. In contrast

---

[2] Ward does not discuss cases in which the second clause is negated, as in (6b). As far as we can tell these cases are the negative counterparts of proposition affirmation, but the question deserves further study.

to proposition affirmation, the evoked proposition must follow from the preceding discourse." (757) These cases are characterized by VP-Top in an *if*-clause, e.g. Ward's (31a):

(10) *Mark finished his thesis late, if finish it he did.*

From our perspective there are two significant aspects of these characterizations of the discourse function of VP-Top. One is that preposing the VP isolates the remnant as a focus, typically one of reaffirmation, new information or contrast. (7) is an instance of Verum Focus, (8) is Verum Focus with new information (*Monday in Chicago and the Cook County suburbs*), and (9) is Verum Focus. In the case of (10), *did* marks the focus, but since it is in the scope of *if*, the focus is not interpreted as affirmation but as suspension.

The other significant aspect of English VP-Top is that in affirmation, what is topicalized is given, and in suspension, what is topicalized is accepted for the sake of further comment. Thus, even in these two uses of VP-Top, we can see that there is no uniform discourse interpretation of the topicalized phrase. Rather, what is common to these varieties of VP-Top is that the predicate is evoked by the context.

A second construction is *though*-attraction (11).[3]

(11) a. *Beneditto now knew what he had long suspected: that he had truly inherited great powers from his father, but, regrettably, he had no knowledge as to how to summon forth these powers.* **Try though he did**, *he remained powerless to free himself from the body of the great tree, neither was he successful in wishing himself a man.*[4]
   b. *The possibility that Freitas, son of the postmaster in the San Joaquin Valley town of Atwater, would climb higher in political office was snuffed out on May 21, 1979, when a jury rejected a first-degree murder conviction for ex-Supervisor Dan White and instead found him guilty of two counts of voluntary manslaughter in the City Hall killings of Moscone and Milk.* **Try though he did in the years that followed**, *Freitas never could distance (...)*[5]
   c. *Poor Charles. He certainly never meant to antagonize anyone, especially not Emma. However,* **try though he might to just get along with**

---

[3] Examples (11b–g) were found in a search of COCA (Davies 2008).
[4] books.google.de/books?isbn=1463405049
[5] http://www.sfgate.com/news/article/Former-D-A-Joseph-Freitas-Jr-dies-in-Paris-at-66-2499610.php

everyone, he still drives her craaaaazy. Without even knowing it, he becomes Emma's greatest enemy; she blames him for pretty much everything, including even meeting her (...)[6]

d. From personally guided trips to dazzling parks for political powerbrokers and their wives to countless cocktails downed in the name of business, Hartzog gave to get. And he sweated the small stuff. When, for instance, news broke that South Carolina senator Strom Thurmond's wife had given birth, Hartzog rang them up and delivered hearty congratulations. **Jaunty and joshing though he often was around legislators and his own conference room table**, the joke-loving Hartzog was also a brusque taskmaster with a short fuse when dealing with underlings. Utley, for one, says his boss could be "a tyrant" when staff failed to do precisely what he wanted.[7]

e. Yet mannerist painters of the early 16th century had painted mountains with an excitement that was not "loathing" at all. Pieter Bruegel, partly inspired by them, and partly by his deliberate route through the Alps on his way home to Flanders from Italy in the early 1550s, drew the mountains with an appreciative objective accuracy and not the slightest hint of distaste. A decade earlier, a Swiss physician, Conrad Gesner, had expressed striking enthusiasm for the Alps: "I sense my spirit struck by these astonishing heights, and ravished in the contemplation of the sovereign architect". Even Leonardo da Vinci, **fascinated though he was with the destructiveness of the earth's elemental forces** (...)[8]

f. **Determined though he was from the start to push ahead with the full reform proposed in the report**, the premier decided to wait until the government was fully (...)[9]

In these examples, both the topicalized material and the remnant are new information. The contrastive function of *though* guarantees that something in the subordinate clause will be in contrast with something in the main clause. For example, in (11f), *determined to push ahead* contrasts with *wait until the government was* (...).

A third construction, found in British English but not American English, shows what appears to be VP topicalization in a simple assertion. The examples in (12) from the BNC illustrate.

---

6 http://www.shmoop.com/madame-bovary/antagonist.html
7 http://www.npca.org/news/magazine/all-issues/2011/summer/the-guardian.html
8 http://www.csmonitor.com/1994/0718/18161.html
9 *The Acadians: In Search of a Homeland*, By James Laxer

(12) a. *He told me that himself. Boasted about it, he did.*
  b. *Said there was nowt like the smell of new-mown grass. Took 'er back to 'er childhood, it did.*
  c. *Well, he's pushed his set right on up through Ragge Down. Come up in the middle of it, he has.*
  d. *He's become an actor! Acting in one of your London theatres, he is!*
  e. *She's a sympathetic woman – trained in London, she was – and she'll help you.*

This construction is quite different from the German and standard English cases that we are considering, because the remnant is not a focus. Moreover, in simple past tense sentences like (12a,b), the past tense is marked on the topicalized VP and the auxiliary. This fact raises the possibility that this is not a variety of VP topicalization, but reduction of the main clause with an emphatic tag – *(He) boasted about it, he did* (Culicover 1971, 1973). Such an analysis is made somewhat more plausible by the existence of cases where the tag shows inversion, e.g. *Hardly boasted about it did he?*[10] We do not have a worked out account of this construction so we will not say anything more about it here.

2.2 Syntax of English VP-Top

We turn now to the syntax. We argue that, contrary to the traditional view, what topicalizes in English VP-Top may be any projection of V, including the head V itself. This conclusion extends naturally to the analysis of German, without requiring an appeal to scrambling in German as part of the explanation of why VP topicalization can leave behind a remnant of the VP.

But first, we consider the landing site. In general, English topicalization can adjoin an XP above a wh-phrase in Spec,CP in main clauses and below the complementizer *that* (Rochemont 1989). The reverse is not possible, however, as the examples in (13)–(14) show.

(13) a. *To Sandy, how many of the books did you give?*
  b. **How many of the books to Sandy, did you give?*

(14) a. *Sandy found out that to Kim, we had given all of the books.*
  b. **Sandy found out to Kim, that we had given all of the books.*

---

10 http://www.not606.com/showthread.php/263872-50-Million-reasons-to-hate-the-Premier-League/page2

These possibilities can be accounted for as plausible stipulations about the linear order of constituents in English, in particular that the complementizer *that* must be clause-initial, and that in sentences with inversion the finite auxiliary must be in second position (Culicover 2013). Furthermore, since multiple extraction produces crossing and nested dependencies, combining topicalization and wh-fronting, or multiple topicalization, typically produces unacceptability that is not necessarily a matter of syntactic well-formedness per se.

For example, (15b) does not appear to violate any ordering constraints, but it is an instance of crossing dependency.

(15) a. *Sandy found out how many of the books$_i$ we had given t_i to Kim.*
 b. **Sandy found out how many of the books$_i$ to Kim$_j$ we had given t_i t_j.*

However, the nested dependency appears to be equally unacceptable.

(16) a. *Sandy found out to whom$_i$ we had given all of the books t_i.*
 b. **Sandy found out to whom$_i$ all of the books$_j$ we had given t_j t_i.*

It may be, then, that extracting over a topic is a subjacency violation, as Rochemont (1989) proposes, or that the unacceptability is due to discourse incompatibility, e.g. between the embedded topic and the interrogative scope. We do not explore the possible options here, but simply assume the standard adjunction sites for English topicalization as realized in the structures above.

We assume for convenience the following structures. We notate heads as X^0 and maximal projections as X^{max}, and we refer in the text to CP (=C^{max}), IP, VP, XP and so on. But crucially, we assume, with HPSG (Pollard and Sag 1994) and the Minimalist Program (Chomsky 1995) that there are no categorial distinctions between various projection levels. Hence a head X^0 and its projections share all categorial features of X^0; the selectional properties at each projection level differ according to the saturation of selectional features.

(17) Root clause

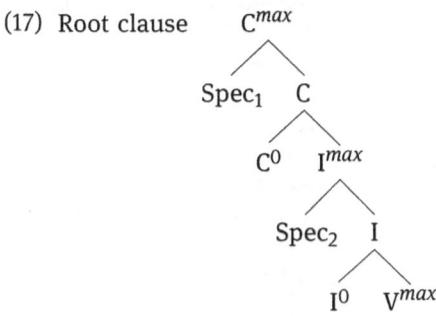

(18) Embedded clause – same as Root clause (17)

(19) Verb phrase (English)

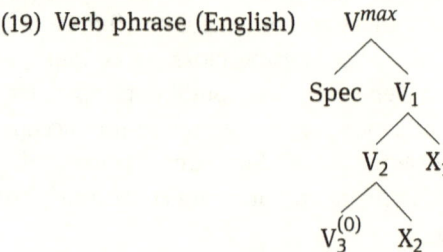

We adopt the conventional assumptions that
- wh-phrases are in Spec,CP in main and subordinate clauses.
- Topicalization is adjunction to IP or CP.[11]
- Inversion in questions is movement of I⁰ to C⁰.
- The subject originates in Spec,VP (the VP Internal Subject Hypothesis).

---

[11] The situation is actually somewhat more complex. Note that it is possible to have a topicalized phrase before either a wh-phrase or a negative phrase, both of which trigger inversion.

(i) a. *To Mary, what did you give?*
    b. *To Mary, not a single thing would I give.*

But unlike a wh-phrase, a negative phrase can trigger inversion in embedded contexts. The following illustrates for an embedded *that*-complement (Culicover 1991).

(ii) *I said that* $\begin{Bmatrix} \text{under no circumstances} \\ \text{only then} \end{Bmatrix}$ *would I agree to something like that.*

Culicover (1991) also observed that it is possible to have negative inversion in relative clauses.

(iii) *a person who* $\begin{Bmatrix} \text{under no circumstances} \\ \text{only then} \end{Bmatrix}$ *would I agree to talk to*

Interestingly, a Web search for "which under no circumstances" comes up with several hits for *which under no circumstances must we* (…) in naturally occurring text.

These cases of inversion in embedded clauses are interesting because they raise the question of how inversion works. If the wh-phrase and the negative-phrase are in Spec,CP, then inversion moves I⁰ to C⁰. But inversion after *that* requires another functional head that has exactly the properties of C⁰ but is between C⁰ and I⁰. Constructions such as these are a major concern of the 'cartographic' approach to the left periphery, e.g. Cardinaletti and Roberts (2002); Rizzi (2004). For simplicity of exposition we assume the simpler structure although it does not in itself account for embedded inversion.

For English, we assume that the structure of a root clause is (17). An embedded clause in English also has this structure. In contrast, an embedded clause in German is VP. Thus it is in the structure of the embedded clause that we see one major difference between English and German. Finally, the structure of VP in German is the same as that of English, except German is left branching while English is right branching.[12]

Now for the central problem: what can topicalize? It has long been held that English VP-Top does not have the same range of partial VP topicalization that German has (e.g. Baltin 2006; Landau 2007; Phillips and Lewis 2013). The main difference appears to be that while the direct object can be stranded in German – see (2) above – it cannot be in English (20)–(22).

(20) a.   (...) and [read a book]$_i$ he did t_i .
    b.   * (...) and read$_i$ he did t_i a book.

(21) a.   (...) and [give a book to Sandy]$_i$, Kim did t_i .
    b.   * (...) and give$_i$ Kim did t_i a book to Sandy.

(22) a.   Though he may visit Sally, it won't matter.
    b.   * Visit$_i$ though he may t_i Sally, it won't matter
      [Baltin 2006]

Observations such as these have led to some interesting accounts. Most prominent is the one due to Müller (1998): German has scrambling, so the direct object can be moved out of VP and stranded by topicalization, while English does not have scrambling, and so the direct object cannot be stranded.

Baltin (2006) remarks that such examples have been attributed to extraposition in earlier work; in his proposal they are stranded by the leftward movement of V. But for Baltin there is a problem with such leftward movement, exemplified by (22): apparently the direct object cannot be stranded. So Baltin concludes in the end that English has scrambling, like German, but if the object is scrambled in English the verb must move to a position to the left of it in order to license it.

Baltin's treatment is criticized by Landau (2007) and Phillips and Lewis (2013) on a number of grounds. Not the least of these is that on Baltin's account, the verb and the direct object must move independently to high positions – giving it the appearance of a topicalized VP – and do not form a

---

[12] Hence we do not adopt the assumption of uniform branching order of Kayne (1994).

constituent. The resulting sequence (which may include more than these two constituents of the original VP) "mysteriously" (Landau's characterization) recapitulates the exact form of a possible VP in situ. When we consider that not only the verb and direct object may constitute a topicalized VP, but in fact any possible VP may be topicalized, with various arguments and adjuncts, the mystery becomes overwhelming.

Note that English in fact has a type of scrambling internal to VP, which is evidenced by the reordering of 'heavy' constituents to the right. Such reordering includes the direct object.

(23) a. *Mary gave [a painting that she found at the art fair] to John.*
b. *Mary gave to John [a painting that she found at the art fair].*

Strikingly, such heavy NPs **can** be stranded under English VP topicalization.

(24) (...) *and give to John she did,* [*a painting that she found at the art fair*].

Such examples, while rare, are attested in corpora.

(25) a. *The other week, I went up to the Compendium bookshop in Camden Town, London NW1, to hear Iain Sinclair read from his latest novel. And read he did,* **the bit about the floating science fiction convention, from towards the end of Radon Daughters.** *The heavy metal lads rushed (...)*[13]
b. *Feb 2, 2006 – If you were not 100% in support of his crusade, you were his enemy to be destroyed and destroy he did* **a lot of good people.** *So we are very (...)*[14]
c. *May 11, 2012 – Mr. Archer's experiences in the legal system gave him much about which to write. And write he did* **(a rather highly acclaimed series, I believe)** *(...)*[15]
d. *May 23, 2009 – And write he did,* **a fair few gems including this one.** *I read it, thought I'd have ago drawing it and here we are. Den Dilworth inked it and I sent it (...)*[16]

---

[13] (Jenny Turner – London Review of Books, http://www.lrb.co.uk/v16/n19/jenny-turner/the-opposite-of-a-dog)
[14] GunAuction.com – Why Do You let People Sell Nazi Crap on this Site? (www.gunauction.com/help/forum/Dis-playForum.cfm?SubjectID=11770)
[15] www.amazon.com/forum/kindledeals/...
[16] https://gcrutchley.blogspot.com/2009/05/

e. *With that kind of eloquence, it is no wonder Jefferson was selected to write the Declaration. And write, he did,* **a document that still shines as bright today as it did** (...)[17]

Moreover, it is possible to strand not only PPs, complements Ss and heavy NPs, but also extraposed complements and adjuncts of NPs.

(26) a. (...) *and make the claim she did* [*that the Yankees would win it all this year*].
b. (...) *and read a book he did* [*that he had taken with him to school*].
c. (...) *and give a book he did to Mary* [*that he had taken with him to school*].
d. (...) *and give a book he did* [*that he had taken with him to school*] *to the girl who was sitting next to him in class.*

(27) a. (...) *and buy a book she did about anti-reconstruction phenomena in Old High German.*
b. (...) *and take a course she did offered by the inter-college consortium for higher learning.*

Given data such as the foregoing, one might well be tempted to conclude that topicalization of a partial VP is possible just in case there are syntactic processes such as scrambling, heavy NP shift and extraposition that can move constituents out of VP and adjoin them higher. But the structure in (19) makes available constituents that can be topicalized without such restructuring, namely V_1, V_2, V_3 and so on. Moreover, at least extraposition in English would have to be vacuous movement to account for examples such as (26a,b,d). In the case of (26d), in fact, extraposition would have to remove the relative clause from the NP and vacuously extrapose it internally in the VP so that it precedes the PP *to the girl who was sitting next to him in class.*

It is clear that such vacuous movement is a way to avoid directly topicalizing V^0 and other sub-constituents of VP, a problem that is resolved by assuming (19) for English and permitting topicalization of any projection of V.[18]

---

17 www.massapequanews.com/holidays.html?, *Holidays – massapequaNEWS.com*
18 Note that this approach requires two assumptions about the relationship between syntactic structure and linear order in the English VP. First, the ordering of heavy NPs, PPs, adjuncts and clausal complements is not derived by movement, but is free. It is subject to constraints on heaviness, information structure, etc. (Wasow 2002). Second, an extraposed relative clause need not be a constituent of the NP that it modifies, but may be a constituent of the VP that

Finally, we note that our analysis predicts the possibility of embedded VP-Top in English, as long as the discourse conditions are satisfied. While embedded VP-Top is rare, it does occur, as the following examples show.[19] Notice that each case has Verum Focus on the tensed auxiliary (Jäger 2018).

(28) a. * At all events, I saw *that go he would not*.
(Hermann Melville, "Bartleby, the scrivener")
b. "*I did not want him to go back to the war for I knew that it would kill him, but I knew that go he must. And he did go and the war did kill him as I was sure that (...)*"[20]
c. "*James would insist that hate him she surely did. But neither hate, nor guilt – nor even lust – had anything to do with Cole's purpose in talking so openly with Jonet*".[21]
d. "*(...) perceiving that there was no remedy, and that die she must, she went out of the dungeon where she was detained, and walked towards the midst of the space*"[22]
e. "*She dashes back just in time, though, holding Billy's bunny and reminding him that love him she surely does*".[23]
f. "*(...) so incredibly beautiful, intelligent and sweet dispositioned could love someone like him – and then confessed, rather bashfully, that love him, she truly did*".[24]

To summarize, English VP-Top is not as constrained as previously thought. Not only is it possible to topicalize the entire VP, it is possible to topicalize the verb alone, or the verb and other constituents of VP, stranding the direct object and other complements, as well as adjuncts. The data thus suggests that the characterization of VP-Top should refer to projections of V, along the lines illustrated in (19).

---

contains the NP. In this case, the extraposed relative clause is then interpreted as predicated of the NP (Dowty 1996).

19 These examples are licensed by the analysis in (17)–(18).
20 Veteran In A New Field – Page 26 – https://books.google.de/books=isbn=061519592X. W. H. Payne – 2013.
21 A Woman Scorned – Page 219 – https://books.google.de/books=isbn=074341778X=Liz Carlyle – 2000
22 Under These Restless Skies: Lady Margaret Pole. under-these-restless-skies.blogspot.com/2014/05/lady-margaret-pole.html
23 See Mom Work Books. — Mommy Tracked. www.mommytracked.com/see-mom-work-books
24 Eleanor Bergstein – Mort Shuman. www.mortshuman.com/eleanor_bergstein.php

3 German VP Topicalization

3.1 Syntax of German VP-Top

We turn now to the syntactic analysis of German VP-Top. We focus first on the syntax, and identify precisely where the differences between German and English lie: (i) the German VP is left branching, while the English VP is right branching, and (ii) in German, any XP may appear in Spec,IP (and not just the external argument, as in English). The two languages differ more dramatically, however, in the discourse conditions on topicalization as discussed in section 3.2: it is relatively free in German, but severely restricted in English.

There is, of course, a vast literature on German constituent order. Much of the literature is devoted to exploration of interactions between the *Vorfeld*, that is, 'topicalized' material, V2 in main clauses and ordering in the *Mittelfeld* (scrambling phenomena). There is a nice range of not entirely consistent proposals about how these orderings are derived, reflecting various assumptions about the inventory of maximal projections in main and subordinate clauses, the underlying position of subjects, triggering of movement, and so on. There is a smaller but robust literature as well concerning the discourse properties of various positions in the German sentence.

Looking back on the history of this part of the field, what is particularly salient is that to a considerable extent, the sorts of proposals that are most prominent are those that are most compatible with the 'standard' views about syntax at the time, to some extent independently of empirical considerations. So, for example, in early work it was argued that the reason that German permits topicalization of part of the VP but English doesn't is that German has scrambling and English doesn't have scrambling (e.g. Müller 1998). But then more recently it has been argued that partial VP fronting in German does not depend on scrambling because scrambling is not licensed in the Minimalist Program, given that it is not plausibly triggered by the need to discharge a feature (Fanselow 2002). As observed by Culicover and Jackendoff (2005), this sort of evolution is not atypical of contemporary syntactic theory, where a substantial part of the development has been driven by aesthetic considerations of uniformity and economy, with no small amount of sociological pressure and historical inertia.

We make these observations in order to contrast the usual approach to the phenomena in question with the one that we take here, which we would characterize as more 'pragmatic'. It turns out that Fanselow's conclusion that scrambling is not involved in partial VP fronting is indeed the right position to take. This can be demonstrated empirically, as we discuss below, and it is the position that we took for the analysis of comparable phenomena in English in section 2.2. More generally, we focus in this piece more on the empirical phenomena and leave questions of conformity to a particular theoretical framework to another venue.

The first decision to make is whether topicalization in German is to Spec,CP with V2 positioning of the verb in C^0 (Evers 1975), or to Spec,IP with V2 positioning of the verb in I^0 (Diesing 1988, 1990; Reinholtz 1991; Rögnvaldsson and Thráinsson 1990; Santorini 1989). The former position is motivated by the fact that V2 does not occur in subordinate clauses – presumably the overt complementizer *dass* blocks V2, but the empty C^0 in the main clause does not.

On the other hand, there is also inversion (that is, V2) in wh-questions in German. Either a wh-phrase and a topicalized XP are in the same location, that is, Spec,CP, or the wh-phrase is in a higher position than the topicalized constituent. Since wh-phrases go into initial position in subordinate clauses but there is no topicalization in subordinate clauses, the simplest assumptions are the following[25]:

- Wh-phrases are in Spec,CP in main and subordinate clauses (as in English).
- In a main clause the complement of C^0 is IP, and a topicalized XP is in Spec,IP (in contrast to English, where XP is adjoined to IP).
- V2 is movement of V^0 to I^0 (as in English).
- Inversion in questions is movement of I^0 to C^0.
- The subject originates in Spec,VP (as in English).
- Crucially, the complement of C^0 in the subordinate clause is VP, not IP (Travis 1991; Sternefeld 2006). Hence there is no V2 in a (non-root) subordinate clause, on the assumption that V2 is movement of the tensed V to I^0.

These assumptions give us the following preliminary structures for German sentences.

---

25 A complication would be the possibility of topicalizing VP in subordinate clauses. Reis (1991) cites the following example, which is marked.

(i) *Obwohl ein Buch gelesen keiner hat, wollte jeder seine Meinung dazu äußern.*
    although a book read nobody has wanted everybody his opinion about it give
    'Although nobody had read a book, everybody wanted to give his opinion.'

See also Haider and Rosengren (2003). We leave open here the questions of whether this apparent topicalization is scrambling, and how scrambling fits into our general framework.

(29) Root clause

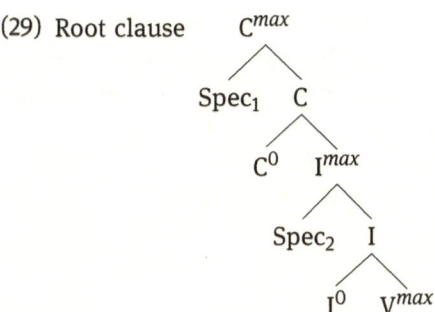

(30) Embedded clause

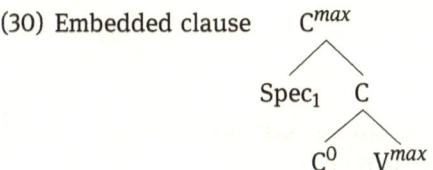

(31) Verb phrase (German)

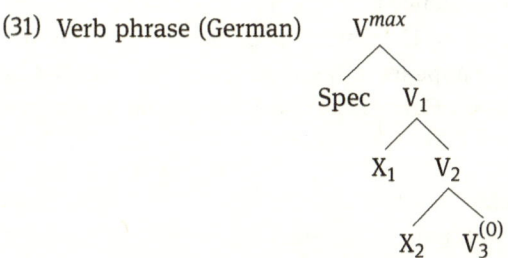

Finally, there is the requirement in German that Spec,IP be occupied by some XP. This position is not thematic; hence it is an A' position in the traditional sense, although it is internal to IP. In English, however, the corresponding requirement is that Spec,IP must be occupied by the constituent that gets some θ-role governed by the verb.[26]

The derived structure of a German main clause and an English main clause is thus the same just when what is moved to Spec,IP in German is the thematic subject and what appears in I^0 is a modal or auxiliary. In both languages an unfilled Spec,IP must be realised overtly as an expletive, *es* in German (von Fintel 1990) and *it* in English. But otherwise, the structures are rather different, particularly with respect to the 'topicalized' constituent.

---

26 This statement is slightly too strong, in view of English extraposition, which leaves behind an expletive in subject position. However, we can treat the pair consisting of the expletive *it* and the extraposed S as the argument (cf. Safir 1985) and understand 'occupied' as referring to at least one element of such a chain.

An interesting piece of evidence that is consistent with the proposal to put the topicalized constituent in German in Spec,IP but the English topic in an adjoined position is due to Marga Reis (p.c.), who points out that topicalized constituents in German can be echoed, while English topics cannot; see (32).

(32) a. *John, I saw.*
 b. **Who* ↗*, you saw?*
 c. *Fritz habe ich gesehen.*
   Fritz have I   seen
   'I have seen Fritz.'
 d. *Wen* ↗ *hast du gesehen?*
   Who   have you seen
   'Who have you seen?'

The assumption that topicalization moves any phrase in German to Spec,IP, combined with the assumption that there is no categorial distinction between heads and projections, has the consequence that any projection of V, including the head, may be topicalized in German (Fanselow 2002; Haider 2010; Hinterhölzl 2002, 2009). This consequence appears to be correct, as demonstrated by many examples from the literature on German partial VP movement, a representative sample of which is given in (33).

(33) a. [$_{VP}$ *Geküsst*] *hat sie Peter nicht.*
     kissed   has she Peter not?
   'She has not kissed Peter.'
   (Fanselow 2002)
 b. [$_V$ *Verkaufen*] *wird er das Pferd.*
     sell.INF   will he the horse
   'He will sell the horse.'
   (De Kuthy and Meurers 2001: 143)
 c. [$_V$ *Zu verkaufen*] *versuchte er das Pferd.*
     to sell   tried   he the horse.
   'He tried to sell the horse.'
   (De Kuthy and Meurers 2001: 155)
 d. [$_V$ *Gekauft*] *hat die Allreal das Areal   für 2,65 Millionen*
     bought   has the Allreal the property for 2.65 million
   Franken.
   francs
   'Allreal bought the property for 2.65 million francs.'
   (COSMAS: A13/JAN.04057 St. Galler Tagblatt, 12.01.2013)

Moreover, since the subject originates in VP, and since there are no restrictions on what can appear in Spec,IP, it should be possible to topicalize a VP with its subject. The following well-known example from the literature confirms this expectation.

(34) [Ein　　Außenseiter　gewonnen] hat　hier　noch　nie.
　　　a.NOM　outsider　　won　　　has　here　still　never
　　　'An outsider has never won here yet.'
　　　(Haider 1990: 94)

To summarize, for German, as for English, it is possible to account for the range of VP-Top possibility without assuming that scrambling out of VP is involved. VP-Top in both language can be accounted in terms of topicalization of any projection of V, leaving behind the rest of VP in situ.

3.2 Discourse Interpretation

We conclude our survey of German VP-Top with an analysis of the discourse properties of examples found in corpora. We show that there is no uniform discourse function of the topicalized VP – it can be explicitly or implicitly contrastive or non-contrastive. The remnant is focus, as we have argued for the comparable English construction. It may be a contrastive focus, or a new information focus, again as the discourse allows.

There are three primary information structural types of VP-topicalization, depending on the discourse function of the topicalized VP, and the remnant.[27]

Type 1. (VP-Top: Contrast. Remnant: Contrastive Focus)

Type 1 is characterized by the fact that the topicalized VP is contrastive. It is a contrastive topic in the sense of Büring (1997, 2016); Jacobs (1997); Krifka (1998); Molnár (1998).

(Type 1a) VP-Top (object and verb)

---

27 Anonymous reviewers observe that other configurations may be possible, e.g. *GeREGnet hat es* 'it has rained' in the context of an alternative question, *Hat es geregnet oder geschneit?* 'Has it rained or snowed?', or *GeREGnet HAT es, aber nicht besonders stark.* 'It has rained, but not particularly hard.' in the context of *Hat es geregnet?* 'Has it rained?'. We leave such cases to future research.

(35) [*Eine Medaille ge*↗*WONnen*] *hat KEI*↘*ner.*
　　 a　　medal　　 won　　　　　 has　nobody
　　 'Nobody has won a medal.'

The schematic representation of the information structural relations are given in (36).

(36) [$_{\text{VP-Top}}$ Contrast (↗)] [$_{\text{remnant}}$ Contrastive Focus (↘)]

(37) *Der US-Amerikaner Paul Krugman ist zweifellos ein blitzgescheiter*
　　 the US-American　Paul Krugman　is doubtless　a　sharp.as.a.tack
　　 Mann – sonst　　wäre　　der prominente Wirtschaftsforscher wohl
　　 man – otherwise would.be the prominent economist　　　　 well
　　 nicht mit　dem Nobelpreis ausgezeichnet worden. Die Klugheit
　　 not　with　the　Nobel.Prize distinguished　been　　the wisdom
　　 gepachtet hat Krugman damit　　allerdings noch lange nicht.
　　 leased　　 has Krugman with.this however　 still　 long　not
　　 'The American Paul Krugman is no doubt sharp as a tack – otherwise the prominent economist would not have been granted the distinction of the Nobel Prize. Despite this fact, Krugman does not have a monopoly on wisdom by a long shot.'

In the more complex (37) there is a contrastive focus on the remnant. *Noch LANge nicht* 'not by a long shot' is contrasted with the affirmation of *ist ZWEIfellos* (...) 'is doubtless (...)' and a contrast on the topicalized VP *Die Klugheit gePACHtet* ('the wisdom leased'), where being smart is contrasted with not having a monopoly on being wise.

Some other examples that show a similar double contrast are given in (38) and (39).

(38) *Zwei Jahre harren　　　 sie　hier　aus. Die Heimat verlassen*
　　 two　years stay.and.wait they here out. The home　 leave
　　 wollte　keiner von ihnen, die meisten bleiben ihr　treu.
　　 wanted　none　of　them, the most　　remain to.it faithful.
　　 'They stay and wait here for two years. None of them want to leave home, most of them stay faithful to it.'

(39) a. *Die Wahl geschafft haben gerade einmal zwei von ihnen.*
　　　　 the vote achieved　have　only　　　　 two　of　them
　　　　 'Managing to get the vote were only two of them.'

b. *Die Wahl geschafft hat auch diesmal keiner der*
the vote achieved has also this.time none of.the
Nachwuchspolitiker.
young.politicians
'Managing to get the vote this time as well were none of the young politicians.'

(Type 1b) VP-Top (subject and verb)

In (35) to (39), the topicalized constituent is the VP (verb plus object). There are, however, well-known cases of VP-top in German where the highest projection of V⁰ is topicalized along with the subject (see e.g. Haider 1990; Höhle 1991). The relevant observation here is that the subject VP-topicalization cases seem to obey the same discourse requirements that are specified for type 1. The topicalized VP contains a contrastive constituent, the remnant must contain a contrastive remnant, preferably a negative indefinite as a response to a positive indefinite (contrast between *je(mals)* vs *nie(mals)* / 'ever' vs. 'never') in the context question, as given in (40):

(40) A. *Hat hier je ein Außenseiter gewonnen?*
has here ever an.NOM outsider won
'Did an outsider ever win here?'
B. [*Ein* ↗*AUßenseiter gewonnen*] *hat hier noch* ↘*NIE*
an outsider won has here still never
'An outsider has never won here yet.'

The schematic relation is given in (41):

(41) [$_{\text{VP-Top}}$ Contrast (↗)] [$_{\text{remnant}}$ Contrastive Focus (↘)

The intonation pattern of type 1 is a prototypical contrastive topicalization contour also referred to as I(ntonational) Topic in the nominal domain (e.g. Büring 1997; Büring 2016; Höhle 1991; Jacobs 1997; Krifka 1998; Molnár 1998). There is a rise on the contrastive element in the VP-Top in the constituent and a fall on the contrastive focus.[28]

---

[28] The best idealized context for this construction is a yes-no-question that contains a positive polarity item, e.g. *jemand* 'someone' vs. *niemand* 'no one', or *je* 'ever' vs. *nie* 'ever', as in the context in (40).

Depending on the context, the topicalized VP can contain either the object(s) or the subject. Further restrictions must be obeyed by the subject-VP-top cases; the verbs prefer to be unaccusative verbs, the subjects prefer to be nonspecific (cf. De Kuthy and Meurers 2003; Grewendorf 1989; Lee-Schoenfeld and Lunden 2017). We observe in our corpus data that the discourse status of the topicalized VP is given (c-construable or entailed) and the rise marks the contrastive element. This can be seen in example (40) (from De Kuthy and Meurers 2003: 99). The yes-no question mentions the topicalized VP. Therefore, in the answer the discourse status must be given. However, the rise on *Außenseiter* 'outsider') sets up a contrast to an implicit set of competitors (at least insiders and outsiders).

Type 2: VP-Top: Contrast. Remnant: Focus new (presentational focus)

Type 2 contains a contrastive element in the topicalized VP. The remnant contains a new information focus, which is often referred to as presentational focus (see Culicover and Rochemont 1983; Rochemont 1986), as schematically represented in (42):

(42) [$_{\text{VP-Top}}$ Contrast (↗)] [$_{\text{remnant}}$ New Information Focus (↘)]

Idealized Context:

(43) A: *Wer gehört denn jetzt zu dem Komitee?*
Who belongs then now to the.DAT committee
'Who belongs to the committee now?'
B: *Dem Komitee ↗BEIgetreten sind, der kantonale*
the committee joined are the cantonal
Ge↘WERKschaftsbund, die SP die Partei der Arbeit (…)
federation the SP the Party GEN Labour (…)

The specific prosodic property of type 2 is that there is a rise on the contrastive element in the topicalized constituent, here on the verb *beigetreten*. The focus of the constituent is not on a quantificational expression as in type 1, but on the new information focus. The remnant is typically heavy and presentationally focused. A H*-pitch accent appears on each item of the list.

(44) *Das Kantonale Komitee* "*Stoppt den Rentenklau*" *unterstützt*
the cantonal committee "Stop the Retirement.theft" supports
deshalb das Referendum und organisiert die
therefore the referendum and organizes the

Unterschriftensammlung in der Region. Dem Komitee beigetreten
signature.collection in the region. the committee joined
sind der Kantonale Gewerkschaftsbund St. Gallen, die SP,
are the cantonal federation.of.trade.unions St. Gallen, die SP,
die Partei der Arbeit (...)
the Party GEN Labour (...)
'The cantonal "Stop the Retirement Theft" Committee therefore supports the referendum and is organizing the signature collection in the region. Joining the committee are the cantonal Federation of Trade Unions of St. Gallen, the SP, the Party of Labour (...)'

In this example the topicalized VP *dem Komitee beigetreten* 'joining the committee' is implicated by the existence of the committee as described in the preceding sentence. It is thus contrastive, in the sense that the exact makeup of the committee is different from its existence and function. The list of participants joining the committee is new information focus, and is postposed because it is long compared to the predicate. The non-topicalized variant (45) has the list of groups joining the committee first and the predicate following it. While grammatical, it is more awkward, as is the English counterpart.

(45) a. *Der Kantonale Gewerkschaftsbund St. Gallen* (...)
  b. The cantonal Federation of Trade Unions of St. Gallen (...)
  sind dem Komitee beigetreten.
  are the committee joined

Another example with the same relation to discourse is (46). In contrast to example (44), the contrastive set of alternatives are explicitly mentioned in the context in which (46) occurs.

(46) *Das Rettungskorps ver/ˊLASSen hat nach 23 Jahren der neue*
  the rescue.corps leave.past.prt has after 23 years the new
  alt Kommandant Milo ˋGOLDener.
  former commander Milo Goldener
  'Leaving the rescue corps after 23 years was the new former commander Milo Goldener.'

This example shows a contrast on the topicalized VP, where leaving the rescue corps is contrasted with various ways of entering or staying in it. In this example, the other events in the set of alternatives are explicitly mentioned in the newspaper article. The remnant contains the new information focus, namely the DP denoting the individual that leaves the committee after 23 years.

A third example with similar structure is (47). This example presents the contrastive set of alternatives in a hierarchical order.

(47) *Bei den Jugendlichen ging der Medaillensatz an Jessica*
by the youth went the medal.set to Jessica
Hollenstein (...) Das Finale er/REICHT hat auch Michael \SCHERrer
Hollenstein (...) the final reached has also Michael Scherrer.
'As for the youths, the medal set went to Jessica Hollenstein. Also reaching the final was Michael Scherrer.'

In this example the topicalized VP is contrastive. The two VPs denote two different things that typically happen in a competition – some achieve medals, some reach the final. The name *Michael Scherrer* is a new information focus and perhaps also has a contrastive reading. In a competition, the winners and almost winners are in contrast. In all three examples, the topicalized VP is contrastive. However, the set of alternatives from which it is chosen is either explicitly mentioned in the discourse or it is only implicated.

Type 3. VP-Top: no Contrast. Remnant: Contrastive Focus (Verum Focus).

Type 3 differs from type 1 and 2 in that the topicalized VP does not contain a contrast. This is the type that comes closest to the English type where the discourse status of the topicalized VP is simply given, as schematically illustrated in (48).

(48) [VP-Top no Contrast] [remnant contrastive focus (\)]

The straightforward case in German is one where the topicalized VP is anaphorically reduced. In the example in (49) it can be seen that the VP-anaphor *das* ('do this') is used. In more colloquial varieties, topic drop can occur and the topicalized VP is not realized at all (Fries 1988).

(49) A: *Hat ihr Hund schon einmal/jemals ein Kind angebellt?*
has your dog PARTICLE once/ever a child barked.at
'Has your dog ever barked at a child?'
B: *Nein, (das) hat er noch nie.*
no do.this has it PRT never
'No, it never has.'

The intonational contour on the VP-anaphor (*das*) is flat.[29]

When the focus falls on a marker of truth value, such as finite tense in English (50) or negation (51), we get Verum Focus.

(50) (...) *and read a book, he DID.*

(51) *Alle   hatten   nach dem   Sieg   eine Feier   erwartet.*
     everyone have.PL   after the.DAT victory a celebration expected
     Aber ein Fest   gefeiert,   hat der TV Mähringen NICHT.
     but a   festival celebrated has the TV Mähringen NOT
     Stattdessen (...)
     instead   (...)
     'TV Mähringen did NOT hold a party. Instead, (...)'

In the German example, the topicalized VP simply evokes the VP implied by the preceding sentence – there is no contrast. The remnant has focal accent on negation *nicht*, and is thus interpreted as contrasting truth value: not having a celebration versus having one.

In the following example, on the other hand, the topic is non-contrastive and the focus is new information. In this example the focus accent is placed on the name *Ellenberger*.

(52) *Nach dem letztjährigen Erfolg   findet zum   zweiten Mal das*
     after the last.year   success takes   for the second time the
     Liechtensteiner Tanzfestival   Tanz+"   statt. Das Programm
     Liechtensteiner dance.festival "Dance+" place the program
     zu ⁄SAMmengestellt hat Barbara \ELLenberger, Leiterin des
     assembled   has Barbara   Ellenberger director of the
     Theaters am Kirchplatz (TaK) in Schaan.
     theater at Kirchplatz (TaK) in Schaan
     'After the success of the previous year, the Liechtensteiner dance festival "Dance+" takes place for the second time. Barbara Ellenberger, the director of the theatre at Kirchplatz (TaK) in Schaan, has assembled the program.'
     (A09/MAR.05562 St. Galler Tagblatt, 18.03.2009, S. 30; Tanz+ in Vaduz)

---

[29] It can also be realized alternatively with a rise. If it is realized with a rise, it is implicated that the dog didn't bark, but that it did something else. In the case of deletion of the VP-anaphor, the negative indefinite in the remnant constituent has falling intonation.

What we have done in this section is provide evidence to support our hypothesis that one of the functions of VP-Top in German is to isolate a subject focus in sentence-final position. Moreover, topicalization establishes discourse either by expressing contrast or by continuing the discourse topic.

4 Conclusions

Let us summarize. We have hypothesized that VP-Top in general is movement of a projection of V to the left edge in both English and German. Topicalization can be explained (in part, at least) in terms of the alignment of the focus under the intonation center at the right edge of the phonological phrase (modulo the branching structure of English and German). The syntax doesn't constrain the type of focus – it constrains where the focus is realized.

We have proposed that the discourse function of the contextual and topicalized material is determined by its intonational properties and links to the discourse, and not by its position in the syntactic structure. Crucially, the topic is not moved to agree with any particular functional feature.[30] It can be contrastive or old information, as the context demands. And how it links to the prior discourse is quite free, as long as the connection with discourse is coherent. Thus, the topic must be 'c-construable', in the sense of Culicover and Rochemont (1983). Focus on the right edge is contrastive or non-contrastive, also as dictated by the discourse context. And, finally, VP-Top in German overlaps in function with varieties of English focus inversion; they both isolate focus, albeit in different ways.

The picture of grammatical architecture that emerges as we work through the details of this account locates the explanation for the phenomenon outside of syntactic representation proper. Broadening the notion of well-formedness to take into account correspondences between syntactic structure, phonological form and meaning, including discourse function, is characteristic of certain constructional approaches to grammar; see for example Culicover and Jackendoff (2005). On such an approach, an expression with a particular syntactic structure is well-formed not simply because it satisfies some licensing conditions imposed by grammatical principles, rules or constructions, but also because it satisfies the requirements of the syntax/information structure interface, as well as the well-formedness conditions on the structural arrangement of constituents.

---

30 It is of course possible to use a formal feature to make the topic move. But this feature does not correspond to any particular interpretation. Therefore, the feature is just a technical and more opaque way of saying that topicalization is a possible construction.

Note: We are grateful to two anonymous reviewers for constructive and critical comments on this paper that have contributed substantial improvements. Thanks as well to the participants in the Workshop on the Architecture of Topic at the University of Lund, December 12–14, 2014, for their questions, comments, suggestions and much helpful discussion, especially Andreas Konietzko, Michael Rochemont, Valéria Molnár, Hans-Martin Gärtner, Verner Egeland, Werner Frey, Roland Hinterhölzl, and Augustine Speyer. We are grateful to the Alexander von Humboldt Stiftung and the German Research Foundation (DFG, SFB833) for financial support. Naturally, any errors are our responsibility.

References

Baltin, Mark. 2006. The nonunity of VP-preposing. *Language* 82(4). 734–766.
Büring, Daniel. 1997. *The meaning of topic and focus: the 59th street bridge accent*. London and New York: Routledge.
Büring, Daniel. 2016. (Contrastive) topic. In Catherine Féry & Shinichiro Ishihara (eds.), *The handbook of information structure*, 64–85. Oxford: Oxford University Press.
Cardinaletti, Anna & Ian Roberts. 2002. Clause structure and X-second. In Guglielmo Cinque (ed.), *Functional structure in DP and IP: The cartography of syntactic structures*, 123–166. Oxford: Oxford University Press.
Chomsky, Noam. 1995. Bare phrase structure. In Gert Webelhuth (ed.), *Government binding theory and the minimalist program*, 383–439. Oxford: Oxford University Press.
Culicover, Peter W. 1971. *Syntactic and semantic investigations*. Cambridge, MA: Massachusetts Institute of Technology dissertation.
Culicover, Peter W. 1973. On the coherence of syntactic descriptions. *Journal of Linguistics* 9. 35–51.
Culicover, Peter W. 1991. Topicalization, inversion, and complementizers in English. In Denis Delfitto (ed.), *Going Romance and beyond*, 1–43. Utrecht: Research Institute for Language and Speech, OTS, University of Utrecht.
Culicover, Peter W. 2013. *Grammar and complexity: Language at the intersection of competence and performance*. Oxford: Oxford University Press.
Culicover, Peter W. & Ray Jackendoff. 2005. *Simpler syntax*. Oxford: Oxford University Press.
Culicover, Peter W. & Michael Rochemont. 1983. Stress and focus in English. *Language* 59. 123–165.
Culicover, Peter W. & Susanne Winkler. 2008. English focus inversion. *Journal of Linguistics* 44. 625–658.
Davies, Mark. 2008. *The corpus of contemporary American English: 560 million words, 1990-present*. Available online at http://corpus.byu.edu/coca/.
De Kuthy, Kordula & Walt Detmar Meurers. 2001. On partial constituent fronting in German. *Journal of Comparative Germanic Linguistics* 3(3). 143–205.
De Kuthy, Kordula & Walt Detmar Meurers. 2003. The secret life of focus exponents, and what it tells us about fronted verbal projections. In Stefan Müller (ed.), *Proceedings of the 10th*

International Conference on Head-Driven Phase Structure Grammar, 97–110. Stanforf, CA: CSLI Publications.
Diesing, Molly. 1988. Bare plural subjects and the stage/individual contrast. In Manfred Krifka (ed.), *Genericity in natural language: Proceedings of the 1988 Tübingen conference*, 107–154. Seminar für Natürlich-Sprachliche Systeme, University of Tübingen, Germany. Report SNS-Bericht 88–42.
Diesing, Molly. 1990. Verb movement and the subject position in Yiddish. *Natural Language and Linguistic Theory* 8. 41–80.
Dowty, David R. 1996. Toward a minimalist theory of syntactic structure. In Harry Bunt & Arthur van Horck (eds.), *Discontinuous constituency*, vol. 6, 11–62. Berlin & New York: Mouton de Gruyter.
Evers, Arnold. 1975. *The transformational cycle in Dutch and German*. Bloomington, Indiana: Indiana University Linguistics Club.
Fanselow, Gisbert. 2002. Against remnant VP-movement. In Artemis Alexiadou (ed.), *Dimensions of movement*, 91–127. Amsterdam: John Benjamins.
Fries, Norbert. 1988. Über das Null-Topik im Deutschen. *Sprache und Pragmatik* 3. 19–49.
Grewendorf, Günther. 1989. *Ergativity in German*. Dordrecht: Foris Publications.
Haider, Hubert. 1990. Topicalization and other puzzles of German syntax. In Günther Grewendorf & Wolfgang Sternefeld (eds.), *Scrambling and barriers*, 93–112. Amsterdam: John Benjamins.
Haider, Hubert. 2010. *The syntax of German*. Cambridge: Cambridge University Press.
Haider, Hubert & Inger Rosengren. 2003. Scrambling: Nontriggered chain formation in OV languages. *Journal of Germanic Linguistics* 15(03). 203–267.
Hinterhölzl, Roland. 2002. Remnant movement and partial deletion. In Artemis Alexiadou, Elena Anagnostopoulou, Stef Barbiers & Hans-Martin Gärtner (eds.), *Dimensions of movement*, 127–149. Amsterdam & Philadelphia: John Benjamins.
Hinterhölzl, Roland. 2009. Predicate doubling and VP-topicalisation in German. *Theoretical Linguistics* 35(2/3). 261–267.
Höhle, Tilman N. 1991. On reconstruction and coordination. In Hubert Haider & Klaus Netter (eds.), *Representation and derivation in the theory of grammar*, 139–198. Dordrecht: Kluwer Academic Publishers.
Horn, Laurence R. 1991. Given as new: When redundant affirmation isn't. *Journal of Pragmatics* 15(4). 313–336.
Jacobs, Joachim. 1997. I-Topikalisierung. *Linguistische Berichte* 168. 91–133.
Jäger, Marion. 2018. An experimental study on freezing and topicalization in English. In Jutta Hartmann, Marion Jäger, Andreas Konietzko & Susanne Winkler (eds.), *Freezing: Theoretical approaches and empirical domains*, 430–450. Berlin & New York: Mouton de Gruyter. 430–450.
Kayne, Richard S. 1994. *The antisymmetry of syntax*. Cambridge, MA: MIT Press.
Krifka, Manfred. 1998. Scope inversion under the rise-fall contour in German. *Linguistic Inquiry* 29(1). 75–112.
Landau, Idan. 2007. Constraints on partial VP-fronting. *Syntax* 10(2). 127–164.
Lee-Schoenfeld, Vera & Anya Lunden. 2017. Syntax, information structure, and prosody of German and "VP"-fronting. Unpublished ms.
Molnár, Valéria. 1998. Topic in focus. on the syntax, phonology, semantics and pragmatics of the so-called 'contrastive topic' in Hungarian and German. *Acta Linguistica Hungarica* 45 (1/2). 1–77.

Müller, Gereon. 1998. *Incomplete category fronting: A derivational approach to remnant movement in German*. Dordrecht, Boston & London: Kluwer Academic Publishers.
Ott, Dennis. 2017. VP-fronting: movement vs. dislocation. Unpublished ms.
Phillips, Colin & Shevaun Lewis. 2013. Derivational order in syntax: Evidence and architectural consequences. *Studies in Linguistics* 6. 11–47.
Pollard, Carl & Ivan A. Sag. 1994. *Head-Driven Phrase Structure Grammar*. Chicago, Illinois: University of Chicago Press and CSLI Publications.
Reinholtz, Charlotte. 1991. Verb-second in Mainland Scandinavian: A reanalysis. In Aaron L. Halpern (ed.), *The Proceedings of the ninth West coast conference on formal linguistics*, 459–476. Stanford, California: Center for the Study of Language and Information.
Reis, Marga. 1991. Zur Topikalisierung in deutschen Verbletzt-Sätzen: Vorläufige Beobachtungen und Konsequenzen. Unpublished ms., University of Tübingen.
Rizzi, Luigi. 2004. On the cartography of syntactic structures. In Luigi Rizzi (ed.), *The structure of CP and IP*, 3–15. Oxford: Oxford University Press.
Rochemont, Michael. 1986. *Focus in generative grammar*. Amsterdam: John Benjamins.
Rochemont, Michael. 1989. Topic islands and the subjacency parameter. *Canadian Journal of Linguistics – Revue Canadianne de Linguistique* 34(2). 145–170.
Rögnvaldsson, Erikur & Höskuldur Thráinsson. 1990. On Icelandic word order once more. In Joan Maling & Annie Zaenen (eds.), *Modern Icelandic syntax* (Syntax and Semantics 24), 3–40. San Diego, California: Academic Press.
Safir, Kenneth. 1985. *Syntactic chains*. Cambridge: Cambridge University Press.
Santorini, Beatrice. 1989. *The generalization of the verb-second constraint in the history of Yiddish*. Philadelphia: Graduate School of Arts and Sciences, University of Pennsylvania dissertation.
Sternefeld, Wolfgang. 2006. *Syntax: eine morphologisch motivierte generative Beschreibung des Deutschen*. Tübingen: Stauffenburg.
Travis, Lisa deMena. 1991. Parameters of phrase structure and verb-second phenomena. In Robert Freidin (ed.), *Principles and parameters in comparative grammar*, 339–364. Cambridge, MA: MIT Press.
von Fintel, Kai. 1990. Licensing of clausal specifiers in German. In Denis Meyer, Satoshi Tomioka & Leyla Zidani-Eroglu (eds.), *Proceedings of the first meeting of the Formal Linguistics Society of Midamerica (FLSM 1)*, 98–113. Madison, WI: University of Wisconsin Press.
Ward, Gregory L. 1990. The discourse functions of VP preposing. *Language* 66. 742–763.
Wasow, Thomas. 2002. *Postverbal behavior*. Stanford, CA: Center for the Study of Language and Information.

Kordula De Kuthy, Andreas Konietzko
Information-structural Constraints on PP Topicalization from NPs

Abstract: In this paper, we discuss PP extraction from complex NPs such as *[Aus Tübingen]$_i$ haben [mehrere Studenten t_i] am Forschungswettbewerb teilgenommen.* ('From Tübingen have several students in the research contest participated'). Extractions from complex NPs are difficult to capture since they are subject to various restrictions related to the syntactic status of the extracted PP, the semantic relation between the verb and the complex NP, and the type of verb involved. In this paper, we will concentrate on one particular kind of extraction, the PP topicalization from NPs. This PP topicalization has been shown to be dependent on an appropriate context. In order to account for the discourse properties of the construction, we present an account based on the Questions under Discussion (QUD) approach to information structure. Modeling QUDs is starting to emerge as a fruitful way to define an explicit hinge between the properties of the sentence and the nature of the discourse in which the sentence can function. The proposed QUD analysis is based on attested data from corpora, which is supplemented by experimental evidence.

Keywords: information structure, syntax, QUD, extraction, contrastive topic

1 Introduction

This article presents an information-structural account of PP topicalization from NPs arguing that many of the factors which previous literature has tried to explain in terms of syntactic restrictions on movement are in fact derivable from discourse factors related to contrastive topics.

The type of PP topicalization from NPs under discussion is exemplified in (1). We underline topicalized constituents in our examples; the host NPs appear in brackets.

(1) *Über Syntax hat Sarah sich [ein Buch] ausgeliehen.*
    about syntax has Sarah self a   book   borrowed
    'Sarah borrowed a book on syntax.'

Kordula De Kuthy, Andreas Konietzko, University of Tübingen

https://doi.org/10.1515/9781501504488-007

The construction has often been referred to as extraction of PPs from NPs because one of the possible syntactic explanations for the fronting of the PP *über Syntax* in (1) is that the PP has been extracted from the NP *ein Buch*, of which the PP is a dependent.

As has often been observed in the literature (cf. Fanselow 1991; Müller 2010; Pafel 1995; De Kuthy 2002; Schmellentin 2006 among others), grammatical examples of PP topicalization from NPs such as the one we saw in (1) depend on the meaning of the selecting verb.

(2) *<u>Über Syntax</u> hat Sarah [ein Buch] geklaut.
 on syntax has Sarah a book stolen
 'Sarah stole a book on syntax.'

The only difference between the sentence in (1) and the one shown in (2) is that the verb *ausleihen* ('to borrow') is replaced by the verb *klauen* ('to steal').

A second important property was discussed by De Kuthy (2002), who in agreement with Fanselow (1991) observed that supposedly unacceptable examples of the kind illustrated by (2) are in fact acceptable in an appropriate context, as illustrated in (3).

(3) *Gestern wurde in der Bibliothek eine Anzahl von Linguistikbüchern geklaut. Vor allem Semantikbücher verschwanden dabei.*
 'Yesterday, a number of linguistics books were stolen from the library. Mostly books on semantic disappeared.'

 a. <u>Über Syntax</u> wurde jedoch [nur ein einziges Buch] geklaut.
 on syntax was however only one single book stolen
 'There was, however, only one book on syntax stolen.'

In this article, we want to argue that a unified discourse-based explanation for both types of examples becomes available in an approach that makes the information structure of a sentence explicit in terms of Questions under Discussion (QUD; Roberts 2012; Büring 2003; Velleman and Beaver 2016), serving as a link between the sentence and the discourse structure. We propose that partial constituents always involve particular information structure requirements. To empirically ground our approach, we present authentic data containing the above discussed PP topicalization and show that the contexts in which these authentic examples occur all have the necessary properties required by our information-structural analysis.

A relevant example from the Stuttgart 21 corpus, the transcript of a panel discussion broadcasted on German TV, is for example shown in (4).

(4) *Ich habe nur nach dem Ablauf der heutigen Diskussion schon auch den Eindruck, dass viele der Fragen, die wir heute jetzt hier diskutiert haben, und auch die Auswirkungen in nicht unerheblichem Maße durchaus auch bei K21 auftauchen. Weshalb ich nochmal dafür werben würde, das Thema Neubaustrecke, (...), eigentlich eher hinter die Diskussion über die beiden Konzepte zu stellen, weil ich glaube, das wäre, sagen wir mal, wenn ich mir überlege, was sind die Konzepte,*

'I got the impression after today's discussion that many of the questions which we discussed today and also implications occur to a not insignificant extent regarding the traditional train station K21. That is why I want to propose again to postpone the topic of the new railroad tracks after the discussion about the two concepts, because I believe, if I think about what are the concepts, '

a. <u>über Neubaustrecke</u>   besteht zumindest in großen Teilen
   about new railroad tracks exists at least   in large   parts
   immer noch [die Einigkeit], dass man sie bauen möchte.
   still   the consensus   that one it build wants
   'There is at least to a considerable extent a consensus about the new railroad tracks that people want to build them.'

The example showcases the topicalization of a PP, *über Neubaustrecke* ('new railroad tracks') originating from a definite subject NP, *die Einigkeit* 'the consensus'. Interestingly, this is a type of PP topicalization that has mostly been argued to be unacceptable, since the remnant NP, of which the fronted PP *über Neubaustrecke* is a dependent, is a definite subject NP. Both, definite NPs and subject NPs, are usually argued to be islands for extraction. If the topicalized PP is extracted, then such examples should normally be ungrammatical. Another interesting characteristic of this example is the cooccurrence of *Einigkeit* 'consensus' and *besteht* 'exists', which is usually considered to be a support verb construction. Unfortunately, in this paper we will not be able to further investigate in which way such special noun verb combinations influence the acceptability of the PP topicalization, for a discussion of this aspect see De Kuthy (2002: 31).

In addition to naturally occurring data from corpora and to further strengthen our approach, we present the results of a rating study showing that a context that supports the required information structure significantly improves the acceptability of PP topicalizations.

Whatever the assumed underlying process for the above construction is, it thus has to account for the fact that PP topicalization from complex NPs is not only constrained by supposedly syntactic factors. One of the decisive factors are the information structure requirements of this particular word order.

2 Accounts of PP Extraction

Previous approaches to PP extraction from NPs have revealed that extraction of this type is determined by syntactic, semantic, lexical, as well as contextual factors. Syntactic factors involve (i) the syntactic status of the NP (subject vs. object), (ii) its position in the middle field, and (iii) the syntactic status of the extracted PP (adnominal adjunct vs. adnominal argument). We turn to these factors further below. Semantic factors mainly involve the semantics of the verbal predicate (cf. the discussion in Section 1). Lexical factors involve the type of verbal predicate which selects the NP from which extraction takes place. It has also been observed that PP extraction improves under certain discourse conditions. We spell out a specific instance of such conditions in Section 3. Let us first turn to the syntactic factors that have been observed in connection with PP extraction. The purpose of this section is to show that many of the so-called generalizations in the literature are not absolute. Speakers' judgments often vary, and for some cases counter examples from corpora can be given.

Let us consider the type of verbal predicate first. It has been argued in the literature that subextraction from direct object NPs is more acceptable than subextraction from subjects. Extraction from subjects is unproblematic in the case of passives (5a), unaccusatives (5b), and stage predicates, while extraction from agentive subjects is not possible (cf. Diesing 1992; Haider 1993; Pafel 1995; Müller 2010; Schmellentin 2006; Fanselow 2001):

(5) a. *Über wen wurde ein Buch gelesen?*
    about whom was a book read
    'A book about whom was read (by someone)?'
  b. *Über wen ist ein Buch erschienen?*
    about whom is a book appeared
    'A book about whom appeared?'

However, this generalization is not absolute and extraction from agentive subjects is also possible. Examples (6a), which is slightly marked as indicated by the '§', and (6b) are taken from Pafel (1995: 148–149), (6c) is attested:

(6) a. § *Von der ZEIT hat ihn der Chefredakteur angerufen.*
   of the ZEIT has him the chief-editor called-up
   'The chief editor of the ZEIT called him up.'
   b. *Von Wittgenstein haben die Erben protestiert.*
   of Wittgenstein have the heirs protested
   'The heirs of Wittgenstein protested.'
   c. *Aus den neuen Ländern und Berlin treten morgen 7950*
   from the new federal-states and Berlin take-up tomorrow 7950
   Rekruten ihren Wehrdienst bei der Bundeswehr an.
   recruits their military-service with the Bundeswehr
   '7950 recruits from the new federal states and Berlin will take up their military service in the German army tomorrow.'

Example (6a) contains extraction from a subject of the transitive verbal predicate *anrufen* ('call'). It is noteworthy that the example contains a pronominal object which has scrambled over the subject NP. We turn to this issue further below. Note, however, that in (6b-c) extraction is acceptable from a subject of an unergative predicate. This indicates that extraction from agentive subjects cannot be solely dependent on the availability of object scrambling, although scrambling seems to improve extraction from subjects, an effect which has been observed for PP extraction as well as for *was-für* splits (cf. Jurka 2010; Müller 2010: and references therein). The following data taken from Müller (2010: 61) illustrate this effect:

(7) a. * *Über wen hat ein Buch den Fritz beeindruckt?*
   about whom has a book the Fritz impressed
   'A book about whom impressed Fritz?'
   b. *Über wen hat den Fritz ein Buch beeindruckt?*
   about whom has the Fritz a book impressed

It is noteworthy that the difference between (7a) and (7b) is not undisputed. Winkler, Radó, and Gutscher (2016) report that extraction from subjects in *was-für* splits in structurally parallel cases to (7a) improves in a context where the subject is contrastively focused. Moreover, cases like (7b) have also received mixed ratings in the literature. Schmellentin (2006), for instance, assigns a '*' to PP topicalizations in a structurally parallel case to (7b):

(8) * *Über Glauser haben Anna viele Artikel beeindruckt.*
   about Glauser have Anna many articles impressed
   'Many articles about Glauser impressed Anna.'

These mixed ratings indicate that extraction from subject NPs cannot be fully explained in purely syntactic terms and evidence suggests that this phenomenon is partly context dependent. In the next section, we sketch an approach based on QUD which captures this context sensitivity. Before we do, let us take a look at the syntactic status of the extracted PP and the role it plays for acceptability. It has been noted in the literature that extraction of modifiers is more degraded than extraction of arguments. Pafel (1995) classifies *von*-PPs and *über*-PPs as arguments (cf. 6a, 6b and 7a), the *mit*-PP in (9), which is taken from Pafel (1995: 147), is taken to be a modifier:

(9) * *Mit rotem Einband habe ich ein Buch gelesen.*
 with red cover have I a book read
 'I read a book with a red cover.'

However, De Kuthy (2002) observed that even PP extraction of such modifiers improves considerably with context, illustrated in (10).

(10) *Auf der gestrigen Modenschau wurden auch die neuesten Frisuren der Saison vorgestellt.*
 'Yesterday at the fashion show also the newest hair cuts were presented.'

 a. <u>*Mit kurzen Haaren*</u> *wurden nur* [*drei Modelle*] *gezeigt.*
  with short hair were only three models presented
  'Only three models with short hair were presented.'

In this section, we have discussed a number of syntactic and lexical constraints on PP extraction. The data show that each of the syntactic generalizations faces counterevidence. In Section 3, we will lay out a discourse-based approach which connects the PP extraction to specific information-structural requirements.

3 The Proposal: A QUD based Approach

We have observed that in an appropriate context the allegedly ungrammatical PP topicalizations are fully acceptable and that many corpus examples show patterns (as for example a subject NP) that have been argued to be ungrammatical due to syntactic constraints. In order to be able to explain why PP topicalization examples are acceptable only in an appropriate context, we need to establish what the exact properties of such embedding contexts are and which properties of the sentence itself must match the context. This lends itself to an information-structural analysis of the construction, as has already been proposed in De Kuthy (2002). Under her account, splitting a PP dependent from an NP is only possible if "the NP and the PP are not both part of the same focus projection and if they are not both part of the background" (De Kuthy 2002: 149). Taking example (3), repeated here as (11), what is the information structure of the sentence and which factors of the preceding discourse support this information structure?

(11) *Gestern wurde in der Bibliothek eine Anzahl von Linguistikbüchern geklaut. Vor allem Semantikbücher verschwanden dabei.*
 'Yesterday, a number of linguistics books were stolen from the library. Mostly books on semantic disappeared.'

   a. <u>*Über Syntax*</u> *wurde jedoch*   [*nur ein einziges Buch*] *geklaut.*
       on   syntax was   however   only one single book stolen
       'There was, however, only one book on syntax stolen.'

In order to connect the information structure of sentences to the overall structure of the discourse, an analysis in terms of Questions under Discussion is proving to be a useful tool. According to Roberts' (2012) account, natural discourse in general serves to answer hierarchically ordered Questions under Discussion (QUDs). These implicit QUDs can be used to account for the information structure of utterances in context: the part of a sentence contained in the formulation of the current question is called the *background*, while the part which provides the actual answer is the *focus*. Since the formulation of such QUDs should not be an arbitrary process, we base our analysis on the approach developed by Riester, Brunetti, and De Kuthy (2018) in terms of both discourse and information structure, integrating an explicitly spelled out notion of QUDs. Explicit pragmatic principles support the formulation of the relevant QUD for an utterance in the discourse. One of their central principles for the formulation of QUDs is the principle of Q-Givenness stating that "implicit QUDs can only consist of given (or highly salient) material" (Riester, Brunetti, and De Kuthy 2018: 10).

An analysis including an implicit QUD for the PP topicalization is shown in (12).

(12) *Gestern wurde in der Bibliothek eine Anzahl von Linguistikbüchern geklaut.*
Vor allem Semantikbücher verschwanden dabei.
'Yesterday, a number of linguistics books were stolen from the library. Mostly books on semantic disappeared.'

Q_1: How many books on which topics were stolen from the library?
$Q_{1.1}$: How many books on syntax were stolen?
$A_{1.1}$: [<u>*Über Syntax*</u>]$_{CT}$ wurde jedoch   [*nur* [*ein einziges*]$_F$ *Buch*]
on   syntax   was   however   only   one single   book
geklaut.
stolen
'There was, however, only one book on syntax stolen.'

There are two interesting observations that help us to precisely characterize the connection between the context and our PP extraction example: The first observation is, that the context introduces two alternative sets, which are picked up by the fronted PP and the remnant NP: an alternative set for the number of books that were stolen and an alternative set for the kinds of books that were stolen. Secondly, a question about some entity (here about the number of linguistic books that were stolen) is not answered directly but is broken down into answers about smaller parts or elements of that entity. Following the account of Büring (2003), these parts are called *contrastive topics*. This idea is also included in the pragmatic principles guiding the formulation of QUDs in Riester, Brunetti, and De Kuthy (2018) as the *Parallelism Constraint*, in which for two or more parallel sentences with two variable positions each, the common QUD should establish the semantically common material of the answers as the background. This common QUD can then be further divided into two or more partial questions. One of the positions in the answers to these partial questions is then a contrastive topic, the other a focus. In our case, one of the subquestions of Q_1 in example (12) asks about the number of syntax books, another subquestion could ask for example about another kind of books that were stolen, as for example books about morphology. The fronted PP and the part of the remnant NP contain the answers to this question, i.e. the fronted PP *über Syntax* 'about syntax' is a contrastive topic, whereas the specifier *ein einziges* 'one single' of the remnant NP is the focus of the sentence. This analysis is in line with the pragmatic constraint formulated by De Kuthy (2002): One part of the split NP is a contrastive topic, the other a focus, i.e. they are not both part of the same focus or the background in the entire clause.

Our analysis nicely carries over to an observation already made by Fanselow (1991: 185). He observes that certain PP extractions from NPs are only acceptable in an appropriate context and the context he provides for his example (13) exhibits similar properties as the one of our example in (11).

(13) *Schau her, was Britt, deine Tochter, mit meiner Biographiensammlung angestellt hat! Die Bücher sind zerissen, bemalt und mit Brei bekleckert! Zwei meiner Bände über Carnap sind entzwei. Drei von meinen Biographien über Bloomfield sind zerfetzt, und (...)*
'Look, what Britt, your daughter, did with my collection of biographies! The books are torn, painted and stained with food! Two of my volumes about Carnap are destroyed. Three of my biographies about Bloomfield are torn up, and (...)'

a. <u>über</u>   Chomsky   hat   sie   sogar   [alle Bücher]   zerrissen.
   about   Chomsky   has   she   even   all   books   torn
   'all books about Chomsky are torn.'

Again, the context in (13) introduces two alternative sets: The number of books that have been destroyed and the set of authors whose books are among the destroyed books. We can thus introduce a similar QUD structure as in (12), as shown in (14).

(14) *Schau her, was Britt, deine Tochter, mit meiner Biographiensammlung angestellt hat! Die Bücher sind zerissen, bemalt und mit Brei bekleckert! Zwei meiner Bände über Carnap sind entzwei.*
'Look, what Britt, your daughter, did with my collection of biographies! The books are torn, painted and stained with food! Two of my volumes about Carnap are destroyed.'

Q_7:   How many books has   she   destroyed?
$Q_{7.1}$: How many books about Bloomfield has she destroyed?
$A_{7.1}$: [Drei]$_F$ von meinen Biographien über Bloomfield sind zerfetzt
       three of   my   biographies about Bloomfield are   torn
       und
       and
       'Three of my biographies about Bloomfield are torn up, and'

$Q_{7.2}$: How many books about Chomsky has she destroyed?
$A_{7.2}$: [<u>über   Chomsky</u>]$_{CT}$ hat   sie sogar [alle]$_F$ Bücher zerrissen.
       about Chomsky   has   she even   all   books torn
       'she has torn up all books about Chomsky.'

Following from the question-answer congruence between the QUD $Q_{7.2}$ and the answer $A_{7.2}$, the topicalized PP *über Chomsky* 'about Chomsky' is the contrastive topic and the specifier *alle* 'all' of the remnant NP *alle Bücher* 'all books' functions as the focus.

This type of analysis is also readily supported by naturally occurring data exemplifying the phenomenon. Topicalized PPs and their immediate context we found in corpora nicely pattern with the just observed information-structural restrictions.

As already briefly discussed in Section 1, example (15) (Stuttgart 21 corpus) involves a PP topicalization originating from a definite subject NP.

(15) *Ich habe nur nach dem Ablauf der heutigen Diskussion schon auch den Eindruck, dass viele der Fragen, die wir heute jetzt hier diskutiert haben, und auch die Auswirkungen in nicht unerheblichem Maße durchaus auch bei K21 auftauchen. Weshalb ich nochmal dafür werben würde, das Thema Neubaustrecke, (...), eigentlich eher hinter die Diskussion über die beiden Konzepte zu stellen, weil ich glaube, das wäre, sagen wir mal, wenn ich mir überlege, was sind die Konzepte,*
'I got the impression after today's discussion that many questions which we discussed today and also the implications also occur with the traditional train station K21. That is why I want to propose again to postpone the topic of the new railroad tracks after the discussion about the two concepts, because I believe, if I think about what are the concepts,'

    a. <u>Über Neubaustrecke</u>   *besteht zumindest in großen Teilen*
       about new railroad tracks exists at least in large parts
       immer noch [die Einigkeit], dass man sie bauen möchte.
       still the consensus that one it build wants
       'There is to at least a considerable extent a consensus about the new railroad tracks that people want to build them.'

Example (16) shows a possible QUD analysis of the respective sentence containing the topicalized PP *über Neubaustrecke* ('about new railroad tracks').

(16) Q_1: *Which discussion basis exists in relation to which train station concept?*
     $Q_{1.1}$: *Which discussion basis exists in relation to the concept of building new railroad tracks?*
     $A_{1.1}$: [<u>Über Neubaustrecke</u>]$_{CT}$ *besteht zumindest in*
         about new railroad tracks exists at least in

großen Teilen immer noch [die Einigkeit, dass man sie bauen möchte.]$_F$
large parts always still the consensus that one it build
wants

'There is to at least a considerable extent a consensus about the new railroad tracks that people want to build them.'

Again, two alternative sets are introduced in the context: a set containing the different alternative building concepts, and the other set consists of the different discussion viewpoints about which kind of train station should be built. The QUD Q_1, to which the sentence $A_{1.1}$ containing the topicalized PP provides an answer, asks about the discussion basis and the train station concepts, and in the more specific subquestion $Q_{1.1}$, an answer to the train station concepts is already included. This PP *über Neubaustrecke* ('about new railroad tracks') thus serves as the contrastive topic and the NP *die Einigkeit* ('the consensus') provides an answer to question about the discussion basis and thus functions as the focus in this sentence.

In a parallel example, (17) from the TAZ newspaper (5.5.1999: 4), two alternative sets are introduced: one about the different kinds of strategies in connection with the war in Serbia, and one about the opinions about these strategies.

(17) *Deshalb werde es zunächst eine 24-stündige Feuerpause geben, die verlängert werde, wenn sich die serbische Seite weiter zurückziehe. Die Luftschläge würden eingestellt, wenn zudem von serbischer Seite die Kampfhandlungen und Vertreibungen beendet würden.*

'Therefore, there will be a preliminary cease of fire for 24 hours, which will be prolonged, if the Serbs retreat further. The air strikes will be stopped if in addition the Serbs stop any fighting and displacement.'

Q: *Which opinion exists about which procedure among the western G8 countries?*

A: *[Über diese Vorgehen]$_{CT}$ bestehe [Einigkeit]$_F$ unter den westlichen*
about these procedures consists agreement among the Western
G8-Staaten.
G8 countries

'There is agreement about these procedures among the western G8 countries.'

A QUD analysis of this example shows that the fronted PP *über dieses Vorgehen* ('about this procedure') is a contrastive topic and the remnant NP *Einigkeit* ('agreement') is the focus (it refers to one of the points of view regarding the strategies in the contrastive topic and provides an answers to the QUD).

Interestingly, such a fine-grained QUD analysis can also account for cases where only part of the fronted PP picks up an element from the discourse alternative set, as exemplified in (18) from taz Bremen (14.10.1995: 29).

(18) *Und Sonntag ist Filmtag: Schon in der Matinee um 11 Uhr im Bürgerhaus Weserterassen läuft "Und täglich grüßt das Murmeltier" (...) Weniger prosaisch die Filme von Velu Viswanadhan.*
'Sunday is movie day: Already at 11 a.m. the movie "Groundhog Day" is showing (...) Less prosaic are the movies from Velu Viswanadhan.'

Q: *What is opening in which respect to the Indian painter in the movie theater?*

A: [*Über den indischen Maler und Filmemacher*]$_{CT}$ *eröffnet um 12*
about the Indian painter and film maker opens at 12
Uhr im Kino 46 [*eine Ausstellung*]$_F$.
o'clock in the cinema 46 an exhibition
'An exhibition about the Indian painter and film maker will open at 12 o'clock in the cinema.'

As before, the context in (18) introduces two alternative sets, one set consists of the relation in which the Indian filmmaker stands to films, exhibitions etc., i.e. a film *about* him, a film *of* him, the other set consists of things, events related to a filmmaker, i.e. films, exhibitions etc. In the proposed QUD analysis the matching QUD for the sentence in (18) thus asks about this relation and about an element from the second set. The preposition *über* ('about') in (18) provides an answer to the relation, and is thus the contrastive topic, the remnant NP *eine Austellung* ('an exhibition') answers the other part of the question and thus functions as the focus in this sentence.[1]

As observed in De Kuthy (2002), PP topicalization from an NP is not only acceptable in contexts where the fronted PP (or parts of it) functions as a contrastive topic, and the remnant NP functions as the focus. She provides

---

[1] An anonymous reviewer points out that the topicalized PP in (18) is not necessarily interpreted as a contrastive topic. Contrastive topics typically carry rising accents which is not necessarily the case in this example. We leave this option open for future research since a detailed analysis of the intonational contours would be needed.

examples where the context introduces two alternative sets such that other material than the remnant NP can function as the focus. In example (19) it is the main verb *ausgeliehen* ('borrowed') at the end of the sentence that functions as the focus.

(19) Q: *Hat Detmar ein Buch über Mozart gekauft?*
'Did Detmar buy a book about Mozart?'
A: [*Über MOZART*]$_{CT}$ *hat Detmar ein Buch* [*AUSGELIEHEN.*]$_F$
about Mozart has Detmar a book borrowed
(*und über Bach hat er eins gekauft.*)
and about Bach has he one Bought
'Detmar has borrowed a book about Mozart and bought one about Bach.'
(De Kuthy 2002: 132)

The parallel example in (20) exhibits this pattern involving PP topicalization from a subject NP (De Kuthy 2002: 134).

(20) Q: *Wo stehen die Porzellanfiguren aus den berühmten Sammlungen?*
'Where are the porcelain figurines from the famous collections?'
A: [*Aus der ROTHSCHILD-Sammlung*]$_{CT}$ *steht eine Porzellanfigur*
from the Rothschild collection is a porcelain figurine
[*in der VITRINE.*]$_F$
in the display
'From the Rothschild collection, there is a porcelain figurine in the display.'

Again, two contrastive alternative sets are established via the question context. The topicalized PP *aus der Rothschildsammlung* ('from the Rothschild collection') selects an element from one of the context sets, the verbal argument PP *in der Vitrine* ('in the display') picks up an element from the other alternative set, while the remnant NP *eine Porzellanfigur* ('a porcelain figurine') is part of the background of the entire clause.

As motivated by the example analyses in this section, PP topicalization resulting from a complex NP involves particular information-structural requirements: The context establishes two alternative sets, such that the fronted PP (or parts of it) functions as a contrastive topic, and the remnant NP or some other constituent from the rest of the clause functions as the focus. In consequence, this must thus also be true of sentences lacking an explicitly provided context such as (1) – an appropriate QUD must then be sufficiently salient based on the lexical material in the sentence alone.

Making this QUD analysis concrete, it means that when reading (1), one can readily accommodate the QUD to obtain the question-answer pair in (21), supporting the occurrence of the partial constituent. For the example (2), on the other hand, the QUD needed to license the partial constituent is so unusual, as illustrated in (22), that the QUD is not readily accommodated without an explicit textual context, such as the one we saw in (3).

(21) Q: *What did Sarah borrow about which topic?*
A: [*Über Syntax*]$_{CT}$ *hat Sarah sich* [*ein Buch*]$_F$ *ausgeliehen.*

(22) Q: *What did Sarah steal about which topic?*
A: [*Über Syntax*]$_{CT}$ *hat Sarah* [*ein Buch*]$_F$ *geklaut.*

In sum, a discourse-based approach formulated in terms of QUD is capable of providing a discourse-based explanation for the occurrence of partial constituents, such as the here discussed PP topicalization, and the role that information structure plays in this regard.

4 Experimental Evidence

In this section, we provide experimental evidence for the account presented in Section 3. In particular, we test the hypothesis that PP extraction from NPs is licensed by contexts that provide two sets of alternatives: one for the extracted PP and one for the remnant NP. Moreover, we have established in Section 3 that the remnant NP is typically focused. This account makes two kinds of predictions. First, under the information-structural conditions spelled-out above, we would predict that PP extraction should benefit more from an adequate context than the corresponding condition without PP extraction. We assume that a sentence without PP extraction cannot receive a contrastive topic interpretation. Second, since we expect the remnant NP to be focused, we also predict a difference with respect to the word order in the middle field. Focused material is realized preverbally in the German middle field (Höhle 1982), hence we would expect that a remnant NP should be dispreferred in a scrambled position in the middle field relative to a second constituent that is discourse given. The sensitivity of subextraction from NPs to the relative order of constituents in the middle field has been noted in the literature (cf. Müller

2010). Under the present approach these differences fall out from information-structural constraints which determine the distribution of focal material in the middle field. In the following section, we specify these effects with an experimental design and derive predictions which will be tested in a rating study.

4.1 Method

4.1.1 Design and Materials

In this experiment we test two aspects of PP extraction. The first concerns the contextual licensing, i.e. the question how the discourse has to be set up for PP extraction to be licensed. The second question concerns the relative position of the host NP in the middle field. To investigate the first question, we compare PP extraction to PP in situ with and without context. Moreover, we manipulate the relative order of constituents in the middle field to see whether this has an effect on extraction. We concentrate on extraction from subject NPs, which is the most controversial case.

Let us concentrate first on the set-up of the context. Recall from Section 3 that PP-extraction from NPs is particularly felicitous if two contrastive sets are contextually salient, one which provides context alternatives for the extracted PP and a second which provides alternatives for the remnant NP from which extraction took place. A PP extraction case with such a context is given in (23) below:

(23) Context:
Daniel liest gerne Bücher über amerikanische Geschichte. Insbesondere interessieren ihn Bürgerrechtler.
'Daniel likes reading books about the history of the US. He is particularly interested in civil rights activists.'

Target item:
Über Marin Luther King hat den Daniel ein Roman
about Martin Luther King has the Daniel a novel
fasziniert.
fascinated
'Daniel was fascinated by a novel about Martin Luther King.'

In the target item in (23) the PP *über Martin Luther King* 'about Martin Luther King' is extracted from the complex subject NP *ein Roman über Martin Luther King* 'a novel about Martin Luther King'. The context introduces a set of alternatives 'books about the history of the US' for the the NP 'novels' and a set of alternatives for the PP: 'civil rights activists'. We pursue two research questions with this context manipulation. First, is there a difference between the PP extraction and the PP in situ with respect to context sensitivity? If PP extraction is context sensitive, as hypothesized in this study, we should observe that PP extraction improves if presented with the context given in (23) while no such effect should be observed with PP in situ. Second, does the context manipulation interact with word order in the middle field? If the host NP from which extraction takes place must contain a focus we would predict that the subject should directly precede the verb in the middle field since this is the position where focus in the middle field is typically realized. We thus arrive at a 2x2 design for the within factors 'extraction' (split vs. base) and middle field 'word order' (SO vs. OS). The conditions are given below:

(24) Conditions:
Context: Daniel liest gerne Bücher über amerikanische Geschichte. Insbesondere interessieren ihn Bürgerrechtler.
'Daniel likes reading books about the history of the US. He is particularly interested in civil rights activists.'

1. *Über Martin Luther King hat ein Roman den Daniel*
   about Martin Luther King has the Daniel a novel
   fasziniert. (SO/split)
   fascinated

2. *Über Martin Luther King hat den Daniel ein Roman*
   about Martin Luther King has the Daniel a novel
   fasziniert. (OS/split)
   fascinated

3. *Neulich hat ein Roman über Martin Luther King den Daniel*
   recently has a novel about Martin Luther King the Daniel
   fasziniert. (SO/base)
   fascinated

4. *Neulich hat den Daniel ein Roman über Martin Luther King*
   recently has the Daniel a novel about Martin Luther King
   fasziniert. (OS/base)
   fascinated

To investigate the effect of context, one group of participants saw the items with and another group without context. This makes 'context' a between subjects factor. The overall design is thus 2x2x2.

4.1.2 Participants and Procedure

Two experimental studies were conducted over the web using the OnExp software for data collection. A total of 96 self-declared native speakers of German participated in the studies. Most of them were students at the University of Tübingen. 43 individuals completed the experiment without context, 53 individuals completed the version with context. Acceptability ratings were collected using a 7-point scale, '1' corresponding to completely unacceptable and '7' to fully acceptable. At the beginning of the experiment, participants identified their age, gender and language background. Each experimental session started with a practice block, where participants saw four practice items to familiarize themselves with the task. Overall, we constructed 16 experimental items according to the design in (24). They were distributed over four different lists according to a Latin square design. In total, participants rated 66 sentences, which were presented in a randomized order, 16 experimental items and 50 fillers.

4.2 Results

We conducted an ANOVA analysis with the factors 'extraction' and 'word order' as within factors and 'context' as a between factor. We concentrate on two questions. First, does the context manipulation have a stronger effect on extraction than on PP in situ? Second, can we observe an effect of context on the word order in the middle field? The results are illustrated in Figure 1. We observe that the extraction conditions benefit from the context manipulation more than the base conditions.

The interaction of the factors 'extraction' and 'context' was significant [$F1(1,94) = 5.5$; $p < .05$; $F2(1,15) = 8,5$; $p < .05$]. This interaction is based on the fact that the split conditions received significantly higher ratings with context than without [$t1(1,94)=3.1$; $p <.01$; $t2(1,15)=6,8$; $p <.001$], while there was no significant improvement for the base conditions. With respect to the context sensitivity of the word order in the middle field, we observed an interaction of the factors 'extraction, and 'word order' that was significant by subject and marginal by items [$F1(1,94) = 7.1$; $p < .001$; $F2(1,15) = 3,9$; $p < .07$]. This interaction corresponds to a context sensitivity which is present for OS word order [$t1(1,94)=2,6$; $p <.01$; $t2(1,15)=3,9$; $p <.001$] but absent for SO word order.

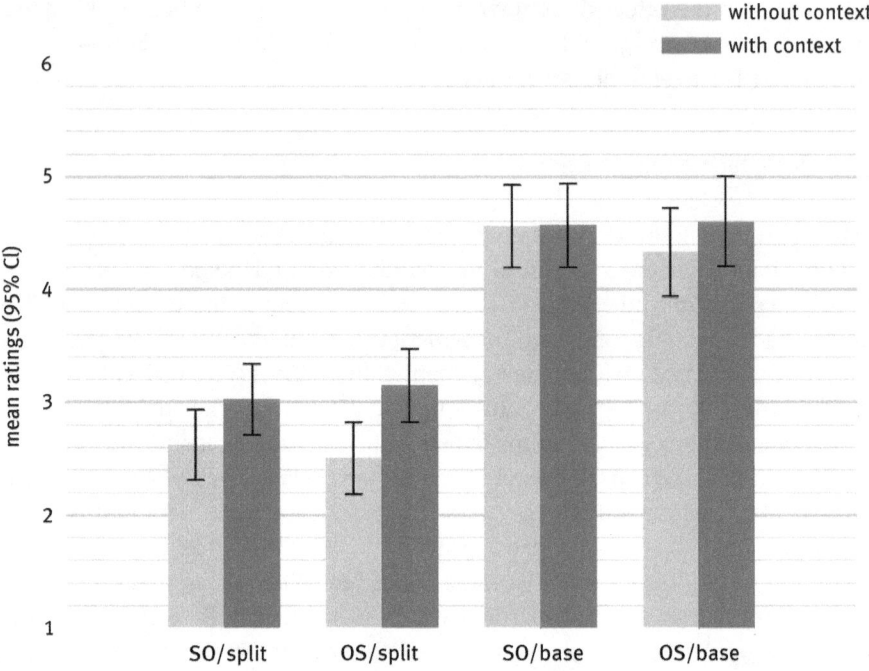

Figure 1: Experimental Results.

4.3 Discussion

Our experimental results prvide evidence for the context sensitivity of PP topicalization from complex subject NPs compared to PPs in situ. This effect was shown to occur under specific discourse conditions which support the information-structural requirements of the NP split as discussed in Section 3. More importantly, we were able to show that this discourse effect is sensitive to word order. Extraction from subject NP receives higher ratings if the subject is preceded by a scrambled object, which results in a OS word order in the middle field. This suggests that extraction from subjects is particularly felicitous if the subject NP occupies a focal position. Under such conditions the subject NP is transparent for extraction. The experimental results thus provide evidence for the information-structural account laid out in this paper. This account links the information-structural requirements of the sentence, which are determined by its focus structure, to the discourse structure. Our results support the view that extraction becomes possible if the information-structural requirements of the sentence converge with the discourse structure, which has to provide the appropriate QUD.

5 Conclusion

In this article, we have presented a discourse-based account of PP topicalization from NPs which shows that supposedly syntactic restrictions on extraction from NPs instead follow from particular information-structural conditions. We have spelled out a detailed account of the discourse properties of PP topicalization based on a QUD and information-structural analysis of this particular word order phenomenon. As a result of this detailed information-structural analysis we were able to show that PP-extraction from NPs is particularly felicitous if two contrastive alternative sets are contextually salient. In this case the topicalized PP (or parts of this PP) functions as a contrastive topic. This account is in line with an approach already presented in De Kuthy (2002), which includes an information-structural requirement for PP topicalization stating that "not both, the fronted PP and the remnant NP, can be part of the same focus in an utterance". Such specific conditions of the information structure of PP topicalization impose requirements on the preceding context of the construction, for example that the appropriate alternative sets for the fronted PP and the remnant NP have to be introduced. If these conditions are met, extraction becomes possible, even for subject NPs. Under this view, additional constraints for subjects, which have been formulated in syntactic terms in the literature, can be dispensed with. Our account is supported empirically by corpus and experimental evidence and provides an explanation for the diverging judgments for NP splits in the literature. They follow from the context dependency of PP extraction, i.e. how easy it is to come up with a context for a given sentence. These context requirements are quite complex and articulate, as we have shown. Our approach also opens up a way to explain language-specific differences with respect to island phenomena. It has been observed in the literature that subject NPs in German are to a far lesser extent opaque for extraction than e.g. in English (for discussion cf. Haider 2010). The transparency of subjects for extraction follows if the language has an option to provide a way that the subject can end up in a focal position, e.g. via scrambling of the object over it, as in German. The possibility of extracting from the subject thus follows from independent syntactic properties of the language and whether these properties have a consequence for the information-structural set-up of the clause.

Acknowledgments: This research was carried out by projects A4 'Comparing Meaning in Context: Generalization of Information Structure and Reference Text' and A7 'Focus and Extraction in Complex Constructions and Islands' of the SFB

833 'The Construction of Meaning', funded by the German Research Foundation (DFG). We would like to thank Detmar Meurers, Susanne Winkler, Lorenz Geiger, Robin Hörnig, Marion Jäger, Andreas Kehl, and two anonymous reviewers for comments, help and suggestions. All remaining errors are ours.

References

Büring, Daniel. 2003. On D-trees, beans, and B-accents. *Linguistics and Philosophy* 26(5). 511–545.
De Kuthy, Kordula. 2002. *Discontinuous NPs in German — a case study of the interaction of syntax, semantics and pragmatics*. Stanford, CA: CSLI Publications.
Diesing, Molly. 1992. Bare plural subjects and the derivation of logical represertations. *Linguistic Inquiry* 23. 353–380.
Fanselow, Gisbert. 1991. *Minimale Syntax – Untersuchungen zur Sprachfähigkeit*. Passau: Universität Passau Habilitationsschrift. (Groninger Arbeiten zur Germanistischen Linguistik 32). Rijksuniversiteit Groningen.
Fanselow, Gisbert. 2001. Features, θ-roles, and free constituent order. *Linguistic Inquiry* 32(3). 405–437.
Haider, Hubert. 1993. *Deutsche Syntax — generativ: Vorstudien zu einer projektiven Grammatik*. Tübingen: Gunter Narr Verlag.
Haider, Hubert. 2010. *The syntax of German*. Cambridge: Cambridge University Press.
Höhle, Tilman N. 1982. Explikationen für 'normale Betonung' und 'normale Wortstellung'. In Werner Abraham (ed.), *Satzglieder im Deutschen*, 75–153. Tübingen: Gunter Narr Verlag.
Jurka, Johannes. 2010. *The importance of being a complement: CED effects revisited*. College Park, MD: University of Maryland dissertation.
Müller, Gereon. 2010. On deriving CED effects from the PIC. *Linguistic Inquiry* 41(1). 35–82.
Pafel, Jürgen. 1995. Kinds of extraction from noun phrases. In Uli Lutz & Jürgen Pafel (eds.), *On extraction and extraposition in German*, vol. 2 (Linguistik aktuell 11), 145–178. Amsterdam & Philadelphia: John Benjamins.
Riester, Arndt, Lisa Brunetti & Kordula De Kuthy. 2018. Annotation guidelines for questions under discussion and information structure. In Evangelia Adamou, Katharina Haude & Martine Vanhove (eds.), *Information structure in lesser-described languages: Studies in prosody and syntax*, 403–443. Amsterdam & Philadelphia: John Benjamins.
Roberts, Craige. 2012. Information structure in discourse: Towards an integrated formal theory of pragmatics. *Semantics and Pragmatics* 5(6). 1–69.
Schmellentin, Claudia. 2006. *PP-Extraktionen: Eine Untersuchung zum Verhältnis von Grammatik und Pragmatik* (Linguistische Arbeiten 507). Tübingen: Max Niemeyer Verlag.
Velleman, Leah & David Beaver. 2016. Question-based models of information structure. In Caroline Féry & Shinichiro Ishihara (eds.), *The Oxford handbook of information structure*, 86–107. Oxford: Oxford University Press.
Winkler, Susanne, Janina Radó & Marian Gutscher. 2016. What determines 'freezing' effects in was-für split constructions? In Sam Featherston & Yannik Versley (eds.), *Firm foundations: Quantitative approaches to grammar and grammatical change* (Trends in Linguistics: Studies and Monographs 290), 207–231. Berlin & New York: Mouton de Gruyter.

Nomi Erteschik-Shir
Stage Topics and their Architecture

Abstract: All focus sentences have implicit "stage" topics indicating the spatio-temporal parameters of the sentence, the here-and-now of the discourse. Such topics can provide the main topic of the sentence and can also appear as the topics of subordinate clauses. This paper is about the role of stage topics in grammar including the distinction between stage and individual level predicates, anaphora in sentences with verbs of perception, the definiteness effect in existentials and extraction out of picture noun phrases and relative clauses.

Keywords: thetic sentence, truth-value, stage-level predicates, existentials, the definiteness effect, information structure, extraction, perception predicates

1 Introduction

Do all-focus or thetic sentences have a topic? Gundel (1974) argues that the topic of such sentences is "the particular situation (time and place) about which it is asserted", a "stage" topic in my terms. This paper outlines the properties of such stage topics and argues that they play an important role in accounting for a wide range of syntactic and semantic problems. The next section defines stage topics as the pivot for truth-value assessment. The following section argues that stage-level predicates are distinguished from individual level predicates by having stage topics. This affords an explanation of why it is not just the lexical properties of predicates that matters but also the context in which they are uttered. Section 4 introduces the Information Structure (IS) framework within which stage topics are to be understood. The topic of section 5 is existentials and the definiteness effect. It is shown that the contextual parameters of stage topics predict whether or not the definiteness effect applies. Section 6 deals with the lexical selection of stages by intensional and perception predicates. Section 7 argues that the presence of stage topics with certain verbs explains extraction out of their picture noun phrase complements and the relative clauses modifying their complements. The concluding section summarizes the properties of stage topics argued for in the paper and comments on an architecture of grammar that includes them.

Nomi Erteschik-Shir, Ben-Gurion University

https://doi.org/10.1515/9781501504488-008

2 What is a Stage Topic?

Topics are what the sentence is 'about' and the truth value of a sentence is determined with respect to them (Reinhart 1981, Strawson 1964). Since sentences may have more than one topic, the 'main' topic (often the syntactically highest one, i.e., a subject or one that is topicalized) is the pivot for truth value assessment. Depending on context, however, any one of the topics in a sentence can play this role. Only referential expressions serve as topics. Topics are prototypically referential DPs with a discoursal antecedent. Weak (unstressed) pronouns are therefore by definition topics and can be used to test which constituent types may function as a topic. Just as the availability of weak personal pronouns indicates that referential DPs qualify as topics, the existence of temporal and locative pronouns (*then, there*) show that spatio-temporal expressions may function as topics. Although topics are necessarily given or presupposed, not all presupposed elements are topics.

Since the topic is the pivot for truth value assessment every sentence must contain at least one topic. This must also be the case for all-focus or thetic sentences. Erteschik-Shir (1997) analyzes such sentences as having an implicit or overt "stage" topic indicating the spatio-temporal parameters of the sentence (the here-and-now of the discourse). Gundel (1974) proposes "(...) that the given element and hence also the topic of sentences (...) which answer some implicit question like *What happened?*, is the particular situation (time and place) about which it is asserted (questioned, etc.). Since this element is almost always recoverable in the context in which the sentence is uttered, it may be deleted, and thus need not be overtly represented in surface structure at all", In the following interchange the question 'what happened?' questions an event taking place in the current here-and-now indicating that the question itself has an implicit stage topic. The answer, then, illustrates an all-focus sentence with a stage topic:

(1) Q: *What happened?*
    A: *John broke the vase.*

The answer must be evaluated with respect to the stage topic (the current here-and-now defined by the question). Evaluation with respect to *John* or *the vase* is in principle also possible, but would contradict the context specified by the question. I use sTOP$_t$ to indicate a stage topic. 's' and 't' indicate the spatial and temporal parameters of the stage.[1] The Information Structure (IS) of the answer in (1) is therefore:

(2) sTOP$_t$ [John broke the vase]$_{FOC}$

Some sentences *must* be predicated of a stage topic independently of context, since they have no other arguments which can play the role of a topic. This is shown in (3).

(3) sTOP$_t$ [It's snowing]$_{FOC}$

The truth value of such sentences can only be evaluated with respect to the stage topic indicating the current here-and-now.

Stage topics can also be overt. Compare (4a) and (4b):

(4) a. sTOPt$_i$ [There's a cat [outside the door]$_i$]$_{FOC}$
     b. [Outside the door]$_{sTOPt}$ [there's a cat]$_{FOC}$

(4a) is evaluated with respect to the implicit stage topic, the current time and location of the discourse. *Outside the door* modifies this location (note coindexing), so the sentence will be true only if the cat is outside the door (here-and-now). In (4b), the PP is topicalized and as any topic requires previous mention of this location. This renders the interpretation that it is true of the location 'outside the door' of the here-and-now that a cat is there. The two sentences are therefore equivalent in truth value.[2]

3 Individual and Stage Topics

According to Kratzer (1989, 1995), stage level predicates may, but need not have a spatio-temporal argument. (5a) illustrates a stage level predicate. Stage level predicates are ambiguous. Either the sentence is predicated of the stage topic, that is, it is evaluated with respect to the current here-and-now or else it indicates a property of firefighters, whereas (5b) with the individual level predicate 'intelligent' only

---
[1] Although both 's' and 't' are indices of the stage. I place the 's' in front of TOP for ease of visibility.
[2] Further explanation for how this comes about is offered in Section 4.

has the latter meaning, i.e., intelligence is interpreted as a property of the subject, the dog.

(5) a. *Firefighters are (always) available.*
    b. *The dog is intelligent.*

According to Kratzer, the spatio-temporal argument is represented in logical structure as a variable which is supplied with a value by the context of use.

If instead of a spatio-temporal argument we view the sentence as having a stage topic, as proposed in Erteschik-Shir (1997), then this would follow from the nature of topics which are always determined by the context of use.[3] The spatio-temporal parameters of the discourse are always available and can therefore play the role of a topic. The IS of each of the interpretations of (5a) is given in (6a) and (6b) and the single IS of (5b) is given in (7).

(6) a. sTOP$_t$ [Firefighters are available]$_{FOC}$
    b. [Firefighters]$_{TOP}$[are (always) available]$_{FOC}$

(7) [the dog]$_{TOP}$ [is intelligent]$_{FOC}$

(7) offers a plausible IS of a sentence with an I-level predicate but requires a constraint on such predicates that they cannot select a stage topic. An alternative analysis follows from the observation that sentences with I-level predicates are true of ALL times and places. This result can be derived if we assume a generic (unindexed) reference time and location. One approach to blocking the possibility of a *contextual* stage topic, indexed with the current time and place, is to have one of the arguments be identified or indexed with this generic stage. The IS would then be the one shown in (8).

(8) [the dog]$_{sTOP}$ [is intelligent]$_{FOC}$

The individual topic of individual level predicates is thus viewed as taking on the spatio-temporal parameters of a generic stage topic.[4] The interpretation

---

3 É. Kiss (1999: 685) similarly proposes that thetic sentences are about the event: "(...) thetic judgments can be analyzed as covert predication structures predicating about a phonologically empty, but deictically or anaphorically bound event argument, that is, about 'here-and-now', or 'there and then'. This would explain why individual-level predicates, possessing no event argument, cannot participate in thetic judgments".
4 Generic stage topics are introduced in section 4.

which follows is that it is true of *the dog*, at any reference time and any location, that *it is intelligent*. In this way the individual dog will not get its locative and temporal parameters from context and the sentence is true of all times and places in which this individual occurs. Evidence for this analysis follows from the interpretation of sentences with I-level predicates in the past tense:

(9) [the dog]$_{sTOP}$ [was intelligent]$_{FOC}$

One interpretation of such a sentence is that *the dog* must be in the past, i.e., the dog is dead. This follows because the past tense modifies the stage to be in the past. The interpretation that the dog was intelligent sometime in the past is not available since the past tense fixes the temporal parameter of the stage to the past identifying the dog as being in the past. As a reviewer pointed out, the context in (10) which puts the current stage in the past, renders the interpretation that it is a property of the dog at that time to be intelligent as in (8).

(10) *We had a family come to visit us last week. The dog was intelligent; the family was not.*

S-level predicates also allow I-level interpretations as shown in (6b). I-level predicates, however, are generally restricted to this interpretation. A parsimonious grammar should allow free assignment of ISs to sentences, allowing for contextual stage topics with I-level predicates as shown in (11), rendering the interpretation that the dog, at the current here-and-now is intelligent.

(11) sTOP$_t$ [the dog is intelligent]$_{FOC}$

Such an interpretation could be feasible in the context of a science fiction scenario and should not be excluded. Allowing for both ISs for I-level as well as S-level predicates also does not necessitate constraints on the type of topic selected by I-level predicates thus simplifying both the lexicon and the grammar. Another benefit of this approach is a simple account of the following well-known examples:

(12) a. *Pigs have red eyes.*
b. *John has red eyes.*

Both sentences allow for both ISs. The interpretations that pigs' eyes are red at a certain time and place is excluded by world knowledge. Similarly the interpretation that John's eyes are permanently red, is also excluded by world knowledge. Both these interpretations can of course be contextualized (pigs in a children's story, John is not human, etc.).[5]

I conclude that all sentences have stage topics and that stage topics can be indexed or not. In the latter case the parameters of the stage topic are associated with an argument as in (9). It follows that the subject of an intransitive I-level predicate, in a normal context, is necessarily interpreted as the topic of the sentence. Intransitive individual level predicates therefore provide an excellent test for topichood. Any element that can function as a subject of such sentences must qualify as a topic. As expected definites are possible topics.

(13) a. *The little boy is intelligent.*
 b. *He is intelligent.*
 c. *John is intelligent.*

As shown in (14) (capitals indicate stress) indefinites are also possible topics. Only non-generic indefinites are excluded:

(14) a. #*A boy is intelligent.*
 b. *Dogs/a dog are/is intelligent.* (only generic)
 c. *A student I know is intelligent.* (specific)
 d. *A DOG is intelligent, a CAT is not.* (contrastive)
 e. *TWO/SOME (of) the students are intelligent.* (partitive)

These facts can be accounted for within a theory of information structure (IS) which is both sensitive to definiteness and which also keeps track of those discourse referents that are 'given' and can be topics and also allows for the introduction of new potential topics as presented in the next section.

4 Topic, Focus and File-Change

Topics, as presented in the introduction, are what the sentence is about.[6] Incorporating Reinhart's (1981) basic insight into their nature, topics represent existing

---

[5] A much more detailed account of the stage/individual level distinction is given in Cohen and Erteschik-Shir (1992) in the context of an analysis of the interpretation of bare plurals.
[6] This section provides an outline of the file-change system. I refer the reader to Erteschik-Shir (1997) for details including an account of how intonation is accounted for within this system.

cards which must both be old *and* "prominent" in the discourse and these cards provide the locus for truth value assignment. According to Reinhart, the common ground is represented by a set of file cards. Each file card represents a discourse referent.

In Erteschik-Shir (1997) this system was adapted to incorporate the notion of focus. The set of file cards are viewed as partially ordered, with the cards for potential topics positioned prominently on top of the stack of cards. Permanently available on top of the stack are the cards for the current stage, as well as the cards for the speaker and the hearer. This is what allows these referents to be topics in the initial utterance of a conversation. Additional cards are added to the top of the stack when the card (the referent it represents) is focused. This follows implicitly from the definition of focus:

(15) The Focus of a sentence S = the (intension of a) constituent c of S which the speaker intends to direct the attention of his/her hearer(s) to, by uttering S. (Erteschik-Shir 1973, Erteschik-Shir and Lappin 1979)

The focus is, according to its definition here, the constituent to which the hearer's attention is drawn. Translated into the file system, this means that focused cards are placed prominently in the file. Utterances are conceived of as a set of instructions by a speaker to a hearer to update and organize a file so that the file will contain all the information the speaker intends to convey. The file consists of indexed cards which represent existing (old) discourse referents and information pertaining to this heading is entered on the card. The system also incorporates a basic idea from Heim (1982) that indefinites trigger the construction of new cards and definites presuppose the existence of old ones.

(16) a. The card is selected from among the already existing file cards if it is definite and therefore represents an existing referent.
b. The hearer is required to make out a new card for an indefinite.

The file system thus involves locating cards on top of a stack (topics) or positioning them there (foci). Additionally, each card is updated with the information predicated of it in the sentence. In many languages foci are marked by stress.

Let me illustrate with the sequence of sentences in (17).

(17) a. I_{TOP} [know a student]$_{FOC}$
b. She$_{TOP}$ [is intelligent]$_{FOC}$

The card for the speaker, first person topic of (17a) is located on top of the file and is therefore licensed as a topic. The focus rule applies to 'a student', a referential element within the focus domain and this constituent is stressed.[7] Since this is an indefinite, a new card is made out for this referent and is then positioned on top of the file. This card therefore licenses the topichood of the coreferential subject of (17b).

The spatio-temporal parameters of the card for the current stage, permanently available on top of the file, change according as the discourse proceeds. If, for example, a location is introduced as in (18a), it can provide the topic for further discourse as in (4b) (repeated here as (18b).

(18) a. *What's outside the door?*
 b. [Outside the door]$_{STOPt}$ [there's a cat]$_{FOC}$

When locations and times are introduced into a context the card they introduce takes on the spatio-temporal parameters of the card for the current here-and-now constraining 'outside the door', in this case, to be at the current location and at the current time This is indicated by the stage index on the PP.

When an individual is introduced into the discourse, it automatically allows generic reference as well. (19) is a natural continuation of (18b).

(19) *Cats can be very independent.*

Individual cards on top of the file thus allow not only individual topics, but also generic ones. This holds true of stage topics as well. Since a card for the current here-and-now is available on top of the file, so is the generic stage which refers to all times and places. Generic topics where introduced in the previous section in the analysis of individual level predicates.

In this system the notions topic and focus are defined discoursally. Participants in a discourse update their common ground according to the rules of IS outlined here. Topics and focus in this framework do not project syntactic structure à la Rizzi (1997), but are rather integrated at the PF interface. For discussion of various aspects of this issue, see Erteschik-Shir and Lappin (1987), Erteschik-Shir (2005b, 2006a, 2006b).

Topics, as defined above, are the pivot for truth value assessment. It follows that topics necessarily take wide scope. The scopal consequences of this

---

[7] For the details of how stress is assigned to complex focused constituents see Erteschik-Shir and Lappin (1983) and Erteschik-Shir (1997: Chapter 4).

view are discussed in Erteschik-Shir (1997, 1999). Endriss (2009), a recent proponent of this view, offers a comprehensive account of the quantificational properties of topics tying together their semantic, structural, and prosodic properties.

The interpretation of Foci differs from that of Rooth (1985, 1992) for whom a focus (informally) involves selection from a set of alternatives. In Erteschik-Shir (1997) I argue that foci may range over a discourse defined set of alternatives, but that this is not a property of foci as such. Foci which do range over a discourse defined set of alternatives (including contrastive foci) have different distributional properties from those which do not.[8]

The main difference between the approach advocated here and syntactic and semantic approaches to IS proposed elsewhere, is the requirement that all IS properties (syntactic, semantic and prosodic) are derivable from the two IS primitives, topic and focus as defined here. These are the only IS primitives required. Elements which are unmarked for topic or focus, do not have any status with respect to IS. This is the case for *eat* in "I_{TOP} ate an apple$_{foc}$" in the context of "What did you eat?" in which the verb is introduced in the question.

We are now ready to examine the distribution of actual topics in (13) and (14). The definite referents are acceptable in the examples in (13) if they have been introduced as foci in the discourse previous to the utterance of the sentences and following (16a), have been selected from the existing file cards and positioned on top of the stack. Similarly, (14b) is acceptable with the generic reading, since generics, like names, are definite. Since no card is available for the singular indefinite in (14a), however, it cannot provide a topic for the sentence. The distinction between singular indefinites which do not provide valid topics and the specific, contrastive and partitive indefinites in c, d, and e, follows naturally from the rules assuming that more than one topic and focus can be assigned within a sentence. This is also the way specificity is derived in cases like (14c) repeated here including its IS:

(20) [[a student]$_{foc}$ [I_{TOP} know e]]$_{TOP}$ [likes linguistics]$_{foc}$

The manipulations of the card file for (20) is identical to that of the sequence of sentences in (17). 'I' and 'a student' are "subordinate" topics and foci, respectively triggering the positioning of a new card for 'a student' with the entry 'I

---

8 See, for example, the properties of wh-phrases that range over discourse defined sets with respect to extraction out of embedded questions (Cinque 1990), to extraction over negation and to superiority effects (Erteschik-Shir 1997).

know e' on top of the file. This allows the modified indefinite to be the main topic of the sentence with 'likes linguistics' as its focus.[9]

Contrast is particularly relevant here because stage topics can also be contrastive. In order to produce a contrastive element, the context has to include a contrast set. So in order to say (21b), for example, the context has to include a sentence such as (21a).

(21) a. *Which day did John arrive, Sunday or Monday?*
    b. *He arrived on MONDAY.*

In (21b) the contrastive stage answers the wh-question and provides the focus of the sentence. Contrastive elements can, however, also provide the topic of the sentence as shown in the interchange in (22) in which MONDAY provides a contrastive stage topic.

(22) *Tell me why you came on Monday instead of Sunday*:
    MONDAY I got up on time (SUNDAY I didn't).

Note that both contrastive foci and contrastive topics are marked by stress. These properties are derived employing the topic and focus primitives and associated file system rules defined above.

In both (21) and (22), the contextually available set {Sunday,Monday} represents a 'set' card on the top of the stack and is therefore available as a topic (Sunday and Monday). One of the members of this set can however be focused: It is selected to be positioned on top of the stack by itself. As a *focus*, it will be stressed and can function as the focus of the sentence. As a member of a topic set, the same constituent will be able to provide a *topic*. All contrastive elements therefore have the following structure:

(23) $\{X_{foc}, Y\}_{TOP}$

(23) signifies the topic set X,Y with X selected as the focus. The card for this topic set is, by definition prominent on top of the stack. X is focused which means that it is selected from within this set and placed, by the focus rule, on top of the stack by itself. We have thus chosen X and not Y. X is stressed as are all foci. The information structures of (21) and (22) follow in (24) and (25), respectively.

---

[9] For more details, see Erteschik-Shir (1997: Chapter 1).

(24) He~TOP~ arrived on [{MONDAY~foc~, ~~Sunday~~}~TOP~]~foc~

(25) [{MONDAY~foc~,~~Sunday~~}~TOP~]~TOP~ [I got up on time]~foc~

The focused element *Monday* is stressed in both examples by the focus rule. The other member of the contrast set is not pronounced (unless negated). This follows because there is no independent card for *Sunday* available. It only appears as a member of the discoursally available set.[10]

The rules for Topic and Focus consequently trigger manipulations on the file, updating files according to the sentences as they are uttered. The same rules also apply to subordinate Topics and Foci.

5 Existentials

One way of 'marking' a sentence as being all focus and having a stage topic is for a non-topic to occupy the left peripheral position. According to É. Kiss (2004) and Holmberg (2000), existentials employ exactly this strategy. As argued in Erteschik-Shir (2007, 2013), the outcome is an all-focus sentence predicated of a stage topic. (A parenthesized spatial or temporal index is one which is not specified contextually):

(26) a. (s)TOP~t~[There is a/*the dog in my garden]~foc~
 b. sTOP~(t)~[There is a/*the meeting at two o'clock]~foc~
 c. (s)TOP~t~[There are many/*all people who like icecream]~foc~

In such an IS, the full sentence is entered on the card for the current here-and-now which provides the stage topic and an all-focus sentence is derived. What is special about the stage topic in existentials is that it is lacking in contextual definition: either the place or the time are not taken from the current stage and a 'new' stage is defined by adding these parameters to it. This can be seen in (26). In (26a) the location is not given contextually and in (26b) the time is missing in the context. In (26c) no locative parameter is contextually available, yet this parameter is not provided in the sentence either, the new stage is accommodated to mean the whole world. The definition of a new stage requires new inventory. Definites presuppose a referent associated with a location. Located

---

[10] Molnár (2006) similarly views contrast as "superimposed" on topics and foci.

referents are therefore incompatible with the interpretation of a new stage. This is the explanation for the Definiteness Effect (DE) in existentials.[11]

The definition of a *new* stage in this way, also provides an explanation for *when* the definiteness effect applies. (27) illustrates examples in which it does not hold[12]:

(27) a. *There's the city hall, the museum, and the park.*
 b. *There's the meeting at 2 o'clock and the office event at 4.*

Such existentials generally provide a list of elements contained in a certain place, or time: (27a) could be a description of the sights in a given town. (27b) could be a response to a request for the day's schedule at the office. In both cases, the context must include reference to the stage in question, namely the town, and the office events, respectively, but what's special about these stages is that they are unpopulated. The inventory which is listed in the existential may be given, yet it is new to the stage in question. An obvious difference between the sentences in (26) and (27) is that the former lack at least one of the parameters of the stage, the latter require full contextual specification of the stage (e.g., for (27a), a particular city, and for (27b), a particular day at work). Since the stage is not new, the inventory on it need not be new either. The definiteness effect is therefore predicted to hold only of new stages.

The contextual difference between existentials of the first type in which the DE holds and those of the second type in which it doesn't, also plays a role in the IS of the sentence as a whole. Whereas the first type is predicated of an (at least partially) unindexed stage, one for which the spatio-temporal parameters are not contextually specified, the stage topic of the second type is fully specified contextually. It follows, that as part of the focus in the first kind, the

---

[11] The same definiteness effect is also found in locatives such as (i) and (ii) but not in possessives such as (iii):

i. My soup$_{top}$ [has a/*the fly in it]$_{foc}$
ii. John$_{top}$ [has a/*the hat on]$_{foc}$
iii. John$_{top}$ [has a/the hat (in his hand)]$_{foc}$

In (i) and (ii) the subjects are interpreted as locations and therefore function as stage topics. Their IS is therefore parallel to that of the sentences in (26) in that these stage topics also require the filling in of the location by a prepositional phrase. (iii) differs in that the subject is interpreted as a possessor and not as a location. The definiteness effect does not apply and the addition of a locational prepositional phrase is optional.

[12] The literature on the definiteness effect, originating with Milsark (1974), is vast and will not be reviewed here.

missing spatio-temporal parameter(s) must be specified which is why such sentences are incomplete without their "coda". This is illustrated in (28) for the examples (26).

(28) a. *(s)TOP$_t$[There is a dog]$_{foc}$
 b. *sTOP$_{(t)}$[There is a meeting]$_{foc}$
 c. *(s)TOP$_t$[There are many people]$_{foc}$

(28c) is somewhat different from the other two. It can easily be completed by a locative, but the coda, in (26c) is a relative clause. What is wrong with (28c) is therefore not that a missing locative must be filled in, but that without some added information the sentence is incomplete, it is missing a contentful focus.[13] One way to remedy this is to add a location, another is to add a relative clause and a third is to supply a contrastive context in which *many people* is contrasted with *few people*, in which case *many* will be stressed. Existential sentences which are subject to the DE therefore generally include a coda as part of the focus.

As shown in (27a) this is not a requirement for existentials of the second kind. Here the location is part and parcel of the stage, and the focus introduces the inventory on this unpopulated but given stage. No coda is therefore required. In (27b) a coda is (optionally) present. This coda is however packaged differently with respect to IS. Compare (29) and (30):

(29) sTOP$_t$ [There's [the meeting at 2 o'clock]] $_{foc}$

(30) sTOP$_{(t)}$ [There is a meeting at 2 o'clock]$_{foc}$

In (29), "the meeting at 2 o'clock" is the element introduced on stage. In the existential in (30), however, what is introduced on the new stage is "a meeting", the coda "at 2 o'clock" functions to specify the missing temporal parameter of the stage.[14]

The fine-tuned view of the properties of stage topics developed here provides a way of distinguishing the different types of existentials and their properties.

---

[13] A reviewer points out that (28b) is fully acceptable in the context of a question such as "Where is everyone?" In such a context the sentence does not merely assert the existence of a meeting but is interpreted as "Everyone is at a meeting".
[14] See Leonetti (2008, 2016) for a cross-linguistic explanation in terms of IS as to whether or not definites of this sort appear in existentials.

6 Lexical Selection of Stages

6.1 Intensional Predicates

Intensional predicates (*find, look for*...) receive an opaque (de dicto) as well as a transparent (de re) reading:

(31) *Bill is looking for a doctor.*

The opague reading – Bill is looking for any doctor – follows from a subordinate IS in which the object is predicated of an unindexed stage as shown in (32).

(32) NP V [sTOP[NP]$_{FOC}$]

The interpretation which follows from this IS is: Bill is looking for a stage, a location where a doctor is to be found. This analysis is very much along the lines of a proposal by Carlson (1977: 192) who treats these verbs "as making an existential claim about stages of the direct object, yet at the same time creating an intensional context in which this existential claim is being made". Evidence that intensional predicates select an unindexed stage as their complement is the fact that individual level predicates are blocked from occurring in the complements of those intensional predicates which select indexed stages.

(33) a. **John tried to fear snakes.*
     b. **John tried to know French.*

Intensional predicates, which select an unindexed generic stage as their complement, *do* allow individual level predicates:

(34) *John wants to own more houses than his father.*

Generic stages are set up via lexical properties of certain predicates and modals as well as conditionals. As noted in Section 3, it is possible to view individual level predicates as allowing a generic stage, but not (without contextual coercion) an indexed one.

If *a doctor* in (31) is introduced on a stage, he will be unique, but not specific, rendering the opaque (de dicto) reading in which *any* doctor will do as the goal of the search. As shown in section 2.1, with example (20), a specific reading results from a subordinate IS. Specificity can be induced on stage by (implicit or overt) context. This analysis predicts that the specific reading must be discoursally implied. If (31), for example, is uttered in a context in which the speaker is reporting an event in which s/he has seen Bill in search of a particular doctor, only the transparent reading is possible. The transparent reading is therefore the more marked one for these predicates since it requires a particular context.

6.2 Perception Verbs

Whereas intensional predicates select unindexed stage topics, perception verbs, such as *hear, see,* etc. select indexed stage topics:

(35) a. *John heard Peter*
b. NP V [sTOP$_t$[NP]$_{FOC}$]

In (35) Peter's existence on the 'stage' is heard by John. In (36) the perception verb is followed by a small clause. In (36a), what Peter hears is the event of Peter's singing on the stage. This interpretation follows from the IS in (36b).

(36) a. *John heard Peter sing.*
b. NP V [sTOP$_t$[NP V]] $_{FOC}$

One piece of evidence for this analysis is the lack of scopal ambiguity found under verbs of perception. (37) has at least three readings. One in which the subject has wide scope (up to six boys are arrested), one in which the object takes wide scope (up to six girls are doing the arresting) and an unscoped reading in which exactly two girls arrest three boys.

(37) *Two girls arrested three boys.*

These readings follow under the assumption that topics take wide scope and that either the subject or the object can be the topic. Alternatively, the sentence is all-focus with a stage topic resulting in the unscoped reading. Now examine (38):

(38) *John saw two girls arrest three boys.*

(38) is not ambiguous. It only gets the unscoped reading. This follows from the small clause being the focus of a stage topic.

An interesting fact about Dutch anaphora also follows nicely.[15] Note the difference between the distribution of anaphors in (39) with direct objects and those in (40) with small clauses. The only possible direct object is the subject oriented anaphor 'zichzelf' in (39c). With the small clauses in (40), the picture changes. There both the pronoun 'zich' and the anaphor 'zichzelf' are licensed as shown in (40b) and (40c).

(39) a. *$Henk_1$ hoorde hem_1.
    Henk heard him
b. *$Henk_1$ hoorde $zich_1$.
    Henk heard SE
c. $Henk_1$ hoorde $\underline{zichzelf_1}$
    Henk heard himself

(40) a. *$Henk_1$ hoorde [hem_1 zingen]
    Henk heard [him sing]
b. $Henk_1$ hoorde [$zich_1$ zingen]
    Henk heard [SE sing]
c. $Henk_1$ hoorde [$\underline{zichzelf_1}$ zingen]
    Henk heard [himself sing]

This data follows from an IS oriented theory of Binding as well as the IS structures assigned to verbs of perception as argued in Erteschik-Shir (1997: 206–11). There "I-dependencies" are argued to hold between anaphors and their antecedents. The dependent in an I-dependency characteristically does not trigger the construction of a new card, instead its 'identity' is fixed by the dependency. I-dependencies include, wh-trace dependencies, the dependency between wh-phrases in sentences with multiple wh-phrases and anaphora. Bound anaphora instantiates the basic idea behind the notion of an I-dependency, namely that the bound noun phrase is identified for the hearer by means of the noun phrase upon which it is dependent. I-dependencies are constrained by the Subject Constraint which requires, grosso modo, that syntactic structure be aligned with IS, such that the subject and topic are aligned and the predicate and focus are aligned or alternatively that the IS consists of a Stage topic and an all focus sentence. In both cases the dependent is

---

[15] The Dutch data are from Reinhart and Reuland (1993). Similar data exists in Scandinavian languages.

contained in the focus domain and the syntactic structure and the IS are aligned[16]:

(41)
$$\left\{ \begin{array}{c} \text{subject}_{top} \\ _s\text{top}_t \end{array} \right\} [...x...]_{foc}$$

The SE pronouns (*zich* (Dutch), *sig* (Danish)) are I-dependent: they are restricted to focus constituents and select a subject topic as their antecedent.

The *zelf/selv* morphemes imposes further locality restrictions: They require an antecedent within the minimal predication. The minimal predication is the minimal IS which includes *minimally* and *maximally* one topic and its focus. Pronouns without *zelf/selv* are excluded within the minimal IS.[17]

The Dutch data in (39) and (40) is now accounted for. In all the grammatical examples, the pronoun is bound to the subject-topic, hence dependent (*zich*). The direct object pronoun in (39) is local (within the minimal predication) excluding the pronouns without *zelf*. (39b) and c show that the pronoun can be viewed as both local and non-local. Compare the three examples in (42):

(42) a. [Henk$_1$]$_{TOP}$ [hoorde sTOP$_t$[a1] $_{FOC}$]$_{FOC}$ a = *zichzelf*
 b. Henk$_1$ hoorde sTOP$_t$[[a1] $_{TOP}$ [zingen]$_{FOC}$]$_{FOC}$ a = *zich*
 c. [Henk$_1$]$_{TOP}$ [hoorde sTOP$_t$[a1] $_{FOC}$ zingen]$_{FOC}$ a = *zichzelf*

---

16 See Erteschik-Shir (1997: Chapter 6) for a detailed account of I-dependencies showing that the Subject Constraint (a processing constraint) obviates the need to invoke c-command and syntactic constraints on extraction.

17 This account separates binding (the subject constraint) and locality (the mnimal predication) and thus allows for both I-dependent pronouns and non-dependent pronouns to be restricted locally or to be free. The Danish data in (i) cannot be accounted for without such a separation.

(i) Anne$_i$ hørte Susan$_k$ snakke med Tina$_m$ om   sig$_i$
                                                  sig selv$_k$
                                                  hende$_i$/$_o$
                                                  hende selv$_m$

Anne heard Susan talk   to   Tina   about   her(self)
Anne heard Susan talk   to   Tina   about   her/herself

In (i) both the I-dependent *sig selv* and the non-dependent *hende selv* are restricted to occur within their minimal predications whereas *sig* and *hende* are not. Since English doesn't have two kinds of pronouns as does Danish, the need for separating out locality as a separate constraint did not appear necessary in initial accounts of binding.

As noted in the previous section, perception verbs involve a subordinate IS with a stage topic. In (42a), a_1's existence on the 'stage' heard by Henk is asserted. In (42b) the event of a_1's singing on the stage is asserted to take place. The two ISs differ, however, in what counts as a minimal predication for the anaphor. The subordinate IS in (42a) has the noun phrase predicated of a stage. This kind of predication does not itself count as a minimal predication since the stage topic is not overt. Therefore the minimal predication includes the subject resulting in a *zelf*-marked pronoun. In (42b), however, the subordinate IS consisting of the topic a_1 and the focus *zingen* is a minimal predication. The antecedent is therefore non-local rendering the non-*zelf*-marked pronoun. The same sequence also allows a *zelf*-marked pronoun as shown in (42c). This results from an IS parallel to (42a). The difference between the ISs in (42b) and (42c) is that in the former a_1 is the topic of a subordinate IS and in the latter it is the focus of a stage topic. The two options are available because verbs of perception select stage topics and the focus of this stage topic is either the whole complement or just the noun phrase. With an overt stage topic as shown in (43), the minimal predication is defined by the stage and the pronoun rendering the non *zelf*-marked pronoun:

(43) Henk hoorde zich op de tape
 Henk heard SE on the tape
 'Henk heard himself on the tape.'

7 Stage Topics and Extraction

The trace in a wh-phrase-trace dependency is I-dependent on a par with anaphors and is also conditioned by the Subject Constraint in (41) (minus locality). The dependent is therefore restricted to the focus constituent. This is how Island Constraints are accounted for in Erteschik-Shir (1973, 1997, 2007). Picture noun phrases illustrate clearly the role of stage topics in predicting extractability. The predicates which license extraction out of picture noun phrases are either 'light' verbs such as *see* which select stages or creation verbs which make a stage come into existence (Erteschik-Shir 1981). Examine the well-known data in (44).

(44) a. *Who did John see pictures of?*
 b. **Who did John see the picture of?*
 c. **Who did John see Susan's picture of?*

Extraction is possible with indefinites as in (44a) but not with definites as shown in (44b) and (44c). The ISs in (45) distinguish the example in (45a) from those in (45b) and (45c):

(45) a. John$_{TOP}$ [saw sTOP$_t$ [pictures of X]$_{FOC}$]$_{FOC}$
 b. John$_{TOP}$ [saw sTOP$_t$ [[the picture]$_{TOP}$ [of X]$_{FOC}$]$_{FOC}$]$_{FOC}$
 c. John$_{TOP}$ [saw sTOP$_t$ [[Susan's]$_{TOP}$ [picture of X]$_{FOC}$]$_{FOC}$]$_{FOC}$

Predicates which allow I-dependencies with picture noun phrases are predicates which select stages.[18] The IS in (45a) is akin to (42a) for which it was argued that the implicit subordinate stage does not count in defining the minimal predication. Neither does it play a role in terms of the Subject Constraint. An I-dependency is therefore licensed taking X as the dependent. Hence extraction is predicted to be grammatical. In the ISs in (45b) and (45c), however, the definite subjects of the picture noun phrases provide topics. The dependent, X, can therefore form an I-dependency within this (subordinate) IS blocking the formation of the I-dependency in the higher IS, hence blocking extraction.

This analysis also predicts the following distribution of anaphors:

(46) a. *John saw Susan's picture of herself/*himself.*
 b. *John saw pictures of himself.*

Extraction from relative clauses in Danish (and other Scandinavian languages) provides additional support for the role played by Stage topics in accounting for extraction.[19]

(47) a. *Det   er   der   mange der   kan   lide.*
       that are   there many   that can   like
       'There are many (people) who like that.'
   b. *Det   hus   kender jeg en   mand som har   købt.*
       that house know   I   a   man   that has   bought
       'I know a man who had bought that house.'

---

18 See Erteschik-Shir (1981) and Diesing (1992) for discussion of the lexical properties of the predicates which license extraction. These predicates are either creation verbs or other 'light' verbs such as *see* which select stages. Creation verbs, for example, make a stage come into existence.
19 Data from Erteschik-Shir (1973).

c. *Det   har   jeg   set   mange der   har   gjort.*
   that have I   seen   many that have done
   'I have seen many (people) who have done that.'
d. *Det   har   jeg   mødt   mange der   har   gjort.*
   that have I   met   many that have done
   'I have met many (people) who have done that.'
e. *Det   har   jeg   let   af   mange der har   gjort.*
   that have I   laughed at   many that have done
   'I have laughed at many (people) who have done that.'
f. **Det har   jeg   drillet mange der   har   gjort.*
   that have I   made-fun-of many that have done

The property that distinguishes these relative clause constructions from the ones that do not allow extraction is that the matrix must serve merely to introduce the head of the relative clause into the discourse (Erteschik-Shir 1982). An existential matrix does so by introducing a noun phrase onto a stage. The other predicates which license extraction are predicates which select indexed or unindexed stages. As the matrix clause becomes harder to interpret as merely introducing the head of the relative clause acceptability declines as shown in (47e) and (47f).[20]

The analysis of extraction out of relative clauses of this type is similar to the one offered for picture noun phrases above. Here the stage topic takes the relative clause as its focus making it the main focus of the sentence as shown in (48).

(48) Det har jeg set sTOP$_t$ [mange der har gjort t]$_{FOC}$

Extraction is therefore licensed in these cases because it does not violate the subject constraint. Since the subject constraint is viewed as a processing constraint, one might predict that extraction out of relative clauses of this sort should be possible cross-linguistically, in particular in a language such as English which is otherwise quite similar to Scandinavian. This prediction is in fact born out as the following examples from Erteschik-Shir (1973) show:

---

20 According to Lindahl (2017), Swedish examples with extraction over matrix verbs such as *beundra* 'admire' and *störa sig på* 'be annoyed at' have been found in her corpus. Matrix clauses with these verbs do not lend themselves to the analysis offered here. Interestingly extractions from complements of these verbs receive the worst ratings by informants according to Lindahl (2017: 211).

(49) a. *?This is the kind of weather that there are many people who like.*
b. *??This is the kind of weather that I know many people who like.*
c. **This is the kind of weather that he made fun of many people who like.*

Although extraction in these cases is degraded compared to Danish, the acceptability rate declines in the same way it does in Danish. One explanation of why the cut-off point for extraction is so much higher in English than in Danish, as suggested in Erteschik-Shir (1982) is the fact that topicalization occurs with great frequency in Danish but not in English. This, I argue, facilitates the processing of the connection between the fronted item and its gap,

8 Conclusion

As we have seen, stage topics are akin to other topics in having the properties listed in (50) but different in the properties listed in (51).

(50) Properties of Stage topics common to all topics in general
   a. the pivot for truth value assignment
   b. overt or implicit
   c. may function as main or subordinate topics
   d. may topicalize
   e. may be contrastive

(51) Properties special to Stage topics
   a. may have both spatial and temporal indices, only one or may be unindexed
   b. sentences with implicit stage topics are unscoped
   c. may be selected by verbs

As indicated in section 4, a card for the current here-and-now is available on the top of the file. Its time and place indices are derived from context and are updated with each successive utterance and is modified by tense. Unindexed or generic stage topics are also available and as shown in section 3 render an interpretation of individual level predicates without recourse to lexical selection. Stage topics may also lack only one of their spatio-temporal parameters allowing for the violation of the DE in existentials as shown in section 5. Since topics determine scope, sentences with such topics will be unscoped. Section 6 argues that verbs may select stage topics: intensional predicates select unindexed stage topics, explaining their de dicto interpretation. Perception verbs select indexed stage topics. This explains the fact that their complements are unscoped and also predicts the distribution of anaphors in their complements in Dutch.

One property that stage topics have in common with other topics is that they can be implicit. The rules for topic-drop are language specific: some languages hardly ever allow topics to drop (e.g., English). Other languages allow only subjects-topics to drop (e.g., Italian). Still others allow object topics to drop as well (e.g., Chinese).[21]

In Erteschik-Shir, Ibnbari and Taube (2013), we offer an account of missing objects as topic drop inspired by Sigurðsson and Maling (2008) and Sigurðsson (2011). Their approach is particularly relevant to the current discussion in that it takes Information Structure into account.[22] Since it is generally the case that missing objects can be replaced by pronouns, and since pronouns are necessarily topics, being replaced by an overt pronoun provides clear evidence that the missing argument is a topic. For us, null arguments thus enter the computation as a bundle of unvalued φ-features:

$$\begin{bmatrix} \alpha & person \\ \beta & number \\ \gamma & gender \end{bmatrix}$$

The PF interface accesses the discourse file and valuation of the feature bundle occurs by matching with a (topic) card from the top of the file, thereby also providing a reference. The assumption that the features are unvalued, forces a process of valuation where the only source of such valuation is the discourse. It is therefore not necessary to mark missing arguments with a topic feature. Topichood follows from the need for valuation.

The cards permanently available on the top of the file are, in addition to the current stage, cards for the speaker and the hearer (see section 3). These are the actors in the speech act and should receive an integrated analysis. Therefore, on a par with null arguments, null stages are viewed as entering the computation as a bundle of unvalued s,t-features:

---

[21] No distinction is made here between the various types of null-arguments.
[22] According to Sigurðsson and Maling (2008: 14) "all pronominal arguments are syntactically computed feature bundles that may or may not be spelled out in PF, depending on PF parametric options and/or language-specific low-level PF spell-out rules and constraints".

$$\begin{bmatrix} \alpha & time \\ \beta & space \end{bmatrix}$$

Access of the discourse file and valuation of the feature bundle occurs by matching with the stage-topic card from the top of the file. Here it is possible to value one of the features or both or to leave them unvalued, generating the unindexed stage topic.[23] This approach to null arguments is however quite different from that of Sigurðsson and Mailing (2008) and Sigurðsson (2011). One difference is that for us the interpretation of the feature bundle is available in situ: It is interpretable if a suitable topic is available on top of the file (and does not involve feature matching with left peripheral elements). Another difference is that for us overt and null pronouns are computed somewhat differently: Whereas a fully specified feature bundle is computed syntactically in the case of overt pronouns, null topics are merged as a set of unvalued φ-features.

The properties of stage topics outlined in this paper strongly argue for a non-syntactic account of IS. Take for example the selection by verbs of implicit stage topics. Such selection must be integrated in a theory of the lexicon.[24] Another example is the subordinate ISs involved in contrast. One would be hard put to make these fit within current syntactic theory. Syntactic theories of IS such as Rizzi (1997) and the following research based on his initial insights, require a plethora of often language-specific IS features to explain word order across languages. In section 7 and elsewhere I argue that extractability is constrained by the processing ease of matching syntactic structure and information structure. Furthermore variation in how IS is marked in a particular language has an impact on this mapping. Pursuing this line of thought may lead to a simpler computational system, freeing it from the onus of explaining such gradient data and (cross-linguistic) variation. Clearly, a coherent view of Information Structure and its integration into a model of grammar is required to fulfill this mission.

References

Carlson, Greg. 1977. *Reference to kinds in English*. Amherst: University of Massachusetts PhD thesis.
Cinque, Guglielmo. 1990. *Types of A'-dependencies*. Cambridge, MA: MIT Press.

---

[23] Overt stages are merged by adjunction as are adverbs (to IP or VP). They are linearized at PF. (See Erteschik-Shir 2005a). Implicit stages are merged in the same way, are valued but do not linearize.
[24] For an initial attempt at such integration see Erteschik Shir (2007: 210–212).

Cohen, Ariel & Nomi Erteschik-Shir. 2002. Topic, focus and the interpretation of bare plurals. *Natural Language Semantics* 10. 125–165.
Diesing, Molly. 1992. *Indefinites*. Cambridge, MA: MIT Press.
É. Kiss, Katalin. 1998. Discourse-configurationality in the languages of Europe. In Anna Siewierska (ed.), *Consitutent order in the languages of Europe*, 681–728. Berlin & New York: Mouton de Gruyter.
É. Kiss, Katalin. 2004. The EPP in a topic-prominent language. In Peter Svenonius (ed.), *Subjects, expletives, and the EPP*, 107–124. Oxford: Oxford University Press.
Endriss, Cornelia. 2009. *Quantificational topics: A scopal treatment of exceptional wide scope phenomena* Berlin: Springer.
Erteschik-Shir, Nomi. 1973. *On the nature of island constraints*. Cambridge, MA: MIT PhD thesis.
Erteschik-Shir, Nomi & Shalom Lappin. 1979. Dominance and the functional explanation of island phenomena. *Theoretical Linguistics* 6. 41–85.
Erteschik-Shir, Nomi. 1981. On extraction from noun phrases (picture noun phrases). In Adriana Belletti, Luciana Brandi & Luigi Rizzi (eds.), *Theory of markedness in generative grammar: Proceedings of the 1979 GLOW Conference*, 147–169. Pisa: Scuola Nomale Superiore di Pisa.
Erteschik-Shir, Nomi. 1982. Extractability in Danish and pragmatic principle of dominance. In Elisabet Engdahl & Eva Ejerhed (eds.), *Readings on unbounded dependencies in Scandinavian languages*, pages. Sweden: Umeå.
Erteschik-Shir, Nomi & Shalom Lappin. 1983. Under stress: a functional explanation of sentence stress. *Journal of Linguistics* 19. 419–453.
Erteschik-Shir, Nomi & Shalom Lappin. 1987. Dominance and modularity. *Linguistics* 25. 671–686.
Erteschik-Shir, Nomi. 1997. *The dynamics of focus structure*. Cambridge: Cambridge University Press.
Erteschik-Shir, Nomi. 1999. Focus structure and scope. In Georges Rebuschi & Laurice Tuller (eds.), *The grammar of focus*, 119–150. Amsterdam & Philadelphia: John Benjamins.
Erteschik-Shir, Nomi. 2005a. Sound patterns of syntax: object shift. *Theoretical Linguistics* 31. 47–93.
Erteschik-Shir, Nomi. 2005b. What is syntax? *Theoretical Linguistics* 31. 263–274.
Erteschik-Shir, Nomi. 2006a. What's what? In Caroline Féry, Gisbert Fanselow, Matthias Schlesewsky & Ralf Vogel (eds.), *Gradience in grammar*, 317–335. Oxford: Oxford University Press.
Erteschik-Shir, Nomi. 2006b. On the architecture of topic and focus. In Valéria Molnár & Susanne Winkler (eds.), *The architecture of focus*, 33–57. Berlin & New York: Mouton de Gruyter.
Erteschik-Shir, Nomi. 2007. *Information structure: The syntax-discourse interface: syntax and morphology*. Oxford: Oxford University Press.
Erteschik-Shir, Nomi. 2013. Information structure and (in)definiteness. In Patricia Cabredo Hofherr & Anne Zribi-Hertz (eds.), *Crosslinguistic studies on noun phrase structure and reference*, 23–51. Leiden: Brill.
Erteschik-Shir, Nomi, Lena Ibnbari & Sharon Taube. 2013. Missing objects as topic drop. *Lingua* 136. 145–169.
Gundel, Jeanette K. 1974. *The role of topic and comment in linguistic theory*. Austin: University of Texas PhD thesis.

Heim, Irene. 1982. *The semantics of definite and indefinite noun phrases*. Amherst, MA: University of Massachusetts, Amherst PhD thesis.
Holmberg, Anders. 2000. Scandinavian stylistic fronting: how any category can become an expletive. *Linguistic Inquiry* 31. 445–483.
Kratzer, Angelika. 1989. Stage-level and individual-level predicates. In *Papers on Quantification*. Amherst: Department of Linguistics, University of Massachusetts.
Kratzer, Angelika. 1995. Stage-level and individual level predicates. In Gregory. N. Carlson and Francis Jeffry Pelletier (eds.), *The generic book*. Chicago: University of Chicago Press.
Leonetti, Manuel. 2008. Definiteness effects and the role of the coda in existential constructions. In Alex Klinge & Henrik Høeg Müller (eds.), *Essays on nominal determination: from morphology to discourse management*, 131–162. Amsterdam & Philadelphia: John Benjamins.
Leonetti, Manuel. 2016. Definiteness effects: The interplay of Information structure and pragmatics. In Susann Fischer, Tanja Kupisch & Esther Rinke (eds.), *Definiteness effects: bilingual, typological and diachronic variation*. Cambridge: Cambridge Scholars.
Lindahl, Filippa. 2017. *Extraction from relative clauses in Swedish*. Institutionen för svenska språket. Göteborg: Göteborgs universitet PhD thesis.
Milsark, Gary, L. 1974. Existential sentences in English. Cambridge, MA: MIT PhD thesis.
Molnár, Valéria. 2006. On different kinds of contrast. In Valéria Molnár & Susanne Winkler (eds.), *The architecture of focus*. Berlin & New York: Mouton de Gruyter.
Reinhart, Tanya. 1981. Pragmatics and linguistics: an analysis of sentence topics. *Philosophica* 27. 53–94.
Reinhart, Tanya & Eric Reuland. 1993. Reflexivity. *Linguistic Inquiry* 24. 657–720.
Rizzi, Luigi. 1997. The fine structure of the left periphery. In Liliane Haegeman (ed.), *Elements of grammar*, 281–337. Dordrecht: Kluwer.
Rooth, Mats. 1985. Association with focus. *Reproduced by GLSA*. Amherst: University of Massachusetts PhD thesis.
Rooth, Mats. 1992. A theory of focus interpretation. *Natural Language Semantics* 1. 75–116.
Sigurðsson, Halldór Ármann & Joan Maling. 2008. Argument drop and the empty left edge condition (ELEC). *Working Papers in Scandinavian Syntax* 81. 1–27.
Sigurðsson, Halldór Ármann. 2011. Conditions on argument drop. *Linguistic Inquiry* 42. 267–304.
Strawson, P. F. 1964. Identifying reference and truth-values. *Theoria* 30. 86–99.

Halldór Ármann Sigurðsson
Topicality in Icelandic: Null Arguments and Narrative Inversion

Abstract: This paper discusses topicality in Icelandic grammar as realized in several phenomena: referential third person *pro* drop in Old Icelandic, diverse types of topic drop in Old and Modern Icelandic, and Narrative Inversion (declarative VS clauses), also in both Old and Modern Icelandic. These phenomena all involve aboutness topics, given topics or both, thus showing that distinct types of topicality are active in Icelandic. However, in contrast to Italian, Icelandic does not provide evidence that different topic types have different structural correlates, a fact that suggests that topicality types are not generally structuralized in language (while not excluding that a topicality hierarchy may be PF-licensed by externalization properties specific to languages like Italian). Topicality is presumably a universally available category or phenomenon, but it is plausibly an interface third factor phenomenon (in the sense of Chomsky 2005), not provided by Universal Grammar but interacting with it in the shaping of externalized grammar, differently so in different languages.

Keywords: Icelandic, narrative inversion, *pro* drop, topic drop, topicality, verb-initial declaratives

1 Introduction: Types of Topicality

A multiple left edge topic approach is developed in several works by Frascarelli, Hinterhölzl, and Bianchi (Frascarelli 2007; Frascarelli and Hinterhölzl 2007; Bianchi and Frascarelli 2009, Bianchi and Frascarelli 2010; Frascarelli 2011). When no further specification is called for, I refer jointly to these works as *Frascarelli et al.* and to the approach as the *Frascarelli et al. approach*. At the core of the approach is the claim that the clausal (CP) left edge contains distinct topic positions that are located between the Force and the Fin categories postulated in Rizzi (1997). The topic categories are labeled somewhat differently in the

---
Halldór Ármann Sigurðsson, Lund University

https://doi.org/10.1515/9781501504488-009

different works of Frascarelli et al.; (1) shows the categories and their order as presented in Frascarelli (2011: 4).[1]

(1) AS-Topic > C-Topic > AG-Topic > FamG-Topic
  [= Aboutness-Shift topic, Contrastive Topic, Aboutness-Given Topic, Familiar-Given Topic]

If each of the topic categories head their own projection (as argued in Frascarelli 2007), we get roughly the hierarchy in (2) (see Frascarelli 2007: 701, with slightly different labels, though).

(2) [$_{ForceP}$ [$_{ASiftP}$ ... [$_{ContrP}$ [$_{FocP}$ [$_{AGivP}$ [$_{FGivP}$ [$_{FinP}$ ...

A striking result of Frascarelli et al. is that Italian third person null-subjects are always coreferential with a newly established or a maintained AS-Topic. Thus, these subjects are given topics at the narrow clausal level, simultaneously as they are coreferential with an AS-Topic at the local discourse level. The term Aboutness-Given Topics in Frascarelli (2011) seems to be coined to capture this double nature. However, to the extent possible, I will try to keep the clausal and discourse levels apart.

The Frascarelli et al. approach makes some non-innocent claims. One claim, explicitly stated by Bianchi and Frascarelli (2010: 54; cf. also Frascarelli and Hinterhölzl 2007: 89), is that "there is a systematic correlation between the formal properties of topics and their function in the discourse, which is encoded in a strict hierarchy in the C-domain (*contra* a free recursion analysis of TopP projections, cf. Rizzi 1997)" – remarkable, if true. Another claim, implicit, is that the different topic categories are heads in the sense of X-bar theory, taking overt topics as specifiers (in the spirit of Rizzi 1997; Cinque 1999). A third claim, also implicit, is that there is a one-to-one correlation between the linear order of elements in the C-edge and their hierarchical relations: if Top_α c-commands Top_β then Top_α also precedes Top_β.

These claims are not easily reconciled with recent development of minimalist thinking (Chomsky 2013 and related work), where there is a growing consensus

---

[1] Hanging topics (as in highest Left Dislocation in Germanic, see Grohmann 1997) are not part of the hierarchy; they "have distinct formal and discourse properties with respect to the Aboutness-shift Topic and are located in a specific (higher) position in the C-domain" (Frascarelli 2007: 698, fn. 13). "Topicalization" or movement (of arguments) to Spec,CP and Left Dislocation (and Contrastive Dislocation) in Icelandic (see Thráinsson 1979) commonly relate to contrast. I set these constructions aside here.

that there is no ordering in deep narrow syntax and also that X-bar theory, with its notion of specifiers, was on the wrong track and should be given up in favor of a simple Agree, Merge and Labeling approach. If that is a step in the right direction, as I believe it is, then the structural claims of Frascarelli et al. cannot be maintained as claims about Universal Grammar (UG) or even narrow syntax (while they can presumably be upheld as claims about Italian externalized grammar). Phase edges, rather than being distinct heads in the X-bar theoretic sense, are plausibly *fuzzy* (cf. Sigurðsson 2004 et seq.), containing an "array of functional categories" (Chomsky 2001: 43, note 8) that are each below the level of materialization but may be jointly materialized (or not materialized at all, as for example C in regular English declarative subordinate vs main clauses: *that* vs. Ø). Chomsky (2008: 9) remarks that "C is shorthand for the region that Rizzi (1997) calls the "left periphery", possibly involving feature spread from fewer functional heads (maybe only one)".

Regardless of the configurational details of the C-edge (if any), it seems that we need to assume a number of sub-lexical or non-lexical topic categories, in the spirit of Frascarelli et al. The correlations between phonology and topic types laid out in Frascarelli and Hinterhölzl (2007) and Frascarelli (2007) provide compelling evidence in favor of this conclusion, and so do multiple topic constructions, such as the ones in (3) and (4), from Franscarelli and Hinterhölzl (2007: 96).

(3) **Io**, inglese non l' avevo mai fatto.
 I English not it have never done
 'I never studied English before.'

(4) **Io**, una cosa che ho trovato positiva, è stata la comprensione.
 I one thing that have found positive is been the comprehension
 'As for me, something that I considered as positive was the comprehension part.'

In the analysis of Frascarelli and Hinterhölzl (2007) the boldfaced *Io* is an Aboutness-Shift topic in both examples, whereas the underlined constituents are a familiar topic in (3) (*inglese*) vs. a contrastive one in (4) (*una cosa che ho trovato positive*). According to Frascarelli and Hinterhölzl (2007: 97) "shifting topics occupy the highest topic position in the left periphery".

My interpretation is that multiple topic constructions are PF-licensed by externalization properties specific to Italian (and some other languages), thus not justifying conclusions about putative universal configurational characteristics of the C-edge while at the same time providing evidence that we need to distinguish between diverse types of topics. Plausibly, topicality is a universally available category or property, but not everything that is universal or universally available to language comes with UG.[2]

Icelandic bears on the status of topicality in grammar in an interesting way, but different from that of Italian. As Icelandic is a rather strict verb-second language, it does not generally allow multiple overt C edge topics, thus presumably having only a single general Top feature in its C edge.[3] However, it has other constructions that are sensitive to topicality and givenness. First, Old Icelandic/Old Norse had *referential pro drop* of both subjects and objects. Second, Icelandic, old and modern, has the Germanic type of *topic drop* (Sigurðsson 1989, 1993, 2011a). Third, Icelandic has verb-initial (Verb-Subject, VS) declarative order, *Narrative Inversion*, NI (Sigurðsson 1990, 1994; see also Braune 1894; Nygaard 1900 and many others before and after). These constructions are exemplified in (5)–(9). As will be discussed in section 2, the distinction between *pro* drop and topic drop is not trivially obvious, but for the present I adopt the understanding in Sigurðsson (1993) without discussion; the Old Icelandic texts are from the 13th and the 14th centuries (preserved in younger copies).

(5) *Referential pro* (Old Icelandic)[4]:
    a. *þá   skar Rognvaldr **hár hans**$_i$, en áðr   var ___$_i$ úskorit*
       then cut   R   hair his   but before was   uncut

---

[2] Given a minimalist biological view of the language faculty (Berwick and Chomsky 2011), the natural assumption is that UG is not only computationally minimal but also item minimal (where functional categories count as items), providing the general premises for item building rather than the items themselves (Sigurðsson 2011b, 2012; see also the concluding discussion in section 4).

[3] Possibly, TP-, VoiceP- and vP-internal given, familiar and contrastive topics each enter an Agree relation with a distinct silent Top(ic) feature in the C edge (unordered in the Icelandic type of languages, but presumably ordered at spell-out in Italian). Alternatively, low phases have silent edge Top features of their own, these lower Top features being "coordinated" with the C Top feature at CP spell-out (see the discussion of multiple Person computation in Sigurðsson 2017). I do not take a stand on this moot issue here.

[4] (5a): Subject drop (from Spec,TP or Spec,vP) in a main clause with a filled Spec,CP.
    (5b): Subject drop in an adverbial clause.
    (5c): Direct object drop in a relative clause.
    (5d): Prepositional object drop in an adverbial clause.

'Then Rognvaldr cut *his hair*, but (*it*) had been uncut before.'
(Heimskringla; Nygaard 1906: 10)

b. ok   kom   **hann**$_i$ þangat ok   var   Hoskuldr uti,   er   ___$_i$ reið
   and   came he   there and was   H.   out   when   rode
   í   tún
   in   field
   'And *he* came there and Hoskuldr was outdoors when (*he*) rode into the heyfield.'
   (Njals saga/Reykjabók; Sigurðsson 1989: 154)

c. dvergrinn   mælti, at   **sá**   **baugr**$_i$ skyldi   vera   hverjum
   dwarf-the   said   that that   that ring   should   be   (to) anybody
   höfuðsbani, er   atti   ___$_i$
   headbane   who   possessed
   'The dwarf said that *that ring* should bring death to anybody who possessed (*it*).'
   (Snorra-Edda; Nygaard 1906: 17)

d. ætla   ek, at   þú   nýtir   eigi **boga** **minn**$_i$
   believe I   that you   (can-)use   not   bow   my
   þóttu   spyrnir fótum   í   ___$_i$
   even-if-you   push   with-feet in
   'I believe that you cannot use *my bow* even if you push with your feet in (*it*).' (i.e., use your feet to stretch it)
   (Heimskringla; Nygaard 1906: 20)

(6) *Topic drop* (Old Icelandic):

a. setnaði þá   kurrinn,   ok _ slitu   við þat
   abated then grumbling-the   and   ended.3PL   at   that
   þingit
   gathering-the
   'Then the grumbling diminished and (*the involved*) ended the gathering at that.'
   (Flateyjarbók; Nygaard 1906: 12)

b. **Herra biskup**$_i$ vaknar (...) ___$_i$ hefir   [sik] upp til kirkju
   sire bishop   wakens   takes   self   up   to   church
   ok   ___$_i$ tekr   skrýddr   heilaga dóma,   ___$_i$ gengr svá (...)
   and   takes in_canonincals sacred   things   walks so
   'Sire bishop wakens, (*he*) takes himself to the church and (*he*) takes "sacred things" (dressed) in canonicals, (*he*) walks like that (...)'
   (Saga Guðmundar Arasonar, Hóla-Biskups; Hjartardóttir 1993: 52)

(7) *Topic drop* (Modern Icelandic):
   a.   __ *Sé   þig á   morgun.*
          see.1SG you on morrow
          '(*I*'ll) see you tomorrow.'
   b. *Kemur hún?* __ *Veit'é(g) ekki.*
      comes she   know-I not
      'Will she come? I don't know (*that*) / (*That*,) I don't know.'
   c. ***Hún**$_i$ kom seint heim.* __$_i$ *Opnaði   dyrnar.* __$_i$ *Læddist   inn.*
      she came late home   opened.3SG door-the   sneaked.3SG in
      'She came home late. (*She*) opened the door. (*She*) sneaked in.'

(8) *Narrative Inversion* (Old Icelandic):
   Þjóstólfr hafði barit   húskarl Hǫskulds$_i$; **rekr** *hann$_i$ Þjóstólf í braut*
   Þ.   had beaten houscarl H.'s   drives he   Þ.   in way
   'Þjóstólfr had beaten Hoskuldr's servant. He drives Þjóstólfr away.'
   (Njals saga/Reykjabók; Sigurðsson 1994: 131)

(9) *Narrative Inversion* (Modern Icelandic):
   Johan Cryuff$_i$ (...) Fyrsti leikur hans$_i$ fyrir Barcelona var í   október
   J.C.   first   game his for B.   was in October
   1973 og **skoraði** *hann$_i$ strax   tvö mörk í 4-0*
   1973 and scored   he immediately two goals in 4-0
   sigri á   Granada.
   victory on Granada
   'Johan Cryuff (...) His first game for Barcelona was in October 1973 and he immediately scored two goals in a 4-0 victory over Granada.'
   (https://is.wikipedia.org/wiki/Johan_Cruyff, 2016-08-24)

The subject in Narrative Inversion is a given topic at the clausal level, typically with a preceding coreferential AS-Topic at the discourse level. I will consider this further in section 3. In the next section, I discuss argument drop, distinguishing, first, between drop from argument positions (*pro*) and topic drop, and, second, between three different types of topic drop.

2 Argument Drop

Icelandic (old and modern) has non-referential *pro* of several sorts, not considered here (Sigurðsson and Egerland 2009). In addition, Old Norse had the following *referential* argument drop types (Nygaard 1906; Hjartardóttir 1993; Sigurðsson 1993):

Old Norse referential argument drop types – Type A vs Type B:

(10) **Type A** (analyzed as *pro* drop in Sigurðsson 1993):
General but not highly frequent drop of (mainly third person) subjects and objects *from argument positions* in both main and subordinate clauses. It seems that this type of drop was only possible *under coreference* with a preceding DP (Hjartardóttir 1993; Sigurðsson 1993).[5]

(11) **Type B** (analyzed as topic drop in Sigurðsson 1993):
Argument drop of subjects and objects *from Spec,CP in verb-initial root clauses* (commonly conjoined *ok* 'and' clauses) – *with or without* a coreferential antecedent in discourse.

Notice that the types overlap when subjects that have a coreferential antecedent are dropped in verb-initial root clauses; such examples can either be analyzed as topic drop from Spec,CP or as a direct drop from Spec,TP (or Spec,vP) in a V1 Narrative Inversion clause.[6]

Due to its distributional properties (confined to Spec,CP in verb-initial root clauses), Sigurðsson (1993) analyzed Type B as involving topic drop, common to many Germanic varieties. Type A, in contrast, involved drop from argument positions and could be found in both root and non-root clauses, which lead Sigurðsson (1993) to the conclusion that it involved *pro* drop. However, if Sigurðsson (2011a) is right in his minimalist criticism of Government and Binding (GB) approaches to null arguments, there is no inherent or "lexical" difference between "distinct types" of null arguments. Nulls must be interpretable (recoverable), but their interpretability depends on their environment and not on

---

5 Kinn, Rusten, and Walkden (2016) argue that this is an incorrect characterization and that there are some cases of referential *pro* without a coreferential antecedent. However, the nulls in question are either arbitrary/generic or expletive or found in idiomatic expressions, and nulls of these sorts are also found in Modern Icelandic texts, in contrast to clearly referential nulls like the ones in (5a–d). Kinn et al. base their conclusions on statistics drawn from the historical IcePaHC corpus. However, one cannot rely on the IcePaHC tagging when it comes to analyzing the many types of argument nulls in Old Norse; one must read the texts word by word to develop reliable intuitions about the nature of the examples being studied.

6 As will be discussed in section 3, topic drop and Narrative Inversion are partly functionally different but also partly interchangeable. In subject topic drop there are silent copies of the subject in both Spec,CP and Spec,TP (as well as in Spec,vP). One could speculate that NI also has a silent subject copy in Spec,CP, only differing (syntactically) from subject topic drop in spelling out a lower copy of the subject in Spec,TP. Alternatively, Spec,CP contains an operator in NI clauses, the subject being blocked by it from moving to Spec,CP. I do not take a stand on this issue here (it is unimportant for my present purposes).

their putative "lexical" or inherent properties. However, for expository ease, I will occasionally refer to Type A and Type B drop as *pro* drop and topic drop, respectively.

The question of recoverability or interpretability is indeed the central problem related to null-arguments (and other systematic silence patterns in language). Simply and very generally stated: Does "meaningful silence" require some sort of licensing or is it the other way around, such that silence is the unmarked and expected strategy, prevailing unless blocked by some extra factors? The licensing approach has been standard in generative syntax for many decades (Chomsky 1981; Rizzi 1986, etc.), but I adopt the opposite approach, where arguments are null unless their silence is blocked by some structural or contextual hindrance (commonly some type of intervention). This general idea, call it the *Happy Null Generalization*, HNG, is stated as follows in Sigurðsson (2004: 254, n. 27):

> Lexicalization is arguably the last resort whenever a meaningful feature cannot be conveyed in a message by any other means than the costly means of overtly expressing some item that carries the feature. Thus, instead of looking for a "license" to stay empty a category is "happy" with whatever "excuse" it has not to get lexicalized.

Given HNG there are no inherent differences between the nulls themselves in types A and B (such as that between variables and *pro* in GB-theoretic approaches). That is also the natural minimalist (and minimal) assumption (see Sigurðsson 2011a; Kinn, Rusten, and Walkden 2016), expected if language developed as a tool of thought and if externalization for communicative and other social purposes is ancillary (Berwick and Chomsky 2011). Nevertheless, it is clear that Types A and B reflect different interpretative or recoverability strategies: Type A nulls (*pro*) are excused under coreference, while type B nulls are excused when as close to the context as possible, namely in Spec,CP in root clauses. And that is not all there is to this – a more fine-grained analysis is required, as I will discuss in the following sections.

2.1 Type A: Pro Drop

Type A, as stated in (10), involved general drop of arguments from *argument positions* in both main and subordinate clauses *under coreference* with a preceding DP in discourse. That is to say: under control, loosely speaking. This type has disappeared from the language, examples like (5a–d) are thus ungrammatical in Modern Icelandic. As pointed out by Hjartardóttir (1993) and also by Sigurðsson (1993) this kind of argument drop was evidently not recovered by agreement, as suggested, first, by the fact that it applied to objects (no agreement) as well as subjects (verb agreement), and, second, by the fact that verb agreement is about equally as rich in Modern Icelandic as it was in Old Norse (with 4–6 distinct forms in the present indicative, depending on conjugations). Identification of *pro* under control across finite C-T boundaries is blocked in Modern Icelandic, presumably by an intervention effect that was absent in Old Norse (see the general analysis in Sigurðsson 2011a).

Examples such as those in (5) show that Old Norse, like Italian, could operate with two topics simultaneously. Consider this for (5b), repeated here as (12), with an added immediately preceding context.

(12) *Referential pro* (Old Icelandic):
[En snemma um morguninn sendir Hoskuldr eptir Hrúti$_i$]
[and early in morning-the sent H. for Hr.]
ok kom **hann**$_i$ þangat ok var Hoskuldr uti, er ___$_i$ reið í tún
and came he there and was H. out when rode in field
'And *he* came there and Hoskuldr was outdoors when (*he*) rode into the heyfield.'
(Njals saga/Reykjabók)

Hoskuldr is an aboutness topic in the wider discourse preceding (12) and a given topic within its clause. The pronoun *hann* 'he' is a reestablished AS-Topic, referred to by the null-subject across the given topic. This is further illustrated in (13).

(13) [*Hoskuldr sent for Hrútr$_i$ and*]
    he$_i$ came there and *Hoskuldr* was outdoors when ___$_i$ rode into the heyfield
    AS   Given   Ø
    |_____|

As seen, the null refers to the closest preceding AS-Topic, other types of topics not interfering with or disrupting the AS-Topic chain (as expected, under the Frascarelli et al. approach).

As indicated by (13), Type A nulls are sometimes found in passages with two overt topics in Old Norse.[7] The two topics are not clause mates, so the Icelandic facts do not bear on the structural claims of Frascarelli et al. However,

---

[7] As one would expect, Type A nulls are most commonly found in Old Norse structures with only a single overt topic (an AS-Topic anteceding the null).

like the data discussed by Frascarelli et al., they show that grammar distinguishes between different types of topics. In addition, Type A nulls (*pro*) in Old Norse are like Italian third person null subjects in Frascarelli's analysis (2007) in that they are usually coreferential with a preceding AS-Topic (maintained or reestablished).

It has been repeatedly observed that null arguments in Old Norse were predominantly in the third person (see, most recently, Kinn, Rusten, and Walkden 2016 and the references there, including Nygaard 1906). As for referential *pro* or Type A nulls, this is precisely what we expect if such nulls had to be anteceded by an AS-Topic.[8] First and second person arguments are typically non-topics or given topics rather than AS-Topics, thus not usually counting as proper or "excusing" antecedents for *pro*.[9] When anteceded or controlled by an AS-Topic, Old Norse *pro* gets a topical referential reading, otherwise getting a non-referential (arbitrary, generic or expletive) interpretation. This latter, impersonal strategy is still widely applicable in Modern Icelandic (Sigurðsson and Egerland 2009).

---

[8] For a rather different suggestion, see Kinn (2016). Following Déchaine and Wiltschko (2002), Kinn argues that first and second person pronouns are "bigger" than third person pronouns (the former being full-fledged DPs, while the latter are argued to be mere "phi-Ps", lacking a D edge) – hence resisting drop, in contrast to the "smaller" third person pronouns. One of the arguments that have been taken to support this is that first and second person pronouns often head full DPs more easily (*we linguists, you linguists*) than do third person pronouns (**they linguists*, %*them linguists*). However, this argument does not carry over to Icelandic, neither old nor modern (e.g., *þeir Gunnar*, lit. 'they Gunnar', roughly 'Gunnar and his (male) companion(s)', *þær systur(nar)*, 'they sisters(-the)', i.e., 'the sisters; they, the sisters'; see also the criticism in Stausland Johnsen 2016). Third person pronouns are in fact commonly "bigger" than first and second person pronouns in that they express gender distinctions, and in Icelandic this applies in the plural as well as the singular (see masc. *þeir* vs. fem. *þær* in the preceding examples). One could counter this argument by saying that first and second pronouns are "big" in the sense that they positively match the logophoric agent/patient linkers in the edge linking approach in Sigurðsson (2011a, 2014) and related work. Crucially, though, third person pronouns corefer with full DPs. I adopt the standard view that all nonreduced pronouns are DPs (see further Sigurðsson 2017).

[9] With some sporadic exceptions. Obviously, though, first and second person pronouns *can* be AS-topics, in Italian (see (3)–(4)) and Icelandic as well as more generally. Given the approach in Sigurðsson (2011a), first and second person pronouns match Top in addition to the logophoric edge linkers in the absence of another more prominent Top matcher.

2.2 Type B: Topic Drop from Spec,CP

All instances of Type B topic drop are structurally uniform in that they cannot normally contain any overt items in Spec, CP (the pre-verbal initial position), as has been repeatedly illustrated (Sigurðsson 1993, 2011a; Sigurðsson and Maling 2010). Consider (14a–b) in comparison with (7a, c), repeated here.

(7) *Topic drop* (Modern Icelandic):
    a.   __   Sé   þig   á   morgun.
                see.1SG   you   on   morrow
                '(I'll) see you tomorrow.'
    c.   **Hún$_i$** kom   seint   heim.   __$_i$ Opnaði   dyrnar.   __$_i$
        she   came   late   home   opened.3SG   door-the.PL
        Læddist inn.
        sneaked.3SG *in.*
        'She came home late. (<u>She</u>) opened the door(s). (<u>She</u>) sneaked in.'

(14) a. **Þig sé   __   á   morgun.*
         you see.1SG   on   morrow
         Intended: '(I'll) see you tomorrow.'
    b.   **Hún$_i$** kom   seint   heim.
        she   came   late   home
        *Dyrnar   opnaði   __$_i$.
        door-the.PL   opened.3SG
        Intended: 'She came home late (and <u>she</u>) opened the door(s).'

In other words: Not only the argument position of the null-argument must be empty but also Spec,CP.

Despite this structural uniformity of Type B null constructions, they are functionally disparate. At least three distinct types can be discerned: constructions 1) with unspecified discourse topics, 2) with specified conjunction reduction type topics, 3) with speech event topics, commonly but not exclusively referring to the speaker.

Type 1, with *unspecified discourse topics*, is exemplified in the Old Icelandic (6a), illustrated again in (15) (with added context).[10]

---

[10] For more examples of this sort, see Hjartardóttir (1993: 54–55).

(15) *Sigurðr* (...) *the farmers* (...)
then the grumbling abated and __ ended.3PL at that the gathering
(i.e., the involved, Sigurðr, the farmers, and others at the gathering, ended it at that)

This type has no clearly coreferential antecedent but the third person plural form of the verb indicates that the null stands for some group of people. The type has disappeared from the language; to my knowledge no examples of this sort have ever been reported for any Modern Icelandic texts or discourse.

Type 2, *with specified conjunction reduction type topics*, is exemplified in the Old Icelandic (6b), illustrated again in (16).

(16) **sire bishop**$_i$ *wakens, __$_i$ takes [self] up to (the) church*
and __$_i$ takes (...) *sacred things __$_i$ walks so*

This type plainly involves regular conjunction reduction, with or without an overt conjunction. It is cross-linguistically widespread, perhaps universal.[11] It is exemplified for Modern Icelandic in (7c), and it is easily found in various kinds of modern texts. See (17) and (18), from a 2015 novel (*Tvöfalt gler* by Halldóra Thoroddsen, pp. 6, 7).

(17) **Hún**$_i$ (...) __$_i$ *Vaknar um miðja nótt* (...) __$_i$ *Sest við*
 she wakens in middle night sits_down at
 suðurgluggann (...) __$_i$ *Horfir yfir sofandi borgina.*
 south_window looks over sleeping city-the
 'She (...) (<u>She</u>) wakens in the middle of the night. (<u>She</u>) sits down at the southern window (...) (<u>She</u>) looks over the sleeping city.'

(18) **Hún**$_i$ *hefði átt að bjóða honum inn* (...) __$_i$ *Hefði ekki átt*
 she had ought to invite him in had not ought
 að (...)
 to
 'She should have invited him in (...) (<u>She</u>) should not have (...)'

The type applies to AS-Topics, in the early as well as the modern language. However, in contrast to Type A nulls (*pro*), it cannot usually refer to its antecedent across another topic, i.e., the antecedent-null relation is subject to strict

---

[11] Regular conjunction reduction in Scandinavian is subject to much the same structural conditions as other types of Germanic Type B drop (as distinct from Type A *pro* drop), as illustrated in Sigurðsson and Maling (2010).

minimality, violated by intervention of another overt topic (AS or given). This is illustrated for Modern Icelandic in (19), where the first person subject is an intervening given topic (to the best of my knowledge the same is true of all earlier stages of the language).[12]

(19) **Hún**$_i$ (...) __$_i$ Vaknar um miðja nótt (...)__$_i$ Sest   við suðurgluggann (...)
    she   wakens in middle night   sits_down at south_window-the
    Ég er   við norðurgluggann.
    I   am at norhern_window-the
    ??__$_i$ Horfir   yfir sofandi borgina.
            looks.3SG over sleeping city-the
    Intended: 'She (...) (<u>She</u>) wakens in the middle of the night. (<u>She</u>) sits down at the southern window (...) I am at the northern window. (<u>She</u>) looks over the sleeping city.'

Type 3, with *speech event null topics*, is exemplified for Modern Icelandic in (7a–b) and illustrated again in (20).

(20) a. __ see.1SG you on morrow (= '<u>I</u>'ll see you tomorrow.')
    b. comes she? __ know-I not (= 'I don't know (<u>that</u>) / (<u>That</u>,) I don't know.')

This type is widespread across most colloquial (and informal written) modern Germanic varieties (see Sigurðsson 1989; Haegeman 1990; Mörnsjö 2002; Thráinsson 2007; Sigurðsson and Maling 2010; Sigurðsson 2011a; Nygård 2013). It has not been observed in Old Norse texts. It may have been non-existent in the language, but I doubt that very much. Rather, I believe, it is absent from the preserved texts because it is not compatible with the formal style of saga dialogues; these dialogues are of course not recorded spoken language, instead they involve fictive scene settings of verbal events that supposedly took place two or three centuries before they were first shaped in writing, in the style of formally trained and educated scribes.

Speech event null topics are typical of informal spoken language answers (i.e., speaker shift contexts), while the other types of null-topics we have been

---

[12] Thus, coreference in Spec,CP (Type B, in Old as well as Modern Icelandic) cannot easily circumvent strict Topic minimality, whereas coreference in an argument position could do so in Old Icelandic (Type A). Presumably, being in an A-position facilitated argument interpretation over distance in Old Icelandic (across subordinate C as well as intervening given topics). It is unclear why this property has gone lost (but see the discussion of Chinese, Finnish and Germanic null arguments in Sigurðsson 2011a).

looking at are confined to speaker (or writer) bounded contexts ("monologues"). So, despite being structurally uniform in V2 Germanic, Type B null-topics are functionally disparate. As we have seen, at least three types can be discerned for Icelandic, as explicitly stated in (21).

(21) a. Unspecified discourse topics in Old Icelandic, without a clearly coreferential antecedent but usually with roughly the plural reading 'those involved in the situation or the event' (distinct from generic readings).
  a. Specified conjunction reduction (CR) type topics, with or without an overt conjunction but with a clearly coreferential antecedent.
  b. Speech event topics, typical of informal spoken language answers.

While type (21a) has disappeared, types (21b–c) seem to be getting more frequent in the written language (cf. Kinn, Rusten, and Walkden 2016), presumably as a side effect of much increased use of informal written style. These drop types cannot always be easily distinguished from one another when the null argument is a subject. For objects, however, they are clearly distinct. Type (21b), the conjunction reduction type, cannot apply to objects in Modern Icelandic, while type (21c) with null objects, as in (7b)/(20b), is natural, provided that the null object is in the third person.[13]

In Modern Icelandic, the conjunction reduction type behaves much like conjunction reduction in English and other related languages – largely confined to subjects that are dropped or non-lexicalized under identity with a preceding coreferential subject. This subject-subject symmetry requirement did not apply in Old Norse, where subjects could be dropped under identity with a preceding object and vice versa (see Nygaard 1906: 10–11). This is illustrated for an object/null-subject chain in (22); similar chains have been documented for Old Italian, in contrast to Modern Italian (Poletto 2017).

(22) Síðan fekk   hon   **honom**$_i$ hit sœmilegsta sęti
    then gave she him   a   respectable seat
    ok   __$_i$ var með konungi um   vetrinn vel   metinn
    and   was with king   through winter   well appreciated.MASC
    'Then she allotted him a respectable seat and (*he*) stayed at the King's in the winter, well appreciated.'
    (14th century, Njals saga/Reykjabók, Sigurðsson 1994: 46)

---

[13] Commonly corresponding to a *það* 'it' or a *þetta* 'that, this' that refers to a proposition rather than to an argument; see the discussion of the Cardinaletti Puzzle in Sigurðsson (2011a).

In general, third person DPs of all sorts could be dropped rather freely in Old Norse, suggesting, as mentioned above, that null DPs do not require any special formal "licensing", although they are recovered in various structural positions under various conditions in various languages. The recovering conditions have changed in the history of Icelandic, such that the Type A strategy (referential drop from argument positions under coreference) has disappeared, in contrast to the Type B strategy (referential drop from Spec,CP). A similar development seems to be partly taking place in present-day colloquial Chinese (see Sigurðsson 2011a: 298).

3 Narrative Inversion (and Other V1 Declaratives)

The clausal word order typology of Icelandic is in many ways similar to that of other Scandinavian languages (see Thráinsson 2007). The major differences are that Icelandic is a semi-null-subject language, with non-referential (expletive/impersonal) subject drop, and usually has verb raising (to T) in subordinate clauses (and infinitives).[14] **SV**X is the neutral order in declarative clauses. Fronting of non-subjects yields a verb-second "inversion", typically X**VS**Y for definite subjects, with the subject next to the finite verb, X**VYS** for indefinite subjects, with the subject in a low or late position, and X**VY** in impersonal subjectless clauses. In addition, however, Icelandic has *declarative V1* orders: **VS, VXS** and subjectless **V**X. See (9), repeated here, and (23).

(9) *Johan Cryuff*$_i$ (...) *Fyrsti leikur hans*$_i$ *fyrir Barcelona var í október*
J.C.   first game his for B.   was in October
1973 og **skoraði** *hann*$_i$ *strax   tvö mörk í 4-0 sigri*
1973 and scored he   immediately two goals in 4-0 victory
á Granada.
on Granada
'Johan Cryuff (...) His first game for Barcelona was in October 1973 and he immediately scored two goals in a 4-0 victory over Granada.'
(https://is.wikipedia.org/wiki/Johan_Cruyff, 2016-08-24)

---

14 SVX thus being the canonical order in declarative subordinate clauses. XV(Y)S (V2 type) orders ("then left she", "then left probably some of the guests") are infrequent and often ungrammatical in subordinate clauses, as opposed to main clauses, and subordinate interrogatives have *wh*-SV order ("when she left"), whereas main clause interrogatives have the V2 type *wh*-VS order ("When left she?"). The common assumption that Icelandic is a symmetric V2 language is thus incorrect.

(23) *Enginn dómari var mættur kl.   4, þegar leikurinn   átti   að hefjast.*
 no   referee was arrived clock 4 when match-the ought to begin
 Var beðið *eftir dómara til kl.   5.30.*
 was waited after referee till clock 5.30
 Voru þá   *nokkrir drengjanna farnir í   burtu.*
 were then some   boys-the   gone in way
 'No referee had arrived at 4, when the match was supposed to begin. The involved waited for a referee until 5.30. Some of the boys had then left.'
 (http://timarit.is/view_page_init.jsp?pageId=3260235)

I specifically refer to the VS type in (9) as *Narrative Inversion*, NI (distinguishing it from the other V1 types, following Sigurðsson 1990, 1994). It has a number of typical traits, as listed in (24).

(24) a. The subject follows immediately after the initial finite verb: VS.
   b. The subject is a given topic at the clausal level, commonly referring to an already established aboutness topic at the discourse level.
   c. It is most frequent for first person subjects, then for pronominal third person subjects, and least frequent for non-pronominal subjects (second person arguments are rare in narrative texts and disregarded here). Thus, in the narrative text counts in Sigurðsson (1990: 45), 47% of the relevant clauses (VS and SV root clauses) with a first person subject had VS order, while that ratio was 22% for pronominal third person subjects and 10% for non-pronominal DP subjects (overwhelmingly most of these, in turn, had a definite DP subject).
   d. It is almost exclusively confined to root clauses and is all but nonexistent in non-root environments.[15]
   e. It is common in *og-* 'and' conjuncts (as in (22)), but virtually nonexistent in adversative *en-* 'but' conjuncts.

The other two declarative V1 types (VXS and subjectless VX) differ from NI. First, they are incompatible with pronominal subjects (i.e., they either contain no subject or only a non-topical subject), and, second, they are grammatical in many non-root contexts. One trait all three V1 types have in common is (24e): they are all frequent in *og-* 'and' conjuncts but almost nonexistent in *en-* 'but' conjuncts. The common denominator for all three types is that V1 declaratives

---

[15] A few examples of embedded NI are reported in Sigurðsson (1994: 74–75, 154; see also Thráinsson 2007: 29).

involve discourse continuity and cannot usually contain any unexpected or adversative information (in relation to previous discourse). V1 declaratives are thus typical of certain narrative texts (including, e.g., sports reports) and some reasoning texts (scientific, political). As for NI, the subject is a given topic, regardless of person; a third person NI subject, in turn, typically refers to an already established aboutness topic at the discourse level, either a maintained aboutness topic, as in (9) above, or a reestablished aboutness topic, as in the Old Icelandic (8). Consider also the Old Icelandic (25), with two subsequent NI clauses with distinct reestablished topics. The broad context is that Hallgerda marries Glum, brother of Thorarin. The immediate context is given in English within square brackets (from the 1861 translation by George W. Dasent).

(25) [*Hallgerda kept her temper down that winter, and they liked her well enough. But when the spring came, the brothers talked about their property, and Thorarin said – "I will give up to you the house at Varmalek, for that is readiest to your hand, and I will go down south to Laugarness and live there, but Engey we will have both of us in common". Glum was willing enough to do that.*]

Fór Þórarinn suðr byggðum en þau bjoggu þar eptir.
went Þ. south district but they stayed there behind
Réð Hallgerðr sér hjón (...)
hired H. herself servants
'So Thorarin went down to the south of that district, and they [Hallgerda and Glum] stayed behind there. Hallgerda hired servants.'
(Njals saga/Reykjabók; Sigurðsson 1994: 139)

In Old High German, in contrast, "V1-clauses serve to introduce a new discourse referent (...) and therefore are typically used in presentational sentences, foremost in the beginning of texts or episodes" (Hinterhölzl and Petrova 2010: 316).[16] This is orthogonal to Icelandic, where declarative V1 never initiates an episode, neither in longer narratives nor in short jokes and anecdotes. In view of this sharp contrast between German and Icelandic declarative V1, it is tempting to speculate that the Icelandic type is part of the Celtic heritage in Iceland, as Celtic

---

16 This characterization is taken to hold for Modern German as well, to the extent that it applies declarative V1 (see Önnerfors 1997; Hinterhölzl and Petrova 2010: 316, fn. 1). However, the "Icelandic" type *und haben wir* 'and have we' (i.e., 'and (thus) we have') does occur, albeit rarely (Gisbert Fanselow, p.c.).

languages are generally VSX.[17] Around 65% of the original female population in the country is believed to have come from Ireland and other Celtic parts of the British Islands (Helgason et al. 2009) and Early and Medieval Irish culture is renowned for its strong narrative tradition. The tellers or creators of the Old Icelandic sagas are all anonymous, while Scandinavian skaldic poetry is crowded with hundreds of names of male scalds. That is perhaps not a coincidence. It does not imply that the scribes of the sagas were women, but it might suggest that the saga tradition was considered to have "unmanly" roots and thus less prestigious than the highly esteemed skaldic tradition.

NI is almost exclusively a root phenomenon, like Type B topic drop. The conjunction reduction type of Type B and NI are partly interchangeable. However, this only holds when the subject refers to an aboutness topic (overt or silent) in an immediately preceding clause (the topic drop construction being subject to strict minimality, violated by intervention of an overt topic, AS or given, cf. (19)). Consider the example in (26).

(26) *Maximus hélt   með her   sinn til Ítalíu árið 387*
     M.   went with army his to Italy year 387
     og **neyddist** *Valentinianus þá   að flýja til Theodosiusar.*
     and was_forced V.   then to flee to Th.
     Theodosius$_i$ leit   á Valentinianus sem bandamann sinn
     Th.   looked at V.   as ally   his
     og **fór** *hann$_i$ því með her til Ítalíu*
     and went he   thus with army to Italy
     og ___$_i$ mætti Maximusi í orrustu
     and   met   M.   in battle
     og ___$_i$ sigraði hann
     and   defeated him

'Maximus went with his army to Italy in the year 387 and then Valentinian was forced to flee to Theodosius. Theodosius considered Valentinian to be an ally of his, and therefore he went with an army to Italy and (<u>he</u>) met Maximus in a battle and (<u>he</u>) defeated him.'
(https://is.wikipedia.org/wiki/Theodosius_1, 29 December 2016)

---

17 This idea might seem to be undermined by the fact that NI occurs in texts that are usually taken to be Old Norwegian rather than Old Icelandic (see examples in Kinn 2016). However, the Old Norse saga genre is overwhelmingly Icelandic, so the saga style in Old Norwegian texts might very well be strongly influenced by the Icelandic narrative tradition.

Here we have two cases of NI ("and was_forced Valentinian", "and went he") followed by two cases of topic drop. The first NI case is not interchangeable with topic drop (as a dropped subject would have to be coreferential with 'Maximus'), but the second one is, and both topic drop cases are interchangeable with NI (which would yield the types "and met he Maximus" and "and defeated he him").

As seen in "and was_forced Valentinian" in (26) and in the Old Icelandic examples in (25), NI subjects (like subjects in regular subject-initial clauses) *can* be coreferential with a non-local antecedent. More commonly, however, NI subjects are coreferential with the closest possible antecedent. Consider (27) and (28).

(27) *Narrative Inversion:*
Ólafur Jónsson (...) Bróðir Ólafs er Jón Jónsson háskólanemi
Ó.   J.   brother Olaf's is J. J.   student
og **er** unnusta hans María Pálsdóttir.
and is fiancé his M. P.
'O. J. (...) O's brother is **J. J. student**$_i$ and his$_i$ fiancé is M.P.'

(28) *Subject-initial order:*
Ólafur Jónsson (...) Bróðir Ólafs er Jón Jónsson háskólanemi
Ó.   J.   brother Olaf's is J. J.   student
og unnusta hans **er** María Pálsdóttir.
and fiancé his is M. P.
'**O. J.**$_i$ (...) **O's**$_i$ brother is J. J. student and his$_i$ fiancé is M.P.'

As seen, the subject ('his fiancé') in the NI example in (27) refers to an immediately preceding AS-Topic, *Jón Jónsson*, whereas the subject in the subject-initial order in (28) refers to a prominent discourse topic, across the potential topic *Jón Jónsson*.[18] Overt subjects in clause-initial position (Spec,CP on standard accounts) thus have a stronger context-scanning capacity than both null subjects in Spec,CP and overt subjects in NI.

---

18 The opposite coreference relations are much degraded, but the appropriate marking would be # (semantically or pragmatically infelicitous) rather than * (ungrammatical). The example in (27) is modelled on a parallel example in an obituary in *Morgunblaðið* 11 February 2017 (with different names).

4 Concluding Discussion

Icelandic does not provide evidence for distinct structural positions for different topic types (disregarding hanging topics). However, referential third person *pro* drop in Old Icelandic (Type A), several types of topic drop (Type B) in Old and Modern Icelandic, and Narrative Inversion, also in both Old and Modern Icelandic, are all phenomena that are sensitive to topicality, either involving Aboutness-Shift topics or given topics or both, thus showing that different types of topicality are active in this language.

Topicality has effects at the clausal level, but it is contextually preconditioned, reflecting relations between discourse (the common ground) and the C edge (plus the inner CP phase). It is thus a category of *broad syntax* (in the sense of Sigurðsson 2014), rather than merely of narrow CP-internal syntax. If Universal Grammar is defined as narrowly as in recent minimalist work topicality is plausibly not part of it or provided by it. Nevertheless, it seems uncontroversial that topicality is a universally available category or phenomenon, suggesting that it is an interface third factor phenomenon (in the sense of Chomsky 2005). That is, a phenomenon stemming from some universal capacity that is distinct from Universal Grammar but interacts with it in the shaping of externalized grammar, differently so in different languages. Thus, while the work of Frascarelli et al. suggests that Italian has developed distinct structural C edge correlates with distinct topic types, this has not happened in Icelandic. The fact that distinct types of topicality are nevertheless operative in Icelandic grammar is one of many facts that raise the central question of what principles steer the molding processes that build individual grammars from the scratch of Universal Grammar and other conceptual/biological subsystems.[19]

Acknowledgments: For helpful comments and discussions many thanks to anonymous reviewers and Mara Frascarelli, Gisbert Fanselow, Werner Abraham, Verner Egerland, and Valéria Molnár. The research for this paper is part of a project on pronouns and pronoun features, partly funded by a grant from Riksbankens Jubelumsfond, P15-0389:1.

---

[19] I intentionally disregard linguistic input here (the second factor in Chomsky 2005). As argued in Sigurðsson (2011b) and related work, linguistic input is secondary in the development of language.

References

Berwick, Robert C. & Noam Chomsky. 2011. The biolinguistic program: The current state of its development. In Anna Maria Di Sciullo & Cedric Boeckx (eds.), *The biolinguistic enterprise: new perspectives on the evolution and nature of the human language faculty*, 19–41. Oxford: Oxford University Press.
Bianchi, Valentina & Mara Frascarelli. 2009. The dark side of the phase: cyclic access is not 'blind'. Paper presented at GLOW 32, Nantes.
Bianchi, Valentina & Mara Frascarelli 2010. Is topic a root phenomenon? *Iberia: An International Journal of Theoretical Linguistics* 2. 43–88.
Braune, Wilhelm. 1894. Zur Lehre von der deutschen Wortstellung [Contribution to the study of German word order]. *Forschungen zur deutschen Philologie*, 34–51. Leipzig: Verlag von Veit & Comp.
Chomsky, Noam. 1981. *Lectures on government and binding*. Dordrecht: Foris.
Chomsky, Noam. 2001. Derivation by phase. In Michael Kenstowicz (ed.), *Ken Hale: a life in language*, 1–52. Cambridge, MA: The MIT Press.
Chomsky, Noam. 2005. Three factors in language design. *Linguistic Inquiry* 36. 1–22.
Chomsky, Noam. 2008. On phases. In Robert Freidin, Carlos P. Otero & Maria Luisa Zubizarreta (eds.), *Foundational issues in linguistic theory. Essays in honor of Jean-Roger Vergnaud*, 133–166. Cambridge, MA: The MIT Press.
Chomsky, Noam. 2013. Problems of projection. *Lingua* 130. 33–49.
Cinque, Guglielmo. 1999. *Adverbs and functional heads: a cross-linguistic perspective*. Oxford: Oxford University Press.
Déchaine, Rose-Marie & Martina Wiltschko. 2002. Decomposing pronouns. *Linguistic Inquiry* 33. 409–442.
Frascarelli, Mara. 2007. Subjects, topics and the interpretation of referential pro. An interface approach to the linking of (null) pronouns. *Natural Language & Linguistic Theory* 25. 691–734.
Frascarelli, Mara. 2011. Discourse features in the interface interpretation of topics: a phase-based compositional account. Paper given at Workshop on prosody and syntax, University of Venice, September. 2011. http://asit.maldura.unipd.it/prosynt/Handout%20Frascarelli.pdf. (accessed 1 November 2016).
Frascarelli, Mara & Roland Hinterhölzl. 2007. Types of topics in German and Italian. In Susanne Winkler & Kerstin Schwabe (eds.), *On information structure, meaning and form*, 87–116. Amsterdam & Philadelphia: John Benjamins.
Grohmann, Kleanthes. 1997. On left dislocation. *Groninger Arbeiten zur germanistischen Linguistik* 40. 1–33.
Haegeman, Liliane. 1990. Understood subjects in English diaries. *Multilingua* 9. 157–199.
Helgason, Agnar, Carles Lalueza-Fox, Shyamali Ghosh, Sigrún Sigurðardóttir, Maria Lourdes Sampietro, Elena Gigli, Adam Baker, Jaume Bertranpetit, Lilja Árnadóttir, Unnur Þorsteinsdottir & Kári Stefánsson. 2009. Sequences from first settlers reveal rapid evolution in Icelandic mtDNA pool. *Journal of Population Genetics* 5 e1000343. doi:10.1371 (accessed 1 November 2016).
Hinterhölzl, Roland & Svetlana Petrova. 2010. From V1 to V2 in West Germanic. *Lingua* 120. 315–328.

Hjartardóttir, Þóra Björk. 1993. Getið í eyðurnar [Guessed into the gaps]. Reykjavík: Institute of Linguistics.
Kinn, Kari. 2016. Null arguments in Old Norwegian: interaction between pronouns and the functional categories of the clause. *Cambridge Occasional Papers in Linguistics* 9. 108–129.
Kinn, Kari, Kristian A. Rusten & George Walkden. 2016. Null subjects in Early Icelandic. *Journal of Germanic Linguistics* 28. 31–78.
Mörnsjö, Maria. 2002. *V1 declaratives in spoken Swedish*. Lund: Studentlitteratur.
Nygaard, Marius. 1900. Verbets stilling i sætningen i det norröne sprog [The position of the verb in the clause in Old Norse]. *Arkiv för nordisk filologi* 16. 209–241.
Nygaard, Marius. 1906. *Norrøn syntax* [Old Norse syntax]. Oslo: H. Aschehoug & Co (W. Nygaard).
Nygård, Mari. 2013. *Discourse ellipsis in spontaneously spoken Norwegian: Clausal architecture and licensing conditions*. Trondheim: Norwegian University of Science and Technology doctoral dissertation.
Önnerfors, Olaf. 1997. *Verb-erst-Deklarativsätze. Grammatik und Pragmatik*. Stockholm: Almquist & Wiksell International.
Poletto, Cecilia. 2017. Null subjects in Old Italian. Ms., Frankfurt am Main: Goethe-Universität.
Rizzi, Luigi. 1986. Null objects in Italian and the theory of *pro*. *Linguistic Inquiry* 17. 501–557.
Rizzi, Luigi. 1997. The fine structure of the left periphery. In Liliane Haegeman (ed.), *Elements of grammar. Handbook in generative syntax*, 281–337. Dordrecht: Kluwer.
Sigurðsson, Halldór Ármann. 1989. *Verbal syntax and case in Icelandic*. Lund: University of Lund PhD dissertation. https://ling.auf.net/lingbuzz/002361 and https://babel.hathitrust.org/cgi/pt?id=mdp.39015016997390;view=1up;seq=7
Sigurðsson, Halldór Ármann. 1990. V1 Declaratives and verb raising in Icelandic. In Joan Maling & Annie Zaenen (eds.), *Modern Icelandic syntax*, 41–69. San Diego: Academic Press.
Sigurðsson, Halldór Ármann. 1993. Argument drop in Old Icelandic. *Lingua* 89. 143–176.
Sigurðsson, Halldór Ármann. 1994. *Um frásagnarumröðun og grundvallarorðaröð í forníslensku* [On narrative inversion and basic word order in Old Icelandic]. Reykjavík: Institute of Linguistics.
Sigurðsson, Halldór Ármann. 2004. Meaningful silence, meaningless sounds. *Linguistic Variation Yearbook* 4. 235–259.
Sigurðsson, Halldór Ármann. 2011a. Conditions on argument drop. *Linguistic Inquiry* 42. 267–304.
Sigurðsson, Halldór Ármann. 2011b. On UG and materialization. *Linguistic Analysis* 37. 367–388.
Sigurðsson, Halldór Ármann. 2012. Thoughts on cartography and universality. In Valentina Bianchi & Cristiano Chesi (eds.), *Enjoy linguistics! Papers offered to Luigi Rizzi on the occasion of his 60th birthday*. http://www.ciscl.unisi.it/gg60/ (accessed 1 November 2016).
Sigurðsson, Halldór Ármann. 2014. Context-linked grammar. *Language Sciences* 43. 175–188.
Sigurðsson, Halldór Ármann. 2017. Who are we – and who is I? About Person and SELF. In Laura R. Bailey & Michelle Sheehan (eds.), *Order and structure in syntax II: subjecthood and argument structure* (Open Generative Syntax series 1), 199–221. Berlin: Language Science Press.

Sigurðsson, Halldór Ármann & Verner Egerland. 2009. Impersonal null-subjects in Icelandic and elsewhere. *Studia Linguistica* 63. 158–185.
Sigurðsson, Halldór Ármann & Joan Maling 2010. The empty left edge condition. In Michael T. Putnam (ed.), *Exploring crash-proof grammars*, 59–86. Amsterdam & Philadelphia: John Benjamins.
Stausland Johnsen, Sverre. 2016. Kari Kinn, Public defense for PhD degree. http://folk.uio.no/sverrej/talk_files/2016/march/uio/stausland.johnsen.march.2016.uio.pdf (accessed 1 November 2016).
Thráinsson, Höskuldur. 1979. *On complementation in Icelandic*. New York: Garland.
Thráinsson, Höskuldur. 2007. *The syntax of Icelandic*. Cambridge: Cambridge University Press.

Verner Egerland
Apropos the Topic

On Topic-introducing Expressions in Swedish

Abstract: The inquiry into topicality calls for a deeper understanding of explicit "topic markers" such as *apropos* and *concerning*, which are found in many if not all the languages of Europe. From a syntactic perspective, phrases introduced by such expressions are not identifiable with any of the construction types that alter the information structure of the clause involving the left periphery. Thus, *apropos* and *concerning* do not introduce a syntactically topicalized element, nor a dislocated element, nor a hanging topic, given some commonly assumed criteria. Instead, it is argued here that phrases introduced by *apropos* and *concerning* represent a fourth such construction type. From the view point of information structure, *apropos* and *concerning*, and presumably similar topic-marking expressions, differ in the sense that they lexicalize pragmatic features such as *aboutness* and *givenness* in different ways. The argumentation is based on Swedish data and limited to two such expressions: *apropå* 'apropos' and *beträffande* 'concerning'.

Keywords: topicalization, dislocation, left dislocation, hanging topic, givenness, aboutness.

1 Introduction

While topicalization and dislocation have attracted much attention in the generative literature, less has been written about such lexical expressions that are used to explicitly mark or introduce a topical element. Well-studied Germanic and Romance languages have a rather considerable repertory of such expressions, as for instance English *with respect to x, with regard to x, apropos x, concerning x, as for x, speaking of x, regarding x, as far as x is concerned*, just to mention some of them. In traditional treatments, there has been a tendency to list such topic markers as one rather homogeneous class, because they fall "within the same general area of meaning" (Quirk et al. 1985: 706). If this had been the exhaustive characterization of such a category, it would constitute a rather unusual case of lexical redundancy. It is clear, however, that different subclasses can and should be recognized within

---

Verner Egerland, Lund University

https://doi.org/10.1515/9781501504488-010

this group of expressions. Such a categorization is of some importance for the future inquiry into topic-related issues. It has been suggested, for instance, that a topic test can be based on the substitution of the topic by expressions such as *as for x*, or embedding of the utterance in *about*-sentences (Reinhart 1981: 64–65). Such testing will presumably give variable results depending on which expressions are used, and we might expect subtle cross-linguistic differences as well.

In this article, I discuss such ideas based on Swedish data. From a purely intuitive viewpoint, which remains to be spelled out in detail, the Swedish words *apropå* 'apropos' and *beträffande* 'concerning' introduce topicalization as in (1)–(2).

(1) *Apropå Johan, han kommer imorgon.*
     APROPOS John   he   comes   tomorrow
     'Speaking of John, he's coming tomorrow.'

(2) *Beträffande Johan, han kommer imorgon.*
     CONCERNING John   he   comes   tomorrow
     'As far as John is concerned, he's coming tomorrow.'

The purpose of this study is two-fold: First, I show that these expressions do not straightforwardly correspond to those topicalization and dislocation structures that have been identified and analyzed in the syntactic literature. Second, from the perspective of information structure, I argue that the expressions in question are grammatical markers of pragmatic notions such as *aboutness* and *givenness*.

Swedish *beträffande* comes from German *betreffen*, while *apropå* is a borrowing from French *à propos*. Both words, and *apropå* in particular, have several cognates among Germanic and Romance languages. Even if some basic properties of such expressions are consistent across the languages where such words are attested, there may of course be cross-linguistic variation with respect to some syntactic and pragmatic patterns. The comparative analysis, however, goes beyond present aims: Although some comparative remarks will be made as we proceed, the argumentation presented here is based on Swedish data. [1]

From now on and throughout this paper, I refer to the fronted constituent introduced by *apropå* in (1) as the APROPOS TOPIC (APT), and that of (2) as the CONCERNING TOPIC (CNT).[2] Section 2 presents an overview of the syntactic

---

[1] Hence, I will not explore to what extent these topic introducers are similar to topic markers such as *wa* in Japanese (cf. Kuno 1973, and subsequent work).

[2] In the glosses, I have chosen to translate *apropå* with English *apropos* and *beträffande* with *concerning*. This choice serves practical purposes, but is not intended to mean that I expect the English words to be equivalents to the Swedish ones in every regard. Part of the interest in this

properties of APTs and CNTs in Swedish, while section 3 contains a discussion of their pragmatic properties.

2 The Syntactic Properties of APT/CNT

In 2.1, I first discuss some general properties of these constructions, showing that both APTs and CNTs can be realized sentence externally and sentence internally.[3] In 2.2–2.3, I argue that the APT/CNT does not unambiguously correspond to any of the three topicalization strategies commonly recognized in the syntactic literature: they are neither topicalizations, dislocations, nor hanging topics.

2.1 The Two Surface Realizations of APT/CNT

To begin with, consider that the APT and the CNT in Swedish are compatible with two different word order patterns. In (3a-b), the introducing APT/CNT is followed by unmarked word order (subject-verb) in the matrix. In (4a-b), on the other hand, we see subject inversion triggered by the APT/CNT.[4]

(3) a. *Apropå Johan, han kommer imorgon.*
    APROPOS John   he comes tomorrow

---

field of research lies precisely in the fact that, at present, we do not know to what extent these words are each other's equivalents.
3 The term "construction" will be used throughout in a purely descriptive fashion, without implications as to the theoretical status of the concept "construction".
4 As pointed out to me by Elisabeth Engdahl (p.c.), and other native speaker consultants, some speakers prefer inserting the adverbial element *så* between the APT and the finite verb in an example such as (i), corresponding to (4a), though not in (ii), which corresponds to (3a).

(i)   *Apropå Johan så träffar jag honom imorgon.*
      APROPOS John so see   I   him   tomorrow
      'Apropos John, I'll meet him tomorrow.'

(ii) **Apropå Johan, så jag träffar honom imorgon.*
      APROPOS John   so I   see   him   tomorrow

I believe the status of (i) and (4a) is a matter of rather idiosyncratic variation, which has no bearing on the following discussion. It should be noticed that the element in question, *så*, in many Scandinavian varieties frequently attaches to the finite verb when the sentence-initial position is occupied by adverbial elements (Egerland and Falk 2010; Nordström 2010; Eide 2011).

b. *Beträffande Johan, han kommer imorgon.*
   CONCERNING John he comes tomorrow

(4) a. *Apropå Johan kommer han imorgon.*
       APROPOS John comes he tomorrow
    b. *Beträffande Johan kommer han imorgon*
       CONCERNING Johan comes he tomorrow
       'Apropos/concerning John, he's coming tomorrow.' = (3a-b), (4a-b)

There are two surface differences between (3a-b) and (4a-b), namely word order and intonation. In (3a-b), there is a prosodic break between the APT/CNT and the following matrix that is, typical of a left dislocation or a hanging topic structure. In examples (4a-b), on the other hand, there is no such break, but rather we find the intonation contour of topicalization. There is no prosodic difference between APT and CNT: The intended intonation patterns corresponding to (3a-b) and (4a-b) are those illustrated in (5) and (6), respectively:

(5)

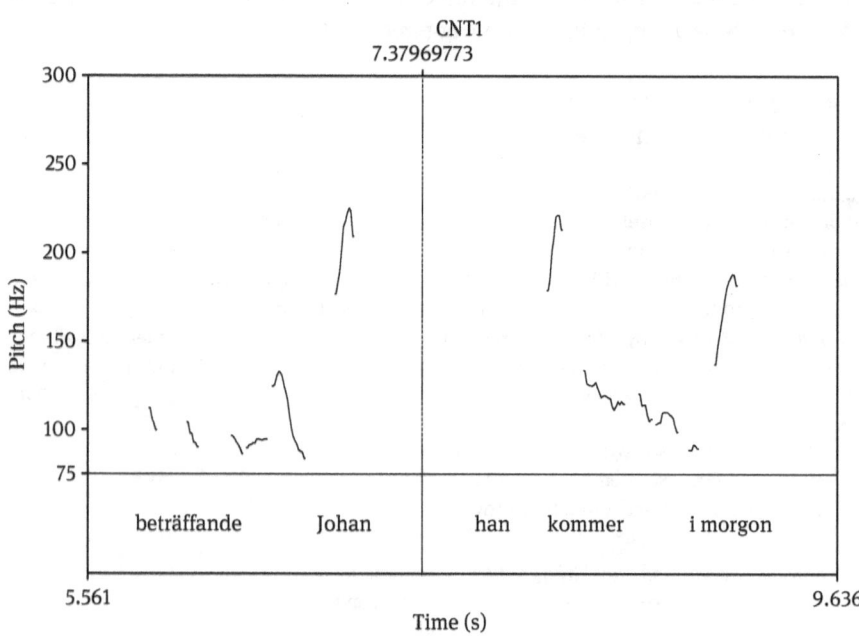

(6)

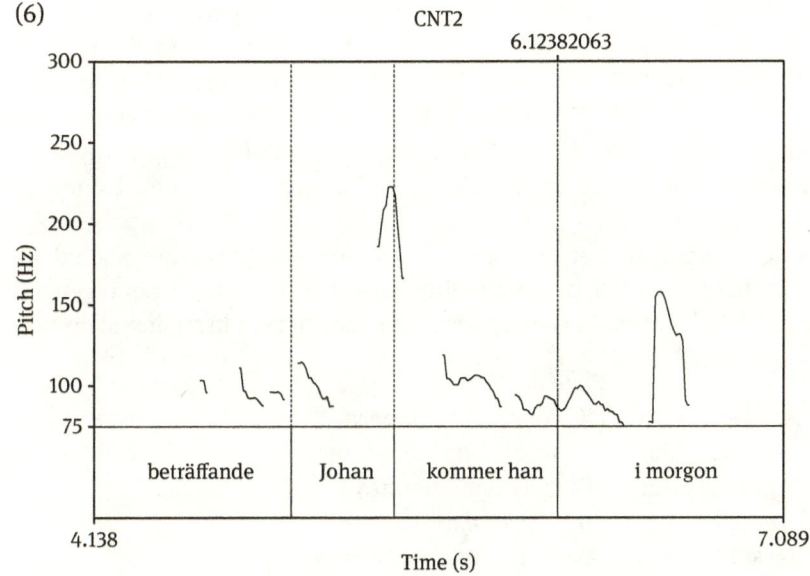

In (5), the introductory constituent and the following matrix have separate pitch accents. Observe the fall-raise contour on *Johan* as well as on the main verb *kommer*. On the contrary, in (6), the clausal pitch falls only on the DP (*Johan*).[5] Assuming that such patterns translate into syntactic structure, I suggest that this distinction be spelled out as in the two structures in (7) and (8). Thus, in (7) the APT/CNT are external to the clausal structure while in (8), they are integrated into it:

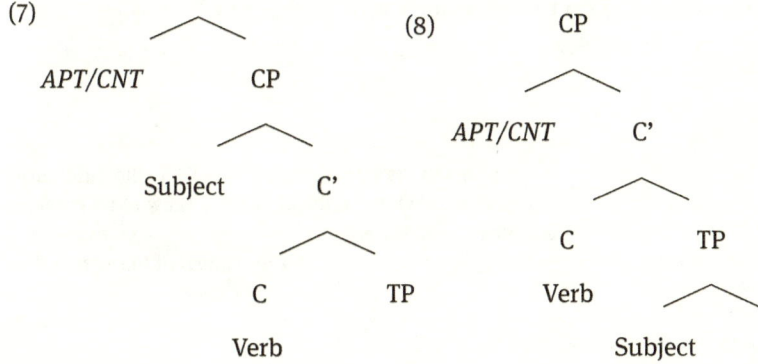

---

5 In addition, there may or may not be an accent on the final PP *imorgon* 'tomorrow'. This is not directly relevant for the present discussion.

I assume that, in (7), the APT/CNT is situated in a left peripheral position, which, for the moment, I assume is a Topic Phrase external to the nuclear clause (cf. Rizzi 1997), though the precise nature of this projection remains unclear. In (8), given that Swedish is a V2 language, the subject-verb inversion is an indication that APT/CNT is in [Spec,C] following the analysis of Swedish sentence structure of, for example, Platzack (1986) and Holmberg and Platzack (1995).

Although here I do not attempt a cross-linguistic survey, it should be pointed out that the double possibility illustrated in (7) and (8) is not a general property of V2-languages. In German, for instance, subject inversion as in (9b) is not acceptable:[6,7]

(9) a. *Apropos Johan, ich treffe ihn morgen.*
    APROPOS John I meet him tomorrow
    'Apropos John, I will meet him tomorrow.'
  b. **Apropos Johan treffe ich ihn morgen.*
    APROPOS John see I him tomorrow

There is a further difference between Swedish and German on this point: in Swedish, APT/CNT can appear in an embedded clause, as in (10):

(10) *Hon sa att hon apropå/beträffande Johan*
    she said that she APROPOS/CONCERNING John
    inte ville träffa honom igen.
    not wanted to-see him again
    'Apropos John, she said that she didn't want to see him again.'

---

[6] Despite the fact that the contrasts illustrated in (3a-b) and (4a-b), as well as the differences between Swedish and German mentioned in the text, are quite obvious, I know of no previous treatment of this phenomenon in the syntactic literature.

[7] An anonymous reviewer points out that (i) is acceptable in his/her variety of German, unlike the example (9b):

(i) *Hans betreffend werde ich mit Maria reden.*
    Hans concerning will I with Maria speak
    'Concerning Hans, I will speak with Mary (about him).'

This fact may be taken to suggest that, in the relevant variety of German, *Hans betreffend* ('concerning Hans') can be topicalized when it is selected by a verb such as *reden* 'to speak (about)'. I will not pursue this idea in this article.

Such a construction is ungrammatical in German, as in (11):

(11) *Sie sagte, dass sie apropos Johan
 she said that she APROPOS John
 ihn nicht mehr sehen wollte
 him not anymore to-see wanted

It should be noticed that the Swedish example (10) has the word order of a subordinate clause: the finite V appears lower than negation (Holmberg and Platzack 1995). That this is indeed a case of subordination is further suggested by the fact that the interpretation of APT/CNT in embedded environments is subject to logophoric shift in the sense of, for example, Speas and Tenny (2003), and Reuland (2006). In (12), the APT/CNT is speaker oriented: trivially, APT/CNT relates to the speaker's discourse. On the other hand, in (13), where APT/CNT are embedded in the complement of the verb *say*, both relate to the grammatical subject's previous discourse:[8]

(12) Apropå / beträffande Johan, hon träffade honom igår.
 APROPOS / CONCERNING John she met him yesterday
 speaker orientation

(13) Hon sa att hon apropå/beträffande Johan
 she said that she APROPOS/CONCERNING John
 hade träffat honom dagen innan.
 had met him day-DET before
 subject orientation

---

[8] Note that such shifting typically occurs when the governing verb is a verb of saying, as in (13)–(14). If, as in (i), the main clause predicate is *she did not regret*, for instance, the logophoric shift is blocked.

(i) ??Hon ångrade inte att hon apropå/beträffande Johan
 she regretted not that she APROPOS/CONCERNING John
 hade träffat honom dagen innan.
 had met him day-DET before
 'She didn't regret that she, apropos John, had seen him the day before.'

To the extent that such a reference can be established, the APT/CNT of (i) relates to the speaker and not to the embedded subject. However, the acceptability of (i) is downgraded in my opinion.

Interestingly, when the APT/CNT appears in clause initial position, (hence, in [Spec,C] by assumption) both interpretations are available as given in (14):

(14) *Apropå/beträffande Johan sa   hon att   hon*
     APROPOS/CONCERNING John said she that she
     hade träffat honom dagen   innan.
     had met   him   day-DET before
     subject/speaker orientation
     'Apropos John, she said that she had met him the day before.'

This can be taken to suggest that the surface structure of (14) is compatible with two different derivations: One in which the APT/CNT belongs to the main clause, where it refers to the speaker, and one in which the APT/CNT, instead, has moved from the subordinate clause. In its surface position, then, the APT/CNT maintains the interpretation it acquires under embedding and is thus reconstructed in its basic position.[9]

Hence, by assumption, the acceptability of (14), in its relevant reading, is linked to that of (13), while both of (13) and (14) are acceptable because of the possibility of integrating the APT/CNT into the syntactic structure, as in (4). It thus makes sense that the examples (4), (13), and (14) are all possible (as in Swedish) or are all excluded (as in German).

Lastly, note that the intonational contour illustrated in (5) and (6) is compatible with the claim of, for example, Jacobs (1984), Krifka (2001), and Bianchi and Frascarelli (2010), that certain instances of topic can be regarded as illocutions, assuming that "topic selection is (...) an initiating speech act that requires a subsequent speech act, like an assertion, question, command, or curse about the entity that was selected" (Krifka 2001: 25). In fact, when the APT/CNT appears in the left periphery, [Spec,C] remains available for *wh*-elements. APT/CNT, thus, can introduce questions as in (15):

(15) *Apropå/beträffande Johan, vem har sett   honom på sistone?*
     APROPOS/CONCERNING John, who has seen him   lately
     'Apropos John, who has seen him lately?'

---

[9] In this sense, there is a certain similarity between the derivation of the ATP/CNT in (14) and the formal movement of scrambled elements to the Comp-field in Frey's (2006) account, as well as Holmberg's (2006: 560) analysis of Stylistic Fronting. It is not excluded that the surface position of APT/CNT in (14), a high position of the midfield, can be identified with the target site of scrambled elements in German. However, this possibility will not be explored further here.

On the other hand, the APT/CNT integrated in sentence structure appears to have the distribution of an adverbial phrase.

The question then arises whether APT/CNT can be identified with any of the topicalization or dislocation constructions that have been thoroughly discussed and analyzed in the syntactic literature. These are briefly presented in section 2.2, and subsequently compared with APT/CNT in 2.3.

2.2 Topicalization, Dislocation, and Hanging Topics

Following standard assumptions (Ross 1967; Cinque 1990; van Riemsdijk 1997; Alexiadou 2006, among many others), I assume that there are three major construction types that alter the information structure of an assertive sentence by involving the left periphery: topicalization, dislocation, and hanging topics.

First, syntactic topicalization structures are analyzed as an A'-dependency holding between the topicalized element in sentence initial position and its trace, licensed as a variable. In a V2 language such as Swedish, topicalization obligatorily triggers subject inversion. In Swedish, the structure is associated with contrast:

(16) *Johan$_i$ träffar jag t$_i$ imorgon.*
 John$_i$ meet I t$_i$ tomorrow
 'John, I will meet tomorrow.'

Second, the dislocation structure does not involve the nuclear clause; for instance, it has been analyzed as base generation in the left periphery (Cinque 1990) or as displacement at PF (Erteschik-Shir 2006, 2007). The dislocated element is repeated by a resumptive pronoun internal to the clause. The following matrix clause has the canonical subject-verb word order:

(17) *Johan, jag träffar honom imorgon.*
 John I see him tomorrow
 'John, I will meet him tomorrow.'

Third, the hanging topic is placed in the left periphery but, unlike dislocation, does not need to be syntactically connected with the matrix (e.g. Alexiadou 2006). Thus, in an example such as (18), the hanging topic is not introduced by a preposition despite the fact that it refers to an oblique argument in the matrix:[10]

(18) *(Ja) den där restaurangen (ja), dit går jag gärna tillbaka.*
(yes) that there restaurant-DET (yes) there go I willingly back
'Well, that restaurant, I'd like to go back there.'

At the surface, the APT/CNT in the peripheral position of (7) is similar to dislocation or hanging topics, while the APT/CNT in [Spec,C] in (8) superficially looks like topicalization. However, neither of these analyses can be defended as argued in 2.3–2.5.

2.3 APT/CNT and Topicalization

In section 2.1, I speculated that the APT/CNT can undergo movement from an embedded clause to the matrix. However, the topical element itself, *John* in (19), clearly does not undergo A'-movement. First, *John* does not leave behind a trace analyzed as a variable:

(19) **Apropå/beträffande Johan$_i$ träffade jag t$_i$ igår.*
APROPOS/CONCERNING John$_i$ met I t$_i$ yesterday

Second, the APT/CNT does not give raise to weak crossover effects (Postal 1971). Take for instance example (20), in which the possessive *his* cannot be interpreted as referring to the topicalized argument *Dickens*. In the APT/CNT-construction in (21) there is no such effect:

(20) **Dickens$_i$ gjorde hans$_i$ roman om Pickwick t$_i$ berömd.*
Dickens$_i$ made his$_i$ novel about Pickwick t$_i$ famous

(21) *Apropå/beträffande Dickens$_i$*
APROPOS/CONCERNING Dickens$_i$
gjorde hans$_i$ roman om Pickwick honom$_i$ berömd.
made his$_i$ novel about Pickwick him$_i$ famous
'Apropos Dickens, his novel about Pickwick made him famous.'

---

10 The hanging topic in Swedish is often introduced by some marker such as *ja* 'yes' which can appear on either side of the topic as is shown in (18) (cf. English *well* in the gloss of (18)).

Hence, the APT/CNT does not involve an A'-dependency.

Third, recall that the APT/CNT in Swedish can appear inside an embedded clause, as in (10), here repeated as (22). Topicalization cannot target this position, as shown in (23):

(22) Hon sa att hon apropå Johan inte ville träffa honom igen.
 she said that she APROPOS John not wanted meet him again
 'Apropos John, she said that she didn't want to see him again.'

(23) *Hon sa att hon JOHAN inte ville träffa igen.
 she said that she JOHN not wanted meet again

Hence, we can conclude that the embedded APT/CNT appears in a position which is not available for topicalized elements. I conclude from this that APT/CNT is not a topicalization structure.

2.4 APT/CNT and Left-Dislocation

As we have seen, the APT/CNT in its left peripheral position is superficially similar to left dislocation, but this analysis can be excluded as well. The APT/CNT is not syntactically connected with the following matrix. Consider the examples in (24)–(27):

(24) Apropå/beträffande Johan, jag är trött på att låna honom pengar.
 APROPOS/CONCERNING John I am tired of to lend him money
 'Apropos/concerning John, I'm tired of lending him money.'

(25) Apropå/beträffande Maria,
 APROPOS/CONCERNING Mary
 jag kom på att jag måste köpa henne en present.
 I came on that I must buy her a gift
 'Apropos/concerning Mary, it came to my mind that I have to buy her a gift.'

(26) *Apropå/beträffande till Johan,
 APROPOS/CONCERNING to John
 jag är trött på att låna honom pengar.
 I am tired of to lend him money

(27) *Apropå/beträffande till Maria,
　　 APROPOS/CONCERNING to　 Mary
　　 jag kom　på att　jag måste köpa henne en present.
　　 I　 came on that I　 must　buy　 her　 a　gift

The APT/CNT in (24)–(25) is not introduced by prepositions although the corresponding elements in the nuclear clause are PPs.

A PP is not entirely excluded, namely in a case such as (28), in which the PP *till Maria* 'to Mary' echoes the PP from the immediately preceding discourse. In (28), the prepositional APT is slightly marginal but not unacceptable in my opinion:

(28) A: *I går　　ringde jag till Maria.*
　　　　 yesterday called I　 to Mary
　　 B: ?*Apropå till Maria, jag måste köpa henne en present.*
　　　　 APROPOS to Mary　 I　 must　buy　 her　 a　gift

Example (28), when considered in contrast to the examples (26)–(27), shows two things: First, the PP in the APT is not syntactically connected with the following matrix, but rather is retrieved from the previous context. Second, any restriction on the lexical items appearing in the construction does not derive from selectional properties of the APT/CNT.

I conclude from this section that the APT/CNT is not an instance of dislocation.

2.5 APT/CNT and Hanging Topic

Having excluded that the APT/CNT is a case of topicalization or dislocation, the remaining alternative is that it is a hanging topic.[11] But such an analysis, too, faces problems when confronted with the data. Hanging topics are subject to a

---

11 An anonymous reviewer suggests that the Left Dislocation and the Hanging Topic may not be radically different "constructions", as argued in Altmann (1981). I do not believe such a distinction is crucial for the present argumentation: Regardless of whether the two are to be understood as one construction or two distinct ones, it is quite clear that APT/CNT is structurally different from both.

restriction of ordering in the sense that they only appear in the sentence initial position (29), as discussed by e.g. Benincà, Salvi and Frison (1988: 133).

(29) *Den där restaurangen, jag går gärna tillbaka dit.*
   that there restaurant-DET I go willingly back there
   'That restaurant, I'd go back there.'

(30) **Jag går gärna tillbaka dit, den där restaurangen.*
   I go willingly back there that there restaurant-DET

On the contrary, the APT can appear not only to the left but also to the right of the matrix, as in (31):

(31) *Jag går gärna tillbaka dit, apropå/beträffande den där*
   I go willingly back there APROPOS/CONCERNING that there
   restaurangen
   restaurant-DET

Furthermore, recall that the APT/CNT can appear in a sentence internal position, as in (32). Again, the difference with respect to the hanging topic (33) is obvious:

(32) *Hon sa att hon apropå/beträffande lägenhet hade hittat en*
   She said that she APRS/CONC apartment had found one
   i centrum.
   in centre
   'Apropos an apartment, she said that she had found one in the town center.'

(33) **Hon sa att hon, lägenhet, hade hittat en i centrum.*
   she said that she apartment had found one in centre

Such a contrast excludes a hanging topic analysis of the APT/CNT.

2.6 Summary

The APT/CNT-constructions cannot unambiguously be identified with any of the three syntactic dependencies taken into consideration. The APT/CNT is neither topicalized through A'-movement, nor dislocated, nor a hanging topic.

The crucial syntactic properties that have been assumed as criteria are summarized in the following Table 1[12]:

Table 1: Syntactic Properties of Topicalization and Dislocation Constructions.

	Involves A'-movement	Shows syntactic connectedness with the following matrix	Can appear clause-finally	Can appear clause-internally (in an embedding)
Topicalization	+	+	–	–
Dislocation	–	+	+	–
Hanging Topic	–	–	–	–
APT/CNT ex. (7)	–	–	+	–
APT/CNT ex. (8)	–	–	–	+

As is clear from this table, along with the three construction types that are commonly assumed to alter the information structure by involving the periphery, the APT/CNT must be recognized as a fourth type. Within this category, a further distinction can be made between the two syntactic realizations illustrated in (7) and (8). It is evident that the APT/CNT cannot be reduced to any of the former three constructions. I now turn to the pragmatic interpretation of the APT/CNT.

3 The Pragmatic Properties of *apropos*-topics and *concerning*-Topics

From a syntactic view point, there are no differences between the APT and the CNT. However, the two expressions show pragmatic differences in a way

---

12 The table summarizes the empirical observations on Swedish. It should be noted that, in Swedish, topicalization can target the position immediately to the right of the subordinater *att* 'that', as in (i):

(i)   Hon   sa   att   JOHAN   vill   hon   aldrig   träffa   igen.
       she   said   that   JOHN   wants   she   never   meet   again
       'She said that, John she never wants to see again.'

But the acceptability of (i) is irrelevant here: The word order in the clause following the topicalization is clearly that of a main clause (see e.g. Julien 2015 and references cited therein). Hence, (i) is not an example of topicalization in an embedding.

that justifies a distinction between two different classes of topic markers. These two classes differ systematically with regard to information structure, as is discussed in *3.1–3.2*.

3.1 "Explicit" Givenness

The first difference resides in the fact that CNTs can introduce a new element, a kind of subtopic, into the discourse, whereas APTs do not have any such property. Consider the following two examples in relation to the context:

[Context: *We had a lovely week in Greece. The weather was beautiful and the food was good, and (...)*]

(34) (...) *beträffande hotellet var det utmärkt.*
      CONCERNING hotel-DET was it   excellent
     '(...) concerning the hotel, it was excellent.'

(35) *(...) *apropå hotellet var det utmärkt.*
      APROPOS hotel-DET was it   excellent
     '(...) apropos the hotel, it was excellent.'

In the context of (34)–(35), the hotel has not actually been mentioned. It is a discourse-new element, at most inferred from the general description and could perhaps count as "old information" by virtue of predictability (e.g. Prince 1981: 226). Note however, that what CNT introduces is not actually Topic Shift: If the overarching topic of the discourse is the trip to Greece, some information about the hotel may be expected and, say, given by association. However, this associative link to the context is not sufficient to introduce the *hotel* as an APT. It seems that the *apropå*-construction actually requires explicit mention of the topic in the preceding discourse. This in turn means that, by these two expressions, the APT and the CNT, a distinction is lexicalized between topics that are given in the sense of being explicitly mentioned, and those that are merely inferred, such as *hotel* in (34)–(35).

3.2 Aboutness

The second difference between APTs and CNTs has to do with the *aboutness* topic of the following matrix (Reinhart 1981: 63). The APT gives a deviant answer to a question such as (36):

(36) A: *Vad kan du berätta om Johan?*
       what can you tell   about John
       'What can you tell me about John?'
   B: ?*Apropå Johan (kan jag berätta att) han har nytt jobb*
       APROPOS John (can I tell that) he has new job
       'Apropos John, I can tell you that he's got a new job.'

The CNT, on the other hand, provides a perfectly acceptable answer in the same context:

(37) B: *Beträffande Johan (kan jag berätta att) han har nytt jobb*
       CONCERNING John (can I tell that) he has new job
       'Concerning John, I can tell you that he's got a new job.'

The CNT is clearly preferred over the APT if the following sentence is actually *about* John.

Furthermore, consider examples such as (38)–(39). Here, the APT presents a Topic, *John*, which must have been previously mentioned but has a purely associative link with the content of the matrix.

(38) *Apropå Johan träffade jag Maria igår.*
     APROPOS John met I Mary yesterday
     'Speaking of John, yesterday I met Mary.'

(39) *Apropå Johan, nu regnar det igen.*
     APROPOS John now rains it again
     'Speaking of John, now it's raining again.'

The example (38) implies that there is some connection between John and Mary, while (39) suggests that I for some reason associate John with poor weather. In other words, there is no requirement on aboutness continuity with regard to the matrix (Prince 1998, Frascarelli and Hinterhölzl 2007). Importantly, such a radical shift is not acceptable with the CNT, as is clear from (40)–(41):

(40) **Beträffande Johan träffade jag Maria igår.*
     CONCERNING John met I Mary yesterday

(41) **Beträffande Johan, nu regnar det igen.*
     CONCERNING John now rains it again

This means that, if I start out by saying *beträffande Johan* 'concerning John', whatever follows must be about *John*. A further consequence of this difference is that the APT can introduce a thetic sentence while the CNT cannot.[13]

It appears, then, that one of the constructions is the mirror image of the other: The referent of the APT must have been mentioned in the previous discourse; it may or may not be present in the following matrix. The referent of the CNT may or may not have been previously mentioned; it must be present in the following matrix. Syntactically, the generalization can be formally expressed as in (42)–(43):

(42) x_i (...) [APT TOPIC$_i$ [$_{CP}$ ... (x_i) ...]]

(43) (x_i) (...) [CNT TOPIC$_i$ [$_{CP}$ ... x_i ...]]

From the view point of information structure, the difference between the APT and the CNT lies in the topical features that they lexicalize. Consider that Frascarelli and Hinterhölzl (2007), as well as Bianchi and Franscarelli (2010), distinguish between three different types of Topics: Aboutness Topics, Contrastive Topics, and Given Topics. What (42)–(43) translates into, essentially, is a claim that the APT is associated with a feature of Givenness, while the CNT comes

---

[13] In fact, the idiomatic expression *apropå ingenting* 'apropos nothing' is used to introduce an entirely new sentence under maximal focus, as in (i):

(i) *Apropå   ingenting   solen   skiner.*
    APROPOS nothing   sun-DET   shines
    'Apropos nothing, the sun is shining.'

The equivalent construction with the CNT is unacceptable:

(ii) **Beträffande   ingenting,   solen   skiner.*
     CONCERNING   nothing   sun-DET   shines

The expression in (i) is rather exceptional in that it seems to contradict the generalization that the APT is always retrieved from preceding discourse. However, the expression in this case is used to signal a "radical aboutness shift", in the sense that *nothing* in the preceding discourse is directly relevant for the following statement.

That (i) indeed exemplifies an idiomatic usage is further suggested by the fact that non-referential expressions cannot productively be used in such a context.

(iii) **Apropå   vemsomhelst,* (...)
      APROPOS   anybody

with a feature of Aboutness, in the sense of *Aboutness continuity* with regard to the matrix. *Aboutness Shift*, on the contrary, is compatible with the APT. Interestingly, none of these expressions easily combine with contrastiveness. Consider the examples in (44)–(45):

(44) ?*Apropå Johan såg jag honom inte. Men Maria.*
 APROPOS John saw I him not but Mary
 'Apropos John, I didn't see him. But Mary.'

(45) ?*Beträffande Johan såg jag honom inte. Men Maria.*
 CONCERNING John saw I him not but Mary
 'Concerning John, I didn't see him. But Mary.'

In (44)–(45), the APT/CNT is retrieved by a weak pronoun in the matrix. It is indeed difficult in these cases to construct the intended contrast between John and Mary.[14] If, instead, strong pronouns are used, as in (46)–(47), the contrast is easily interpretable:

(46) *Apropå Johan såg jag inte HONOM. Men Maria.*
 APROPOS John saw I not HIM but Mary
 'Apropos John, I didn't see HIM. But Mary.'

(47) *Beträffande Johan såg jag inte HONOM. Men Maria.*
 CONCERNING John saw I not HIM but Mary
 'Concerning John, I didn't see HIM. But Mary.'

Not unexpectedly, this shows that the relevant contrastive feature lies in the nature of the pronoun, not in the APT/CNT. In other words, the content of APT/CNTs is not contrasted with anything in the sentence.

There is, however, no evidence in Swedish for a hierarchical ordering of such features, and in this sense, Swedish differs from the analysis of Italian in Frascarelli (2007) and Frascarelli and Hinterhölzl (2007). It is clear, by now, that the APT and the CNT, despite their pragmatic differences, have the same distribution, both in the matrix and in the subordinate clause.

---

14 Rather, in my opinion, both of (44) and (45) tend to the irrelevant reading 'I didn't see John, but Mary did'. Hence a contrast is established with the matrix subject, not with the APT/CNT.

6 Final Remarks

The survey of topic marking expressions in Swedish has been limited to two classes of expressions, *apropå* 'apropos' and *beträffande* 'concerning', defined APT and CNT respectively. The APT and the CNT share the same syntactic and intonational properties. In particular, they have two surface realizations: One of these is integrated into the clause, it has essentially the distribution of an adverbial and is not attested in a closely related V2-language such as German. The other one, which is structurally more similar to its equivalents in German (as well as many other languages) is external to the nuclear clause structure, and perhaps analyzable as an independent speech act.

None of these realizations can be identified with any of the construction types that are commonly assumed to alter the information structure of a sentence by involving its peripheries: Topicalization, Dislocation, and Hanging Topic. Therefore, APT/CNT-structures must be recognized as a fourth class of such expressions.

The difference between the APT and the CNT lies in the way they lexicalize pragmatic features: the CNT imposes *aboutness continuity* with regard to the main clause, whereas the APT signals *givenness* and *aboutness shift*.

A cross-linguistic survey is left for future research. It remains to be seen to what extent some general observations on topic marking expressions in Swedish may to carry over to other Germanic and Romance languages. Lastly, it is clearly possible that we can identify not only two but more subclasses among such topic markers that have not been discussed in this paper.

References

Alexiadou, Artemis. 2006. Left dislocation (including CLLD). In Martin Everaert & Henk van Riemsdijk (eds.), *The Blackwell companion to syntax*, vol. II, 668–699. Oxford: Blackwell.
Altmann, Hans. 1981. *Formen der »Herausstellung« im Deutschen. Rechtsversetzung, Linksversetzung, Freies Thema und verwandte Konstruktionen*. Tübingen: Niemeyer.
Benincà, Paola, Giampaolo Salvi & Lorenza Frison. 1988. L'ordine delle parole e le costruzioni marcate. In Lorenzo Renzi (ed.), *Grande grammatica italiana di consultazione*, 115–225. Bologna: Il Mulino.
Bianchi, Valentina & Mara Frascarelli. 2010. Is topic a root phenomenon? *Iberia: An International Journal of Theoretical Linguistics* 2. 43–88.
Cinque, Guglielmo. 1990. *Types of A'-dependencies*. Cambridge, MA: MIT Press.
Egerland, Verner & Cecilia Falk. 2010. *Si* och *så*. Mellan narrativitet och grammatik. In Gunilla Burman, Anna Gustafsson & Henrik Rahm (eds.), Svensson och svenskan. Festskrift till Jan Svensson den 24 januari 2010, 60–72. Lund: Lunds Universitet.
Eide, Kristin Mellum. 2011. Norwegian (non-V2) declaratives, resumptive elements, and the Wackernagel position. *Nordic Journal of Linguistics* 34. 179–213.

Erteschik-Shir, Nomi. 2006. On the architecture of topic and focus. In Valéria Molnár & Susanne Winkler (eds.), *The architecture of focus*, 33–57. Berlin & New York: Mouton de Gruyter.
Erteschik-Shir, Nomi. 2007. *Information structure. The syntax-discourse interface*. Oxford: Oxford University Press.
Frascarelli, Mara. 2007. Subjects, topics and the interpretation of referential pro. An interface approach to the linking of (null) pronouns. *Natural Language and Linguistic Theory* 25. 691–734.
Frascarelli, Mara & Roland Hinterhölzl. 2007. Types of topics in German and Italian. In Susanne Winkler & Kerstin Schwabe (eds.), *On information structure, meaning and form*, 87–116. Amsterdam and Philadelphia: John Benjamins.
Frey, Werner. 2006. The grammar-pragmatics interface and the German prefield. In Valéria Molnár & Susanne Winkler (eds.), *The architecture of focus*, 235–264. Berlin & New York: Mouton de Gruyter.
Holmberg, Anders. 2006. Stylistic fronting. In Martin Everaert, Henk van Riemsdijk, Rob Goedemans & Bart Hollebrandse (eds.), *The Blackwell companion to syntax*, 532–565. Oxford: Blackwell.
Holmberg, Anders & Christer Platzack. 1995. *The role of inflection in Scandinavian Syntax*. Oxford-New York: Oxford University Press.
Jacobs, Joachim. 1984. Funktionale Satzperspektive und Illokutionssemantik. *Linguistische Berichte* 91. 25–58.
Julien, Marit. 2015. The force of V2 revisited. *The Journal of Comparative Germanic Linguistics* 18. 139–181.
Krifka, Martin. 2001. Quantifying into question acts. *Natural Language Semantics* 9. 1–40.
Kuno, Susumu. 1973. *The structure of the Japanese Language*. Cambridge, MA: The MIT Press.
Nordström, Jackie. 2010. The Swedish så-construction. A new point of departure. *Working Papers in Scandinavian Syntax* 85. 37–63.
Platzack, Christer. 1986. The position of the finite verb in Swedish. In Hubert Haider & Martin Printzhorn (eds.), *Verb second phenomena in Germanic languages*, 27–47. Dordrecht: Foris.
Postal, Paul M. 1971. *Cross-over phenomena*. New York: Holt, Rinehart and Winston.
Prince, Ellen F. 1981. Toward a taxonomy of given-new information. In Peter Cole (ed.), *Radical pragmatics*, 223–255. New York: Academic Press.
Prince, Ellen F. 1998. On the limits of syntax, with reference to left-dislocation and topicalization. In Peter Culicover & Louise McNally (eds.) *The limits of syntax* (Syntax and Semantics 29), 281–302. New York: Academic Press.
Quirk, Randolph, Sidney Greenbaum, Geoffrey Leech & Jan Svartvik. 1985. *A comprehensive grammar of the English language*. London-New York: Longman.
Reinhart, Tanya. 1981. Pragmatics and linguistics: an analysis of sentence topics. *Philosophica* 27. 53–94.
Reuland, Eric. 2006. Logophoricity. In Martin Everaert & Henk van Riemsdijk (eds.), *The Blackwell companion to syntax*, vol. III, 1–20. Oxford: Blackwell.
Riemsdijk, Henk van. 1997. Left dislocation. In Elena Anagnostopoulou, Henk C. van Riemsdijk & Frans Zwarts (eds.), *Materials on left dislocation*, 1–10. Amsterdam & Philadelphia: John Benjamins.
Rizzi, Luigi. 1997. The fine structure of the left periphery. In Liliane Haegeman (ed.), *Elements of grammar*, 281–337. Kluwer, Dordrecht.
Ross, John R. 1967. *Constraints on variables in syntax*. Cambridge, MA: MIT PhD dissertation.
Speas, Peggy & Carol Tenny. 2003. Configurational properties of point of view roles. In Anna Maria Di Sciullo (ed.), *Asymmetry in grammar, vol. 1. Syntax and semantics* 315–343.

Valéria Molnár, Hélène Vinckel-Roisin
Discourse Topic vs. Sentence Topic Exploiting the Right Periphery of German Verb-second Sentences

Abstract: Exploring the interface between discourse structure and syntax, the present study addresses the relationship between discourse topicality and marked word order in German V2-sentences. It takes as its point of departure two manifestations of a highly marked syntactic structure at the right periphery of the German sentence: the 'extraposition' (also called 'unbracketing', *Ausklammerung* in German grammars) and the 'right-dislocation' (*Rechtsversetzung*). In both cases, verbless constituents like PPs and NPs appear beyond the right frontier of the sentence (created by a closure-marking final element), in the 'extended postfield' (*Nachfeld*).

On the basis of a corpus collected from German contemporary newspapers (*Frankfurter Allgemeine Zeitung* and *Süddeutsche Zeitung*), we will show that these two right-peripheral syntactic strategies 'extraposition' and 'right-dislocation' can have the same discourse function, despite different syntactic and prosodic/typographic features. They indicate that the referent of the right-peripheral constituent (NP or PP) is salient and highly relevant for the whole discourse. It functions as the 'discourse topic referent', i.e. the discourse referent that is most stably activated in the mental representation of each discourse segment. We claim that both investigated strategies are relevant 'forward-looking' devices (often in a combination with 'backward-looking' strategies), guaranteeing referential coherence in discourse by imposing certain constraints on the subsequent and/or previous discourse segment(s).

Keywords: discourse topic, sentence topic, postfield, (mental) salience, extraposition, unbracketing, right-dislocation

1 Introduction

In our study we will discuss the notion of *discourse topic* at the interface of discourse and syntax, demonstrating its relevance for creating a coherent text and

---

Valéria Molnár, Lund University
Hélène Vinckel-Roisin, Sorbonne University

https://doi.org/10.1515/9781501504488-011

investigating its relation to certain language specific syntactic and prosodic means in German. The notion of discourse topic is, however, an elusive concept in text linguistics and in information structural research. The difficulties in its definition arise both from the discourse perspective and from the interface perspective, since it is very hard to identify its functional load and to find systematic patterns for the formal realization of this notion. We will, however, argue that the right-peripheral position outside the verbal bracket of the German sentence – the so-called 'postfield' (*Nachfeld*) – can play a prominent role in marking discourse topicality and contribute to strengthening of coherence relations in texts.

The structures under investigation can be considered as the two most important right peripheral syntactic phenomena of the German sentence, 'unbracketing' (*Ausklammerung*) and 'right-dislocation' (*Rechtsversetzung*). Unbracketed and right-dislocated constituents are placed in different parts of the postfield in the German sentence as a result of different syntactic operations: movement or base-generation. Movement is assumed to be relevant only for unbracketing where similarly to 'extraposition' (possible in other languages like English) a constituent is pushed to the right edge of the sentence leaving behind a trace. In contrast, right-dislocated constituents are base-generated sentence-externally and are connected to a pronominal copy in the middle field or in the prefield of the sentence.

Sentential constituents like subordinated sentences with object function are often 'extraposed',[1] and the placement on the right periphery is also the preferred alternative for relative clauses. According to a generally accepted claim, no special discourse effects arise in these cases of preferred or "grammaticalized" postfield placement. In contrast, unbracketed or right-dislocated NPs and PPs in the postfield or in the so-called 'extended postfield'[2] are regarded as marked structures with special discourse functions (see the discussion below in section 3).

In our study we will focus on the two above mentioned types of postfield-structures – unbracketing and right-dislocation of non-sentential constituents in German contemporary newspapers – illustrated below in examples (1)

---

1 Unbracketing is typical for subordinated sentences (see Inaba 2007, *Duden 4. Die Grammatik* 2016: 897–898 § 1386). The occurrence of sentential constituents in the middle field is highly marked and in case of finite sentential constituents without correlates often ungrammatical (see for example Zifonun, Hoffmann, and Strecker 1997: 1651).
2 See Zifonun's (2015) proposal for the differentiation of the postfield and for the introduction of the notion "extended postfield" in section 3 below.

and (2).³ By analysing attested instances of these right-peripheral structures we will reconsider their functional load from the 'global', textual perspective, paying special attention to their impact on the development of the discourse. In example (1) the unbracketed PP *mit Christian Wulff* on the right periphery displays a high degree of integration into the rest of the sentence, both on the syntactic and on the prosodic level, here supported by the lack of use of the punctuation mark comma.⁴ (Postfield constituents are marked in boldface.)

(1)　　*Man　kann　Mitleid　　　haben* **mit　Christian　Wulff.**
　　　　one　can　compassion　have　　with　Christian　Wulff
　　　　'One can have compassion with Christian Wulff.'
　　　　(sueddeutsche.de, 05.01.2012) ⁵

In example (2) the right-dislocated NP *der Kanzlerkandidat der SPD* can be regarded as an 'apposition equivalent' in the sense of Zifonun (2015: 40), since it is both coreferent and case congruent with the pronoun *er* 'he' in the middle field (also in boldface).⁶

(2)　　*Was　hat* **er** *eigentlich gesagt,* **der Kanzlerkandidat　　der　SPD**?
　　　　what　has　he　really　　said　　the　chancellor candidate GEN SPD
　　　　'What did he really say, the chancellor candidate of SPD?'
　　　　(faz.net, 30.12.2012)⁷

---

3 Unbracketed constituents in the postfield are generally prepositional phrases. However, the investigation of their discourse function in this study concentrates on the referential and discourse properties of the NP within the PP.
4 Cf. for example Lambert (1976), Altmann (1981: 46), Hoberg (1981: 188), Zahn (1991), Filpus (1994), Zifonun, Hoffmann, and Strecker (1997: 1649–1650), *Duden 4. Die Grammatik* (2016: 897 § 1386).
5 Example (1) is embedded in the following text:
　　(1 §) Man kann Mitleid haben **mit Christian Wulff.** *Er ist nicht, wie es seinem Amtseid entspräche, damit beschäftigt, Schaden vom Volk abzuwenden, sondern Schaden von sich selbst. Er verbraucht all seine Kraft damit, sich zu erklären und seine Fehler zu entschuldigen.*
　　(1 §) 'One can have compassion **with Christian Wulff.** He is not, as would be in keeping with his oath of office, occupied with averting harm from the people, but with averting harm from himself. He expends all his energy on vindicating himself, and excusing his mistakes.'
6 This phenomenon is subsumed under the category *Thematisierungsausdruck* ('thematizing expression') in the IDS-Grammatik (Zifonun, Hoffman, and Strecker 1997: 1647).
7 Example (2) is embedded in the following text:
　　(1 §) Was hat **er** *eigentlich gesagt,* **der Kanzlerkandidat der SPD**? (...)

The right-dislocated NP is generally separated from the host sentence prosodically, indicated by a (micro-)pause in front of the right-dislocated NP in oral language and a comma in written language. As argued by Averintseva-Klisch (2007 and 2009) this structure has generally two basic types; it can be used for the clarification of referential identity (as *Rechtsversetzungs-Nachtrag*), or for discourse topic marking (as *Rechtsversetzung* in the strict sense).[8] Since the referent of the NPs is already introduced in the first sentence of the text in the above-mentioned case, the function of right-dislocation cannot simply be the disambiguation of pronominal reference; rather, in example (2), the marking of the discourse topic seems relevant.

Our claim is that particularly short non-sentential constituents in the postfield of the German sentence, both in case of right-dislocation and unbracketing, can have relevance for the whole text or for larger sections of it. In our paper, we would like to concentrate on the common functional features of these two marked right-peripheral structures, despite certain above-mentioned syntactic and prosodic differences.[9] From the 'local' perspective they are both related to the host sentence, and are relevant for marking prominence in it (see also sections 6 and 7 below). The right-peripheral constituent can either carry the nuclear focus of the sentence or mark a postnuclear secondary focus in both structures. They are also very similar with respect to their discourse function since they can both indicate discourse topicality.[10]

The specific discourse function of non-sentential postfield constituents is, however, dependent on the location of the sentence (containing the postfield

---

(2 §) *Peer Steinbrück* beklagt sich über die zu niedrige Vergütung des Jobs, den er im kommenden Herbst anstrebt, heißt es nun. (...)

(11 §) *Steinbrück* und das liebe Geld – der Kanzlerkandidat wird das Thema einfach nicht los. (...) Das ist umso prekärer, als er es im Wahlkampf mit einer Kanzlerin zu tun bekommt, die ihm auch in dieser Hinsicht keine Angriffsfläche bietet.

(1 §) 'What did **he** really say, **the chancellor candidate of the SPD**? (...)

(2 §) *Peer Steinbrück* complains about the low salary of the job that he is aiming for next autumn, it is now said (...)

(11 §) *Steinbrück* and the dear money – the chancellor candidate simply cannot get away from this topic. This is all the more awkward as in the election campaign he will have to deal with a chancellor who presents him with no weak spot in this respect either.

8 "Afterthought" is also mentioned as a possible function of right-dislocation by Averintseva-Klisch (2007) and Truckenbrodt (2016).
9 In this article we will focus on the *common discourse function* of unbracketing and right-dislocation since this aspect has not been investigated in research yet.
10 It is important to point out that the assumed function of postfield constituents as discourse topic markers is only one of several possible functions (see for an overview section 3.2. below). However, other discourse functions are not taken into consideration in this study.

constituent) in relation to other sentences in the text. As our empirical analysis will show, in a sentence at the beginning of a text, noun phrases or prepositional phrases in the postfield announce the discourse topic and serve as *forward-looking devices*, imposing constraints on the continuation of the subsequent segments. In contrast, in a sentence concluding a text, noun phrases or prepositional phrases in the postfield are *backward-looking devices*, marking the return to the discourse topic of the previous segments and providing it with special prominence.

According to our claim, the two investigated cases of right-peripheral structures 'unbracketing' and 'right-dislocation' seem to be extremely conclusive for the *information packaging* in text, since they demonstrate a strong correlation between the right-edge position and the highest possible degree of *salience* of the discourse referents. Our hypothesis is that the postfield placement of NPs and PPs in German written texts should be regarded as a contextually adequate, coherence-strenghtening and salience-maximizing linearization strategy for indicating the maximal degree of salience achievable in the given discourse. Our hypothesis is anchored in the *Mental Salience Framework* (MSF) of Chiarcos (2003, 2005, 2010 and (2011a/b), providing an appropriate textlinguistically based model for the explanation of the functional relevance of the right-peripheral placement in the German sentence. Especially the notion of 'speaker salience' elaborated in Chiarcos' model and the development of salience metrics for the prediction of contextually adequate realization preferences within the NLG (Natural Language Generation) systems seem to be crucial for the functional analysis of unbracketed PPs and right-dislocated NPs in German (see below section 5). As empirical base of the present study we use articles from prominent German contemporary newspapers *Frankfurter Allgemeine Zeitung* and *Süddeutsche Zeitung*.

The paper is structured as follows: After the introductory section, section 2 argues for the distinction between 'discourse topic' and 'sentence topic', and analyses the relation between these two concepts which require operationalization on different levels at the syntax-discourse interface. Section 3 discusses the relevance of sentential edge positions for the expression of different types of topichood and focuses on the functional load of the left- and right-periphery of German sentences. In section 4, the 'global' and 'local' constraints of information structuring will be discussed with reference to key notions like 'coherence', 'referential movement' and 'salience', suggested in influential approaches of linguistic research. Section 5 presents the theoretical framework for the investigation of discourse topicality at the interface of discourse and syntax where special attention will be payed to Chiarcos' Mental Salience Framework, emphasizing the relevance of different types of salience for information packaging. The following two sections (6 and 7) contain our qualitative analysis of selected examples with unbracketed and right-dislocated non-sentential constituents in different textual positions, at the beginning of a text (section 6) and at the end of the text (section 7). In our analysis of the functional properties of postfield placement, we include information packaging both *within the sentence* and *within the whole discourse*. The final section of our article (section 8) contains the conclusions of our study and a short discussion of its possible theoretical and methodological extensions in future research.

2 Discourse Topic *vs.* Sentence Topic at the Discourse-syntax Interface

The central pragmatic concept of this article is the notion of *topichood*. Topics are generally claimed to contribute to the organization of information in discourse in a decisive manner and function as "sort keys" to file and access information (Kuno 1972). Topichood has been investigated during the last six decades both from the micro-perspective, i.e. perspective of the sentence, and from the macro-perspective of the text. However, there is no doubt that the notion of topichood on the sentence level has recieved considerably more attention in research than topichood on the discourse level, also called "discourse topic" (Reinhart 1982, Brown and Yule 1983), "quaestio", the notion of "what a text, a narrative is about" (Klein and Stutterheim 1991, 2002), or *"question under discussion" (QUD)* (Roberts 1996a/b).

We claim that the analysis of information structure requires the investigation of both local and global constraints on the structure of sentences and discourse. We will argue that discourse topics should be distinguished from sentence topics and that these two types of topichood are relatively independent notions, operating on different levels of discourse.

2.1 Sentence Topics

The notion of "sentence topic" is regarded as one of the core notions of information structure, which contributes to the binary division of sentences together with its complementary notion called "comment" or "focus". The most influential definition of sentence topics is suggested on the basis of the *aboutness*-relation typical for predicative constructions. According to Hockett (1958/²1963: 201), "[t]he most general characteristic of predicative constructions is suggested by the terms «topic» and «comment» for their ICs [intermediate constituents]:

the speaker announces a topic and then says something about it. Thus *John / ran away; That new book by Thomas Guernsey / I haven't read yet*. In English and the familiar languages of Europe, topics are usually also subjects, and comments are predicates: so in *John / ran away"*. The definition of topics based on aboutness is advocated in several important functionally anchored works on information structure (Reinhart 1982; Gundel 1988; Lambrecht 1994; Molnár 1998; Jacobs 2002; Bianchi and Frascarelli 2010).

The view of topichood based on "what the sentence is about" is, however, rejected by Chafe (1976: 51), who defines "real" topics (present in topic prominent languages) as setting "a spatial, temporal, or individual framework within which the main predication holds". Frame-setting for topichood is also considered as relevant in other works (Jacobs 1984, 2002, Molnár 2006, and Krifka 2007 suggesting for these cases the notion "delimitation"), even if in these approaches the topic definition is not restricted to this dimension.

There are also widely diverging views in research on the relevance of the discourse-semantic feature *givenness* for topichood. Whereas stronger or weaker versions of context-dependence (*givenness* and/or *familiarity*) are regarded as obligatory topic correlates in many approaches (cf. Gundel 1974; Lambrecht 1994; *Centering Theory*), the possibility of context-independence is argued for in Reinhart (1982), Frey (2004), Krifka (2007), and Büring (2016). Krifka (2007: 39–40) claims that "(...) in many cases, topic constituents are "old" in the sense of being inferable from the context. But there are certainly cases of new topics". He illustrates this with the following appropriate discourse-initial sentence:

(3)   [*A good friend of mine*]$_{Topic}$ [*married Britney Spears last year*]$_{Comment}$

Concerning the formal indicators of sentence topics morphological means as the particle *-wa* in Japanese and the specific intonational pattern fall-rise (Molnár 1998, 2002, 2006; Büring 2016) received much attention in research. In most approaches, though, specific syntactic positions (the sentence-initial or early placement) and different topic structures (hanging topic, left dislocation) are regarded as the most important topic marking devices (see the discussion below in section 3).

2.2 Discourse Topics

Not only the notion of sentence topic is controversial, but also the definition of discourse topicality seems to be a challenge for the theory on information structure. As discussed by Stede (2004: 242), there are several approaches to the

notion of 'discourse topic' which "are not entirely unrelated but nonetheless quite distinct:
1. DT1: An entity (a discourse referent) talked about in the discourse, which plays a particular prominent role – the discourse can be said to be 'about' this entity.
2. DT2: an over-arching 'theme' that might not be explicitly mentioned in the discourse but has ramifications for certain aspects of its structure.
3. DT3: An 'ideal question' that readers can construct for each sentence in the discourse, and that is answered by a sentence.
4. DT4: A proposition that readers have to actively construct when processing a sentence or a sequence thereof, and that has specific consequences for subsequent processing".
(Stede 2004: 242)

The definition proposed in Stede (2004) under *discourse topic (DT1)* corresponds best to the approach advocated in our analysis. We understand *discourse topic* here as the discourse referent that is most stably activated in the mental representation of each discourse segment; as such, DT is the default goal of coherence relations. This can be illustrated by examples (1) and (2) mentioned in the introductory part of this article where unbracketing und right-dislocation serve as important structural devices of marking the referent of a right-peripheral NP or PP as the discourse topic. In these examples the referents – *Christian Wulff* in (1) and *Peer Steinbrück* in (2) – are placed at the right periphery in the first sentence of each text. This placement of the NP and the PP is highly marked in written German, which makes it possible to draw special attention to these referents. The special highlighting (as narrow focus and/or part of the focus) at the right periphery on the sentence level can also anticipate special relevance of these referents for the whole text. The expectation can be fulfilled later in discourse; the *forward-looking center* can thus be guaranteed both on the sentence level and on the textual level identifying the discourse topic of text, i.e. the most persistent element in the following segment(s) (see footnotes 5 and 7 above). As will be demonstrated later in section 7, persistency of an entity and discourse relevance can also be combined with postfield placement of a constituent in the concluding part of a text.

2.3 The Relation between Discourse Topic and Sentence Topic

As the information structural analysis of the right-peripheral non-sentential constituents *Christian Wulff* and *Peer Steinbrück* in examples (1) and (2) indicate, the relation between sentence topic and discourse topic is not a straightforward matter. Importantly, discourse topicality is not dependent on the sentence topic status of a constituent. We will elaborate this issue by analysing the short dialogues in (4)–(6) below. The discourse topic *Bob Dylan's new album* is specified in the questions in all three cases, and is taken up in the answers by *it* in (4-A$_1$) and (5-A$_2$) and by one of the discs *Til The Sun Goes Down* in (6-A$_3$) (underlined in the sentences). The discourse topic does, however, only correspond to the sentence topic in (4-A$_1$) where it stands in the sentence initial position. In (5-A$_2$) it is embedded in the comment part as a given element, and in (6-A$_3$) it belongs to the focus of the sentence. Cf.:

(4) Q: *What about **Bob Dylan's new album**?*
     A$_1$: *It includes three discs with 30 songs by American songwriters.*

(5) Q: *What about **Bob Dylan's new album**?*
     A$_2$: *I haven't heard about it.*

(6) Q: *What about **Bob Dylan's new album**?*
     A$_3$: *I like one of the discs Til The Sun Goes Down very much.*

This shows that the "What about *x*?" test is only adequate to specify topichood of a constituent *x* on the discourse level since the sentence internal structure into topic and comment is based on different criteria. For sentence topics the appropriate marking of topichood within the sentence (aboutness or frame setting for the predication) is essential, motivating not only the preference for discourse-semantic features like givenness, familiarity (and also referentiality, specificity) of the entity but requiring also early mentioning for processing. In contrast, discourse topics are operating beyond the sentence level; consequently, discourse topicality requires the consideration of more complex discourse properties. It is mainly based on the relevance of a referent for the whole text, indicated by its persistency, i.e. its occurence in a large number of segments of the text.

It is important to emphasize that this prominent discourse role does not necessarily need the use of special syntactic or prosodic means or specific information structural roles within the sentence. As we have seen above, discourse topicality can be combined with topichood marking on the sentence level (primarily by sentence-initial or early placement), but the constituent referring to the discourse topic can also be integrated in the later comment-part of the sentence. However, as claimed in connection with the analysis of examples (1) and (2) strategically relevant segments of the text (especially in initial and final textual positions) provide optimal conditions for indicating their discourse relevance prospectively or regressively. The choice of specific syntactic positions and marked structures at the right periphery of the sentence, connected to implicit prosodic patterns in written texts (construction of default prosodic structures and covert assignment of focal accents during silent reading) can signal unambiguously the relevance of the referent (denoted by an NP or PP) for the whole discourse or at least for larger segments of the text.

We also assume that the degree of relevance and prominence of a constituent both on the sentence and on the discourse level correlates with the degree of markedness of the mapping between syntactic function, degree of determination and position (see also Chiarcos' proposal below in section 5). The expression of the prominent discourse role of a referent can be supported by its information structural status in the sentence which in case of NPs and PPs placed to the right of the verbal bracket often means nuclear focus or secondary focus.

3 The Relevance of Edge Positions for the Expression of Topichood

The claim is often made in linguistic research that edge positions have a special status in information structuring: Besides their contribution to the division of the sentence into foregrounded and backgrounded material they play a key role in integrating the information of a sentence into a greater discourse context. In the discussion of textual coherence, special attention was payed to the left periphery of the sentence, often by reference to the universality of the so-called "TOPIC before FOCUS"-constraint (or some of its versions).[11] The cognitively and functionally based argumentation is appealing: Constituents related thematically to the preceding discourse (the so-called "topics") come first, while constituents with new ("focused") information appear later. The specific functions of the left and right periphery are, however, dependent on the typological features of languages, where especially the opposition between verb-initial (VSO, VOS) and non-verb-initial (SVO, SOV) languages is of high relevance (see Herring's 1990 "Word Order Type Principle"). It seems though uncontroversial that in non-verb-initial (SOV, SVO) languages the function of the left periphery is mainly related to the function of establishing coherence in discourse. The linear

---

11 See Gundel's (1988: 229) *Given Before New Principle,* and Tomlin's (1986: 37) *Theme First Principle.*

syntactic structure is assumed to mirror iconically the dichotomy based on the two main constraints of information structuring – constraint of coherence and constraint of informativeness, by preferring *given* or *known* elements at the left edge and adding *new, informative* elements later in the sentence, closer to the right periphery.[12]

3.1 Left Periphery vs. Right Periphery of the German V2-Sentence

As mentioned above, topichood is claimed to have a strong affinity to givenness, i.e. the discourse given or referential status of the element which makes it easier for the hearer / reader to anchor the new information in the later part of the sentence. According to Halliday (1967, 1970) the leftmost position of the sentence is reserved for the *topic* function (in his terminology *theme*), defined as "the point of departure for the clause as a message" (Halliday 1967: 212) and called "the peg on which the sentence is hung" (Halliday 1970: 161). This claim has been questioned later in research. However, even theories of information structure which do not argue for a 1:1 correlation between the sentence-initial position and topichood consider the first – or an early – position for topics as optimal for the creation of "file cards" and expression of "aboutness".

The relevance of the left periphery (or early mentioning) for sentence topics seems to be accepted also for the analysis of German. The prefield, i.e. the position in front of the finite verb creating the first part of the verbal bracket (e.g. Molnár 1993, 1998, Filippova and Strube 2007, see also Chiarcos' claims below in section 5) or the leftward positions in front of the position of sentence adverbials in the middle field (Frey 2004, 2006, 2007) are suggested to be necessary preconditions for the formal realization of topichood. Even approaches emphasizing the cataphoric function of sentence topics (i.e. the relevance of anchoring the predication in the initial part of the sentence) claim that topics have a high degree of responsibility for the connection of the sentence with previous segments of the discourse and for functioning as backward-looking centers. Grammatical features of sentence topics like the marking of discourse givenness by pronouns or definiteness of the noun phrases are often mentioned as relevant properties of topics, contributing to the formal expression of their anaphoric or backward-looking character.

---

[12] See the discussion of the edge positions and the relevant discourse-pragmatic principles in Molnár (2012).

In contrast, the right periphery of the German sentence can be claimed to have a different discourse function – at least on the sentential level. German is a language with a basic SOV-order and a verbal bracket (created by the finite verb and non-finite parts of the predicate), showing a strong preference for the placement of the nuclear focus of the sentence at the end of the clause (either on the last constituent of the middle field or on the closing part of the verbal bracket). The placement of the focused element in the right periphery is especially relevant in written texts, where discourse relevance and prominence can only be indicated by syntactic means in the absence of explicit prosody.

3.2 Postfield

Right peripheral placement of a constituent is also possible in the German postfield, outside of the verbal bracket. The notion of postfield (*Nachfeld*) was introduced in the "two-field-theory" (*Zwei-Felder-Theorie*' by Drach (1937/²1939) identifying the position after the finite verb in declarative sentences (cf. '*Grundplan*' in Drach ²1939: 17). The model of Drach has, however, been modified; since Engel (1970a/b, 1972) the proposals for the topological division of the German sentence take also the verbal bracket into consideration. The position(s) preceeding the final part of the verbal bracket belong to the 'middle field' (*Mittelfeld*), whereas the position following the verbal bracket constitutes the 'postfield' (*Nachfeld*). This view is further elaborated in the IDS-Grammatik (Zifonun, Hoffman, and Strecker 1997: 1644–1675, cf. also Wöllstein 2014: 73–76, *Duden*-Grammatik 2016: 897–898). The right periphery outside of the verbal bracket is divided in two positions, the 'postfield' (*Nachfeld*) and the 'right outfield' (*rechtes Außenfeld*) on the basis of the criterion of 'syntactic integration'. This criterion has, however, been questioned by Zifonun (2015) who argues against a bipartite structure in the right periphery and instead suggests the notion of 'extended postfield' (*erweitertes Nachfeld*). She regards the extended postfield after the verbal bracket as a single field with 'reduced syntacticity' (*verminderte Syntaktizität*).

The discourse function and the information structural markedness of the right peripheral non-sentential constituents can, however, vary depending on a number of grammatical factors (see Eisenberg 1999: 391–392). Syntactic function (objects vs. adverbials), morphological realization (noun phrases vs. prepositional phrases, pronouns vs. adverbs) and also length have an impact on the degree of grammaticality and appropriateness of the placement at the right periphery. The right peripheral placement of case marked arguments (subjects and objects) is highly marked (Zifonun, Hoffmann, and Strecker 1997: 1660,

Eroms 2000), whereas non-obligatory adverbials realised as prepositional phrases occur more frequently in the postfield and are less marked. Short pronominal arguments in the postfield are borderline cases or ungrammatical (see Eisenberg 1999; Frey 2015). The increase of constituent length by coordination or the insertion of a cataphoric element (contributing to right-dislocation) can improve the grammaticality of right peripheral placement also for case marked nominal phrases (see Zifonun, Hoffmann, and Strecker 1997: 1651; Eroms 2000: 380; Truckenbrodt 2016).

Several functional analyses of the right periphery in German emphasize its relevance for focusing of the postfield constituent (cf. Vinckel 2006a; Zifonun, Hoffmann, and Strecker 1997). The righthand placement of constituents in the final sentence position outside of the verbal bracket shows, however, a functional diversity both in written texts and in interactions.[13] It is used for extension of information by precision, explication and addition of information as well as for exemplification and repair.[14] Rhetorical strategies, stylistic figures (Vinckel 2006a: 171–178) and the *afterthough*-effect (this however in unaccented cases, Truckenbrodt 2016) and its special functions in spoken language (Auer 1991, 1996) are also discussed in research. Indicating discourse topicality can thus only be claimed as one of the discourse functions of postfield placement (also mentioned as a relevant discourse function in earlier stages of German, see Coniglio and Schlachter 2015).

This discourse function is, however, dominating in the collected newspaper texts where postfield or the 'extended postfield' contains not only a prominent constituent of the sentence but also on the discourse level. Using a marked structure at the right periphery makes the narrow focus reading of a non-sentential constituent outside the verbal bracket possible.[15] This is often related to further interpretational components: with emphatic, contrastive interpretation or with marking of textual persistence and special discourse relevance. Since this last mentioned interpretational feature is characteristic for discourse topics, we can assume that a narrow focus in the two marked syntactic structures on the right periphery is an optimal device for the expression of discourse

---

13 See also Vinckel (2006a/b), Vinckel-Roisin (2011a/b and 2012a), Vinckel-Roisin (2015) and Molnár's (2014) report on the conference "Das 'Nachfeld' im Deutschen zwischen Syntax, Informationsstruktur und Textkonstitution: Stand der Forschung und Perspektiven".
14 See also the contributions in Vinckel-Roisin (2015).
15 In case of right dislocation, the isolated sentence external structure requires prominence (even if it does not exclude focus on sentence internal constituents at the same time). Focus on the right periphery is, however, only a (preferred) option in unbracketings where the nuclear focus can also be assigned to the right peripheral part of the verbal bracket.

topicality. Whereas a sentence with postfield placement in the initial segment of a text (or a text segment) can be used for announcing the discourse topic and signalling its persistence in the later segments of the text, postfield mentioning of a constituent in a sentence appearing in the final part of the text can draw attention to the persistency of its referent in earlier segments and contribute to strengthening its relevance for the whole discourse.

4 'Global' and 'Local' Constraints of Information Structure

As mentioned above, the study of discourse topicality requires the consideration of organizing principles in language that account for the ordering of information in discourse beyond the level of sentence. Investigations of the *textual perspective* depart generally from the discourse context and are either interested in *locally* manifested connections of discourse segments or in the *global* structure of texts. Studies focusing on the local constraints of text and/or discourse have mostly addressed the question, how *preceeding* discourse segments influence word order and information structure within the sentence and which syntactic and lexical choices can guarantee textual coherence in an optimal way.

One of the most influential proposals for the organization of information in texts was developed by Daneš (1970, 1974) in the so-called "thematic progression" model, claiming that the organization of information in texts is determined by "the choice and ordering of utterance themes, their mutual concentration and hierarchy as well as their relation to the hypertheme of the superior text units (such as paragraph, chapter [...]) to the whole text, and to the situation" (Daneš 1974: 114). In this model, special attention was payed to the local strenghtening of textual relations, by the investigation of the connection between the "theme" of utterances and the "theme" and the "rheme" in the immediately preceeding utterances.[16]

The local and global constraints on textual coherence have also been examined on the basis of the concept of "referential movement" suggested by Klein and Stutterheim (1991) in the so-called "Quaestio model". Klein and Stutterheim (1991, 2002) argue that a coherent text is not an arbitrary set of

---

[16] The most important local patterns discussed by Daneš are (i) "simple linear progression" (where the *theme* of the later utterance is derived from the *rheme* of the previous utterance), and (ii) the "continuous theme" (where the *themes* of two neighboring utterances are identical).

utterances and it involves a 'referential movement' within various semantic domains (called 'referential domains'), such as persons, place, time, circumstances, modality, and others. Importantly, this model also pays attention to the text as a whole and is mostly interested in the question how the local constraints follow from the global ones. The basic idea is that a coherent text is an answer to a question "What happened (to you) at this time at this place?" and contains utterances which "in their entirety serve to express, for a given audience and to a given end, a complex set of information, a *Gesamtvorstellung*" (Klein and Stutterheim 1991: 1). Global constraints resulting from the *Gesamtvorstellung* and the *Quaestio* ("text question") "(...) can be stated as restrictions on possible referential movement and, as a consequence, of the appropriate language-specific means to express this referential movement" (Klein and Stutterheim 1991: 3).

The relevance of questions for discourse structure and coherence in discourse has also been discussed in terms of a *Question under Discussion* (QUD) developed by Ginzburg (1996) and Roberts (1996a/b). This approach claims that discourse proceeds by continually raising explicit or implicit questions, and that each sentence in discourse addresses an (often implicit) QUD either by answering it, or by bringing up another question that can help answering that QUD. If the interlocutor accepts the question, it becomes the QUD, a narrowed set of alternatives to be addressed. A QUD can thus be regarded as a partially structured set of questions which discourse participants are mutually committed to resolve at a given point in time.

The QUD-proposal is based on the intuition which also lies behind the question-answer test used already by the Prague School theorists for detecting the focus (in their terminology the "rheme") of sentences. An answer to a question is appropriate only if its focused constituent corresponds to the *wh*-phrase of the question. For example, (8-a) with a nuclear pitch accent and narrow focus on the subject (indicated by small caps) is an appropriate answer only to (7-a), whereas (8-b) only fits the question in (7-b) by assigning accent and focus to the direct object.

(7) a. *Who received the Peace Nobel Prize 2015?*
 b. *What did the Tunisian National Dialogue Quartet receive 2015?*

(8) a. [*The TUNISIAN NATIONAL DIALOGUE QUARTET*]$_F$ *received the Peace Nobel Prize 2015.*
 b. *The Tunisian National Dialogue Quartet received* [*THE PEACE NOBEL PRIZE*]$_F$.

QUDs provide essential contextual information and explicate strategies of inquiry. The approaches based on the notions of *Quaestio* and *QUD* have also created a bridge between the global structure of discourse and the local characteristics of sentences, and make the clarification of the relation between the discourse topic (on different textual levels) and the topic-focus articulation of sentences possible.

A further relevant notion for the analysis of referential coherence and information structuring in discourse in functional, cognitive and computational approaches is the cognitively based notion of 'salience'. Linguistic salience describes (i) the accessibility of entities in a speaker's or hearer's memory and (ii) how this accessibility affects the production and interpretation of language.[17] The notion of salience, defined in psychology and neurobiology as a gradual assessment of attentional states, has, however, led to considerable confusion in linguistic theory by referring to different, incompatible aspects of attention. As Chiarcos (2010: 33) points out, it has been used "as a near-synonym of 'givenness' (Sgall et al., 1986, p.54f.), but also as a near-synonym of 'newness (for the hearer)' (Davis and Hirschberg, 1988), or 'degree of interest (of the speaker)' (Langacker 1997, p.22)".

5 Theoretical Framework – Mental Salience Framework

In the *Mental Salience Framework* (MSF) Chiarcos (2010) developed a two-dimensional model of salience in order to resolve the terminological and theoretical problems connected with this problematic notion and to make its formalization possible in the NLG systems. He distinguishes two independent dimensions of salience in discourse associated with different roles regarding the flow of attention in discourse, *speaker salience* and *hearer salience*: "speaker salience represents the attentional states of the speaker (that express her intentions to guide the hearer's focus of attention), and hearer salience represents the speaker's approximation of the attentional states of the hearer" (Chiarcos 2010: 34). Chiarcos also claims that from the perspective of an NLG system, especially the 'attentional states' of the speaker are decisive for

---

17 Theories of linguistic salience had to explain how the salience of entities affects the form of referring expressions (cf. the *Givenness Hierarchy* in Chafe 1976; Givón 1992; Gundel, Hedberg, and Zacharski 1993), or how it affects the local coherence of discourse (cf. *Centering Theory* in Grosz, Joshi, and Weinstein 1995).

discourse planning. This does not mean that the hearer-related perspective can be neglected: "(...) a cooperative speaker takes the perspective of the addressee into consideration, i.e. she acts according to her assumptions about the attentional states of the hearer (Prince 1981). Generating text that is both coherent (for the hearer) and goal-directed (for the speaker) requires both perspectives" (Chiarcos 2010: 34).

In his model, Chiarcos elaborates earlier salience-related approaches where Givón's (1983, 2001) two-dimensional analysis of 'topicality' and the distinction between different attention centers proposed in the framework of *Centering Theory* play a prominent role. Hearer salience and speaker salience show namely similarity to Givón's notions of 'anaphoric topicality' of a referent (measured by the distance from its last mention) and 'cataphoric topicality' (measured by its persistence (frequency) within the subsequent utterances). The distinction between the attentional states of hearer and speaker is also closely related to the proposal of *Centering Theory*: "(...) assumed attentional states of the hearer can indeed be characterized as being primarily backward-looking (the preceding discourse allows to approximate the attentional states of the hearer), whereas attentional states of the speaker involve a forward-looking aspect (subsequent discourse can unveil the speaker's earlier intentions to elaborate on a particular issue)" (Chiarcos 2010: 34).[18]

Another basic feature of mental salience is according to Chiarcos its dynamic character. This leads to the possibility and necessity of its ranking dependently of the development of discourse, cf. Chiarcos (2010: 120):

> *Mental salience is a dynamic property of representations within a mental model; mental salience characterizes the attentional state of a given mental representation relative to the attentional states of other mental representations within this mental model. Thereby, mental salience induces a ranking (partial or total order) over the representations in the mental model (...).*

Ranking of speaker and hearer salience affects information packaging and is essential for the use of appropriate formal means in discourse. The calculation of salience degree decides about the choice of referential expressions, assignment of grammatical roles[19] and word order options. Speaker salient (forward-looking) referents are prototypically realized with oblique nouns, accompanied

---

18 See especially the discussion of two centering theories in Chiarcos (2010: 77–95): the *Centering Theory* of Grosz, Joshi, and Weinstein (1995) and the *Functional Centering Theory* of Strube and Hahn (1999). See also the discussion of the forward-looking centers in German sentences in Vinckel-Roisin (2012b).
19 Chiarcos (2010: 33) uses the term 'grammatical roles' for syntactic functions.

by the indefinite articles, placed in later positions (as the underlined constituent in (9)). In contrast, constituents with low speaker salience (and high hearer salience) are often subjects, indicated by a definite article in (10) or a pronoun in (11). They often stand initially or in early sentence internal positions (as the italicized constituents in examples (10) and (11)):

(9) Turkey and Greece were hit <u>by a strong earthquake.</u>

(10) <u>The Aegean eartquake</u> killed two tourists in July 2017.

(11) <u>It</u> also injured 500 people.

According to Chiarcos, non-canonical alignments of syntactic functions and positions as in (12) where the definite object is topicalized are marked (contrastive) and indicate higher speaker salience. Non-canonical structures as left-dislocation in (13) are also marked and appropriate means for indicating high speaker salience. (The marked left-peripheral structures are underlined):

(12) <u>The strong earthquake,</u> many people will never forget.

(13) <u>As for the Aegean eartquake,</u> many people will remember it.

Chiarcos develops a formalization of salience degree within the NLG-system and the proposed model for salience metrics includes both the hearer salience score and the speaker salience score calculated on the basis of the type of referring expression (definite or indefinite noun phrase, proper name, pronoun), grammatical role, and word order. An important task for the salience metrics is to predict preferences for information packaging. *Chiarcos argues that the choice between unmarked and marked structures is mainly dependent on the speaker salience score.* In German, higher degree of speaker salience is primarily connected to expectations of a marked word order – as formulated in Principles 10 and 11 below[20]:

- *Principle 10 (Speaker salience and marked word order)*
  The more speaker salient a discourse referent is, the greater is its potential to induce marked word order.
  (Chiarcos 2010: 193)

---

[20] See a more detailed discussion of the relation between *salience and word order* in Chiarcos (2010: 188–196).

- *Principle 11 (Salience and word order in German main clauses)*
  The more hearer salient a given referent is, the greater is the preference for an unmarked position within the core of the clause.
  The more speaker salient a discourse referent is, the greater is the preference to be placed in a marked position outside the core of the clause.
  (Chiarcos 2010: 194–195)[21]

According to Chiarcos, the principles of markedness hierarchy have consequences for the left periphery of German sentences: The degree of newsworthiness or relevance of a referent for the speaker motivates prefield placement or left-dislocation, corresponding to the distributional markedness hierarchy of topological fields (cf. Chiarcos 2010: 157).

Chiarcos does not take, however, the postfield placement and its alternative realizations into consideration. Our aim is to fill this gap of information structural and syntactic research[22] by highlighting the discourse function of two marked postfield-structures in German. Based on the MSF-framework special attention will be payed to the specification of both dimensions of salience (backward-looking hearer salience, and forward-looking speaker salience) not only at the sentence level, but also at the textual level. Thus concentrating on the interface between discourse and grammar, Chiarcos' ideas will be relevant both concerning the "packaging hierarchies, i.e., rankings of grammatical devices for different packaging phenomena. (...), that are aligned with cumulated salience scores calculated from hearer salience and speaker salience" (Chiarcos 2011b: 33) and the principles for the mapping between packaging hierarchies and salience scores.

We also claim that the investigation of texts from the global perspective should include factors related to genre, since the patterns which are manifest in a discourse are constrained by genre considerations. The term 'genre' is used here in the sense defined by Dudley-Evans (1987: 1): "a typified society recognized form that is used in typified society recognized circumstances. It has characteristic features of style and form that are recognized, either overtly or covertly, by those who use the genre". According to Lüger (1995a: 54), press texts with monologue format are thoroughly planned and especially *press commentaries* prefer "*meinungsbetonte Darstellungsformen*" ('opinion emphasizing

---

[21] The notions *core* und *clause* are used in Chiarcos (2010) in the sense of *Role and Reference Grammar*: CORE includes the verb and its "base generated" arguments (here *core* corresponds to the middle field), CLAUSE includes Vorfeld ("pre-core slot"), CORE and PERIPHERY. See the detailed discussion in van Valin (1993: 10) and the overview in van Valin (2009).
[22] See also Chiarcos (2003: 56).

ways of presentation'). The high degree of planning results in a high degree of "intentionality", which contributes to the foregrounding of the addressee's side and the intention of a manipulative influencing of the addressee.[23]

6 Establishment of the Global Discourse Topic in the Initial Part of the Text

The discourse function of the 'extended postfield' of the German sentence will be the main topic of the following sections analysing different empirically attested cases of postfield placement in the German sentence. We will show that the specific type of narrow focusing in the right periphery is an excellent device for the explicit linguistic marking of the discourse topic – the most salient element in the discourse.

Our analysis is structured correspondingly to the position of the sentence containing a postfield non-sentential constituent in the discourse. We will demonstrate that the discourse strategies can vary depending on the initial or final position of the sentence in the investigated newspaper texts: announcement of the discourse topic is possible in the beginning of the discourse whereas reinforcement of discourse topicality can be provided in the concluding part. Due to limitations of space, cases of postfield placement occurring in sentences with "intermedial textual position", i.e. in openings and endings of specific paragraphs cannot be included in our analysis. Earlier analysis of unbracketing (Vinckel-Roisin 2011a: 393–394, 2012a: 153–155) and right-dislocation in German (Averintseva-Klisch 2009: 159–160), as well as our recently collected postfield corpus show that both unbracketed and right-dislocated constituents can be used as discourse structuring devices on the intermediate level. As topic-announcing expressions they mark the topic-shift in the intermediate position in an unambiguous way in this case.

6.1 Material – Method

The relevance of the postfield for the establishment of the discourse topic will be discussed on the basis of recent examples for both unbracketing and

---

[23] Cf. Lüger's original formulation in German (1995a: 54): "die Intentionalität, die den adressatenbezogenen Aspekt von Pressetexten in den Vordergrund rückt und nicht zuletzt eine manipulative Beeinflussung intendieren kann". See also Lüger (1995b, 2001, 2005) and the 'nearness-distance' model of Koch and Oesterreicher (1990).

right-dislocation. The data were collected manually und are taken from *Süddeutsche Zeitung* and *Frankfurter Allgemeine Zeitung*.[24] Our analysis can confirm the results of earlier investigations of unbracketing in German carried out by Vinckel-Roisin (2011a/b and 2012a), claiming the relevance of the postfield for discourse topic marking on the basis of a comprehensive corpus-based study.[25] Concerning the discourse function of the right-dislocation the results of our analysis support also the claims of Averintseva-Klisch (2009).

We wish to make a qualitative analysis of selected cases without a statistical evaluation of the corpus in this study. Based on theoretical consideration related to the interface between syntax and information structure, our primary goal is to account for the information structural status of the NPs and PPs in the postfield, both on the sentential level and on the level of discourse. We will thereby clarify certain obligatory and possible correlations between discourse topicality and the discourse status of postfield constituents within the sentence.

Our argumentation will be motivated both by the formal and functional features of the attested examples and on different displacement tests (placement in the prefield and middle field within the sentence and change of the word order of constituents in the subsequent segment(s)). The evaluation of different versions elicited in informal acceptability judgments by native informants can provide evidence for the superiority of the postfield placement in the given text both from the perspective of the sentence and the whole text. As will be shown, the acceptability judgments confirm that only the postfield placement of a PP or NP can trigger expectations concerning the continuation of the discourse in an unambiguous way and guarantee the preservation of attention on these referents.[26]

As mentioned above in section 3, the analysis of newspaper texts should also take genre-specific constraints into consideration. One of the most striking features of press texts is the special pattern for the introductory part of newspaper articles required by genre conventions. The 'headline', the 'title' and the 'lead' are obligatory and constitutive parts of this text type, and generally, they

---

[24] Our data collection contains 50 recent examples for unbracketing and 30 examples for right-dislocation which were elicited in order to show the use of discourse topic announcement and reinforcement in German newspapers.
[25] This study was financially supported by the Humboldt-Foundation 2009/2010 and carried out at the Humboldt Universität zu Berlin (Lehrstuhl Syntax).
[26] For this paper the acceptability judgments were elicited by informal discussions with 3 native speakers of German. The judgments of the interviewed persons seem to show a complete (100%) identity. However, we are aware of the fact that further acceptability judgments and experiments (e.g. eye-tracking studies) are needed for the confirmation of our results (see below section 8).

are inserted later by the journalist or the redaction, based on the content of the article.[27] All examples investigated in detail below (examples (14)–(17)) follow this typical pattern.

6.2 Analysis of Unbracketed Constituents

Example (14) demonstrates unbracketing of a PP in the first sentence of the text, where the PP *für Sepp Blatter* 'for Sepp Blatter' is placed after the verbal bracket. (The postfield constituents are boldfaced in the examples and the relevant elements of the referential chain are underlined):

(14) (HEADLINE) *Fifa-Präsident*
(TITEL) *Blatter hätte das Bundesverdienstkreuz eigentlich nicht bekommen dürfen*
(LEAD) *Sepp Blatter, der derzeit gesperrte Präsident des Fußball-Weltverbands Fifa, hat sein Bundesverdienstkreuz am Ende der WM 2006 unter fragwürdigen Umständen bekommen.*

(1 §) *Mit dem Friedensnobelpreis hat es nicht geklappt **für Sepp Blatter**.*[28] *Der inzwischen suspendierte Chef des Fußball-Weltverbandes Fifa hätte diese Auszeichnung gerne entgegengenommen, <u>er</u> hätte sie aus <u>seiner</u> Sicht auch völlig verdient. <u>Blatter</u> betrachtet den Fußball ja als globale Friedensbewegung, <u>sich selbst</u> hat <u>er</u> schon mal mit dem Papst auf eine Stufe gestellt. (...)*
(sueddeutsche.de, 23.11.2015)

'(HEADLINE) President of FIFA
(TITLE) Blatter should not have received the "Bundesverdienstkreuz" prize
(LEAD) Sepp Blatter, the currently suspended president of the football world confederation FIFA, received his award Bundesverdienstkreuz at the end of the 2006 world cup in dubious circumstances.

---

[27] See Schneider and Raue (1998: 170), Sauer (2007: 164) and the overview in Szakmary (2002: 164).
[28] (14) (1 §) *Mit dem Friedensnobelpreis hat es nicht geklappt* ***für Sepp Blatter**.*
      with the Peace Nobel Prize has it not worked out for Sepp Blatter
      'The Nobel Peace prize did not work out for Sepp Blatter.'

(1 §) The Nobel Peace Prize did not work out **for Sepp Blatter**.
The, in the meantime suspended, president of the football world confederation FIFA would have wished to receive this award, and from his perspective he would have fully deserved it too. Blatter regards football as a global peace movement, and he has already placed himself on the same level as the pope (...).'

According to our claim, the right peripheral position of the unbracketed PP has the function of indicating discourse topicality of the denoted referents and is motivated by the high degree of their salience. Interestingly, the degree of speaker salience seems to be crucial for discourse topicality. Consequently, the central question of our analysis is how the high mental salience from the perspective of the speaker can be identified and calculated. This requires the specification of the relevant cognitive, pragmatic and grammatical factors, which influence or decide about the values, both from the perspective of text production and text perception.

In Chiarcos' model (2010: 134–137) the measurement of speaker salience is not only based on cognitive factors (on perceptual aspects of salience, cf. Pattabhiraman 1993), but also on linguistic and textual features. The most important indicator of speaker salience is the frequency of occurrences in the text, i.e. persistence (corresponding to the "topic persistence (TP) of referents" suggested by Givón 2001: 457). The frequency of mentioning in the subsequent discourse (e.g. in form of pronominal anaphors) seems to have special relevance for calculating speaker salience in a certain part of the text. (However, as discussed in section 7 below, persistence in the previous part of the discourse has the same impact on the values). Crucially, the relevant value of salience includes the cumulated salience scores calculated from speaker salience and hearer salience (see Chiarcos' proposal in section 5 above).

All those above mentioned factors which indicate a very high degree of speaker salience are attested in example (14). Not only the textinitial position of the sentence containing the unbracketed PP in (14) is of importance for structuring the whole discourse, but also the fact that this sentence makes use of special syntactic structures and a marked alignment of grammatical role and syntactic position using specific syntactic structures. In addition, the discourse referent of the short postfield constituent 'Sepp Blatter' in (14) is activated already in the beginning of the text, in close vicinity to the sentence with the postfield structure, indicating high degree of hearer salience of the referent.

It is relevant to point out that the marked combination of the speaker and hearer salience is also based on the requirements of the genre, including "headline – titel – lead" of the article (introducing these entities) and imposing expectation on the elaboration of the information in the subsequent text.

The assumption of the discourse topical character of the referent 'Sepp Blatter' in the article and its *newsworthiness* (a relevant speaker salience factor, discussed in Chiarcos' (2010) model) is confirmed by the development of discourse in (14), by the repeated name *Blatter, Sepp Blatter, Blatter* and the explicit anaphoric elements *Fifa-Präsident (president of Fifa), der* 'definite article', *sein* 'his'.

Consequently, the attested high salience scores for 'Sepp Blatter' are motivated both by factors lying behind speaker salience (marked position, highlighting by marked alignment of grammatical roles and syntactic position, and persistence in the text) and by hearer salience (namely the previous mentioning of these referents in the introductory headline-titel-lead part of the article and short distance to previous mentioning). The combination of the high degree of speaker salience and the high scores for hearer salience contribute to the highest possible salience in these cases, accounting for the optimal discourse topicality marking by the postfield constituents.[29]

In the following discussion, we will show the effect of different displacements and other strategies on the information structure of the sentence and the text by the detailed analysis of different positions of the PP *für Sepp Blatter* in the introductory sentence of text (14). This PP, which is unbracketed in the original version of example (14a), can be either placed in the middle field (surrounded by the verbal bracket) as in (14b) or moved to the prefield, in front of the finite verb as in (14c) below on the next page.

The syntactic structure of (14a) is marked from the beginning due to the placement of the PP *(mit) dem Friedensnobelpreis* in the prefield, identifying a highly marked [+discourse new; +hearer new] (in Prince's 1992 terminology) sentence topic with contrastive function. The unbracketing of the PP *für Sepp Blatter* results in an additional, syntactically marked structure, where prosodic highlighting of this highly salient discourse referent seems to be the preferred version. In (14b) the placement of the PP *für Sepp Blatter* in the middle field position in front of the negation particle leads to a change of the information structural status of this PP:

(14a) *Mit dem Friedensnobelpreis hat es nicht geklappt **für Sepp Blatter**.*

(14b) *Mit dem Friedensnobelpreis hat es **für Sepp Blatter** nicht geklappt.*

Due to the presence of the negation particle (attracting accent and focus) the placement of the PP in (14b) can indicate the background status of the referent of *Sepp*

---

[29] According to Chiarcos, the salience scores for the speaker also include the salience scores calculated for the hearer.

Blatter, thereby strongly reducing its potential to function as a discourse topic in the subsequent text. However, in spoken language, an additional focus accent on the PP would be compatible with the (secondary) focus reading of this constituent (this could be marked typographically by capitals). Importantly, this word order option (with different prosodic patterns) does not make the continuation of the text inappropriate with the choice of the same referent ('Sepp Blatter') as the topic of the subsequent sentence as attested in example (14a). Both the background reading or a (possible, but in the written version not preferred) focus reading of 'Sepp Blatter' in the first sentence of the text can be compatible with the topic function of this referent in the second sentence (corresponding to the patterns "continuous themes" and "linear progression" suggested by Daneš 1970, 1974). This new sentence topic (in this case 'Sepp Blatter', realized as the NP *der inzwischen suspendierte Chef des Fußball-Weltverbandes Fifa*) can principally also be sustained in the following sentences of the texts. However, neither options of the PP-placement within the middle field of the sentence (with or without prominence) would guarantee the triggering of further expectations on the continuation of the text.

Turning to the potential prefield position of the PP *für Sepp Blatter* as illustrated in (14c), we can note that this also seems to be problematic from the point of view of the information structure in the given discourse (appearing as the first sentence of the text):

(14c) ? **Für Sepp Blatter** hat es mit dem Friedensnobelpreis nicht geklappt.

The PP *für Sepp Blatter* as a potential sentence topic is ambiguous between a 'continuous, given topic' (without pitch accent) and a 'contrastive topic' reading (with pitch accent) within the sentence. However, neither of these readings is optimal for triggering expectations on discourse topicality in the given text. Even if the first mentioned reading is compatible with discourse topicality of 'Sepp Blatter', it is not appropriate for manipulating attention and marking of high speaker salience of the referent. The latter (contrastive topic) is also ruled out in the discourse, since there are no competing alternatives to 'Sepp Blatter' in the previous or following text segments. (As demonstrated in the original example (14a) above, only 'Sepp Blatter' is mentioned as referent in the introductory part of the text and the topic of the following sentences is the same referent 'Sepp Blatter').

As the comparison between the postfield, middle field and prefield positions of the PP *für Sepp Blatter* above shows, the placement of a specific constituent in the prefield, middle field or postfield has consequences for focussing options and for the information structural division of the sentence. Further, the choice of the most appropriate information structural pattern in a sentence is dependent on both contextual factors related to the global discourse stucture and genre specific factors.

In order to show the impact of the postfield placement on information structure for the subsequent discourse, we would like to discuss two other instances of displacement in (14d) and (14e), where the immediately following sentence (S2) has been changed. The difference between the two test-cases is the position of the PP *für Sepp Blatter* in the first sentence (S1): the middle field placement of this PP in (14d) is contrasted to its postfield placement in (14e). Let's start with the analysis of example (14d) where the PP *für Sepp Blatter* stands within the verbal bracket:

(14) [S1] *Mit dem Friedensnobelpreis hat es **für Sepp Blatter** (auch) nicht geklappt.*
with the peace Nobel prize has it for Sepp Blatter (also) not worked out
'The Nobel Peace Prize did not work out for Sepp Platter.'

[S2] *Geklappt hat es dieses Jahr für das tunesische Quartett,*
worked out has it this year for the Tunisian Quartet
das aus dem tunesischen Gewerkschaftsverband (UGTT),
that from the Tunisisian trade union (UGIT),
tunesischen Gewerkschaftsverband (UGTT), dem
Tunisisian trade union (UGIT), the
Arbeitgeberverband (UTICA), der Menschenrechtsliga (LTDH)
working union (UTICA), the human rights league (LTDH)
und der Anwaltskammer besteht.
and the bar association consists.'
'It has worked out for the Tunisian Quartet that consists of the trade union (UGIT), the working union (UTICA), the Human Rights League (LTDH) and the Bar Association.'

The word order in the first sentence of (14d) leads to a coherent connection between (S1) and (S2) which is established by the continuity of the predicate *geklappt* 'worked out'. The conditions for contrast are also fulfilled partly by contrasting different polarities of the predicate (*nicht geklappt* and *geklappt*), and partly by the comparison of the referents in focus 'Sepp Blatter' and 'tunesisches Quartett'. Consequently, the topic shift in (S2) after (S1) (i.e. shifting from the PP *mit dem Friedensnobelpreis* to *geklappt*) is appropriate when (S1) is realized without the exploitation of the postfield.

In contrast, the unbracketing of the PP *für Sepp Blatter* leads to inappropriateness of the contrastive topicalization of the predicate *geklappt* and contrastive focusing of the constituent *für das tunesische Quartett* 'the Tunisian Quartet', since these contradict the expectations triggered by the unbracketing of the PP *für Sepp Blatter*:

(14e) *Mit dem Friedensnobelpreis hat es nicht geklappt **für Sepp Blatter**.*
   ?? *Geklappt hat es (aber) dieses Jahr für das tunesische Quartett, (...)*

The expectation in (S2) of the example (14e) is a continuation of the discourse topic 'Sepp Blatter', announced by the marked word order in (S1). This discourse-topic announcing strategy explains why a shift to another referent is evaluated as problematic by native informants.

The comparison of the sentences (14a), (14b) and (14c) with the PP *für Sepp Blatter* in different syntactic positions as well as the contrast between (14d) and (14e) indicate the following: the unmarked word order with this PP in the middle field (with background or focus reading of the PP) opens up for more possibilities in the continuation of the text than the marked placement of the PP in the postfield. The postfield placement triggers specific expectations for the hearer not only with respect to the choice of the following sentence topic but also for the establishment of the discourse topic. The choice of the contextually most appropriate textual pattern attested in the original version of the sentence in (14a) can also be related to genre. As discussed above in section 5, the high degree of planning typical for press texts resulting in a high degree of "intentionality" turns the foregrounding of the addressee's side – and thereby the manipulative influencing of the addressee – to the optimal strategy.

6.3 Analysis of Right-dislocated Constituents

Example (15) demonstrates the right-dislocation of the NP *die Fußballvereine*, which is coreferent with the pronoun *sie* standing in the prefield of the same sentence.

(15) (HEADLINE) *Bundesliga-Kommentar*
   (TITEL) *Neuer Mut tut meistens gut*
   (LEAD) *Die Beförderung von Julian Nagelsmann oder anderen zu Bundesliga-Cheftrainern beweist: Die alte Gleichung im Berufsbild eines Coaches gilt nicht mehr. Doch das Modell, auf den großen Unbekannten zu setzen, hat auch seine Tücken.*

   (1 §) ***Sie** sind mutiger geworden, **die Fußballvereine**.*[30]
   So mutig wie nun die TSG Hoffenheim war überhaupt noch kein Klub. Mitten in der Saison die auch noch stark abstiegsgefährdete Mannschaft nicht nur

---

30 (15) (1 §) ***Sie** sind mutiger geworden, **die Fußballvereine**.*
   they are braver become   the football leagues
   'They have become more brave, the football leagues.'

einem Trainerneuling in der Bundesliga, sondern mit Julian Nagelsmann gleich einem Coach anzuvertrauen, der bislang nur Erfahrung mit Jugendmannschaften besitzt (...) – das ist ungewöhnlich für <u>*eine Branche, die, (...) gerne auf Bewährtes setzt und Neuerungen erst einmal gründlich misstraut.*</u>
(...)
(faz.net, 15.02.2016)

'(HEADLINE) Bundesliga-comment
(TITLE) New courage often does good
(LEAD) The promotion of Julian Nagelsmann and others to Bundesliga coaches confirms: The received wisdom regarding the professional image of a coach is no longer valid. However, the model of betting on the big "unknown", is also deceitful.

(1 §) **They** have become braver, **the football leagues**.
No club has ever been as brave as the <u>TSG Hoffenheim</u>. To entrust <u>the strongly relegation-threatened team</u> in the middle of the season to not just a coaching novice but, in Julian Nagelsmann, to a coach who until now only has experience with youth teams (...) – this is unusual in <u>a business that (...) prefers to bet on the well-tried and deeply mistrusts novelties (...)</u>.

We claim that postfield placement also in this case has a relevant function for attention manipulation and for the indication of information structural prominence both on the level of sentence and on the level of discourse. The marked alignment of grammatical role and syntactic position (here by mentioning the referent of the subject *sie* in a later position), the (at least implicit) accent assignment combines two dimensions: *Calling* attention to a certain constituent (by narrow focusing) locally and predicting the *sustainment* of attention on this constituent during a longer discourse segment, i.e. turning this constituent to discourse topic of the text or text segment (see also Averintseva-Klisch 2009 on right-dislocation). The information structural analysis of different types of displacements and the results of acceptability judgments using displacement tests show convincingly that the unambiguous marking of the combination "focus status and discourse topicality" seems to be only possible by placement in the postfield – not only in case of unbracketing (as discussed above in section 6.2.), but also in the right-dislocated structures.

There are, however, relevant word order differences between example (14) and example (15). In example (15) the word order is unmarked with a subject pronoun in the prefield followed by the predicate. Here "only" the right-dislocation of the NP *die*

Fußballvereine 'the football leagues' and its separation from the sentence result in a marked alignment of grammatical role and position. The syntactic separation leads to the creation of a separate prosodic phrase requiring an obligatory accent (also relevant for the implicit prosody), and consequently to a high degree of speaker salience. (In the above discussed example (14) with unbracketing, the syntactic structure was marked already in the beginning of the sentence, due to the placement of the PP (*mit) dem Friedensnobelpreis* '(with) the Nobel Peace Prize' in the prefield.)

As for the analysis of the alternatives to the text-initial sentence containing a right-dislocation in the original version (15a), the displacement strategies are more complicated than in the unbracketed cases. Since the right-dislocated NP *die Fußballvereine* in (15a) has a pronominal copy in the sentence, this pronominal copy should be replaced first by the right-dislocated constituent. Whereas (15b) shows the replacement of the personal pronoun by the reference-identical NP in the prefield, (15c) contains the NP in its base position in the middle field, moving instead the predicative *mutiger* 'braver' into the prefield:

(15a) **Sie** *sind mutiger geworden,* **die Fußballvereine***.*

(15b) **Die Fußballvereine** *sind mutiger geworden.*

(15c) ?*Mutiger sind* **die Fußballvereine** *geworden.*

It is easy to realize not only the relevant syntactic differences between the variants (15a), (15b) and (15c), but also the effects of the syntactic changes on the information structure. (15b) has an unmarked word order with the subject in the prefield, making the reading with maximal focus domain possible. This means that the whole sentence can be new information and none of its constituents is specially highlighted in information structural sense (the sentence accent is assigned in the default way to the focus exponent, which is in this case the predicative *mutiger*).[31] This option does not exclude the possibility that the NP *die Fußballvereine* can function both as a sentence topic and a discourse topic, it does however not trigger any expectations. Compatibility with discourse topicality does not mean unambiguous marking of this discourse function. As discussed above, discourse topicality requires highlighting with highest possible speaker salience scores, which can only be indicated by narrow focus structures (achieved by marked alignments of

---

[31] Changes of default prosody can only be marked in written texts by the use of different typographical strategies (caps, italics) – without additional marking the nuclear accent falls on the focus exponent.

positions and grammatical roles) or by marked special structures (dislocation, cleft), and which optimally includes also high degree of speaker salience.

The result of the displacement of the subject in the second modified case, in (15c), is strange in the given context. Not only a predicative in the prefield of a discourse initial sentence is marked, but also the placement of the subject in the middle field position immediately before the closing part of the verbal bracket, which normally hosts the focus or focus exponent of the sentence. Since both constituents appear in marked positions – the predicative in the prefield and the subject in the middle field – they both trigger a highlighted, focused or contrastive reading. However, the conditions for contrast are not fulfilled in the context of the original example in (15a); this explains why the sentence is odd in the given discourse. The conclusion is that the original option with right-dislocation (and narrow focusing) is the optimal choice, since it is *not only compatible* with the discourse topic function of the NP *die Fußballvereine*, but it can also *guarantee* the highest possible salience score for this NP and the unambiguous marking of its discourse topicality. The subsequent text in (15) confirms this claim: the right-dislocated NP *die Fußballvereine* serves as a discourse topic, licencing the referential chain of the related NPs in the following sentences of the text *die TSG Hoffenheim, die auch noch stark abstiegsgefährdete Mannschaft* 'the strongly relegation-threatened team', *Jugendmannschaften* 'youth teams' und *eine Branche, die* 'a business that' (...).

To sum up, our analysis has shown that the postfield placement of NPs and PPs in the investigated newspaper texts announces the discourse topic of a text or text segment in an unambiguous and optimal way, which would not be possible without the exploitation of this sentence position. We argued that the marked syntactic alignment of grammatical role and sentence position at the right periphery can indicate the highest possible degree of salience of a referent within the sentence. The high salience score based on the focus status of the constituent in unbracketing and right-dislocation has consequences for the discourse structure by triggering the expectation that the referent is highly relevant for the whole discourse.

7 Returning to the Global or Local Discourse Topic – Text-final Placement

Concluding the investigation of the postfield in the German sentence and its relevance for marking discourse topicality, we will discuss some cases of high speaker salience manifested by postfield placement, where the referent is serving primarily as a backward-looking center. In this cases, the unbracketed or right-dislocated constituent appears in the final segment of the text. Similarly to the above discussed examples (14) and (15) unbracketing and right-dislocation are important rhetorical strategies for this text type, anchored in a high degree of "intentionality" of use which serves the manipulation of the addressee's attention. The placement in the marked right-peripheral position signals the return and reinforcement of the discourse topic, by re-activating and focusing a [+discourse old; +hearer old] referent, showing a high degree of persistency in the text.

The texts presented in (16) and (17) below demonstrate the efficiency of postfield placement also for marking the return to the discourse topic. In (16) the PP um *VW* 'around VW' is standing to the right of the verbal bracket in the first sentence of the last paragraph of the press commentary. Due to its persistency in the text (marked by underlining of the relevant items) it can be assigned high hearer salience in this final part of the text; however, due to its placement triggering prominence (both in prosodic and information structural sense) it also receives high speaker salience scores. The combination of the high salience values from both the hearer and the speaker perspective leads to the highest possible degree of salience for the postfield constituent making its function as the discourse topic possible.

(16) (HEADLINE) *Nach Abgasmanipulation*
(TITEL) *So viel Dummheit von VW ist unentschuldbar*
(LEAD) *Mit der Klage der US-Regierung gegen Volkswagen bekommt der Abgas-Skandal eine völlig neue Dimension. Eine, die zeigt: Das Schlimmste steht dem Unternehmen noch bevor.*

(1 §) *Zu den vielen unentschuldbaren Dummheiten des <u>VW</u>-Skandals gehörte vom ersten Tag an der Umstand, dass <u>der Konzern</u> nicht nur die Käufer <u>seiner</u> Diesel-Pkw in Europa und Fernost jahrelang belog, sondern auch jene in den USA. (...)*

... (2 §) ... (5 §) ...

(6 §) *Einige Institute haben bereits ausgerechnet, wie viele Menschen – rein statistisch gesehen – wegen der unzulässigen <u>VW</u>-Abgasemissionen an Atemwegs- und Herzerkrankungen gestorben sind, (...)*

(7 § / last paragraph)

> *Es war einige Zeit ruhig geworden **um VW** – zu ruhig, wie sich jetzt zeigt:*[32]
> *Alle, die geglaubt haben, das Schlimmste sei für den Konzern bereits ausgestanden, werden nun eines besseren belehrt. Das Schlimmste, es steht erst noch bevor.*
> (sueddeutsche.de, 05.01.2016)

> '(HEADLINE) After the exhaust manipulation
> (TITLE) So much stupidity by VW is inexcusable
> (LEAD) With the complaint by the US government against Volkswagen, the exhaust scandal gains a completely new dimension. One which shows: The worst is yet to come for the company.
>
> (1 §) Among the many inexcusable stupidities of the VW-scandal was from day one the fact that the conglomerate was lying for many years not only to buyers of their diesel cars in Europe and the Far-East, but also to those in the USA. (...)
>
> ...(2 §)...(5 §)...
>
> (6 §) Some institutes have already calculated how many people – purely statistically – have died of respiration and heart diseases because of the unpermitted VW exhaust emissions, (...)
>
> (7 §) For some time it has been quiet ***around VW*** – too quiet, as it has now turned out: all those who believed that the worst had already passed for must now think again. The worst is yet to come for VW.'

In text (17) below, the politician *Rainer Brüderle* is in the center of interest. Interestingly, in the final paragraph the referent is mentioned in the two last sentences of the press commentary. The right-dislocated NPs, *der kalauernde Bierzeltrhetoriker* and *Rainer Brüderle*, indicate in both cases the role of this referent as discourse topic.

(17) (HEADLINE) *Brüderle-Rede auf FDP-Parteitag*
    (TITEL) *Fehlprogrammierter Mittelstürmer*

---

32 (16) (7 § / last paragraph)
    *Es war einige Zeit ruhig geworden **um**   VW – zu ruhig, wie sich jetzt zeigt:*
    it was some time quiet become around VW too quiet as itself now shows
    'For some time it has been quiet around VW – too quiet, as it has now turned out:'

(LEAD) *Rainer Brüderle macht ab sofort den Miro Klose der FDP. Doch auf dem Parteitag der Liberalen in Berlin präsentiert sich ein müder, abgekämpfter Stürmer, der nur selten seine Fähigkeiten durchblitzen lässt – und so redet, als stünden die Russen noch vor der Tür.*

(1 §) *Es dauert eine Stunde und sechs Minuten, bis* <u>Brüderle</u> *mal etwas lauter wird.* (...)

...(2 §) ... (12 §)...

(13 §) *Manche Scherze verunglücken irgendwie: "Ich mache für die FDP die Sturmspitze wie Miro Klose", sagt* <u>er</u> *und redet danach davon, dass der jetzt in anderen Ländern aushelfe. Will* <u>Brüderle</u> *auswandern?*

(14 § / last paragraph) *Erst in den letzten Minuten fängt* <u>er</u> *plötzlich nochmal aus dem Nichts heraus an, den Saal niederzubrüllen: "Wir überlassen diesen Fuzzis, diesen fehlprogrammierten Typen nicht unser Land!"*
Da war <u>er</u> *wieder,* **der kalauernde Bierzeltrhetoriker Brüderle.**[33] *Der, der einen Marktplatz in eine liberale Kampfarena verwandeln kann. An diesem Tag* <u>seiner</u> *Kür zum Spitzenmann aber wirkte nur* <u>einer</u> *völlig fehlprogrammiert:* **Rainer Brüderle.**[34]
(sueddeutsche.de, 10.03.2013)

'(HEADLINE) Brüderle speech at FDP-party conference
(TITLE) Misprogrammed centre forward
(LEAD) Effective immediately, Rainer Brüderle will play as the Miro Klose of the FDP. However, at the party conference of the liberals in Berlin, a tired and exhausted striker presents himself, whose skills only

---

[33] (17) (14 §/last paragraph)
    Da war <u>er</u> *wieder,* **der kalauernde Bierzeltrhetoriker   Brüderle.**
    here was he again   the bantering   beer tent rhetorician B
    'Here he was again, the bantering   beer tent rhetorician Brüderle.'
[34] (14 §/last paragraph)
    An diesem Tag <u>seiner</u> *Kür   zum Spitzenmann aber wirkte nur* <u>einer</u> *völlig*
    on this   day his   election to   standout   but   acted only one   totally
    fehlprogrammiert: **Rainer Brüderle.**
    misprogrammed R   B
    'However, on this day of his election as leader only one *person* appeared totally misprogrammed: Rainer Brüderle.'

seldom shine through – and who speaks as if the Russians stood before the door.

(1 §) It takes one hour and six minutes before <u>Brüderle</u> grows somewhat louder. (...)

...(2 §) ... (12 §)...

(13 §) Some jokes fail somehow: "I will be the forward for the FDP like Miro Klose", <u>he</u> says, and then speaks of how the latter now helps out abroad. Does <u>Brüderle</u> want to emigrate?

(14 §) Not until the final minutes does <u>he</u> suddenly out of nowhere resume shouting down the hall: "We do not surrender our country to these freaks, these misprogrammed characters!" Here <u>he</u> was again, *the bantering beer tent rhetorician Brüderle*. <u>The one who</u> can transform a market place into a liberal battle arena. However, on this day of <u>his</u> election to leader <u>only one person</u> appeared completely misprogrammed: **Rainer Brüderle**.'

With the examples discussed in this section we wanted to show that the placement of an NP or a PP in the right periphery at the end of German newspaper texts can also be used for marking a backward-looking center combined with high speaker salience. This strategy seems relevant for the stabilization of coherence relations and fulfilling special textual-rhetorical function ("Pointierung", Lüger 1995b: 220). Interestingly, both examples taken from our press corpus illustrate another relevant rhetorical strategy for this genre, called "Rahmenkomposition" ('frame composition'). As Kurz, Müller, and Pötschke (2000: 138) point out, this strategy "gehört im Journalismus zu den älteren Mitteln, auch in der Argumentation" ('belongs in journalism to the older devices, also in the argumentation'). In the above discussed cases the 'frame composition' is supported by the unbracketed and right-dislocated constituent appearing in a sentence in the final section of the text, creating the other pillar of the frame introduced in the headline, title and/or lead. Thereby it contributes not only to the unambiguous marking of the discourse prominence of the constituent in the postfield, but also to the strengthening of the argumentative force of the press commentary.

8 Conclusion

The main goal of the present study was to discuss different types of topichood and their relation to the edge positions of the German sentence at the syntax-discourse interface. Special attention was payed to the discourse-pragmatic properties of two right-peripheral structures, called unbracketing and right-dislocation, and their relevance for the expression of topichood. The discussion was based on the key notion of 'mental salience' and its different types as suggested by Chiarcos (2010) in *Mental Salience Framework*. Our main claim was that non-sentential constituents in the German postfield as a result of an unbraketing or a right-dislocation can have the same discourse function in our corpus: equipped with the highest possible degree of salience (including both hearer and speaker salience), they are in both cases highly relevant for the whole discourse. Consequently, they can function as discourse topics at the global text structure.

The distinction of different aspects of salience as suggested in Chiarcos' framework and the estimation of salience scores in dependence on different contextual and linguistic factors seemed fruitful for the clarification of the cognitive and linguistic aspects of discourse topicality. Whereas hearer salience is backward oriented and primarily based on the degree of givenness of a certain constituent, also related to the distance of its previous mention, speaker salience is forward-looking and requires prominence in the linguistic context. On the global textual level, this can be guaranteed by the high degree of persistence; however, we have also argued that certain requirements should be fulfilled on the local level of information packaging in order to make the strong or unambiguous marking of the prominent textual function as discourse topic possible. Prominence and discourse relevance can be indicated by the marked alignment of a given grammatical role (subject, object, adverbial) to an edge position, accompanied by explicit or implicit prosody. This fact indicates a close relation of discourse topicality to sentential focus, which – especially when realized in marked syntactic structures as narrow focus at the right periphery of the sentence – can contribute to the maximization of salience scores. Besides high speaker salience, high hearer salience value can also be important for guaranteeing the highest possible salience score value in a certain discourse.

As we have emphazised in this article, the right periphery beyond the verbal bracket of the German sentence is – at least in case of non-sentential constituents – a syntactically non-obligatory, and thus entirely pragmatically ruled position. This position can be considered as the preferred position for the expression of discourse topicality in press texts, by creating optimal conditions for marking the highest degree of the combined hearer and speaker salience. It can thereby serve the unambiguous marking of discourse topicality – either the announcement of the discourse topic or the return to this most prominent referent of the discourse.

In future research, the discourse relevance of syntactic structures at the right-periphery of the sentence should also be investigated by extending the range of methodological and theoretical issues. Concerning the methodological dimension, further corpus studies and more extensive acceptability judgments could contribute to research in this field, relying also on quantificational and statistical evaluation of the empirical data. The methodological tools for the calculation of saliency scores and the statistical analysis are already developed in Chiarcos' model, which could be applied to the analysis of postfield structures. The results could be confirmed and further examined by the application of modern psycholinguistic experiments, where eye-tracking studies seem to be especially important and conclusive.

As for the cross-linguistic perspective of the investigation of the relation between discourse topicality and structures at the edge of the sentence further contrastive, comparative studies (for example based on the results of Ashby 1988, Lambrecht 2001, Grobet 2002 for French, Grosz and Ziv 1998 for English, and Averintseva-Klisch 2009 for German) and typologically anchored studies would be of great interest, leading to the establishment of language specific patterns and universally relevant cognitive and pragmatic principles in this field.

References

Altmann, Hans. 1981. *Formen der 'Herausstellung' im Deutschen: Rechtsversetzung, Linksversetzung, freies Thema und verwandte Konstruktionen*. Tübingen: Niemeyer.
Ashby, William J. 1988. The syntax, pragmatics, and sociolinguistics of left- and right-dislocations in French. *Lingua* 75. 203–229.
Auer, Peter. 1991. Vom Ende deutscher Sätze – Rechtsexpansionen im deutschen Einfachsatz. *Zeitschrift für germanistische Linguistik* 19. 139–157.
Auer, Peter. 1996. On the prosody and syntax of turn-continuations. In: Elizabeth Couper-Kuhlen & Margret Selting (eds.), *Prosody in conversation: interactional studies*, 57–100. Cambridge: Cambridge University Press.
Averinteva-Klisch, Maria, 2007. Anaphoric properties of German right-dislocation. In Monika Schwarz-Friesel, Manfred Consten & Mareile Knees (eds.), *Anaphors in Text. Cognitive, formal and applied approaches to anaphoric reference*, 165–182. Amsterdam & Philadelphia: John Benjamins.
Averintseva-Klisch, Maria. 2009. *Rechte Satzperipherie im Diskurs. Die NP-Rechtsversetzung im Deutschen*. Tübingen: Stauffenburg.

Bianchi, Valentina & Mara Frascarelli. 2010. Is topic a root phenomenon? *Iberia: An International Journal of Theoretical Linguistics* 2. 43–88.
Brown, Gillian & George Yule (eds.). 1983. *Discourse analysis*. Cambridge: Cambridge University Press.
Büring, Daniel. 2016. (Contrastive) Topic. In Caroline Féry & Shinichiro Ishihara (eds.), *The Oxford handbook of information structure*, 64–85. Oxford: University Press.
Chafe, Wallace L. 1976. Givenness, contrastiveness, definiteness, subjects, topics, and point of view. In Charles Li (ed.), *Subject and topic*, 25–55. New York: Academic Press.
Chiarcos, Christian. 2003. Eine Satzplanungskomponente für die Textgenerierung. *GLDV – Journal for Computational Linguistics and Language Technology* 18(1). 53–67.
Chiarcos, Christian. 2005. Mental salience and grammatical form: Generating referring expressions. In Manfred Stede, Christian Chiarcos, Michael Grabski & Luuk Lagerwerf (eds.), *Salience in discourse. Proceedings of the 6th Workshop on Multidisciplinary Approaches to Discourse*, 17–26. Amsterdam, Stichting & Münster: Nodus.
Chiarcos, Christian. 2010. *Mental salience and grammatical form. Toward a Framework for salience in natural language generation*. Potsdam: University of Potsdam PhD dissertation. http://www.academia.edu/785120/Mental_Salience_and_Grammatical_Form_Toward_a_Framework_for_Salience_Metrics_in_Natural_Language_Generation (accessed 14 October 2018).
Chiarcos, Christian. 2011a. The mental salience framework: context-adequate generation of referring expressions. In Christian Chiarcos, Berry Claus & Michael Grabski (eds.), *Salience. Multidisciplinary perspectives on its function in discourse*, 105–140. Berlin & New York: Mouton de Gruyter.
Chiarcos, Christian. 2011b. Evaluating Salience Metrics for the Context-Adequate Realization of Discourse Referents. *Proceedings of the 13th European Workshop on Natural Language Generation (ENLG)*, 32–43. Nancy: Association for ComputationalLinguistics.
Coniglio, Marco & Eva Schlachter. 2015. Das Nachfeld im Deutschen zwischen Syntax, Informations- und Diskursstruktur. Eine diachrone, korpusbasierte Untersuchung. In Hélène Vinckel-Roisin (ed.), *Das Nachfeld im Deutschen: Theorie und Empirie*, 141–163. Berlin & New York: Mouton de Gruyter.
Daneš, Frantisek. 1970. Zur linguistischen Analyse der Textstruktur. *Folia Linguistica* 7. 72–78.
Daneš, Frantisek. 1974. Functional sentence perspective and the organization of the text. In Frantisek Daneš (ed.), *Papers on Functional Sentence Perspective*, 106–128. Prague: Academia/The Hague: Mouton.
Davis, Dames Raymond & Julia Hirschberg. 1988. Assigning intonational features in synthesized spoken directions. In *Proceedings of the 26th Annual Meeting of the Association for Computational Linguistics* (ACL 1988), 187–193. SUNY, Buffalo, New York.
Drach, Erich. ^{1}1937 / ^{2}1939. *Grundgedanken der deutschen Satzlehre*. Frankfurt am Main: Diesterweg.
Duden 4. Die Grammatik. Unentbehrlich für richtiges Deutsch. 9. vollständig überarbeitete und aktualisierte Auflage, 2016. Berlin: Dudenverlag.
Dudley-Evans, Tony. 1987. Introduction from editor: "Genre analysis and ESP". *ELR Journal* 1. 1–9. (English Language Research, Birmingham University).
Eisenberg, Peter. 1999. *Grundriss der deutschen Grammatik. Bd. 2. Der Satz*. Stuttgart, Weimar: Metzler.

Engel, Ulrich. 1970a. Studie zur Geschichte des Satzrahmens und seiner Durchbrechung. In Hugo Moser (ed.), *Studien zur Syntax des heutigen Deutsch. Paul Grebe zum 60. Geburtstag*, 45–61. Düsseldorf: Schwann.

Engel, Ulrich. 1970b. Regeln zur Wortstellung. *Forschungsberichte des Instituts für Deutsche Sprache* 5. 7–148.

Engel, Ulrich. 1972. Regeln zur 'Satzgliedfolge'. Zur Stellung der Elemente im einfachen Satz. *Linguistische Studien* 1. 17–76.

Eroms, Hans Werner. 2000. *Syntax der deutschen Sprache*. Berlin & New York: Mouton de Gruyter.

Filippova, Katja & Michael Strube. 2007. The German Vorfeld and local coherence. *Journal of Logic, Language and Information* 16(4). 465–485.

Filpus, Raija. 1994. *Die Ausklammerung in der gesprochenen deutschen Sprache der Gegenwart*. Tampere: Universität Tampere.

Frey, Werner. 2004. A medial topic position for German. *Linguistische Berichte* 198. 153–190.

Frey, Werner. 2006. Contrast and movement to the German prefield. In Valéria Molnár & Susanne Winkler (eds.), *The architecture of focus*, 235–264. Berlin & New York: Mouton de Gruyter.

Frey, Werner. 2007. Some contextual effects of aboutness topics in German. In Andreas Späth (ed.), *Interfaces and interface conditions*, 329–348. Berlin & New York: Mouton de Gruyter.

Frey, Werner. 2015. Zur Struktur des Nachfelds im Deutschen. In Hélène Vinckel-Roisin (ed.), *Das Nachfeld im Deutschen: Theorie und Empirie*, 53–75. Berlin & New York: Mouton de Gruyter.

Ginzburg, Jonathan. 1996. Dynamics and the semantics of dialogue. In Jerry Seligman & Dag Westerståhl (eds.), *Language, logic, and computation*, vol. 1 (CSLI Lecture Notes 58), 221–257. Stanford, CA: CSLI Publications.

Givón, Talmy. 1983. *Topic continuity in discourse*. Amsterdam & Philadelphia: John Benjamins.

Givón, Talmy. 1992. The grammar of referential coherence as mental processing instructions. *Linguistics* 30(1). 5–56.

Givón, Talmy. 2001. *Syntax: A functional-typological introduction*, 2nd edn., vol. 2. Amsterdam & Philadelphia: John Benjamins.

Grobet, Anne. 2002. *L'identification des topiques dans les dialogues*. Bruxelles: Duculot.

Grosz, Barbara J., Aravind K. Joshi & Scott Weinstein. 1995. Centering: a framework for modelling the local coherence of discourse. *Computational Linguistics* 21(2). 203–225.

Grosz, Barbara J. & Yael Ziv. 1998. Centering global focus and right-dislocation. In Marilyn A. Walker, Aravind K. Joshi, & Ellen F. Prince (eds.), *Centering in discourse*, 293–307. Oxford: Clarendon Press.

Gundel, Jeanette K. 1974. *The role of topic and comment in linguistic theory*. Austin: University of Texas at Austin, PhD dissertation.

Gundel, Jeanette K. 1988. Universals of topic-comment structure. In Michael Hammond, Edith A. Moravcsik & Jessica Wirth (eds.), *Studies in syntactic typology* (Typological Studies in Language 17), 209–242. Amsterdam & Philadelphia: John Benjamins.

Gundel, Jeanette K. Nancy Hedberg & Ron Zacharski. 1993. Cognitive status and the form of referring expressions in discourse. *Language* 69(2). 274–307.

Halliday, Michael A. K. 1967. Notes on transitivity and theme in English. Part 2. *Journal of Linguistics* 3(2). 199–244.

Halliday, Michael A. K. 1970. Language structure and language function. In John Lyons (ed.), *New Horizons in Linguistics*, 140–165. Harmondsworth: Penguin Books.
Herring, Susan 1990. Information structure as a consequence of word order type. In Kira Hall, Jean Pierre Koenig, Micahel Meacham, Sondra Reinman & Laurel Sutton (eds.), *Proceedings of the sixteenth annual meeting of the Berkeley Linguistic Society*. February 16–19, 1990, 163–174. Berkeley /California: Berkely Linguistic Society.
Hoberg, Ursula. 1981. *Die Wortstellung in der geschriebenen deutschen Gegenwartssprache*. München: Hueber.
Hockett Charles F. 1958/³1963. *A course in modern linguistics*. New York: Macmillan.
Inaba, Jiro. 2007. *Die Syntax der Satzkomplementierung. Zur Struktur des Nachfeldes im Deutschen*. Berlin: Akademie-Verlag.
Jacobs, Joachim. 1984. Funktionale Satzperspektive und Illokutionssemantik. *Linguistische Berichte* 91. 25–58.
Jacobs, Joachim. 2002. Dimensions of topic-comment. *Linguistics* 39. 641–681.
Klein, Wolfgang & Christiane von Stutterheim. 1991. Text structure and referential movement. *Arbeitsberichte des Forschungsprogramms Sprache und Pragmatik* 22, 1–32. Lund.
Klein, Wolfgang & Christiane von Stutterheim. 2002. Quaestio and L-perspectivation. In Carl Friedrich Graumann & Werner Kallmeyer (eds.), *Perspective and perspectivation in discourse*, 59–88. Amsterdam & Philadelphia: John Benjamins.
Koch, Peter & Wulf Oesterreicher. 1990. *Gesprochene Sprache in der Romania* (Romanistische Arbeitshefte 31). Tübingen: Niemeyer.
Krifka, Manfred. 2007. Basic notions of information structure. In Caroline Féry & Manfred Krifka (eds.), *Interdisciplinary studies in information structure 6*, 13–56. Potsdam: Universitätsverlag.
Kuno, Susumo, 1972. Functional sentence perspective. *Linguistic Inquiry* 3. 269–320.
Kurz, Josef, Daniel Müller & Joachim Pötschke. 2000. *Stilistik für Journalisten*. Wiesbaden: VS Verlag für Sozialwissenschaften.
Lambert, Pamela Jean. 1976. *Ausklammerung in Modern Standard German*. Hamburg: Buske.
Lambrecht, Knud. 1994. *Information structure and sentence form. Topic, focus, and the mental representations of discourse referents*. Cambridge: Cambridge University Press.
Lambrecht, Knud. 2001. Dislocation. In Martin Haspelmath, Ekkehard König, Wulf Oesterreicher & Wolfgang Raible (eds.), *Language typology and language universals*, 1050–1078. Berlin & New York: Mouton de Gruyter.
Langacker, Ronald W. 1997. Constituency, dependency, and conceptual grouping. *Cognitive Linguistics* 8. 1–32.
Lüger, Heinz-Helmut. 1995a. *Pressesprache*. 2. neu bearbeitete Auflage. Tübingen: Niemeyer.
Lüger, Heinz-Helmut. 1995b. Presseanalysen: Meinungsbetonte Texte. *Beiträge zur Fremdsprachenvermittlung* 29. 111–137.
Lüger, Heinz-Helmut. 2001. Akzeptanzwerbung in Pressekommentaren. In Ulrich Breuer & Jarmo Korhonen (eds.), *Mediensprache – Medienkritik*, 207–224. Frankfurt am Main, Bern, Bruxelles, New York, Oxford & Wien: Lang.
Lüger, Heinz-Helmut. 2005. Optimierungsverfahren in Pressetexten. Aspekte einer kontrastiven Analyse (deutsch-französisch). In Hartmut E. H. Lenk & Andrew Chestermann (eds.), *Pressetextsorten im Vergleich – Contrasting text types in the press*, 1–34. Hildesheim, Zürich & New York: Olms.
Molnár, Valéria. 1993. Zur Pragmatik und Grammatik des TOPIK-Begriffes. In: Marga Reis (ed.), *Wortstellung und Informationsstruktur*, 155–202. Tübingen: Niemeyer.

Molnár, Valéria. 1998. Topic in focus. On the syntax, phonology, semantics and pragmatics of the so-called 'contrastive topic' in Hungarian and German. *Acta Linguistica Hungarica* 4 (1–2). 1–77. Dordrecht: Kluwer Academic Publishers & Budapest: Akadémiai Kiadó.

Molnár, Valéria. 2002. Contrast – from a contrastive perspective. In Hilde Hasselgård, Stig Johannson, Bergljot Behrens & Cathrine Fabricius-Hansen (eds.), *Information structure in a cross-linguistic perspective*. 147–161. Amsterdam & New York: Rodopi.

Molnár, Valéria. 2006. On different kinds of contrast. In Valéria Molnár & Susanne Winkler (eds.), *The architecture of focus*, 197–233. Berlin & New York: Mouton de Gruyter.

Molnár, Valéria. 2012. Zur Relevanz der linken Peripherie für die Strukturierung der Information. Kontrastive und typologische Überlegungen. In Lutz Gunkel & Gisela Zifonun (eds.), *Deutsch im Sprachvergleich. Grammatische Kontraste und Konvergenzen. Jahrbuch des Instituts für deutsche Sprache 2011*, 383–416. Berlin & New York: Mouton de Gruyter.

Molnár, Valéria. 2014. Das 'Nachfeld' im Deutschen zwischen Syntax, Informationsstruktur und Textkonstitution: Stand der Forschung und Perspektiven. *Zeitschrift für Germanistische Linguistik* 42(2). 326–337.

Pattabhiraman, Thiyagarajasarma. 1993. *Aspects of salience in natural language generation*. Vancouver B.C.: Simon Fraser University PhD thesis. http://citeseerx.ist.psu.edu/viewdoc/summary?doi=10.1.1.45.5809 (accessed 14 October 2018).

Prince, Ellen F. 1981. Toward a taxonomy of given-new information. In Peter Cole (ed.) *Radical pragmatics* (Syntax and Semantics 14), 223–255. New York: Academic Press.

Prince, Ellen F. 1992. The ZPG letter. Subjects, definiteness, and information-status. In Sandra Thompson & William Mann (eds.), *Discourse description: diverse analyses of a fund raising text*, 295–325. Amsterdam & Philadelphia: John Benjamins.

Reinhart, Tanya. 1982. Pragmatics and linguistics: An analysis of sentence topics. *Philosophica* 27. 53–94.

Roberts, Craige, 1996a. Information structure in discourse: Towards an integrated formal theory of pragmatics. *Papers in semantics*. OSU *Working Papers in linguistics* 49, Department of Linguistics, 91–136. The Ohio State University, Columbus.

Roberts, Craige, 1996b. The QUD model of discourse. Guest lecture in CSCI 9/24/13. http://cs.brown.edu/courses/csci2951-k/papers/QUD_Lecture_Robotics.pdf. (accessed 14 October 2018).

Sauer, Moritz. 2007. *Weblogs, Podcasting & Online-Journalismus*. Köln: O'Reilly.

Schneider, Wolf & Paul-Josef Raue. 1998. *Handbuch des Journalismus*. Hamburg: Rowohlt.

Sgall, Peter, Eva Hajičova & Jarmilla Panenova. 1986. *The meaning of the sentence in its semantic and pragmatic aspects*. Dordrecht, Boston, Lancaster & Tokyo: Reidel.

Stede, Manfred. 2004. Does discourse processing need discourse topic? *Theoretical Linguistics* 30(2–3). 241–253.

Strube, Michael & Udo Hahn. 1999. Functional centering. Grounding referential coherence in information structure. *Computational Linguistics* 25(3). 309–344. http://www.aclweb.org/anthology/J99-3001 (accessed 14 October 2018).

Szakmary, Corinna. 2002. *Personenreferenz und Textplanung: eine textlinguistische Untersuchung über den Einfluss von Textplanungsprozessen auf die sprachliche Realisierung von Personenreferenzen*. Frankfurt am Main, Berlin, Bern & Wien: Lang.

Tomlin, Russell S. 1986. *Basic word order. Functional principles*. London, Sydney, Wolfeboro & New Hampshire: Croom Helm.

Truckenbrodt, Hubert. 2016. Some distinctions in the right periphery of the German clause. In Werner Frey, André Meinunger & Kerstin Schwabe (eds.), *Inner-sentential propositional proforms. Syntactic properties and interpretative effects*, 105–145. Amsterdam & Philadelphia: John Benjamins.

van Valin, Robert D. Jr. (ed.) 1993. *Advances in role and reference grammar*. Amsterdam & Philadelphia: John Benjamins.

van Valin, Robert D. Jr. 2009. An overview of Role and Reference Grammar. https://pdfs.semanticscholar.org/7e76/32c6c6b827a45c03292e109ccc2b0fa481c8.pdf (accessed 14 October 2018).

Vinckel, Hélène. 2006a. *Die diskursstrategische Bedeutung des Nachfeldes im Deutschen. Eine Untersuchung anhand politischer Reden der Gegenwartssprache*. Wiesbaden: DUV.

Vinckel, Hélène. 2006b. Zur interaktionalen Relevanz verbfreier Nachfeldbesetzungen. Eine Untersuchung anhand von Talkshow-Dialogen. In Arnulf Deppermann, Reinhard Fiehler & Thomas Spranz-Fogasy (eds.): *Grammatik und Interaktion. Untersuchungen zum Zusammenhang von grammatischen Strukturen und Gesprächsprozessen*, 295–318. Radolfzell: Verlag für Gesprächsforschung.

Vinckel-Roisin, Hélène. 2011a. Wortstellungsvariation und Salienz von Diskursreferenten: Die Besetzung des Nachfeldes in deutschen Pressetexten als kohärenzstiftendes Mittel. *Zeitschrift für germanistische Linguistik* 39(3). 377–404. Berlin & New York: Mouton de Gruyter.

Vinckel-Roisin, Hélène. 2011b. Ende gut, alles gut – oder: Wie gewinnt und erhält man die Aufmerksamkeit des Lesers? Neue Forschung zu Wortstellungsvariation und Textverstehen. *Sprachreport* 2. 17–24. Mannheim: IDS.

Vinckel-Roisin, Hélène, 2012a. Das ‚Nachfeld' im Deutschen: Rechte Satzperipherie und Diskurstopik-Auszeichnung. *Studia Linguistica XXXI*. 143–163. Wroclaw: TOTEM.

Vinckel-Roisin, Hélène, 2012b. Les 'centres anticipateurs' dans les théories du Centrage: modèle grammatical *vs.* modèle fonctionnel. *Verbum XXXIV*(1). 99–130.

Vinckel-Roisin, Hélène (ed.). 2015. *Das Nachfeld im Deutschen: Theorie und Empirie*. Berlin & New York: Mouton de Gruyter.

Wöllstein, Angelika. 2014. *Topologisches Satzmodell. 2. Auflage*. Heidelberg: Universitätsverlag Winter.

Zahn, Günther. 1991. *Beobachtungen zur Ausklammerung und Nachfeldbesetzung in gesprochenem Deutsch*. Erlangen: Palm und Enke.

Zifonun, Gisela. 2015. Der rechte Rand in der IDS-Grammatik: Evidenzen und Probleme. In Hélène Vinckel-Roisin (ed.), *Das Nachfeld im Deutschen: Theorie und Empirie*, 25–51. Berlin & New York: Mouton de Gruyter.

Zifonun, Gisela, Lugder Hoffmann & Bruno Strecker. 1997. *Grammatik der deutschen Sprache*. Berlin & New York: Mouton de Gruyter.

Sources

faz.net
sueddeutsche.de

PART III: **Topics from the Diachronic Perspective**

Augustin Speyer
Topichood and the Margins of the German Clause from a Historical Perspective

Abstract: German sentence structure offers two clause-peripheral positions, the left-peripheral prefield and the right-peripheral postfield. The content of both is determined by information structural constraints. The prefield especially is often seen as topic position. A closer look into the history reveals that the prefield started as a position specialized for familiar aboutness topics in pre-Old High German, but became more permissive over time, eventually allowing for anything that establishes a link to the context. Likewise, the postfield, a designated position for constituents bearing presentational focus, widened its application range to anything that bears some focus (including contrastive foci). The development of the fields towards less information structural specialization is interpreted as a process of 'bleaching', in that the semanto-pragmatic feature content of elements that are compatible with the fields is reduced, until only few features are left.

Keywords: aboutness topic, prefield, postfield, focus, Old High German, Early New High German, bleaching

1 Introduction

Often, German clause structure is described using the so-called topological field model (e.g. Wöllstein 2010). This model is particularly appropriate for descriptive reasons, because it covers the observable generalizations in a clear manner, and one need not subscribe to a particular theoretic framework when working with it. This might be the reason why it has been used under varying theoretical auspices; since its origins in the early days of German linguistics (Herling 1821) and its rediscovery in the age of structuralism (Drach 1937), it experienced a new heyday in the age of generativism (e.g. Höhle 1986). This might have to do with the fact that it mirrors important insights arrived at in the generative paradigm (e.g. Dürscheid 1989; Sabel 2000).

The basic conception can be seen on example (1).

Augustin Speyer, Saarland University

https://doi.org/10.1515/9781501504488-012

(1)		prefield	| LSB |	middle field	| RSB	| postfield
a.		Gestern	| hat	| Uller seiner Kollegin	| gesagt	| dass (...)
		yesterday	has	U. [his colleague]-DAT	said	that
b.		Uller	| hat	| gestern seiner Kollegin	| gesagt	| dass (...)
		U.	has	yesterday [his colleague]-DAT	said	that
c.		Seiner Kolleg.	| hat	| Uller gestern	| gesagt	| dass (...)
		[his coll.]-DAT	has	U. yesterday	said	that

The abbreviations 'LSB' and 'RSB' stand for 'left sentence bracket' and 'right sentence bracket' respectively. The sentence brackets are the positions for verbal material; all non-verbal material is positionally defined relative to them. There are more fine-grained analyses on the market, but for our purposes this degree of granularity is sufficient. The postfield here contains a subordinate clause which of course has a topological structure on its own which is neglected here.

I concentrate on the margins of the clause, the prefield and the postfield.[1] In purely syntactic terms, the generalization that holds for the prefield is that exactly one constituent – in a generative framework, it would be a maximal projection – can occupy it, regardless of its syntactic function (barred are only finite verb forms).[2] This can be seen in (1): In (1a), a temporal adverbial is in the prefield, in (1b), the subject, in (1c), the indirect object. Which constituent may be placed in the prefield is not syntactically restricted, and it has been recognized for a long time that the filling of the prefield is information structurally determined (e.g. Molnár 1993; Hoberg 1997). For the postfield, it is not as easy to arrive at a generalization. One important difference from the prefield is that it is only optionally filled, whereas the filling of the prefield depends on the sentence type (or *Satzmodus*, to use the more constrained German term). In declarative clauses and wh-interrogative clauses, it needs to be filled, in yes-no-interrogative clauses and imperative clauses, it cannot be filled, at least not with overt material (see e.g. Brandt et al. 1992). If it is realized at all, it rarely contains more than one constituent. Often we find 'heavy' constituents in the postfield, for instance clauses that are integrated into the matrix clause (e.g. Reis 1997), but prepositional phrases or

---

[1] As I am approaching the matter here from a descriptive perspective, I avoid the term periphery in this instance; the postfield is anyway not a 'periphery' in the same sense as the prefield / left periphery that corresponds to defined functional projections.

[2] There are some cases of multiple prefield-filling, but this is a marginal phenomenon. The analysis of multiply filled prefields is not clear on the whole. Some propose a remnant movement analysis of a partially emptied VP (e.g. Müller 2003), while others advocate the view that there is really more than one phrase before the verb (= C°), and couch this often in terms of a cartographic approach (e.g. Speyer 2008b).

noun phrases also appear there occasionally (e.g. Hoberg 1997). As with the prefield, the postfield is not syntactically restricted and whether it is filled (and if so, by what) is mainly determined by information structural factors.

Both the prefield and the postfield were subject to changes in the history of German. In the case of the prefield, it seems to have originated as part of the general development of the verb second syntax in Germanic languages. While this development predates the earliest documentary evidence of German, traces of the development process are still visible in Old High German (henceforth abbreviated OHG; cf. Hinterhölzl and Petrova 2010, 2011). As for the postfield, it was used more readily in earlier stages of German, especially with non-clausal constituents (e.g. Schildt 1976). As we see a clear change of usage here,[3] a diachronic study of this issue is likely to be fruitful in order to better understand the conditions which account for re-ordering operations.

The question that will be investigated in this paper is to what extent the information structural conditions under which constituents appear in the prefield or postfield have changed during the history of German, especially with respect to topichood. Specifically, it will be discussed whether the observable changes are due to a loosening of association of the prefield and the postfield with information structural values, or rather the contrary. To that end, a more precise description of the prefield and postfield in Modern German (abbreviated ModG) under an information structural perspective is offered (section 2). Based on this, two studies on the information structural properties of the prefield (section 3) and the postfield (section 4) in earlier stages of German are presented. A short summary (section 5) ends the paper.

---

[3] A word might be in place whether it is adequate to use the field model for earlier stages of German. In principle, versions of the field model can be used for any language with two designated, not necessarily adjacent verbal positions. This applies to older stages of German. One has to just bear in mind that the generalizations made with respect to the fields may be subject to change. So the generalization that only one constituent occupies the prefield holds largely for ModG, but it does not, however, hold (or at least: it covers less cases) for OHG, where we often find verb first clauses and occasionally multiply filled prefields (see Speyer 2015 for a more thorough discussion). A more interesting issue is what the field model translates to in structural-generative terms. There is evidence that the clausal structure did not undergo radical change from OHG to ModG (see e.g. Axel 2007), so what we describe as prefield and which corresponds to SpecCP in generative terms (Dürscheid 1989) was already in existence in this form in OHG. Changes may pertain to the exact realization of SpecCP, that is, if there is a cascade of C-projections in the style of Rizzi (1997) whose singular projections were more freely accessible in earlier stages of German.

2 The Fields and Information Structure

2.1 The Prefield and Topichood

Many studies have been devoted to the influence of information structure on the prefield position in the ModG declarative clause (e.g. Molnár 1993, 2012; Eroms 2000; Jacobs 2001; Frey 2004b, 2006; Speyer 2007, 2008a, 2009a, 2010; Roberts 2011). It is clear from these studies that it is not possible to pinpoint one information structural property of prefield constituents. There are at least three properties; a constituent (or, rather, the referent of the constituent) should possess at least one of these in order to be put to the prefield. In Speyer (2008a, 2009a), they have been described as follows (examples (2) taken from Speyer 2008a):

- scene setting elements (2a), printed in the examples in small capitals, that is, expressions that delimit the situation in which the proposition is evaluated with respect to its truth value (cf. Jacobs 2001),
- poset elements (2b), printed in the examples underlined, that is, expressions whose referents are members of a set which is evoked in the discourse either explicitly by mentioning the set or implicitly by mentioning another member of the same set (cf. Vallduví and Vilkuna 1998; Prince 1998),
- aboutness topics (2c) in the sense of Reinhart (1982), printed in the examples in bold. Normally, they are discourse-old. Newly introduced referents are permissible only if they are macrostructurally relevant, i.e. if the topic is chosen as sentence topic at least in one more sentence (cf. Daneš 1970; Vater 1994).

(2) a. SCHON IM VORJAHR (...) waren **die vielen** (...) **Briefe**
even in year. before were the many letters
geschrieben (...) worden.
written become
'The many letters of invitation had already be written in the previous year.'

b. Dem SPD-Kanzlerkandidaten Gerhard Schröder hielt **Waigel**
[the SPD-chancellor-candidate G. S.]-DAT held W.
vor, (...). Alt-Bundespräsident Richard von Weizsäcker warf
PTC ex-federal president R. v. W.]-DAT threw
Waigel eine "(...) Verharmlosung" der SED-Nachfolgepartei vor.
W. a trivialization of.the SED-successor party PTC

'Waigel confronted the chancellor candidate of the SPD (labour) G. Schröder (...) Waigel accused former federal president R. v. Weizsäcker of trivializing the successor party of the SED.'

c. ***Verteidigungsminister Peter Struck (SPD)*** *hat gestern sein*
defence minister P. S. (SPD) has yesterday his
Sparprogramm bekannt gegeben. ***Er*** *sieht darin auch einen*
cut program known given he sees therein also a
Schritt zur Reform der Bundeswehr
step to.the reform of.the federal army
'Secretary of Defense P. Struck announced his plans for budget cuts yesterday. He also sees this as a contribution to a reform of the federal army.'

A common denominator for these properties is that they all relate somehow to the concept of topic. Topic is understood here not as an atomic concept, but rather as a group of properties that a referent (and hence the constituent which refers to this referent) can have. Frascarelli and Hinterhölzl (2007) distinguish at least three types of topics, aboutness topics, contrastive topics and familiar topics. As they show, they behave differently syntactically and prosodically, so it is evident that they should be distinguished in principle. Scene setting elemens are then topical in the sense that they establish a link to a situation, that is, they locate a proposition in a local or temporal, that is, extralinguistic, context.[4] What is termed here as poset element is grosso modo equivalent to contrastive topic in Frascarelli and Hinterhölzl (2007), the aboutness topics as used here are an intersection of aboutness topics and familiar topics. The fact that we have an intersection leads to a different way of viewing topichood: It is not several types of topics (such as 'aboutness topic', 'contrastive topic') that can be defined in a categorical, mutually exclusive way, but they can be seen as bundles of properties that are represented as

---

[4] Scene-setting elements are not to be confused with frame topics as keywords that activate a particular frame in Fillmore's sense (e.g. Bigi and Morasso 2012; Busse 2012: 644–687). They do not evoke frames but specify the situation under which an event is evaluated (definition following e.g. Jacobs 2001). Krifka (2007) sees a connection to contrastive topics in that situations are delimited which implies that there are other situations possible in which other truth value assignments are possible.

feature bundles in the syntactic derivation.[5] For example, 'aboutness topics' share with 'contrastive topics' that they determine the 'filecard' (to quote Heim's metaphor) to which the clause adds information (= aboutness). So both kinds of topics have a feature [aboutness]. 'Contrastive topics' have, in contrast to 'aboutness topics', another feature, in that they represent members of a situationally or textually evoked set of alternatives. They share this feature (let us call it [set membership]) with foci. 'Familiar topics' have necessarily a feature [familiarity] which means that their referents are already textually or situationally evoked. Another type of topic, which is not discussed in Frascarelli and Hinterhölzl (2007) (but see e.g. Roberts 2011) is the 'discourse topic' that refers to the entity that an entire textual passage is 'about'. The difference in comparison to 'aboutness topics' is that it represents the 'filecard' to which a whole stretch of discourse / text adds information, rather than only a clause. In order to distinguish these two kinds of topic, we might add another feature, [question under discussion] (adopting Roberts' (2011) term). An aboutness topic may refer to the discourse topic (then having two features, [aboutness] and [question under discussion]), but need not do so.

Let us now move away from topics in a general sense and look at the properties of the preferred prefield elements. All three types of prefield elements have in common that they establish a link to the linguistic and extralinguistic context. In fact, this seems to be the defining quality of all sorts of 'topics', which have been defined as "instructions to the hearers on *where* the propositional content expressed by the assertion act should fit in the C[ommon] G[round]" (Bianchi and Frascarelli 2010: 47, cf. also Krifka 2007). We may term this property as [bridging]. Scene-setting elements instruct the hearer, as to what the specifications of the situation are, under which the propositional content is evaluated, thereby establishing a link to the extralinguistic context. Sentence adverbials such as *leider* 'unfortunately' or *natürlich* 'of course' have a similar function, but it is not the situation that is specified but rather other extra-linguistic aspects such as the epistemic value of the propositional content (in the view of the speaker) or the speaker's estimation of the proposition. Even contrastive topics can be defined as contributing to common ground management, not by adding information to a filecard, but by indicating the implicit question under discussion (Bianchi and Frascarelli 2010, following Büring 2003 and Krifka 2007). Furthermore, poset elements and aboutness topics have in common that they name the referent the sentence is 'about'. Whether [aboutness] is only strictly local for this

---

[5] This is in line with Büring's (2003: 512) assumption about topics that they have several properties, some of which hold for the case he discusses, namely contrastive topics.

discourse segment, as in poset elements, or is continued as such on a longer stretch of discourse, as in aboutness topics in the sense used here is irrelevant.

Here a word on locality and potential impacts beyond the local level are in place. Poset elements tend to be local in that the poset element provides the filecard for only one clause, the next clause having another referent (from the same set) as filecard, and so on. But the fact that several members of a set serve as filecards in a row adds a component that goes beyond pure locality; typically it is a stretch of discourse, consisting of a number of sentences, that is defined by the set. Topics are often seen as having some macrostructural effect, in that discourse stretches are defined by topic continuity (see 'continuing topic' in Frascarelli and Hinterhölzl 2007). Poset elements have a similar quality, but on another level: it is not a single topic that defines a discourse stretch, but a single set from which members are taken that serve as local topics in the discourse stretch. Finally, aboutness topics standing in the prefield tend to be given; [familiarity] is a property that prefield elements can have, regardless of what their exact function is. Poset elements and scene setting elements can be familiar, but need not be; aboutness topics are often familiar, but they can also be non-familiar entities. There are examples in which it is a newly introduced entity that is referred to in the prefield, which turns out to be the aboutness topic of the sentence. However, in these cases, this element is used in the following sentences as aboutness topic as well.

In cases in which the sentence contains more than one constituent with properties that could lead to prefield positioning, the prefield is filled according to a ranking: if a scene-setting element is present, it is most likely placed in the prefield. Otherwise, if a poset element and an aboutness topic are present, it is the poset element that has a higher likelihood of being moved to the prefield (Speyer 2008a). In (2a, b), we see such cases of competition. In Table 1, taken from Speyer (2008a), the frequencies from a corpus of newspaper texts, comprising roughly 500 declarative verb second sentences, are given.[6]

Note that these numbers suggest that the prefield is not the archetypical position of an aboutness topic, which is at the left edge of the middle field (Frey 2004a). The fact that the topic is found relatively often in the prefield is due to the fact that cases in which an aboutness topic is in competition with either a scene-setting element or a poset element are not frequent. Hence, often the aboutness

---

[6] The abbreviations in this and other tables are: S = scene-setting elements, P = poset elements, A = aboutness topic. "S > P" and the like mean: cases in which the sentence contains a scene-setting element and a poset element and in which the scene-setting element, not the poset element, is in the prefield. "% P: A" and the like mean: the percentage of cases, in

Table 1: Relative frequencies of potential prefield fillers in competition cases, ModG.

2 competitors	S > P	S > A	P > A	P > S	A > S	A > P
	12	25	20	3	4	9
% P: A			69 %			31 %
% S: A		86 %			14 %	
% S: P	80 %			20 %		
3 competitors	S > P, A		P > A, S		A > S, P	
	6		1		0	
% S: P, A	86 %		14 %		0 %	

topic is the only constituent that has the necessary properties to be put into the prefield.

Is it possible to draw conclusions as to the structural analysis of the prefield from this data? The fact that potential prefield fillers are a heterogeneous group indicates a rich left periphery in the sense that there are several positions available which are determined by singular information structural features. There is an ongoing discussion on this issue, ranging from one information structurally determined position for contrastive elements and an underspecified position filled by formal movement from the middle field (Frey 2004b, 2006) to assuming Rizzi's whole cascade as available in principle (Grewendorf 2002; Speyer 2008b). Assuming a rather rich left periphery rather than resorting mostly to formal movement has the advantage that it covers more cases. Take for example sentences in which there is a sentence adverbial and a topic present. Sentence adverbials can be counted under the definition of scene setting elements. In a system with one special position for scene setting elements and one for aboutness topics in the left periphery, we would sometimes expect that the sentence adverbial and sometimes the aboutness topic may be placed into the prefield, and that the frequency is an outcome of the ranking. In a system in which scene setting elements and topics are both only movable to the prefield by formal movement, we would expect that topics exclusively or sentence adverbials occur in the prefield in cases of competition, depending on which

---

which one of the two possible permutations (in this case of aboutness topics and poset elements) occurs, as indicated by the column title.

one is assumed to be in a higher position. Corpus studies show, however, that the distribution is not categorical (see Speyer 2017).

If there is more than one prefield position available, the question arises how it comes about that usually only one of these positions is filled. Another question is, how the frequencies can be modelled in an analysis of the prefield. In Speyer (2008a, b, 2009a) it was suggested that the actual prefield-filling can be modelled by a stochastic optimality theoretic approach.[7] The constraints are the following, given in their actual ranking:

(3) 1-VF ≫ SCENE -VF ≫ POSET-VF ≫ TOPIC-VF

  1-VF: Only one constituent occupies the prefield.
  SCENE-VF: The prefield is occupied by a scene-setting element.
  POSET -VF: The prefield is occupied by a poset element.
  TOPIC-VF: The prefield is occupied by an aboutness topic.

The ranking is not categorical in *Stochastic Optimality Theory*. As the ranking values of the constraints are not seen as a discrete number, but rather as high points on a Gaussian bell curve, every now and then a paradox ranking can appear. This is the case if the actual value of a higher-ranked constraint is lower than the actual value of a lower-ranked constraint in a special assignment. The observed frequencies are an outcome of the numeric ranking values of the constraints, the closer the ranking values are, the more often paradox rankings occur.

2.2 The Postfield

Also with respect to the postfield, several studies have been devoted to the relationship of information structure and the postfield in ModG (e.g. Hoberg 1997; Vinckel 2006, 2011; Molnár 2014). Again, postfield constituents can show several information structural properties that are hard to characterize as a single property, the common denominator being at least that it usually has a function

---

[7] In Stochastic Optimality Theory, the grammar is built as in classical OT, in that a generative module generates a certain number of possible candidates from the deep-structural input, and subsequently an evaluation module selects the optimal candidate according to a set ranking of constraints. The difference is that in Stochastic Optimality Theory, the relative value of the constraints can differ and therefore the relative ranking of any two given constraints may sometimes be reversed.

associated with the concept of 'comment'. Typical information structural properties of postfield constituents are:

- High informational content, either due to the sheer mass of information mashed into one constituent (a potential rationale of the 'heaviness' effect) or to the quality of information, e.g. if it is mostly new information (4a, from Hoberg 1997: 1670).[8] Either way, the information is hard to process; disentangling of information by putting a constituent with high informational content into the postfield eases processing for both the speaker and the hearer (cf. Hoberg 1997). The postfield is marked with a dash and the index PoF. It should be noted that extraposition to the right for reasons of 'heaviness' or otherwise difficult processing is not limited to German. Other languages, like English, exhibit this as well (see e.g. Hawkins 1994; Wasow 2002; Taylor and Pintzuk 2012).
- Focus (4b, from Hoberg 1997: 1673), in the sense that the set requirements defined by Rooth (1985) as condition for focus (which, incidentally, are similar to the poset requirements put forward by Vallduví and Vilkuna 1998 and Prince 1998) hold and there is some emphasis put on the constituent (cf. Hoberg 1997; Vinckel 2006).[9] Postfield positioning can thus be seen as a foregrounding strategy, which is in line with what Rochemont (1986) observes about constructional focus, that is: syntactic operations connected to the notion of focus, be it presentational (as in the case of new elements) or contrastive.
- Introduction of discourse topics (4c, from Vinckel 2011: 391). Vinckel (2011) identifies cases in which discourse topics are introduced for stylistic reasons in the postfield and reiterated in the next sentence in the prefield. Note that this is a very special case of topic positioning; in principle, the postfield is not a topic position.

(4) a. *Hier soll nun die Frage gestellt werden* |$_{PoF}$ *nach den*
here shall now the question posed become after the
historisch gewordenen, nachweisbaren und weiterwirkenden
historically originated detectable and still-operating

---

[8] In this and the following examples, the left edge of the postfield is indicated with a stroke and the subscript abbreviation PoF.
[9] Note that focus and emphasis are not necessary conditions of each other (cf. e.g. Rochemont 1986).

       Formen, in denen der Mensch Zeit gerechnet, und das
       forms   in which the human time calculated and that
       heißt: Zeit gegliedert hat
       means time segmented has
       'Let us now ask about the forms, historically originated, detectable and still in operation, in which human beings calculated time, and at the same time: segmented time.'
- b. *Dieses Grab   mag befunden werden*
    this   sepulchre may seen   become
    |$_{PoF}$ *als endgültig verschlossen oder als offenes Grab.*
          as finally closed   or as open   sepulchre
    'One might think of this sepulchre as a sealed or an open sepulchre.'
- c. *Man mag schon   fast   Mitleid haben* |$_{PoF}$ **mit Adolf**
    one may already almost pity   have   with A.
    Sauerland. *Er ist ein Bild   des Jammers.*
    S.   he is a   picture of grief
    'One might almost feel pity for AS. He is the personification of grief.'

The function of introducing a discourse topic illustrated in (4c) shares with the focus function that it is a foregrounding strategy. In contrast to the focus function, however, the referents are obligatorily deaccented. Note that referents that are introduced into the discourse in the described manner are not brand-new, but situationally evoked, in the sense that the referent is the subject of an ongoing discussion. The example in (4c) works only because *Adolf Sauerland* (then mayor of Duisburg, Germany) has been mentioned earlier in the context of reports on the stampede at the Love Parade in Duisburg.[10] Consequently, postfield positioning can be seen not only as a foregrounding strategy, but also as a strategy to indicate that the referent is currently under discussion in the newsfeed. We might assume that journalists employ this strategy deliberately to mark some piece of information as being relevant for the ongoing discourse. We will see that sources of this usage can be detected already in Early New High German (henceforth abbreviated ENHG), although there are some differences.

---

10 The stampede in a tunnel was caused by insufficient security personnel; Sauerland was made responsible for assigning too little personnel to the place of the event.

2.3 Expectations

We saw that both peripheral fields in the German sentence, the prefield, and the postfield, are filled according to information structural considerations, but not unambiguously associated with singular information structural values. Roughly, the fields serve broadly to establish a topic-comment structure, in the sense that the functions of prefield elements can be described as flavours of 'topic', whereas elements that can be moved to the postfield serve functions subsumable under the concept of 'comment'.[11] Yet not all kinds of topics can appear in the prefield, and not everything in the postfield is automatically part of the comment. This indicates that the features responsible for movement to the prefield and postfield respectively are rather fine-grained and do not only cover features of the type 'topic' or 'focus'. The fact that more than one information structural value allows for prefield- or postfield-movement might be an epiphenomenon of structural differences between the cases with different prefield-filling, either in a Rizzian way or in the way Frey (2004a, 2004b, 2006) describes it, or might be the outcome of a scenario with competing constraints on prefield (and postfield) filling, as described at the end of 2.1.

In attempting a diachronic study of the peripheral fields, a question to be asked in the context of information structure in general and topichood in particular is, whether the association of the fields with different information structural values was somewhat tightened or somewhat loosened over the history of the language. In other words: Should we assume that the fields were originally associated with singular, fine-grained information structural values, and more values became possible over time (loosening of association), or should we assume that the fields were originally associated with a broad cover value and became specialized to flavours of those values in the course of the history (tightening of association)? An attempt to answer this question will be made in the remainder of this paper.

---

[11] Leaving aside special cases such as the echoing of salient material in the postfield (like *Ich kann diesen Idioten nicht ausstehen, diesen Idioten* 'I can't stand this moron') or the stylistic topic presentation demonstrated in (4c).

3 The Prefield in Earlier German

3.1 Former Studies

Hinterhölzl and Petrova (2010, 2011) developed a scenario on how the prefield could have originated. The background is that the Proto-Indoeuropean predecessor of German most likely had a verb-final syntax, so something like a prefield (if it is defined stictly as a position of non-verbal constituents to the left of a left peripheral verb) did not exist. However, that does not mean that there was no left periphery at all. We may assume information structurally motivated fronting operations, the target of which might have been positions in a C-architecture (cf. e.g. Speyer 2009b), but importantly, the verb did not regularly partake in such operations. The Proto-Indoeuropean predecessor was also most probably a topic-drop language, which has implications for Hinterhölzl and Petrova's scenario.

The scenario might have been as follows (based on Hinterhölzl and Petrova (2010, 2011), but in some cases differing from their account): It was possible even in Proto-Indoeuropean to front the verb for reasons of emphasis. In the dialect that would eventually develop into Proto-Germanic, this verb fronting operation (whose target might have been a C-head) was employed inflationarily. This means the verb was fronted even when the emphasis on it was weak to nil. Inflationary usages of this kind are rather common in e.g. grammaticalization processes,[12] so this is plausible. Eventually, the normal way to form a declarative clause came to be verb first clauses (stage 1). The topic was zero in these cases, if it was retrievable from the context. If it needed to be expressed, e.g. in cases of topic shift, it was done by way of a construction similar to the Hanging Topic construction: first, the topic was named, then the clause offering the comment to the topic was uttered. Note that the Hanging Topic is an orphan, it does not occupy a position in the clause structure (cf. Shaer and Frey 2004). In the second stage, the topic-drop character of the language was eventually lost. In this context, an expression referring to the topic, i.e. a pronoun, was necessary in the clause proper.

So a serialization in terms of clarifying the topic/comment structure of the clause has developped. The position in which to put the topic was in the left part of the clause, before the verb. The verb signaled the beginning of the comment part. In cases in which there was a hanging topic, the topic pronoun was

---

[12] See on grammaticalization e.g. Hopper and Traugott (2003); Roberts and Roussou (2003); van Gelderen (2011); Eckardt (2012).

coreferential with the hanging topic. In all cases, the prefield pronominals served as bridges to the context. From such a situation it is easy to perceive that the hanging topic could optionally be integrated into the clause (instead of the pronoun) in the left periphery (stage 3). 'Integrated' means that it occupies a position within the clause. If we assume that verb fronting targeted C°, the position of the 'integrated' topic would be SpecCP. If non-pronominals are allowed in the left periphery, other non-pronominals that serve a bridging function could be put there as well, e.g. scene-setting elements, and in this way, the prefield in the sense we know it, would have come into being.

Note that under this scenario we would expect the prefield to originally only host topics, and this is the line Hinterhölzl and Petrova (2010, 2011) take. From stage 3 onwards, the prefield could host anything that had some bridging quality. We would then have a loosening of association, in that the prefield would have become more permissive over time.

Hinterhölzl and Petrova (2010, 2011) acknowledge the presence of scene-setting elements in the prefield. We have seen that these can be subsumed under bridging expressions. We have also seen that this is also possible with contrastive (or poset) elements. Consequently, other studies (e.g. Lötscher 2009; Lühr 2009; Schönherr 2012) find focalized elements, for instance contrastive elements, in the prefield. It is not easy to judge from their examples if those are contrastive topics (Büring 1997), having a sorting-key character (Kuno 1982), but in any case they would not be covered easily under Hinterhölzl and Petrova's definition. So the prefield in OHG probably was as permissive as the ModG prefield. If there was a change, it could only be a 'weak' change in frequency of prefield fillers (which would be an effect of the ranking of the constraints leading prefield movement, see Speyer 2008a, 2008b) and not a 'hard' structural change. By 'weak change' I mean a change that does not imply structural changes, but only a change in the frequency of alternatives, which can be modelled as a change in ranking values of constraints in an (stochastic) optimality theoretic framework.

3.2 The Prefield Ranking in Old High German

In order to decide this question, a small study was undertaken in which the prefields of a sample of an OHG text were investigated with respect to their information structural content. The text chosen was the translation of *Isidor* because, unlike other translation texts, this OHG text is relatively independent of the Latin original. 131 verb-second declarative clauses from chapters 1–4 were analyzed. The results are represented in Table 2.

Table 2: Relative Frequencies of Potential Prefield Fillers in Competition Cases, OHG.

2 competitors	S > P	S > A	P > A	P > S	A > S	A > P
	7	2	3	0	3	23
% P: A			12 %			88 %
% S: A		(40 %)			(60 %)	
% S: P	(100 %)			(0 %)		
3 competitors	S > P, A		P > A, S		A > S, P	
	1		0		2	
% S: P, A	(33 %)		(0 %)		(67 %)	

Two things can be observed. First, poset elements are not preferred prefield fillers. In competition with aboutness topics, aboutness topics account for almost 9 out of 10 cases, and scene-setting elements oust them in all cases. Second, the strong preference for scene-setting elements over topics for the prefield is not as pronounced as it is in ModG; if at all, there is a slight preference for aboutness topics over scene-setting elements. Example (5a: Isidor 2.3) shows a sentence in which the aboutness topic is preferred over the poset element as prefield filler, and in (5b: Isidor 2.2) we see an example of an aboutness topic ousting a scene-setting element.

(5) a. **Dhaz** ni saget *apostolus* (noh forasago ni bifant
       That not says apostle neither prophet not thought
       noh *angil gotes* ni uuista).
       neither angel of-God not knew
       'The apostle doesn't say this, nor does the prophet know it, nor does the angel of God know it.'
   b. **mit imu** was ich DANNE al thiz frummenti
       with him was I then all this creating
       'I created at that time all this with him'

So obviously there are some differences from the ModG ranking: the aboutness topic is ranked about as high as scene-setting elements, and poset elements are ranked low, as far as we can judge based on the limited data. This result corroborates the scenario outlined by Hinterhölzl and Petrova (2010, 2011), as the association between the prefield and aboutness topics is much more clearly visible than in ModG.

3.3 The Prefield-ranking in Early New High German

Another study was carried out on texts that were written roughly halfway between the composition date of the Isidor and today, that is, in the middle of the 15th century (ENHG). Texts from two dialect areas were analysed, namely East Central German (Saxonian and Thuringian) and East Upper German (Middle Bavarian). Furthermore, texts from three text types were selected, namely chronicle, free narrative, and sermon. For each dialect/text type pairing, 100 verb-second declarative clauses were analysed, totalling 600 sentences.[13] The differences in text type and dialect were negligible, so all results are conflated in Table 3.

Table 3: Relative frequencies of potential prefield fillers in competition cases, ENHG.

2 competitors	S > P	S > A	P > A	P > S	A > S	A > P
	53	70	34	1	2	16
% P: A			68 %			32 %
% S: A		97 %			3 %	
% S: P	98 %			2 %		
3 competitors	S > P, A		P > A, S		A > S, P	
	8		0		0	
% S: P, A	(100 %)		(0 %)		(0 %)	

Examples of the majority types are given in (6). In (6a: Kazmair §130), a scene-setting element is preferred over a poset element, in (6b: Pilgerfahrt p.161), a scene-setting element ousts an aboutness topic, and in (6c: Predigt Leipzig, p.5), a poset element wins over an aboutness topic in prefield filling.

(6) a. (*Herzog Steffan kam...*) AM ANDERN TAG FRUE kam
      duke S. came at.the other day early came
      Herzog Ernst und mein Frau geen Landsperg.
      duke E. and my lady to Landsberg
      'The next day, in the morning, duke Ernst and my lady came to Landsberg.'

---

[13] For an exact overview of the texts constituting the corpus see Speyer (in prep.).

b. (Aboutness topic in the preceding context: Prince Wilhelm v. Thüringen)
   V̄FF MYTTEWOCHIN NACH CRUCIS INUENTIONE *fuer* **der**
   on Wednesday after elevation-of-the-cross travelled the
   furste (…) *zcu Venedie.*
   prince   to Venice
   'On Wednesday after Elevation the prince travelled to Venice.'

c. (context: *Judas gink mit Petro zu* **dirre herschaft**)
             Judas went with Peter to this government
   Petrus nam **dar an** *daz ewige leben*,
   Peter   took thereon the eternal life
   Judas der nam **dar an** *den ewigen tot*.
   Judas he took thereon the eternal death
   Judas went with Peter to this disciplehood. Peter gained from it eternal life, Jude gained from it eternal death.'

We see that the modern ranking is already in operation in ENHG: Scene-setting elements are strongly preferred as prefield-fillers, and there is a slight preference for poset elements over aboutness topics. These frequencies even are somewhat clearer than in ModG. We also see that the establishment of the ModG prefield ranking is not a matter of one dialect (at least not in the 15th century), but a common phenomenon.

3.4 Development of the Prefield

Let us summarize the findings of the diachronic survey of the prefield. The prefield in OHG is very clearly associated with aboutness topics. So nothing speaks against the hypothesis that the prefield originated as a position specialized for aboutness topics. This association of prefield and aboutness topics loses impact between 800 AD (around when the Isidor is thought to have been written) and 1450 AD, at which time the investigated ENHG texts were composed. We can interpret this finding in such a way that the special information structural assignment of this position was being lost in that period. So the prefield develops into a position that is less specified with respect to information structure: it is sufficient that the prefield element is somewhat topical, but it need not be an aboutness topic. The beginning of this development is in fact visible even in OHG where we find other types of topics in the prefield, but only marginally. Still, all possible elements have in common that they have some context-linking force, so what probably happened in terms of the information structural specification of the prefield is that the feature content of the prefield was minimized. Whereas hitherto only elements that possessed all the information structural features [aboutness], [familiar] and [bridging] were allowed in the prefield, in ENHG and ModG it is sufficient that an element has the feature [bridging] for it to be eligible for the prefield.

4 The Postfield in Earlier German

4.1 Former Studies

The postfield has been the subject of several studies with a more or less information structural viewpoint. From a purely quantitative point of view, Borter (1982) finds that even in OHG there was a tendency of the postfield to be filled by heavy elements. Information structural studies in the strict sense only came about later, e.g. with Lötscher (2009), Lühr (2009), Petrova (2009), and Schlachter (2012). Petrova (2009) finds examples in the *Tatian*-translation where a Latin order Verb > Object was changed to OHG Object > Verb (that is: where the postfield was avoided), if the object was anaphoric or otherwise discourse-old. She concludes from that that the postfield could not host discourse-old elements. She, Lühr (2009) and Schlachter (2012) agree that the postfield is a position specialized for informational foci, which again fits well with constructional focus, interpreted as presentational focus, associated with rightward movement according to Rochemont (1986), or new elements in general. Lötscher (2009), trying to interpret the findings in the light of a topic-comment structure, finds that the postfield can only host parts of the comment. So the common denominator of these studies is that the postfield in OHG is specialized for both new and non-topical elements.

This state of affairs persists to some extent into the ENHG period. Several studies (e.g. Bies 1996; Sapp 2007, 2014; Light 2012) describe the postfield position in ENHG as a designated focus position. They narrow down the function to narrow focus and informational focus; in the latter case even subjects can be moved to the postfield.

When comparing the studies, it becomes apparent that a slight change seems to have occurred between OHG and ENHG, in that contrastive foci begin to be permitted. So there is some increase in the information structural interpretations compatible with postfield positioning. As a consequence, the postfield becomes less specified. So far, this development is somewhat parallel to the development in the prefield and constitutes a loosening of association.

4.2 Study on the Postfield in Early New High German

In order to assess this more precisely, I undertook an analysis of several postfields in the ENHG era. To that end, texts from two dialect areas, East Central (Thuringian) and East Upper German (Bavarian), and across two time spans, around 1450 and 1550, were selected and the postfields gathered manually.[14] Preference was given to texts that are as close to the vernacular as possible, in order to keep the results comparable to ModG, where postfield positioning is largely a matter of oral speech.[15] Only postfields with non-clausal content were taken into account.

To quantify the information structural content of the postfields, the ratio of new referents in both the postfields and the middle fields of the clauses containing a postfield were calculated and compared. 'New' referents were defined as in Prince (1981) as not being mentioned in the previous context and not inferable from other, already mentioned referents. Table 4 shows the numbers and ratios.

Table 4: Ratio of New Referents, ENHG.

		Bavarian: Postfield	Bavarian: Middle field	Thuringian: Postfield	Thuringian: Middle field
1450	number of referents	57	52	80	48
	number of new ref.	13	5	36	7
	ratio of new ref.	*22.8*	*9.6*	*45.0*	*14.6*
1550	number of referents	83	58	81	47
	number of new ref.	61	12	57	16
	ratio of new ref.	*73.5*	*20.7*	*70.4*	*34.0*

It is evident that there is a correlation between the postfield and new information, in that the ratios of new referents are higher in the postfields than in the middle fields. For the earlier period, the effect is more clearly visible in Thuringian than in Bavarian, In the later period, the difference between the dialect

---

14 The texts were: East Central German: Rothe (1421), Bange (1599); East Upper German: Kottanerin (1445), zu Herberstein (1557).
15 Postfield positioning is also used as a stylistic device e.g. in newspapers, but this kind of postfield positioning follows quite different constraints. See e.g. Vinckel (2011).

areas dwindles, which may be due to the beginning usage of the East Central German based standard in this period.[16]

Two examples for postfields in ENHG are given in (7). In (7a), an example from earlier Thuringian (Bange 3.2.11f.), the typical case is illustrated. The postfield contains new information, and the aboutness topic of the clause is in the middle field (*er* 'he'). But there are also counterexamples, especially in Bavarian. In (7b), taken from Kottanerin (11.14f.), the postfield contains information that is given, indeed highly salient (the sentence is taken from a report of the fire in the queen's bedroom), whereas *der poes veint*, 'the evil enemy (= the devil)' has not been mentioned in the text. Although the information in the postfield is not the most informative bit in the clause, it is not the topic, as which counts *die* 'her' = the queen in the prefield.

(7) a. *Da   must   er vber Meer fliehen* |$_{PoF}$ *mit Zwantzig Tausendt*
       then   needed he over sea escape   with twenty   thousand
       gewapneter Man.
       armed-GEN man
       'Then he had to escape over sea, with 20.000 armed men.'
   b. (context: The maid of the queen had risen from bed and did not notice that the candle had tumbled down and that there was fire in the room)
       die hiet der poes veint   gern   gelaidigt |$_{PoF}$ *mit der pruenst.*
       Her had the evil enemy willingly hurt   with the fire
       'The evil enemy would have liked to hurt her by means of the fire.'

If there was a correlation between new information and the postfield, we would likewise expect the ratio of given, especially salient, referents to be low in the postfield, relative to the middle field. Table 5 shows that this expectation is born out. A working definition of 'salient' information is as follows: referents are regarded as salient, if they are contextually given and if there are no more than 10 other referents mentioned between the present and the previous mention of the same referent. The consideration underlying this definition is that the short-term memory can only keep 5 to 10 elements. So, we can be rather sure that if more than 10 referents have been evoked between the present mentioning and the last mentioning the referent is not any more in the short term memory.

---

[16] Significant distributions are 15th cent. Thuringian (p = 0.0004; χ^2 = 12.442), 16th cent. Bavarian (p = 0; χ^2 = 46.682), 16th cent. Thuringian (p = 0.00006; χ^2 = 16.017). Non-significant (but almost) is 15th cent. Bavarian (p = 0.06; χ^2= 3.432). The χ^2-calculation was done using Preacher (2001).

Table 5: Percentage of given/salient referents, ENHG.

		Bavarian: Postfield	Bavarian: Middle field	Thuringian: Postfield	Thuringian: Middle field
1450	number of referents	57	52	80	48
	number of salient ref.	20	39	19	35
	percentage of salient ref.	*35.1*	*75.0*	*23.8*	*72.9*
1550	number of referents	83	58	81	47
	number of salient ref.	9	31	9	26
	percentage of salient ref.	*10.8*	*53.4*	*11.1*	*55.3*

The ratio of salient information is significantly lower in the postfield as compared to the middle field. Again, the effect is stronger in the later period, where the dialect areas behave identical, and in the earlier period the effect is clearer in Thuringian than in Bavarian.[17]

If we concentrate not on given or given/salient information in general, but rather on given/salient information that counts at the same time as aboutness topic (which is a subset of the data in Table 5), we see the same picture (Table 6).

Table 6: Percentage of given Topical Referents, ENHG.

		Bavarian: Postfield	Bavarian: Middle field	Thuringian: Postfield	Thuringian: Middle field
1450	number of referents	57	52	80	48
	number of topical ref.	6	20	5	16
	percentage of topical ref.	*10.5*	*38.5*	*6.3*	*33.3*
1550	number of referents	83	58	81	47
	number of topical ref.	3	17	2	17
	percentage of topical ref.	*3.6*	*29.3*	*2.5*	*36.2*

Note, however, that, although the ratio is very low around 1550, the postfield still contains a relatively high proportion of topics in the earlier period,

---

[17] Significant distributions are 15th cent. Bavarian (p = 0.00003, χ^2 = 17.446), 15th cent. Thuringian (p = 5e^{-8}; χ^2 = 29.734), 16th cent. Bavarian (p = 3e^{-8}, χ^2 = 30.497), 16th cent. Thuringian (p = 6e^{-8}; χ^2 = 29.258). The χ^2-calculation was done using Preacher (2001).

especially in Bavarian, where about one tenth of postfields is topical. In (8), from Kottanerin 10.3, an example is given in which the discourse topic *die Heiligen Kron* 'the holy crown' is in the postfield. The example is taken from a passage about the safe storage of the crown. It is questionable whether the local aboutness topic of the clause is the crown or rather the omitted subject 'I'. The information in the postfield constitutes the discourse topic at any rate and shows topical features such as 'linking' and 'familiar'.

(8) (Context: Many Hungarian lords took the crown with them and carried them into a vault)
und wol sach, wie, wo man hin tët |$_{\text{PoF}}$ *die Heiligen Kron,*
and well saw how where one to-did the holy crown
'and I saw well where they put the holy crown,'

This usage in some ways foreshadows the modern journalistic usage of highlighting a discourse topic (see Vinckel 2011), but it does not seem to be connected to a special foregrounding strategy. The modern journalistic usage might, however, stem from this state of affairs, when the postfield was not associated to new or focused material.

Summarizing the study on ENHG postfields, one can conclude that the postfield seems to be a information structurally specialized position in this period, especially in Thuringian. In Bavarian, this specialization is less visible, but it develops to match the Thuringian state of affairs; in the later period, the specialization on new information and only parts of the comment is very pronounced.

If we compare this to OHG, as investigated in several studies mentioned in the preceding section, we notice some difference. ENHG around 1450 seems more permissive than OHG, which speaks for a loosening of association, similarly to the prefield. Unexpected in this context is the development 'back' towards a more restrictive use around 1550. Whether this is a real change or only an epiphenomenon of changing influences on the written language cannot be decided.

4.3 Study on the Postfield in Modern German Dialects

As the non-clausal postfield is mostly a vernacular phenomenon in ModG, dialect texts (which per se are close to the vernacular, or at least try to be) from the same dialect areas, composed around 1850, were investigated in the same manner as the ENHG texts.[18]

The tendencies that were visible in ENHG around 1450 pertain. Table 7 shows the ratio of new referents in the texts. The ratios of the ENHG periods are repeated to ease comparison.

Table 7: Percentage of New Referents, ModG Dialects.

		Bavarian: Postfield	Bavarian: Middle field	Thuringian: Postfield	Thuringian: Middle field
1450	percentage of new ref.	22.8	9.6	45.0	14.6
1550	percentage of new ref.	73.5	20.7	70.4	34.0
1850	number of referents	24	18	16	16
	number of new ref.	9	5	11	2
	percentage of new ref.	37.5	27.8	68.8	12.5

The correlation of new information and the postfield remains strong in Thuringian at about the level reached around 1550, and is stronger in Bavarian than in 1450, but less than in 1550. This supports the hypothesis that the correlation is mostly an East Central German dialect feature not adopted in the Bavarian vernacular. Example (9) shows typical cases: new information in the postfield and given in the middle field of a Thuringian text (9a: Kürsten 1906: 32), and the opposite, given information in the postfield and new information in the middle field in Bavarian (9b: Reitzenbeck 1846: 114f.). The information in the postfield is given and at the same time represents the discourse topic for this subdiscourse.

(9) a. (context: and they took... [four quite honourable citizens as hostages]$_1$ to the Bietersberg (castle))

on an 1. November da worden **se$_1$** alle bsamm
and on 1st November there became they all together
äigesteckt |$_{PoF}$ en anne donkle Kasematte,
in-put into a dark dungeon
'and on November 1, they all were thrown into a dark dungeon,'

---

[18] The texts were: Thuringian: Kürsten (1906); Bavarian: Reitzenbeck (1846).

b. (context: *Only one thing makes me nervous at such a fair, the large number of beggars$_1$,...*)
Dö Wirth' solln liaber án Groschn Eintritt begehrn
The landlords should rather a dime fee set
|$_{PoF}$ *für dö Bedlleut$_1$.*
for the beggars
'The landlords should rather set an entrance fee of a dime for the beggars.'

The same essentially holds for given/salient and topical referents (Tables 8, 9).

Table 8: Percentage of given/salient Referents, ModG dialects.

		Bavarian: Postfield	Bavarian: Middle field	Thuringian: Postfield	Thuringian: Middle field
1450	percentage of sal. ref.	35.1	75.0	23.8	72.9
1550	percentage of sal. ref.	10.8	53.4	11.1	55.3
1850	number of referents	24	18	16	16
	number of sal. ref.	10	12	1	10
	percentage of sal. ref.	41.7	66.7	6.3	62.5

Table 9: Percentage of Topical Referents, ModG Dialects.

		Bavarian: Postfield	Bavarian: Middle field	Thuringian: Postfield	Thuringian: Middle field
1450	percentage of top. ref.	10.5	38.5	6.3	33.3
1550	percentage of top. ref.	3.6	29.3	2.5	36.2
1850	number of referents	24	18	16	16
	number of top. ref.	2	4	0	6
	percentage of top. ref.	8.3	22.2	0	37.5

It is easy to see that in Thuringian, the ratio of salient and also of topical referents in the postfield decreases even more in the ModG dialect text. On the other hand, the Bavarian text more or less replicates the numbers from 1450. On the whole, we can interpret these findings such that Bavarian was more permissive with respect to the information structural configurations, in which the postfield was used. This might be an effect of a different syntactic status of the postfield in Bavarian versus Thuringian (and the standard variety of German). But more work needs to be done in order to assess this question (for a preliminary discussion see Speyer 2016). It is however clear that mere 'heaviness' in terms of structural complexity or number of words / constituents / information bearing units is not the decisive factor for postfield positioning.

5 Syntactic Change by Feature Reduction (Vulgo: 'Bleaching')

5.1 Overview over the Changes

On the whole we can see that with both the prefield and the postfield the originally strict correlation to information structural values is loosened. Most importantly, the frequency of aboutness topics as prefield elements in OHG is strikingly higher than in later stages of the language.

The prefield presumably started out as a position specialized for topics (probably more precise: given aboutness topics, but only after a topic shift occurred) and becomes more permissive over time: In addition to aboutness topics, scene-setting elements and poset elements are allowed in Modern German, and we witness the increasing loosening of the association in the documented history of the language. The only elements that are not preferred in the prefield currently are new elements, if they have no topical value. Note that these classes of elements are attested already in OHG as prefield elements, but the frequency of aboutness topics is strikingly higher in OHG.

In both periods, OHG and ModG, we have variation in the prefield, which has been modelled further below using stochastic OT. Note that the change between OHG and ModG is not a structural change, but rather a change in frequencies of different sorts of prefield elements and in the preference for prefield elements of certain sorts if they are in competition with each other. This can be interpreted as a change in the ranking value of the prefield fillers (or, more precisely, of the constraints that select such candidates as the optimal ones). The constraint that would select the candidate with the topic in the prefield (TOPIC-VF) had the highest ranking value in OHG compared to the constraint selecting poset elements (POSET-VF) and the one selecting scene-setting elements (SCENE-VF). So the OHG ranking is as in (10), assuming that the generalization that the prefield can host only one element was more or less valid also in OHG (see Axel 2007):

(10) 1-VF ≫ Topic-VF ≫ Scene-VF ≫ Poset-VF

The ModG ranking was already presented under (3) in section 2.1. In ModG the constraint selecting the scene-setting candidate is ranked highest and the constraint selecting the candidate with the topic in the prefield is lowest, even a bit below the constraint selecting poset elements.

The postfield presumably started as a positon specialized for information foci. In ENHG, especially in Bavarian, it appears to be more permissive than in OHG in that all sorts of elements, most notably contrastive foci but also given elements, even discourse topics come to be allowed. In East Central ENHG (Thuringian), elements that are given, let alone topics, continue to not be preferred. As there is a large impact of East Central German on all varieties of German from the 16th century onward, the postfield in other varieties seemingly develops 'back' to a more restrictive position.

The above interpretation of the changes leads to some considerations about potential mechanisms of syntactic change beyond the 'hard' structural changes that result from reanalysis during language acquisition (e.g. Clark and Roberts 1993; Lightfoot 1999). We will see that syntactic changes can come about also by changes in frequencies, which in turn are reflexes of changes in the feature content of certain positions, and this is where information structure as a trigger for syntactic change may play a role.

5.2 Feature Reduction in the Prefield

How can we account for the change in the information structural content of the two positions? The OT analysis given for the prefield already presupposes that there are variants available, but OHG seems to give a glimpse of a pre-OHG stage where no variation was possible. The change in information structural content can be captured as a consequence of loss of features that trigger movement. Let us exemplify this with the prefield. The original feature content of the prefield (or, rather, the relevant projection in the C architecture) was a junction of the topical features [aboutness], [given] and [bridging].[19] In OHG, the feature content was already simplified so that in the end only [bridging] was left. This

---

19 The features are to be thought as features that can trigger movement. The information structural propoerties on the elements, say, aboutness topics etc., are coded as features of the type given in the text. These features correspond to features in the left periphery positions. The difference to 'normal' feature driven movement is that the derivation does not crash if the feature-driven movement does not happen. This is more or less the mechanism that is

means that every phrase which is marked with the feature 'bridging' can be moved to the prefield. This goes for aboutness topics of the sort described, but also for scene setting elements and poset elements, as each of those bears some relationship to the linguistic or extralinguistic context.

The change in frequency is another matter which is rather independent of the feature content of the relevant C projection. But for the question of which phrases can be moved at all, the presence of a [bridging] feature is crucial. So what happens is that the feature content of the prefield position is reduced, and because of that more sorts of elements can automatically be moved to the prefield. In some ways this is related to 'bleaching' as it is known from grammaticalization processes. Bleaching in grammaticalisation – as well as in semantic change in general – can be captured as a reduction of semantic features (discussed in e.g. Langacker 1977: 84–87; Sweetser 1988; Lehmann 1995: 127; Eckardt 2012).

Similarly, information structural bleaching can occur if a bundle of features that trigger movement is reduced. Especially with pragmatic notions a bleaching scenario is plausible, as there the reduction of features can be caused by an inflationary usage of some expression, a rather common process in general (e.g. Hentschel 1998). We might assume that the originally pragmatically restricted realization of a prefield was also subject to this kind of inflationary usage. In terms of features, inflationary usage means that a mode of expression, as e.g. the prefield, is used by language users even in cases in which the full feature content of prefield movement is not satisfied. For instance, a speaker might move a phrase that is marked for [bridging] and [given], but not [aboutness], to the prefield. This over-usage has consequences for language acquisition. So, a language learner of a learner generation F might pick out only some features that are relevant for prefield movement from the output provided by speakers of the parental generation P. If we view topichood in general as a feature bundle that might be variable in different languages, containing e.g. [aboutness], [bridging], [given], [discourse topichood] etc., language learners of generation F might pick out only some features as relevant for prefield movement, e.g. [bridging]. In that way other elements that also contain [bridging] in their information structural feature content are allowed, e.g. scene setting or poset elements. Thus, the inflationary usage by generation P, which originally stemmed from riding dead a specialized construction with novelty effect, might lead to the analysis of this construction as one with reduced feature content.

---

described in Rizzi (1997) for the informational structural features responsible for optional movement to TopP, FocP etc.

In the case of the prefield, this kind of feature reduction was relatively easy to originate. We may assume that some C-architecture was even present in Proto-Indoeuropean and also in Proto-Germanic (Speyer 2009b), so several prefabricated C-projections were available. The only structural change was that verb movement to the C-architecture became compulsory, resulting in the Germanic verb second syntax. The development of the prefield and its proliferation went hand in hand with the movement of the verb to the C-projection.

The feature reduction scenario outlined above might translate into a cartographic C-architecture approach in the style of Rizzi (1997). Originally, movement targeted only one C-projection (the one with the fitting feature content), whereas after feature reduction, other C-projections that are compatible with the reduced feature content might be targeted as well. An aboutness topic, for instance, carries the features [aboutness] and [bridging] (possibly among others). There is a position in the left periphery that is specified for [aboutness] and [bridging], so the topic can be moved there. It cannot be moved into other positions which are specified for [bridging] and something else, e.g. [contrast]. After feature reduction, the topic can be moved to all positions that are specified for [bridging], as they are underspecified with respect to other information structural properties.

In Modern German, a phrase must still have some minimal feature content in order to be moved to the prefield. Otherwise you would never expect to get prefield expletives: If prefield expletives are used exactly in those cases in which no suitable phrase that can be moved to the prefield is available, this implies that phrases must still have some properties that make them movable to the prefield. Note that aboutness topics in German sentences with prefield expletive typically lack the bridging quality (see Speyer 2009a).

5.3 Feature Reduction in the Postfield

With the postfield, the reanalysis scenario is necessarily different as there are no prefabricated positions. The postfield is not part of the functional overlay a clause has anyway (such as the C-architecture), but is either a consequence of a variable head parameter or a case of ad-hoc adjunction. Consequently, the development of the postfield is rather different both from a descriptive and a structural point of view. Descriptively, we do not see an inflationary usage; if anything, the postfield is used even more rarely.[20] The fact that the postfield is

---

20 This is in contrast to the English postfield. Here we had inflationary usage which eventually led to a generalization to the VO-syntax (cf. e.g. Taylor and Pintzuk 2012).

not used frequently is a direct consequence of its information structural specialization as a focus position. First, focus is used in general less often than, say, topic. Second, the postfield is not the only focus position in the German clause: Elements at the right edge of the middle field can be interpreted as foci as well. In terms of features, this infrequent usage means that bleaching does not occur on the same scale as in the case of the prefield. The postfield is still a fairly specialized position. Structurally, the ongoing infrequent usage did not trigger any reanalysis towards an analysis in which the postfield is a regular syntactic option, e.g. by reanalysing the head parameter of the verb phrase categorically to left-headedness.[21] So, an analysis of the postfield as an 'expensive' construction (which involves for instance building up extra structure) is not prevented. In fact, it might even be triggered by the fact that it is relatively rare: A language learner might come to the conclusion that the rarity of this construction is a consequence of its costly syntax.[22]

6 Summary and Final Remarks

The history of the prefield and the postfield in the history of German was outlined with respect to the information structural interpretation of the fields. With respect to the prefield, it could be showed that the prefield became more permissive with respect to information structural content. It started as a position designated for aboutness topics, and it is nowadays a position that can host anything as long as it has one property of topics, namely the property to anchor the proposition to the context (what we referred to as bridging). With respect to the postfield, a different development took place. Although an extension of possible information structural properties of postfield material is visible, the use of the postfield became less frequent over time. The developments were interpreted as a bleaching process in that the stock of information structural features that were necessary for movement to either field was reduced so that in the end only one relatively general feature (such as [bridging] for the prefield) needed to be satisfied by prefield movement.

---

[21] This might have happened and did happen e.g. in languages such as Middle English (Kroch and Taylor 1997).
[22] In Speyer (2016) it was argued that Bavarian might have had a variable head parameter, such as e.g. Old English seems to have had (cf. Petrova and Speyer 2011); this might have been reanalyzed to adjunction as the more 'costly' variant by such considerations.

The question about the 'architecture of topic' is answered here in a way reminiscent of lexical semantics in the tradition of Katz and Fodor (1963), in that topichood is seen as a bundle of semanto-pragmatic features. Many flavors of topichood are in use in the research tradition of the past 40 years – aboutness, givenness, lack of (prosodic) prominence, to name but a few – and it seems sometimes as a matter of personal preference, which flavor is ennobled with the term 'topic' and which flavors have to fobbed off with some other term. There are many advantages of the interpretation of topichood as a feature bundle. One is that it is easily transmitted to syntactic views of information structurally induced movement as feature-driven movement: A 'topic' consisting of a bundle of semanto-pragmatic features provides the features necessary for movement. Another advantage is that all flavors of topic indeed are to be seen as topic-like – they all correspond to possible features, some of which constitute an archetypical topic in one language, some other selection constitutes an archetypical topic in another language. One of the main advantages of this view, however, is that it allows to trace the development of some aspect of topichood – in the present case: the properties an element must have in order to be placed in a 'topic' position like the prefield – to a general process of feature loss. Similar processes can be used fruitfully to model the semantic side of grammaticalization, so this might be a general process in semantic or pragmatic changes of any kind.

Note: This paper goes back to two talks given at Lund University in December 2014, in the context of the Grammar Seminar and of the workshop 'Architecture of Topic', and a talk given at the Università Ca' Foscari di Venezia in April 2016. The data for the postfield study was collected with the aid of my Göttingen research assistant Marten Santjer, whose work I gratefully acknowledge. I want to thank furthermore the audiences of these talks, especially Peter Culicover, Lars-Olof Delsing, Werner Frey, Hans-Martin Gärtner, Giuliana Giusti, Roland Hinterhölzl, Gunlög Josefsson, Valéria Molnár, Michael Rochemont, and Halldór Sigurðsson for interesting discussions. I thank also Jonathan Watkins for correcting my English. All remaining errors are my own.

Sources

Bange, Johann. 1599. *Thüringische Chronick oder Geschichtsbuch*. Mühlhausen: Hantzsch. http://www.korpora.org/Fnhd/ (accessed July 15 2016).
Pilgerfahrt: In: Erben, Johannes. 1961. *Ostmitteldeutsche Chrestomathie*. Berlin: Akademie-Verlag.

Isidor v. Sevilla. 1964. *Der althochdeutsche Isidor: nach der Pariser Handschrift und den Monseer Fragmenten*. Ed. by Hans Eggers. Tübingen: Niemeyer. http://titus.uni-frankfurt.de/texte/etcs/germ/ahd/isidor/isido.htm (accessed July 15 2016).

Kazmair, Jörg. 1403. Jörg Kazmair's Denkschrift über die Unruhen zu München in den Jahren 1397–1403. In: Hegel, C. 1878. *Die Chroniken der baierischen Städte: Regensburg, Landshut, Mühldorf, München* (Die Chroniken der Deutschen Städte Bd. 15). Leipzig: Hirzel.

Kottanerin, Helene. 1445 [1971]. *Die Denkwürdigkeiten der Helene Kottanerin*. Ed. by Karl Mollay. Wien: Österreichischer Bundesverlag für Unterricht, Wissenschaft und Kunst. http://www.korpora.org/Fnhd/ (accessed July 15 2016).

Kürsten, Otto. 1906. *Lustige Geschichten in Thüringer Mundart*. Erfurt: Körner.

Predigt Leipzig. In: Schönbach, Anton E. 1886. *Altdeutsche Predigten*. Graz: Styria. http://korpora.org/Fnhd/ (accessed July 15 2016).

Reitzenbeck, Heinrich. 1846. *Glimmer. Bd. 1: Lieder und Briefe in österreichischer Volksmundart*. Regensburg: Manz.

Rothe, Johannes. 1421. Düringische Chronik des Johann Rothe. Hg. von R. v. Liliencron. Jena: Frommann, 1859. http://www.korpora.org/Fnhd/ (accessed July 15 2016).

Zu Herberstein, Siegmund. 1557. *Moskouia oder Hauptstadt der Reissen*. Wien: Zimmermann. http://www.korpora.org/Fnhd/ (accessed July 15 2016).

References

Axel, Katrin. 2007. *Studies on Old High German syntax*. Amsterdam & Philadelphia: John Benjamins.

Bianchi, Valentina & Mara Frascarelli. 2010. Is topic a root phenomenon? *Iberia* 2 (1). 43–88.

Bies, Ann. 1996. *Syntax and discourse factors in Early New High German: Evidence for verb-final order*. Philadelphia: University of Pennsylvania MA thesis.

Bigi, Sarah & Sara Greco Morasso. 2012. Keywords, frames and the reconstruction of material starting points in argumentation. *Journal of Pragmatics* 44(10). 1135–1149.

Borter, Alfred. 1982. *Syntaktische Klammerbildung in Notkers Psalter*. Berlin & New York: Mouton de Gruyter.

Brandt, Margareta, Marga Reis, Inger Rosengren & Ilse Zimmermann. 1992. Satztyp, Satzmodus und Illokution. In Inger Rosengren (ed.), *Satz und Illokution I*, 1–90. Tübingen: Niemeyer.

Büring, Daniel. 1997. *The meaning of topic and focus. The 59th street bridge accent*. London & New York: Routledge.

Büring, Daniel. 2003. On D-trees, beans, and B-accents. *Linguistics and Philosophy* 26. 511–545.

Busse, Dietrich. 2012. *Frame-Semantik. Ein Kompendium*. Berlin & New York: Mouton de Gruyter.

Clark, Rob & Ian Roberts. 1993. A computational model of language learnability and language change. *Linguistic Inquiry* 24. 299–345.

Daneš, Frantisek. 1970. Zur linguistischen Analyse der Textstruktur. *Folia Linguistica* 4. 72–78.

Drach, Erich. 1937. *Grundgedanken der deutschen Satzlehre*. Frankfurt/M.: Diesterweg.

Dürscheid, Christa. 1989. *Zur Vorfeldbesetzung in deutschen Verbzweit-Strukturen*. Trier: Wissenschaftlicher Verlag Trier.
Eckardt, Regine. 2012. Grammaticalization and semantic reanalysis. In Claudia Maienborn, Klaus von Heusinger & Paul Portner (eds.), *Semantics: An international handbook of natural language meaning*, 2675–2702. Berlin & New York: Mouton de Gruyter.
Eroms, Hans-Werner. 2000. *Syntax der deutschen Sprache*. Berlin & New York: Mouton de Gruyter.
Frascarelli, Mara & Roland Hinterhölzl. 2007. Types of topics in German and Italian. In Kerstin Schwabe & Susanne Winkler (eds.), *On information structure, meaning and form. Generalizations across languages*, 87–116. Amsterdam & Philadelphia: John Benjamins.
Frey, Werner. 2004a. A medial topic position for German. *Linguistische Berichte* 198. 153–190.
Frey, Werner. 2004b. The grammar-pragmatics interface and the German prefield. *Sprache & Pragmatik* 52. 1–39.
Frey, Werner. 2006. Contrast and movement to the German prefield. In Valéria Molnár & Susanne Winkler (eds.), *The architecture of focus* (Studies in Generative Grammar 82), 235–264. Berlin & New York: Mouton de Gruyter.
van Gelderen, Elly. 2011. *The linguistic cycle: language change and the language faculty*. Oxford: Oxford University Press.
Grewendorf, Günther. 2002. *Minimalistische Syntax*. Tübingen & Basel: Francke.
Hawkins, John. 1994. *A performance theory of order and constituency*. Cambridge: Cambridge University Press.
Hentschel, Elke. 1998. Die Emphase des Schreckens: *Furchtbar nett* und *schrecklich freundlich*. In Theo Harden & Elke Hentschel (eds.), *Particulae particularum*, 119–132. Tübingen: Stauffenburg.
Herling, S.H.A. 1821. Ueber die Topik der deutschen Sprache. *Abhandlungen des frankfurtischen Gelehrtenvereines für deutsche Sprache* 3. 296–362; 364.
Hinterhölzl, Roland & Svetlana Petrova. 2010. From V1 to V2 in West Germanic. *Lingua* 120. 315–328.
Hinterhölzl, Roland & Svetlana Petrova. 2011. Rhetorical relations and verb placement in Old High German. In Christian Chiarcos, Berry Claus & Michael Grabski (eds.), *Salience. Multidisciplinary perspectives on its function in discourse*, 173–201. Berlin & New York: Mouton de Gruyter.
Hoberg, Ursula. 1997. Die Linearstruktur des Satzes. In Gisela Zifonun, Ludger Hoffmann & Bruno Strecker (eds.), *Grammatik der deutschen Sprache*. vol. 2, 1496–1680. Berlin & New York: Mouton de Gruyter.
Höhle, Tilman. 1986. Der Begriff 'Mittelfeld'. Anmerkungen über die Theorie der topologischen Felder. In Walter Weiss, Herbert Wiegand & Marga Reis (eds.), *Kontroversen, alte und neue*, vol. 3, 329–340. Tübingen: Niemeyer.
Hopper, Paul & Elizabeth Closs Traugott. 2003. *Grammaticalization*. 2nd edn. Cambridge: Cambridge University Press.
Jacobs, Joachim. 2001. The dimensions of topic-comment. *Linguistics* 39. 641–681.
Katz, Jerrold & Jerry Fodor. 1963. The structure of a semantic theory. *Language* 39. 170–210.
Krifka, Manfred. 2007. Basic notions of information structure. In Caroline Féry, Gisbert Fanselow & Manfred Krifka (eds.), *Interdisciplinary studies on information structure*. (Working Papers of the SFB 632 6), 13–55. Potsdam: University of Potsdam.

Kroch, Anthony & Ann Taylor. 1997. Verb movement in Old and Middle English: Dialect variation and language contact. In Ans van Kemenade & Nigel Vincent (eds.), *Parameters of morphosyntactic change*, 297–325. Cambridge: Cambridge University Press.
Kuno, Susumu. 1982. The focus of the question and the focus of the answer. In Robinson Schneider, Kevin Tuite & Robert Chametzky (eds.), *Papers from the parasession on nondeclaratives*, 134–157. Chicago: Chicago Linguistics Society.
Langacker, Ronald W. 1977. Syntactic reanalysis. In Charles Li (ed.), *Mechanisms of syntactic change*, 57–139. Austin: University of Texas Press.
Lehmann, Christian. 1995. *Thoughts on grammaticalization*. München: Lincom.
Light, Caitlin. 2012. The information structure of subject extraposition in Early New High German. *UPenn Working Papers in Linguistics* 18. 169–177.
Lightfoot, David. 1999. *The development of language. Acquisition, change, and evolution*. Malden & Oxford: Blackwell.
Lötscher, Andreas. 2009. Verb placement and information structure in the OHG *Gospel Harmony* by Otfrid von Weissenburg. In Roland Hinterhölzl & Svetlana Petrova (eds.), *Information structure and language change*, 281–321. Berlin & New York: Mouton de Gruyter.
Lühr, Rosemarie. 2009. Translating information structure: A study of Notker's translation of Boethius's Latin *De Consolatione Philosophica* into Old High German. In Roland Hinterhölzl & Svetlana Petrova (eds.), *Information structure and language change*, 323–366. Berlin & New York: Mouton de Gruyter.
Molnár, Valéria. 1993. Zur Pragmatik und Grammatik des TOPIK-Begriffes. In Marga Reis (ed.), *Wortstellung und Informationsstruktur*, 155–202. Tübingen: Niemeyer.
Molnár, Valéria. 2012. Zur Relevanz der linken Peripherie für die Strukturierung der Information: kontrastive und typologische Überlegungen. In Lutz Gunkel & Gisela Zifonun (eds.), *Deutsch im Sprachvergleich* (Jahrbuch des Instituts für deutsche Sprache 2011), 383–416. Berlin & New York: Mouton de Gruyter.
Molnár, Valéria. 2014. Das Nachfeld im Deutschen zwischen Syntax, Informationsstruktur und Textkonstitution: Stand der Forschung und Perspektiven. *Zeitschrift für germanistische Linguistik* 42. 326–337.
Müller, Stefan. 2003. Mehrfache Vorfeldbesetzung. *Deutsche Sprache* 31. 29–62.
Petrova, Svetlana. 2009. Information structure and word order variation in the Old High German Tatian. In Roland Hinterhölzl & Svetlana Petrova (eds.), *Information structure and language change*, 251–279. Berlin & New York: Mouton de Gruyter.
Petrova, Svetlana & Augustin Speyer. 2011. Focus movement and focus interpretation in Old English. *Lingua* 121. 1751–1765.
Preacher, Kristopher J. 2001. Calculation for the chi-square test: An interactive calculation tool for chi-square tests of goodness of fit and independence. http://quantpsy.org (accessed 29 June 2016).
Prince, Ellen F. 1981. Toward a taxonomy of given-new information. In Peter Cole (ed.), *Radical pragmatics*, 223–255. New York: Academic Press.
Prince, Ellen F. 1998. On the limits of syntax, with reference to topicalization and left-dislocation. In Peter Culicover & Louise McNally (eds.), *The limits of syntax*, 281–302. New York: Academic Press.
Reinhart, Tanya. 1982. Pragmatics and linguistics: an analysis of sentence topics. *Philosophica* 27. 53–94.

Rizzi, Luigi. 1997. The fine structure of the left periphery. In Liliane Haegeman (ed.), *Elements of grammar*, 281–337. Dordrecht: Kluwer.
Roberts, Craige. 2011. Topics. In Claudia Maienborn, Klaus von Heusinger & Paul Portner (eds.), Semantics: An international handbook of natural language meaning, 1908–1934. Berlin & New York: Mouton de Gruyter.
Roberts, Ian & Anna Roussou. 2003. *Syntactic change: a minimalist approach to grammaticalisation*. Cambridge: Cambridge University Press.
Rochemont, Michael S. 1986. *Focus in generative grammar*. Amsterdam & Philadelphia: John Benjamins.
Rooth, Mats E. 1985. *Association with focus*. Amherst: University of Massachusetts PhD dissertation.
Sabel, Joachim. 2000. Das Verbstellungsproblem im Deutschen. *Deutsche Sprache* 28. 74–99.
Sapp, Christoper. 2007. Focus and verb order in Early New High German: Historical and contemporary evidence. In Sam Featherston & Wolfgang Sternefeld (eds.), *Roots. Linguistics in search of its evidential base*, 299–318. Berlin & New York: Mouton de Gruyter.
Sapp, Christopher. 2014. Extraposition in Middle and New High German. *The Journal of Comparative Germanic Linguistics* 17. 129–156.
Schildt, Joachim. 1976. Zur Ausbildung der Satzklammer. In Gerhard Kettmann & Joachim Schildt (eds.), *Zur Ausbildung der Norm in der deutschen Literatursprache auf der syntaktischen Ebene*, 235–284. Berlin: Akademie-Verlag.
Schlachter, Eva. 2012. *Syntax und Informationsstruktur im Althochdeutschen*. Heidelberg: Winter.
Schönherr, Monika. 2012. Zur Interdependenz von Wortstellung und Informationsstruktur im Althochdeutschen. *Sprachwissenschaft* 37. 125–155.
Shaer, Benjamin & Werner Frey. 2004 ‚Integrated' and ‚non-integrated' left-peripheral elements in German and English. In Benjamin Shaer, Werner Frey & Claudia Maienborn (eds.), *Proceedings of the Dislocated Elements Workshop, ZAS Berlin, November 2003* (ZASPiL 35,2), 465–502. Berlin: ZAS.
Speyer, Augustin. 2007. Die Bedeutung der Centering Theory für Fragen der Vorfeldbesetzung im Deutschen. *Zeitschrift für Sprachwissenschaft* 26. 83–115.
Speyer, Augustin. 2008a. German Vorfeld-filling as constraint interaction. In Anton Benz & Peter Kühnlein (eds.), *Constraints in discourse*, 267–290. Amsterdam & Philadelphia: John Benjamins.
Speyer, Augustin. 2008b. Doppelte Vorfeldbesetzung im heutigen Deutsch und im Frühneuhochdeutschen. *Linguistische Berichte* 216. 455–485.
Speyer, Augustin. 2009a. Das Vorfeldranking und das Vorfeld-*es*. *Linguistische Berichte* 219. 323–353.
Speyer, Augustin. 2009b. Versuch zur Syntax im Protoindoeuropäischen. In Elisabeth Rieken & Paul Widmer (eds.), *Pragmatische Kategorien. Form, Funktion und Diachronie. Akten der Arbeitstagung der Indogermanischen Gesellschaft vom 24. bis 26. September 2007 in Marburg*, 287–305. Wiesbaden: Reichert.
Speyer, Augustin. 2010. Filling the Vorfeld in spoken and written discourse. In Sanna-Kaisa Tanskanen, Marja-Liisa Helasvuo, Marjut Johansson & Mia Raitaniemi (eds.), *Discourses in interaction* (Pragmatics & Beyond New Series 203), 263–290. Amsterdam & Philadelphia: John Benjamins.

Speyer, Augustin. 2015. Auch früher wollte man informieren – Zum Einfluss der Informationsstruktur auf die Syntax in der Geschichte des Deutschen. *Zeitschrift für germanistische Linguistik* 43(3). 485–515.
Speyer, Augustin. 2016. Die Entwicklung der Nachfeldbesetzung in verschiedenen deutschen Dialekten: Informationsdichte und strukturelle Verschiedenheit. In Augustin Speyer & Philipp Rauth (eds.), *Syntax aus Saarbrücker Sicht 1* (Zeitschrift für Dialektologie und Linguistik, Beiheft 165), 137–157. Stuttgart: Steiner.
Speyer, Augustin. In prep. *Vorfeld-Studien*. To appear in the series Linguistische Arbeiten. Berlin: & New York: Mouton de Gruyter.
Sweetser, Eve. 1988. Grammaticalization and semantic bleaching. In Axmaker, Shelley, Annie Jaisser & Helen Singmaster (eds.), *Proceedings of the 14th Annual Meeting of the Berkeley Linguistic Society*, 389–405. Berkeley: Berkeley Linguistic Society.
Taylor, Ann & Susan Pintzuk. 2012. Rethinking the OV/VO alternation in Old English: The effect of complexity, grammatical weight, and information status. In Terttu Nevalainen & Elizabeth Closs Traugott (eds.), *The Oxford handbook of the history of English*, 835–845. Oxford: Oxford University Press.
Vallduví, Enric & Maria Vilkuna. 1998. On rheme and kontrast. In Peter Culicover & Louise McNally (eds.), *The limits of syntax* (Syntax and Semantics 29), 79–108. New York: Academic Press.
Vater, Heinz. 1994. *Einführung in die Textlinguistik*. 2nd edn. München: Fink.
Vinckel, Hélène. 2006. *Die diskursstrategische Bedeutung des Nachfelds im Deutschen. Eine Untersuchung anhand politischer Reden der Gegenwartssprache*. Wiesbaden: Deutscher Universitätsverlag.
Vinckel, Hélène. 2011. Wortstellungsvariation und Salienz von Diskursreferenten. Die Besetzung des Nachfelds in deutschen Pressetexten als kohärenzstiftendes Mittel. *Zeitschrift für germanistische Linguistik* 39. 377–404.
Wasow, Thomas. 2002. *Postverbal behavior*. Stanford: CSLI Publications.
Wöllstein, Angelika. 2010. *Topologisches Satzmodell*. Heidelberg: Winter.

Valéria Molnár
Stylistic Fronting at the Interface of Syntax and Discourse

Abstract: This paper presents a novel analysis of the discourse properties of the phenomenon called "Stylistic Fronting" (SF). The widely held view according to which Stylistic Fronting has no discourse-semantic effects in Icelandic, but is related to topic or focus interpretation in Romance, is challenged. It is argued that SF is not simply triggered by formal features but has relevance for information structure (IS) in both Romance and Scandinavian. The impact of SF on discourse interpretation is, however, dependent on the type of syntactic derivation.

In Icelandic, the "stylistic" movement can be either a locally (and information-structurally) restricted "formal movement" *(STYL-inversion)* into the subject gap without changing the IS-properties of the moved constituent or a "true" discourse-triggered movement *(STYL-preposing)* with an obligatory contrastive effect. Since SF also seems to vary with respect to syntactic properties and discourse interpretation in Romance, the triggers and interpretive properties of SF in Scandinavian seem not to be as different from those in Romance as generally suggested in the literature.

Keywords: stylisting fronting, stylistic inversion, stylistic preposing, topicalization, focus movement, formal movement, coherence feature, EPP-movement

1 Introduction

This paper discusses the discourse properties of the phenomenon called "Stylistic Fronting" (SF) in Scandinavian and Romance languages and makes the proposal that this kind of movement has interpretive effects in both language groups. Thus, the widely held view according to which Stylistic Fronting has no discourse-semantic effects in Icelandic, but is related to topic or focus interpretation in Romance, will be challenged. It will, however, be argued that the impact of SF on discourse interpretation is dependent on the type of syntactic derivation.

Since Joan Maling's (1980) seminal work on "Inversion in embedded clauses in Modern Icelandic", Stylistic Fronting has received considerable attention in linguistic research. In this work Maling brought to attention an old

Valéria Molnár, Lund University

phenomenon, already present in Old Icelandic: a special type of fronting movement through which predicative ("small") elements – not typically available for Topicalization – can occupy a vacant subject position. As observed by Maling, the inversion of a postverbal element (negation *ekki*, past participle) and the finite verb is possible (but not obligatory) in certain syntactic environments (cf. examples (1) and (2) from Gestur Pálsson's "Tilhugalíf"). The fronted constituent is given in boldface type.

(1) *og nú   eigum   við að vita (...) hvort   **ekki**$_i$ finnst t$_i$ meira*
    and now   ought   we to know   whether   not   finds   more
    þýfi   hjá piltinum
    stolen-goods on the.boy
    'and now we are supposed to find out whether any more stolen goods can be found where the boy lives'
    (Maling 1980)

(2) *Honum   mætti standa á   sama, hvað **sagt**$_i$ væri t$_i$ um   hann*
    him-DAT might stand   on same what   said   was   about him
    'It might be all the same to him what was said about him.'
    (Maling 1980)

Maling (1980) originally claimed that SF – as opposed to Topicalization – applies to head-like categories like past participles, predicative adjectives, verbal particles and adverbs. However, it has been recognized in later research that Topicalization and SF do not operate on disjunctive sets of categories and that phrasal categories like DPs and PPs can also undergo SF (Holmberg 2000; 2006; Ott 2009, etc.). Consider the authentic examples in Wood (2011) from the *Ístal* corpus (3), which includes informal conversations, and from the *Alþingi* corpus (4), which contains unprepared parliament speeches:

(3) *ég veit bara að sá   sem **Steini**$_i$[1] var með t$_i$ hann*
    I   know just that the.one who Steinn.DAT   was with   he/it
    var   alveg finn (...)
    was   just great
    'I just know that the one who was with Steinn, he was just great (...)'
    (Wood 2011)

---

[1] As Wood (2011: 55, note 4) points out, "the case marking of *Steini* 'Steinn.DAT' shows that it is the object of the preposition *með* 'with' and not the subject of the clause".

(4) sem að **um málið**$_i$ á   að véla   t$_i$
    who that about the.issue should to address
    'who should address the issue'
    (Wood 2011)

As argued in several works (e.g. Holmberg 2000; Ott 2009), SF of both predicative and phrasal elements obeys the same type of syntactic constraints and should therefore be analyzed in a uniform manner. The two instances of SF are also claimed to be identical with regard to their interpretation, which is said to lack semantic and pragmatic implications. The discourse behavior of the stylistic movement is, however, much more complex. As will be argued in this paper, SF should not be regarded as a semantically vacuous movement, and (at least) two interpretively distinct subtypes should be distinguished: (i) a movement which can apply in non-specified contexts in neutral cases (like in examples (1) and (2)) and (ii) a movement which is obligatorily associated with emphasis and contrastive interpretation (cf. examples (3) and (4)).

SF is also attested in Romance languages and is especially common in some Old Romance varieties. The Romance data indicate that fronting is possible in the case of both predicative and phrasal elements, as illustrated here by examples taken from Old Catalan (5), Old French (6) and Sardinian (7):

(5) que **feta**$_i$ aviets t$_i$ la corona del Emperi
    that made had   the crown of-the emperor
    'who had made the crown of the emperor'
    (Desclot, 297, quoted by Fischer and Alexiadou 2001)

(6) S'ont   trovee la sale overte qui **de tiules**$_i$ estoit
    self-have.3PL found the room open that of tiles   be.PAST.3SG
    coverte t$_i$
    covered
    'They found the room open whose roof was covered with tiles.'
    (Le Chevalie la Charrette 991–992, quoted by Mathieu 2006)

(7) **Arrivatu**$_i$ est t$_i$ a sa festa.
    arrived   is   at the party
    'He has arrived at the party.'
    (Jones 1993)

Concerning the discourse effects of fronting in Modern and Old Romance languages and varieties, it is claimed in the literature (cf. Fischer and Alexiadou

2001; Jones 1993; Mathieu 2006) that SF expresses a kind of emphasis (5), has topic interpretation (6) or Fronting is an instance of focus movement (7). However, the (exclusively) topic/focus/emphasis-related analysis of the discourse behavior of SF in Romance seems to contradict the empirical facts (cf. the Italian data in Cardinaletti 2003 and Franco 2009). The main task of the present article will be to provide a more differentiated analysis of the functional load of SF in Romance and Scandinavian showing that the type of SF occurring in neutral cases should be distinguished from the obligatorily emphatic cases in both language groups.

The paper is structured as follows. Section 2 starts out with the central theoretical issue of the present paper by discussing the trigger(s) of Stylistic Fronting. After the presentation of the relevant diagnostics of SF in Icelandic in section 3, the discourse-based analysis of SF is presented in the following two sections: after providing syntactic motivation for the split of stylistic movement into two different types in section 4, the discourse effects of the proposed structural split are discussed in more detail in section 5. The structural and functional differences between SF and the other information-structurally relevant movements – Topicalization and Focusing – are summarized in section 6. Section 7 discusses apparent structural and functional differences between SF in Romance and Scandinavian, but section 8 shows that Scandinavian and Romance seem similar as to the variation with respect to the discourse effects of stylistic movement despite certain parametric differences between these languages. Section 9 concludes the paper.

2 The Triggers of "Stylistic Movement" – Formal vs. Discourse-semantic Features

As documented in linguistic research, SF was highly productive at earlier stages of Scandinavian and Romance languages (in Old Danish, Middle Danish, Old Swedish, Old Italian, Old French, and Old Catalan), whereas it is less frequent in modern "Insular Scandinavian" (e.g. Modern Icelandic, Faroese), no longer (or less) productive in Romance varieties and not attested in modern Mainland Scandinavian languages. Following Maling's work, SF in Scandinavian and Romance has been studied in a large number of syntactic approaches from both a diachronic and a synchronic perspective.

The key questions of SF-research have been related to the trigger(s) of this syntactic operation. "Triggers" are defined by Breitbarth and van Riemsdijk (2004) as "requirements of some sort that cause syntactic effects, most notably displacement". According to Chomsky (1995, 2001) different types of formal features are required for displacement such as the *ϕ-features* (gender, person, number) of Infl and *v*, the *Case features* of DP and the *EPP-feature/Edge feature*[2] of Comp, Infl and *v*. These features are regarded as uninterpretable features which must be eliminated before the derivation reaches an interface (LF or PF). Otherwise the derivation crashes and violates the requirements of the *Principle of Full Interpretation*. Since the elimination (checking) of uninterpretable features is possible by displacement, these features are triggers for movement. Peripheral, extra-syntactic features related to information structure and prosody (like [+*wh*], [*topic*] / [*focus*]) are also claimed to belong to the set of triggers, where the same status is assigned to them as to regular morphosyntactic features. Crucial for the trigger-based approach is also the claim that independently of the type of triggers, displacement is forced to apply if the abovementioned features are present. Whether the checking of regular and peripheral morphosyntactic features applies overtly or covertly is a matter of cross-linguistic variation.

There are different options for the explanation of the displacement type which is represented by Stylistic Fronting in the trigger-based framework. One option is to relate it to the *Extended Projection Principle* (EPP), which requires that a predicational entity must take a subject. If the EPP-feature is assigned to a head, the overt displacement of phrasal material to the specifier position of this head is obligatory. In this case, however, the stylistic movement is triggered by the properties of the target (by *Attract*, cf. Chomsky 1995, chapter 4) and not by the category being moved. As demonstrated below, this type of analysis is adopted predominantly for SF in Scandinavian. The other possibility – triggering of movement by the discourse properties of the displaced category – is most often taken into account in the analysis of SF in Romance. However, only operator(-like) features such as [topic] and [focus] (and the related feature "emphatic") are discussed among the relevant discourse properties of the SF-moved constituents in Romance.

As argued in this paper, the inventory of information-structurally based features should also be extended to other types of discourse features, primarily to those which relate to the role in discourse linking, like [givenness] and [contrast]. These features – which guarantee coherence in discourse (also called "C(oherence)-features", cf. Molnár 2003; Molnár and Winkler 2010) – differ from the abovementioned operator features in several respects and work orthogonally to topicality and focusing, both overlapping and cutting

---

2 Platzack (2008: 7) claims that both the EPP-feature and the Edge feature (EF) may trigger movement. However, there is an important difference: "EPP is a demand that an Agree-relation must be visible at the SM [Sensory-Motor] interface, the edge feature a demand that a phase head must have an A' specifier. Hence, visibility at SM holds for EPP but not necessarily for EF".

across these two other established notions of information structure. Both topics and foci can – but do not need to – guarantee coherence, either by the contextually recoverable (given) status of a constituent or by contrasting a (given or new) constituent to another constituent in a contextually given set. The "C-feature" seems to be relevant for fronting strategies also in Scandinavian languages, which observe the "C-Constraint" suggested by Molnár (2003: 236): "Place a 'C'-marked element in the left peripheral – sentence internal (or sentence external) – position".

The question arises, though, as to whether the triggering mechanism can be restricted to these two complementary options or whether there are more complex cases. A very intriguing problem is the question of whether the target position of SF should only be related to 'regular' formal features or whether it is also connected to/constrained by pragmatic features (e.g. [focus], the C-feature). Since the choice of the fronted constituent is dependent on certain contextual and semantic factors, the restriction to exclusively formal properties of the target position seems not to correspond to the empirical facts: fronting also requires compatibility with certain semantically and contextually based requirements. Consequently, it is plausible to assume that Stylistic Fronting is not only triggered by formal properties of the target but also by the category being moved. Further, it also seems necessary to take additional factors – e.g. prosodic properties – into consideration as relevant conditions for this fronting operation (cf. Wood 2011).

The discussion of possible SF-triggers also requires a comparison of SF with two major types of A-bar-movement – Topicalization and Focus movement. It has to be clarified whether SF is a distinct, totally different type of movement, i.e. if it is possible to distinguish SF from Topicalization and Focus movement on structural and/or functional grounds. A comparison of languages where SF is attested also leads to the question of whether SF can be regarded as a uniform movement in Romance and Scandinavian, triggered by the same feature(s) and similar with regard to its structural and interpretive properties.

This paper aims to provide an answer to the above questions by investigating SF at the interface of narrow syntax and information structure from a contrastive perspective. I will compare SF with Topicalization and Focusing and discuss its peculiarities in different Scandinavian and Romance languages. Despite a large amount of work, a satisfactory discussion of SF at the syntax-pragmatics interface is still missing in linguistic research. As will be shown below in more detail, the claims concerning the discourse relevance of SF are contradictory, with regard to both Scandinavian and Romance. Regarding SF in the Romance languages (mainly in Old Romance varieties), SF is most often related to either Focus or Topic interpretation, although a less categorical position is taken by Cardinaletti (2003) and Franco (2009). In the analysis of the discourse properties of SF in

Scandinavian (concentrating on Icelandic) the dominant view is that SF is a movement that fulfills some condition which purely concerns form – for example satisfying the EPP or triggered by the Edge feature (cf. Holmberg 2000, 2006; Ott 2009; Platzack 2009). It is explicitly claimed by Holmberg (2006: 560) that the term "stylistic" does not refer to the discourse relevance of SF but is motivated by the optionality and the "formal, even archaic" character of this movement. This view is also supported by Angantýsson (2009), who argues that SF is more common in written language and in a formal style of speech.

The main claim of this paper is that SF – similarly to Topicalization and Focusing – is a discourse-semantically relevant and/or contextually restricted movement in both Romance and Scandinavian. The trigger of SF cannot be reduced to the target, but is also related to semantic-pragmatic features of the moved constituents driving dislocation in narrow syntax. Further, it will be argued that the impact of SF on discourse interpretation is dependent on the type of syntactic derivation in both language groups:

1. The Icelandic data require a distinction to be made between two major types of stylistic movement: a "true fronting" (*STYL-preposing*) triggered by contrast,[3] and a locally more strictly restricted "formal movement" into the empty subject position (*STYL-inversion*). Crucially, this latter type is also visible at the interface between syntax and semantics/pragmatics since it is arguably restricted by semantic and discourse constraints. These two types of SF have partially different discourse effects (they do not create disjunctive sets), which can be regarded as a consequence of different syntactic configurations or derivational histories. Whereas STYL-preposing is a contrast-related movement with obligatory accent, STYL-inversion often appears in contextually not specified (i.e. "unmarked") cases with a maximal focus domain, even though optional backgrounding, conditioned by the givenness of the fronted element, or contrastive focusing is also possible.

2. The split of stylistic movement into a type with obligatory emphasis and a type with optional emphasis and interpretive variation also has interesting consequences for the comparison of languages. The proposed distinction of two SF-types makes it possible to analyze stylistic movement in Scandinavian and Romance in a uniform manner. I will argue below that it is not the case that SF in Scandinavian and Romance is different in the sense that it lacks discourse relevance in Scandinavian while it has discourse effects in Romance; rather, both language groups seem to have (at least) two structurally and functionally distinct varieties.

---

[3] The obligatory character and connected problems will be discussed in more detail below in the syntactic and pragmatic analysis of SF (see sections 4 and 5).

3 Stylistic Fronting – Selected Diagnostics of SF in Icelandic

As Maling points out in her article from 1980, SF in Icelandic is different from Topicalization in several respects and the suggested dichotomy has by and large been confirmed in later SF-research. The most important syntactic asymmetries are related to the type of the fronted elements, the target position, and the (ir)relevance of locality restrictions.

The *prototypical elements* that undergo SF are heads or head-like elements – participles, infinitives, but also particles, adverbs, negation, predicative adjectives, and predicative nominals – in contrast to phrases, which are typical for Topicalization. SF of DPs and PPs is restricted, but not excluded. The variation in Icelandic with regard to the moved elements is illustrated in the examples (1–4), with fronting of "heads" (1–2) on the one hand, and with movement of full DPs and PPs in (3–4) on the other.

The *target position* of SF is according to Maling (1980), Platzack (2009), Rögnvaldsson and Thráinsson (1990), and Holmberg (2000, 2006) the position immediately preceding the finite verb – Spec,TP or Spec,IP – as opposed to Topicalization, which targets Spec,CP (an A-bar-position). Since Spec,TP is the canonical subject position, SF can only apply if there is no overt subject in this position. As the grammaticality contrast of the following examples (8-a) and (8-b) indicates, preverbal subjects are ungrammatical in Icelandic sentences with SF:

(8) a. *hún sem **fyrst**$_i$ var t$_i$ til að lýsa stílfærslu*
    she that first was PREP to [describe] Stylistic Fronting
    'she who was first to investigate Stylistic Fronting'
b. **afleiðslan sem hún **fyrst**$_i$ var t$_i$ til að lýsa*
    the-construction that she first was PREP to [describe]
    'the construction that she was first to [describe]'
    (Holmberg 2006)

The so-called *subject gap condition* also has consequences for typical SF-contexts. In Scandinavian, SF often appears in subject extraction contexts and is thus dominant in embedded clauses, e.g. in subject relative clauses (see examples (2), (3), (4) above). However, SF is also possible in different types of impersonal (main or embedded) clauses (see (9), (10)) or in main or embedded clauses with a "late" subject (see (11), (12)):

(9) **Tekin**$_i$ hefur verið t$_i$ erfið ákvörðun.
    taken has been difficult decision
    'Difficult decision was taken.'
    (Holmberg 2000)

(10) Það fór að rigna, þegar **búið**$_i$ var t$_i$ að borða.
     EX went to rain when finished was to eat
     'It began to rain when we had finished eating.'
     (Holmberg 2006)

(11) **Fallið**$_i$ hafa t$_i$ margir hermenn í þessu stríði.
     died have many soldiers in this war
     'Many soldiers died in this war.'
     (Jónsson 1991)

(12) Ég hélt að **kysst**$_i$ hefðu t$_i$ hana margir stúdentar.
     I thought that kissed had her many students
     'I thought that many students have kissed her.'
     (Jónsson 1991)

In addition to the *subject gap condition*, **locality restrictions** are of decisive relevance for SF since SF is regarded as a movement of the closest element to T obeying the "accessibility hierarchy". This hierarchy, which was first observed by Maling (1980) and later modified by several researchers (Hrafnbjargarson 2003, 2004a; Holmberg 2006), partly corresponds to *Attract Closest* suggested by Chomsky (1995: 311). The order "negation *ekki*/sentence adverb > past participle/verb particle > predicative adjective" regulates the possible movements of elements if there are several candidates for SF and predicts that negation and sentence adverbs will always block SF of elements lower in the hierarchy (cf. (13-b)):

(13) a. (...) þegar **ekki** var t$_i$ **búið**$_i$ að borða.
        when not was finished to eat
     b. *(...) þegar **búið**$_i$ var **ekki** t$_i$ að borða.
        when finished was not to eat
        (Holmberg 2006)

The "accessibility hierarchy" is, however, only operative in the case of SF, in contrast to Topicalization, where locality restrictions do not play a role.

The syntactic status of the target position is also indicated by the fact that SF is clause-bound. Stylistic Fronting – as opposed to Topicalization – is an A-movement, and does not license operator chains. As example (14-b) below shows, SF from a complement clause to the matrix clause is generally ruled out (see also Maling 1980; Sigurðsson 1989: 58; Thráinsson 2007: 374):

(14) a. þeir sem halda að **farið**$_i$ verði t$_i$ á morgun eru bjartsýnir.
     they who think that left   will-be   tomorrow are optimists
     'They who believe that they will leave tomorrow are optimists.'
   b. *þeir sem **farið**$_i$ halda að verði t$_i$ á morgun (...)
      they who left   think that will-be tomorrow
      (Egerland 2013)

The most intriguing property of SF is the fact that it can apply to a heterogeneous set of categories. In Maling's (1980) original proposal, only "small elements" were taken into consideration regarding SF. However, Holmberg's (2000, 2006) argumentation seems convincing when he shows that not only "heads" but also phrasal elements may undergo SF in Icelandic. Fronting of DPs and PPs is restricted by the same constraints as fronting of adverbs and predicative elements (see the effect of the subject gap condition in example (15) and the relevance of the locality restriction ("shortest move") in example (16) below):

(15) *þeir sem **í Danmörku**$_i$ hann hafði hitt t$_i$ (...)
     those who in Denmark   he   had   met
     'Those whom he had met in Denmark (...)'
     (Thráinsson 2007)

(16) *þeir sem **í Danmörku**$_i$ hafa ekki verið t$_i$ (...)
     those that in Denmark   have not been
     'Those who have not been in Denmark (...)'
     (Thráinsson 2007)

The variation with respect to the SF-moved category has, however, led to different syntactic analyses in Scandinavian. In addition to the hybrid view represented by Hrafnbjargarson (2003, 2004a), according to which SF is either a head or a phrasal movement depending on the fronted element, the dominant approach to the analysis of SF in Icelandic data is a uniform treatment. Jónsson (1991), for example, consistently accounts for all SF as head movement, while others (e.g. Ott 2009) argue for the analysis of all instances of SF as phrasal movement. The latter approach stipulates remnant movement of the head-like categories, which means that in these cases "incomplete" categories containing traces are moved (see Ott 2009 and the reference to Webelhuth and den Besten 1987 therein).

Of special interest for the present analysis of SF are the differences between SF and Topicalization with respect to *discourse effects*. According to Maling (1980), Topicalization requires emphasis or focus on the fronted constituent, whereas emphasis or focus is not necessarily present on the fronted element in the case of SF. In later analyses the differences between the discourse properties of SF and Topicalization are often more sharply separated, resulting in the claim that SF has no semantic and pragmatic implications (Rögnvaldsson and Thráinsson 1990; Jónsson 1991; Holmberg 2006; Thráinsson 2007; Ott 2009; Platzack 2009). Commenting on fronting of "small elements" like particles and non-finite main verbs, Thráinsson (2007: 372) claims that "there is no focussing involved. The particle *fram* 'forth' cannot possibly have any kind of focus reading in [... [(17)] (...) and by *komið* 'come' in (...) [(18)] ...] it is not being implied, for instance, that other students had 'gone' or whatever". Consider:

(17) **Fram**$_i$ *hefur komið* t$_i$ *að* **fiskað**$_j$ *hefur verið* t$_j$ *í leyfisleysi* (...)
forth has   come   that   fished   has   been   illegally
'It has been revealed that illegal fishing has taken place (...)'
(Holmberg 2006)

(18) **Komið**$_i$ *höfðu* t$_i$ *margir stúdentar á bókasafnið* (...)
come (sup.) had   many   students   to library
'There had come many students to the library.'
(Thráinsson 2007)

The claim of semantic / pragmatic vacuity of SF in Icelandic is also supported by the fact that impersonal Icelandic sentences allow for an alternation with the expletive ((17'-a) vs. (17'-b)). According to Holmberg (2006: 549) SF can be regarded as a kind of expletive movement: "The category fronted by SF is an expletive in its derived position".

(17') a. **Fram**$_i$ *hefur komið* t$_i$ *að* (...)
forth   has   come   that
b. **Það** *hefur komið fram að* (...)
EXPL   has   come   forth   that
(Holmberg 2006)

Also Sigurðsson (2010b) maintains the dominant view regarding Icelandic: "SF often has (formal) stylistic flavor to it, but it does not correlate with propositional semantics, (...) it generally has vague or even non-detectable semantic effects".[4]

The alleged sharp contrast between the discourse functions of Topicalization and Stylistic Fronting is, however, problematic and there are good reasons to take a closer look at the functional differences between Topicalization and Stylistic Fronting. Topicalization in Scandinavian is only typically but not necessarily connected to emphasis. If one also reads Maling's description of the pragmatic role of SF carefully, then it becomes clear that Topicalization and SF are functionally not as different as generally claimed in the literature. Crucially, emphasis or focus is not excluded in SF in Maling's or Holmberg's analyses. Both types of fronting operations can thus appear with and without emphasis and focus, and the alleged "atypical" cases are quite common: (i) even if not mentioned by Maling and other researchers, emphasis is often absent in the case of Topicalization of subjects or certain types of adverbials, and (ii) stylistically fronted elements with emphasis should not be regarded as unexplainable exceptions either (contrary to Holmberg 2006). Consequently the question arises: is it really justified to distinguish Topicalization and SF in Scandinavian on functional grounds? This question can, however, only be answered if SF is clearly defined and syntactically delimited from other types of fronting, and its relation to the two most important functionally loaded A-bar-movements – Topicalization and Focus movement – is properly accounted for. This will be the aim of the following sections.

4 A Discourse-based Proposal – A Syntactically Motivated Split with Interpretive Effects

We will argue that the discourse effects of SF in Scandinavian are not as different from the functions of Topicalization as claimed in the literature, and consequently, the view that SF is a semantically and pragmatically vacuous movement does not seem to be justified. On the contrary, it is plausible to assume that SF can have different discourse properties both in Scandinavian and Romance. Concerning the relation between SF and discourse, one of the main questions is which types of interpretations can be identified. In a study looking at the interface between

---

4 However, in a recent study, Sigurðsson (2017) points out the preference for choosing contextually anchored, deictic SF candidates.

syntax and information structure it is also essential to ask whether the different discourse effects of SF in the same language can be justified by different structural configurations.

In order to answer the above questions, the interpretive potential of SF in Icelandic will be revisited and scrutinized in this section, leading to a new proposal accounting for at least two syntactically distinct SF-types with different interpretive properties. In a later section (section 7) the parametric differences between Scandinavian and Romance will be discussed and it will be shown that despite structural differences SF in the two language groups has considerable similarities concerning its discourse interpretation.

The main challenge in the analysis of the discourse relevance of SF in Icelandic is to explain the apparently contradictory SF-behavior:

i. On the one hand, it is desirable to account for the information-structural "neutrality" of SF, i.e. the rather common cases with "reconstruction effects" which also provide the main motivation for Holmberg's analysis of Stylistic Fronting as a PF-phenomenon. According to Holmberg (2006: 560) "[t]he fronted constituent (...) is presumably 'reconstructed' in the sense that it is interpreted in its pre-movement position".

ii. On the other hand, it is necessary to explain the possibility or necessity of emphasis/focus in certain cases which in Holmberg's (2006) analysis are considered as exceptions to the rule.

According to the proposal made in this paper both tasks are made possible by splitting SF in Icelandic into two types: STYL-inversion and STYL-preposing. First, I will argue that these two types have partly different discourse effects: for STYL-inversion focusing and emphasis are not typical and not necessary, although they are possible (a claim which is compatible with Maling's and Holmberg's analyses), whereas STYL-preposing (in the sense defined here) bears obligatory contrastive accent. Second, I claim that the observed interpretational difference is due to syntactic differences. Third, it seems reasonable to assume semantic and/or discourse visibility and relevance in both cases.

4.1 Two Types of Topicalization: Formal Movement and A-bar-movement

The present proposal is based on earlier approaches distinguishing different fronting types in verb-second (V2) languages. Since all Scandinavian languages belong to this language type, the distinction of fronting operations is highly relevant for the analysis of SF. Several works within the generative framework argue that "fronting" in V2-languages (e.g. the case of the filling of the so-called "prefield" in German) is not a uniform phenomenon (cf. Frey 2006, also Fanselow 2002, Bhatt 1999). According to Frey's view the prefield in German can be filled in different ways and movement comes in two varieties: (i) In the case of "Formal Movement" the highest constituent of the middle field is moved into the prefield preserving whatever pragmatic property the constituent has "acquired" in the middle field. (ii) The other type of fronting – a "true" A-bar-movement – goes together with an obligatory contrastive interpretation of the moved item. In contrast to Formal Movement, this movement does not need to observe the locality restrictions.

Formal movement (FM), affecting the highest constituent in the middle field, can be applied both to base generated and scrambled phrases. According to Frey the unmarked case is when base generated items are moved by FM, which Frey illustrates with examples (19-a) and (19-b). Since the base position of the frame adverbial is the highest position of the middle field (shown in 19-a), this sentence is unmarked. After applying FM to the frame adverbial the resulting sentence (19-b) is also unmarked simply because (19-a) is unmarked.

(19) a. *(dass) fast   überall   Jungen gerne Fußball spielen*
    that   almost everywhere boys   gladly soccer play
    'that boys like to play soccer almost everywhere'
  b. *Fast   überall$_1$ spielen t$_1$ Jungen gerne Fußball.*
    almost everywhere play   boys   gladly soccer
    'Almost everywhere, boys like to play soccer.'

As Frey points out, FM in German (a language with basic OV-order) can also be applied to a scrambled phrase if the scrambled phrase occupies the highest position in the middle field. However, a constituent which is scrambled to the highest position in the middle field (shown in 20-b) induces pragmatic markedness, i.e. it cannot constitute a part of a maximal focus domain. It can either be interpreted as backgrounded or in special cases as contrastive focus. But if a scrambled phrase is moved to the prefield by FM – as is the case in (20-c) – the markedness status of the construction will be preserved:

(20) a. *(dass) Otto mit der Axt den Baum gefällt hat*
    that   Otto with the axe the tree chopped has
    '(that) Otto cut down the tree with the axe'

b. *(dass) mit der Axt₁ Otto t₁ den Baum gefällt hat*
   that with the axe Otto the tree chopped has
   '(that) Otto used the axe to cut down the tree'
c. *Mit der Axt₁ hat t₁' Otto t₁ den Baum gefällt.*
   with the axe has Otto the tree chopped
   'With the axe Otto cut down the tree.'

On the other hand, the application of true A-bar-movement has quite different interpretive consequences and is always bound to contrast. True A-bar-movement is the only way for certain elements (like predicative phrases, modal adverbials) to target the prefield since these elements cannot be scrambled and thus cannot get to the highest position of the middle field (see the ungrammatical examples (21-a) and (22-a)). Movement of a predicative (in 21-b) and a modal adverbial (in 22-b) into the prefield always results in a marked (contrastive, emphatic) reading of the fronted elements:

(21) a. **dass Maria grün₁ die Tür t₁ streichen wird*
       that Maria green the door paint will
       'that Maria will paint the door green'
   b. *Grün wird Maria die Tür streichen.*
       green will Maria the door paint
       'Maria will paint the door GREEN.'

(22) a. **dass Otto unfreundlich₁ sehr oft t₁ gewirkt hat*
       that Otto unfriendly very often seemed has
       'that Otto often came across as unfriendly'
   b. *Unfreundlich hat Otto sehr oft gewirkt.*
       unfriendly has Otto very often seemed
       'Otto often came across as unfriendly.'

The main syntactic difference between Formal Movement and true A-bar-movement is thus that in the former case the movement from IP to Spec, CP is EPP driven and is restricted by locality requirements (*Minimal Link*; cf. also *Attract Closest*) whereas the latter can (cyclically) move any constituent in the middle field to the prefield without locality restrictions. Crucially, the syntactic difference has interpretive consequences according to Frey's claim: Formal Movement has no semantic and pragmatic effect in contrast to true A-bar-movement, which always induces a contrastive interpretation of the moved item (cf. Frey 2006: 241; see also Frey 2010 on the notion of emphasis).

Frey's analysis of German suggests that complements of verbs can undergo formal movement in a structure with basic OV-order thanks to the visibility of their fronting in the middle field (Scrambling). Consequently, Topicalization of non-subjects in these languages is not bound to contrast or emphasis. The assumption that Topicalization in an OV-language is more easily available is also supported by Håkansson's (2010) study of Swedish, which shows that the degree of variation in the prefield is dependent on the variation in the "middle field" in Old Swedish – which as an OV-language is similar to German. By contrast, Topicalization of non-subjects in Modern Swedish (a VO-language) is more restricted, less frequent and connected with markedness (emphasis, contrast) (cf. Molnár and Winkler 2010).

4.2 Two Types of SF

Inspired by Frey's (2006) analysis of fronting in German, it will be suggested in this work that Stylistic Fronting in Icelandic (and in Scandinavian languages) should be divided into two types, based not primarily on the types of the moved categories or on the different target positions (as argued for in previous "hybrid analyses"), but on the type of derivation of the fronting. The most important claims of this article concerning the syntax and discourse behavior of Stylistic Fronting in Icelandic can be summarized as follows:
1. The target position of Stylistic Fronting is Spec,TP.
2. Filling the Spec,TP-position by stylistic movement is, however, not a uniform syntactic phenomenon.
3. It is not the category of the moved element but the type of derivation that decides the discourse properties of stylistic movement.
4. The function of SF cannot be reduced to a movement fulfilling only the EPP/EF-feature requirement associated with the empty subject position and thereby applied at the Phonological Form as claimed by Holmberg (2000, 2006).

In the following discussion the abovementioned issues will be taken up in more detail.

4.2.1 The Target Position of SF

The target position of Stylistic Fronting is *Spec,TP*, which is to be regarded as an A-position, or alternatively as a mixed A- and A-bar-position. *Movement to this position by SF is possible in two different contexts*: either in clauses with a subject trace or in clauses with a non-trace subject gap. Importantly, SF is apparently optional in both cases, but it alternates with different options: in subject extraction cases with a subject trace in the Spec,TP ((23-a), (23-b)), and in impersonal clauses with the overt expletive *það* obligatorily required in this context according to Holmberg (2006); see (24-a), (24-b), (25-c)):

(23) a. *Hver heldur þú að* _____ *hafi **stolið** hjólinu?*
 who think you that has stolen the-bike
 'Who do you think has stolen the bike?'
 b. *Hver heldur þú að **stolið**₁ hafi t₁ hjólinu?*
 who think you that stolen has the-bike
 'Who do you think has stolen the bike?'
 (Holmberg 2006)⁵

(24) a. *Ef **það** er gengið eftir Laugaveginum (...)*
 if EXPL is gone along Laugavegur
 'If one walks along Laugavegur (...)'
 b. *Ef **gengið**₁ er t₁ eftir Laugaveginum (...)*
 if gone is along Laugavegur
 'If one walks along Laugavegur (...)'
 c. * *Ef er **gengið** eftir Laugaveginum (...)*
 (Holmberg 2006)⁶

The optional character of movements is, however, a considerable problem for the trigger-based movement theory. In order to confirm the traditional conception of triggers it is thus necessary to show that SF is non-optional. In the case of impersonal clauses where SF has complementary distribution with *það*, SF could be claimed to be obligatory in some sense. Holmberg's (2006: 533) claim that either SF or insertion of an expletive pronoun must apply in impersonal clauses is, however, contradicted by the empirical data of Sigurðsson (2010b, 2017) who shows in his investigation that V1 is also an acceptable option in these sentence type.⁷

---

[5] The example is taken from Jónsson (1991).
[6] The example is taken from Rögnvaldsson and Thráinson (1990).
[7] Sigurðsson's (2017: 329) empirical investigation indicates that "SF is still the most common of the three competing word order types in impersonal clauses in the written language, much more common than V1 and það-V together in all the clause types checked".

The problem of optionality in the case of subject extraction clauses is, also intriguing, but needs a different explanation. In this case, the position in front of the finite verb apparently contains the trace of a subject, satisfying the EPP-requirement. According to Ott (2009), however, this is only one of two available syntactic options in clauses with relativized *wh*-extracted subjects in Icelandic. Besides this option, where T raises the phrase (the subject) it agrees with and where after movement to Spec,CP this position hosts a deleted copy of the subject, there is another possibility: C can raise the subject directly, and in this case Spec,TP must be filled by some other element (the closest element). Thus, in these latter mentioned cases of subject extraction the filling of Spec,TP by SF is obligatory.[8]

4.2.2 Non-uniformity of SF

Filling the Spec,TP-position by stylistic movement is, however, *not a uniform phenomenon* since this movement shows both syntactic and interpretive differences. This motivates the Stylistic Fronting split into (i) a type called STYL-inversion, which is locally strictly restricted and not necessarily bound to emphasis, and (ii) a movement called "true" STYL-preposing, which shows differences with regard to the locality requirements and obligatorily induces emphasis (and different types of contrast).

The above claim, however, contradicts the claim that fronting of phrasal and head-categories is subject to identical locality constraints. Both Holmberg (2000, 2006) and Ott (2009) argue for the equal accessibility of predicative elements and complements to SF and the equidistance of the two categories. According to Holmberg (2006), this is probably a special case of a more general phenomenon (with regard to the relation of a head and its complement), whereas Ott (2009) explains the optionality of the choice between a predicative element and the XP in a "remnant movement approach". The proposal is based on Chomsky's "phase

---

[8] Ott's proposal is based on Chomsky's (2008) idea concerning parallel chain formation. Chomsky argues that T and C are parallel probes and can attract XPs to their specifiers at the same derivational step. "A-chains (triggered by attraction by T) and A´-chains (triggered by attraction by C) are fronted *simultaneously* when both heads enter the derivation. (...) This view entails that C can raise A´-moved subjects directly from their base position (Spec,*v*) since the A-chain formed by T raising the subject to its specifier is invisible to C" (Ott 2009: 168).

theory", where it is suggested that the movement of a complement XP to the edge of *v*P (which is regarded a phase) is required for further operations.

According to this theory, phrases (complement XPs) which start out as sisters of V in VP must be moved first to the outer edge of *v*P in order to be available for further operations. This derivation is possible if one assumes that *v* can be optionally endowed with an EPP-property that triggers this movement to the *v*P-edge (cf. Ott 2009). Ott emphasizes that SF of complements, which he regards as parasitic on this edge-driven movement, still fulfills the locality requirements of SF. This is because the moved XP and the *v*P are equidistant from T after the movement of XP to the outer edge of *v*P, since they are sisters and neither asymmetrically c-commands the other. Importantly, movement of predicative elements is also analyzed by Ott as an instance of phrase movement ("remnant movement") "with evacuation movement of the object triggered by *v*P's edge property" (2009: 158). There are good reasons to adopt the suggested remnant movement analysis since it also explains why the choice between moving of XPs or predicative elements is possible.

However, Ott overlooks one important factor in his analysis in claiming that "movement of an XP complement of V to the phase edge leads to equidistance, in that either the XP at the edge of *v*P or *v*P itself can raise to Spec,T" (2009: 167). His emphasis on the equivalence of the two options seems to contradict the empirical facts. As pointed out in SF-research, SF of non-predicative elements is much more restricted than SF of predicative elements and the two options show considerable differences with regard to frequency, acceptability and markedness (cf. Sigurðsson 2010b, 2017).

According to the proposal of this paper the decisive distinguishing factor should be related to the status of the *v*P-edge and/or to the fact that this position can be reached by different kinds of operations, depending on the directionality parameter (OV vs. VO). If we adopt the approach based on the special edge property of the *v*P, phrasal elements can only reach the *v*P-edge by a true, discourse-driven movement with obligatory contrastive effect in modern Icelandic, a VO-language, (cf. (25)). This discourse effect is preserved in the last step of the derivation. By contrast, predicative elements can undergo Stylistic Inversion, i.e. formal movement of the remnant *v*P to the Spec,TP.

(25)

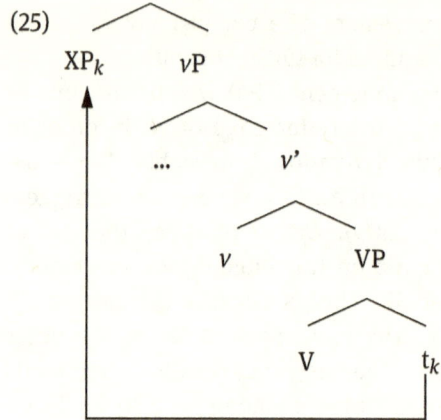

In OV-languages (German, Old Scandinavian), phrasal elements can be target the *v*P-edge by formal movement (cf. (26)):

(26)

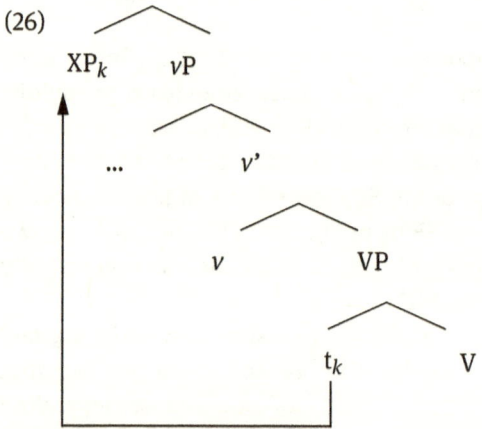

The apparent difference between the OV- and VO-type of languages could also accounted for by the visibility of the *v*P-edge. As suggested by Poletto (2006), the OV-order is important for the active status and visibility of the *v*P periphery in a V2-grammar, making a locally restricted "formal" movement easily available. In contrast, the invisibility of the *v*P-edge in VO-languages blocks the possibility of this option and requires true XP-movement to the Spec,TP.

4.2.3 The Relevance of the Derivation Type

Concerning the syntactic differences between the two kinds of stylistic operations, it is, however, relevant *not to equate fronting of DPs and PPs with true STYL-preposing and the movement of head-like elements with STYL-inversion*. Since the type of phrasal SF is dependent on the directionality parameter, in OV-languages not only predicative elements but also complements of verbs can undergo formal movement to the *v*P-edge and/or to Spec,TP. Thus, crucially, it is not the category of the moved element (NP, PP vs. predicative element in the remnant *v*P), but the type of derivation that decides the discourse properties of stylistic movement – even though this is not apparent in Modern Scandinavian, which exhibits VO-order.

The correlation between the basic OV-order and the frequency/adequacy of SF-movement of phrases is also attested in Old Swedish, which is a (head-final) OV-language. STYL-inversion was not only available for predicative elements but also for phrases, although this option does not exist in Modern Scandinavian (due to its basic VO-order, see below). The Old Swedish data referred to by Delsing (2001: 165, 166) support this analysis: "The possibility to move objects in MIcel. [Modern Icelandic] is very limited (...). On the contrary, OSw. [Old Swedish] frequently fronts objects by SF. According to Petterson (1987), they are the second most likely category to be fronted by SF (after negation) (...). The difference between MIcel. and OSw. with regard to fronting of objects by SF can possibly be connected to the basic word order of these languages (...). The idea is that, in an OV-language, the object is found to the left of the verb, and it should also be accessible to SF". As we will see below, the availability of the OV-configuration in Modern Icelandic contributes to the acceptability and unmarkedness of XP-fronting (cf. example (37)), i.e. XP-fronting can also be regarded as an instance of STYL-inversion in certain cases in Icelandic.[9]

4.1.4 The Interpretive Effect of SF

As to the *interpretive properties* of different kinds of stylistic movement, the main claim is that this type of movement cannot be reduced to a movement fulfilling only the EPP/EF-feature requirement associated with the empty subject position and thereby applied at the Phonological Form as suggested by Holmberg (2000, 2006). This claim is supported by the following arguments:

---

9 Concerning the decline and the loss of OV in Icelandic (see Hróarsdóttir (2001).

a. The distinction between true vs. formal movement – motivated by the different relevance of locality constraints for the syntactic derivation in the two instances – contributes to an empirically adequate account of the functional load of SF: The discourse effect of the stylistic movement operation is dependent on the movement type: contrast/emphasis is obligatory in the case of STYL-preposing. Emphasis/focusing – connected to contrast – is also possible in the case of STYL-inversion.
b. The target position of the stylistic movement is also subject to discourse constraints in the sense that it is "coherence"-related.
c. Further, semantic constraints are operative as well, since stylistic movement targets meaningful elements with lexical semantics (see however footnote 12 below). This movement is also related to scope differences or has specificity effects (connected to "C-relatedness").

5 The Discourse Function of SF in Icelandic

In order to account for the discourse effects of SF in a systematic way, it is, however, necessary to specify the range of possible information-structural interpretations of elements in the left periphery of different clause types (both main clauses and embedded clauses).

5.1 Two Main Requirements of Discourse

The claim is that a distinction needs to be made between *informativeness* and *coherence*. Informativeness in discourse is guaranteed primarily by two different types of focus, whereas coherence in discourse is guaranteed by *background* and *contrast*.[10]

---

[10] A relevant information-structural category is also the notion *topic*. However, the function of topic is more complex, since topic not only contributes to the establishment of coherence of discourse, but can be informative (contain new information). Concerning the functions of topic, cf. Molnár (1991, 1998, 2006).

5.1.1 Two Types of Focus

In neutral contexts, i.e. in contextually unspecified utterances answering the general informative question *What happened?*, the focus domain (i.e. the domain of new information) extends over the whole sentence. In these contexts, the constituent on the left periphery constitutes a part of a maximal focus domain. In this case, focusing of the clause-initial element (or other constituents) is "merely" connected to new information. This kind of focusing – called *information focus* by É. Kiss (1998) – seems to be relevant for SF in Icelandic.

However, focus can also be an instance of quantificational operation – operation on a set of contextually possible alternatives – which is typical for the Focus operator in Hungarian, Italian, etc. and induces the presence of an operator [focus] feature. This type of focus – the so-called *identificational focus* (É. Kiss 1998) – is both pragmatically and syntactically narrowed down, and is complemented by a presupposed and/or contextually given background part (this part can also be eliminated in certain contexts). The function of this operator focus is extensively discussed in both semantic theories (based on Rooth's 1985 influential work) and syntactically oriented approaches to information structure (cf. É. Kiss 1998, 2006; Kenesei 2006; Molnár 2006, etc.). For our present purposes it may suffice to say that this kind of focus is not necessarily related to contrast and already contextually present alternatives (cf. Molnár 2006). Evidence for this claim is the fact that a sentence in Hungarian (a language with a designated operator focus position) containing identificational focus can be an exhaustive answer to a *wh*-question, but does not need to operate on (and exclude) contextually present alternatives (27-b):

(27) a. (Context: *What did you buy?*)
    b. [Focus *Egy biciklit*] *vettem.*
            a   bicycle   bought-1SG
       'I bought a BICYCLE.'

The presence of alternatives in the context and the contrastive reading are, however, not excluded: (27-b) can also be an answer to the question *Did you buy a car or a bicycle?* Identificational focus (which is not dependent on explicitly or implicitly anchored contextual alternatives), also has relevance for certain types of (SF-related) fronting. I will though argue below in section 7, that this function can only come into question for fronting of constituents in certain Romance languages.

5.1.2 Background and Contrast

As will be demonstrated below, besides the abovementioned types of focus, at least two other discourse functions of the left peripheral constituents should be taken into consideration: *backgrounding and contrast*. As opposed to the two focusing types, these functions are context-related ("C-related") and contribute to the establishment of coherence in discourse in different ways (cf. Molnár 2003; Molnár and Winkler 2010). C-relatedness is either guaranteed by the contextually known or given status of a constituent (by the identity or similarity of the constituent with generally known or previously mentioned elements in discourse) or by relating a (given or new) constituent to another constituent in a contextually given set. The former function is typical for backgrounding, and the latter for contrast. The C-relatedness of the moved constituent – its backgrounding or contrastive character – seems extremely relevant for SF in Scandinavian in those cases where the focus domain of the clause is narrowed down. In these cases the SF-moved constituent at the left periphery of the main or embedded clause is either backgrounded or contrasted.

This indicates that the *target position of stylistic movement is also subject to discourse constraints* in the sense that it is "coherence-" ("C-")related. As argued in Molnár (2003) and Molnár and Winkler (2010), preferably "C"-marked (coherence establishing) elements are moved to the left edge position of CP and TP (cf. the C-Constraint or Coherence-Constraint[11] in SV-languages, to which all Germanic languages belong). The proposed C-Constraint also predicts the ungrammaticality and inappropriateness of the stylistic movement of non-C-marked elements, which is typical for non-contrastive (narrow) foci. Those focus constituents in Spec,CP or Spec,TP that are integrated into a larger (or maximal) focus domain (as typical for all-new utterances) are, however, acceptable since default C-marking is assumed in these cases.

5.2 Stylistic Inversion and Stylistic Preposing in Discourse

As was argued above in section 4, two types of SF should be distinguished in Icelandic (and other Scandinavian languages: STYL-inversion and STYL-preposing. In the following, the discourse properties of these two SF-movements and the differences between them will be investigated in more detail. We

---

11 Cf. Molnár (2003: 236): "Place a 'C'-marked element in the left peripheral – sentence internal (or sentence external) – position".

should, however, keep in mind that these two syntactic types do not create disjunctive sets with respect to their functions.

As will be demonstrated below, STYL-inversion – as a type of formal movement – can preserve the original interpretive function of the moved element. It is compatible with the information focus status of the constituent in the left peripheral position in neutral contexts, and it can relate to both C-marked functions: backgrounding and contrast. STYL-preposing is, however, as a "true" fronting operation, bound to contrast (emphasis). Thus the distribution of the information-structural functions shows a more complex pattern, since STYL-inversion and STYL-preposing not only differ, but also share certain properties with respect to contrast.

There is a further functional similarity between the two SF-types. As predicted by the C-Constraint, both SF-types should be restricted to those information-structural functions which are C-related in some sense, and the stylistic movement of an element to the left peripheral Spec,TP-position can guarantee coherence in discourse. It is thus expected that identificational focus (the quantificationally based focus type) should be excluded in both SF-types.

The pattern of information-structural functions for SF in Icelandic is given in (28):

(28) The discourse functions of the two SF-types:

STYL-INVERSION	STYL-PREPOSING
contrast	contrast
backgrounding	? * backgrounding
information focus	? * information focus
* identificational focus	* identificational focus

As discussed above, in Icelandic – a language with a VO-basic word order – STYL-Inversion is particularly frequent with adverbs and predicative elements, whereas STYL-Preposing is typical for phrasal elements (DPs and PPs). The asymmetry between the acceptability and frequency of the two SF-types is striking, and indicates that the formal movement type is more easily available (despite the equidistance of predicative elements and their complements) and is contextually much less restricted that the true stylistic movement.

The empirical data discussed in SF-research and the evaluation of their discourse effects support the suggested analysis. As to the discourse function of the formal type of SF, it is emphasized that it does not need to have a focusing effect (see examples (17) and (18) above) and can occur without contextual specification, i.e. in discourse initial contexts (29), such as introducing news in a broadcast (cf. Egerland 2013). In these cases, the fronted constituent is, however, still part of a maximal focus domain and can be regarded as information focus:

(29) **Smyglað**$_i$ hefur verið t$_i$ miklu magni   af áfengi til landsins
     smuggled   has   been   large amount of alcohol to country-the
     frá í haust.
     in autumn
     'A large amount of alcohol has been smuggled to the country during the autumn.'
     (Sigurðsson, p.c.)

As Egerland (2013) argues, the fronted element can also be backgrounded. He gives no context for the evaluation of the discourse function of the SF-moved constituent in the following impersonal sentence, but the sentence could be uttered in the context of a question like *What should be built next?* (Sigurðsson, p.c.):

(30) **Byggja**$_i$ má nýa brú   t$_i$ ef viljinn væri fyrir hendi.
     build   may new bridge   if will is at hand
     'A new bridge could be built íf there is willingness.'
     (Egerland 2013)

Importantly, SF of non-finite verbal elements can be – but is *not necessarily* – related to backgrounding. As the sentences (17), (18) and (29) quoted above after Holmberg, Thráinsson and Sigurðsson show, SF can also occur discourse-initially and be related to focus within a maximal focus domain. Consequently, information focus is compatible with SF. The focus type which is excluded is the quantificationally based identificational focus. The infelicity of this type of focusing in a sentence answering the question *Is there no bridge to the mainland?* (in (31)) is also argued for by Egerland (2013):

(31) * Nei, en **byggja**$_i$ má hana t$_i$.
       no but build   may it
       'No, but they/we could build one.'
       (Egerland 2013)

Contrast, however, seems to license stylistic fronting of narrowly focused elements. As pointed out by Sigurðsson (1997) and later by Holmberg (2006: 548), a predicative element can be fronted (32-b) if it is contrastively focused:

(32) a. (...) sem ___ hafa **GERT** eitthvað,   en ekki bara talað.
              that   have DONE something and not only talked
              'that they DID something and not only talked.'

b. (...) sem **GERT**$_i$ hafa t$_i$ eitthvað, en ekki bara talað.
   (Holmberg 2006)[12]

Also Hrafnbjargarson (2003) claims that focusing of the SF-moved element requires contrast: according to him fronting of the past participle *lesnar* in (33-a) is only adequate if the sentence is "contrasted with a situation where books have not been read" and *lesnar* is contrastive (called *verum* focus by Hrafnbjargarson in this special case). Example (33-b), where *lesnar* is focused without SF, should, on the other hand, be acceptable without contrast; this sentence is regarded by Hrafnbjargarson (2003: 161) as only "a description about books being read".

(33) a. **Lesnar**$_i$ hafa   verið t$_i$ bækur. [13]
        read   have   been   books
        'Books have been read.'
     b. Bækur hafa verið **lesnar**.
        books have been read
        'Books have been read.'
        (Hrafnbjargarson 2003)

The C-Constraint can be assumed to be operative even in cases of stylistic fronting of DPs, where the specificity requirement indicates the necessity of the contextual anchoring of the SF-moved phrase. As Holmberg points out (2006: 548) "there is some evidence that the fronted category, if it is a DP, cannot be nonspecific". Consider example (34) quoted by Holmberg after Maling (1980)[14]:

---

12 Sigurðsson (2017, footnote 22) emphasizes that "[a]ccentuation may for instance apply in rare cases of clear contrasts, as in [32-b], (...) but comparable examples without a contrast or accentuation are fine too (*sem gert hafa ýmislegt fyrir byggðarlagið*, 'who done have various things for the district', etc.)".
13 According to the judgment of an anonymous reviewer (a native speaker of Icelandic) there is "no obligatory contrast induced by SF in [(33-a)]". This is, however, not a problem for the present analysis, since fronting of the predicative elements (being a formal instance of SF-movement) does not require contrast. The C-Constraint only predicts the ungrammaticality of contextually not anchored (non-contrastive) narrow focusing (identificational focus). Hrafnbjargarson's analysis seems to correspond to this claim: if the fronted participle is a narrow focus, it must induce contrast.
14 Maling (1980), who subsumes only fronting of predicative elements under SF, classifies fronting of DPs as an instance of Topicalization.

(34) *hundurinn sem **minkinn**$_i$ /****minka**$_i$ drap* t$_i$
 the.dog.N that the.mink / minks.A killed
 'the dog who killed the mink/*minks'
 (Holmberg 2006)

The specificity requirement in (34) is, however, regarded by Holmberg as a problematic case and as "an exception to the generalization that SF has no semantic effect."

Wood (2011: 31) is right in maintaining that "the conditions governing the acceptability of fronting DPs are extremely subtle, and not fully understood. Definiteness (Maling 1980) and abstractness (Sigurðsson 1997) have been suggested to have an effect". A closer look at the evaluation of different cases of phrasal SF-movement seems, however, to help us to discern a certain pattern. It appears that both structurally based and/or pragmatically anchored properties of the clause or of the moved constituent play a role in the judgment of acceptability of phrasal SF-movement: the "closeness" of the noun to the verbal head in the structure of the VP, the availability of the OV-order, and formally also indicated C-related features (contextual anchoring by deictic elements, contrast-inducing structures) seem to contribute to a higher degree of acceptability.

Let's start the discussion with the structural aspects of the issue. The relevance of the feature *abstractness* can probably be motivated by the fact that the SF-moved noun in the evaluated cases is a derived noun *nomen actionis* which creates a complex predicate together with a "light verb" in the VP. This "predicative" character of abstract verbal nominals explains not only the suggested acceptability contrast between (35-a) and (35-b) (see Holmberg 2006: 562, footnote 14), but also the absence of a specificity effect in (35-c), which is regarded as a problem by Holmberg:

(35) a. *Þeir sem **þessa erfiðu ákvörðun**$_i$ verða að taka* t$_i$
 those that this difficult decision have to take
 'those who have to take this difficult decision'
 b. ? *Þeir sem **þessa leiðinlegu bók**$_i$ verða að lesa* t$_i$
 those that this boring bok have to read
 'those who have to read this boring book'
 c. *Þeir sem **erfiðar ákvarðanir**$_i$ verða að taka* t$_i$
 those that difficult decisions have to take
 'those who have to take difficult decisions'
 (Holmberg 2006)

The availability of OV-structure in certain contexts is also a factor favoring fronting, since XP-fronting in these cases can be regarded as formal movement (like in Old

Swedish). Negative fronting in Old Icelandic shows clear residual OV-effects: as pointed out by Delsing (2001: 157) "in sentences with a negative object, the object must occur to the left of the verb" (cf. (36)):

(36) a. Ég hef **enga bók** keypt
       I have no   book bought
  b. *Ég hef keypt **enga bók**
       I have bought no   book
    'I have not bought any books.'

Delsing emphasizes that in these constructions it is clearly possible to front objects by SF in Modern Icelandic:

(37) Sá sem **enga bók**$_i$ hefur lesið t$_i$
    he who no   book has read
    'he who has read no book'

The higher degree of acceptability also seems to show a correlation with the formal realization of different C-related features – e.g. by contrast-inducing structures and the use of deictic elements.

Concerning the impact of contrast, Wood (2011: 50) mentions in connection with adjective fronting in subject relatives (XPs are not included in his analysis) that the use of "comparative and superlative forms (...) often improves otherwise marginal examples of adjective fronting", cf. example (38):

(38) Það sem að **alvarlegast**$_i$ er t$_i$ (...)
    it   which that most.serious is
    'What is most serious (...)'
    (Wood 2011)

Hrafnbjargarson (2003: 180) also discusses the acceptability difference between cases of XP-fronting with and without contrast-inducement. According to him, cases like (39), where the noun has the definite article suffix, are rather marked (he mentions, however, in a footnote that his informants did not agree on the grammaticality of the sentence):

(39) ?? Það var hún sem **flöskunum**$_i$ hafði stolið t$_i$
      it was her that bottles-the had   stolen
    'It was her that had stolen the bottles.'
    (Hrafnbjargarson 2003)

Sentence (40) is judged more acceptable because "the full DP is not unique but picked out of a set" (Hrafnbjargarson 2003: 180). As pointed out by Sigurðsson (p.c.), the use of *allir* generally increases the degree of acceptability. This fact receives an explanation in the proposed C-related approach, since the creation of a subset implies the relevance of other subsets and induces contrast (cf. (40)). The main point here is that *the set of those who have drunk homebrewed aquavit* is a subset and can be contrasted to another *set of people who have drunk something else*:

(40) ? *Allir sem **heimabryggað brennivín**$_i$ hafa drukkið t$_i$ vita þetta*
     all   that homebrewed   aquavit   have drunk   know this
     'Everyone who has drunk homebrewed aquavit knows this'
     (Hrafnbjargarson 2003)

Interestingly, contrast marking by the C-feature also makes the fronting of a non-specific noun possible. This indicates that not the specificity requirement is crucial (as argued by Holmberg, see example (34) above) but C-marking of the phrase. As required by the C-Constraint, C-marking is possible not only by the "C-continuity" feature (based on/correlating with specificity, givenness, definiteness) but also with "C-contrast." In this way, the intuition of an anonymous reviewer (a native speaker of Icelandic) that "the contrast between the definite and indefinite cases reported for [(34)] is quite weak" can also receive an explanation.

The same reviewer has also pointed out that XP-fronting (see example (35)) is not obligatorily bound to contrast. This judgment – the lack of contrast – can, however, also be accounted for in the proposed framework by the distinction of STYL-inversion and STYL-preposing. Assuming that the obligatory contrast reading is only motivated in VO-structures where the movement of an XP is an instance of true SF-movement, one could argue that the lack of contrast on the moved item indicates that SF of phrases is treated by the speaker as formal movement similarly to SF of heads. This variation in speaker judgments can possibly be related to the *Double Basis Hypothesis* suggested by Kroch (1989), the relevance of which for SF is discussed in more detail in Egerland (2013). According to this hypothesis, "an old grammatical system is continuously reinforced in the language community if the speakers are exposed to evidence for it, along with evidence for the new system" (Egerland 2013: 75). This is the case in Icelandic, where fronting structures – "reestablishing" the OV-configuration – are frequently used, making the formal movement analysis of XP-fronting understandable.[15]

The formal movement of XPs seems, however, to be triggered and/or restricted by the C-constraint. In a recent corpus study Sigurðsson (2017: 336) argues for the influence of contextual anchoring on the choice of SF "candidates": he shows that "indexical or deictic elements [DPs, PPs and AdvPs] with their reference depending on properties of the speech event (...) seem to front more readily than do other DPs and PPs/AdvPs". According to Sigurðsson's (2017:322) empirical study, "the effect of the presence of *þar* 'there' is striking" in the subject relative *sem þar hafa búið* 'who there has lived' as compared to *sem í Danmörku hafa búið* 'who í Denmark has lived', with 20 (vs. 1) hits in *Google* and 196 (vs. 0) instances in *Timarit.is*. The relevance of the deictic character of the SF-fronted elements is also attested in several other cases: "Thus, searching *Timarit.is* (July 6, 2015) for *sem við mig hafa talað* 'who with me have spoken' gave 47 hits, whereas its "competitors", *sem hafa talað við mig* and *sem talað hafa við mig* yielded 56 and 24 hits respectively". A systematic examination of these C-related factors for SF in the case of XP-movement could be an interesting task for further research.

The requirement of obligatory contrastive interpretation for the SF-moved DP or PP would also contradict another important, widely accepted claim made in SF-research, according to which "heavy constituents resist SF more strongly than "lighter" constituents" (Ott 2009: 149).[16] Contrastive phrases bear (contrastive) accent and thus can be claimed to have a higher phonological weight. This correlates with a higher information-structural weight. The effect of phonological and information-structural "heaviness" in contrastive cases is clear: fronting of XPs is marked and strongly restricted. Phonological

---

15 Cf. Hróarsdóttir (2001: 56): "Although Modern Icelandic is generally assumed to have SVO surface order (...), there still exist three constructions in Modern Icelandic exhibiting some sort of SOV order: Negative (and quantified) phrase construction, Object Shift, and Stylistic Fronting".

16 According to Sigurðsson (2017: 323) "(...) 'lightness' rather than focus/accentuation seems to favor SF. Wood presents evidence from spoken language corpora that "constituents with 1 syllable highly favor fronting, those with 2 syllables weakly disfavor fronting, and those with 3–5 strongly disfavor fronting" (2011: 45). Deictic elements are also "light" in another sense: they are presupposed in a given speech event and thus "informationally light". As many indexicals are monosyllabic and often deaccentuated, informational lightness and phonetic lightness commonly overlap, and it is not always easy to tell these factors apart. However, when they can be teased apart, there is some evidence that mere phonetic lightness is not a strongly promoting or favoring factor".

weight includes, though, not only accent but also other formal aspects, like length. This explains the clear contrast between (41-a) and (41-b) in Sigurðsson's (2010b) judgment, which also correlates with the clear quantitative difference between the attested frequency of the two uses in Google:

(41) a. OK *sem **þessa ákvörðun**$_i$ tóku* t$_i$
            that this   decision   took
            'that took this decision'
    b. ? *sem **þessa erfiðu ákvörðun**$_i$ tóku* t$_i$
            that this   difficult decision   took
            'that took this difficult decision'

This "lightness" constraint on SF (in both a phonological and an information-structural sense) is also referred to by Egerland (2013) to explain another intriguing fact in connection with SF in Icelandic, namely the ban on SF-movement of those VPs where the non-finite verb would be moved together with its complement, as discussed by Holmberg (2006), Ott (2009) and Egerland (2013). Consider (42-a) and (42-b):

(42) a. * *sá sem **skrifað þessa bók**$_i$ hefur* t$_i$
           he that written this   book has
    b. * *kosningar   sem **farið fram**$_i$ hafa* t$_i$
           the.elections that gone forth have
           (Holmberg 2006)

Since phrases can be moved by SF and the remnant movement analysis should also predict the possibility of the cases illustrated above in (42), there is no structural reason for the fact that movement is excluded in these cases. The heaviness of the moved item (as suggested by Ott 2009) cannot, however, render a satisfactory explanation either, since heavier constituents with a more complex internal structure ((35-a), (41-a)) can be SF-moved while VP movement including the complement is ungrammatical in the case of shorter elements as in (42). Heaviness can thus be claimed "only" to reduce the acceptability of SF-movement but not to exclude it. A reason for the ungrammaticality of this movement could possibly be related to the VO-structure within the VP. This prohibits the SF-movement of VP since it does not correspond to the basic requirement of SF: the reconstruction or preservation of an OV-configuration.

Before summarizing the discussion on the interpretive effects of SF in Icelandic, one more argument for the semantic and discourse relevance of SF must be mentioned. As observed by Jónsson (1991) and discussed in later research (e.g. Holmberg 2006; Egerland 2013), fronting cannot apply to the copula or passive auxiliary *vera*:

(43) a. þetta er versta bók   sem **skrifuð**$_i$ hefur verið t$_i$
       this   is worst   book that written   has   been
       'This is the worst book that has been written.'
   b. *þetta er versta bók   sem **verið**$_i$ hefur t$_i$ skrifuð
       this   is worst   book that been   has   written
       'This is the worst book that has been written.'
       (Holmberg 2006)

This fact that SF-movement is restricted to contentful verbal elements while auxiliaries cannot be SF-moved (43-b) is also consistent with the proposal of the present work to not regard SF as a pure PF-phenomenon.[17]

We can thus conclude that SF in both cases – not only STYL-preposing but also STYL-inversion – has pragmatic and/or semantic effects and/or is restricted by semantic and pragmatic constraints. The two types show, however, certain differences with regard to their interpretation, motivated by the type of syntactic movement applied for their derivation. As argued above, in the case of STYL-inversion only the identificational (and not the C-related narrow) focus interpretation is deviant, whereas the inducement of contrast is obligatory for STYL-preposing and all other interpretations are excluded. According to the present proposal, the syntactic and interpretive distinction between the formal and the "true" type of SF should not simply be related to the category of the moved item but to other factors as well. The availability of the OV-structure was regarded as the most relevant distinguishing feature between the two types of syntactic derivations of SF, motivating their interpretive differences. The higher degree of availability of the OV-register could thus also contribute to the formal analysis of the movement when the moved item was a DP and PP (cf. the comment of the anonymous reviewer). It was also shown that SF-movement is always restricted by the C-Constraint, which has the consequence that the movement of quantificational narrow focus without contextual anchoring (C-feature) and that of items without semantic-pragmatic visibility is excluded.

The facts discussed above indicate that Holmberg's analysis (2000, 2006), according to which SF is to be interpreted as movement of only phonological

---

[17] However, according to Sigurðsson (2017) SF of progressive *vera* (comparable with *be –ing* in English) is common. In the Icelandic equivalents of cases like 'who was reading' is SF possible: *sem verið var að lesa*.

features, cannot be on the right track. The relevance of the semantic and pragmatic constraints for SF discussed above calls the expletive character of this syntactic movement into question.

6 SF Compared to Focusing and Topicalization

The accuracy of Holmberg's claim concerning the interpretation of SF has been challenged by Hrafnbjargarson, who takes quite a different position in this discussion based on cases where the semantic and discourse relevance of SF is apparent. The "overestimation" of the semantic and pragmatic effects of SF in Icelandic leads Hrafnbjargarson (2004a), however, to conclude that SF is *Focus movement* in Icelandic: "The claim is that SF has semantic effects. This could be reflected in an analysis where SF is a feature-driven movement operation into two positions: XP undergo SF into FocusP and heads undergo SF into Focus°. (...) The feature [F] on Focus° may be any kind of a formal feature alpha. It might be an EPP feature, or some kind of focus/topic feature. I will not try to identify the feature here".

Hrafnbjargarson's claim is, however, problematic, even though it has the advantage that it makes a hybrid treatment of SF possible by opening up two positions, a Spec- and a head-position in the Focus projection (see examples (33) and (40)). Yet several questions are unsatisfactorily answered and problems remain unsolved in this approach:

i. How can we account for cases of SF without focusing? Hrafnbjargarson's proposal, according to which the checking of the Focus feature is "open for either an expletive or a stylistically fronted XP", where the expletive is regarded as "a semantically empty focus element that is inserted into FocusF-Spec to check the focus feature on F°" (Hrafnbjargarson 2003: 164), seems rather ad hoc.
ii. The fact that narrow focus in SF is always bound to contrast although focusing (operator focus) is not obligatorily contrastive (as pointed out by Molnár 2006 among others) is not taken into consideration.
iii. There is no clear evidence for a split C-domain in V2-languages, although subsequent work by Hrafnbjargarson and Wiklund seems to be on a promising path in this direction (cf. Hrafnbjargarson and Wiklund 2009).
iv. The main syntactic requirements of SF – the locality constraints and the subject gap condition – are definitely not present in Focus movement, which strengthens the impression that the parallel syntactic analysis of these two movements is not convincing.

As argued above, the claim of discourse relevance and the possibility of focusing in the case of SF can be integrated into an approach where SF is regarded as a special type of syntactic operation in Icelandic. The claim of the present work is thus that SF should be distinguished not only from Focus movement but also from *Topicalization*, both on structural and functional grounds. This claim is partly consistent with Maling's original analysis, where the distinction between SF and Topicalization was introduced and argued for; the differences between SF and Topicalization regarding their discourse interpretation, however, have not been further elaborated on until the present work.

Thus, in the current proposal Topicalization and SF are still regarded as two different syntactic movements, distinguished primarily not by the type of the moved category but rather by the difference with respect to the role of the empty subject position and the accessibility hierarchy (cf. section 2). Functionally, however, the two movement types seem to be more closely related, as recognized by Maling, even if they do differ with regard to their "typical" function. The range of the possible functions is identical in both cases; their distribution, however, is different if only Topicalization of non-subjects is taken into consideration.

The main discourse differences should thus not be located between Stylistic Fronting and Topicalization, but along the lines of "formal" vs. "true" movement, both in the case of Topicalization and stylistic movement. This analysis consequently contradicts a previous claim by Rögnvaldsson and Thráinsson (1990: 28), according to which "[TOP and SF] are syntactically a unified process, even though they are certainly different functionally (...)", emphasizing the syntactic similarities between SF and Topicalization, and also subsuming certain instances of SF under Topicalization. Thráinsson explicitly suggests in a later work that the relevant distinguishing factor is the discourse function of the movement: "Every time a constituent is fronted for focusing purposes it is an instance of Topicalization. If the fronting has no focusing effect it is an instance of SF" (Thráinsson 2007: 369).

7 SF in Scandinavian and Romance

So far the syntactic and functional analysis of SF has concentrated on the Icelandic data, and the proposal made above in section 5 was only related to Scandinavian languages. From a cross-linguistic perspective there are still two important issues regarding SF, which will be taken up in the following discussion.

The main questions relating to language comparison are (i) whether there are common structural prerequisites of the stylistic movement in Romance and Scandinavian that justify its separation from Topicalization and Focusing in both language groups, and (ii) whether it is possible to reach a cross-linguistically valid generalization regarding the interpretive effects of these syntactic operations in the different languages. The structural aspects of SF in Romance will be discussed in 7.1., followed by a presentation of the dominant view concerning the discourse function of SF in Romance in 7.2. The question of other possible interpretations in Romance will be addressed in 7.3.

7.1 Syntactic Requirements

The diversity of the moved categories is also attested in Romance languages, where similarly to Scandinavian, SF comes in two basic variants. The examples in the introductory section of this paper taken from Old Catalan (5) and Old French (7) show both types of fronting possibilities in Old Romance, however, these patterns are also encountered in Modern Romance languages and dialects. According to Cardinaletti (2003) both predicative elements (44) and DPs (45) can be stylistically fronted in Italian:

(44) *Lo studente que **via**$_i$ andò t$_i$ senza dire niente a*
 the student that away went without saying anything to
 nessuno.
 anybody
 'the student that went away without saying anything to anybody'
 (Cardinaletti 2003)

(45) *Merito di John Elderfield, que **questa espozione**$_i$ ha voluto e*
 merit of John Elderfield who this exhibition has wanted and
 curato t$_i$
 edited
 'John Elderfield's merit, who wanted and edited this exhibition'
 (Cardinaletti 2003)

The observed categorical variation with respect to the fronted element in SF – which is apparently present in both Romance and Scandinavian – has, however, been analyzed in quite a different way by Fischer and Alexiadou (2001). Instead of accounting for both varieties in Romance and Scandinavian, they argue for a parametric difference between the SF-syntax of Scandinavian and that of Romance, which in their view is the reason behind the different discourse behavior of SF in these language groups (2001: 136f.): "Now the analysis we proposed in the previous section for Old Catalan and the one adopted here for Icelandic are straightforwardly unified under the XP vs. X° parameter. If we are right in suggesting [that] SF in Old Catalan involves X° (information structure related) movement, and we maintain Holmberg's analysis that SF in Icelandic involves XP (EPP) topic-related movement, then the relevant difference is again one of XP vs. X°. SF involves head raising in Old Catalan, but involves XP raising in Icelandic".

There are, however, "real" differences between Scandinavian and Romance with respect to the basic syntactic requirements of Stylistic Fronting and also concerning the discourse relevance of this movement.

The *subject gap condition* – one of the most crucial syntactic prerequisites of SF – seems to be obligatory in Scandinavian languages (e.g. in Old and Modern Icelandic, Old Swedish) but not in Romance (Old Catalan, Italian, etc.).[18] Whereas the grammaticality contrast of the examples (8-a) and (8-b) discussed above indicates the relevance of the subject gap condition for SF in Icelandic, a preverbal subject is apparently acceptable in Old Catalan (46) (subjects are underlined):

(46) e   adonchs con amà   Deu e   serví   Déu
     and so   with love.3sg God and serve.3sg God
     de que Déus **donat**$_i$ li   havia   t$_i$
     of that God given   him had.3sg
     (Fischer and Alexiadou 2001)

Fischer and Alexiadou (2001: 122) point out that "Old Catalan SF seems to have been an optional operation, applying independently of verb second requirements and the necessity of a subject gap, unlike Icelandic SF".

Stylistic Fronting can appear with preverbal subjects in Old and Modern Italian as well, as illustrated in examples (47) and (48) below:

(47) Il   saver   dell' arme   color di Cartagine **difender**$_i$
     the know.INF of.the weapon those of Carthage defend.INF
     non potè   t$_i$
     not could.3sg
     'The knowledge of warcraft could not defend the people of Carthage'
     (Franco 2009)

---

18 The subject gap condition is, however, relevant for Sardinian.

(48) La ragione per la quale si può dire che il problema
the reason for the which SI can say that the problem
risolto$_i$ non è t$_i$
solved not is
'The reason for which one can say that the problem is not solved'
(Cardinaletti 2003)

Further "deviations" from the basic syntactic patterns required for SF in Scandinavian are discussed in the analysis of fronting data in Sardinian (Jones 1993; Egerland 2013). Fronting of predicative elements seems to be an A-bar-movement supported by the possibility of extraction of the moved item (49-b) as opposed to the clause boundedness property of SF in Icelandic (see example (14) above):

(49) a. Creu ka est arribau.
I(think) that (he)is arrived
'I think he arrived.'
 b. **Arrivatu**$_i$ creu ka esti t$_i$
arrived (I)think that (he)is
(Egerland 2013)

7.2 The Discourse Relevance of SF in Romance

Concerning the discourse effects of SF in Modern and Old Romance languages and varieties, it is often claimed in the literature that SF expresses a kind of emphasis and is either bound to focus or to topic interpretation.

In Sardinian, fronting of the participle in main and embedded clauses like (50) and (51) is claimed by Jones (1993) to require obligatory narrow focus on the fronted participle and to have the same information-structural interpretation as Focus movement:

(50) **Arrivatu**$_i$ est t$_i$ a sa festa.
arrived is at the party
'He has arrived at the party.'
(Jones 1993)

(51) Appo natu ki **arrivatos**$_i$ sun t$_i$ (...)
said sg.1. that arrived are
'I said that they have arrived (...)'
(Jones 1993)

Egerland (2013) discusses the Sardinian data at length and shows convincingly that this type of fronting in Sardinian shares certain syntactic properties with SF in Icelandic (the subject gap condition, which, however, has different sources in these two languages, and the ungrammaticality of fronting of purely functional elements), but also differs from SF Icelandic with respect to some fundamental syntactic properties: this type of fronting is not clause-bound (49), shows no definiteness effect, and has focus interpretation. Since in this case the quantificational type of focusing is involved, this kind of movement is regarded by Egerland (following Jones 1993) as Focus movement. Consider example (52) in a context where the VP – verb and direct object – is new information (narrow focus), and the rest of the sentence is backgrounded:

(52) (Context: *What did you do for his birthday?*)
  Arregallau unu libru$_i$ dd'   appu   t$_i$
  given   is   a   book   to-him   (I)have
  'I have given him a book.'
  (Egerland 2013)

As generally claimed, focus movement is compatible with contrast even if contrast is not required. Thus fronting in Sardinian can also be appropriate in contexts inducing contrast (cf. Jones 1993; Egerland 2013):

(53) a. **Arregordaus**$_i$ si   funt   t$_i$?
    remembered   REFL   (they)are
    'I they are remembered.'
  b. *Nou,* **scarèscius**$_i$ si   funt   t$_i$?
    no   forgotten   REFL   (they)are
    'No, they are forgotten.'
    (Egerland 2013)

As Egerland shows, fronting in Sardinian is not acceptable (54-a) in the context of a question like *What happened?*, where the whole answer is information focus, without containing a focus-background-partition. In this case, only the answer without fronting is felicitous (54-b):

(54)   (Context: *What happened?*)
  a. * **Perdiu su trenu**$_i$ ari   t$_i$ Gianni
      missed the train   has   John
  b. *Gianni ari perdiu su trenu.*
      John   has missed the train
      'John has missed the train'
      (Egerland 2013)

Concerning SF in Old Catalan, Fischer and Alexiadou (2001: 127–128) argue that "SF in Old Catalan contributes to information structure" and describe this contribution as "emphatic affirmation". In their view SF is used "in order to express something which needs to be emphasized, which is unexpected/unforeseen or outstanding in the development of the text". They illustrate their claim with the following example:

(55) [Context:
Longament consider   lo   hermit en la   demanda que li
long   considered the hermit in the question that him
hac   feta   Fèlix (...)
had.3sg made Fèlix
'For a long time the hermit considered the question that Felix had asked him...']
Continuation:
Fèlix, se   meravell   à   del hermità
Fèlix ref. surprised of the hermit
*com no li   responia   a la demanda [que **feta**$_i$ li   havie t$_i$]*
how not him answered to the question   that made him had.3sg
'Felix was surprised that the hermit did not answer him to the question he had asked him.'
(Llull/24, quoted by Fischer and Alexiadou 2001)

According to Fischer and Alexiadou (2001: 127) the preposed element *feta* clearly indicates the emphasis of the unforeseen – in the given context the fact that *Fèlix* had not expected that the hermit would not be able to answer his question: "In our interpretation the inverse word-order here, clearly emphasizes the surprise Fèlix felt, and the reader feels" (ibid: 127–128). However, the analysis of the information structure of this example – and thereby also the discourse interpretation of the SF-moved constituent – is not convincing: the surprise is rather motivated by the polarity of the sentence (55) and consequently the emphasis should be related to the negation adverb *no*.

Mathieu (2006) also suggests that SF in Old French has significance for discourse interpretation. Its discourse effects are, however, related to the notion of Topic (56) (see also example (7) above):

(56) Quant les dames et les damoiselles qui **avec le reine**$_i$
    when the ladies and the young-girls who with the queen
    estoient assises t$_i$
    be.PAST.3PL sat
    'When the ladies and the young girls who sat with the queen'
    (Mathieu 2006)

Concerning the evaluation of the discourse effects of SF in Romance, there seems to be considerable agreement in the literature. As opposed to the dominant view in Scandinavian linguistics, according to which the trigger of SF is some version of the EPP requiring that the Spec,TP-position of finite clauses be filled, SF in Romance is most often claimed to have information-structural functions. These are, however, subject to cross-linguistic variation: as discussed above, the expression of "emphatic affirmation" in Old Catalan, focusing in Sardinian and topicality in Old French are suggested as different options. The difference with regard to the information-structural behavior of SF in Scandinavian and Romance is thus widely accepted in SF-research. Comparative studies analyzing the parametric differences between the two language groups in detail also contribute to this picture by relating the different syntactic properties of SF to differences with respect to its discourse behavior (cf. Fischer and Alexiadou 2001; Franco 2009).

7.3 Revision of the Dominant View

The analysis of SF in Romance presented above has, however, been challenged in two works on stylistic movement in Italian. Cardinaletti (2003: 47) suggests that "Italian SF displays the same properties as SF in Icelandic" referring to Maling's (1980) and Holmberg's (2000) analyses. She claims that not only the syntactic properties of SF in Modern Italian (with respect to the type of the fronted item (44, (45), the accessibility hierarchy, clause boundedness, etc.) are reminiscent of SF in Icelandic,[19] but also its discourse properties: "While a focalized element always needs contrastive focus contrastive focus (CF)and gives rise to a marked word order (Rizzi 1997), this is not the case for the SF-constituent". According to Egerland (2013: 75), "Cardinaletti (2003) provides a convincing analysis of fronting in

---

[19] Cardinaletti argues, however, that the subject gap condition is not operative in Italian (cf. example (48)), since Italian is not a V2-language (see also the discussion of the V2-parameter and its effects on SF in section 8.2. below).

Old and Renaissance Italian. (...) Whether it is the accurate desription of *modern* Italian, however, is a matter of controversy". Franco (2009: 67) does not share Cardinaletti's view concerning the productivity of SF in modern language usage and "accept[s] only some cases as instances of (old) literary style".[20]

Franco's analysis of Old Italian data is, however, compatible with Cardinaletti's claim. She shows on the basis of an extensive empirical investigation that different positions – and consequently also different interpretive options – are available for stylistically fronted elements in Old Italian. Although her analysis is restricted to the examination of SF in "unmarked" cases, her data and conclusions are novel. The restriction to fronting of predicative elements (e.g. participles, infinitives) seems necessary, primarily in order to avoid the problem of apparent overlap between SF and Focus movement or Topic movement in the case of fronting of phrases. Franco's examples, taken from three Old Italian corpora, show, based mainly on evidence from the placement of clitics, that there are two different target positions for stylistically fronted predicative elements in the CP-field of Old Italian: ModP and FinP (located in the following way: (FocP >) ModP > FinP (> SubjP)). Nominal predicates and adjectives (parasitically) target ModP in the CP-domain (57), a non-quantificational position which according to Rizzi (2001) is dedicated to adverb preposing. By contrast, participles and infinitives are located in FinP after stylistic movement (58):

(57) **Bisogno**$_i$ fa   t$_i$ che noi lo   ritroviamo.
     need   makes   that we 3s.CL.ACC find
     'It is necessary that we find him.'
     (Franco 2009, FR, 47, 13)

(58) *Per una grande pioggia che* **venuta**$_i$ *era* t$_i$
     for a   big   rain   that   come   was
     'because of a lot of rain that had come'
     (Franco 2009, N, 31, 11)

Franco argues that the distinction of (at least) two types of SF is required for predicative elements since they differ not only with respect to syntax (targeting different positions and showing different frequency in main and subordinate clauses) but also functionally. They check different features at different structural levels and this fact explains why they occur differently in main and subordinate clauses: SF

---

[20] Concerning the explanation of the difference between Cardinaletti's and Franco's judgments, see also Egerland (2013).

to ModP is preferred in main clauses, and SF to FinP in subordinated contexts. And importantly, they are also bound to different interpretations: she argues that emphatic stress is only required in the case of movement to ModP. Although the details of her analysis regarding information structure must be worked out in more detail, her proposal of SF-split shows interesting similarities to the analysis of SF suggested for Icelandic in this paper.

8 Parametric Differences between Scandinavian and Romance – their Effect on SF

The following discussion will show how the parametric differences and similarities between the two language groups play a role in SF. As discussed above, the most important structural properties of / prerequisites for SF are the following: (i) the *subject gap condition* related to the inflectional properties and the presence of pro-drop, (ii) the *V2-property*, and (iii) the *directionality parameter* (OV- vs. VO-configuration). These are summarized in (59) below. It is, however, important to point out that these properties also show considerable synchronic and diachronic variation (cf. Franco 2009). In order to capture the main similarities and differences between the two language groups, the details regarding the variation at different developmental stages will not be specified in (59). However, the following discussion will also take some relevant aspects of the attested variation into consideration.

(59) **ROMANCE**   **SCANDINAVIAN**
     pro-drop   only partial pro-drop
     "relaxed V2"/ non-V2   V2
     VO/OV   OV/VO

8.1 Subject Gap – the Pro-drop-parameter

Concerning the issue of the structural prerequisites of stylistic movement, the *subject gap condition* seems to have the highest priority. This is the common syntactic denominator for different instances of SF in Romance and Scandinavian, motivating the structural distinction between SF and Topicalization.

The possibility of a subject gap providing a target position for SF as well as the frequency of this are, however, related to certain parametric properties of the languages: (i) to *rich agreement* and V°-to-I°-movement (Falk 1993) since the checking of the phi-features in I° is necessary and can be satisfied by verbal morphology (subject-agreement suffixes) if there is no nominal element in the subject position, and (ii) to the *pro-drop property*, which licenses a subject in Spec,IP without overt realization and also makes a subject gap possible in main clauses with any subject.

The parametric differences with respect to the pro-drop property explain the contrast between Romance and Scandinavian concerning the subject gap. The pro-drop property of Romance shows, however, certain variation. As Franco (2010) demonstrates, Old Italian has an asymmetric pro-drop pattern where pro-drop can only be licensed in main clauses by V-to-C-movement. Full pro-drop in Modern Italian makes a subject position without an overt subject possible in both main and subordinate clauses and as such creates optimal conditions (at least with respect to pro-drop) for SF.

In contrast to Italian, pro-drop is much more restricted in Icelandic and can apply only in the case of expletive subjects and quasi-arguments in impersonals (cf. Sigurðsson 2010a). The pro-drop property of Romance is thus essential for creating empty subject positions in more types of environments (both in main and subordinate clauses) than is the case in Scandinavian languages, where SF typically appears in subordinated clauses.

8.2 The V2-parameter

The restriction on the cooccurrence of a raised subject and an SF-constituent in Icelandic requires, however, that the setting of the V2-parameter also be taken into consideration. As argued in the literature, this restriction is due to constraints on V2 (cf. Cardinaletti 2003; Franco 2009, 2010). As discussed above in sections 3 and 7, SF in Scandinavian is only possible where no visible overt subject is present in the subject position whereas overt subjects are not necessarily obstacles to SF in Romance. Since in non-V2-languages more subject projections are available, SF is possible with realized definite subjects in Italian. The subject gap can be attested in Romance languages in clauses with definite subjects preceding the empty subject position, leading to a completely unthinkable SF-configuration in Scandinavian.

In Scandinavian languages, thus, the *verb-second property* is regarded as a crucial prerequisite for stylistic movement. Maling (1980: 71) claims that "(...) this kind of fronting can [...] be viewed as a generalization of V2 to clauses that would otherwise begin with the finite verb". It is uncontroversial that V2 has a greater significance in Scandinavian languages than in Romance. The dominant view regarding Scandinavian languages, including Old and Modern varieties, is that they all belong to the V2-language type and show a "strict" V2-order.[21] According to Franco's (2010) claim, Old Romance languages have a "relaxed type" of V2-order since more than one element can precede the finite verb in the C-domain. V2 is asymmetric, though, since the verb moves to the CP only in main clauses, not in subordinate ones. (As Franco also points out, this explains why pro-drop is not licensed in subordinate clauses, where overt subject pronouns are found instead.) V2, however, has been lost in the Modern Romance languages, including Modern Italian, which is thus a non-V2-language.

In the generative framework the abovementioned differences regarding the V2-property between languages and/or developmental stages are accounted for in the following way: V2 in (Old) Scandinavian means that after the V°-to-I°-movement into the C-domain, movement of I° to C° is required (cf. Falk 1993). Concerning Old Catalan with the Romance-type of V2 (relaxed V2 or non-V2), Fischer and Alexiadou (2001) suggest an additional movement into the so-called Σ^0-projection located between IP and CP, for hosting an SF-moved constituent with an emphatic reading. According to their analysis, the operation of SF in Old Catalan is therefore to be regarded as the head movement I°-to-Σ^0 (in contrast to XP-movement in Scandinavian), differing from SF in Scandinavian both with respect to syntax and information structure (cf. subsection 7.1. above). However, as discussed above, for the analysis of SF in Old Italian, Franco makes a different proposal following Rizzi's "Split-CP model" (Rizzi 1997): SF can target certain functional projections within the "articulated" C-domain: not only the operator positions in TopicP and FocusP are available for this movement but also ModP and FinP (located before the SubjP).

Based on this difference between Romance and Scandinavian, another relevant difference can also be observed between these two language groups. The C-Constraint related to the left peripheral positions of main or embedded clauses is only relevant in Scandinavian, which belongs to the V2-type languages, and is not operative in Romance. This explains why focusing in Romance does not require contrast as opposed to in Scandinavian – focus is realized by Focus movement and results in the creation of a quantificational type of focus showing relevant differences both to the non-quantificational "information focus" and contrastive instances of focusing not necessarily bound to an operator type (A-bar) Focus movement.

---

21 A somewhat different proposal is made by of Hrafnbjargarson and Wiklund (2009), who argue against this view on the basis of Modern Icelandic data. Examples from Early Runic and Old Norse (cf. Eythórsson 1996; Faarlund 2008 referred to in Franco 2009) also serve as evidence for a more relaxed V2 in Scandinavian.

8.3 The Directionality Parameter – OV- vs. OV-configuration

A further significant parametric difference between Romance and Scandinavian and between different stages of these languages can be traced back to the setting of *the OV–VO-parameter*. The relevance of OV for stylistic movement is connected to the "easier" frontability of different lexical elements from the lower phrasal domain, since these are locally closer to the SF-probe in the basic OV-configuration (cf. Franco 2010).

With respect to the basic word order the main differences are not between Romance and Scandinavian, but are instead related to the availability of OV in the older varieties of these languages. As pointed out in works on Old Romance, OV is a frequent configuration despite the VO-character of these languages. OV seems possible for any type of constituent (arguments, adverbials, verbal modifiers) with the "lack of specialization" typical of left peripheral positions (Poletto 2006). According to Egerland (1996), OV results from direct object agreement, i.e. object movement to AgrOP in Old Italian. In Modern Romance, OV is more restricted and residual OV is regarded as typical for the literary register (cf. Egerland 2010).

The Scandinavian languages, which were originally all OV-languages, have, however, lost the OV-property to a greater extent than Romance. As mentioned above in the introductory section, SF was quite frequent in for example Old Swedish, partly due to the OV-character of this language. There is one relevant exception, though, as to the presence of OV in Modern Scandinavian, namely Icelandic. Icelandic preserved a basic OV much longer than the other Scandinavian languages and turned to VO as late as 1800. As argued by Poletto (2006), the importance of OV-order in a V2-grammar is related to the active status and visibility of the low *v*P periphery at the end of the main phrase, causing the locally restricted "formal" version of SF to be much more easily available in an OV-language. The late change of OV to VO in Icelandic and Iceland's influential literary tradition may have contributed to the "activity" of OV-order in Modern Icelandic. SF can be regarded as an excellent means in Icelandic of reconstructing the traditional OV-configuration, giving an archaic flavor to sentences where the structural requirements of SF can be satisfied (cf. Egerland's 2013 discussion on the *Double Basis Hypothesis*).

We can conclude that the frequency of SF and its importance in Romance and Scandinavian are linked to the abovementioned parametric differences, also discussed in the literature. The positive setting of the pro-drop parameter contributes to a wider availability of the vacant subject positions required for SF, and the OV-property of languages creates symmetry between the high left periphery (CP) and the low one (*v*P), enabling the frontability of SF-moved elements (by observing the locality restrictions onmovements). Finally, the differences with regard to the V2-parameter contribute to the difference in the significance of the subject gap condition in the sense that overt subjects can precede the SF-moved constituent in Romance, an option which is not available in Scandinavian since fronting in a V2 language is restricted to a single constituent.

8.4 Interpretive Effects of SF in Scandinavian and Romance

The differences concerning the interpretive properties of SF are also generally attributed to the V2-parameter. In most approaches, verb-second in Scandinavian serves as the main motivation for an analysis according to which SF in Scandinavian is only conditioned by EPP-requirements (or by the Edge feature) without any relevance for discourse. As argued earlier in this work (cf. section 5) this proposal seems unable to account for the complexity of information-structural possibilities in Icelandic. Instead, a distinction was suggested between two different subtypes of SF (STYL-preposing and STYL-inversion), which show different discourse behavior due to the different derivations of the stylistic movement. However, as emphasized in section 5, both types of stylistic movement must respect the C-Constraint.

Concerning Romance, this splitting up of Stylistic Fronting also seems to be supported by the empirical facts. As Franco argues, SF is not uniform in Old Italian and can have different interpretations depending on the type of features which are checked at different structural levels. However, in standard treatments, the variation in the interpretive effects of SF in Romance is often disregarded. Fischer and Alexiadou's (2001) claim of the discourse relevance of SF in Old-Catalan, i.e. "emphatic affirmation" as a consequence of movement to ΣP located between CP and IP and triggered by a strong Topic feature on ΣP, cannot capture all relevant interpretive options of SF in Romance. Nor can Mathieu's (2006) analysis of Old French data, which also claims a discourse relevance of SF – in this case the Topic-interpretation – be the whole story. And even if Cardinaletti's (2003) analysis of SF in Modern Italian deviates from the widely held view of discourse relevance of SF in Romance, the variation with regard to the interpretation is not accounted for.

In addition to cases which are reminiscent of "true" stylistic movement (STYL-Preposing) in Icelandic and require emphasis, there are also cases (documented by Cardinaletti and Franco) where the function of Stylistic Fronting is quite different. In these cases SF is analyzed by Franco (2010: 22) as "an interface requirement to license subject extraction/drop, by checking the relevant features on the lower complementizer position (FinP); cf. Sigurðsson and Maling 2008". Following Rizzi (2004) and Rizzi and Shlonsky (2007), Franco relates these cases to the Subject Criterion, by which the "classical EPP," the requirement that clauses have subjects, is restated as a criterial requirement, the Subject Criterion, formally akin to the Topic Criterion and the Focus Criterion (cf. Franco 2009, 2010). These latter instances of SF, which are reminiscent of STYL-inversion, indicate, however, that the dominant view of the functional load of SF in Romance should be revisited and modified.

9 Conclusion

As the comparison of the stylistic movement in Romance and Scandinavian presented above shows, the evaluation of the functional load of SF is quite problematic in linguistic research. Mainly cases related to emphasis (with Topic or Focus interpretation) have been taken into consideration in works on Romance, while research in Icelandic has focused on unmarked, functionally neutral instances of SF. The exaggeration of the dominant cases regarding both language groups – in combination with unmotivated or problematic judgments – has led to the conclusion that the discourse behavior of SF in the Scandinavian and Romance languages is quite different.

The main aim of this paper has been to call the parametric difference between Romance and Scandinavian regarding the discourse effect of SF into question and to provide a modified account of the interpretive properties of Stylistic Fronting. It has been argued that SF in Romance and Scandinavian is more similar than hitherto suggested in the literature, and it has also been claimed that stylistic movement comes in (at least) two varieties in both language groups. Despite relevant parametric differences between Romance and Scandinavian with respect to the verb-second parameter, basic word order (VO vs. OV) and pro-drop property, SF can have different discourse effects within the language groups in both cases. It can appear as a Formal Movement (here called STYL-inversion) in unmarked cases, primarily satisfying the requirements of the EPP, Edge feature or "Subject Criterion", but in V2-languages also respecting the C-Constraint. "True" stylistic fronting (STYL-preposing) with a marked information-structural effect is also possible in both language groups and is not restricted to the Romance languages. This proposal, based on earlier ideas on the relevance of locality restrictions for Topicalization developed within the generative framework (cf. Frey 2006), is also compatible with a recent analysis of SF in Old Italian suggested by Franco (2009, 2010).

Another important aspect of the comparative approach presented here is that the differences in the discourse function of SF within and between languages and developmental stages are – similarly to previous proposals – attributed to syntactic differences. However, it is not primarily the type of the SF-moved category that is regarded as the main reason for the different interpretation but rather the differences in the derivational history and the influence of the locality constraints.

Concerning Icelandic it has been argued that "true" stylistic movement (STYL-preposing) is a contrast-related movement (with obligatory emphatic accent), whereas the discourse behavior of the locally strictly restricted STYL-inversion shows a greater diversity. Contrast is also optional in these cases and backgrounding is possible. Crucially, this type of SF is also compatible with the unmarked cases where the whole sentence – thus also the fronted element – belongs to the maximal focus domain. As argued in this paper, the C-Constraint is observed by all these cases whereas the violation of this constraint which occurs in the presence of narrow focus without contrast is infelicitous.

The different options of SF claimed for Romance are according to this proposal also related to the syntactic differences between the SF-types. In this case the discourse interpretation is decided by the feature and its checking in different structural layers of the left periphery. SF can appear in Romance as a criterial operator movement to the higher CP-domain, which is focus related and bears obligatory accent (as is the case in Sardinian, and presumably also in Italian), or as a non-operator movement to lower projections at the left periphery, leading to different interpretational effects. The movement to ModP or FinP correlates with different prosody, and in the former case (moving predicatives, especially in V2-contexts) it is related to nuclear accent, whereas particles and infinitives typically lack an accent in the FinP-position.

The cross-linguistic analysis of SF at the interface of narrow syntax and discourse interpretation proposed in this paper leaves open many issues which should be investigated in more detail and on the basis of much more linguistic data, from both a synchronic and a diachronic perspective. However, by challenging the dominant view on the functional load of SF and claiming a more detailed distinction of functional types both in Romance and Scandinavian, the purpose of this new perspective on SF is to contribute to an empirically more adequate analysis of this phenomenon, which is necessary for further theoretical generalizations concerning stylistic movement operations.

References

Angantýsson, Ásgrímur. 2009. Stylistic fronting and expletive insertion: Some empirical observations. Paper given at the Maling Seminar. Ráðstefna til heiðurs Joan Maling 30 at the University of Iceland. November/December 2009.

Bhatt, Rakesh Mohan. 1999. *Verb movement and the syntax of Kashmiri*. Dordrecht: Kluwer.
Breitbarth, Anne & Henk van Riemsdijk. 2004. The role of triggers in linguistic theory: Some introductory remarks. In Anne Breitbarth & Henk van Riemsdijk (eds.), *Triggers*, 1–13. Berlin & New York Mouton de Gruyter.
Cardinaletti, Anna. 2003. Stylistic fronting in Italian. In Lars-Olof Delsing, Cecilia Falk, Gunlög Josefsson & Halldór Ármann Sigurðsson (eds.), *Grammar in focus. Festschrift for Christer Platzack*, 47–55. Lund: Wallin and Dalholm.
Chomsky, Noam. 1995. *The minimalist program*. Cambridge, MA: MIT Press.
Chomsky, Noam. 2001. Derivation by phase. In Michael Kenstowitz (ed.), *Ken Hale. A life in language*, 1–52. Cambridge, MA: MIT Press.
Chomsky, Noam. 2008. On phases. In Robert Freidin, Carlos P. Otero & Maria-Luisa Zubizarreta (eds.), *Foundational issues in linguistic theory*, 133–166. Cambridge, MA: MIT Press.
Delsing, Lars-Olof. 2001. Stylistic fronting. Evidence from Old Scandinavian. *Working Papers in Scandinavian Syntax* 68. 141–171.
Egerland, Verner. 1996. *The syntax of past participles. A generative study of nonfinite constructions in Ancient and Modern Italian* (Études Romanes de Lund 53). Lund: Lund University PhD dissertation.
Egerland, Verner. 2010. The double basis for stylistic fronting. Paper given at the conference on Focus, contrast and givenness in interaction with extraction and deletion at the Max Planck Institute in Tübingen, March 2010.
Egerland, Verner. 2013. Fronting, background, focus. A comparative study of Sardinian and Icelandic. *Lingua* 136. 63–76.
Eythórsson, Thórhallur. 1996. Functional categories, cliticization and word order in the early Germanic languages. In Höskuldur Thráinsson, Samuel D. Epstein & Steve Peter (eds.), *Studies in Germanic syntax II*, 109–139. Dordrecht: Kluwer,
Faarlund, Jan Terje. 2008. *The syntax of Old Norse*. Oxford: Oxford University Press.
Falk, Cecilia. 1993. *Non-referential subjects in the history of Swedish*. Lund: Lund University PhD dissertation.
Fanselow, Gisbert. 2002. Quirky subjects and other specifiers. In Ingrid Kaufmann & Barbara Stiebels (eds.), *More than words*, 227–250. Berlin: Akademie Verlag.
Fischer, Susann & Artemis Alexiadou. 2001. On stylistic fronting: Germanic vs. Romance. *Working Papers in Scandinavian Syntax* 68. 117–145.
Franco, Irene. 2009. *Verbs, subjects and stylistic fronting*. Siena: University of Siena PhD dissertation.
Franco, Irene. 2010. Verbs, subjects and stylistic fronting. Talk given at the Centre for Languages and Literature in Lund, February 2010.
Frey, Werner. 2006. The grammar-pragmatics interface and the German prefield. In Valéria Molnár & Susanne Winkler (eds.), *The architecture of focus* (Studies in Generative Syntax 82), 235–264. Berlin & New York: Mouton De Gruyter.
Frey, Werner. 2010. A-bar movement and conventional implicatures: About the grammatical encoding of emphasis in German. *Lingua* 2010 (120–6), 1416–1435.
Håkansson, David. 2010. Svenskans topikalisering i diakron belysning. In Cecilia Falk, Andreas Nord & Rune Palm (eds.), *Svenskans beskrivning* 30, 133–143. Stockholm: Institutionen för nordiska språk.
Holmberg, Anders. 2000. Scandinavian stylistic fronting. How any category can become an expletive. *Linguistic Inquiry* 31(3). 445–483.

Holmberg, Anders. 2006. Stylistic fronting. In Martin Everaert, Henk van Riemsdijk, Rob Goedemans & Bart Hollebrandse (eds.), *The Blackwell companion to syntax*, 532–565. Oxford: Blackwell.
Hrafnbjargarson, Gunnar Hrafn. 2003. On stylistic fronting once more. *Working Papers in Scandinavian Syntax* 72. 153–205.
Hrafnbjargarson, Gunnar Hrafn. 2004a. Stylistic fronting. *Studia Linguistica* 58. 88–134.
Hrafnbjargarson, Gunnar Hrafn. 2004b. Stylistic fronting. Talk given on January 8, 2004.
Hrafnbjargarson, Gunnar Hrafn & Anna-Lena Wiklund. 2009. General embedded V2: Icelandic A, B, C, etc. *Working Papers in Scandinavian Syntax* 84. 21–51.
Hróarsdóttir, Þorbjörg. 2001. *Word order change in Icelandic: From OV to VO* (Linguistik Aktuell/Linguistics Today 35). Amsterdam & Philadelphia: John Benjamins.
Jones, Michael Allan. 1993. *Sardinian syntax*. New York: Routledge.
Jónsson, Jóhannes Gísli. 1991. Stylistic fronting in Icelandic. *Working Papers in Scandinavian Syntax* 48. 1–43.
Kenesei, István. 2006. Focus as identification. In Valéria Molnár & Susanne Winkler (eds.), *The architecture of focus* (Studies in Generative Syntax 82), 137–168. Berlin: & New York: Mouton De Gruyter,.
É. Kiss, Katalin. 1998. Identificational focus versus information focus. *Language* 74. 245–273.
É. Kiss, Katalin 2006. Focussing as predication. In Valéria Molnár & Susanne Winkler (eds.), *The architecture of focus* (Studies in Generative Syntax 82), 169–193. Berlin: & New York: Mouton De Gruyter.
Kroch, Anthony. 1989. Reflexes of grammar in patterns of language change. *Language Variation and Change* 1. 199–244.
Maling, Joan. 1980. Inversion in embedded clauses in Modern Icelandic. *Íslenskt mál og almenn málfræði* 2: 175–193. Also published as Maling, Joan. 1990. Inversion in embedded clauses in Modern Icelandic. In Joan Maling & Annie Zaenen (eds.), *Modern Icelandic syntax*, 71–91. San Diego: Academic Press.
Mathieu, Eric. 2006. Stylistic fronting in Old French. *Probis* 18. 219–266.
Molnár, Valéria. 1991. *Das TOPIK im Deutschen und im Ungarischen* (Lunder Germanistische Forschungen 58). Stockholm: Almquist & Wiksell International.
Molnár, Valéria. 1998. Topic in focus. On the syntax, phonology, semantics and pragmatics of the so-called 'contrastive topic' in Hungarian and German. *Acta Linguistica Hungarica* 45. 89–166.
Molnár, Valéria. 2003. "C". In Lars-Olof Delsing, Cecilia Falk, Gunlög Josefsson & Halldór Sigurðsson (eds.), *Grammar in focus. Festskrift till Christer Platzack, Vol. II*, 235–248. Institutionen för nordiska språk, Lunds universitet.
Molnár, Valéria. 2006. On different kinds of contrast. In Valéria Molnár & Susanne Winkler (eds.), *The architecture of focus* (Studies in Generative Syntax 82), 197–233. Berlin: & New York: Mouton De Gruyter.
Molnár, Valéria & Susanne Winkler. 2006. Exploring the architecture of focus in grammar. In Valéria Molnár & Susanne Winkler (eds.), *The architecture of focus* (Studies in Generative Syntax 82), 1–29. Berlin: & New York: Mouton De Gruyter.
Molnár, Valéria & Susanne Winkler. 2010. Edges and gaps: Contrast at the interfaces. *Lingua: Special issue: Contrast as an information structural notion in grammar* 2010 (120). 1392–1415.
Ott, Dennis. 2009. Stylistic fronting as remnant movement. *Working Papers in Scandinavian Syntax* 83. 141–178.

Pálsson, Gestur. 1970. *Sögur*. Almenna Bókafélagið. Reykjavík.
Pettersson, Gertrud. 1987. Bisatsledföljden i svenskan eller Varifrån kommer BIFF-regeln? *Arkiv för nordisk filologi* 1988, 157–180. Lund: Lund University Press.
Platzack, Christer. 2008. The edge feature on C. Unpublished manuscript, October 2008.
Platzack, Christer. 2009. Old wine in new barrels. The edge feature in C, topicalization and Stylistic Fronting. Paper given at the "Maling Seminar. Ráðstefna til heiðurs Joan Maling 30" at the University of Iceland. November/December 2009.
Poletto, Cecilia. 2006. Parallel phases: A study on the high and low left periphery of Old Italian. In Mara Frascarelli (ed.), *Phases of interpretation*, vol. 91, 261–295. Berlin: & New York: Mouton de Gruyter.
Rizzi, Luigi. 1997. The fine structure of the left periphery. In Liliane Haegeman (ed.), *Elements of grammar*, 281–337. Dordrecht: Kluwer.
Rizzi, Luigi. 2001. On the position ‚Int(errogative)' in the left periphery of the clause. In Guglielmo Cinque & Giampaolo Salvi (eds.), *Current studies in Italian linguistics*, 287–296. Amsterdam: Elsevier.
Rizzi, Luigi. 2004. On the form of chains: Criterial positions and ECP effects. In Lisa Cheng, Lai-Shen & Norbert Corver (eds.), *On movement*, 97–133. Cambridge, MA: MIT Press.
Rizzi, Luigi & Ur Shlonsky. 2007. Strategies of subject extraction. In Hans-Martin Gärtner & Uli Sauerland (eds.), *Interfaces + recursion = language?* 115–160. Berlin. & New York: Mouton de Gruyter.
Rögnvaldsson, Eiríkur. 1984. Icelandic word order and það-insertion. *Working Papers in Scandinavian Syntax* 8. 1–21.
Rögnvaldsson, Eiríkur. 1996. Word order variation in the VP in Old Icelandic. *Working Papers in Scandinavian Syntax* 58. 55–86.
Rögnvaldsson, Eiríkur, and Höskuldur Thráinsson. 1990. On Icelandic word order once more. In Joan, Maling & Annie Zaenen (eds.) *Modern Icelandic syntax*, 3–40. San Diego: Academic Press.
Rooth, Mats. 1985. *Association with focus*. Amherst: University of Massachusetts at Amherst: PhD dissertation.
Sigurðsson, Halldór Ármann. 1989. *Verbal syntax and case in Icelandic*. Lund: Lund University PhD dissertation.
Sigurðsson, Halldór Ármann. 1997. Stylistic fronting. Ms. University of Iceland.
Sigurðsson, Halldór Ármann. 2010a. On EPP effects. *Studia Linguistica* 64. 159–189.
Sigurðsson, Halldór Ármann. 2010b. On stylistic fronting. Paper given at the conference on Focus, contrast and givenness in interaction with extraction and deletion at the Max Planck Institute in Tübingen, March 2010.
Sigurðsson, Halldór Ármann. 2017. Stylistic fronting in Corpora. In Höskuldur Thráinsson, Caroline Heycock, Hjalmar P. Petersen & Zakaris Svabo Hansen (eds.,) *Studies in Germanic linguistics*, 307-338. John Benjamins.
Sigurðsson, Halldór Ármann & Joan Maling. 2008. Argument drop and the empty left edge condition (ELEC). Talk given at the XXXII IGG, Florence, March 2006.
Thráinsson, Höskuldur. 2007. *The syntax of Icelandic*. Cambridge: CUP.
Webelhuth, Gert & Hans den Besten. 1987. Remnant topicalization and the constituent structure of VP in the Germanic SOV languages. Paper presented at GLOW, Venice.
Wood, Jim. 2011. Stylistic fronting in spoken Icelandic relatives. *Nordic Journal of Linguistics* 34. 29–60.

Index

aboutness 11, 12, 27, 34, 36, 37, 97, 98, 120, 127, 129, 131, 133, 145, 148, 264, 265, 266, 289, 290, 303, 340, 341, 342, 343, 344, 351, 353, 361, 363, 364, 365
aboutness topic (A-topic) 12, 27, 34, 36, 37, 97, 98, 120, 127, 129, 131, 133, 264, 265, 266, 289, 340, 341, 342, 343, 344, 351, 353, 361, 363, 364, 365
acceptability judgment 313, 320, 327
accessibility hierarchy 381, 407, 413
adverb 11, 21, 96, 105, 110, 120, 130, 140, 150, 151, 160, 303, 342, 344, 374, 380, 381, 384, 397
adverbial 11, 21, 96, 105, 110, 120, 130, 140, 150, 160, 303, 342, 344, 384
adverbial clause 34, 110, 111, 113, 130, 140, 144, 145, 150, 151, 152, 153, 154, 155, 156, 157, 158, 159, 160, 161, 162, 163, 164, 165
AdvP 164
affirmation 87, 177, 178, 192
agentive subject 206, 207
Agree 84, 251
all-focus sentences 35, 224, 233
Alternative Semantics 6, 146
American English 179
anaphora 7, 15, 68, 238
ANOVA analysis 219
apropos topic (APT) 274
argument 3, 54, 58, 67, 69, 72, 90, 91, 102, 150, 151, 152, 153, 156, 159, 226, 228, 254, 255, 256, 258, 259, 282, 305, 404
argument drop 254
assertion 18, 89, 90, 101, 104, 105, 117, 121, 122, 128, 141, 142, 146, 150, 153, 280, 342

backward 303, 309, 311, 323, 326, 327
backward looking 303, 309, 311, 323, 326
bare plural 228
binding 32, 33, 67, 68, 71, 74, 75, 76, 77, 78, 79, 83, 84, 85, 89, 91, 99, 113, 115, 238
bleaching 38, 363, 365

bridging 148, 350, 363
British English 179

C-Constraint 378, 396, 397, 399, 402, 403, 405, 417, 419–421
C-domain 27, 33, 67, 69, 92, 129, 141, 142, 144, 145, 147, 148, 149, 155, 156, 157, 161, 162, 163, 165, 250, 406, 417
Caribbean English 48
causal clause 111, 113, 153
Centering Theory 29, 309
central adverbial clause (CAC) 82, 102, 153, 156, 157, 158, 159, 162, 164, 165
Chinese 8, 263
clitic left dislocation (CLLD) 22
codetermination 78
coherence 1, 35, 115, 294, 297, 300, 302, 303, 306, 307, 308, 326, 377, 378, 394, 396, 402, 405
coherence feature (C-feature) 378, 402, 405
comment 8, 48, 298, 348
commitment 101, 120, 122, 177
Commitment Phrase (CmP) 122
common ground content (CG content) 6, 7, 10, 47, 144, 149
common ground management (CG management) 6, 7, 144
common ground (CG) 5, 6, 141
communication 1, 4, 5, 6, 7, 8, 10, 129
complementizer 155, 160, 161, 188
complex NP 35, 206, 215
concerning topic (CNT) 274
concessive clause 153, 154, 164, 165
conditional clause 151, 152, 153, 154, 165
ConjP 164
conjunction reduction (CR) 259, 260, 262, 264, 266
continuing topic 343
contrast 1, 2, 20, 31, 73, 139, 147, 232, 265, 290, 318, 379, 388, 396, 397, 421

contrastive focus (CF) 59, 87, 88, 89
contrastive topic / C-topics (CT) 19, 33, 86, 91, 132, 143, 146, 148, 156, 157, 161, 163, 213, 214, 216, 341
conversational dynamics 18, 34, 140, 144, 145
coreference 33, 49, 51, 52, 64, 67, 68, 69, 70, 71, 74, 75, 76, 77, 79, 84, 91, 92, 256
coreference rule 68, 75, 77
CP 164, 182, 188, 249, 255, 256, 259, 380, 387, 390, 396, 417, 419
creation verbs 240

Dahl's puzzle 71, 77, 78, 83, 85, 91
Danish 35, 241, 243
de dicto / de re 14, 15, 236, 244
deaccenting 33, 47, 48, 49, 50, 51, 52, 53, 57, 58, 63, 64
declarative 36, 111, 119, 128, 140, 146, 251, 252, 304, 338, 352
definite 48, 49, 205, 223, 228, 229, 231, 233, 234, 310, 402, 411, 416
definiteness effect 223, 234, 411
dependent clauses, types of 101, 113, 114
discourse 1, 4, 10, 22, 24, 29, 32, 35, 37, 38, 47, 49, 51, 54, 70, 71, 79, 82, 83, 91, 129, 139, 140, 141, 144, 145, 154, 163, 176, 177, 178, 191, 198, 217, 230, 265, 287, 293, 294, 296, 297, 300, 301, 304, 305, 306, 308, 311, 312, 313, 315, 316, 317, 319, 320, 321, 322, 327, 358, 375, 379, 384, 385, 394, 396, 397, 406, 407, 412, 420, 421
discourse categories 139, 140, 141, 144, 154
discourse coherence 35
discourse function 4, 22, 37, 163, 176, 177, 191, 198, 294, 296, 304, 305, 311, 312, 313, 321, 327, 384, 396, 397, 407, 420
discourse interpretation 38, 178, 379, 385, 407, 412, 421
discourse operator 70, 71, 79, 82, 83, 91
discourse referent (DR) 10, 37, 49, 70, 71, 79, 265, 300, 315, 316
discourse topic 29, 37, 47, 49, 51, 293, 294, 296, 297, 300, 301, 306, 308, 312, 313, 317, 319, 320, 322, 327, 358

discourse triggered movement 38
discourse update 230
discourse-semantic effects 24, 38
dislocation 154, 159, 163, 273, 274, 275, 281, 282, 284, 291, 379
doxastic attitude 102, 103
DP 12, 71, 73, 98, 99, 113, 147, 155, 164, 165, 256, 264, 277, 377, 403, 405
Dutch 238, 239, 244

Early New High German (ENHG) 347
East Central German 352, 356, 359, 362
embedded clause 34, 82, 96, 101, 105, 107, 124, 130, 131, 132, 139, 141, 182, 183, 282, 283, 396, 410, 417
emotive factive verb 109
English 2, 6, 7, 8, 9, 15, 21, 22, 25, 30, 33, 34, 35, 48, 49, 92, 104, 159, 175, 198, 299
entailment 33, 49, 51, 52, 53, 54, 64
epistemic 14, 101, 105, 121, 342
EPP-movement 409
evidential 101
exceptional rule of codetermination (ERC) 76
existential F-closure 54, 61
existentials 72, 73, 233, 234, 235, 236, 242
experimental evidence 35, 221
expressives 96, 100, 101, 102, 108, 127, 129
Extended Projection Principle (EPP) 377
extraction 35, 204, 205, 206, 207, 216, 217, 218, 219, 220, 221, 223, 241, 242
extraposition 37, 183, 185

F-marked 54, 55, 56, 61
factive verb 124
familiarity 29, 33, 47, 48, 49, 51, 63, 64, 301
file-change 228
focus 8, 35, 174, 198, 298, 376, 378, 384, 406, 407, 410, 411, 414, 417
focus inversion 174, 198
focus isolation 35, 198
focus movement 376, 378, 384, 406, 407, 410, 411, 414, 417
Force 34, 47, 58, 115, 117, 249

formal movement (FM) 38, 280, 379, 386, 387, 388, 391, 393, 394, 397, 400, 402, 403, 420
forward looking 37, 309, 327
frame setting 2, 11, 26, 165, 299
free theme 98
French 153, 274, 328
fronting 150, 151, 152, 153, 159, 163, 204, 263, 349, 376, 378, 386, 397, 400, 408

G-marked 61, 62, 63
GB (Government and Binding) 255
gender 98, 219, 258, 376
German 12, 21, 22, 27, 30, 33, 34, 35, 37, 69, 96, 97, 98, 100, 101, 103, 104, 119, 133, 143, 174, 175, 176, 180, 183, 187, 189, 191, 198, 219, 221, 265, 291, 294, 296, 297, 300, 303, 304, 305, 311, 312, 313, 313, 322, 326, 327, 365
German hanging topic (GHT) 98, 133
German left dislocation (GLD) 133
German newspapers 313
German press commentaries newspapers 326
given 2, 13, 27, 28, 29, 30, 33, 34, 36, 47, 48, 49, 51, 52, 54, 56, 57, 58, 60, 63, 131, 140, 148, 149, 157, 158, 159, 160, 161, 162, 163, 228, 261, 274, 301, 303, 308, 378, 379, 396
givenness 2, 13, 27, 28, 29, 33, 34, 47, 48, 49, 51, 54, 56, 57, 58, 63, 131, 148, 149, 157, 158, 159, 160, 161, 162, 163, 274, 301, 303, 308, 379
givenness topic / G-Topic 27, 28, 34, 131, 148, 149, 157, 158, 159, 160, 161, 162, 163
grammatical coding of topicality 28
grammaticalization 363

hanging topic 8, 22, 36, 112, 133, 276, 281, 282, 282, 284, 285, 291
happy null generalization (HNG) 256

Icelandic 36, 38, 252, 258, 263, 265, 268, 380, 382, 384, 385, 388, 390, 396, 407, 413, 416, 418, 419, 420, 421

illocution 18, 31, 32, 33, 34, 96, 115, 117, 118, 119, 125, 127, 129, 131, 133, 141, 144, 146, 149, 151, 162, 163, 165, 280
illocutionary force 18, 31, 32, 33, 34, 96, 115, 117, 118, 119, 125, 127, 129, 131, 133, 141, 144, 146, 149, 151, 162, 163, 165
imperatives 111, 119, 144, 338
individual-level (I-level) (predicate) 225, 226
information 1, 2, 3, 4, 5, 7, 10, 16, 20, 22, 23, 29, 35, 36, 38, 85, 86, 89, 91, 140, 144, 148, 159, 179, 191, 194, 195, 196, 197, 198, 205, 206, 209, 221, 223, 225, 228, 229, 235, 245, 274, 281, 286, 289, 291, 294, 298, 299, 302, 303, 306, 307, 308, 311, 313, 315, 316, 317, 318, 321, 340, 342, 346, 356, 358, 377, 378, 385, 395, 415
information packaging 5, 6, 297, 298, 309, 310, 327
information structure (IS) 1, 3, 4, 5, 7, 10, 16, 20, 22, 29, 35, 36, 38, 85, 91, 140, 144, 205, 206, 209, 221, 223, 225, 228, 245, 274, 281, 286, 289, 291, 298, 299, 303, 306, 313, 316, 317, 318, 321, 340, 377, 378, 385, 415
inherently negative verb 109, 112, 132
integration, degrees of 295
intensional predicate 245
interface 4, 5, 18, 32, 34, 36, 77, 83, 140, 144, 268, 293, 294, 297, 378, 379, 384
interface analysis 140
interface root restriction 18, 34, 144
interface rule 77
interjection 34, 106, 107, 117, 128
intervention effect 151, 154, 159
intonation 98, 99, 158, 160, 162, 193, 276
inversion 23, 24, 182, 263, 374
IP 59, 189, 387, 416, 417, 419
island constraints 240
Italian 21, 22, 27, 30, 33, 34, 36, 69, 142, 150, 154, 251, 252, 257, 258, 268, 395, 413, 416, 419

Judgement Phrase (JP) 121, 122, 123, 124, 125, 127
judgment 154, 156, 157, 399, 400, 402

lambda operator 70, 79
left dislocation 9, 22, 25, 32, 36, 98, 142, 159, 276, 283, 284
left edge 21, 198, 249, 303, 396
left periphery 20, 26, 29, 31, 36, 37, 127, 149, 151, 153, 154, 159, 163, 281, 302, 303, 311, 344, 349, 350, 364, 395, 396
left sentence bracket (LSB) 338
LF 4, 15, 33, 73, 80, 81, 377
location 158, 165, 188, 225, 226, 227, 233, 235, 236, 296
locative inversion 142
logophoricity 279

main clause phenomena (MCP) 130, 131
Malaysian English 48
marked word order in German 310
mental salience framework (MSF) 297, 308
middle field 12, 20, 21, 22, 96, 97, 98, 129, 206, 216, 217, 218, 219, 220, 294, 295, 303, 304, 313, 316, 317, 318, 319, 321, 322, 343, 344, 386, 387, 388
Mittelfeld 187, 304
modal particle (MP) 34, 101
MoodP 164
Movement 35, 38, 69, 142, 154, 165, 175, 203, 250, 282, 285, 294, 297, 377, 379, 381, 382, 390, 393, 394, 404, 407
movement of VP 404

Nachfeld 294, 304
narrative inversion 36, 252, 254, 255, 264, 268
narrow focus 17, 305, 307, 321, 327, 354, 405, 406, 410, 421
Natural Language Generation (NLG) 297
new 6, 13, 23, 30, 56, 60, 233, 234, 302, 303, 396
newness 6
non-integrated dependent clause (NonIC) 104

NP 17, 20, 35, 37, 205, 206, 209, 210, 212, 213, 214, 215, 216, 217, 218, 220, 221, 296, 300, 313, 317, 319, 320, 321, 326
null arguments 244, 245, 255, 258
null object 262
null subject 258
number 10, 20, 26, 29, 31, 76, 156, 183, 208, 210, 211, 304, 377

Old Catalan 375, 408, 409, 412, 413, 417
Old French 375, 376, 408, 412, 413, 419
Old High German (OHG) 37, 265, 339
Old Icelandic 36, 252, 265, 266, 268, 401
old information 47, 287
Old Norse 252, 254, 257, 258, 261, 262, 263
only 7, 56, 57, 62
operator 14, 18, 55, 57, 70, 101, 141, 151, 152, 155, 164

parallelism 71, 72, 73, 74, 75, 80, 83, 84, 85, 86, 87, 88, 89, 91, 210
parallelism constraint 83, 85, 91, 210
parallelism requirement 80, 87
parallelism 71, 72, 73, 74, 75, 80, 83, 84, 85, 86, 87, 88, 89, 91, 210
parameters 223, 228, 233, 234
particle 7, 13, 19, 20, 24, 87, 96, 97, 101, 108, 111, 113, 127, 128, 129, 133, 299, 380, 383, 421
partitive 49, 231
passive 206, 405
past participle 374, 399
perception 102, 103, 223, 237, 240, 244, 315
perception predicates 223
perception verbs 237, 240, 244
peripheral adverbial clauses (PAC) 34, 102, 150, 159, 160, 161, 162, 163, 164, 165
persistence 306, 315, 327
person 36, 69, 89, 105, 131, 230, 250, 258, 260, 261, 262, 263, 264, 265, 268, 307, 376
PF 161, 165, 230, 244, 245, 281, 377
poset elements 342, 343, 351, 353, 361, 362, 363

postfield 38, 100, 294, 297, 298, 300, 311, 312, 313, 314, 317, 318, 319, 322, 327, 338, 338, 339, 354, 355, 362, 364, 365
PP 35, 37, 123, 175, 185, 203, 225, 230, 284, 294, 295, 297, 300, 302, 313, 314, 315, 316, 317, 318, 319, 321, 322, 323, 326, 374, 380, 382, 403, 405
PP topicalization 35, 203
pragmatic adverbial clause 113
predicate 9, 16, 50, 55, 60, 68, 79, 102, 123, 132, 142, 146, 178, 195, 206, 207, 223, 226, 229, 230, 234, 236, 237, 238, 240, 241, 242, 243, 279, 299, 318, 320, 400
predicative adjective 380
predictability 53, 287
prefield 22, 37, 97, 98, 99, 103, 104, 114, 115, 125, 126, 294, 303, 311, 316, 317, 319, 320, 321, 322, 338, 339, 340, 342, 343, 344, 345, 348, 349, 354, 356, 358, 361, 362, 363, 364, 365, 386, 387, 388
pro drop 36, 252, 255, 256, 268
proper name 310
proposition suspension 177
prosodic domain 59, 117
prosody 31, 57, 58, 60, 304, 327, 377, 421
Proto-Germanic 349, 364

Q-givenness 209
quaestio-model 306
question under discussion (QUD) 87, 298, 307, 342

referentiality 31
relative clause 17, 60, 131, 151, 165, 185, 223, 235, 241, 242, 294, 380
remnant movement 338, 382, 391, 404
resumptive pronoun (RP) 22, 98, 281
rheme 8, 306
right dislocation 32, 100, 112, 113, 127, 129, 129, 133, 305, 314
right periphery 37, 100, 149, 153, 163, 305
right periphery of German verb-second sentences 37
right sentence bracket (RSB) 338

Romance languages 38, 273, 274, 291, 375, 376, 378, 395, 408, 416, 420
root 30, 96, 100, 101, 102, 103, 107, 108, 110, 111, 113, 116, 118, 119, 123, 127, 133, 139, 140, 142, 143, 183, 255, 256, 266
root clause 96, 102, 103, 140, 142, 143, 183, 255, 256
root phenomena (weak, strong) 102, 103, 107, 110, 113, 118, 119, 127
root sensitivity 96, 100, 101, 102, 108, 111, 113, 133

salience 33, 36, 47, 48, 49, 50, 51, 63, 64, 297, 308, 315, 316, 317, 327
Sardinian 375, 410, 411, 413
Saxonian 352
scene-setting 341, 342, 343, 350, 351, 352, 353, 361
scope 14, 15, 24, 72, 90, 102, 121, 123, 129, 143, 153, 181, 230, 237, 243, 394
scrambling 180, 183, 184, 185, 187, 191, 207
SE pronouns 239
second occurrence focus (SOF) 33, 48, 56, 57
semantic parallelism 71, 73, 74, 85
semantics 6, 14, 18, 55, 112, 115, 126, 141, 206, 366, 379, 384, 394
sentence topic 7, 19, 26, 29, 30, 37, 49, 98, 122, 297, 298, 299, 301, 303, 316, 317, 319, 321
sentential adverbial (SADV) 96
small clause 237, 238
spatio-temporal argument 225, 226
speech act 18, 71, 80, 82, 85, 90, 100, 101, 117, 119, 120, 121, 122, 124, 125, 126, 128, 146, 244, 280, 291
speech act phrase (ActP) 122
stage topic (sTOP) 35, 223
stage-level (S-level) (predicate) 223, 227
stochastic optimality theory 345
stress 55, 86, 116, 229, 232, 415
stylistic fronting 38, 280
stylistic inversion (STYL-inversion) 153, 391, 396
stylistic preposing (STYL-preposing) 396
subject constraint 238, 239, 240, 241, 242

subject gap condition 380, 382, 406, 409, 411, 415, 419
subjective epistemics 101, 121
Swedish 21, 22, 36, 274, 275, 278, 279, 281, 283, 286, 290, 291, 388
syntactic derivation 38, 342, 379, 394, 405
syntax 20, 36, 61, 68, 70, 76, 79, 120, 122, 125, 150, 180, 187, 198, 210, 251, 256, 293, 297, 313, 326, 339, 364, 365, 379, 385, 388, 414, 417
syntax-discourse interface 297, 326
syntax-information structure interface 198

tag 104, 105, 133
textual persistence 305
theme 7, 19, 29, 300, 306
thetic sentence 17, 26, 224
though-attraction 178
Thüringian 355, 357, 358, 360, 361, 362
time 151, 164, 225, 226, 307
topic 3, 7, 9, 10, 13, 21, 22, 25, 28, 29, 34, 36, 100, 101, 131, 140, 159, 181, 185, 187, 193, 198, 231, 232, 243, 244, 250, 252, 254, 255, 255, 256, 259, 266, 267, 268, 273, 275, 276, 280, 281, 286, 291, 357, 366, 374, 376, 378, 380, 382, 383, 384, 388, 407, 420
topic drop 36, 244, 252, 254, 255, 256, 259, 266, 267, 268
topic marking constructions 34, 100, 101
topic typology 3
topicalization 9, 21, 22, 25, 34, 36, 159, 181, 185, 187, 198, 243, 250, 273, 275, 276, 281, 286, 291, 374, 376, 378, 380, 382, 383, 384, 388, 407, 420
TopP (Topic Phrase) 250
TP 115, 120, 123, 255, 315, 380, 390, 392, 393, 396

trace 81, 84, 240, 281, 294, 383, 389, 390
transfer of information 5
truth condition 7, 100
truth value 16, 48, 224, 225, 230

unaccusative 194, 206
unbracketing 32, 294, 296, 297, 300, 312, 313, 314, 316, 318, 320, 321, 322, 326
Upper German 355

V1 (verb first) 185, 255, 264, 265, 389
V2 (verb second) 21, 125, 142, 143, 185, 187, 188, 262, 263, 278, 281, 291, 385, 386, 392, 416, 417, 419
vehicle change 88
verb of saying / verbum dicendi 103, 104, 132, 279
verum focus 399
Vorfeld 187
VP 33, 35, 59, 63, 67, 71, 72, 73, 74, 75, 77, 78, 80, 82, 83, 85, 86, 88, 89, 90, 91, 92, 174, 175, 176, 180, 183, 190, 193, 197, 391, 404
VP movement 190, 404
VP topicalization (VP-Top) 35, 174, 176, 180, 183
VP-ellipsis 33, 67, 71, 72, 73, 74, 75, 77, 78, 80, 82, 83, 85, 86, 88, 89, 90, 91, 92

was für-split 207
wh-phrase 180, 182, 188, 238, 307
word order 21, 36, 206, 216, 218, 219, 220, 221, 275, 276, 279, 281, 286, 306, 310, 313, 317, 318, 319, 320, 321, 393, 413, 418, 420

www.ingramcontent.com/pod-product-compliance
Lightning Source LLC
Chambersburg PA
CBHW021941240426
43668CB00037B/266